Communications in Computer and Information Science 1808

Rationale

The CCIS series is devoted to the publication of proceedings of computer science conferences. Its aim is to efficiently disseminate original research results in informatics in printed and electronic form. While the focus is on publication of peer-reviewed full papers presenting mature work, inclusion of reviewed short papers reporting on work in progress is welcome, too. Besides globally relevant meetings with internationally representative program committees guaranteeing a strict peer-reviewing and paper selection process, conferences run by societies or of high regional or national relevance are also considered for publication.

Topics

The topical scope of CCIS spans the entire spectrum of informatics ranging from foundational topics in the theory of computing to information and communications science and technology and a broad variety of interdisciplinary application fields.

Information for Volume Editors and Authors

Publication in CCIS is free of charge. No royalties are paid, however, we offer registered conference participants temporary free access to the online version of the conference proceedings on SpringerLink (http://link.springer.com) by means of an http referrer from the conference website and/or a number of complimentary printed copies, as specified in the official acceptance email of the event.

CCIS proceedings can be published in time for distribution at conferences or as post-proceedings, and delivered in the form of printed books and/or electronically as USBs and/or e-content licenses for accessing proceedings at SpringerLink. Furthermore, CCIS proceedings are included in the CCIS electronic book series hosted in the SpringerLink digital library at http://link.springer.com/bookseries/7899. Conferences publishing in CCIS are allowed to use Online Conference Service (OCS) for managing the whole proceedings lifecycle (from submission and reviewing to preparing for publication) free of charge.

Publication process

The language of publication is exclusively English. Authors publishing in CCIS have to sign the Springer CCIS copyright transfer form, however, they are free to use their material published in CCIS for substantially changed, more elaborate subsequent publications elsewhere. For the preparation of the camera-ready papers/files, authors have to strictly adhere to the Springer CCIS Authors' Instructions and are strongly encouraged to use the CCIS LaTeX style files or templates.

Abstracting/Indexing

CCIS is abstracted/indexed in DBLP, Google Scholar, EI-Compendex, Mathematical Reviews, SCImago, Scopus. CCIS volumes are also submitted for the inclusion in ISI Proceedings.

How to start

To start the evaluation of your proposal for inclusion in the CCIS series, please send an e-mail to ccis@springer.com.

Abolfazl Mirzazadeh · Babek Erdebilli ·
Erfan Babaee Tirkolaee ·
Gerhard-Wilhelm Weber · Arpan Kumar Kar
Editors

Science, Engineering Management and Information Technology

First International Conference, SEMIT 2022
Ankara, Turkey, February 2–3, 2022
Revised Selected Papers, Part I

Editors
Abolfazl Mirzazadeh
Kharazmi University
Tehran, Iran

Babek Erdebilli
Ankara Yıldırım Beyazıt University
Ankara, Türkiye

Erfan Babaee Tirkolaee
Istinye University
Istanbul, Türkiye

Gerhard-Wilhelm Weber
Poznań University of Technology
Poznań, Poland

Arpan Kumar Kar
Indian Institute of Technology Delhi
New Delhi, India

ISSN 1865-0929 ISSN 1865-0937 (electronic)
Communications in Computer and Information Science
ISBN 978-3-031-40394-1 ISBN 978-3-031-40395-8 (eBook)
https://doi.org/10.1007/978-3-031-40395-8

This Springer imprint is published by the registered company Springer Nature Switzerland AG
The registered company address is: Gewerbestrasse 11, 6330 Cham, Switzerland

Preface

International Conference on Science, Engineering Management and Information Technology (SEMIT 2022) was held virtually in Ankara, Turkey. The 2022 event was executed in two sections with different structures and programs meanwhile the same subjects and approaches. The first section was held on 2–3 February 2022 and the second was held on 8–9 September 2022, both online. The following is the book for the former event (SEMIT 2022-Feb.)

It provided an energetic knowledge-transferring atmosphere for participants (as several feedbacks revealed).

SEMIT 2022 attracted the attention of students and professionals internationally. The covering subjects included, but not limited to "IT and EM based case studies of manufacturing/service industries (including automotive, food, tourism, petroleum, healthcare, insurance and banking, energy, etc.)", "E-government, E-commerce, E-learning", "Marketing and E-marketing for resources management", "Data science, big data, data mining and knowledge management in EM", "Decision making and support systems in an uncertain environment and risk management", "Industry 4.0, supply chain 4.0, and logistics 4.0", "Supply chain management (green SCM, sustainable SCM, agile SCM, JIT SCM, global SCM, etc.)", "Optimization and decision making: methods and algorithms", "Applied soft computing in engineering management", "Metaheuristic algorithms and applications", "Project management", "Blockchain in engineering management", "Artificial intelligence and expert systems", "Digital city", "Internet of things (IoT)", "Other fields of study related to EM and IT".

SEMIT 2022-Feb. was honored to be enriched by outstanding keynote speakers from Italy, Japan, Poland, Spain and India. In this event, seven universities from UK, France, Czech Republic, Brazil, India, Morocco and Turkey were present as scientific sponsors.

The conference included participation of 42 countries. The geographical diversity of international scientific committee members was from 21 countries.

The conference team received 138 English and Turkish papers, which were reviewed by at least three international reviewers (single blind reviews). Considering the reviewers' comments in the first round of review, the papers have been reviewed once more with stricter criteria to select the most appropriate ones for Springer's Publication. Finally, the two-round review process resulted in the selection of 29 papers (around 21%) for this book series.

The review criteria in this step were: content; originality; relevance; contribution to the professional literature; significance and potential impact of the paper; language accuracy; study validity; accuracy of methodology and analysis; paper organization, required relevant data, citations and references; adequate referring of the background information; consistency of references, symbols and units throughout the paper; quality and clarity of tables and figures.

The papers in SEMIT 2022-Feb. were presented in 15 panel sessions: "supply chain management", "internet data and MIS for risk management strategy in the concept of sustainability in industry 4.0", "optimization algorithms for data science, decision making and transportation", "decision making & support systems in an uncertain environment and risk management", "competing in the era of globalization based on industrial engineering and management techniques", "recent developments in decision making situations and their potential on cooperative games, operations research and disaster management", "case studies of manufacturing/service industries", "artificial intelligence and expert systems", "human factors engineering in contemporary research", "towards smart systems based blockchain technologies for enhancing cybersecurity and building resilience", "internet data and mis for risk management strategy in the concept of sustainability in industry 4.0", "inventory control, production planning and scheduling + optimization and decision making: methods and algorithms", "engineering optimization and artificial intelligence", "industry 4.0 and information systems: innovations, optimization and decision support systems", "models and computational intelligence approaches for transportation, logistics and manufacturing systems".

SEMIT 2022-Feb. included four applied workshops by outstanding lecturers with a good number of audiences. The workshop titles were very well received by the participants which were: "evaluating the environmental efficiency of OECD countries with DEA in the context of the circular economy"; "collaborative logistics with combinatorial auctions"; "importance of circular economy for sustainable development"; "a hybrid evaluation approach for social sustainability performance measures in warehousing hub"

December 2022

Abolfazl Mirzazadeh
Babek Erdebilli
Erfan Babaee Tirkolaee
Gerhard-Wilhelm Weber
Arpan Kumar Kar

Organization

Conference Chairs

Abolfazl Mirzazadeh	Kharazmi University, Iran
Babek Erdebilli	Yildirim Beyazit University, Turkey

Conference Coordinator

Leyla Chehrghani	Kharazmi University, Iran

Ankara Yildirim Beyazit University Authorities

Ibrahim Aydinli (Rector)	
Hasan Okuyucu	Dean of Faculty of Engineering and Natural Sciences
Mete Gundogan	Head of IE Department

Technical and Editorial Chairs

Abolfazl Mirzazadeh	Kharazmi University, Iran
Babek Erdebilli	Yildirim Beyazit University, Turkey
Erfan Babaee Tirkolaee	Istinye University, Turkey
Gerhard-Wilhelm Weber	Poznan University of Technology, Poland
Arpan Kumar Kar	Indian Institute of Technology Delhi, India

Scientific Committee Members

Jai Acharya	Principal Consultant, International Maritime Management & Consultancy Services, Singapore
Maher Agi	Rennes School of Business, France
Ali Allahverdi	Kuwait University, Kuwait
Sirma Zeynep Alparslan Gok	Suleyman Demirel University, Turkey

Fayçal Belkaid	Abou Bekr Belkaid University of Tlemcen, Algeria
Marilisa Botte	University of Naples, Italy
Kevin Cullinane	University of Gothenburg, Sweden
Alexandre Dolgui	IMT Atlantique (Former Ecole des Mines de Nantes), France
Leopoldo Eduardo Cárdenas-Barrón	School of Engineering and Sciences, Tecnológico de Monterrey, Mexico
Ergun Eraslan	Yildirim Beyazit University, Turkey
Serap Ergun	Isparta University of Applied Sciences, Turkey
Paulina Golinska	Poznan University of technology, Poland
Maria Grazia Speranza	University of Brescia, Italy
Josef Jablonsky	University of Economics and Business, Czech Republic
Mehmet Kabak	Gazi University, Turkey
Marzieh Khakifirooz	Tec de Monterrey, Mexico
Sankar Kumar Roy	Vidyasagar University, India
Fabiana Lucena Oliveira	Amazonas State University, Brazil
Nasr Hamood Mohamed Al-Hinai	Sultan Qaboos University, Oman
Beata Mrugalska	Poznan University of Technology, Poland
Mustapha Oudani	International University of Rabat, Morocco
Eren Ozceylan	Gaziantep University, Turkey
Ayse Ozmen	Committee Member on IFORS Web-Based Resources on OR for Development
Sujan Piya	Sultan Qaboos University, Oman
Ruben Ruiz Garcia	University of Polytechnics, Spain
Sadia Samar Ali	King Abdul Aziz University, Saudi Arabia
Yavuz Selim Ozdemir	Ankara Science University, Turkey
Kathryn Stecke	University of Texas at Dallas, USA
Tatiana Tchemisova	University of Aveiro, Portugal
Chefi Triki	University of Kent, UK
Abdullah Yildizbasi	Ankara Yildirim Beyazit University, Turkey
Ibrahim Yilmaz	Ankara Yildirim Beyazit University, Turkey

Keynote Speakers

Mitsuo Gen	Tokyo University of Science, Japan
Arpan Kumar Kar	Indian Institute of Technology Delhi, India
Sankar Kumar Roy	Vidyasagar University, India
Ruben Ruiz Garcia	University of Polytechnics, Spain
Maria Grazia Speranza	University of Brescia, Italy
Gerhard-Wilhelm Weber	Poznan University of Technology, Poland

Reviewers

Khawar Abbas	Xian Jiaotong University, China
Mohammad Abdel-Aal	King Fahd University of Petroleum and Minerals, Saudi Arabia
Charles Adusei	Garden City University College, Ghana
Oludele Afolabi	Modibbo Adama University Yola, Nigeria
Vankesh Agarwal	Dr Vishwanath Karad MIT World Peace University, India
Houda Ait Aabdelmalk	Mohammed v University, Morocco
Adeyinka Ajayi	Redeemer's University, Nigeria
Erol Aktay	Gazi University, Turkey
Sadia Samar Ali	King Abdul Aziz University, Saudi Arabia
Omid Aligholipour	Gazi University, Turkey
Luma Al Kindi	University of Technology, Iraq
Sirma Zeynep Alparslan Gok	Suleyman Demirel University, Turkey
Minwir AlShammari	University of Bahrain, Bahrain
Shabnam Amirnezhad Barough	Yildirim Beyazit University, Turkey
Melisa Antonio	Middle East College, Oman
Evgeny Averin	Trade Representation of Russia in Turkey
Nadi Serhan Aydin	Istinye University, Turkey
Erfan Babaee Tirkolaee	Istinye University, Turkey
Eric Bang	Broad Institute of MIT and Harvard, USA
Sanjib Biswas	Calcutta Business School, India
Maide Cakir	Yildirim Beyazit University, Turkey
Yavuz Can	Friedrich Alexander University, Germany
Ibrahim Chaloob	Al Esraa University College, Iraq
Mouna Derbel	University of Sfax, Tunisia
Erkan Dogan	Manisa Celal Bayar University, Turkey
Skalli Dounia	Hassan 1st University, Morocco
Tugrul Erdem	Manisa Celal Bayar University, Turkey
Suresh Garg	DTU University, India

Peiman Ghasemi	University of Calgary, Canada
Alireza Goli	Isfahan University, Iran
Karnik Gulati	Institute of Chartered Accountants, India
Parul Gupta	Global Institute of Technology and Management, India
Doha Haloui	Moulay Ismail University, Morocco
Gholamreza Haseli	Shiraz University, Iran
Jorge Hernandez Lopez	University of Ibague, Colombia
Asmaa Houar	Abou Bekr Belkaid University, Algeria
Mahamed Houasni	Kemis Miliana University, Algeria
Abdellah Houmz	Mohammed V University of Rabat, Morocco
Yusuf Tansel Ic	Baskent University, Turkey
Mehmet Kabak	Gazi University, Turkey
Yavuz Kahraman	Gaziantepe University, Turkey
Bilal karroumi	National School of Applied Science, Morocco
AllaEldin Kassam	University of Technology, Iraq
Ali Kazemi	Kish University of Management, Iran
Sarika Keswani	Symbiosis University campus, India
Rakesh Kumar	Namibia University of Science and Technology, Namibia
Sara Lahlou	International University of Rabat, Morocco
Eloisa Macedo	University of Aveiro, Portugal
Abdelkader Mechaacha	Abou Bekr Belkaid University, Algeria
Abolfazl Mirzazadeh	Kharazmi University, Iran
Srikanta Mohapatra	Chitkara University, India
Beata Mrugalska	Poznan University of Technology, Poland
Saja Nahoo	University of Technology, Iraq
Hasanian Nasser	University of Technology, Iraq
Kanthavelkumar Natesan	Anna University, India
Narjisse Nejjari	Mohammed V University, Morocco
Ammar Odeh	Princess Sumaya University of Technology, Jordan
Ozge Onat	Isparta University of Applied Science, Turkey
Mohanned Oudah	University of Technology, Iraq
Aybike Ozyuksel Ciftcioglu	Manisa Celal Bayar University, Turkey
Ayse Ozmen	Committee Member of IFORS web-based Resources on OR for Development
Osman Palanci	Suleyman Demirel University, Turkey
Anil Pandey	NITIE Mumbai University, India
Duy Pham	University of Economics, Vietnam
Adem Pinar	Gazi University, Turkey
Prakash Sarangi	Lovely Professional University, India

Noucaiba Sbai	Mohammed V University, Morocco
Eftal Sehirli	Karabuk University, Turkey
Halima Semaa	University of Hassan 1st, Morocco
Mohd Rizaimy Shaharudin	University of Technology, Malaysia
Esra Sipahi Dongol	Aksaray University, Turkey
Karuppiah S. P.	Anna University, Iceland
Aditi Srivastava	Noida International University, India
Moch Sulistio	Yonsei University, South Korea
Jighjigh Tamber	Benue State University, Nigeria
Tatiana Tchemisova	University of Aveiro, Portugal
Chefi Triki	University of Kent, UK
Murchhana Tripathy	TA Pai management Institute, India
Yagmur Turkkan	Yildirim Beyazit University, Turkey
Anak Agun Gde Satia Utama	University of Airlangga, Indonesia
Katike Uttam	National Institute of Technology, India
Fatma Unal	Hitit University, Turkey
Vidhisha Vyas	IILM University, India
Abdullah Yildizbasi	Yildirim Beyazit University, Turkey
Ibrahim Yilmaz	Yildirim Beyazit University, Turkey

Scientific Sponsors

Kent Business School

International University of Rabat

Vidyasagar University

Prague University of Economics and Business

Ankara Science University

Amazonas State University

Rennes School of Business

Contents – Part I

Application of Computer Science and Technology in Operations and Supply Chain Management

Advances of Engineering Technology and Artificial Intelligence in Application Management

Contents – Part II

Application of Computer Science and Technology in Operations and Supply Chain Management

Developing an Optimization Model to Determine Fleet Size of Automated Guided Vehicle

Deniz Esen Erdogan(✉) and Seren Ozmehmet Tasan

Dokuz Eylul University, 35390 Izmir, Turkey
denizesen.erdogan@ogr.deu.edu.tr

Abstract. This paper considers the problem of defining the optimum number of diverse types of Automated Guided Vehicles (AGVs). AGVs are mobile robots that are used for automatic material handlings, such as for finished items, raw materials, and products. Due to the high degree of unpredictability and the various variables involved, the design and operation of AGV systems are extremely complicated. Well-designed AGV systems will reduce product damage, enhance workplace safety by eliminating human errors, will provide a long-term profit to the business.

The determination of AGV fleet size plays a decisive role in the performance of production systems. There are several studies focusing on the fleet size of AGV. However, it has been seen that most of these studies only dealt with the fleet size problem of a single type of AGV although the use of different types of AGVs operating on the same route in enterprises has become popular. Therefore, in this study, a mixed integer model was developed to determine the fleet size of multitype of AGVs. The aim of this proposed model is to optimize the fleet size under cost constraints and real system constraints. The model was applied with the data of a real manufacturing system in an electronic sector. As a result, the number of two types of AGVs that should be used in the real system were determined with a minimum cost of $194.578.

Keywords: Handling System · Automated Guided Vehicle Systems · Mixed Integer Programming

1 Introduction

Material flow control has become one of the critical concerns for system efficiency as industrial systems have expanded in size and complexity and determining the number of vehicles necessary is a significant issue in the design of AGV (Automatic Guided Vehicle) systems for automated material flow management. AGVs are unmanned electric vehicles that move materials from one point to another. They move on fixed routes that require infrastructure and need pre-programmed software for operating instructions. An AGV system is a sophisticated material handling system that consists of a driverless vehicle that follows a path (virtual or guided) and is controlled by a computer or microprocessor [1]. The frame, batteries, electrical system, driving unit, steering, precision stop unit, onboard controller, communication unit, safety system, and work platform are typical components of an AGV.

A. Mirzazadeh et al. (Eds.): SEMIT 2022, CCIS 1808, pp. 3–17, 2023.
https://doi.org/10.1007/978-3-031-40395-8_1

AGV systems are primarily used for material distribution in warehouse environments, as well as for transporting materials from production areas and storage areas in industrial facilities. To develop an effective AGV system, it is necessary to make the right design first and then make operational decisions [2, 3]. It must be choosing most suitable AGV type and navigation system, then calculate the fleet size of AGVs.

The aim of this study is to design the AGV system that can work in the most effective way, to create a safe work environment within the factory while minimizing the cost. The most suitable type of AGV and navigation system for the enterprise will be selected. Then, the appropriate AGV navigation method will be selected. Finally, how many of each AGV type will be calculated. To solve this design and organization problem, a mixed integer model will be constructed. In this model, it will be determined how many of which type of vehicle should be used to meet the need. Finally, the optimal solution will be implemented in a real-life project.

The structure of the paper is organized as follows. In section two, a theoretical background of AGV systems is given together with a review of literature that is performed to identify the problems related to AGV designs in manufacturing system while introducing recent studies. In section three, the fleet sizing of multitype of AGV problem is defined in detailed and the proposed mixed integer model is constructed. In section four, the proposed model is applied with the data of a real manufacturing system in an electronic sector. Finally in section five, concluding remarks and future research directions are given.

2 Automated Guided Vehicles

The expansion of flexible manufacturing systems, the large-scale use of robots and other computer-controlled machines, is a huge demand for the use of automated vehicle systems. Although AGV systems which have a major place among Material Handling Systems, were first designed in the United States, they were used as driverless tractors in Europe for the first time after World War II. The first introduction of automatic vehicle systems was made in 1953 on a line in the warehouse, and since 1959 it has been used extensively in factories and warehouses [4, 5].

2.1 Characteristics

AGVs are unmanned electric vehicles that move materials from one point to another. They move on fixed routes that require infrastructure and need pre-programmed software for operating instructions. An AGV system is a sophisticated material handling system that consists of a driverless vehicle that follows a path (virtual or guided) and is controlled by a computer or microprocessor. The frame, batteries, electrical system, driving unit, steering, precision stop unit, onboard controller, communication unit, safety system, and work platform are typical components of an AGV.

AGV systems are primarily utilized for material distribution in warehouse environments, as well as material moving to and from production areas and storage areas in industrial facilities. Other non-manufacturing uses of AGV systems include, but are not limited to, delivering mail, messages, and goods in offices and meals and laundry in hospitals.

There are four AGV types commonly used. They are unit type, lurking type, fork type and towing type. Standard one-way carrying, unit type AGV, it can place commodities like tray, material rest and work bin on the AGV body to conduct delivery or drag the material skip behind the AGV. This type of AGVs need a platform to take the load. Their carrying capacity is limited. It is locked to the materials with the pin on the lurking type AGV and opens and leaves the pin in the appropriate place. This type of AGV transports the material by pulling. In this way, more than the carrying capacity can be loaded. Transport trolleys are required for the use of this type of AGV. Forklift type AGVs are usually created by modifying existing pallet trucks or forklifts and making them human-independent. This type of AGV can pick up the product and drop it on the ground. Maneuverability is limited. The Towing type AGV can tow a series of trolleys attached one after the other. Their carrying capacity is quite high. It can take a large number of products to the relevant station at one time. However, it cannot be used in layout structures with hard turns.

The technology used by the AGV to find its route is called navigation. Along with the developing technology, various kinds of navigation technologies have started to be used in AGVs. The most preferred navigation technologies are magnetic tape tracking, laser navigation and natural navigation. Magnetic lane navigation technology AGVs find their way by following the lanes laid on the ground. This technology is inexpensive but is not recommended for businesses with frequent layout changes. Magnetic tapes can wear out quickly. It is not recommended to be used in areas open to forklift and pedestrian traffic. In laser navigation technology, reflectors are placed in certain areas in the enterprise. These reflectors allow to reflect the laser beam back. The AGV continuously sends a laser beam and finds its route from the reflected beams. If there are many glossy surfaces and dusty conditions in the business, it becomes difficult for the AGV to find direction. Laser navigation is not recommended for businesses with these conditions. Finally, natural navigation enables AGVs to find their way with the help of Wi-Fi. This system does not require any construction. It is quite easy to install but requires a good network system and is quite expensive.

2.2 Literature Review

AGV systems are frequently reviewed in the literature in recent years. Handling operations play a significant role and has impacted overall performance, efficiency, and effectiveness of final product cost [6]. Reduction in handling operation costs will have a significant impact on overall costs. With the expansion of flexible manufacturing systems, the large-scale use of robots such as AGVs and other computer-controlled machines has become popular. According to Gotting [7] over 20.000 AGVs using in all around the world for different purposes. The reasons for being extremely popular these systems, they significantly reduce labor cost, are much safer than forklifts also increase transportation cost.

Well-designed AGV systems provide cost optimization but developing the AGV system is extremely complex because there are many decisions to make that directly affect system performance. To develop an effective AGV system, many factors have to be taken into account. Several of these factors are number of units to be transported, points in time at which units can be or need to be transported, capacity of the vehicle, speed of the vehicle, costs of the system, layout of the system and guide path, traffic congestion, vehicle dispatching strategies, number and location of pick-up and delivery points [8]. In this study, three main AGV system problems are investigated. These are routing, scheduling, and fleet sizing problems. Alternative solution methods have been applied to these problems in the literature. In this section, the studies and methods that are used examined.

When the literature is reviewed from the routing perspective, the selection of a certain route mainly effects the performance of the system. The longer it takes to transport a job, the fewer the jobs that can be handled within a certain time [9]. Main purpose of the routing problems minimizing the total travel distance of an AGVs. Xing et al. [10] is used novel tabu search algorithm for improve the efficiencies of picking goods of automated guided vehicles. Soylu [11] applied neural network approach to find the shortest tour for a single AGV. Bi-Level Path Planning Algorithm is presented for avoiding the AGV path conflicts by Yuan [12]. Rocak et al. [13] used a dynamic programming method for supervisory control of multiple automated guided vehicles that are traveling within a layout of a given warehouse. The route planning problem to minimize the total transportation time is formulated by Nishi and Maeno [14]. They proposed the petri net decomposition approach to reduce computational complexity.

When the literature is reviewed from the scheduling perspective, it is necessary to prioritize the intersecting paths in systems where more than one AGV is used. At the same time, prioritization of critical components service is also important for the performance of production systems. Zou applied iterated greedy algorithm for minimize the total cost of the system.[15] Xue solved the scheduling problem with reinforcement learning method. Aim of this study was minimize the average job delay and total makespan. [16]. Nishi et al. [17] developed a mixed integer programming model to minimize the total weighted tardiness of the set of jobs related to these tasks. Goli, Tirkolaee and Aydın [18] designed a new cellular manufacturing system which used a set of automated guided vehicles (AGVs) which were responsible for transporting parts between cells. They developed a hybrid genetic algorithm and a whale optimization algorithm. Mousavi et al. [19] developed a mathematical model and integrated with evolutionary algorithms (genetic algorithm particle swarm optimization, and hybrid) to optimize the task scheduling of AGVs with the objectives of minimizing makespan and number of AGVs while considering the AGVs' battery charge.

When the literature is reviewed from the fleet sizing perspective, one of the most important factors in implementing an automation is the cost of that system. The main goal of every business is to maximize the profits from the product sold. The less money spent on the production, transportation, and other activities of the product, the greater the profit will be. Accurate calculation of the fleet size is especially important for AGV systems, as the fleet size will directly affect the initial investment cost, maintenance, and repair costs. If more AGVs are purchased than the need, the cost will increase, if less AGVs are purchased, the need will not be met. In the literature, the studies conducted to determine the fleet size were examined. Pjevcevic et al. [20] simulated a real system and changing the metrics of the AGVs found the fleet size of AGV system. Rahimikelarijani,

Mehrabad and Barzinpour [21] developed a non-linear mathematical model for reduce system penalty cost up by using the multiple load AGV instead of single load AGV. Rjeb, Gayon and Norre [22] concluded the optimal types and number of robots for multiple types by formulating an integer linear model.

As seen from this literature review, initial studies were only focusing on routing of one AGV where the main aim is to decide on the path whereas recent studies are focusing on multiple AGVs where main aim on decide on the path and AGV priority of the intersecting paths. Technology has seen great advance in the last years. By these advances, new types of AGV used in facilities to meet unique needs. It has become common for businesses to use several types of AGVs on the same route. While initial studies have focused on determining the fleet size of one type of AGV, recent studies have focused on determining the fleet size of multiple types of AGVs. Our study will also focus on determining the fleet size of multiple types of AGVs.

3 Problem Definition

The precise selection of choosing the suitable AGV from several models and technological possibilities has a direct influence on the cost and overall performance of the unmanned system to be deployed. The decision problem is the most important aspect influencing the cost and overall performance of the unmanned system to be installed. Vehicle brand and model specs, parameters, and qualities must be digitalized and appraised within a consistent systematic consistency.

Various supplies and pieces are transferred from warehouses by AGVs to assembly lines. For this purpose, several types of AGVs can be used. The production department's operator governs the assembly line's output rate count and line balance. The replenishment cycle of material/parts is determined by the assembly line's production rate, replenishment lot size, AGV speed, and distance between loading point (LP) in the warehouse and drop point (DP) in the assembly lines (See Fig. 1). In this figure as an example 18 assembly lines and two warehouses are used for producing 4 different types of products, i.e., circle, triangle, star and square. According to product type, AGV should get the relevant part from the appropriate warehouse's LP and travel to the allocated assembly line's DP. Several types of products have different DP locations on the assembly line. For example, in Fig. 1, the DP locations of the products shown in circle and square are at the top, whereas for triangles and stars are at the bottom. For each replenishment cycle, the AGV travel time from LP to DP and then back from DP to LP must be less than the part consumption rate determined by production rate and replenishment lot size. The AGV service time is the amount of time it takes to transit from LP to DP and back. The component demand generated by manufacturing lines that prompts the transfer of things to DPs is referred to as "call".

The total time it takes for services to react to calls cannot exceed the AGV available time. Singh [23] below describes this condition. "If Da (aggregate demand) is 1, a single AGV may provide the whole material transfer need." If, on the other hand, Da > 1, it means that a single AGV will be insufficient to provide the overall material transfer need. For example, if 2 Da 3 is used, we know that at least three AGVs will be needed to meet the overall transfer need".

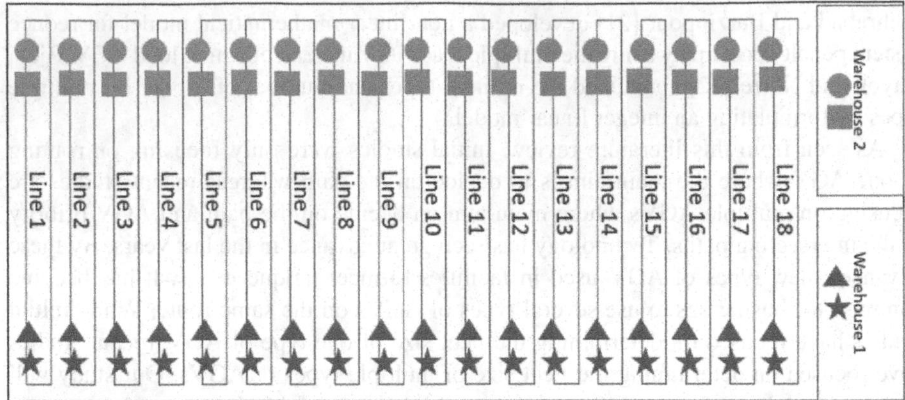

Fig. 1. Layout Plan

The level of inventory is a key factor in the production line side due to work-in-process (WIP). Its value must also be maintained under control to meet the objectives of inventory management policies. The available space at the manufacturing location is highly precious. Because of the efficacy and efficiency concerns of other manufacturing processes, there are severe constraints for the operating area of AGV. As a result, the space designated for LP and DP is limited. The carriage capacity of AGVs, service duration as a function of AGV speed, and needed operating area are all important aspects in decision making. These aspects are fundamental to AGV. Aside from fleet scale, the choice process becomes an issue of technology selection.

Another key factor is deployment of vehicles based on base locations within a specific operation region and delivery duties allocated to be completed. The issue is commonly referred to as fleet allocation and management. A vehicle or fleet of vehicles is allocated several call requests to move things between loading and drop-off sites in a particular time frame. Demand for movements between various locations is frequently imbalanced, implying the need for redistribution of empty vehicles across the network from locations where they have become idle to locations where they can be used [24].

The main aim of the study is to find a proper distribution or usage of AGVs to react to as many calls as feasible. There are 3 main problems to be overcome to design an effective AGV system. First, the appropriate AGV type should be determined, then the guidance system should be determined and finally the feet sizing should be calculated. AGV prices and speeds were determined according to AGV specifications. For each AGV, the operating cost was calculated from costs such as direct, indirect labor and energy. Loading and unloading areas are defined for each material. If the number of AGVs is more than it should be, the amount of space to be allocated increases, the operating cost increases and the unit cost increases. In this case, the products reach the production lines on time, but the cost to the enterprise is quite high. If the number of AGVs is low, the possibility of not being able to grow material increases, the need for operation and space decreases, but there may be a risk of downtime. In this case, it is necessary to find the optimum number of fleets.

3.1 Assumptions

The assumptions of the problem are as follow.

1. Each product is associated with a certain warehouse. Locations of all products' LP are predetermined and same in the warehouse.
2. Each product can be produced in any assembly line. Locations of each product's LP are predetermined and different in the assembly lines.
3. Routes between LP and DP are predetermined.
4. There is a constant number of AGV types used for transportation purposes.
5. AGV speeds are taken as constant. It is assumed that the AGV velocity does not change in the turns. It is assumed that the speed of AGVs is not affected by weight.
6. It is assumed that the AGVs are always fully charged. It was thought that all AGVs were in a working position when there was a request from the lines.
7. The maximum area that can be allocated for the new system is 1000 square meters.
8. AGV prices are assumed to be constant regardless of lot size.

3.2 Mathematical Model

A mixed integer mathematical model is created to seek the feasible and minimal worth of the funding fee by means of AGV technological know-how and model, AGV depend on, and operation duties assigned. For this reason, the mathematical model handles at the same time joint questions of technology selection, fleet sizing and fleet allocation and finds the satisfactory answer. The target function is set to search out minimum value of the sum of initial buying rate, cost of house occupied through loading/unloading areas and operation by using AGVs and maintenance charges. The dispatch and traffic administration software of AGVs are special also the program is capable to manipulate handiest possess company and mannequin AGVs. Only one form AGV can operate in the facility on the customary paths and intersecting routes. Consequently, the visitor's administration software can regulate movement priorities and ready principles.

Notations. The notations used in the model are given below.

Indices
K: Material Type.
s: Size.
r: Available Route.
l: Available Locations.
j: Model of Product.
Parameters
VU: Speed of unit Type AGV.
VF: Speed of Fork Type AGV.
H_k: Annual unit cost of loading area to be occupied by material k.
PU: Purchasing Cost of unit Type AGV.
PF: Purchasing Cost of Fork Type AGV.
SU_k: Total loading-unloading area occupied by U type AGV assigned to transport k.
SF_k: Total loading-unloading area occupied by F type AGV assigned to transport k.
M_{ks}: Transportation capacity of part k of size s.

O_{lsj}: Availability of line l for model j of size s; the availability of the production line is status of the line by means of the production line is status of the line by means of available(open) or unavailable(closed) for the to produce size s of model j. The parameter retrieves binary values of 1 or 0.

P_l: Production rate of line l.

D_{lk}: Distance between loading and unloading station to location l.

OCU: Total operation cost of U type AGV.

OCF: Total operation cost of F type AGV.

M: A Large Number.

FA: Free Area for System.

Decision Variables

NU_k: Quantity of unit type AGV to be purchased to carry material k.

NF_k: Quantity of fork type AGV to be purchased to carry material k.

y: Binary variable. If an AGV purchased y = 1 else y = 0.

Linearization Variables

ZU_k: Linearization variable which is equal to " multiplication of y and NU_k.

ZF_k: Linearization variable which is equal to multiplication of (y–1) and NF_k.

$NU_k > 0$.

$NF_k > 0$.

The Objective Function. In the objective function, it is aimed to minimize the sum of the AGV purchasing cost, operational costs and the annual costs of the area where the materials are placed.

$$\text{MinZ} = \sum{}_k ZU_k PU + ZF_k PF + ySU_k H_k + (1 - y)SF_k H_k + ZU_k OCU + ZF_k OCF \quad (1)$$

Consumption and Speed Calculations. The creation shop floor the place AGVs are going to be applied is busy with pedestrians, operators on duty and different transportation automobiles conveying the miscellaneous accessories, trashes and scraps which are excluded in our assignment. The material replenishment loop of AGV is customarily interrupted by means of these external factors. The delays and waiting instances are inevitable inside the entire process dynamic. The delays and ready occasions and disasters are the fundamental factors which influence efficiency and effectiveness of the unmanned handling procedure.

The term workload (W_{lskj}) is defined to make the compulsion certain in the model. The replenishment frequency of a line can be calculated as production rate divided by transportation capacity (P_l/M_{ks}). The sum of tasks is multiplication of the distances and call frequencies in the material replenishment loop.

$$2O_{ljs} * D_l * \frac{P_l}{M_{ks}} * (1 + \sigma) = W_{lskj} \quad (2)$$

Consumption rate of a material is calculated as division of transportation size by production rate of the line. The fraction is multiplied with sixty to convert unit to minute.

$$60\frac{M_{ks}}{P_l} \quad (3)$$

3.3 Constraints

The speed of the AGV must be at least equal to the line speed so that the production rate of the line is not affected by delays, or the line does not stop. Replenishment time of the material, in other words, travel time of AGV between loading point and drop point and back must be less than consumption rate of the material k.

$$60\frac{M_{ks}}{Pl} \geq 2y\frac{D_{lk}}{VU} + 2(1-y)\frac{D_{lk}}{VF} \tag{4}$$

$$\sum_{l}\sum_{k}\sum_{s}\sum_{j} 2(1+\sigma)\frac{P_1}{M_{ks}}D_{1k}O_{1js} \leq 60ZU_kVU + 60ZF_kVF \tag{5}$$

The inequality (4) is introduced to ensure the total capacity of the procedure will not be violated. The challenge assigned to an AGV is the gap which AGV must journey to carrier that creation line. The complete tasks assigned to a single AGV must not exceed the capacity of AGV. The tasks are strict with the special construction agenda and fixed transportation distances. If the sum of tasks is bigger than AGV potential, the count of AGV required increases by using (1). The period workload (W_{lskj}) is outlined to make the compulsion particular within the model. The replenishment frequency of a line can also calculated as construction fee divided by transportation potential. The sum of tasks is multiplication of the distances and phone frequencies within the fabric replenishment loop. The capacity of an AGV is the total distance can be traveled by AGV in a unit time. The sum of total duties cannot be better than complete distance traveled over by means of an AGV as perform of AGV speed.

$$\sum_{k} \mathrm{SU}_k y \leq \mathrm{FA}\ \mathrm{For}\forall \mathrm{k} \tag{6}$$

$$\sum_{k} \mathrm{SF}_k y \leq \mathrm{FA}\ \mathrm{For}\forall \mathrm{k} \tag{7}$$

The maneuverability and material handling procedure of distinctive AGVs exhibit a discrepancy. Consequently, the requirement of operation field differs according to AGV technological know-how selected for the undertaking. Even though, the objective function of the mannequin tries to cut down the rate of operation house, there occurs a need of a further inflexible limit to make sure the approach is working within allowed operation house. The inequalities (6) and (7) are determined for this motive.

Either-Or Constraints. Either or constraints are as follows.

$$\mathrm{NU}_k \leq \mathrm{My}\ \mathrm{For}\forall \mathrm{k} \tag{8}$$

$$\mathrm{NF}_k \leq M(y-1)\ \mathrm{For}\forall \mathrm{k} \tag{9}$$

This truth forces the choice makers to select just one style of AGV for the service in the field. As a result, binary variable y and big M parameter is said to make either-or determination.

Linearization Constraints. Linearization constraints are as follows.

$$\mathrm{ZU}_k \leq \mathrm{NU}_k\ \mathrm{For}\forall \mathrm{k} \tag{10}$$

$$\mathrm{NU}_k + \mathrm{My} \le \mathrm{ZU}_k + M \text{ For}\forall \mathrm{k} \quad (11)$$

$$\mathrm{ZF}_k \le \mathrm{NF}_k \text{ For}\forall \mathrm{k} \quad (12)$$

$$\mathrm{NF}_k + M\,(y-1) \le \mathrm{ZF}_k + M \text{ For}\forall \mathrm{k} \quad (13)$$

The multiplication of binary variable and decision variable is not allowed in linear solvers. There occurred a need to convert non-linear terms of (y) $\mathrm{NU_k}$ and (1–y) $\mathrm{NF_k}$, thus, $\mathrm{ZU_k}$ and $\mathrm{ZF_k}$ variables are stated. The inequalities (10) and (13) are declared to bound and equalize new variables to the prior non-linear variables. To reduce the complexity of real-time problem and to shorten the time required by optimizer to solve the mathematical model a Mixed-Integer Linear Optimization model is created finally.

4 Case Study and Results

Table 1. Distance of Each Material from LP of Warehouse to DP of Assembly Line

Assembly line number	Components			
	Compressor	Evap	Fan	Gasket
1	180	180	212	250
2	182	182	214	230
3	153	153	185	232
4	155	155	187	212
5	126	126	158	212
6	128	128	160	192
7	100	100	142	192
8	102	102	144	172
9	73	73	105	172
10	75	75	107	152
11	46	46	78	152
12	76	76	60	152
13	96	96	42	112
14	98	98	60	112
15	124	124	62	132
16	126	126	72	132
17	138	138	76	152
18	140	140	88	152

In order to apply the proposed model on a case study, first, relevant data are collected. Some of the data already exists whereas some need to be calculated by applying time study. Second, the model is constructed using these data. Finally, the model is solved and the results are interpreted.

This case study is performed in an electronics manufacturing company located in Turkey with eighteen assembly lines dedicated to one product. The product is made of 4 different components. These components are fan, gasket, EVAP and compressor. There are ten models of the product and fifteen different sizes of each component. The main reason required the usage of AGVs is that these components are extremely sensitive parts in terms of quality and correction of any damage suffered during the transportation process is very costly. EVAP and compressors are in warehouse 1 and Fans and gaskets are located in warehouse 2. For each part, there are 18 LP in each warehouse. When a call request occurred in any line, an AGV will take the parts pallet from the related LP of the warehouse, transport it to the related assembly line and unload the parts pallets at the related DP of the assembly line. Requests can come from any line at any time. The AGV is programmed to respond to the first incoming request.

Product demand from the lines will be created depending on the production speed of each product. The product call of the lines will be the same as the product consumption rate. This speed is calculated by Eq. (3). When the material demand comes, the appropriate AGV will transport the product using the previously determined routes. The distance of the materials to the lines is as in the table below.

There are several types of AGV for the answer this need. It is particularly important to choose the right type of AGV for a system to work properly. AGV type can be selected depending on the type of material to be transported, the surface to be moved, the adequacy of the infrastructure, and the effect of pedestrian traffic. However, in this study, by looking at the layout structure within the company, it was determined that the two most suitable types of AGV were forklift type and lurking type AGVs. While some of the 4 materials to be transported in the company are transported on pallets, the other part is transported in boxes of different sizes. While it is appropriate to use fork type AGV for palletized materials, lurking type AGV is suitable for transporting more materials due to the heavy weight of the materials. Price offers from 4 different companies are considered for this study. AGV speeds that will not pose a risk in terms of occupational health have been determined. While the lurking type AGV can reach a maximum speed of 37 m/min, the fork type AGV can go up to 58 m/min. For several types of AGVs, the number of products it can carry at one time also differs. Fork type AGVs have higher carrying capacities while lurking type AGVs have lower carrying capacities. Carrying capacity information was obtained from the supplier company. In addition, each product has dimensions that vary according to the size of the cabinet in which it is mounted. This affects the number of products that the AGV can overflow at once, depending on the size of that product. Unit type AGV's selling price is $11000 while forklift type AGV is $88000. Considering the direct, indirect, energy and consumable costs of AGVs, it is calculated that the operating cost of the lurking type AGV is around $1320, while the fork type AGV is at the level of $5950 (Table 1).

The AGV is considered to work perfectly in the system. In this case, delays will not be considered. As the AGV operates in an area open to pedestrian traffic, delays are quite possible. To calculate this delay, a partial time study was made. The factor of delay was calculated by time study (see Table 2).

To bring a precise estimation for the determination of the safety factor, we measured the delivery times of an AGV loop (transportation of compressor to production location 1).

Table 2. Partial Time Study

Sample number	Observed time	Sample number	Observed time
1	18,1	13	20,3
2	17,6	14	18,8
3	18,8	15	16,8
4	14,2	16	13,8
5	21,3	17	17,4
6	19,9	18	13
7	13,3	19	11,5
8	13	20	11,7
9	11	21	17,5
10	13,8	22	18,1
11	13	23	13,8
12	20,9	24	13,7

The results of this partial time study shows that the mean of all times measured is 15.9 min whereas the standard deviation of the sample is 3.16. The ratio of sample standard deviation to sample mean ($s/\overline{x}$), Coefficient of Variation (CV), is 19.86. The value of 0.1986 is assigned to factor σ to calculate workload parameter given in Eq. 2.

Annual unit cost of operation calculated for compressor \$23.4, EVAP \$23.4, fan \$25, gasket \$12. The total operation area occupied by lurking type AGV assigned to transfer material compressor 120 m2, EVAP 150 m2, fan 100 m2, gasket 80 m2. The total operation area occupied by forklift type AGV assigned to transfer material compressor 80 m2, EVAP 90 m2, fan 100 m2, gasket 50 m2.

This case study is solved by mixed integer programming model given in Sect. 3. With the help of this model, we aim to find a minimum cost of AGV transportation system. The fleet sizing situation is solved by means of picking out minimal number of AGVs. The result of the mathematical model is as follows; the minimum cost is found to be \$ 194.578, total number of AGVs used in this solution is 15, of which 0 is forklift type and 15 is lurking type AGV, and among forklift type AGVs, model shows there is no need for using fork type AGV for this system. Among lurking type AGVs, 4 AGVs are for transporting compressor, 2 AGVs are for transporting EVAP,5 AGVs are for transporting fan, 4 AGVs are for transporting gasket.

5 Conclusions

AGVs are frequently used to transport materials. AGV ensures the traceability of the transportation systems, reduces the risk of occupational accidents, and increases efficiency. A professionally designed AGV system reduces labor costs and prevents products from being damaged. To provide all these advantages, it is important to design the AGV system correctly. It is necessary to select the AGV type specific to the project and to calculate the optimum fleet size.

There are several studies in literature focusing on the fleet size of AGV. However, it has been seen that most of these studies only dealt with the fleet size problem of a single type of AGV although the use of several types of AGVs operating on the same route in enterprises has become popular. Due to coming into prominence of this subject in recent years, we considered multiple types of AGV while determining the fleet size for transporting varied materials in this study. For this purpose, a mixed integer programming model was developed for calculating the optimum fleet size of AGV system. The model was applied with the data of a real manufacturing system in an electronic sector for transporting the materials from the warehouses to the production lines by considering all the assumptions mentioned in Sect. 3.1. With the help of the model, quantity of each type of AGV should be used was calculated. Thus, the most efficient system was designed with optimum cost.

For future studies, this study a good starting point for discussion and further research. It can serve as a resource for defining the optimum fleet size for multiple types of AGVs. Although the proposed has been developed with some assumptions, some of these assumptions can be relaxed in future studies such as line assignment of AGVs, and alternative routes. In the real manufacturing systems, there could be some lines that allocated for producing a certain product so some of the AGVs could be assign predetermined lines, and the routes for the AGVs can have alternatives. Another future direction is related to the cost. It has been seen in literature review, AGV system cost not only depends on the fleet size, but also defining optimum route and scheduling have a significant impact on the system cost. For this reason, routing and scheduling constraints can also add the model to reduce system cost. On the other hand, today AGV systems have started to give way to recent technology where material handling equipment can move without being directly controlled by an operator on a not predetermined path such as Autonomous Mobile Robot (AMR) systems. These systems have an intelligent algorithm that automatically calculates the shortest distance between two destinations. For this reason, in future studies, this study can be a source for the optimization of the latest technology AMR systems by integrating the scheduling problems and battery consumption optimization problems into the current model. The proposed model can be also modified for determining the fleet size of AMR system to determining the optimum fleet size.

References

1. Hammond, K.J.: A Model of Case-based Planning, AAAI. CHEF, pp. 267–271 (1986)
2. Rahaman, M.A., Jasim, M., Ali, M.H., Hasanuzzaman, M.: Computer vision based bengali sign words recognition using contour analysis. In: 18th International Conference on Computer and Information Technology (ICCIT), pp. 335–340. IEEE, Bangladesh (2015)
3. Arifin, R., Egbelu, P.J.: Determination of vehicle requirements in automated guided vehicle systems: a statistical approach. Prod. Plan. Control **11**(3), 258–270 (2000)
4. Kaspi, M., Kesselman, U., Tanchoco, J.M.A.: Optimal solution for the flow path design problem of a balanced unidirectional AGV system. Int. J. Prod. Res. **40**(2), 389–401 (2002)
5. Jaiganesh, V., Kumar, J.D., Girijadevi, J.: Automated guided vehicle with robotic logistics system. Proc. Eng. **97**, 2011–2021 (2014)
6. Shaik, M.N., Abdul-Kader, W.: Transportation in reverse logistics enterprise: a comprehensive performance measurement methodology. Prod. Plan. Control **24**(6), 495–510 (2013)
7. Prusak, A., Bemshausen, J., Roth, H., Warburg, J., Hille, C., Gotting, H.H., Neugebauer, T.: Applications of automated guided vehicle (AGV) and industry robots with PMD-camera. In: Proceedings of the International Conference on Robotics and Applications, Wurzburg, pp. 29–31 (2007)
8. Vis, I.F.: Survey of research in the design and control of automated guided vehicle systems. Eur. J. Oper. Res. **170**(3), 677–709 (2006)
9. Fazlollahtabar, H., Saidi-Mehrabad, M.: Methodologies to optimize automated guided vehicle scheduling and routing problems: a review study. J. Intell. Rob. Syst. **77**(3), 525–545 (2015)
10. Xing, L., Liu, Y., Li, H., Wu, C.C., Lin, W.C., Chen, X.: A novel tabu search algorithm for multi-AGV routing problem. Mathematics **8**(2), 279 (2020)
11. Soylu, M., Özdemirel, N.E., Kayaligil, S.: A self-organizing neural network approach for the single AGV routing problem. Eur. J. Oper. Res. **121**(1), 124–137 (2000)
12. Yuan, Z., Yang, Z., Lv, L., Shi, Y.: A bi-level path planning algorithm for multi-AGV routing problem. Electronics **9**(9), 1351 (2020)
13. Smolic-Rocak, N., Bogdan, S., Kovacic, Z., Petrovic, T.: Time windows based dynamic routing in multi-AGV systems. IEEE Trans. Autom. Sci. Eng. **7**(1), 151–155 (2009)
14. Nishi, T., Maeno, R.: Petri net decomposition approach to optimization of route planning problems for AGV systems. IEEE Trans. Autom. Sci. Eng. **7**(3), 523–537 (2010)
15. Zou, W.Q., Pan, Q.K., Wang, L.: An effective multi-objective evolutionary algorithm for solving the AGV scheduling problem with pickup and delivery. Knowl.-Based Syst. **218**, 106881 (2021)
16. Xue, T., Zeng, P., Yu, H.: A reinforcement learning method for multi-AGV scheduling in manufacturing. In: IEEE International Conference on Industrial Technology (ICIT), France, pp. 1557–1561 (2018)
17. Nishi, T., Hiranaka, Y., Grossmann, I.E.: A bilevel decomposition algorithm for simultaneous production scheduling and conflict-free routing for automated guided vehicles. Comput. Oper. Res. **38**, 876–888 (2011)
18. Goli, A., Tirkolaee, E.B., Aydın, N.S.: Fuzzy integrated cell formation and production scheduling considering automated guided vehicles and human factors. IEEE Trans. Fuzzy Syst. **29**(12), 3686–3695 (2021)
19. Mousavi, M., Yap, H.J., Musa, S.N., Tahriri, F., Md Dawal, S.Z.: Multi-objective AGV scheduling in an FMS using a hybrid of genetic algorithm and particle swarm optimization. PloS one **12**(3) (2017)
20. Pjevcevic, D., Nikolic, M., Vidic, N., Vukadinovic, K.: Data envelopment analysis of AGV fleet sizing at a port container terminal. Int. J. Prod. Res. **55**(14), 4021–4034 (2017)

21. Rahimikelarijani, B., Saidi-Mehrabad, M., Barzinpour, F.: A mathematical model for multiple-load AGVs in Tandem layout. J. Optim. Ind. Eng. **13**(1), 67–80 (2020)
22. Rjeb, A., Gayon, J.P., Norre, S.: Sizing of a homogeneous fleet of robots in a logistics warehouse. In: 17th IFAC Symposium on Information Control Problems in Manufacturing Hungary
23. López, J., Zalama, E., Gómez-García-Bermejo, J.: A simulation and control framework for AGV based transport systems. Simul. Model. Pract. Theory **116** (2022)
24. Gaskins, R.J., Tanchoco, J.M.: Flow path design for automated guided vehicle systems. Int. J. Prod. Res. **25**(5), 667–676 (1987)

A Multi-objective Optimization Model for Sustainable-Robust Aggregate Production Planning Problem

Erfan Babaee Tirkolaee[1](✉), Nadi Serhan Aydın[1], Iraj Mahdavi[2], and Büşra Çelik[1]

[1] Department of Industrial Engineering, Istinye University, Istanbul 34396, Turkey
erfan.babaee@istinye.edu.tr

[2] Department of Industrial Engineering, Mazandaran University of Science and Technology, Babol, Iran

Abstract. Aggregate production planning (APP) is known as a demand-driven production planning activity using aggregate plans for manufacturing processes. It tries to match supply and demand within a medium-term time horizon. In this work, a sustainable-robust APP problem is modeled through a multi-objective mixed-integer linear programming (MOMILP) model. The objective functions are formulated in a way to simultaneously minimize total cost, minimize total environmental impacts and maximize service level. Then, robust optimization (RO) technique is used to treat the demand uncertainty within the problem. To treat the multi-objectiveness and find the optimal solution, an improved multi-choice goal programing (IMCGP) method is introduced as an extension to the classical goal programming approach (GP). Next, several numerical examples are generated in different scales to assess the validity and applicability of the suggested methodology under deterministic as well as uncertain conditions. Eventually, a set of sensitivity analyses are implemented to assess the behavior of objective functions against real-world uncertainty in model parameters. It is demonstrated that the proposed methodology is capable of modeling, solving and analyzing the sustainable-robust APP problem efficiently. As one of the main findings, although the 1st and 2nd objective functions are sensitive to conservatism level, the 3rd objective function remains neutral.

Keywords: Sustainable aggregate production planning · Service level · Robust optimization · Improved multi-choice goal programing · Sensitivity analysis

1 Introduction

Aggregate production planning (APP) is a production planning activity that is at the center of all production planning operations and tries to match supply and demand in a medium-term planning period of 3 to 11 months. In general, standard APP aims to determine various aspects of production activities, such as production levels, inventory amount, workforce levels, and so on, in order to achieve minimum cost or maximum profit.

A. Mirzazadeh et al. (Eds.): SEMIT 2022, CCIS 1808, pp. 18–34, 2023.
https://doi.org/10.1007/978-3-031-40395-8_2

An accurate and comprehensive APP is very important for organizations carrying out production activities to maintain their presence in the market. Most traditional APP models include only economic purposes and do not consider sustainability criteria. However, in today's world, it is not enough to only include economic dimensions in order to stay competitive in the market. Environmental factors like minimizing environmental damage and societal metrics like employee well-being and customer satisfaction should be included in APP models. In addition, since there are uncertainties and variations in production parameters in the real-world industrial environment, these should also be taken into account in APP models for a more realistic planning.

Therefore, unlike classic APP models, this research aims to formulate a sustainable-robust APP problem that considers sustainability criteria and uncertainty of the parameters in the real world, using a multi-objective mixed integer linear programming (MOMILP) model. This model comprises sustainability criteria in the objective function, by aiming to minimize the total environmental impact and maximize the service level as well as minimize the total cost. To tackle the demand uncertainty, robust optimization (RO) technique is implemented in the model. Furthermore, an improved multiple choice goal programming (IMCGP) technique is used to cope with the multi-objectiveness of the model. Finally, a few numerical examples are employed in the model for testing efficacy of the proposed methodology under both deterministic and uncertain conditions. Besides, a series of sensitivity analyses are implemented to examine the behavior of objective functions against uncertainty in the model parameters.

In conclusion, given the long-term contribution of the sustainability criterion to both economy, environment, and society and the fluctuations and uncertainties in production parameters in the real-world industrial environment, the contributions that we aim to make with our study are given below:

- Offering a novel sustainable APP model to address economic, environmental, and social aspects simultaneously,
- Applying robust optimization technique to deal with demand uncertainty,
- Implementing an improved multi-choice goal programing (IMCGP) method to tackle the tri-objectiveness of the model,
- Performing a set of sensitivity analyses to study the reflection of the objective functions against real-world uncertainty.

According to the structure of the remaining sections, Sect. 2 surveys the most relevant studies in the literature. The suggested problem and model are represented in Sect. 3. Moreover, the robust counterpart model is also elaborated in this section. Section 4 presents the proposed solution method; i.e., IMCGP. The computational results are illustrated in Sect. 5, and eventually, concluding notes and future research opportunities are provided in Sect. 6.

2 Related Studies

The majority of research works on aggregate production planning (APP) have focused on economic objectives rather than sustainability criteria as part of their modeling approach. To fill this gap, Türkay et al. [6] offered a mathematical APP model to cover the three widely accepted aspects of sustainability in the literature: environmental, social, and economic criteria. They used a real-life case study to analyze the outcomes of their model. Rasmi et al. [9] suggested an MOMILP model to formulate APP problem. Unlike traditional APP models, which just evaluate economic factors in a single objective function, the model includes economic, social, environmental, and cultural aspects. They used an illustrative example to demonstrate the model's effectiveness. Hahn and Brandenburg [3] introduced a hierarchical decision-making technique that synthesizes a deterministic linear programming (LP) model and an aggregate stochastic queuing network formulation to offer sufficient decision support for APP in the process industry that contains complex manufacturing operations. They concentrated on carbon emissions, sustainable operation planning, and campaign planning integrated with the operational level. In a case study problem from the chemical industry, they illustrated their approach.

Some other studies addressed energy as part of the production planning process due to the importance of energy as a crucial input for production. Modarres and Izadpanahi [10] proposed an APP model that considers demand, production capacity and energy planning at the same time, with three objective functions to minimize the total cost of the production system. They used the robust optimization method to develop robust solutions - which outperform deterministic solutions - in an environment of uncertainty in product demand due to the uncertainties that may appear in the input data. The study also illustrated the applicability of the proposed method by using a real-life example. On the other hand, Chaturvedi [11] developed an insight-based graphical approach for multi-installation APP that can afford the capital cost and minimize the energy consumption of the production facilities in order to make energy-efficient production planning that incorporates the cost of capital. They tested their approach on illustrative examples and concluded that a considerable energy reduction could be attained.

Furthermore, according to uncertainties and fluctuations in production parameters in a real-world industrial environment, it is also inescapable to take into consideration the effect of uncertainty in APP models. In this regard, for solving a multi-period multi-product multi-site APP problem in a green supply chain with demand uncertainty, a stochastic programming approach was developed by Mirzapour Al-e hashem et al. [4]. They offered a mixed-integer nonlinear programming (MINLP) model to consider waste and greenhouse gas emissions and offered a numerical example to prove the model's validity. Khalili-Damghani and Shahrokh [8] utilized MOMILP and fuzzy sets to create a novel multi-product, multi-period, multi-objective APP model. To treat the model's multi-objectiveness, they utilized a fuzzy goal programming (GP) method and implemented their model in a real-world industrial case study. For APP in a supply chain with demand uncertainty, Gholamian et al. [5] proposed a multi-objective mixed-integer nonlinear programming (MOMINLP) with contradictory objective functions. To treat the model, they employed a fuzzy multi-objective optimization approach. A robust optimization approach was designed by Entezaminia et al. [12] to treat a multi-site, multi- period, multi-product APP problem. They looked at prospective collection and recycling facilities in a green supply chain and, similarly, demonstrated the applicability of the suggested model in a case study. Goli et al. [1] applied an RO approach to an MOMILP model to address demand uncertainty in the APP problem. To control the multi-objectiveness, the GP method was employed. The authors designed two meta-heuristic solution approaches to generate Pareto solutions. Tirkolaee et al. [7] introduced a mixed-integer linear programming (MILP) model to examine a novel fuzzy multi-objective multi-period APP problem under seasonal demand uncertainty, with the major aim of simultaneously minimizing overall cost and maximizing customers' satisfaction level. They utilized the weighted goal programming (WGP) technique to show the validity of their suggested model using CPLEX solver. Darvishi et al. [2] studied supplier selection, logistics decisions, and multi-site APP in the textile industry. They presented an MINLP model under a hybrid fuzzy-stochastic environment and employed a robust two-stage stochastic programming technique to define the optimal policy under a complex uncertainty. Recently, Aydin and Tirkolaee [16] conducted a comprehensive literature survey on APP problems in terms of developed models and solution methods. They also discussed the importance of sustainability along with circularity to be addressed through digitalization. Tirkolaee et al. [17] developed a hybrid bi-objective MINLP formulation relying on continuous-time Markov chain to deal with the inventory decision process. The objectives were to minimize the total cost and total environmental pollution simultaneously. Several illustrative examples were adapted from the literature to analyze the performance of the suggested methodology. Table 1 summarizes the literature review, sorted by year.

According to the surveyed study and Table 1, it is clear that there are still open doors in the literature to address sustainable development along with uncertainty-handling issues in the problem. Accordingly, this work tries to deal with these two important factors in the APP through developing a sustainable-robust methodology.

3 Model Development

The proposed APP is formulated in this section, where three main objectives in each company are as follows:

- Total cost minimization,
- Total environmental impacts minimization,
- Service level maximization.

Finally, the main assumptions and limitations of APP are listed in the following:

- Normal and overtime working time of the workforce should not violate their maximum allowable values,
- Number of the workforce should be limited to its minimum and maximum number in each period,
- Necessary hours for working normally and overtime must be fulfilled in each period,
- Amount of outsourced production should not surpass its maximum allowable value in each period,
- There is a limit on the hiring capacity of the workforce in each period,
- Number of the unemployed workforce must be denoted in each period,
- There are no inventory on-hand and shortage of products at the end of the planning horizon,
- Shortage of final products is permitted,
- Inventory level should be balanced in each period,

Table 1. Comparison of the related works.

Reference	Year	MCDM		Model Type				Uncertainty				Solution				Extra Features				
		m1	m2	t1	t2	t3	t4	u1	u2	u3	u4	s1	s2	s3	s4	e1	e2	e3	e4	e5
Mirzapour Al-e hashem et al. [15]	2013			+						+					+	+	+	+	+	
Khalili-Damghani and Shahrokh [22]	2014		+	+				+								+	+		+	
Türkay et al. [20]	2016			+								+							+	+
Modarres and Izadpanahi [25]	2016		+		+				+										+	+
Gholamian et al. [16]	2016	+	+	+				+							+				+	
Chaturvedi [26]	2017				+									+						+
Entezaminia et al. [27]	2017			+					+	+					+	+	+	+	+	
Hahn and Brandenburg [5]	2018				+					+				+					+	+
Rasmi et al. [24]	2019		+	+										+						+
Goli et al. [1]	2019		+	+					+			+	+							
Tirkolaee et al. [21]	2019		+	+				+									+			
Darvishi et al. [3]	2020						+	+	+			+						+		
Tirkolaee et al. [32]	2022		+	+						+		+				+			+	+
Current Study	2022		+	+					+			+				+	+		+	+

MCDM: m1: MADM, m2: MODM; **Model Type:** t1: MILP, t2: Other Linear, t3: MINLP, t4: Other Nonlinear; **Uncertainty:** u1: Fuzzy/Possibilistic, u2: Robust Optimization, u3: Probabilistic/Stochastic, u4: No Uncertainty; **Solution:** s1: Exact Solution/Solver, s2: Metaheuristic, s3: Heuristic, s4: No Specific Method; **Extra Features:** e1: Multi-product, e2: Multi-period, e3: Multi-site, e4: Case study/Real life example/Numerical example, e5: Sustainability.

- GHG emissions are evaluated at in-house production and subcontractor levels,
- Number of the existing workforce should be balanced in each period.

Tables 2 and 3 illustrate the notations of the developed mathematical model.

Table 2. Indices, sets and parameters.

Notation	Explanation
t	Index of time periods ($t = 1, 2, \ldots, T$)
p	Index of products ($p = 1, 2, \ldots, P$)
c	Index of subcontractors ($c = 1, 2, \ldots, C$)
D_{pt}	Demand of pth product in t^{th} period
CI_{pt}	Internal production cost of of each unit of pth product in t^{th} period
CA_{pct}	Production cost of each unit of pth product by c^{th} subcontractor in t^{th} period
CB_t	Cost per man-hour of the workforce to work normally in t^{th} period
CC_t	Cost per man-hour of the workforce to work overtime in t^{th} period
CD_t	Employment cost of the workforce in t^{th} period
CE_t	Unemployment cost per man-hour of the workforce in t^{th} period
CF_{pt}	Shortage cost of each unit of pth product in t^{th} period
CG_{pt}	Holding cost of each unit of pth product in t^{th} period
R_t	Normal capacity (hours) per worker in t^{th} period
O_t	Overtime capacity (hours) per worker in t^{th} period
WI	Initial number of workers
WL	Minimum number of workers
WU	Maximum number of workers
RM_p	Required man-hour of the worker to produce each unit of pth product
MP_{pt}	Maximum amount of production of pth product permitted to be outsourced in t^{th} period
I_{p0}	Initial inventory amount of pth product at the beginning of the planning horizon
PC_p	Warehouse capacity for p^{th} product in a time period
GA_p	GHG emission for manufacturing a unit of pth product
GH_{pc}	GHG emission for manufacturing a unit of pth product by c^{th} subcontractor
GB_p	GHG emission per p^{th} product held in the inventory in a time period

The developed model is shown as follows:

$$\text{minimize} TC = \sum\nolimits_{p=1}^{P} \sum\nolimits_{t=1}^{T} CI_{pt}(YA_{pt} + YB_{pt}) \tag{1}$$

$$+\sum\nolimits_{p-1}^{P} \sum\nolimits_{c=1}^{C} \sum\nolimits_{t=1}^{T} CA_{pct} YC_{pct} \tag{2}$$

Table 3. Variables of the model.

Notation	Explanation
x_{pt}	Amount of pth product delivered to customers in t^{th} period
YA_{pt}	Amount of the normal manufacturing of pth product in t^{th} period
YB_{pt}	Amount of the overtime manufacturing of pth product in t^{th} period
YC_{pct}	Amount of the manufacturing of pth product outsourced to c^{th} subcontractor in t^{th} period
I_{pt}	Remaining inventory of pth product at the end of tth period
BA_{pt}	Shortage of pth product at the end of tth period
MN_t	Man-hours of the workforce working normally in t^{th} period
MO_t	Man-hours of the workforce working overtime in t^{th} period
NN_t	Number of the workforce working normally in t^{th} period
NO_t	Number of the workforce working overtime in t^{th} period
HM_t	Amount of the employed man-hours of workforce in t^{th} period
HN_t	Number of the employed workforce in t^{th} period
FM_t	Amount of the unemployed man-hours of workforce in t^{th} period
FN_t	Number of the unemployed workforce in t^{th} period
VA_{pt}	Amount of pth product directly delivered to customers in t^{th} period
VB_{pt}	Amount of pth product delivered to customers in t^{th} period to fulfill previous shortages
VC_{pt}	Amount of the covered demand for p^{th} product in t^{th} period, which is fulfilled by productions in that period
VD_{pt}	Amount of the covered demand for p^{th} product in t^{th} period, which is fulfilled by inventory on-hand

$$+\sum_{t=1}^{T} CB_t MN_t \tag{3}$$

$$+\sum\nolimits_{t=1}^{T} CC_t MO_t \tag{4}$$

$$+\sum\nolimits_{p=1}^{P}\sum\nolimits_{t=1}^{T} CG_{pt} I_{pt} \tag{5}$$

$$+\sum\nolimits_{p=1}^{P}\sum\nolimits_{t=1}^{T} CF_{pt} BA_{pt} \tag{6}$$

$$+\sum\nolimits_{t=1}^{T} CD_t HM_t \tag{7}$$

$$+\sum_{t=1}^{T} CE_t FM_t \tag{8}$$

$$\text{minimize}GE = \sum_{p=1}^{P}\sum_{t=1}^{T}\left(GB_pI_{pt} + GA_p(YA_{pt} + YB_{pt}) + \sum_{c=1}^{C}GH_{pc}YC_{pct}\right) \tag{9}$$

$$\text{maximize}SL = \sum_{t=1}^{T}\sum_{p=1}^{P}\frac{D_{pt} - BA_{pt}}{D_{pt}} \tag{10}$$

Subject to :

$$I_{p,t-1} + (YA_{pt} + YB_{pt} + \sum_{c=1}^{C} YC_{pct}) - x_{pt} - BA_{p,t-1} = I_{pt} - BA_{pt} \quad \forall t, p, \tag{11}$$

$$NN_{t-1} + HN_t - FN_t = NN_t \ \forall t, \tag{12}$$

$$\sum_{p=1}^{P} YA_{pt} \times RM_p \leq MN_t \ \forall t, \tag{13}$$

$$\sum_{p=1}^{P} YB_{pt} \times RM_p \leq MO_t \ \forall t, \tag{14}$$

$$WL \leq NN_t \leq WU \ \forall t, \tag{15}$$

$$I_{pt} \leq PC_p \ \forall p, t, \tag{16}$$

$$MN_t \leq R_tNN_t \ \forall t, \tag{17}$$

$$MO_t \leq O_tNO_t \ \forall t, \tag{18}$$

$$\sum_{c=1}^{C} YC_{pct} \leq MP_{pt} \ \forall p, t, \tag{19}$$

$$HM_t \leq HN_t(O_t + R_t) \ \forall t, \tag{20}$$

$$FM_t \leq FN_t(O_t + R_t) \ \forall t, \tag{21}$$

$$\sum_{t=1}^{T} x_{pt} = \sum_{t=1}^{T} D_{pt} \ \forall p, \tag{22}$$

$$VA_{pt} + VB_{pt} = x_{pt} \ \forall p, t, \tag{23}$$

$$VC_{pt} + VD_{pt} = x_{pt} \ \forall p, t, \tag{24}$$

$$VD_{pt} \leq I_{p,t-1} \ \forall p, t, \tag{25}$$

$$VB_{pt} \leq BA_{p,t-1} \; \forall p, t, \tag{26}$$

$$VC_{pt} \leq YA_{pt} + YB_{pt} + \sum_{c=1}^{C} YC_{pct} \; \forall p, t, \tag{27}$$

$$I_{pT} = 0 \; \forall p, \tag{28}$$

$$BA_{pT} = 0 \; \forall p, \tag{29}$$

$$\begin{gathered} x_{pt}, YA_{pt}, YB_{pt}, YC_{pct}, I_{pt}, BA_{pt}, MN_t, MO_t, HM_t, FM_t, VA_{pt}, VB_{pt}, \\ VC_{pt}, VD_{pt} \geq 0; NN_t, NO_t, HN_t, FN_t \in \mathbf{Z}^+ \\ \forall p, t, c. \end{gathered} \tag{30}$$

Minimize the total cost including 8 different terms is defined as the 1st objective function. Formula (1) denotes the in-house production costs. Formula (2) expresses the outsourcing costs. The costs for working normally are given in Formula (3). Formula (4) is in tune with the overtime costs. Formulas (5) and (6) represent the holding costs of raw material and final product, and shortage costs, respectively. Formulas (7) and (8) stand for employment and unemployment costs respectively. The 2nd objective function is shown by Eq. (9) including the minimization of total GHG emission. Equation (10) states the third objective maximizing the service level. Equation (11) stands for the balance of inventory of final the product in each period. Equation (12) expresses the balance of the workforce. Constraints (13) and (14) strike a balance between the required man-hour based on the production amount. Constraint (15) shows the lowerbound and upperbound of the required number of workforce, respectively. Constraint (16) expresses the warehouse capacity limitations of products. Constraints (17) and (18) display the maximum hours required for the workforce to work normally and overtime, respectively. Constraint (19) ensures that the outsourcing amount does not violate the maximum pre-defined and allowed amount. Constraint (20) shows the capacity limitation of the employed workforce in man-hours. Similarly, Constraint (21) indicates the maximum allowed number of unemployed workforce. Equation (22) expresses that the total amount of products sent to the customers should be equal to the overall demand over the whole period. Equation (23) displays the amount of products received from the customers' point of view considering the demand and shortages that happened in previous periods. Equation (24) calculates the amount of products sent from the company's point of view considering the inventory and production amount at each period. Constraint (25) ensures that the amount of products from inventory sent to the customers must not violate the inventory on-hand in the beginning of a specific period. Constraint (26) guarantees that the amount of products sent to the customers in order to cover a must should not violate that shortage amount in the beginning of a specific period. Constraint (27) represents that the amount of products sent to the customers must not surpass the total production capacity of in-house manufacturing and outsourcing. Equations (28) and (29) ensure that no inventory and shortage are allowed in the end of the planning. Constraint (30) defines the types of the variables.

3.1 Robust Counterpart Model

Here, RO technique is employed to treat the uncertainty of supply and demand parameters. Robust optimization seeks for feasible near-optimal solutions (with a high probability). It guarantees the feasibility of solutions by slightly ignoring the optimal objective function value under uncertain conditions [1]. In this research, the demand parameter (D_{pt}) is supposed to be uncertain and change within given symmetric intervals. By implementing the robust optimization approach, the optimal solution incurs the robustness cost considering its feasibility. On the other hand, the output results are more reliable and decision-makers can deal with uncertainty even under the worst case. Our applied robust optimization method is based on the linear formulation offered by Bertsimas and Sim [13].

To do so, $\tilde{D}_{pt}$ as the uncertain supply capacity of suppliers fluctuates in the interval $\left[\overline{D}_{pt} - \widehat{D}_{pt}, \overline{D}_{pt} + \widehat{D}_{pt}\right]$, where $\overline{D}_{pt}$ and $\widehat{D}_{pt}$ are the nominal and deviation values of this parameter. Here, $\widehat{D}_{pt}$ is calculated by $\widehat{D}_{pt} = \rho\overline{D}_{pt}$, where ρ stands for the uncertainty level. In this regard, Eq. (22) and causes uncertainty in the proposed model. Moreover, Γ_p stands for the conservatism levels (budgets of uncertainty) of Eq. (22). These parameters provide a balance between the solution feasibility and the model robustness which take value in accordance with the decision-makers' attitudes. Here, they are defined as $\Gamma_p \in [0, 1]$ [14].

$$\sum_{t=1}^{T} \overline{D}_{pt} - \Gamma_p \sum_{t=1}^{T} \hat{D}_{pt} \leq \sum_{t-1}^{T} x_{pt} \leq \sum_{t=1}^{T} \overline{D}_{pt} + \Gamma_p \sum_{t=1}^{T} \hat{D}_{pt} \; \forall p. \tag{31}$$

Consequently, the robust counterpart model is given as follows in which Constraints (11)–(21), (23)–(30) and (31) are the constraints.

4 Improved Multi-Choice Goal Programming

As a recently-enhanced variant of GP technique, IMCGP was offered by Jadidi et al. [15]. To summarize the main advantages of IMCGP, it considers a priority function and a goal interval in place of an individual goal because in some cases, the objective function may debase the expected or ideal amount, a penalty cost is then applied to the model. This important characteristic has not been addressed by former GP methods [15]. Consequently, the IMCGP approach is employed to solve our suggested MOMILP model. With regard to the IMCGP technique and to build up a final single-objective MILP model, Eq. (32) is given as the single objective function of the model. Furthermore, Constraints (33)–(38) are embedded into the model as new constraints while maintaining Constraints (11)–(21), (23)–(30) and (31):

$$\text{maximize} Z_{IMCGP} = \sum_{k=1}^{3} \left(w_k^{\alpha} \alpha_k - w_k^{\beta} \beta_k \right) \tag{32}$$

Subject to:

$$Z_k = \alpha_k QA_{k,min} + (1 - \alpha_k) QA_{k,max} + \beta_k (QB_k^- - QA_{k,max}) (k = 1, 2), \tag{33}$$

$$Z_k = \alpha_k QB_k^+ + (1-\alpha_k)QA_{k,min} + \beta_k(QB_k^- - QA_{k,min}(k=3), \quad (34)$$

$$\alpha_k \le y_k < 1 + \alpha_k(\mathrm{k} = 1, 2, 3), \quad (35)$$

$$\beta_k + y_k \le 1(\mathrm{k} = 1, 2, 3), \quad (36)$$

$$0 \le \alpha_k, \beta_k \le 1(\mathrm{k} = 1, 2, 3), \quad (37)$$

$$y_k \in \{0, 1\}(\mathrm{k} = 1, 2, 3), \quad (38)$$

Constraints (11)–(21), (23)–(30) and (31),
where α_k stands for a positive factor taking value between 0 and 1; i.e., the normalized distance of kth objective function from QB_k^+. Furthermore, QB_k^+ and QB_k^- show the ideal and unideal values of kth objective function.

Moreover, $[QA_{k,\min}, QA_{k,\max}]$ denotes the desire interval of kth objective function to be identified by the decision maker. Here, $QA_{k,\max}$ as the upper bound of the desire interval is set to QB_k^+, whereas $QA_{k,\min}$ as the lower bound of the desire interval accepts a value larger than or equal to QB_k^-. Actually, the interval $[QB_k^-, QB_k^+]$ is divided into the more pleasant interval $[QA_{k,\min}, QA_{k,\max}]$ and less pleasant one $[QB_k^-, QA_{k,\min}]$. Moreover, β_k denotes the normalized distance of the kth objective function from $QA_{k,\min}$. If the amount of the kth objective function is larger than $QA_{k,\min}$, a penalty cost is then applied to the model fluctuating between 0 and 1. Eventually, y_k is entered as a binary variable, and w_k^α and w_k^β show the weights of the kth objective function concerning α_k and β_k. These weights are tuned are according to the decision-maker's opinion to be assigned to $Z_1 = TC$, $Z_2 = GE$ and $Z_3 = SL$.

5 Findings

Table 4. Scale of the problem.

Notation	Value
T	4
P	3
C	3

This section tries to assess the applicability of the developed methodology using a numerical example as the extension of the example investigated by Goli et al. [1]. In this example, most of the parameters are set using uniform distributions. Accordingly, the scale of the problem is given in Tables 4 and 5 represents the input data. It must be noted that GHG emission data were extracted from Rasmi et al. [9] since they were not applicable in Goli et al. [1]. The weights allocated to the objective functions in the proposed IMCGP model are 0.5, 0.3 and 0.2, respectively. The final model is implemented with the help of CPLEX solver of GAMS.

Table 5. Parameter setting.

Parameter	Value
D_{pt}	uniform(10,100)
CI_{pt}	uniform(10,20)
CA_{pct}	uniform(25,30)
CB_t	uniform(1,2)
CC_t	uniform(1,2)
CD_t	uniform(100,200)
CE_t	uniform(50,75)
CF_{pt}	uniform(5,8)
CG_{pt}	uniform(5,8)
R_t	uniform(8,9)
O_t	uniform(1,3)
WI	uniformint(100,300)
WL	uniformint(10,30)
WU	uniformint(1000,3000)
RM_p	uniform(800,1000)
MP_{pt}	uniform(800,1000)
I_{p0}	uniform(100,200)
PC_p	uniform(10000,20000)
GA_p	uniform(0.0279, 0.0479)
GH_{pc}	uniform(0.0379, 0.0579)
GB_p	uniform(0.0038, 0.0058)
$\overline{D}_t$	0.2 D_t
Γ_p	0.5
w_k^{α}	(0.5, 0.3, 0.2)
w_k^{β}	(0.5, 0.3, 0.2)
$GA_{k,min}$	(2390247.110, 3863.966, 0)
$GA_{k,max}$	(7559.225, 18.651, 1)
GB_k^{+}	(7559.225, 18.651, 1)
GB_k^{-}	(2390247.110, 3863.966, 0)

The final numerical findings are represented in Table 6.

Table 6. Numerical results.

Variable	Z_{IMCGP}	TC	GE	SL	Runtime (s)
Value	0.380	860442.321	23.965	1.000	0.2

The numerical results in Table 6 demonstrate the proficiency of the developed methodology to find the optimal solution in less than 1 s.

Now, a set of sensitivity analyses are implemented on the key parameter of the robust counterpart model and the weights allocated to the objective functions; i.e. conservatism level (Γ_p) and w_k^α and w_k^β, respectively. The aim is to investigate the role of uncertainty and decision-maker's attitude thoroughly. As a consequence, several symmetric change intervals are designed to analyze the applicability of the model. The sensitivity analysis results are displayed in Table 7 and Figs. 1 and 2.

Table 7. Sensitivity analysis results.

Variables	Γ_p				
	– 20%	**– 10%**	**0%**	**+ 10%**	**+ 20%**
Z_{IMCGP}	0.379	0.380	0.380	0.380	0.380
TC	860513.742	860827.281	860442.321	861454.359	861767.898
GE	24.045	24.494	23.965	25.394	25.844
SL	1.000	1.000	1.000	1.000	1.000
Variables	w_k^α **and** w_k^β				
	(0.2, 0.3, 0.5)	**(0.3, 0.4, 0.3)**	**(0.5, 0.3, 0.2)**	**(0.5, 0.2, 0.3)**	**(0.6, 0.3, 0.1)**
Z_{IMCGP}	0.572	0.408	0.380	0.479	0.315
TC	861140.820	861140.820	860442.321	861060.312	861140.820
GE	24.944	24.944	23.965	25.072	24.944
SL	1.000	1.000	1.000	1.000	1.000

As can be inferred from Table 7 and Figs. 1 and 2, there are varying behaviors of the objective functions against various change intervals. Accordingly, the instability of real-world and the attitude of the decision-maker can directly influence the problem and modify the optimal policy. As an example, the applied changes to the convertasim level changed the values of the 1st and 2nd objective functions while there is no influence on Z_{IMCGP} and the 3rd objective function. On the other hand, various combinations of weights assigned to the objective functions influenced Z_{IMCGP}, 1st and 2nd objective function but the 3rd objective function still remained stable and this comes from zero backorders.

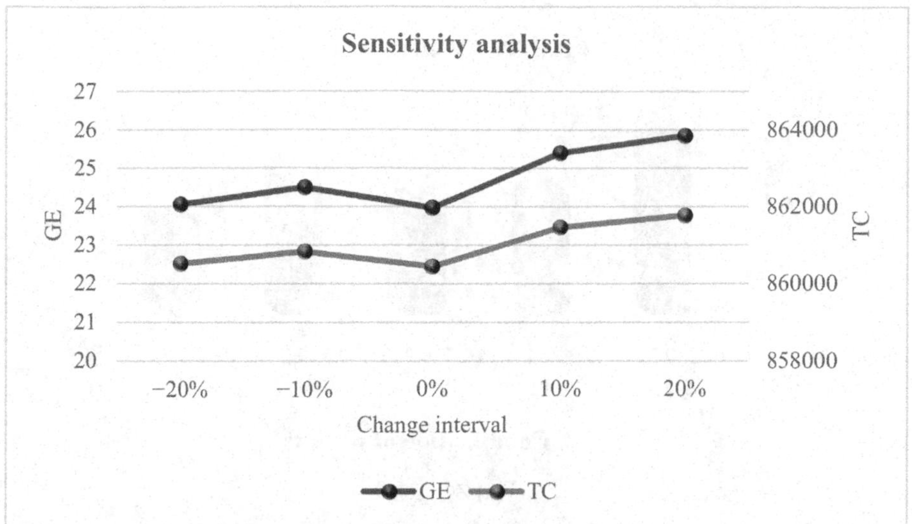

Fig. 1. Sensitivity analysis of the conservatism level.

In accordance with the results, it seems that sensitivity analysis can be regarded as a beneficial tool for managers and decision-makers in order to cope with real-world conditions and determine the required resources within the production system. Furthermore, striking a balance between economic and environmental aspects is known as a managerial challenge to be handled through the potential of a production system. In the current study, there is still room to address this issue and also incorporate more real-world assumptions.

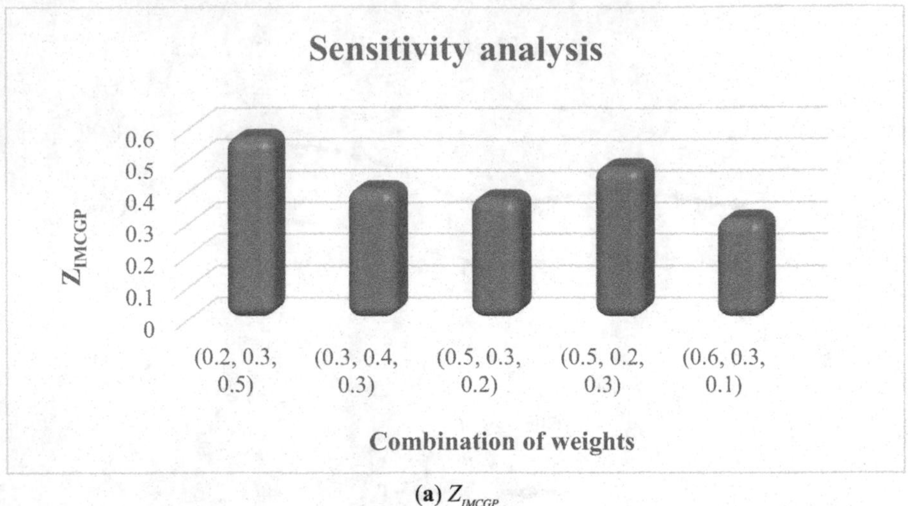

(a) Z_{IMCGP}

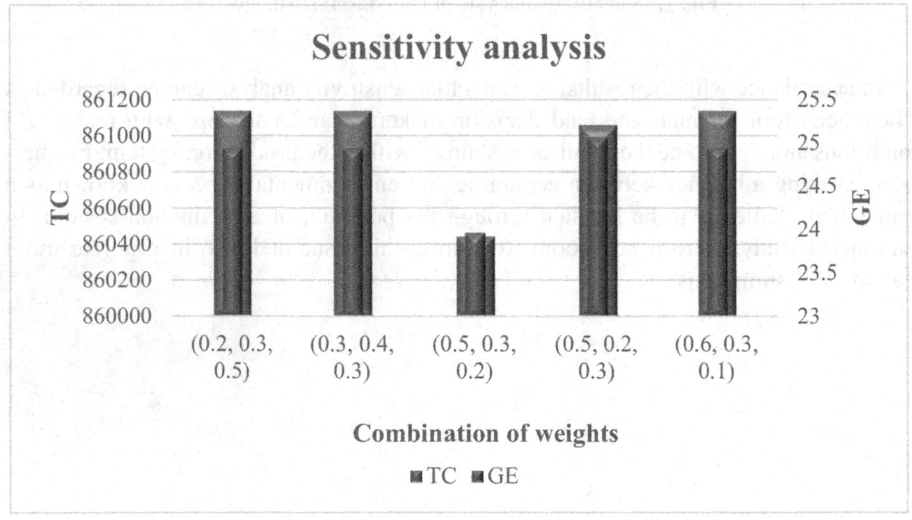

(b) TC vs. GE

Fig. 2. Sensitivity analysis performed on the weights of objective functions.

6 Conclusion and Recommendations for Future

In this research, a sustainable-robust APP was investigated through developing an efficient methodology based on a tri-objective MILP model, robust optimization method and IMCGP technique. Three objective functions of total cost minimization, total pollution minimization and service level maximization were addressed in the model to establish triple bottom line strategy of sustainable development. Then, the robust counterpart model was built based on the Bertsimas' and Sim's model to treat demand uncertainty within a symmetric interval. At the end, the suggested IMCGP approach was applied to the model in order to provide a single-objective robust model. The applicability and validation of the suggested methodology were finally evaluated through a numerical example and a set of sensitivity analyses. It was revealed that our methodology is effectively capable of finding the optimal policy. According to the output results from the sensitivity analyses, it was also demonstrated that the 3rd objective function remains unchanged due to zero backorders in the numerical example.

In accordance with the main limitation of the study such as studying the impacts of human factors, solution algorithm development and social aspacts, the following recommendations are given for future research:

- Implementing other uncertainty handling techniques such as fuzzy programming and grey system in order to be assessed against the suggested RO method,
- Taking into account the suppliers, raw materials and workforce skill levels in the model,
- Considering the rework possibility and scraps in the model which makes the model closer to the real-world situation,
- Developing approximation algorithms to treat the problem complexity in large scales,
- Studying the impact of customer service level maximization as another objective function in the model.

References

1. Goli, A., Tirkolaee, E.B., Malmir, B., Bian, G.-B., Sangaiah, A.K.: A multi-objective invasive weed optimization algorithm for robust aggregate production planning under uncertain seasonal demand. Computing **101**(6), 499–529 (2019). https://doi.org/10.1007/s00607-018-00692-2
2. Darvishi, F., Yaghin, R.G., Sadeghi, A.: Integrated fabric procurement and multi-site apparel production planning with cross-docking: a hybrid fuzzy-robust stochastic programming approach. Appl. Soft Comput. **92**, 106267 (2020)
3. Hahn, G.J., Brandenburg, M.: A sustainable aggregate production planning model for the chemical process industry. Comput. Oper. Res. **94**, 154–168 (2018)
4. Mirzapour Al-e-hashem, S.M.J., Baboli, A., Sazvar, Z.: A stochastic aggregate production planning model in a green supply chain: considering flexible lead times, nonlinear purchase and shortage cost functions. Eur. J. Oper. Res. **230**(1), 26–41 (2013)
5. Gholamian, N., Mahdavi, I., Tavakkoli-Moghaddam, R.: Multi-objective multi-product multi-site aggregate production planning in a supply chain under uncertainty: fuzzy multi-objective optimisation. Int. J. Comput. Integr. Manuf. **29**(2), 149–165 (2016)
6. Türkay, M., Saraçoğlu, Ö., Arslan, M.C.: Sustainability in supply chain management: aggregate planning from sustainability perspective. PLoS ONE **11**(1), e0147502 (2016)
7. Tirkolaee, E.B., Goli, A., Weber, G.W.: Multi-objective aggregate production planning model considering overtime and outsourcing options under fuzzy seasonal demand. In: Hamrol, A., Kujawińska, A., Barraza, M. (eds.) Advances in Manufacturing II. MANUFACTURING 2019. Lecture Notes in Mechanical Engineering. Springer, Cham (2019). https://doi.org/10.1007/978-3-030-18789-7_8
8. Khalili-Damghani, K., Shahrokh, A.: Solving a new multi-period multi-objective multi-product aggregate production planning problem using fuzzy goal programming. Ind. Eng. Manage. Syst. **13**(4), 369–382 (2014)

9. Rasmi, S.A.B., Kazan, C., Türkay, M.: A multi-criteria decision analysis to include environmental, social, and cultural issues in the sustainable aggregate production plans. Comput. Ind. Eng. **132**, 348–360 (2019)
10. Modarres, M., Izadpanahi, E.: Aggregate production planning by focusing on energy saving: a robust optimization approach. J. Clean. Prod. **133**, 1074–1085 (2016)
11. Chaturvedi, N.D.: Minimizing energy consumption via multiple installations aggregate production planning. Clean Technol. Environ. Policy **19**(7), 1977–1984 (2017). https://doi.org/10.1007/s10098-017-1376-3
12. Entezaminia, A., Heidari, M., Rahmani, D.: Robust aggregate production planning in a green supply chain under uncertainty considering reverse logistics: a case study. Int. J. Adv. Manufact. Technol. **90**(5–8), 1507–1528 (2016). https://doi.org/10.1007/s00170-016-9459-6
13. Bertsimas, D., Sim, M.: The price of robustness. Oper. Res. **52**(1), 35–53 (2004)
14. Hatefi, S.M., Jolai, F.: Robust and reliable forward–reverse logistics network design under demand uncertainty and facility disruptions. Appl. Math. Model. **38**(9–10), 2630–2647 (2014)
15. Jadidi, O., Cavalieri, S., Zolfaghari, S.: An improved multi-choice goal programming approach for supplier selection problems. Appl. Math. Model. **39**(14), 4213–4222 (2015)
16. Aydin, N.S., Tirkolaee, E.B.: A systematic review of aggregate production planning literature with an outlook for sustainability and circularity. Environ. Dev. Sustain. 1–42 (2022)
17. Tirkolaee, E.B., Aydin, N.S., Mahdavi, I.: A hybrid Biobjective Markov chain based optimization model for sustainable aggregate production planning. IEEE Trans. Eng. Manag. (2022)

Quality-Based Supplier Evaluation and Improvement Using DEA and SQFE

K. Niazmand[1], A. Mirzazadeh[1](✉), and L. Chehreghani[2]

[1] Department of Industrial Engineering, Kharazmi University, Tehran, Iran
mirzazadeh@khu.ac.ir

[2] Department of Management, Center for European Studies, Ershad Damavand University, Kharazmi University, Tehran, Iran

Abstract. In today's competitive global market, manufacturers should continuously evaluate suppliers in terms of the product quality to ensure that their performance meet the standards. In this direction, SQFE (Suivi Qualite Par le Fournisseur Exterieur) approach is first introduced by three automotive manufacturers: Peugeot, Citroen and Renault to monitor supplier performance by measuring the quality level of the units shipped from a supplier. In this study, using SQFE and data envelopment analysis (DEA), a new methodology is introduced to assess and improve the performance of suppliers which offer the same product at the same price and different quality. To quality-based supplier evaluation, DEA is performed with one dummy input and three output variables, which are the results of SQFE. Apart from ranking suppliers, using SQFE indices as DEA outputs which was not seriously treated by the researchers, we demonstrate how the method can be used for identifying potential improvement in each output variable, for inefficient suppliers. Finally, a numerical example is presented to show the application of the presented model for ranking the suppliers and setting the new targets for suppliers' performance improvement.

Keywords: Supplier selection · SQFE · DEA

1 Introduction

Supplier development has been introduced as "any activity by a manufacturer to enhance the performance of the suppliers". It can be supplier evaluation, supplier training, goal setting, performance measurement, and other related efforts [1]. Strong evidences confirm that today, to improve supplier performance and to maintain the competitive advantage, the companies are turning to pay more attention to supplier development programs [2]. It will lead to the quality improvement which is important in supply chain quality management [3] through attaining levels of performance that are significantly better than any past level [4].

Supplier evaluation involves many advantages that helps managers to concentrate on the priorities and set the new objectives; it provides suppliers with evaluation feedback by which they could implement corrective actions in order to enhance their performance.

A. Mirzazadeh et al. (Eds.): SEMIT 2022, CCIS 1808, pp. 35–49, 2023.
https://doi.org/10.1007/978-3-031-40395-8_3

Moreover, it will improve the employees' motivation through identifying and rewarding to suppliers and people whose performance is at a better-than-normal level [5]; and finally, the most important role of this assessment is that, it ensures that all the manufacturer's requirements and subsequently customers' expectations are at an acceptable performance level and responded consistently [6]. Assessing a group of suppliers is a complex task due to the wide range of factors such as cost, quality, delivery time, service, goodwill and environmental impact to be included in this process [7].

Cooperating with suppliers with high quality goods has always been important for manufacturers [8]. According to Ho et al. [9] that reviewed the literature in the field of the multi-criteria decision making approaches for supplier evaluation between 2000 and 2008, "quality" has been identified as the most popular criterion, used by decision makers in the selection and evaluation of suppliers. They have found various quality related attributes in previous works such as: "compliance with quality", "acceptable parts per million", "documentation and self-audit", "corrective and preventive action system", " total quality management program", "inspection and control", "low defect rate", "net rejections", "number of quality staff", "non-conforming material control system", "perfect rate", "percentage of products or items not rejected upon inspection", "process control capability", "quality planning", "quality assurance production", "quality award", "quality certification", "quality data and reporting", "quality manual", "quality management practices and systems", "reliability of quality", "rejection in incoming quality", "rejection in production line", "service quality experience", "rejection from customers", "service quality credence".

Pearson et al. [10] randomly selected and investigated 210 members of NAPM (National Association of Purchasing Management). They discovered that the most important criterion considered by both the small and large electronic firms for evaluating suppliers, is "quality".

In this regard, SQFE approach, introduced by three automotive companies, Peugeot, Citroen and Renault, is used for quality improvement by supplier monitoring. This approach involves many capacities for both supplier and manufacturer. As a guideline for suppliers' performance improvement, it informs them to implement corrective actions through measuring and monitoring overall quality of their products. It also provides managers with useful data to set the new targets by focusing on the priority areas. As the guidance of quality department audits, it ensures the manufacturer that the materials received from the suppliers meet the quality and reliability requirements. It gives manufacturer the chance to establish improvement objectives compatible with zero defect [11].

Extensive approaches related to multi-criteria decision making have been applied in various studies in literature for supplier evaluation and improvement, some of them are as follows: analytic hierarchy process (AHP), linear programming (LP), data envelopment analysis (DEA), case-based reasoning (CBR), analytic network process (ANP), mathematical programming, data neural networks (NN), multi-objective programming, and fuzzy set theory (FST) methods [12].

Among various quantitative methods, data envelopment analysis (DEA), first presented by Charnes et al. in 1978, is a widely recognized approach to help the buyer by categorizing the suppliers into efficient suppliers and inefficient suppliers [13]. DEA is specifically designed to evaluate the efficiencies of alternative decision making units (DMUs) using multiple inputs and multiple outputs [14]. Efficiency which is defined as the ratio of outputs to inputs, is an operational parameter for short-term decision making [15]. In this regard, some researchers applied DEA to assess the total performance of suppliers with respect to different criteria of inputs and outputs [5, 15–18].

The principal advantages of DEA application are: (1) In original DEA formulations, the evaluated DMUs can freely choose the weights to be assigned to each input and output in order to maximize their efficiency, considering that this system of weights to be feasible for all other DMUs [17]; whereas in MCDM methods, the decision makers should specify the inputs and outputs, that more importance could be attached to them. This is the weakness of MCDM methods, since additional knowledge is needed [19]. (2) DEA does not need any prior assumptions on the underlying functional relationships between inputs and outputs [14]. (3) It can be utilized as a tool in negotiating with inefficient DMUs [13].

Therefore, it can be said that DEA has found its place as a proper approach in measuring the efficiencies related to peer units in case of presenting multiple performance measures [20].

Some studies in this field are listed as below:

- Çelebi and Bayraktar [21] presented a new combination of neural networks and DEA to assess suppliers when the information of evaluation criteria is incomplete.
- Karsak and Dursun [22] integrated quality function deployment (QFD) and data envelopment analysis (DEA) to create a fuzzy multi-criteria group decision making model to enhance the supplier selection. Their model included the effect of inner dependence of supplier evaluation criteria via house of quality (HOQ).
- Dobos and Vörösmarty [23] studied the supplier evaluation methods with green and environmental concerns. They used composite indicators (CI) method to study the traditional methods of supplier selection including environmental concerns. They categorized the criteria in traditional and environmental factors. Then they studied a system in which the decision is affected by green criteria.
- Mahdiloo et al. [24] presented a new approach of green supplier selection by categorizing the efficiency indicators to technical, environmental and eco-efficiency scores. They used linear goal programming to integrate the mentioned categories into multiple objective linear programming (MOLP) DEA model. Consequently, their model provided more valid eco-efficiency indicator of decision-making units (DMUs) by applying a better integration of the technical and environmental efficiency goals comparing the conventional models. Their model identified DMUs as being eco-efficient subject to both technically and environmentally efficiency.
- Zhou et al. [25] presented the type 2 fuzzy DEA model to evaluate the sustainable supplier in which both effectiveness and efficiency are seen to show the suppliers productivity.
- Yousefi et al. [26] considered DEA in determining benchmarks of inefficient decision making units (DMUs). In their study, they proposed dynamic ideal DMU by the application of dynamic DEA and scenario-based model of robust to cover the shortage of benchmarking in improving future efficiency of DMUs.

- Cheng et al. [27] presented a hybrid DEA-Adaboost model to answer the need to data driven DM methods. This study combined the DEA and learner and made a hybrid model to minimize the complexities and time of supplier selection.
- Kumar Jauhar and Pant [28] combined the DEA, DE and MODE to develop an efficient system to evaluate supplier selection. Their model increased the capability of DEA and empowered the results of DEA.
- Amindoust [29] introduced a modular Fuzzy Inference System to consider the sustainability and resilience in supplier selection.
- Dobos and Vörösmarty [30] presented a method to handle the characteristics of management criteria and green criteria. Their methodology examines the management and green criteria and investigates the effect of inventory and EOQ costs on the selected supplier.
- Tavassoli [31] introduced DEA as a proper tool for measuring the suppliers' sustainability. This study presented four models of supplier selection. The paper presented a decision making scheme with the purpose of selecting appropriate model of supplier selection under deterministic, stochastic and fuzzy conditions.
- Ersoy and Nuri [32] measured the performance of 16 suppliers of 5 textile companies. They evaluated the results using two methods of Fuzzy Analytic Hierarchy Process (FAHP) and Fuzzy Data Envelopment Analysis (FDEA)
- Patel et al. [33] studied the selection of right corrugated box supplier in Fiber industry. For this purpose, they proposed hybrid approach of Fuzzy TOPSIS for qualitative criteria evaluation and Grey Relational Analysis for quantitative criteria evaluation for a Fiber industry located in Goa, India.
- Vorosmarty and Dobos [34] summarized all their researches on supplier selection and evaluation using DEA among the papers published between 2009 and 2018. They explained the support of DEA from supplier selection and evaluation in strategic decision making and suppliers management.
- Sadjadi et al. [35] presented two models of supplier selection for complementary, sustainable and conditional products. They formulated two multi-objective mixed-integer non-linear programming models. They used Best Worst Method (BWM) for identified decision making criteria. They presented two case studies to affirm the practical application of the suggested method.

To sum up, since quality is an important issue for most decision makers for suppliers evaluation, it will bring an issue of supplier selection process based on quality and evaluation by SQFE approach into the main focus of this research, which was not seriously considered by the researchers in the literature. For this purpose, SQFE indices are applied as DEA outputs. This methodology provides an opportunity to compare the performance of suppliers offering the same product at the same price and different quality by which apart from ranking suppliers, the new targets will be set for inefficient suppliers.

The organization of this paper is as follows: in Sect. 2, the method of SQFE is briefly described, Sect. 3 presents DEA model considering the SQFE indices for ranking suppliers which is able to specify potential improvements for inefficient suppliers. Section 4 demonstrates the application of the presented models in practice with a numerical example. Finally, the last section concludes the present research.

2 SQFE Approach and the Indices

In order to evaluate the quality of supplier's product, the following steps are advised in effective application of SQFE:

Step 1. First, the quality characteristics, their sample size and sample location must be identified and validated during the product and process control phase by producer with the agreement of supplier. Since the selected samples are representatives of the quality of total goods delivered to manufacturer, inspection and measurement should be performed on products ready to dispatch.

Step 2. In this step, an agreement on demerit rating's criteria is set forth by which every sample is supposed to be rated. The criteria of none measurable quality characteristics, is presented in Table 1, and for measurable quality characteristics, demerit weights should be assigned to each sample as a function of the distance from the center of the tolerance interval (target value). Table 2 presents the overall demerit rating guideline of double limit measurable quality characteristics. This is in accordance with Fig. 1, in which *m* denotes the target.

Table 1. Demerit rating criteria of none measurable quality characteristics.

Demerit weight	Criteria
0	None defect
3	Meriting improvement
5	Meriting rework
15	Imperative rework
55	Recall necessary

Table 2. Demerit rating criteria of double limit measurable quality characteristics

Class	Criteria	Demerit weight
1	$B_L \leq x \leq B_R$	0
2	$A_L \leq x < B_L OR B_R < x \leq A_R$	3
3	$C_L \leq x < A_L OR A_R < x \leq C_R$	Standard rating: 5 If defect requires rework: 15 If defect require recall: 55
4	$x < C_L OR x > C_R$	Standard rating: 15 If defect requires recall: 55

The parameters are defined as follow: T is the tolerance; A_R and A_L are upper and lower specification limits, respectively. Additionally, by using B_R and C_R determined on the right side of target value and B_L and C_L on its left side, the tolerance band is divided to 4 classes in each side, that each sample should be judged based on them. The

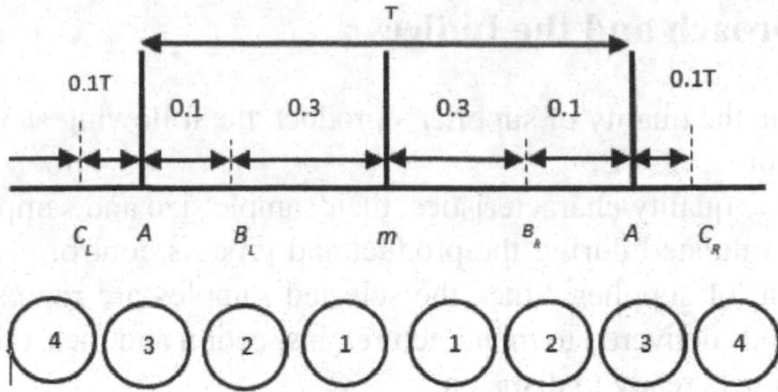

Fig. 1. Division of tolerance band of a double limit measurable quality characteristic.

mathematical formulas are as follows (for one-sided measurable quality characteristics see SQFE, 1993):

$$B_R = m + 0.33T \tag{1}$$

$$C_R = A_R + 0.1T \tag{2}$$

$$B_L = m - 0.33T \tag{3}$$

$$C_L = A_L - 0.1T \tag{4}$$

It is important to note that the manufacturer and the supplier agree on the described criteria in above tables, considering the importance of the part in the performance of final product.

Step 3. The main indices of SQFE utilized measuring the supplier's products quality are as follows:

- Mean unit demerit *(DUM)*
- Level of quality aptitude *(NAQ)*
- Level of none quality *(TNNQ)*

They could be calculated as follows: Let W_{ij} be the demerit weight of j th inspection sample, with respect to i th quality characteristic, which is determined by the judgment on each sample based on the criteria defined in advanced. Therefore, the sum of demerits for i th quality characteristic, denoted by Dr_i will be obtained as follows:

$$Dr_i = \sum_{j=1}^{n_i} W_{ij} \tag{5}$$

Where $i = 1, 2, \ldots, q$, $j = 1, 2, \ldots, n_i$ and n_i is the total number of the samples collected to monitor the i th characteristic. For i th quality characteristic, Dmr_i which indicates the mean demerit, will be obtained by:

$$Dmr_i = \frac{Dr_i}{n_i} \tag{6}$$

The *DUM* for the product will be obtained by:

$$DUM = \sum_{i=1}^{q} Dmr_i \quad (7)$$

As the second index, the level of none quality for each characteristic consists of a four digits number between 0000 and 9999. It compares the different products of the same family. In fact, the number of defects in that category of demerit does not affect the value of *NNQ*, however, it represents the maximum observed demerit category. The rule is summarized in Table 3. Then, the *TNNQ* for the product is calculated by summing the *NNQ*s but limiting to 9 for each class of demerit.

$$TNNQ = \sum_{i=1}^{q} NNQ_i \quad (8)$$

As the third index, the level of quality aptitude for a product is represented by the highest value of the *CAQ*s for all of characteristics as:

$$NAQ = \max_i (CAQ_i) \quad (9)$$

Table 3. The rule of making *NNQ*s.

The maximum observed demerit for *i* th characteristic	NNQ_i
0	0000
3	0001
5	0010
15	0100
55	1000

The *CAQ* that is calculated just for measureable characteristics, affirms the dispersion of sample data within the tolerance interval of each characteristic. It is to mention that when the value of *CAQ* is obtained 1 or greater, it should be represented 0.99. Assume $x_{i1}, x_{i2}, \ldots, x_{in_i}$ are collected randomly sample data regarding *i* th quality characteristic, where T_i represents the tolerance interval and m_i represents the target value of characteristic *i* at the center of tolerance. Hence, *CAQ* is computed as follows for each double limit measurable quality characteristic (for one-sided measurable quality characteristics see SQFE, 1993):

$$CAQ_i = max(\frac{m_i - \min_j(x_{ij})}{T_i/2}, \frac{\max_j(x_{ij}) - m_i}{T_i/2}) \quad (10)$$

Therefore, in this approach, the quality levels of received parts are measured by three main indices as follows: *DUM*, which is the mean number of demerit points for the product, gives a relative value of the products' quality level whereas *TNNQ* and *NAQ*, as the complement to *DUM* are not influenced by the number of defects. *TNNQ* represents the maximum defect category which has been observed during the inspection and *NAQ* indicates the maximum observed deviation from the target value. These tendings towards zero indices, present an opportunity to compare delivered quality during the time to reach the new level of improvement by implementing corrective and preventive actions and setting the new targets (SQFE 1993).

3 Supplier Selection and Evaluation Methodology

Data envelopment analysis (DEA) which was first proposed by Charnes et al. in 1978, is a non-parametric technique for evaluating the relative efficiency of a set of decision making units (DMUs) with multi-inputs and multi-outputs. As a methodology with linear programming base, it assesses the efficiency of each DMU of an estimated production possibility frontier determined by all DMUs [36]. In the algorithm presented by [37], referred to as the CCR model, DEA assigns an efficiency score to each unit, by which DMUs will be classified to efficient and inefficient units. Such inefficiency is to pay attention to the fact that a unit could produce the same level of outputs utilizing fewer inputs than those currently employed by the inefficient unit. The inefficiency also could imply that a unit produces a greater number of outputs using the same level of inputs. [38]. DEA analysis is not new method with the approach of problem solving related to the supplier selection issues. Supplier efficiency is defined as the ratio of the weighted sum of the outputs that is the performance of the supplier to the weighted sum of its inputs that is the costs of the supplier. Through DEA model, the suppliers are evaluated on benefit criteria (outputs) and cost criteria (inputs) [13].

3.1 Supplier Evaluation Model Based on DEA and SQFE

In this step, since the focus is supposed to be on the quality of suppliers' products, the suppliers' inputs are not considered. In order to measure each supplier's efficiency, we assume unitary inputs (dummy) for all units according to Zeydan, Çolpan, & Çobanoglu, 2011. Moreover, supplier performance values obtained through SQFE approach are considered as three output variables of *DUM*, *NAQ* and *TNNQ*. All of these quality indices are expressed by unqualified products; thus they are naturally smaller the better, while an output can be defined as any increase that will cause the increase in efficiency [17]; therefore the supplier evaluation indices are appropriately transferred to bigger the better as follows:

$$\begin{aligned} DUM &\rightarrow {}^{1}/_{DUM} \\ NAQ &\rightarrow 0.99 - NAQ \\ TNNQ &\rightarrow 9999 - TNNQ \end{aligned} \tag{11}$$

Here, an output oriented model is suitable because its objective is to maximize the expansion rates of outputs in order to reach the efficient frontier with the same level of inputs as the unit [39]. Let us assume that n decision making units consume varying amounts of m different inputs to produces p different outputs. Assume that x_{ij} and y_{rj} $(i = 1, \ldots, m)$, (j = 1,…,n), (r = 1,2,…,p) represent, respectively, the input and output of the j th decision making unit (DMU_j). The model we consider here is CCR model (constant returns to scale) in output-oriented version which can be formulated as:

$$\max\theta_k + \varepsilon\left(\sum\nolimits_{i=1}^{m} S_i^- + \sum\nolimits_{r=1}^{p} S_r^+\right) \tag{12}$$

$$s.t. \sum\nolimits_{j=1}^{n} x_{ij}\lambda_j + S_i^- = x_{ik}$$

$$\sum\nolimits_{j=1}^{n} y_{rj}\lambda_j - S_r^+ = \theta_k . y_{rk}$$

$$\lambda_j, S_i^-, S_r^+ \geq 0$$

$$j = 1, \ldots, n, i = 1, \ldots, m, r = 1, \ldots, p$$

Where

$\theta_k \rightarrow$ Efficiency score corresponding to DMU_k in the output oriented model.
$x_{ik} \rightarrow i$ th input of k th DMU.
$y_{rk} \rightarrow r$ th output of k th DMU.
$\lambda_j \rightarrow$ Weights attached to inputs and outputs of k th DMU,
$S_i^- \rightarrow$ Slack corresponding to i th input of k th DMU.
$S_r^+ \rightarrow$ Surplus corresponding to r th output of k th DMU.
$\varepsilon \rightarrow$ a non-Archimedean quantity that is usually given a small positive value, for instance 10^{-8} [39].

In the above model, DMU_k is considered to be efficient comparing to its compatriots if and only if the optimal value$\theta_k = 1, S_i^- 0$ *and* $S_r^+ = 0$, whereas any unit that has a score greater than 1 is considered as inefficient. This model is applied to assess the efficiency of DMUs by utilizing the existing level of inputs while primarily considers to provide suggestions regarding outputs for inefficient DMUs. Since the DEA-CCR model is weak in discriminating between efficient suppliers [40] "Super-efficiency Analysis" was proposed by Andersen and Petersen in 1993 in order to discriminate the performance of efficient DMUs. To this aim, for a complete ranking of efficient units, the weight λ_k of the evaluated unit DMU_k is equated to zero, while this model cannot influence the efficiency score of the inefficient units [39]. For The output oriented super-efficiency DEA, the linear programming model is as follows:

$$\max\theta_k + \varepsilon\left(\sum\nolimits_{i=1}^{m} S_i^- + \sum\nolimits_{r=1}^{p} S_r^+\right)(13)$$

$$s.t. \sum\nolimits_{j=1, j\neq k}^{n} x_{ij}\lambda_j + S_i^- = x_{ik}$$

$$\sum\nolimits_{j=1, j\neq k}^{n} y_{rj}\lambda_j - S_r^+ = \theta_k . y_{rk}$$

$$\lambda_j, S_i^-, S_r^+ \geq 0$$

$$i = 1, \ldots, m, j = 1, \ldots, n, r = 1, \ldots, p$$

3.2 Potential Improvement

An advantage of the DEA approach is that the mentioned model provides target values for inefficient DMUs in order to become efficient by changing the values of the inputs/outputs. The variables S_i^-, S_r^+ express the difference between virtual inputs/outputs and appropriate inputs/outputs of DMU_k. Each unit can be considered to be efficient if the virtual unit is identical with the evaluated unit; it means that there is not a virtual unit with better inputs and outputs [39]. Indeed, a linear combination of other units, defines the relevant portion of the production frontier that the inefficient unit would seek to reach as it strives to become efficient [38]. The model identifies the target values for the outputs of DMU_k to make improvement via the following equation [39]:

$$\begin{aligned} x_{ik}^* &= x_{ik} - S_i^- \\ y_{rk}^* &= \theta_k^*.y_{rk} + S_r^+ \end{aligned} \tag{14}$$

4 Numerical Illustration

To affirm the applicability of the proposed method, a numerical example is presented. For α plant whose quality could be monitored by SQFE approach, 5 quality characteristics has been identified, C_1,C_2,C_3 as 3 measureable quality characteristics and C_4,C_5 as 2 none measurable characteristics. The characteristics and their demerit rating criteria are listed in Table 4. For 5 suppliers which produce α plant, assume that the quality level has been calculated according to the average of SQFE results in a period of time. The results are summarized in Table 5. The parameter values of input which has been assumed unitary for all suppliers and output items of each supplier, which are obtained from the SQFE approach and transferred into bigger the better by using Eq. (11) are listed in Table 6.

The DEA linear programming model, as shown in Eq. (12), is applied to determine suppliers' relative efficiencies. The efficiency scores, and other parameter values which are the results of the linear programming model, obtained by analytical program "LINGO" are summarized in Table 7. Moreover, using Eq. (13) as supper efficiency model, the ranks of all efficient suppliers are calculated and reported in Table 8. According to the result of analysis, two suppliers (S1, S2) are defined as "inefficient" vendors, while other suppliers (S3, S4, S5) are "efficient". At the end of this evaluation process, according to the combination of the actual outputs and inputs of the reference subset of suppliers, for any inefficient supplier, target values are calculated based on Eq. (14) and are shown in Table 9.

Table 4. The quality characteristics, their specification limits and demerit rating criteria

C_i	Specification Limits	Sample size	Sample data	Demerit weight	Sample data	Demerit weight	Sample data	Demerit weight	Sample data	Demerit weight
C_1	3305-3315	20	3306.7-3313.3	0	33.13-3315 Or 3305-3306.7	3	3315-3316 Or 3304-3305	5	Greater than 3316 Or less than 3304	15
C_2	16-17.5	20	16.3-17.2	0	17.2-17.5 Or 16-1.3	3	17.5-17.65 Or 15.85-16	5	Greater than 17.65 Or Less than 15.85	15
C_3	700-840	10	724-840	0	700-724	3	686-700	5	Less than 686	15
C_4		20	Ok	0	Not ok	3				
C_5		20	Ok	0	Not ok	5				

Table 5. The results of SQFE indices

Suppliers	DUM	NAQ	TNNQ
S1	3.05	0.88	0031
S2	2.7	0.91	0102
S3	2.4	0.73	0201
S4	1.05	0.82	0120
S5	1.8	0.95	0004

Table 6. Input and output data for suppliers

Suppliers	Input	Outputs		
	X1	Y1	Y2	Y3
S1	1	0.3278	0.11	9968
S2	1	0.3703	0.08	9897
S3	1	0.4166	0.26	9798
S4	1	0.9523	0.17	9879
S5	1	0.5555	0.04	9995

Table 7. Efficiency of suppliers and other parameters based on the output-oriented CCR model

Suppliers	θ_k	S_1^-	S_1^+	S_2^+	S_3^+
S1	1.002	0	0.226	0	0
S2	1.009	0	0.181	0.029	0
S3	1	0	0	0	0
S4	1	0	0	0	0
S5	1	0	0	0	0

Table 8. The efficient DUMs ranking based on the super efficiency model

Suppliers	θ_k(supper efficiency)	Rank
S1	-	Inefficient
S2	-	Inefficient
S3	0.65	2
S4	0.58	1
S5	0.99	3

Table 9. Potential Improvement of inefficient suppliers

Suppliers	Input		*DUM*		*NAQ*		*TNNQ*	
	Actual	Target	Actual	Target	Actual	Target	Actual	Target
S1	1	1	3.05	1.803	0.88	0.87	0031	0011
S2	1	1	2.7	1.802	0.91	0.88	0102	0013

5 Conclusions

Supply chain quality is an important factor helping manufacturers to achieve competitive advantage. A higher quality level production with the same price, always attracts more consumers in a specified market segment. This paper presented a new technique for evaluation of suppliers which offer the same product at the same price and different quality. This research provided a comprehensive analysis of the suppliers' performance to rank the suppliers as well as to robust the performance of inefficient suppliers. The quality-based supplier evaluation method presented in this paper is able to evaluate suppliers using their quality level obtained from SQFE approach, with the help of DEA which is widely used in the performance analysis in numerous fields in the literature e.g. supplier selection. The ability of making a comparison between suppliers, regarding three indices with different scale, while does not require any specific weights to be assigned to indices, is one of the superiorities of using DEA over the MCDM methods which has been considered in this paper. In addition, data envelopment analysis with its easy and successful application has been used as a practical method for analyzing the SQFE approach results in order to set the new targets to improve inefficient suppliers which is another capability of DEA method. The presented methodology is still applicable to other indices related quality.

References

1. Krause, D.R., Handfield, R.B., Tyler, B.B.: The relationships between supplier development, commitment, social capital accumulation and performance improvement. J. Oper. Manag. **25**(2), 528–545 (2007)
2. Modi, S.B., Mabert, V.A.: Supplier development: improving supplier performance through knowledge transfer. J. Oper. Manag. **25**(1), 42–64 (2007)
3. Xie, G., Wang, S., Lai, K.: Quality improvement in competing supply chains. Int. J. Prod. Econ. **134**(1), 262–270 (2011)
4. Yaqiong, L., Man, L.K., Zhang, W.: Fuzzy theory applied in quality management of distributed manufacturing system: a literature review and classification. Eng. Appl. Artif. Intell. **24**(2), 266–277 (2011)
5. Wu, D.D.: A systematic stochastic efficiency analysis model and application to international supplier performance evaluation. Expert Syst. Appl. **37**(9), 6257–6264 (2010)
6. Wang, W.P.: A fuzzy linguistic computing approach to supplier evaluation. Appl. Math. Model. **34**(10), 3130–3141 (2010)
7. Shu, M.H., Wu, H.C.: Quality-based supplier selection and evaluation using fuzzy data. Comput. Ind. Eng. **57**(3), 1072–1079 (2009)
8. Hsu, B.M., Chiang, C.Y., Shu, M.H.: Supplier selection using fuzzy quality data and their applications to touch screen. Expert Syst. Appl. **37**(9), 6192–6200 (2010)
9. Ho, W., Xu, X., Dey, P.K.: Multi-criteria decision making approaches for supplier evaluation and selection: a literature review. Eur. J. Oper. Res. **202**(1), 16–24 (2010)
10. Pearson, J.N., Ellram, L.M.: Supplier selection and evaluation in small versus large electronics firms. J. Small Bus. Manage. **33**(4), 53–65 (1995)
11. S. M. Quality monitoring by the supplier, direction des Achats Atomobiles Renault, Peugeot and Citroen (1993)
12. Toloo, M., Nalchigar, S.: A new DEA method for supplier selection in presence of both cardinal and ordinal data. Expert Syst. Appl. **38**(12), 14726–14731 (2011)
13. Wu, D.: Supplier selection: a hybrid model using DEA, decision tree and neural network. Expert Syst. Appl. **36**(5), 9105–9112 (2009)
14. Poveda, A.C.: Economic development and growth in Colombia: an empirical analysis with super-efficiency DEA and panel data models. Socioecon. Plann. Sci. **45**(4), 154–164 (2011)
15. Falagario, M., Sciancalepore, F., Costantino, N., Pietroforte, R.: Using a DEA-cross efficiency approach in public procurement tenders. Eur. J. Oper. Res. **218**(2), 523–529 (2012)
16. Reiner, G., Hofmann, P.: Efficiency analysis of supply chain processes. Int. J. Prod. Res. **44**(23), 5065–5087 (2006)
17. Saen, R.F.: Restricting weights in supplier selection decisions in the presence of dual-role factors. Appl. Math. Model. **34**(10), 2820–2830 (2010)
18. Forker, L.B., Mendez, D.: An analytical method for benchmarking best peer suppliers. Int. J. Oper. Prod. Manag. **21**(1–2), 195–209 (2001)
19. Adler, N., Friedman, L., Stern, Z.S.: Review of ranking methods in the data envelopment analysis context. Eur. J. Oper. Res. **140**(2), 249–265 (2002)

20. Liang, L., Yang, F., Cook, W.D., Zhu, J.: DEA models for supply chain efficiency evaluation. Oper. Res. **145**, 35–49 (2006)
21. Çelebi, D., Bayraktar, D.: An integrated neural network and data envelopment analysis for supplier evaluation under incomplete information. Expert Syst. Appl. 1698–1710 (2008)
22. Ertugrul Karsak, E., Dursun, M.: An integrated supplier selection methodology incorporating QFD and DEA with imprecise data. Expert Syst. Appl. 6995–7004 (2014)
23. Dobos, I., Vörösmarty, G.: Green supplier selection and evaluation using DEA-type composite indictors. Prod. Econ. 273–278 (2014)
24. Mahdiloo, M., Saen, R.F., Lee, K.-H.: Technical, environmental and eco-efficiency measurement for supplier selection: an extension and application of data envelopment analysis. Prod. Econ. 279–289 (2015)
25. Zhou, X., Pedrycz, W., Kuang, Y., Zhang, Z.: Type-2 fuzzy multi-objective DEA model: an application to sustainable supplier evaluation. Appl. Soft Comput. 424–440 (2016)
26. Yousefi, S., Shabanpour, H., Fisher, R., Saen, R.F.: Evaluating and ranking sustainable suppliers by robust dynamic data envelopment analysis. Measurement 72–85 (2016)
27. Cheng, Y., Peng, J., Zhou, Z., Gu, X., Liu, W.: A hybrid DEA-adaboost model in supplier selection for fuzzy variable and multiple objectives. IFAC-PapersOnLine 12255–12260 (2017)
28. Jauhar, S.K., Pant, M.: Integrating DEA with DE and MODE for sustainable supplier selection. J. Comput. Sci. 299–306 (2017)
29. Amindoust, A.: A resilient-sustainable based supplier selection model using a hybrid intelligent method. Comput. Indust. Eng. 122–135 (2018)
30. Dobos, I., Vörösmarty, G.: Inventory-related costs in green supplier selection problems with Data Envelopment Analysis (DEA). Economics 374–380 (2019)
31. Tavassoli, M., Farzipoor Saen, R., Mohamadi Zanjirani, D.: Assessing sustainability of suppliers: a novel stochastic-fuzzy DEA model. Sustain. Prod. Consum. 78–91 (2020)
32. Ersoy, Y., Ozgur Dogan, N.: An integrated model of fuzzy AHP/Fuzzy DEA for measurement of supplier performance: a case study in textile sector. Int. J. Supply Oper. Manag. **7**(1), 17–38 (2020)
33. Manjunat Patel, G.C., Nayakappa Patil, A., Shivkumar, K.M., Jatti, S.P., Rivankar, S.N.: Fuzzy TOPSIS and grey relation analysis integration for supplier selection in fiber industry. Int. J. Supply Oper. Manag. **7**(4), 373–383 (2020)
34. Vorosmarty, G., Dobos, I.: A literature review of sustainable supplier evaluation with Data Envelopnemt Analysis. ScienceDirect (2022)
35. Sadjadi, S.J., Forghani, A., Farhang Moghadam, B.: Supplier selection models for complementary, sustainable and conditional products. Int. J. Supply Oper. Manag. **9**(2), 149–161 (2022)
36. Hatami, A.M., Emrouznejad, A., Tavana, M.: A taxonomy and review of the fuzzy data envelopment analysis literature: two decades in the making. Eur. J. Oper. Res. **214**(3), 457–472 (2011)
37. Charnes, A., Cooper, W.W., Rhodes, E.L.: Measuring the efficiency of decision making units. Eur. J. Oper. Res. **2**(6), 429–444 (1978)
38. Nahra, T.A., Mendez, D., Alexander, J.A.: Employing super-efficiency analysis as an alternative to DEA: an application in outpatient substance abuse treatment. Eur. J. Oper. Res. **196**(3), 1097–1106 (2009)

39. Jablonsky, J.: Measuring the efficiency of production units by AHP models. Math. Comput. Model. **46**(7–8), 1091–1098 (2007)
40. Zeydan, M., Çolpan, C.: A new decision support system for performance measurement using combined fuzzy TOPSIS/DEA approach. Int. J. Prod. Res. **47**(15), 4327–4349 (2009)

Airport Situations and Games with Fuzzy Uncertainty

İsmail Özcan(✉) and Sırma Zeynep Alparslan Gök

Faculty of Arts and Sciences, Department of Mathematics, Süleyman Demirel University, 32 260 Isparta, Turkey

ismailozcanmath@gmail.com, zeynepalparslan@yahoo.com

Abstract. Airport situations are widely studied allocation problems, with the aim of providing simple and fair allocation for the landing fees. In the airport situations, different airline firms use the airstrips of different lengths. As expected, a larger plane needs a longer airstrip. In the sequel if a plane is served by an airstrip, then all the other smaller planes are served by the same airstrip. To accommodate all these planes, the airstrip must be long enough for the largest plane. This paper deals with the research area of cooperative games arising from airport situations with fuzzy data. We deal with airport situations, where the costs of the pieces of the runway are chosen as fuzzy intervals. Also, we study some properties of airport situations as an allocation problem. On the other hand we extend Baker-Thompson rule under fuzzy uncertainty and introduce the fuzzy interval Baker-Thompson rule. The main result of this study is to give an axiomatic characterization of this rule.

Keywords: Cooperative games · Uncertainty · Fuzzy intervals · Baker-Thompson rule · Axiomatization

1 Introduction

Recently cooperative game theory is interested in popular research area with several pioneering developments. In these models, the rewards/costs allocated to the coalition of players are known with certainty, but when uncertainty is taken into consideration values of the characteristic functions are not real valued as in the crisp case. Hence, these values capture the uncertainty on the outcome of cooperation in different. For example, stochastic, fuzzy interval, interval, ellipsoidal and fuzzy uncertainty.

Cooperative games with fuzzy intervals are generalization of cooperative game theory with intervals, see [1, 4, 5, 10], in the sense that each coalition has the form of a fuzzy interval of real numbers rather than an interval. The domain of definition of the characteristic function from coalitions to fuzzy coalitions of the set of players is extended in [8] and [11]. Here, studies, the characteristic function assigns to each fuzzy coalition to a real number again. On the other hand [17, 18, 19] are concerned with the uncertainty in the values of the characteristic functions. These models remain the domain of the characteristic function of a game to be the system of deterministic coalitions, but put the worths of the coalitions as fuzzy intervals. Crisp coalitions for games are used in

A. Mirzazadeh et al. (Eds.): SEMIT 2022, CCIS 1808, pp. 50–60, 2023.
https://doi.org/10.1007/978-3-031-40395-8_4

[16], where the worth of the coalition is a fuzzy interval. In [20], the interval Shapley function is considered for interval fuzzy games based on the extended Hukuhara difference. In [15], the general prenucleolus and the least square general prenucleolus over the pre-imputation set are provided for cooperative fuzzy games. Further, cooperative bubbly games are extended to cooperative fuzzy bubbly games in [22]. Equal surplus sharing solutions for cooperative games under fuzzy uncertainty are studied in [23]. Furthermore, big boss fuzzy interval games are studied in [6]. Different applications of fuzzy interval cooperative games are given in [23, 27, 28).

The rest of the paper is organized as follows. Section 2 gives some preliminaries from fuzzy interval cooperative games and the definiton of the Baker-Thompson rule in the classical sense. The model of fuzzy interval Baker-Thompson rule is introduced in Sect. 3. An axiomatic characterization of this rule is given in Sect. 4. Furthermore, an example is given in Sect. 5. Finally, we conclude our study in Sect. 6.

2 Preliminaries

2.1 Fuzzy Intervals

A fuzzy set $\mathcal{F}$ in $\mathbb{R}$ is a function $u_{\mathcal{F}} : \mathbb{R} \to [0, 1]$ where $u_{\mathcal{F}}$ assigns to each point in $\mathbb{R}$ a degree of membership. For any $\alpha \in [0, 1]$, $\alpha-$ level set (α − cut) of $\mathcal{F}$ is defined by [26]:

$$[\mu_{\mathcal{F}}]^{\alpha} = \{x \in \mathbb{R} : u_{\mathcal{F}}(x) \geq \alpha\} = \left[\mu_{\mathcal{F}}^{-}, \mu_{\mathcal{F}}^{+}\right]. \quad (1)$$

If $\alpha = 0$ then $[\mu_{\mathcal{F}}]^0 = cl\{x \in \mathbb{R} : \mu_{\mathcal{F}}(x) > 0\} = supp(\mu_{\mathcal{F}})$.

Here $cl\{x \in \mathbb{R} : \mu_{\mathcal{F}}(x) > 0\}$ is the closure of $\{x \in \mathbb{R} : \mu_{\mathcal{F}}(x) > 0\}$.

A fuzzy set $\mathcal{F}$ in $\mathbb{R}$ is called a fuzzy interval, if the following conditions are hold [12]:

- $[\mu_{\mathcal{F}}]^{\alpha}$ is compact, $\forall \alpha \in [0, 1]$;
- $[\mu_{\mathcal{F}}]^{\alpha}$ is convex, $\forall \alpha \in [0, 1]$;
- $[\mu_{\mathcal{F}}]^{\alpha}$ is normal, that is, there exist $x \in \mathbb{R}$ such that $\mu_{\mathcal{F}}(x) = 1$.

The family of fuzzy intervals are denoted as $\mathcal{F}(\mathbb{R})$. For all $\mathcal{F} \in \mathcal{F}(\mathbb{R})$ there exist $a, b, c, d \in \mathbb{R}$ and $L : [a, b] \to \mathbb{R}$ non-decreasing and $R : [c, d] \to \mathbb{R}$ non-increasing such that the membership function $\mu_{\mathcal{F}}$ is defined by [12]:

$$\mu_{\mathcal{F}}(x) = \begin{cases} L(x) & a \leq x \leq b, \\ 1 & b \leq x \leq c, \\ R(x) & c \leq x \leq d, \\ 0 & \text{otherwise.} \end{cases} \quad (2)$$

If L and R are linear then $\mu_{\mathcal{F}}$ is called trapeziodal fuzzy interval and its membership function is defined by [12]:

$$\mu_{\mathcal{F}}(x) = \begin{cases} \frac{x-a}{b-a} & a \leq x \leq b, \\ 1 & b \leq x \leq c, \\ \frac{x-d}{c-d} & c \leq x \leq d, \\ 0 & \text{otherwise.} \end{cases} \quad (3)$$

The trapeziodal fuzzy interval defined above is denoted by (a, b, c, d) and the set of all trapezoidal fuzzy intervals are denoted by $\mathcal{F}_T(\mathbb{R})$. In this case if $a = b$ and $c = d$, then (a, b, c, d) is a compact interval, if $a = b = c = d$ then (a, b, c, d) is a real number.

For all $\alpha \in [0, 1]$ the α-level set of a trapeziodal fuzzy interval of $\mathcal{F}$ with membership function u is defined as [12]:

$$\begin{aligned}[\mu_{\mathcal{F}}]^{\alpha} &= \left[L^{-1}(0)(1-\alpha) + \alpha L^{-1}(1), R^{-1}(0)(1-\alpha) + \alpha R^{-1}(1)\right] \\ &= [a(1-\alpha) + \alpha b, (1-\alpha)d + \alpha c] \\ &= \left[\mu_{\mathcal{F}}^{-}, \mu_{\mathcal{F}}^{+}\right] \end{aligned} \tag{4}$$

If $\mathcal{F} \in \mathcal{F}(\mathbb{R})$, then the decomposition of $\mathcal{F}$ as follows [12]:

$$\mathcal{F} = \bigcup_{0 \le \alpha \le 1} [\mu_{\mathcal{F}}^{-}, \mu_{\mathcal{F}}^{+}]. \tag{5}$$

Let $\mathcal{F}_1, \mathcal{F}_2 \in \mathcal{F}(\mathbb{R})$, the binary relation $\trianglerighteq$ is defined on $\mathcal{F}(\mathbb{R})$ as follows [12, 13]. For all $\alpha \in [0, 1]$;

$$\mathcal{F}_1 \triangleright \mathcal{F}_2 \Leftrightarrow \left[\mu_{\mathcal{F}_1}\right]^{\alpha} \triangleright \left[\mu_{\mathcal{F}_2}\right]^{\alpha} \Leftrightarrow \mu_{\mathcal{F}_1} \ge \mu_{\mathcal{F}_2}^{-} \text{and } \mu_{\mathcal{F}_1}^{+} \ge \mu_{\mathcal{F}_2}^{+}. \tag{6}$$

Let $\mathcal{F}_1 = (a_1, a_2, a_3, a_4)$ and $\mathcal{F}_2 = (b_1, b_2, b_3, b_4) \in \mathcal{F}_T(\mathbb{R})$ be two trapeziodal fuzzy intervals and $\lambda \in \mathbb{R}^+$, then the following conditions hold [12, 13]:

- $\mathcal{F}_1 + \mathcal{F}_2 = (a_1 + b_1, a_2 + b_2, a_3 + b_3, a_4 + b_4)$,
- $\lambda \mathcal{F}_1 = (\lambda a_1, \lambda a_2, \lambda a_3, \lambda a_4)$,
- $\mathcal{F}_1 \trianglerighteq \mathcal{F}_2 \Leftrightarrow a_1 \ge b_1, a_2 \ge b_2, a_3 \ge b_3$, and $a_4 \ge b_4$ holds.

Let $\mathcal{F}_1, \mathcal{F}_2 \in \mathcal{F}(\mathbb{R})$. If there exist $\mathcal{F}_3 \in \mathcal{F}(\mathbb{R})$ such that $\mathcal{F}_1 = \mathcal{F}_2 + \mathcal{F}_3$, then $\mathcal{F}_3$ is said to be Hukuhara difference between $\mathcal{F}_1$ and $\mathcal{F}_2$ is denoted by $\mathcal{F}_3 = \mathcal{F}_1 -_H \mathcal{F}_2$ [13].

Let $\mathcal{F}_1 = (a_1, a_2, a_3, a_4)$ and $\mathcal{F}_2 = (b_1, b_2, b_3, b_4) \in \mathcal{F}_T(\mathbb{R})$ be two trapeziodal fuzzy intervals. If $a_i - b_i \le a_j - b_j$ then the Hukuhara difference between $\mathcal{F}_1$ and $\mathcal{F}_2$ is defined as:

$$\mathcal{F}_1 -_H \mathcal{F}_2 = (a_1 - b_1, a_2 - b_2, a_3 - b_3, a_4 - b_4), \forall i \le j. \tag{7}$$

In this paper, we use $\mathcal{F}_1 - \mathcal{F}_2$ instead of $\mathcal{F}_1 -_H \mathcal{F}_2$, $\forall \mathcal{F}_1, \mathcal{F}_2 \in \mathcal{F}(\mathbb{R})$.

2.2 Fuzzy Interval Cooperative games

A fuzzy interval cooperative game is a pair $< N, \mathcal{U} >$, where $N = \{1, 2, ..., n\}$ is the set of players and $\mathcal{U} : 2^N \to \mathcal{F}(\mathbb{R})$ is the characteristic function mapping each coalition $S \in 2^N$ into a fuzzy interval $\mathcal{U}(S) \in \mathcal{F}(\mathbb{R})$ with $\mathcal{U}(\varnothing) = 0$. Here, 0 is a fuzzy interval with the membership function defined in [16]:

$$\mu_0(x) = \begin{cases} 1, & x = 0 \\ 0, & x \ne 0 \end{cases}. \tag{8}$$

We denote by $\mathcal{F}(\mathbb{R})^N$ the set of fuzzy payoff vectors and $\mathcal{F}G^N$ the set of fuzzy interval cooperative games.

A fuzzy interval cooperative game $< N, \mathcal{U} >$ is size monotonic, if $< N, |\mathcal{U}| >$ size monotonic. That is, $|\mathcal{U}|(T) \geq |\mathcal{U}|(S)$, $\forall \alpha \in [0, 1]$, $S, T \in 2^N$ with $S \subset T$, where $|\mathcal{U}| = \mu^+_{\mathcal{U}} - \mu^-_{\mathcal{U}}$. We denote by $SM\mathcal{F}G^N$ the class of size monotonic fuzzy interval games.

The Shapley value of a fuzzy interval cooperative game is introduced in [25] as follows:

Let $< N, \mathcal{U} >$ be a size monotonic fuzzy interval game. Then the Shapley value is defined by:

$$\phi(\mathcal{U}) = (\phi_1(\mathcal{U}), \phi_2(\mathcal{U}), ..., \phi_n(\mathcal{U})),$$

where

$$\phi_i(\mathcal{U}) := \sum_{S \subset N \setminus \{i\}} \frac{|S|!(N - 1 - |S|)!}{N!} (\mathcal{U}(S \cup \{i\}) -_H \mathcal{U}(S)). \tag{9}$$

2.3 Airport Situations and the Baker-Thompson Rule

In this part, we study an airport with a runway and assume that planes which are to land are classified into m types [2].

In classical airport problems for each $1 \leq j \leq m$, we denote the set of landings of planes of kind j by N_j and its carnality by n_j. Here, $N = \cup_{j=1}^m N_j$ represents the set of all landings. Let c_j represent the cost of a runway adequate for planes of kind j.

We suppose that the kinds are ordered such that $0 < c_0 < c_1 < ... < c_m$. We suppose that the runway is divided into m consecutive pieces P_j, $1 \leq j \leq m$, where P_1 is adequate for landings of planes of kind 1; P_1 and P_2 together for landings of planes of kind 2, and so on. The cost of the piece P_j, $1 \leq j \leq m$, is the marginal cost $c_j - c_{j-1}$. Hence, every landing of planes of kind j contributes to the cost of the pieces P_k, $1 \leq k \leq j$, equally divided into its users $\cup_{r=k}^m N_r$. Accordingly, [9] and [24] submit the following rule:

$$BT_i = \sum_{k=1}^{j} \left[\sum_{r=k}^{m} n_r \right]^{-1} (c_k - c_{k-1}), \tag{10}$$

whenever $i \in N_j$, which is known as the Baker-Thompson rule.

Formally, an allocation rule for an allocation problem is a map F associating each allocation problem $(N, (c_k)_{k=1,...,m})$, to a unique point $F(N, (c_k)_{k=1,...,m}) \in \mathbb{R}^N$ with

$$\sum_{i \in N} F_i(N, (c_k)_{k=1,...,m}) = c_m. \tag{11}$$

An allocation rule F satisfies individual equal sharing (*IES*) property if for each situation

$$(N, (c_k)_{k=1,...,m}), F_i(N, (c_k)_{k=1,...,m}) \geq \frac{c_r}{m}, \tag{12}$$

for all $i \in N_r$ and $r = 1, ..., m$.

An allocation rule F satisfies collective usage right (CUR) property if for every situation $(N, (c_k)_{k=1,...,m})$,

$$(N, (c_k)_{k=1,...,m}), F_i(N, (c_k)_{k=1,...,m}) \leq c_r \left(\sum_{l=1,...,n} n_l \right)^{-1} \tag{13}$$

for every $i \in N_r$ and $r = 1, ..., m$.

An allocation rule F satisfies consistency on last group ($CLAST$) property if for every situation $(N, (c_k)_{k=1,...,m})$ and for every $h \in N_m$

$$F_i(N, (c_k)_{k=1,...,m}) = F_i(\widehat{N}, (\widehat{c_k})_{k=1,...,m}), i \in N \backslash \{h\}, \tag{14}$$

where $\widehat{N}_l = N_l, l = 1, ..., m-1, \widehat{N}_m = N_m \backslash \{h\}$ and $\hat{c}_l = c_l - F_h(N, (c_k)_{k=1,...,m}), l = 1, ..., m$.

In the following section, we extend these results to by using fuzzy intervals. We inspired by [14].

3 Airport Fuzzy Situations and Their Baker-Thompson Rule

In this part, we study airport situations, where cost of pieces of the runway are fuzzy intervals. Here, we associate such a situation to a fuzzy interval game. Moreover, we extend the results presented above for airport fuzzy interval games. We use a similar approach used in [3, 7, 21].

Let $\mathcal{F} \in \mathcal{F}(\mathbb{R})$, $T \backslash \{\varnothing\}$, also let $u_T^* : 2^N \rightarrow \mathbb{R}$ be the classical dual unanimity game based on T. The fuzzy interval game $< N, \mathcal{F}u_T^* >$ defined as $(\mathcal{F}u_T^*)(S) := u_T^*(S)\mathcal{F}$ $\forall S \in 2^N$ plays a key rule. Note that, $\phi(\mathcal{F}u_T^*)$ for the fuzzy interval game $< N, \mathcal{F}u_T^* >$ is related with the Shapley value $\phi(u_T^*)$ of the crisp game $< N, \mathcal{F}u_T^* >$ as given below:

$$\phi_i(\mathcal{F}u_T^*) = \phi_i(u_T^*)\mathcal{F} = \begin{cases} \mathcal{F}/|T|, & i \in T \\ 0, & i \in N \backslash T. \end{cases} \tag{15}$$

Let the fuzzy $\mathcal{U}_j$ with non-negative finite bounds represent the fuzzy cost of piece P_j, $1 \leq j \leq m$.

Now, we introduce fuzzy interval allocation rule β, which we call fuzzy interval Baker-Thompson rule. For an airport fuzzy interval situation $(N, (\mathcal{U}_k)_{k=1,...,m})$ the Baker-Thompson allocation for each player $i \in N_j$ is defined as:

$$\beta_i = \sum_{k=1}^{j} (\sum_{r=k}^{m} n_r)^{-1} \mathcal{U}_k. \tag{16}$$

Notice that for the piece of P_k the users are $\cup_{r=k}^m N_r$. So, $(\sum_{r=k}^m n_r)^{-1} \mathcal{U}_k$ is the equal fuzzy interval cost share of each user of the piece P_k. So a player $i \in N_j$ contributes to the cost of the pieces $P_1, ..., P_j$.

The cost function $\mathcal{U}$ of the airport fuzzy interval game $< N, \mathcal{U} >$ is given by $\mathcal{U}(\varnothing) = 0$ and $\mathcal{U}(S) = \sum_{k=1}^{j} \mathcal{U}_k$ for all coalitions $S \subset N$ satisying $S \cap N_j \neq \varnothing$ and $S \cap N_k \neq \varnothing$ for all $j + 1 \leq k \leq m$. Next, we give the definition of the airport fuzzy interval game as follows:

$$\mathcal{U} = \sum_{k=1}^{m} \mathcal{U}_k u_{N^*}^*. \tag{17}$$

The following theorem shows that the fuzzy interval Baker-Thompson rule coincides with the fuzzy Shapley value.

Theorem 3.1 *Let* $< N, \mathcal{U} >$ *be an airport fuzzy interval game. Then, the fuzzy interval allocation* β *agrees with the fuzzy Shapley value* $\phi(\mathcal{U})$.

Proof. For $i \in N_j$ we have.

$$\phi_i(\mathcal{U}) = \phi_i(\sum_{k=1}^{m} \mathcal{U}_k u_{N^*}^*)$$

$$= \sum_{k=1}^{m} \phi_i(\mathcal{U}_k u_{N^*}^*)$$

$$= \sum_{k=1}^{j}(\sum_{r=k}^{m} n_r)^{-1}\mathcal{U}_k = \beta_i$$

This is what we wanted to show.

We again consider the aircraft fee problem of an airport with one runway. There is a set of potential airplanes, denoted by $\mathcal{I} \subseteq \mathbb{N}$ where $\mathbb{N}$ is the set of natural numbers. Let $\mathcal{N}$ be the class of non-empty and finite subsets of $\mathcal{I}$. Given $N \in \mathcal{N}$ and $i \in N$, let $\mathcal{U}_i \in \mathcal{F}(\mathbb{R})^N$ be airplane i's fuzzy interval cost, and $\mathcal{U} = (\mathcal{U}_i)_{i \in N}$ the fuzzy interval cost vector. An airport fuzzy interval problem for N is a list $\mathcal{U} \in \mathcal{F}(\mathbb{R})^N$. Let $\mathcal{C}^N$ be the class of all problems for N. A fuzzy interval contribution vector for $\mathcal{U} \in \mathcal{C}^N$ is a vector $\mathcal{U} \in \mathcal{F}(\mathbb{R})^N$. Let $\mathcal{F}(\mathcal{U})$ be the set of all fuzzy interval contributions vectors for $\mathcal{U} \in \mathcal{C}^N$. A fuzzy interval rule is a function defined on ${}_{N \in \mathcal{N}}\mathcal{C}^N$ that associates with each $N \in \mathcal{N}$ and each $\mathcal{U} \in \mathcal{C}^N$ a vector in $\mathcal{F}(\mathcal{U})$. For all $N \in \mathcal{N}$ such that $|N| = n$, let $\eta : N \to \{1, ..., n\}$ be a bijection such that $\mathcal{U}_{\eta^{-1}(1)} \leq \cdots \leq \mathcal{U}_{\eta^{-1}(n)}$. Thus, the airplanes in N are ordered in terms of their costs. For all $N \in \mathcal{N}$ and all $N\prime \subset N$, we define $\mathcal{U}_{N\prime} = (\mathcal{U}_i)_{i \in N\prime}$, $S_{N\prime}(\mathcal{U}) = (S_i(\mathcal{U}))_{i \in N\prime}$, and so on. For a given airport fuzzy interval situation $(N, (\mathcal{U}_k)_{k=1,...,m})$; fuzzy interval Baker-Thompson rule $\beta_i(\mathcal{U})$ is defined as follows:

For all $N \in \mathcal{N}$, all $T \in \mathcal{C}^N$, and $\forall i \in N$, is given by:

$$\beta_i(\mathcal{U}) = \frac{\mathcal{U}_{\eta^{-1}(1)}}{|N|} + \frac{\mathcal{U}_{\eta^{-1}(2)} - \mathcal{U}_{\eta^{-1}(1)}}{|N| - 1} + \cdots + \frac{\mathcal{U}_{\eta^{-1}(k)} - \mathcal{U}_{\eta^{-1}(k-1)}}{|N| - k + 1}, \tag{18}$$

such that $\mathcal{U}_{\eta^{-1}(k)} \trianglelefteq \mathcal{U}_{\eta^{-1}(k+1)}$, where $\eta(i) = k$.

The fuzzy interval cost allocation rule β_i called fuzzy interval Baker-Thompson rule.

Theorem 3.2 *$(N, (\mathcal{U}_k)_{k=1,\ldots,m})$ be an airport fuzzy interval situation. Then fuzzy interval Baker-Thompson rule β for each player $i \in N_j$ is $\beta_i = \left[\beta_i^-, \beta_i^+\right]$.*

Proof. From (5) and (10),

$$\begin{aligned}\beta_i &= \sum_{k=1}^{j} \left(\sum_{r=k}^{m} n_r\right)^{-1} \mathcal{U}_k \\ &= \sum_{k=1}^{j} \left(\sum_{r=k}^{m} n_r\right)^{-1} \left[\mu_{\mathcal{U}_k}^-, \mu_{\mathcal{U}_k}^+\right] \\ &= \left[\sum_{k=1}^{j} \left(\sum_{r=k}^{m} n_r\right)^{-1} \mu_{\mathcal{U}_k}^-, \sum_{k=1}^{j} \left(\sum_{r=k}^{m} n_r\right)^{-1} \mu_{\mathcal{U}_k}^+\right] \\ &= \left[\beta_i^-, \beta_i^+\right]\end{aligned}$$

for all $\alpha \in [0, 1]$. □

In Theorem 3.2, we show that one can calculate the lower/upper bound of the fuzzy interval Baker-Thompson rule by using the left/right $\alpha-$ cuts of fuzzy interval costs for all $\alpha \in [0, 1]$.

4 Discussion

In this section, an axiomatic characterization can be found by using the fuzzy interval uncertainty, which we are inspried by [2] and we use a similar approach used in [3, 7, 21].

We define an interval allocation rule for an airport interval $(N, (\mathcal{U}_k)_{k=1,\ldots,m})$ as a map F associating each allocation situation $(N, (\mathcal{U}_k)_{k=1,\ldots,m})$ to a unique rule

$$F(N, (\mathcal{U}_k)_{k=1,\ldots,m}) = F(N, (\left[\mu_{\mathcal{U}_k}^-, \mu_{\mathcal{U}_k}^+\right])_{k=1,\ldots,m}) \in \mathcal{F}(\mathbb{R})^N \tag{19}$$

with

$$\sum_{i \in N} F(N, (\mathcal{U}_k)_{k=1,\ldots,m}) = \sum_{i=1}^{m} \left[\mu_{\mathcal{U}_k}^-, \mu_{\mathcal{U}_k}^+\right] = \mathcal{U}_i.$$

for each $\alpha \in [0, 1]$.

An allocation rule F satisfies the fuzzy interval individual equal sharing ($\mathcal{F}IES$) property if for every situation,

$$(N, (\mathcal{U}_k)_{k=1,\ldots,m}), F_i(N, (\mathcal{U}_k)_{k=1,\ldots,m}) = \left[\frac{\sum_{k=1}^{j} \mu_{\mathcal{U}_k}^-}{\sum_{r=k}^{m} n_r}, \frac{\sum_{k=1}^{j} \mu_{\mathcal{U}_k}^+}{\sum_{r=k}^{m} n_r}\right] \tag{20}$$

$$\geq \left[\frac{\sum_{k=1}^{j} \mu_{\mathcal{U}_k}^-}{n}, \frac{\sum_{k=1}^{j} \mu_{\mathcal{U}_k}^+}{n}\right]$$

for each $i \in N_r$, $\alpha \in [0, 1]$, $r = 1, ..., m$.

An allocation rule F satisfies the fuzzy interval collective usage right ($\mathcal{F}CUR$) property if for every situation $(N, (\mathcal{U}_k)_{k=1,...,m})$,

$$F_i(N, (\mathcal{U}_k)_{k=1,...,m}) \leq \left[\sum_{k=1}^{j} \mu^-_{\mathcal{U}_k}(\sum_{l=1,...,r} n_l)^{-1}, \sum_{k=1}^{j} \mu^+_{\mathcal{U}_k}(\sum_{l=1,...,r} n_l)^{-1} \right] \tag{21}$$

for each $i \in N_r$, $\alpha \in [0, 1]$, $r = 1, ..., m$.

An allocation rule F satisfies the fuzzy interval consistency on last group ($\mathcal{F}CLAST$) property if for every situation $(N, (\mathcal{U}_k)_{k=1,...,m})$, $(N, (\mu^-_{\mathcal{U}_k})_{k=1,...,m})$ and $(N, (\mu^+_{\mathcal{U}_k})_{k=1,...,m})$ satisfy *CLAST* for each $i \in N_r$,$\alpha \in [0, 1]$, $r = 1, ..., m$.

Proposition 4.1 *The fuzzy interval Baker-Thompson rule β satisfies $\mathcal{F}IES$, $\mathcal{F}CUR$ and $\mathcal{F}CLAST$.*

Proof. The proof is obtained by following the steps of [14] for β_i^- and β_i^+ for each $i \in N_j$ and $j = 1, ..., m$. Then, applying Theorem 3.1, completes the proof.

Next, we give an axiomatic characterization of the fuzzy interval Baker-Thompson rule.

Theorem 4.1 *The fuzzy interval Baker-Thompson rule β is the unique rule satisfying $\mathcal{F}IES$, $\mathcal{F}CUR$ and $\mathcal{F}CLAST$.*

Proof. From Proposition 3.1 we conclude that β satisfies the three properties. We just need to prove the uniqueness. It is obvious by [14] that β_i^- and β_i^+ are the unique allocations satisfying the three properties *IES*, *CUR* and *CLAST* for each $i \in N_j$ and $j = 1, ..., m$. By Theorem 3.2, we see that $\beta_i = \left[\beta_i^-, \beta_i^+\right]$ is unique for every $i \in N_j$ and $j = 1, ..., m$. Hence, β is the unique fuzzy interval allocation satisfying $\mathcal{F}IES$, $\mathcal{F}CUR$ and $\mathcal{F}CLAST$.

5 An Application

In this section, we have an application on an airport situation under fuzzy uncertainty.

Example 5.1 *Let $(N = \{1, 2, 3\}, (\mathcal{U}_k)_{k=1,2,3})$ be an airport fuzzy interval situation with fuzzy interval costs.*

$\mathcal{U}_1 = (30, 60, 90, 150)$, $\mathcal{U}_2 = (60, 90, 120, 180)$ and $\mathcal{U}_3 = (60, 120, 150, 240)$. Then,

$$\mathcal{U}_1 = \begin{cases} \frac{x}{30} - 1 & 30 \leq x < 60 \\ 1 & 60 \leq x \leq 90 \\ -\frac{x}{60} + \frac{5}{2} & 90 < x \leq 150 \\ 0 & \text{otherwise} \end{cases}, \mathcal{U}_2 = \begin{cases} \frac{x}{30} - 2 & 60 \leq x < 90 \\ 1 & 90 \leq x \leq 120 \\ -\frac{x}{60} + 3 & 120 < x \leq 180 \\ 0 & \text{otherwise} \end{cases},$$

$$\mathcal{U}_3 = \begin{cases} \frac{x}{60} + 1 & 60 \leq x < 120 \\ 1 & 120 \leq x \leq 150 \\ -\frac{x}{90} + \frac{8}{3} & 150 < x \leq 240 \\ 0 & \text{otherwise} \end{cases}.$$

We have

$$\mathcal{U}_1 = [\mathcal{U}_1^-, \mathcal{U}_1^+] = [30 + 30\alpha, 150 - 60\alpha]$$

$$\mathcal{U}_2 = [\mathcal{U}_2^-, \mathcal{U}_2^+] = [60 + 30\alpha, 180 - 60\alpha]$$

$$\mathcal{U}_3 = [\mathcal{U}_3^-, \mathcal{U}_3^+] = [60 + 60\alpha, 240 - 90\alpha]$$

for all $\alpha \in [0, 1]$. Then, we obtain fuzzy interval Baker-Thompson rule as follows:

$$\beta_1^- = \frac{\mathcal{U}_1^-}{3} = 10 + 10\alpha$$

$$\beta_2^- = \frac{\mathcal{U}_1^-}{3} + \frac{\mathcal{U}_2^- - \mathcal{U}_1^-}{3-1} = 25 + 10\alpha$$

$$\beta_3^- = \frac{\mathcal{U}_1^-}{3} + \frac{\mathcal{U}_2^- - \mathcal{U}_1^-}{3-1} + \frac{\mathcal{U}_3^- - \mathcal{U}_2^-}{3-2} = 25 + 40\alpha$$

and

$$\beta_1^+ = \frac{\mathcal{U}_1^+}{3} = 50 - 20\alpha$$

$$\beta_2^+ = \frac{\mathcal{U}_1^+}{3} + \frac{\mathcal{U}_2^+ - \mathcal{U}_1^+}{3-1} = 65 - 20\alpha$$

$$\beta_3^+ = \frac{\mathcal{U}_1^+}{3} + \frac{\mathcal{U}_2^+ - \mathcal{U}_1^+}{3-1} + \frac{\mathcal{U}_3^+ - \mathcal{U}_2^+}{3-2} = 125 - 50\alpha.$$

Then we obtain,

$$\beta_i^- = (10 + 10\alpha, 25 + 10\alpha, 25 + 40\alpha),$$

$$\beta_i^+ = (50 - 20\alpha, 65 - 20\alpha, 125 - 50\alpha).$$

Hence,

$$\beta_i = (\beta_1, \beta_2, \beta_3) = ((10, 20, 30, 50), (25, 35, 45, 65), (25, 65, 75, 125))$$

where

$$\beta_1 = \begin{cases} \frac{x}{10} - 1 & 10 \le x < 20 \\ 1 & 20 \le x \le 30 \\ -\frac{x}{20} + \frac{5}{2} & 30 < x \le 50 \\ 0 & \text{otherwise} \end{cases}, \quad \beta_2 = \begin{cases} \frac{x}{10} - \frac{5}{2} & 25 \le x < 35 \\ 1 & 35 \le x \le 45 \\ -\frac{x}{20} + \frac{13}{4} & 45 < x \le 65 \\ 0 & \text{otherwise} \end{cases},$$

$$\beta_3 = \begin{cases} \frac{x}{40} - \frac{5}{8} & 25 \le x < 65 \\ 1 & 65 \le x \le 75 \\ -\frac{x}{50} + \frac{5}{2} & 75 < x \le 125 \\ 0 & \text{otherwise} \end{cases}.$$

Now, let us construct the fuzzy interval cooperative game. Here, $< N, \mathcal{U} >$ is a three-person airport fuzzy interval game corresponding to the airport fuzzy situation. Fuzzy costs of the pieces are given as $\mathcal{U}_1 = (30, 60, 90, 150)$, $\mathcal{U}_2 = (60, 90, 120, 180)$ and $\mathcal{U}_3 = (60, 120, 150, 240)$. Then,

$$\mathcal{U}(\emptyset) = (0, 0, 0, 0)$$

$$\mathcal{U}(\{1\}) = (30, 60, 90, 150)$$

$$\mathcal{U}(\{2\}) = \mathcal{U}(\{1, 2\}) = (60, 90, 120, 180)$$

$$\mathcal{U}(\{3\}) = \mathcal{U}(\{1, 3\}) = \mathcal{U}(\{2, 3\}) = \mathcal{U}(\{1, 2, 3\}) = (60, 120, 150, 240)$$

We illustrate the fuzzy Shapley-value of the game as follows:

$$\phi(\mathcal{U}) = (\phi_1(\mathcal{U}), \phi_2(\mathcal{U}), \phi_3(\mathcal{U}))$$

$$= ((10, 20, 30, 50), (25, 35, 45, 65), (25, 65, 75, 125)).$$

6 Conclusion

Cooperative game theory is built around the question of how to allocate the collective income to the players in a fair and rational way. The use of theory of fuzzy sets can be used in cases, where uncertainty is included.

Uncertainty is the greatest solution for airport difficulties, and in a situation like this, informational environment is decision-making factors on operations collaboration and economics. We take into account the issue of aircraft fees for airports with only one runway. This study demonstrates how Baker-Thompson rule-based fuzzy interval cooperative game theory may assist in distributing landing expenses in a fair and simple manner. For further research, other Operational Research situations can be extended by using fuzzy interval setting. It may be interesting to do studies involving numerical tests and simulations for future work.

References

1. Alparslan Gök, S.Z., Branzei, R., Tijs, S.: Convex interval games. Adv. Decis. Sci. (2009)
2. Alparslan Gök, S.Z.: On the interval Baker-Thompson rule. J. Appl. Math. (2012)

3. Alparslan Gök, S.Z., Branzei, R., Tijs, S.: Airport interval games and their Shapley value. Oper. Res. Decis. **2**(19), 9–18 (2009)
4. Alparslan Gök, S.Z., Branzei, O., Branzei, R., Tijs, S.: Set-valued solution concepts using interval-type payoffs for interval games. J. Math. Econ. **47**(4–5), 621–626 (2011)
5. Alparslan Gök, S.Z., Miquel, S., Tijs, S.: Cooperation under interval uncertainty. Math. Methods Oper. Res. **69**(1), 99–109 (2009)
6. Gök, S.A., Özcan, I.: On big boss fuzzy interval games. Eur. J. Oper. Res. **306**(3), 1040–1046 (2023)
7. Alparslan Gök, S.Z., Qasim, E., Palanci, O., Weber, G.W.: Airport situations and games with grey uncertainty. Int. J. Ind. Eng. Oper. Res. **1**(1), 51–59 (2019)
8. Aubin, J.P.: Cooperative fuzzy games. Math. Oper. Res. **6**(1), 1–13 (1981)
9. Baker, J., Jr.: Airport runway cost impact study. Report submitted to the Association of Local Transport Airlines, Jackson, Mississippi (1965)
10. Branzei, R., Branzei, O., Gök, S.Z.A., Tijs, S.: Cooperative interval games: a survey. CEJOR **18**(3), 397–411 (2010)
11. Butnariu, D.: Fuzzy games: a description of the concept. Fuzzy Sets Syst. **1**(3), 181–192 (1978)
12. Dubois, D.J.: Fuzzy Sets and Systems: Theory and Applications, vol. 144. Academic Press (1980)
13. Dubois, D., Kerre, E., Mesiar, R., Prade, H.: Fuzzy interval analysis. In: Fundamentals of Fuzzy Sets, pp. 483–581. Springer, Boston (2000)
14. Fragnelli, V., Marina, M.E.: An axiomatic characterization of the Baker-Thompson rule. Econ. Lett. **107**(2), 85–87 (2010)
15. Kong, Q., Sun, H., Xu, G., Hou, D.: The general prenucleolus of n-person cooperative fuzzy games. Fuzzy Sets Syst. **349**, 23–41 (2018)
16. Mallozzi, L., Scalzo, V., Tijs, S.: Fuzzy interval cooperative games. Fuzzy Sets Syst. **165**(1), 98–105 (2011)
17. Mareš, M.: Additivities in fuzzy coalition games with side-payments. Kybernetika **35**(2), 149–166 (1999)
18. Mareš, M.: Fuzzy Cooperative Games, Cooperation with Vague Expectations. Physica-Verlag, Heidelberg (2001)
19. Mareš, M., Vlach, M.: Fuzzy classes of cooperative games with transferable utility. Scientiae Mathematicae Japonica **2**, 269–278 (2004)
20. Meng, F., Chen, X., Tan, C.: Cooperative fuzzy games with interval characteristic functions. Oper. Res. **16**, 1–24 (2016)
21. Olgun, M.O., Palanci, O., Gök, S.Z.A.: On the grey Baker-Thompson rule. J. Dyn. Games **7**(4), 303 (2020)
22. Özcan, İ., Gök, S.Z.A.: On cooperative fuzzy bubbly games. J. Dyn. Games **8**(3), 267 (2021)
23. Özcan, I., Gök, S.Z.A.: On the fuzzy interval equal surplus sharing solutions. Kybernetes **51**(9), 2753–2767 (2021)
24. Thompson, G.F.: Airport Costs and Pricing. Ph. D. Thesis submitted to University of Birmingham (1971)
25. Yu, X., Zhang, Q.: An extension of cooperative fuzzy games. Fuzzy Sets Syst. **161**(11), 1614–1634 (2010)
26. Zadeh, L.A.: Fuzzy sets. Inf. Control **8**(3), 338–353 (1965)
27. Özcan, I., Sledzinski, J., Gök, S., Butlewski, M., Weber, G.E.R.H.A.R.D.: Mathematical encouragement of companies to cooperate by using cooperative games with fuzzy approach. J. Ind. Manage. Optim. **19**(10) (2023)
28. Zadeh, L.A.: Fuzzy sets. Inf. Control **8**(3), 338–353 (1965)

Recent Directions of Industry 4.0 Applications in Supplier Ranking Process

Asma A. Mohammed Ali(✉) and AllaEldin H. Kassam

Department of Production Engineering and Metallurgy, University of Technology-Iraq, Baghdad, Iraq
pme.19.15@grad.uotechnology.edu.iq, allaeldin.h.kassam@uotechnology.edu.iq

Abstract. The supplier ranking process has evolved in recent years as a result of the leveraging of Industry 4.0 and digital technologies in the supply chain. Supplier ranking (selection) is one of the most important considerations in influencing the reduction of supply chain costs and increasing overall product and service quality by selecting the most efficient supplier. Therefore, this study presents a review of the potential of Industry 4.0 in the supplier ranking process. Due to the significance of supplier ranking and the novelty of industry 4.0 technologies, a literature study has been prepared to analyze the applications of Industry 4.0 technologies in supplier ranking, by reviewing papers from some structural dimensions: annual distribution of publications, a summary of reviewed publications, type of application, common criteria adopted, and MCDM approach used. The results showed that only (17) papers or about (46%) of the collected papers adopted industry 4.0 technologies in supplier ranking during the period (2016–2021), which were grouped into two groups: the first group of papers applied the Industry 4.0 technologies in the process of supplier ranking. The second group adopted the technologies as criteria for supplier ranking. The most common technologies adopted in the supplier ranking process are big data analytics, the internet of things, and cloud computing. In terms of criteria used, the common criteria used are focused mainly on big data analytics and technological capabilities. The most widely used MCDM approaches are Fuzzy-TOPSIS and Fuzzy-AHP. Finally, the use of uncertainty in supplier ranking in the (I4.0) era is discussed.

Keywords: Industry 4.0 · Supplier Ranking · MCDM Approaches · Systematic Literature Review

1 Introduction

According to rapid and enormous technological progress during the past few years in the manufacturing and service fields, the traditional technique and methods became inappropriate and slow in responding and catching up with this huge scientific explosion. Thus, new technologies have emerged that can keep pace with this explosion of information including Industry 4.0 (I4.0). Therefore, the focus of this section will be on the (I4.0)

A. Mirzazadeh et al. (Eds.): SEMIT 2022, CCIS 1808, pp. 61–80, 2023.
https://doi.org/10.1007/978-3-031-40395-8_5

and its technologies. Smit et al. [1], emphasized that (I4.0) is organizing of technology-based manufacturing processes and equipment that independently communicated with one another in a self-contained manner throughout the value chain, a futuristic intelligent plant model where physical processes are monitored by computer-controlled systems and produce a virtual replica of the real environment, and decentralized decision making based on principles of self-regulation. Hence it can facilitate, accurate and quick response to the business orders in the completion of the globalization era. This study will review the existing research papers to find out what researchers have achieved in this field by systematic literature review. The study consists of five parts; the introduction covers and explores the basics of (I4.0) components to initiate its applications in supplier ranking and selection process in the supply chain. The second part includes the theoretical background of supply chain management and supplier ranking. The third part explains the methodology. The fourth part is results discussions and findings. Finally, the fifth part includes the conclusion and limitations of the study. There are opportunities for adopting the technologies of (I4.0) in the supplier ranking process covered under the field of industrial and management engineering. The common (I4.0) technologies are shown in Fig. 1, include: Big Data, Simulation, Internet of Things, Robotics, Augmented Reality, System Integration, Cloud Computing, Additive Manufacturing and Cyber Security. The technologies will be discussed in general and briefly to clarify the concepts:

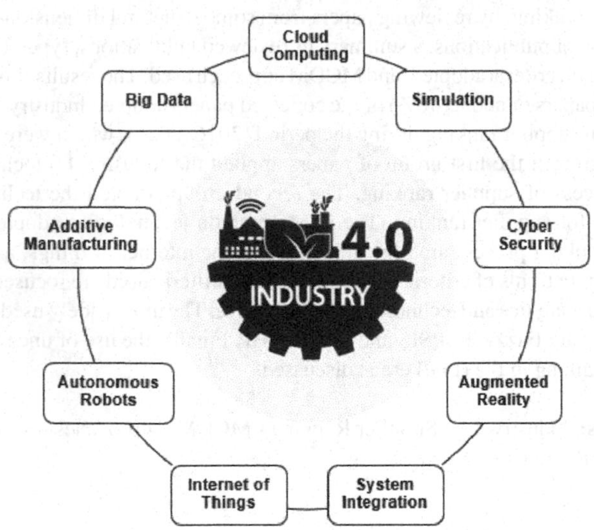

Fig. 1. Industry 4.0 key technologies [2].

1.1 Cloud Computing (CC)

It indicates that data and applications are stored and accessed online instead of the hard disk of the computer [3]. With the use of cloud computing, supply chain users may store and analyze their data on a private cloud or on a server owned by a third party, making the data conveniently available from practically anywhere [4]. In the case of choosing a supplier, the platforms based on the cloud act as a database, storing several data about various providers, resulting in significant savings for businesses that deal with multiple providers. Thus, businesses can nominate their providers based on their capability to supply suitable raw materials or semi-products according to the specifications of the final product and to meet the time limits [5].

1.2 Simulation

Simulation is the process of designing an actual or virtual system to describe and analyze the behavior of the system [6]. Different scenarios in product design, supply chain network, and manufacturing can be analyzed by creating an abstract of a hypothetical model from data raised from the cloud and treated by big data [7]. Simulation can be applied to the supply chain (supplier, factory, and client) to demonstrate known correlations and phenomena to enhance decision-making [8].

1.3 Cyber Security (CS)

Cyber security refers to preserving and protecting the data, software, or hardware in computer systems from spoilage and stealing. Thus, the (CS) protocols are applied to make (I4.0) safe for use by everyone [9]. The dangers and harms to people, businesses, and national security demonstrate the urgent need for corporations to intensify their efforts and investments in cyber security in order to protect not only their business information but also the information of their clients. Whereas, for a business to run successfully and integrate with the community, the security and trustworthiness of interactions and privacy of information, as well as collaborating with trustworthy suppliers, would be of crucial significance [10].

1.4 Augmented Reality (AR)

It can be summarized as the technology of computer graphics in which an artificial virtual object such as CAD model, code, image, and typing, is attached to a video stream in real mode [11]. The purpose of augmented reality (AR) apps is to provide more information to the user by integrating the real-world environment with a computer-generated virtual scene. AR might enhance the performance of employees and companies and transform work by providing real-time information to employees, such as stock on shelf, tasks to be completed, handling conditions etc. [12].

1.5 System Integration

To move the firm to the highest level, all of the components involved must be able to communicate effectively. Therefore to achieve more efficiency in the production process, (I4.0) has vertical, horizontal, and end to end integration systems. [9]. (Gottge & Menzel [13]) described the three different types of cross-linked integration approaches based on [14, 15]:

- Horizontal integration with the company's own components, providers, and clients.

- Vertical integration among levels of organization hierarchy.
- End to end integration towards the whole product life cycle.

The application of horizontal integration through (suppliers, factories, and clients) greatly contributes to the automatic selection of suppliers, through transferring information from clients to the business or suppliers directly through (cloud systems, communication network, or social media interactions).

1.6 Internet of Things (IOT)

Internet of things refers to a global network that connects different physical devices through sensors, standard protocols, and special software, that automatically signals a series of special responses [16]. (IOT) can be defined in supply chain management as a network of digitally connected physical elements to sense, monitor, and interact in the firm, allowing flexibility, tracking, visibility, and data interchange to assist timely planning and control [17]. IoT and blockchain technology can help the supply chain become more transparent and connected, which can help it meet the customers' evolving needs [18].

1.7 Autonomous Robots

All automated machines that receive instructions to create a set of repetitive tasks are represented as autonomous robots, which are machines that can make a decision, communicate, and act without instruction [19]. Improving the flexibility of the logistics system through process automation is essential to rapidly respond to fluctuating demand markets. An agile logistics system can be made possible by deploying automated robots that lowering waste, raise repeatability, and increase productivity [12].

1.8 Additive Manufacturing

It represents the technology that creates a three-dimensional object with the formation of the next layer of material under the control of the computer. Additive manufacturing, is also known as 3D Printing has been explained by (American Society for Testing and Materials (ASTM) [20]) as "the process of joining materials to make objects from 3D-model data, usually layer upon layer, as opposed to subtractive manufacturing methodologies, such as traditional machining". With the help of 3D printing, it is possible to create components that cannot be created by traditional manufacturing methods. By decentralizing the production, these parts may be created everywhere there is a 3D printer. In addition, this technique may enable the production of some products to be cheaper [12].

1.9 Big Data

Recent academic research begins discussing and arguing about different meanings of big data. Some academics suggest that big data is just a vast series of data, while others contend that it is erroneous to define it without taking 'analytics' into account [21].

(Fisher et al. [22]) stated that big data is the process of converting a huge volume of useless data into a small volume of more useful data. The analysis of big data is defined by applying sophisticated analytics approaches to enormous volumes of data to summarize valuable data and make data-driven decisions easier [23]. Some researchers have pointed to the application of big data in procurement, where (Darvazeh et al. [24]) indicated that the analytics of big data can make real-time control easier for data management and supply chain as it enhances the effectiveness of supply chain decisions, where leveraging a vast set of data from different sources like reports, social media data, and event data provides predictability and proactive planning for the supply chain. (Sanders [25]) defined the big data application for "sourcing" in supply chain management by suppliers segmentation, evaluation sourcing channel options, integrating with suppliers, and supporting supplier negotiations.

2 Theoretical Basis

2.1 Supply Chain Management (SCM)

SCM is a collection of techniques used to efficiently integrate vendors, plants, storehouses, and purchasing centers in order to provide clients with the products they need, in the quantities they need, at the times they need them while minimizing chain costs [26]. In a traditional SCM, after the innovation or development of a new product, the raw materials are often bought from major vendors, then the products are produced in the plant. Accomplished goods are then transported to storehouses, where they are stored before being dispatched to retailers, as shown in Fig. 2. Choosing supplier, facilities and instruments, and distributions centers wisely is regarded as one of the most important design considerations for a (SCM) [27]. To be competitive in contemporary business, companies need to provide products with high-quality, low-cost, and quick turnaround. Therefore, choosing the right suppliers becomes one of the essential issues of (SCM). Choosing the appropriate supplier has a direct and positive influence on a company's performance [28].

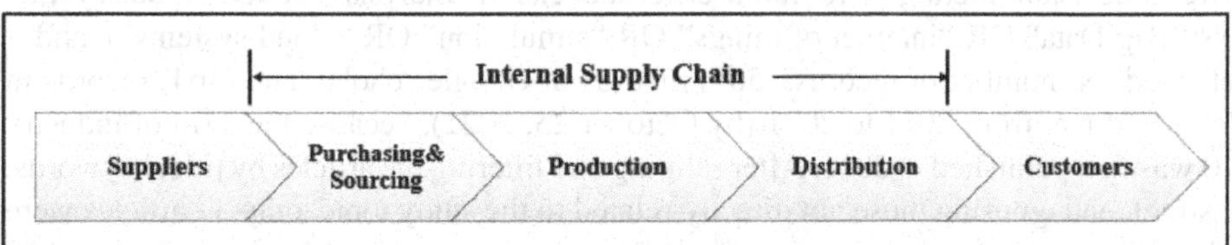

Fig. 2. Traditional supply chain [29].

2.2 Supplier Ranking

Supplier ranking is a process to rank the effective suppliers in (SCM), whereas the supplier selection is a process of selecting the most effective supplier from the ranked suppliers. Supplier ranking is one of the most significant elements in (SCM), which is considered a multi-criteria decision making (MCDM) problem that includes both qualitative and quantitative criteria [30]. Van Weele [31] has pointed out that the supplier ranking process is a part of the procurement and sourcing processes that begins with market research after identifying the functional or technical specifications. Figure 3, shows the sourcing and procurement common process consisting of supplier selection.

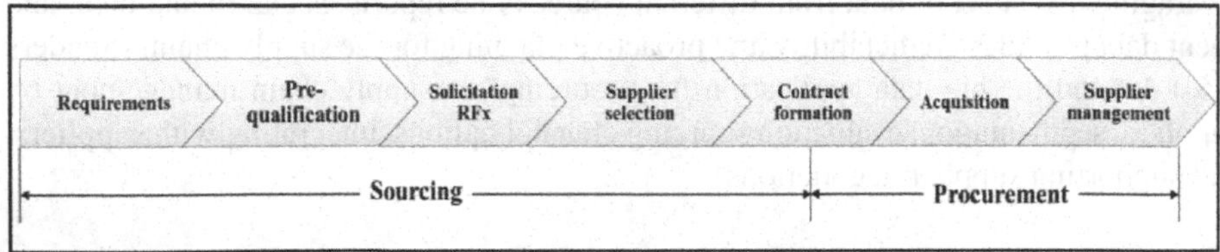

Fig. 3. Sourcing and procurement process [32].

Supplier ranking is usually a problem of deciding on a set of multiple criteria that includes numerous competing criteria about which the decision maker's understanding is normally ambiguous and inaccurate [33]. MCDM approaches are usually used for supplier ranking and choosing the best one, with the goal of providing a recommendation from a limited set of options by evaluating them from multiple criteria [34].

3 Methodology

A systematic literature review has been prepared about (I4.0) applications with (MCDM) methods in the supplier ranking process and collected the most important articles on the subject. Two datasets are used for analyzing and searching are Google scholar and Science direct. Figure 4, illustrates the flow chart of the systematic literature review. The following strategy is used to search the keywords in both Google Scholar and Science direct datasets: ("supplier selection" OR "supplier ranking") AND ("multi-criteria decision making" OR "multi-criteria decision Analysis") AND ("industry 4.0" OR "Big Data" OR "internet of things" OR "simulation" OR "cloud systems"), and it returned (N) number of records, (502) records in Google scholar, and (464) records in Science direct from 2011 to 2021 (by October 23, 2021), because the term of industry 4.0 was first published in 2011. After refining and filtering the articles by title, keywords, abstract, and ignoring those not directly related to the study topic, only 37 articles were selected.

The following structural dimensions were examined in the selected articles: Firstly, the annual distribution of publications and growth data, a summary of reviewed publications, type of application of (I4.0) technologies, criteria adopted in the (I4.0) Era, the MCDM approaches used with (I4.0) in supplier ranking, and finally the uncertain optimization-models adopted in (I4.0) era.

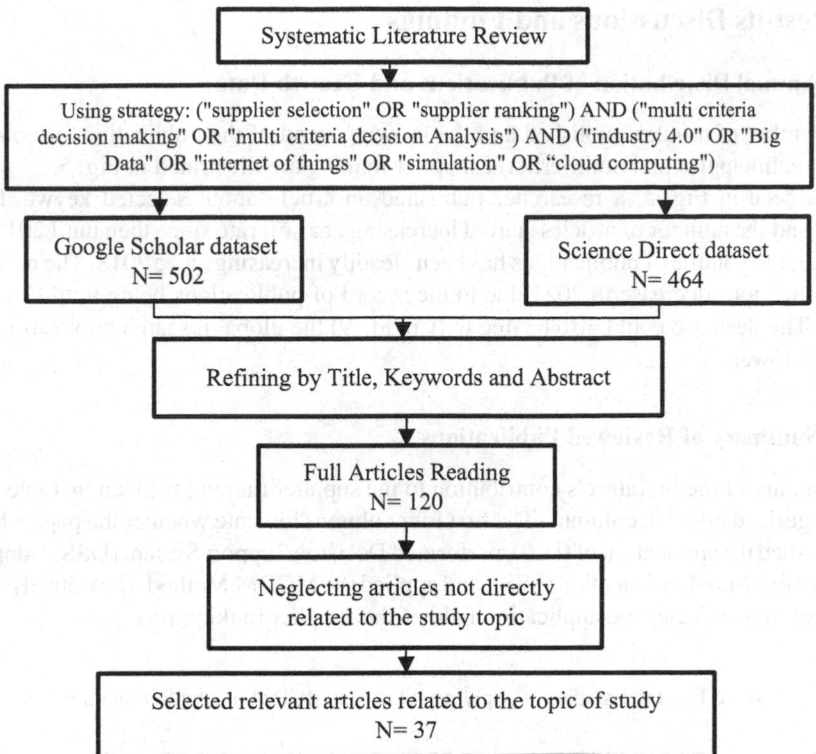

Fig. 4. The outline of the methodology adopted [source: Author]

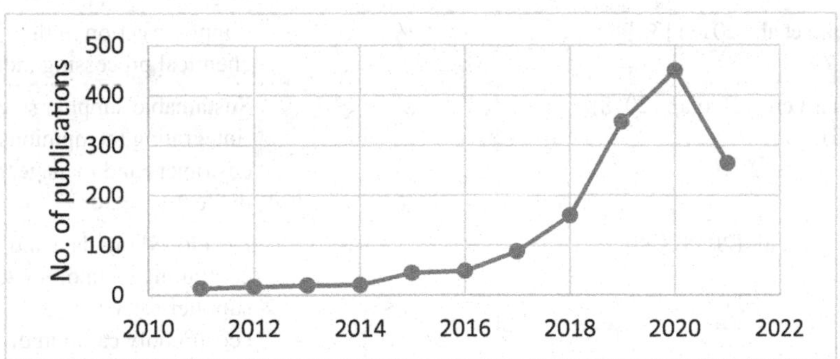

Fig. 5. A number of publications of ("supplier selection" OR "supplier ranking") AND ("multi criteria decision making" OR "multi criteria decision Analysis") AND ("industry 4.0" OR "Big Data" OR "internet of things" OR "simulation" OR "cloud computing") [source: Author based on Google scholar & Science direct datasets].

4 Results Discussions and Findings

4.1 Annual Distribution of Publications and Growth Data

The number of articles published and the growing trend of the publication in terms of (I4.0) technologies and multi-criteria supplier ranking are illustrated in Fig. 5.

As seen in Fig. 5, a researcher published an article about selected keywords in 2011, and the number of articles started increasing at a soft rate since then until 2016. In general, the volume of publications has been steadily increasing since 2018. The number of publications decrease in 2021 due to the record of publications being until October 2021. The decrease could also be due to (Covid 19) the global research publications in general lower.

4.2 Summary of Reviewed Publications

A summary of the literature's contribution to the supplier ranking is given in Table 1. It is categorized into five columns. The first four columns indicate whether the papers have established the application of (I4.0), performed Decision Support System (DSS), adopted Sustainable Supplier Selection (SSS), and applied the MCDM Method, respectively. The fifth column indicates the application field of the supplier ranking process.

Table 1. Major studies of applying (I4.0) and MCDM in supplier ranking

No	References	I 4.0	DSS	SSS	MCDM	Applications
1	Alkhalifah & Ansari (2016) [35]	√				Modelling of E-procurement System using Data Mining Technique for Supplier Performance
2	Quan et al. (2018) [36]			√	√	Supplier section in the chemical processing industry
3	Guarnieri & Trojan (2018) [37]			√	√	Sustainable supplier selection (integrating the opinions of customers and managers) in the textile sector
4	Singh et al. (2018) [38]	√			√	Developed big data and cloud computing technology to supplier selection for eco-friendly cattle in beef abattoir company
5	Sarpong et al. (2019) [39]	√		√	√	Evaluation and selection of sustainable suppliers in Pakistan's textile manufacturing company

(*continued*)

Table 1. (*continued*)

No	References	I 4.0	DSS	SSS	MCDM	Applications
6	Utomo et al. (2019) [40]	√	√			Suppliers selection in (I4.0) era for the manufacturing industry
7	Cavalcante et al. (2019) [41]	√	√			Supplier Selection in digital manufacturing
8	Chen et al. (2019) [42]			√	√	Sustainable vehicle transmission supplier selection
9	Hasan et al. (2019) [43]	√	√		√	The resilient supplier selection in logistic 4.0
10	Drakaki et al. (2019)[44]			√	√	Sustainable supplier selection considering risk factors case study adapted from literature
11	Drakaki et al. (2019) [45]	√		√	√	Order allocation, routing problem, and sustainable supplier selection
12	Sachdeva et al. (2019) [46]	√			√	Selection of suppliers in the era of (I4.0). in the private automobile manufacturer
13	Wilson et al. (2020) [47]				√	Used Machine Learning Algorithms to find out the best supplier by providing data in the manufacturing industry
14	Machesa et al. (2020) [48]			√		Identify and select a sustainable supplier for the paint manufacturing industry
15	Torbacki (2020) [49]	√	√		√	Supplier Selection in (I4.0) Era
16	Uzan (2020) [50]				√	Selection suppliers of the airline (IT) department software for an airline company in Turkey
17	Barrios et al. (2020) [51]			√	√	The mining industry (suppliers of forklift filters.)
18	Jain et al. (2020) [52]			√	√	Supplier section in the Iron and steel industry of India

(*continued*)

Table 1. (*continued*)

No	References	I 4.0	DSS	SSS	MCDM	Applications
19	Özek & Yildiz (2020) [53]	√			√	Supplier section for a company operating in the garment industry
20	Sumanto et al. (2020) [54]				√	selecting equipment supplier for IT VSAT goods
21	Ahmadi et al. (2020) [55]			√	√	Supplier selection for manufacturing industry in Iran
22	Patil et al. (2020) [56]				√	Supplier selection for fibre industry in India
23	Zekhnini et al. (2020) [57]	√		√		Resilient-sustainable supplier selection in the digital era
24	Kannan et al., (2020) [58]			√	√	Sustainable circular supplier selection for wire-and-cable industry in Iran
25	Liu et al. (2020) [59]				√	Evaluation of suppliers based on customers' demand
26	Moghaddam et al. (2020) [60]	√		√	√	Supplier selection in a cloud environment with sustainable criteria
27	Torkayesh et al. (2020) [61]				√	Selection of digital suppliers for an online retail shop in Iran
28	Sharma & Joshi (2020) [62]	√	√		√	Digital supplier selection
29	Wang et al. (2020) [63]				√	Supplier selection in garment and textile industry
30	U-Dominic et al. (2020) [64]			√	√	The effect of Covid-19 pandemic on SSS in manufacturing field
31	Tong et al. (2020) [65]			√	√	Sustainable maintenance supplier performance evaluation in Chinese petrochemical enterprise
32	Yildizbasi & Arioz (2021) [66]	√		√	√	Selection of supplier in new era for sustainability in the electronics industry

(*continued*)

Table 1. *(continued)*

No	References	I 4.0	DSS	SSS	MCDM	Applications
33	Kaya & Aycin (2021) [67]	√			√	Identify key criteria to (I4.0) technologies to selection supplier in the era of (I4.0) for technical textile manufacturer
34	Çalık (2021) [68]	√		√	√	Supplier selection for agricultural tools and machinery company
35	Kaur &Singh (2021) [69]	√			√	Supplier selection and order allocation based on criteria appropriate in (I4.0) era for an automobile company
36	Alavi et al. (2021) [70]		√	√	√	(SSS) in Circular Economy for a petrochemical holding company
37	Strategy et al. (2021) [71]				√	Assessment of suppliers in the case of a circular economy for leading automobile manufacturers in India

As illustrated in Table 1, the number of papers that adopted (I4.0) technologies in the supplier ranking process is (17) papers, only (5) of which have been implemented (DSS). On the other hand, the number of publications that have applied MCDM methods with (I4.0) technologies is (13) papers. While the papers that have adopted (SSS) with (I4.0) are (6) papers only. Figures (Fig. 6 and Fig. 7), show the approaches and the percentage of approaches with (I4.0) applied within collected papers, respectively.

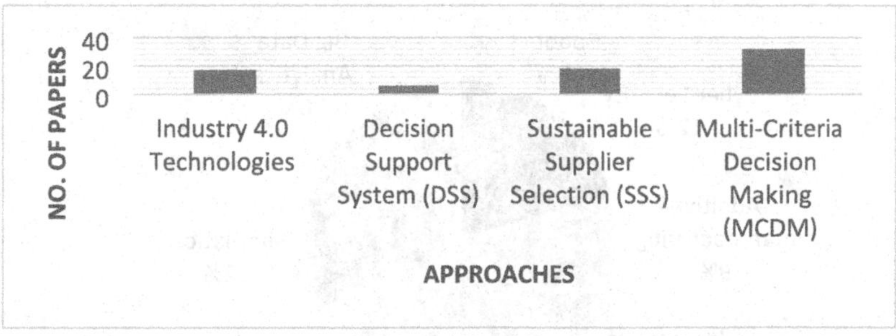

Fig. 6. Approaches applied within collected papers [source: the Author].

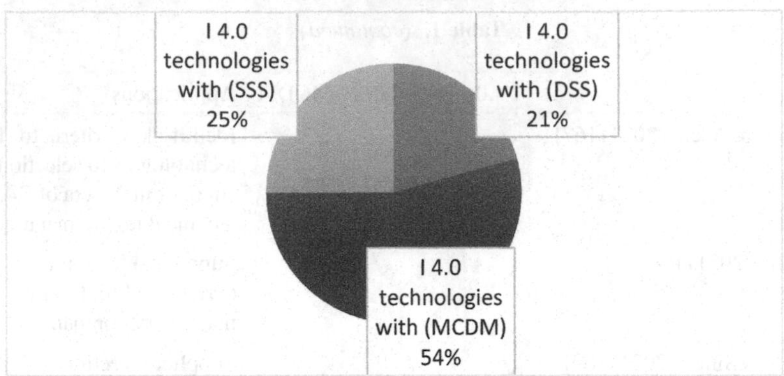

Fig. 7. Percentage of approaches adopted with Industry 4.0 in collected papers [source: the Author].

4.3 Type of the (I4.0) Technologies Applications

According to the literature review, the papers have used the concept of (I4.0) and its technologies in two ways: the first group of papers applied the (I4.0) technologies in the process of supplier ranking such as Singh et al. (2018) [38] developed a framework based on cloud computing and big data to supplier ranking for eco-friendly cattle. Cavalcante et al. (2019) [41] developed a hybrid supplier selection technology that combines machine learning and simulation and examines their applications to support decision making based on data-driven. Yildizbasi et al. (2021) [66] adopted analytics of big data in calculating the frequency of criteria in literature's keywords. The second group of papers adopted the (I4.0) technologies as criteria for supplier ranking such as Çalık (2021) [68], Özek & Yildiz (2020) [53], Kaur & Singh (2021) [69]. Figure 8, shows the percentage of the (I4.0) technologies applied in the supplier ranking considering the papers of two groups. As we can see, the most common technologies adopted in the supplier ranking process are big data analytics, cloud computing, and (IOT), respectively.

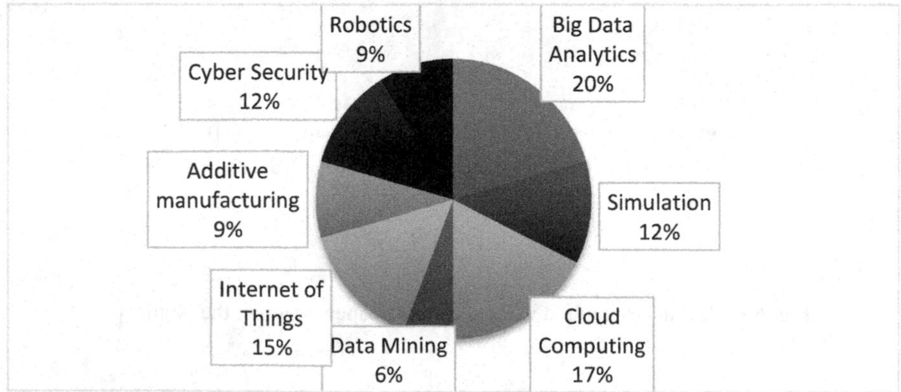

Fig. 8. Percentage of (I4.0) technologies applied in the papers within literature review [source: the Author].

4.4 Criteria Adopted in the (I4.0) Era

In terms of main criteria used in the (I4.0) era, papers focused mainly on big data analytics, and technological capabilities, which were used in 6, and 5 papers, respectively as shown in Table 2. Where the papers Çalık (2021) [68], Özek & Yildiz (2020) [53], Kaur & Singh (2021) [69] are used common criteria of (I4.0) technologies.

Table 2. Criteria used in (I4.0) era for supplier ranking

Criteria	Papers	Frequency
Big Data Analytics	Çalık (2021) [68], Sarpong et al. (2019) [39], Cavalcante et al. (2019) [41], Özek & Yildiz (2020) [53], Sharma & Joshi (2020) [62], Kaur &Singh (2021) [69]	6
Technological capabilities	Sachdeva et al. (2019) [46], Çalık (2021) [68], Cavalcante et al. (2019) [41], Torbacki (2020) [49], Kaya & Aycin (2021) [67]	5
Cyber Security/Information security	Cavalcante et al. (2019) [41], Torbacki (2020) [49], Özek & Yildiz (2020) [53], Kaur &Singh (2021) [69]	4
IoT & CPS	Çalık (2021) [68], Sarpong et al. (2019) [39], Özek & Yildiz (2020) [53], Kaur & Singh (2021) [69]	4
Cloud Computing	Çalık (2021) [68], Özek & Yildiz (2020) [53], Kaur & Singh (2021) [69]	4
Robotics	Çalık (2021) [68], Özek & Yildiz (2020) [53], Sharma & Joshi (2020) [62]	3
3D printing and Augmented Reality	Çalık (2021) [68], Özek & Yildiz (2020) [53], Kaur & Singh (2021) [69]	3
Simulation	Özek & Yildiz (2020) [53], Sharma & Joshi (2020) [62]	2

4.5 MCDM Approaches

In terms of (MCDM) approaches used for supplier ranking in the (I4.0) era, the most used methods in papers are Fuzzy-AHP and Fuzzy-TOPSIS. Where Singh et al. (2018) [38] used Fuzzy AHP, TOPSIS and DEMATEL methods, Hasan et al. (2019) [43] used fuzzy-TOPSIS and MultiChoice Goal Programming (MCGP) methods, Sachdeva et al. (2019) [46] used hybrid intuitionistic fuzzy entropy with TOPSIS. A. Pinar (2020) [72] pointed out that AHP and Fuzzy-TOPSIS are the most widely used methods in supplier selection. Sharma & Joshi (2020) [62] used the weighted aggregated sum product assessment (WASPS) and stepwise weight assessment ratio analysis (SWARA) methods. Özek &

Yildiz (2020) [53] used the interval type-2 fuzzy TOPSIS method, Moghaddam et al. (2020) [60] used Fuzzy DEMATEL and VIseKriterijumska Optimizacija I Kompromisno Resenje (VIKOR) methods, Torbacki (2020) [49] used the DEMATEL method. Kaya & Aycin (2021) [67] used Interval Type 2 Fuzzy AHP and Gray Complex Proportional Assessment (GOPRAS-G) techniques, Çalık (2021) [68] used the Pythagorean Fuzzy with (AHP and TOPSIS). Finally, Kaur &Singh (2021) [69] used Data Envelopment Analysis (DEA) and (FAHP-TOPSIS) methods. Table 3, illustrates the frequency of MCDM approaches used in the reviewed papers that adopted (I4.0).

Table 3. MCDM techniques used in the reviewed papers

MCDM Approaches	Papers	Frequency
Fuzzy TOPSIS	Hasan et al. (2019) [43], Sachdeva et al. (2019) [46], Özek & Yildiz (2020) [53], Çalık (2021) [68], Pinar A. (2020) [72], Jain et al. (2020) [49]	6
Fuzzy AHP	Singh et al. (2018) [38], Kaya & Aycin (2021) [67], Çalık (2021) [68], Kaur & Singh (2021) [69], Wilson et al. (2020) [47], Barrios et al. (2020) [48]	6
DEMATEL	Singh et al. (2018) [38], Torbacki (2020) [49], Uzan (2020) [50], Barrios et al. (2020) [48]	4
TOPSIS	Singh et al. (2018) [38], Kaur & Singh (2021) [69]	2
Goal Programming	Hasan et al. (2019) [43]	1
WASPAS	Sharma & Joshi (2020) [62]	1
Fuzzy DEMATEL	Moghaddam et al. (2020) [60]	1
GOPRAS-G	Kaya & Aycin (2021) [67]	1
DEA	Kaur & Singh (2021) [69]	1
VIKOR	Moghaddam et al. (2020) [60]	1
SWARA	Sharma & Joshi (2020) [62]	1

4.6 Optimization-Models of Uncertainty in the I4.0 Era

The uncertainty (lack of certainty) is defined as a state of limited knowledge in which it is impossible to accurately describe a current state, or the future outcome [73]. The supplier ranking process may involve uncertainty with identifying and selecting the evaluation criteria. Thus, in this section will discuss the papers developed uncertain models in I4.0 era. Table 4, gives a summary of the main uncertain optimization-models developed by the papers and the sources of uncertainty.

As can be seen from Table 4, various optimization models were used by the reviewed papers such as fuzzy models (interval type-2 fuzzy, Pythagorean fuzzy, and intuitionistic fuzzy entropy), grey incidence, and machine learning; to overcome uncertainties in various sources like decision-maker judgments, customer demands, supplier capacity, delivery, cost/price, quality, etc.

Table 4. Uncertain optimization-models in reviewed papers

papers	Uncertain models	Source of uncertainty
Kaur & Singh (2021) [69]	multi stage hybrid model a (mixed integer program)	Demand, price, capacity, delivery
Drakaki et al. (2019) [44]	Fuzzy Axiomatic Design Approach with Risk Factors (RFAD)	Price, productivity, quality, capacity of suppliers, production technology, responsiveness
Cavalcante et al. (2019) [41]	Combining of simulation and machine learning	Delivery, supplier performance, capacity
Zekhnini et al. (2020) [57]	Adaptive Fuzzy Neuro Network	Cost, delivery, quality
Chen et al. (2019) [42]	hybrid rough-fuzzy DEMATEL-TOPSIS	Linguistic vagueness, group preference diversity
Hasan et al. (2019) [43]	Decision support system in the logistic 4.0 environment	Uncertainty of decision relevant information
Çalık (2021) [68]	Integrated Pythagorean Fuzzy (AHP and TOPSIS)	The opinions of decision-makers (delivery, quality)
Sachdeva et al. (2019) [46]	hybrid intuitionistic fuzzy entropy weight with TOPSIS	Uncertainty of judgment (Cost, delivery, quality (rejection rate))
Sharma & Joshi (2020) [62]	Decision support system with integrated SWARA-WASPAS	supplier competency, digital value chain and information sharing
Özek & Yildiz (2020) [53]	Interval Type-2 Fuzzy TOPSIS	Excessive number of decision making criteria, subjective and linguistic judgments of decision makers
Kaya & Aycin (2021) [67]	Interval Type 2 Fuzzy AHP	Cost, delivery, quality, capacity
Quan et al. (2018) [36]	Weighted Grey Incidence	Sparse data and incomplete information (Cost, quality, delivery)

5 Conclusion, Future Directions and Limitation

This study provided an overview of the potential of (I4.0) technologies in the supplier ranking process. In this study, 37 papers were collected on supplier ranking using MCDM and (I4.0) technologies, by using two datasets for analyzing and searching are Google scholar and Science direct. The selected papers were analyzed from different aspects: publication growth trends, application of (I4.0), criteria used, and MCDM methods. Despite the significance of supplier ranking or (selection) and the importance of applying (I4.0) technologies, few publications have attempted to examine the implications of

(I4.0) technologies in supplier ranking. Only (46%) of collected papers adopted (I4.0) technologies in supplier ranking which included two groups: the first group of papers applied the (I4.0) technologies in the process of supplier ranking. The second group adopted the technologies as criteria for supplier ranking. From the results, the most common technologies adopted in the supplier ranking process are big data analytics, cloud computing, and the IoT, with percentages (20%), (17%), (15%) respectively. In terms of criteria used, the study revealed that most of (I4.0) technologies are used as criteria for supplier ranking, where the common criteria used is big data analytics were which appeared in (6) papers. On the other hand, different MCDM methods were used by the researchers with (I4.0) technologies. However, the most used methods are Fuzzy TOPSIS and Fuzzy AHP. The use of uncertainty in supplier ranking in the (I4.0) era is discussed by listing the uncertain optimization-models used by the reviewed papers to overcome uncertainties in various sources. This study serves as a reference for researchers interested in the applications of (I4.0) in supplier ranking (selection). Furthermore, it can help companies looking to implement the (I4.0) applications in their supply chain. The opportunities for future studies can be listed as follows:

1. There is a lack of application of (I4.0) technologies in supplier ranking, therefore, the (I4.0) technologies may applied to supplier ranking field through using the big data analytics with data mining for analyzing customer feedback in supplier evaluation and ranking.
2. According to the fields of applications, there are few or no studies on the service sector as the healthcare sector for example.
3. The Lack of models to uncertainty study using stochastic models in supplier ranking in the I4.0 era.
4. There is no use of the multi objective optimization models such as Pareto optimal solutions in supplier ranking in the I4.0.

Regarding the limitations of the study, firstly, this study focused on applications of (I4.0) with MCDM in supplier ranking, so a more comprehensive study can be done on (I4.0) applications in supplier ranking regardless of the methods used for ranking. Secondly, the study used two databases only in searching for related papers, which may have lost some papers that were not indexed in these two databases. Therefore, additional search databases can be used to increase the range of papers to be analyzed. Lastly, the use of keywords in searching may lead to the loss of some papers, as search results lead to those given in the titles and abstracts of the papers.

References

1. Smit, J., Kreutzer, S., Moeller, C., Carlberg, M.: Policy Department A: Economic and Scientific Policy Industry4.0 (2016)https://doi.org/10.1007/978-3-030-35032-1_18
2. Dalmarco, G., Ramalho, F.R., Barros, A.C., Soares, A.L.: Providing industry 4.0 technologies: the case of a production technology cluster. J. High Technol. Manag. Res. **30** (2019)
3. Mohamed, K.S.: The Era of Internet of Things: Towards a Smart World. Springer, Cham (2019). https://doi.org/10.1007/978-3-030-18133-8
4. Stank, T., Scott, S., Hazen, B.: A savvy guide to the digital supply chain. Glob. Supply Chain Inst. White Paper, 1–56 (2018)

5. Toka, A., Aivazidou, E., Antoniou, A., Arvanitopoulos-Darginis, K.: Cloud computing in supply chain management: an overview. In: E-Logistics and E-Supply Chain Management : Applications for Evolving Business, pp. 218–231 (2013). https://doi.org/10.13140/2.1.2717.2800
6. Scheidegger, A.P.G., Pereira, T.F., de Oliveira, M.L.M., Banerjee, A., Montevechi, J.A.B.: An introductory guide for hybrid simulation modelers on the primary simulation methods in industrial engineering identified through a systematic review of the literature. Comput. Ind. Eng. **124**, 474–492 (2018)
7. Zhong, R.Y., Xu, X., Klotz, E., Newman, S.T.: Intelligent manufacturing in the context of industry 4.0: a review. Engineering **3**, 616–630 (2017)
8. Stich, V., Pause, D., Blum, M., Hinrichs, N.: A simulation based approach to investigate the procurement process and its effect on the performance of supply chains. In: Nääs, I., et al. (eds.) APMS 2016. IAICT, vol. 488, pp. 335–342. Springer, Cham (2016). https://doi.org/10.1007/978-3-319-51133-7_40
9. Kumar, A., Nayyar, A.: si3-industry: a sustainable, intelligent, innovative, internet-of-things industry. In: A Roadmap to Industry 4.0: Smart Production, Sharp Business and Sustainable Development, pp. 1–21 (2020)
10. Kowalkiewicz, M., Safrudin, N., Schulze, B.: The business consequences of a digitally transformed economy. In: Oswald, G., Kleinemeier, M. (eds.) Shaping the Digital Enterprise, pp. 29–67. Springer, Cham (2017). https://doi.org/10.1007/978-3-319-40967-2_2
11. Santi, G.M., Ceruti, A., Liverani, A., Osti, F.: Augmented reality in industry 4.0 and future innovation programs. Technologies **9** (2021)
12. Oswald, G., Kleinemeier, M. (eds.): Shaping the Digital Enterprise. Springer, Cham (2017). https://doi.org/10.1007/978-3-319-40967-2
13. Gottge, S., Menzel, T.: Purchasing 4.0: an exploratory multiple case study on the purchasing process reshaped by industry 4.0 in the automotive industry (2017)
14. Oesterreich, T.D., Teuteberg, F.: Understanding the implications of digitisation and automation in the context of Industry 4.0: a triangulation approach and elements of a research agenda for the construction industry. Comput. Ind. **83**, 121–139 (2016)
15. Smit, J., Kreutzer, S., Moeller, C., Carlberg, M.: Industry 4.0. Brussels Eur. Union (2016)
16. Vaidyaa, S., Ambadb, P., Bhoslec, S.: Industry 4.0–a glimpse. Procedia Manuf. **20**, 233–238 (2018)
17. Ben-Daya, M., Hassini, E., Bahroun, Z.: Internet of things and supply chain management: a literature review. Int. J. Prod. Res. 1–24 (2017)
18. Tirkolaee, E.B., Sadeghi, S., Mooseloo, F.M., Vandchali, H.R., Aeini, S.: Application of machine learning in supply chain management: a comprehensive overview of the main areas. Math. Probl. Eng. (2021)
19. De Conciliis, C.: Industry 4.0 in small and medium enterprises (2018)
20. ISO, A.: Additive manufacturing Design—Requirements, guidelines and recommendations. ASTM International. https://www.astm.org/Standards/ISOASTM52910.htm
21. Arya, V., Sharma, P., Singh, A., De Silva, P.T.M.: Benchmarking: an international journal an exploratory study on supply chain analytics applied to spare parts supply chain article information. Benchmark. Int. J. **24**, 1571–1580 (2017)
22. Fisher, D., DeLine, R., Czerwinski, M., Drucker, S.: Interactions with big data analytics. Interactions **19**, 50–59 (2012)
23. Awwad, M., Kulkarni, P., Bapna, R., Marathe, A.: Big data analytics in supply chain : a literature review big data analytics in supply chain: a literature review. In: Proceedings of the International Conference on Industrial Engineering and Operations Management, pp. 418–425 (2018)
24. Darvazeh, S.S., Vanani, I.R., Musolu, F.M.: Big data analytics and its applications in supply chain management. New Trends Use Artif. Intell. Ind. **4**, 1–26 (2020)

25. Sanders, N.: Big Data Driven Supply Chain Management: A Framework for Implementing Analytics and Turning Information In to Intelligence. Pearson Education Inc., New Jersey (2014)
26. Tirkolaee, E.B., Dashtian, Z., Weber, G., Tomaskova, H.: An integrated decision-making approach for green supplier selection in an agri-food supply chain: threshold of robustness worthiness. Mathematics **9** (2021)
27. Al-zuheri, A.: Cross - comparison of evolutionary algorithms for optimizing design of sustainable supply chain network under disruption risks. Adv. Sci. Technol. Res. J. **15**, 342–351 (2021)
28. Meo, K.N.: Definition of Supplier Selection. scribd https://www.scribd.com/document/217201744/Definition-of-Supplier-Selection (2014)
29. Chen, I.J., Paulraj, A.: Towards a theory of supply chain management: the constructs and measurements. J. Oper. Manag. **22**, 119–150 (2004)
30. Cengiz, A.E., Aytekin, O., Ozdemir, I., Kusan, H., Cabuk, A.: A multi-criteria decision model for construction material supplier selection. Procedia Eng. **196**, 294–301 (2017)
31. Van Weele, A.J.: Purchasing and Supply Chain Management Analysis, Strategy, Planning and Practice. Cengage Learning EMEA, Andover (2014)
32. Sollish, F., Semanik, O.: Strategic Global Sourcing Best Practices. Wiley, Hoboken (2011)
33. Abdul-Razaq, F.F., Al-Zubaidi, S.S., Kassam, A.H.: Fuzzy analytical hierarchy process for embedded risk reduction in selecting the right planning decision. Al-Khwarizmi Eng. J. **15**, 92–105 (2019)
34. Chai, J., Liu, J.N.K., Ngai, E.W.T.: Application of decision making techniques in supplier selection: systematic review of literature. Expert Syst. Appl. **40**, 3872–3885 (2013)
35. Alkhalifah, A., Ansari, G.A.: Modeling of e-procurement system through UML using data mining technique for supplier performance. In: 2016 1st International Conference on Software Networking, ICSN 2016 (2016). https://doi.org/10.1109/ICSN.2016.7501930
36. Quan, J., Bo, Z., Dai, L.: Green supplier selection for process industries using weighted grey incidence decision model. In: Complexity in Industry 4.0 Systems and Networks, pp. 1–12 (2018)
37. Guarnieri, P., Trojan, F.: Decision making on supplier selection based on social, ethical, and environmental criteria: a study in the textile industry. Resour. Conserv. Recycl. **141**, 347–361 (2019)
38. Singh, A., Kumari, S., Malekpoor, H., Mishra, N.: Big data cloud computing framework for low carbon supplier selection in the beef supply chain. J. Clean. Prod. **202**, 139–149 (2018)
39. Kusi-Sarpong, S., et al.: Sustainable supplier selection based on industry 4.0 initiatives within the context of circular economy implementation in supply chain operations. Prod. Plan. Control (2019)
40. Utomo, D.T., Pratikto, Santoso, P.B., Sugiono: Preliminary study of web based decision support system to select manufacturing industry suppliers in industry 4.0 era in Indonesia. Comput. Inf. Sci. **54** (2019)
41. Cavalcante, I.M., Frazzon, E.M., Forcellini, F.A., Ivanov, D.: A supervised machine learning approach to data-driven simulation of resilient supplier selection in digital manufacturing. Int. J. Inf. Manage. **49**, 86–97 (2019)
42. Chen, Z., Ming, X., Zhou, T., Chang, Y.: Sustainable supplier selection for smart supply chain considering internal and external uncertainty: an integrated rough-fuzzy approach. Appl. Soft Comput. J. **87** (2019)
43. Hasan, M.M., Jiang, D., Ullah, A.M.M.S., Noor-E-Alam, M.: Resilient supplier selection in logistics 4.0 with heterogeneous information. Expert Syst. Appl. **139** (2020)
44. Drakaki, M., Goren, H.G., Tzionas, P.: Supplier selection problem in fuzzy environment considering risk factors. In: Proceedings of International Conference on Developments in eSystems Engineering (DeSE), October 2020, pp. 784–788 (2019)

45. Drakaki, M., Gören, H.G., Tzionas, P.: A multi-agent based decision framework for sustainable supplier selection, order allocation and routing problem. In: Proceedings of 5th International Conference on Vehicle Technology and Intelligent Transport Systems, VEHITS 2019, pp. 621–628 (2019). https://doi.org/10.5220/0007833306210628
46. Sachdeva, N., Shrivastava, A.K., Chauhan, A.: Modeling supplier selection in the era of Industry 4.0. Benchmarking **28**, 1809–1836 (2019)
47. Wilson, V.H., Prasad, A.N.S., Shankharan, A., Kapoor, S., Rajan, J.A.: Ranking of supplier performance using machine learning algorithm of random forest. Int. J. Adv. Res. Eng. Technol. **11**, 298–308 (2020)
48. Machesa, M.G.K., Tartibu, L.K., Okwu, M.O.: Selection of sustainable supplier(S) in a paint manufacturing company using hybrid meta-heuristic algorithm. South Afr. J. Ind. Eng. **31**, 13–23 (2020)
49. Torbacki, W.: Analytic method for decision support of blockchain technology supplier selection in industry 4.0 era. Multidiscip. Asp. Prod. Eng. **3**, 296–307 (2020)
50. Uzan, Ş.B.: Analysis of supplier selection process with multi criteria decision making techniques; example of an airline company. Atatürk Üniversitesi İktisadi ve İdari Bilim. Derg. **34**, 315–334 (2020)
51. Ortiz-Barrios, M., et al.: A hybrid fuzzy multi-criteria decision making model for selecting a sustainable supplier of forklift filters: a case study from the mining industry. Ann. Oper. Res. **307**, 443–481 (2020)
52. Jain, N., Singh, A.R., Upadhyay, R.K.: Sustainable supplier selection under attractive criteria through FIS and integrated fuzzy MCDM techniques. Int. J. Sustain. Eng. **13**, 441–462 (2020)
53. Özek, A., Yildiz, A.: Digital supplier selection for a garment business using interval type-2 fuzzy TOPSIS. Tekst. ve Konfeksiyon **30**, 61–72 (2020)
54. Sumanto, S., Indriani, K., Marita, L.S., Christian, A.: Supplier selection very small aperture terminal using AHP-TOPSIS framework. J. Intell. Comput. Heal. Informatics **1**, 39 (2020)
55. Ahmadi, H.B., Lo, H.W., Gupta, H., Kusi-Sarpong, S., Liou, J.J.H.: An integrated model for selecting suppliers on the basis of sustainability innovation. J. Clean. Prod. **277**, 123261 (2020)
56. Patil, A.N., Shivkumar, K.M., Manjunath Patel, G.C., Jatti, S.P., Rivankar, S.N.: Fuzzy TOPSIS and grey relation analysis integration for supplier selection in fiber industry. Int. J. Supply Oper. Manag. **7**, 373–383 (2020)
57. Zekhnini, K., Cherrafi, A., Bouhaddou, I., Benghabrit, Y., Garza-Reyes, J.A.: Supplier selection for smart supply chain: an adaptive fuzzy-neuro approach. In: Proceedings of the 5th NA International Conference on Industrial Engineering and Operations Management, pp. 1–9 (2020)
58. Kannan, D., Mina, H., Nosrati-Abarghooee, S., Khosrojerdi, G.: Sustainable circular supplier selection: A novel hybrid approach. Sci. Total Environ. **722**, 137936 (2020)
59. Liu, A., Liu, T., Mou, J., Wang, R.: A supplier evaluation model based on customer demand in blockchain tracing anti-counterfeiting platform project management. J. Manag. Sci. Eng. **5**, 172–194 (2020)
60. Tavakkoli-Moghaddam, R., Alipour-Vaezi, M., Mohammad-Nazari, Z.: A new application of coordination contracts for supplier selection in a cloud environment. In: Lalic, B., Majstorovic, V., Marjanovic, U., von Cieminski, G., Romero, D. (eds.) APMS 2020. IAICT, vol. 592, pp. 197–205. Springer, Cham (2020). https://doi.org/10.1007/978-3-030-57997-5_23
61. Torkayesh, S.E., Iranizad, A., Torkayesh, A.E., Basit, M.N.: Application of BWM-WASPAS model for digital supplier selection problem: a case study in online retail shopping. J. Ind. Eng. Decis. Mak. **1**, 12–23 (2020)
62. Sharma, M., Joshi, S.: Digital supplier selection reinforcing supply chain quality management systems to enhance firm's performance. TQM J. (2020). https://doi.org/10.1108/TQM-07-2020-0160

63. Wang, C.N., Hoang Viet, V.T., Ho, T.P., Nguyen, V.T., Nguyen, V.T.: Multi-criteria decision model for the selection of suppliers in the textile industry. Symmetry (Basel) **12**, 1–12 (2020)
64. U-Dominic, C.M., Orji, I.J., Okwu, M.O., Mbachu, V.M.: The impact of Covid-19 pandemic on sustainable supplier selection process. In: Advancing Industrial Engineering in Nigeria through Teaching, Research and Innovation (2020)
65. Tong, L., Pu, Z., Chen, K., Yi, J.: Sustainable maintenance supplier performance evaluation based on an extend fuzzy PROMETHEE II approach in petrochemical industry. J. Clean. Prod. **273**, 122771 (2020)
66. Yildizbasi, A., Arioz, Y.: Green supplier selection in new era for sustainability: a novel method for integrating big data analytics and a hybrid fuzzy multi-criteria decision making. Res. Sq. (2021)
67. Kayapinar Kaya, S., Aycin, E.: An integrated interval type 2 fuzzy AHP and COPRAS-G methodologies for supplier selection in the era of Industry 4.0. Neural Comput. Appl. **33**(16), 10515–10535 (2021). https://doi.org/10.1007/s00521-021-05809-x
68. Çalık, A.: A novel Pythagorean fuzzy AHP and fuzzy TOPSIS methodology for green supplier selection in the Industry 4.0 era. Soft. Comput. **25**(3), 2253–2265 (2020). https://doi.org/10.1007/s00500-020-05294-9
69. Kaur, H., Prakash Singh, S.: Multi-stage hybrid model for supplier selection and order allocation considering disruption risks and disruptive technologies. Int. J. Prod. Econ. **231** (2021)
70. Alavi, B., Tavana, M., Mina, H.: A dynamic decision support system for sustainable supplier selection in circular economy. Sustain. Prod. Consum. **27**, 905–920 (2021)
71. Strategy, B., Haleem, A., Islamia, J.M., Khan, S., Luthra, S.: Supplier evaluation in the context of circular economy: a forward step for resilient business and environment concern (2021).https://doi.org/10.1002/bse.2736
72. Pinar, A.: Multiple criteria decision making methods used in supplier selection. J. Turk. Oper. Manag. **4**, 449–478 (2020)
73. Hussain, A., Xu, J., Kashif, M.: Supplier selection under uncertainty: a detailed case study. Int. J. Sci. Basic Appl. Res. **15**, 200–217 (2014)

A Two-Stage Machine Learning-Based Heuristic Algorithm for Buffer Management and Project Scheduling Optimization

Shakib Zohrehvandi[1,3](✉), Roya Soltani[1,2], Dimitri Lefebvre[4], Mehrnoosh Zohrehvandi[3], and Alexandra Tenera[5]

[1] New Technologies Department, Center for European Studies, Kharazmi University, Tehran, Iran
shakibzohrevandi@gmail.com, shakib.zohrehvandi@srbiau.ac.ir, r.soltani@khatam.ac.ir

[2] Department of Industrial Engineering, Faculty of Engineering, Khatam University, Tehran, Iran

[3] Department of Industrial Engineering, Science and Research Branch, Islamic Azad University, Tehran, Iran

[4] GREAH, Le Havre Normandy University, 75 Rue Bellot, 76600 Le Havre, France
dimitri.lefebvre@univ-lehavre.fr

[5] Department of Industrial and Mechanical Engineering, Faculty of Sciences and Technology (FCT), UNIDEMI, Universidade NOVA de Lisboa, Caparica, Portugal

Abstract. One of the main problems that project managers face is that in most cases the projects won't be completed according to predetermined schedules and therefore prolonged delays and losses occur during the project implementation phase. This study aims to propose a predictive buffer management algorithm (PBMA) based on machine learning technology to predict project buffer size and control project buffer consumption in construction projects to be not more than predetermined schedules and consequently prevent delays in projects' completion times. The proposed machine-learning-based heuristic algorithm falls into the category of supervised machine learning algorithms and consists of two main stages. In the first stage, the project critical chain is identified and the appropriate project buffer size is specified. In the second stage, the consumption of the project buffer is monitored and controlled in the project implementation stage. To evaluate the performance of the proposed PBMA, it is coded in MATLAB software and implemented using the data taken from a hypothetical project. The results show that the use of the proposed PBMA improves the productivity of projects, and therefore the projects can be completed according to predetermined schedules. The resulted values for the longest path of the project's critical activities, the duration of the project's critical chain, the buffer duration of the project, and the duration of the project plan are respectively 60, 30, 15, and 45 days. The proposed PBMA can be applied to a variety of projects.

Keywords: Predictive buffer management algorithm (PBMA) · Project scheduling · Machine learning · Construction management · Project time optimization

A. Mirzazadeh et al. (Eds.): SEMIT 2022, CCIS 1808, pp. 81–94, 2023.
https://doi.org/10.1007/978-3-031-40395-8_6

1 Introduction

Project schedules are one of the necessary tools for organizing sequences of activities [1]. One of the important problems that projects and organizations face is that projects last longer than planned schedules. Various project hazards such as unexpected events may lead to project delays, excessive costs, unsatisfactory project results, or even complete failure. Various delays may happen in the implementation phase of projects and most cases, the projects won't be completed according to predetermined schedules.

In a typical project, working times are usually uncertain. Working hours that are longer than expected usually increase project completion time. While shorter working hours than expected can reduce project completion time. The main reason for this asymmetry is Parkinson's law [2], or "work expands to fill the time available to complete it" [3]. As in the case of project management, Parkinson's law states that the time required to complete a task and report on its completion is not less than the amount of time available to it [4]. The effect of Parkinson's law is that the potential benefit of completing the work disappears sooner than expected. It can not compensate for other tasks later than expected. To solve this problem, we describe the Critical Chain Project Management (CCPM) technique, which considers activity interdependence and resource constraints, thereby reducing the impact of Parkinson's law. The CCPM technique modifies the accuracy of projects designs by considering buffers in project scheduling to address fluctuations. CCPM was first proposed by Goldratt (1997) to improve traditional project management methods using a new mechanism for managing uncertainties [5]. Project buffers collect the protection a project needs to reach its deadline (by removing the safety from individual tasks) and allow it to focus on project duration [6]. Theory of constraint (TOC) and critical chain/buffer management are two effective approaches in project management [7]. Since the introduction of the TOC, several researchers have examined its application in project management.

Buffer sizing can be considered the most important step in implementing the critical chain scheduling method in a project. If small buffers are allocated, the project needs to be reprogrammed. There are three types of buffers: project buffer, feeding buffers, and resource buffers. The project buffer presented in the schedule considers uncertainties related to the implementation of critical path activities. One of the useful techniques in determining the optimal size of buffers in project scheduling is the machine learning technique.

Machine learning refers extensively to the process of adapting prediction models to data or identifying information groups within the data [8]. In recent years, intelligent fault diagnosis has attracted the attention of many scientific researchers who are deeply involved in machine learning activities [9, 10]. Traditional machine learning theories in intelligent fault diagnosis have been practiced until the 2010s. Early research related to the machine learning field dates back to the 1950s, and in the 1980s it became one of the hot topics in artificial intelligence and a number of traditional theories were developed during this period [11].

Zohrehvandi et al. (2020) introduced a heuristic algorithm for determining project buffer size and feeding buffers as well as dynamic buffer consumption control, called Fuzzy Overlap Buffer Management Algorithm (FOBMA). In this research, pentagonal fuzzy numbers were used to determine the appropriate amount of project activity resources. In addition, an overlapping method was used to obtain more realistic durations for activities. In this research, buffer consumption is controlled using a dynamic method. Due to different conditions in different stages of a project (i.e. the duration of each stage, the number of resource activities, and the complexity of the network of activities), it is necessary to control the dynamics of buffer consumption. For this purpose, the number of buffers that remain unused in each stage of the project is transferred to the next stage [12]. In another research, Zohrehvandi et al. (2020) introduced an efficient project buffer and resource management (PBRM) model for project resource leveling and project buffer sizing and controlling of project buffer consumption of a wind power plant project to achieve a more realistic project duration [13]. In addition, Zohrehvandi et al. (2021) proposed a project time optimization algorithm that initially calculates project buffers and feeding buffers and then dynamically controls buffer consumption at different stages of a wind farm project to find a more realistic project duration [14].

Pushdar et al. (2018) tested a multi-objective probability-based project buffer sizing method against the records of a bridge construction project. The results were compared to the findings from a numerical analysis obtained by an extensive Monte Carlo study. The comparison indicated the high quality of the proposed method optimization analysis, while it utilizes an approximate combinatorial analytic method to avoid the errors typical of the numerical analysis [15]. Zhang et al. (2018) proposed a buffer control model which operates according to the conditions in various stages of projects [16]. Martens and Venhoucke (2020) improved project time forecasting accuracy by extending exponential smoothing to the project time forecasting using earned value management and time management by integrating corrective actions taken during project progress [17]. Zohrehvandi and Soltani (2022) surveyed the latest models and methods of project buffer management and time optimization of construction projects and manufacturing industries [18].

In this research, through prediction analysis, a machine learning-based approach is proposed to predict the size of project buffers. The purpose of this study is to introduce a predictive buffer management algorithm (PBMA) based on machine learning technology to determine the buffer size of projects and control the buffer consumption in construction projects to finish the projects according to planned schedules as much as possible. One of the advantages of the proposed method is that the required amount of buffer is estimated and a suitable amount is considered for consumption by the project activities. The structure of the rest of the article is as follows: In Sect. 2, a literature review is presented. The proposed method is given in Sect. 3. In Sect. 4, numerical results are presented. Finally, the conclusion is given in Sect. 5.

2 Literature Review

Machine learning with big data technologies and high-performance computations has been emerged to create new opportunities for data-intensive science in the field of multidisciplinary technologies [19]. During the last two decades, significant research has been done using machine learning algorithms, which aims to eliminate the shortcomings of traditional methods, improve the project success rate, and be coordinated with modern project development and project approaches [20].

Kanakaris et al. (2020) proposed a synergistic approach based on a synergy between machine learning techniques and contemporary operational research. They commented on proper coordination between operations research algorithms and related machine learning, paying equal attention to optimization and macro data manipulation issues [21]. Peña et al. (2019) proposed a method to control the project execution process based on soft computing and machine learning approaches and implemented seven algorithms based on space segmentation, neural networks, gradient descent, and genetic algorithms.. Their proposed method makes use of machine learning and tuning of fuzzy inference systems to evaluate projects [22]. Predictive analysis has been used by proposing a machine learning approach to predict the project performance based on criteria of several aspects of entrepreneurial orientation and entrepreneurial attitude of individuals. They examined this machine learning approach using a sample of 185 observations and a range of machine learning algorithms including ropes, ridges, support vector machines, neural networks, and random forests [23].

Chattapadhyay and Putta (2021) developed a risk prediction system based on a cross-analytical machine learning model for large construction projects. A total of 63 risk factors on project cost, time, quality, and scope and initial data were collected from industry experts on a five-point Likert scale [24]. Sousa et al. (2021) presented the application of machine learning techniques for risk assessment in software projects. A Python application was developed using Scikit-learn, two machine learning models, and trained using software project risk data, which is shared by the project partner company, to predict the impact of risk [25].

Đumić et al. (2018) addressed the issue of resource-constrained project scheduling (RCPSP) and the exploratory development of genetic programming-based scheduling. The results showed that this approach is a good option for a custom scheduling method in a dynamic environment, which allows the automatic development of a suitable scheduling exploration [26]. Bourhnane et al. (2020) examined artificial neural networks (ANNs) as machine learning algorithms with genetic algorithms. They deployed their models in a real-world test platform of smart buildings. They used CompactRIO to run ANN [27]. Adamu and Aromolaran (2018) introduced a machine learning priority rule to solve non-preventive RCPSP. The goal was to find a plan for project tasks so that project completion time is minimized by prioritizing the resource constraints. The results showed that the completion time obtained by their proposed algorithm competes favorably with all 13 priority rules in the literature [28].

Zohrehvandi and Khalilzadeh (2019) combined the adaptive approach with the resource constraint (APRT) method with FMEA, which resulted in a short project duration [29]. Öhman et al. (2021) proposed a new solution design plan for aircraft maintenance and provided theoretical insights into buffer management in operations. The airline's field problem was to improve flight reliability for long-haul aircraft without increasing maintenance resources and the use of support aircraft [30]. Zohrehvandi (2022) introduced a heuristic algorithm for scheduling construction projects of a power plant and managing project resources to determine the size of project buffers and feeding buffers. This algorithm consists of three steps: 1) Estimating the duration of project activities, 2) Determining the size of project buffers and feeding buffers, 3) Simulation of the mentioned algorithm [31]. In another research, Zohrehvandi (2022) investigated modeling and optimization in project planning & scheduling in construction management and project time optimization [32].

Takami et al. (2021) evaluated the effectiveness of the Dynamic Buffer Management (DBM) approach for dynamic adjustment of inventory levels to maintain the availability of final goods in distribution systems and to avoid over-storage [33]. Zohrehvandi et al. (2022) introduced a fuzzy project buffer management (FPBM) algorithm that combines APRT methods and fuzzy failure mode and effect analysis (FFMEA) [34]. She et al. (2021) proposed a new method for buffer sizing based on a network that offers logical advantages over the previous ones. This finding shows that this method offers much more accuracy in estimating the duration of the project and optimizing the feeding buffers [35]. Zohrehvandi and Honarmand Shahzileh (2022) introduced an innovative algorithm for more accurate project scheduling and minimizing latency by managing project buffers and suitable buffer sizing. This research presented an exploratory algorithm for determining the size of project buffers, feeding buffers, and resource buffers simultaneously [36].

The purpose of this study is to introduce a predictive buffer management algorithm using machine learning technology to measure project buffer size as well as control project buffer consumption in construction projects so that the projects can be completed according to planned schedules.

3 Methodology

In this research, a machine learning approach is used to propose a two-stage algorithm, PBMA, for predicting and controlling project buffers. The exploratory machine learning algorithm proposed in this research falls into the category of supervised machine learning algorithms. In the first stage, the appropriate buffer size is predicted for a given project. To do so, according to the critical activities of the project, the project critical chain is determined. Then, the project buffer size is predicted and the predicted buffer is allocated to the end of the critical chain of the project. In the second stage, the consumption of the project buffer is controlled and monitored during the project implementation phase. Also, proper monitoring of the project buffer consumption is done in this stage to prevent overuse.

In the second stage, the project buffer consumption phase begins. At this stage, the project enters the implementation phase and the designated project buffer is assigned to the critical chain of the project. During the implementation of the project and also the consumption of the desired buffer, the necessary control and monitoring are done on the consumption of the buffer. If the used buffer is more than the program value, it goes back to the beginning of the buffer sizing step to reset the buffer, otherwise, it goes to the next step. At this stage, if the amount of buffer consumed is less than the programmed value, the algorithm is terminated, otherwise for better control returns to the beginning of the control and monitoring of buffer consumption.

At this stage, the daily critical ratio is plotted on a trend chart. All buffer fluctuations and resource allocation conditions of the project from the beginning to the end are presented in different areas depending on the buffer consumption conditions. Each of these areas corresponds to a ground-rule (i.e. green: ok; yellow: do plan; red: interfere). This guide enables project practitioners to allocate constrained capacity to a place where high benefits are achieved. If a large amount of buffer is consumed, the point is in the red area and the duration of the project's tasks is probably underestimated. If it spends most of its time in the green area, the duration of the project's tasks is probably overestimated.

During the project implementation phase, the amount of buffer consumption is evaluated many times. If the consumption of the project's buffer is more than the project's predicted buffer, the project is re-planned and corrective actions are made to use project resources. Otherwise, if the consumption of the project buffer is less than or equal to the predicted project buffer size, this step will not be considered and monitoring of the project buffer consumption cycle will continue till the project's finished. Figure 1 schematically shows the procedure of the proposed PBMA. This Figure shows the heuristic algorithm of the PBMA. In this algorithm, arrows indicate the priority of the algorithm steps.

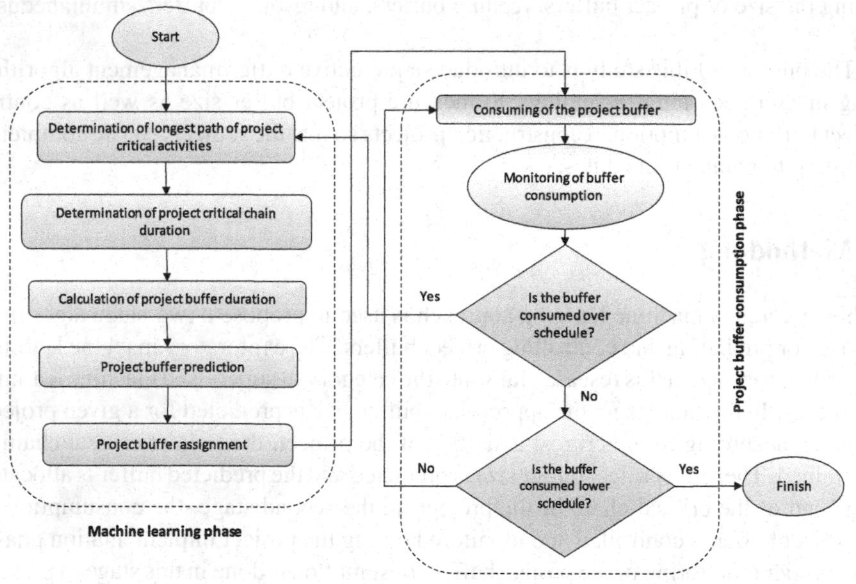

Fig. 1. Illustration of the proposed predictive buffer management methodology

According to the above methodology, the appropriate accuracy to determine the size of the buffer has a significant impact on how the buffer is used in the next phase. For example, if a suitable buffer is determined for the project, in the next phase, the consumption of the specified buffer can be done optimally and more accurately. It should also be noted that both phases of this methodology are directly and closely related to each other and have a direct impact on each other during the project. The methodology presented in this research improves the quality and effectiveness of project measurement and buffer consumption during project implementation.

3.1 The First Stage of the Proposed PBMA

In the first stage of the proposed PBMA, an appropriate buffer size for a given project is predicted. For this purpose, according to the project's critical activities, the project's critical chain is determined. Then the buffer sizing of the project is done and the predicted project buffer is assigned to the end of the project critical chain. To do so, the indices, the parameters, and the variables used to mathematically formulate the proposed problem are as follows.

The indices:

j: Index of the project activity (j = 1,…, m)

The parameters:

PCA_j: The project's critical activity j

The decision variables:

PLPA: The longest path of the project's critical activities
PBD: The buffer duration of the project
CCD: The duration of the project's critical chain
PPD: The duration of the project plan

In this stage, since the project's critical activities are already known, thc project's critical chain can be identified. Equation (1) shows, that the longest path of critical activities of a given project is the sum of the project's critical activities.

$$PLPA = \sum_{j=1}^{m} PCA_j \tag{1}$$

The project's critical chain duration is calculated through Eq. (2), after determining the project's longest path of critical activities.

$$CCD = \sum_{j=1}^{m} (PCA_j) \times 1/2 \tag{2}$$

Afterward, the project buffer size is predicted through Eq. (3).

$$PBD = (\sum_{j=1}^{m} (PCA_j) \times 1/2)/2 \tag{3}$$

Finally, the predicted buffer is assigned to the end of the critical chain of the project. The planned project duration is the sum of the project's critical chain duration and the project's buffer duration according to Eq. (4).

$$PPD = CCD + PBD \tag{4}$$

3.2 The Second Stage of the Proposed PBMA

In the second stage, the buffer consumption of the project is controlled and monitored during the project's implementation phase. At this stage, the daily critical ratio is plotted on a trend chart. All buffer fluctuations and project resource allocation conditions from the beginning to the end of the project are presented in different areas depending on the buffer consumption conditions. Each of these areas corresponds to a ground-rule (i.e. green: ok; yellow: do plan; red: interfere). These ground-rule enable project practitioners to allocate constrained capacity to a place from where high benefits are achieved.

4 Numerical Results

A numerical example is provided to evaluate the performance of the proposed PBMA. A hypothetical project with 15 activities is considered. The initial duration of the project is 60 days. As shown in Fig. 2, activities 1, 2, 3, 7, 8, 9, 12, 13, 14, and 15 are critical and constitute the longest path of the project's critical activities (PLPA). In this figure, the relationship between activities finish to start (FS) is considered. To use this method in real and large projects, you can use all kinds of connections between activities such as finish to start (FS), start to finish (SF), finish to finish (FF), and start to start (SS). In this case, the relevant coding can be done in MATLAB software and used as a case study on the project. Rachidi et al. (2017) proposed a Petri Nets (PNs) based modeling of discrete event systems (DESs) that includes complex temporal constraints. This research transform business process modeling (BPM) that deal with such constraints into PNs and proposes a systematic way to include inter-tasks constraints in PN formalisms [37]. The network of activities in Fig. 2 is usually provided by the project planning and control unit in the projects and can be prepared for different projects.

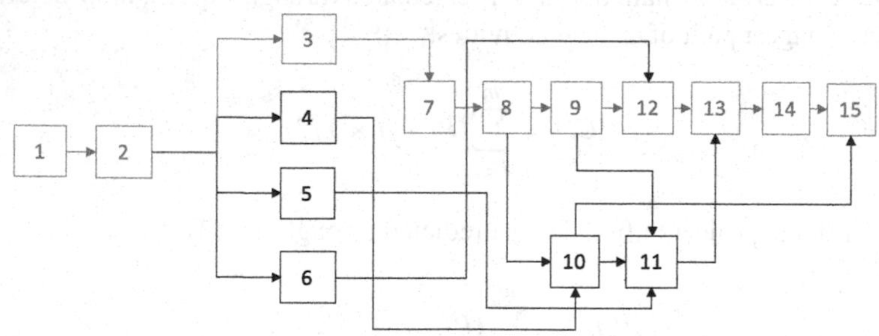

Fig. 2. Network of the project's activities for the numerical example

As mentioned in the literature review of this article, this method is based on the CCPM technique and the critical chain is obtained accordingly. According to the literature review, this method is also used in large projects. There are two major challenges to implementing CCPM, namely buffer size and the level of multiple resources. CCPM does not allocate safety time to each activity. Instead, it creates a collective safety time and places it in specific situations in the critical chain to act as a buffer. The use of buffers, which take into account both priority and resource constraints, helps to shorten project duration and increase project scheduling robustness. Buffers play a key role in CCPM, and determining the size of buffers is critical to increasing their effectiveness and ultimately ensuring successful project program management [38]. Table 1 shows the duration of activities in the numerical example.

Table 1. Duration of project's activities

Activity number	1	2	3	4	5	6	7	8	9	10	11	12	13	14	15
Activity duration	3	4	2	5	3	7	1	5	6	3	2	5	2	8	4

To evaluate the performance of the proposed method, PBMA is encoded in MATLAB software and executed using numerical data of the hypothetical project. In the first step of the proposed PBMA, the size of the project buffer is determined by Eqs. (1) - (4). The resulted values for PLPA, CCD, PBD, and PPD are respectively 60, 30, 15, and 45 days.

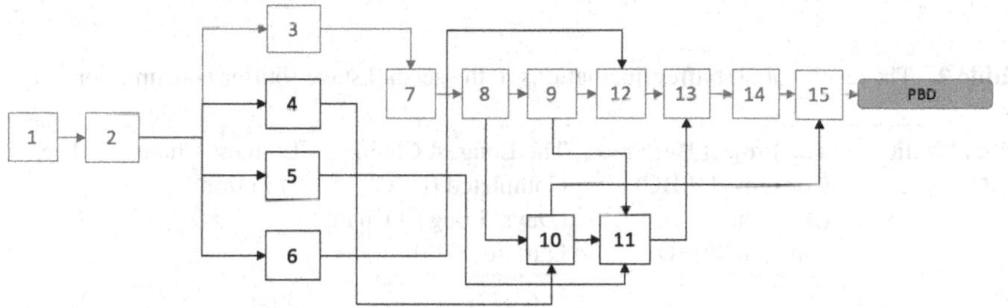

Fig. 3. Allocation of the predicted project's buffer duration

Figure 3 shows the project buffer, which is assigned to the end of the project network in green color. In the second stage of the proposed algorithm, the project enters the implementation phase and the consumption of buffer is controlled. According to the project buffer consumption (PBC) and the longest completed chain (LCC), on the 22nd day of the project, the project buffer conditions (dark spot in Fig. 4) are in the green area, which means that the project buffer size is less than Planned value. The PBC indicates the amount of project buffer consumption during project execution. This value is obtained by dividing the amount of buffer consumed by the buffer duration of the project (amount consumed/PBD). Also, the LCC is the percentage of completion of the longest critical chain of the project obtained by dividing the desired day by the longest critical chain multiplied by 100 (days/longest chain duration*100). Both PBC and LCC values can be calculated at any time during project execution. In this numerical example, 12 times from day 2 to 40 have been calculated, the calculations are given in Table 2. Also, the value of the Critical Ratio is obtained by dividing the LCC by the PBC (LCC/PBC), which can be seen in the last column of this table.

The critical ratio can be plotted daily on a chart, as shown in Fig. 5. In this figure, all buffer fluctuations and project resource allocation conditions from the beginning to the

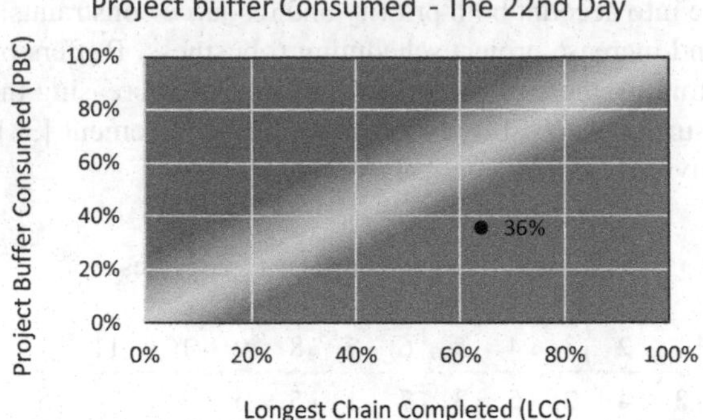

Fig. 4. Consumption of the project's buffer on the 22nd day

end of the project are presented with some points. Depending on the buffer consumption conditions, each point can be located in different areas. In Table 2, as shown in the second column from the left, the duration of the project's critical chain varies from 30 to 40 days.

Table 2. The results of all buffer fluctuations in the second stage (buffer consumption stage)

Critical Ratio (LCC/PBC)	The Project Buffer Consumed (PBC) (Amount consumed/PBD)	The Longest Chain Completed (LCC) (Days/ Longest Chain Duration*100)	Longest Chain Duration	Days
0.10	6.7	6.67	30.0	2
0.15	13.3	19.35	31.0	6
0.16	20.0	31.25	32.0	10
0.18	23.3	43.08	32.5	14
0.18	30.0	53.73	33.5	18
0.17	36.7	63.77	34.5	22
0.17	43.3	73.24	35.5	26
0.15	50.0	76.71	36.5	28
0.15	53.3	81.08	37.0	30
0.14	60.0	86.84	38.0	33
0.14	66.7	94.87	39.0	37
0.14	73.3	100.00	40.0	40

According to the calculated PBC and LCC presented in Table 2, which is obtained from the beginning to the end of the project, for buffer fluctuations presented in Fig. 5, it is determined that initially, the buffer consumption is located in the yellow area. Then it gradually enters the green area and continues in the same way until the middle of the project. Then it gradually gets closer to the yellow area and finally stays in the green area close to the yellow area. The results show that using the proposed PBMA, the project buffer size can be properly calculated and predicted, and the project buffer consumption can be monitored and controlled during the project implementation stage.

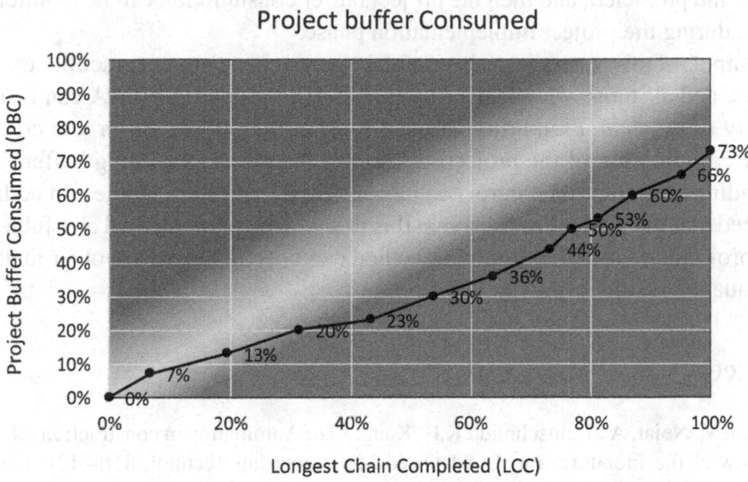

Fig. 5. Buffer fluctuations in the second stage of the proposed PBMA

In the second stage of the proposed PBMA, the daily critical ratio is plotted on a trend chart. All buffer fluctuations and project resource allocation conditions from the beginning to the end of the project are presented in different areas depending on the buffer consumption conditions. Each of the areas corresponds to a ground-rule (i.e. green: ok; yellow: do plan; red: interfere). This guide enables project practitioners to allocate limited capacity to a place/project from where high benefits will be achieved. In addition, buffer fluctuations provide project practitioners with feedback for planning and scheduling future construction projects. If a large amount of buffer is consumed, the point is in the red area and the duration of the project's tasks is probably underestimated. If it spends most of its time in the green areas, less amount of buffer is consumed and the duration of the project's tasks has probably been overestimated.

5 Conclusion

In this study, using predictive analysis, a machine learning-based exploratory approach was proposed to predict the buffer size of projects. For this purpose, a predictive buffer management algorithm based on machine learning technology was proposed to properly predict the buffer size of a given project and control the project buffer consumption in construction projects achieving a more realistic project duration.

The proposed method consists of two stages. In the first stage, the appropriate buffer size is predicted for a given project. In this stage, according to the project's critical activities, the project's critical chain is determined. Then the project buffer size is predicted.

In the second stage, the operation of project implementation begins and the buffer of the project is consumed. Proper controlling and monitoring of the project buffer consumption is done to prevent buffer consumption overuse. The proposed PBMA was implemented with numerical data taken from a hypothetical project. The results showed that by employing the proposed PBMA, first the project buffer size can properly be calculated and predicted, and then the project buffer consumption can be monitored and controlled during the project implementation phase.

The outputs of this research can be useful for researchers, project practitioners, industry owners, and all those who deal with projects. The proposed PBMA can be applied to a variety of projects. Further to the measuring of the project buffer and controlling the buffer consumption of the project, the size of the project's feeding buffers and the corresponding consumption control can be considered for future studies. In addition, it is suggested that the method presented in this research be implemented as a future study in a real project, and also the proposed method can be compared with other methods in terms of quality, results, etc.

References

1. Faghihi, V., Nejat, A., Reinschmidt, K.F., Kang, J.H.: Automation in construction scheduling: a review of the literature. Int. J. Advanced Manufacturing Technol. **81**(9–12), 1845–1856 (2015). https://doi.org/10.1007/s00170-015-7339-0
2. Parkinson, C.N., Lancaster, O.: Parkinson's Law: or the Pursuit of Progress (1958)
3. Parkinson, C.N.: Parkinson's law, Economist (1955)
4. Gutierrez, G.J., Kouvelis, P.: Parkinson's law and its implications for project management. Manage. Sci. **37**(8), 990–1001 (1991)
5. Goldratt, E.M.: Critical Chain. North River Press, New York (1997)
6. Leach, L.P.: Critical Chain Project Management, 2nd edn. Artech House Inc., London (2005)
7. Goldratt, E.M., Cox, J.: The Goal: Excellence in Manufacturing. North River Press (1984)
8. Greener, J.G., Kandathil, S.M., Moffat, L., Jones, D.T.: A guide to machine learning for biologists. Nat. Rev. Mol. Cell Biol. **23**(1), 40–55 (2022). https://doi.org/10.1038/s41580-021-00407-0
9. Duan, L., Xie, M., Wang, J., Bai, T.: Deep learning enabled intelligent fault diagnosis: overview and applications. J. Intelligent & Fuzzy Syst. **35**(5), 5771–5784 (2018). https://doi.org/10.3233/JIFS-17938
10. Liu, R., Yang, B., Zio, E., Chen, X.: Artificial intelligence for fault diagnosis of rotating machinery: a review. Mech. Syst. Signal Process. **108**, 33–47 (2018). https://doi.org/10.1016/j.ymssp.2018.02.016
11. Golge, E.: Brief History of Machine Learning (2016). http://www.erogol.com/brief-history-machine-learning/
12. Zohrehvandi, S., Khalilzadeh, M., Amiri, M., Shadrokh, S.: A heuristic buffer sizing algorithm for implementing a renewable energy project. Autom. Constr. **117**, 103267 (2020). https://doi.org/10.1016/j.autcon.2020.103267
13. Zohrehvandi, S., Vanhoucke, M., Khalilzadeh, M.: A project buffer and resource management model in energy sector; a case study in construction of a wind farm project. Int. J. Energy Sect. Manage. **14**(6), 1123–1142 (2020). https://doi.org/10.1108/IJESM-10-2019-0025
14. Zohrehvandi, S., Khalilzadeh, M., Amiri, M., Shadrokh, S.: Project buffer sizing and dynamic buffer consumption algorithm in power generation construction. Eng. Constr. Archit. Manag. **29**(2), 716–738 (2021). https://doi.org/10.1108/ECAM-08-2020-0605

15. Poshdar, M., González, V.A., Raftery, G.M., Orozco, F., Cabrera-Guerrero, G.G.: A multi-objective probabilistic-based method to determine optimum allocation of time buffer in construction schedules. Autom. Constr. **92**, 46–58 (2018)
16. Zhang, J., Jia, S., Diaz, E.: Dynamic monitoring and control of a critical chain project based on phase buffer allocation. Journal of the Operational Research Society, 1-12 (2018). https://doi.org/10.1080/01605682.2017.1415641
17. Martens, A., Vanhoucke, M.: Integrating corrective actions in project time forecasting using exponential smoothing. J. Manag. Eng. **36**(5), 04020044 (2020). https://doi.org/10.1061/(ASCE)ME.1943-5479.0000806
18. Zohrehvandi, S., Soltani, R.: Project scheduling and buffer management: a comprehensive review and future directions. J. Project Manage. **7**(2), 121–132 (2022)
19. Liakos, K.G., Busato, P., Moshou, D., Pearson, S., Bochtis, D.: Machine learning in agriculture: a review. Sensors **18**(8), 2674 (2018). https://doi.org/10.3390/s18082674
20. Pospieszny, P., Czarnacka-Chrobot, B., Kobylinski, A.: An effective approach for software project effort and duration estimation with machine learning algorithms. J. Syst. Softw. **137**, 184–196 (2018). https://doi.org/10.1016/j.jss.2017.11.066
21. Kanakaris, N., Karacapilidis, N., Kournetas, G., Lazanas, A.: Combining machine learning and operations research methods to advance the project management practice. In: Parlier, G.H., Liberatore, F., Demange, M. (eds.) ICORES 2019. CCIS, vol. 1162, pp. 135–155. Springer, Cham (2020). https://doi.org/10.1007/978-3-030-37584-3_7
22. Peña, A. B., et al.: Method for project execution control based on soft computing and machine learning. In: 2019 XLV Latin American Computing Conference (CLEI), pp. 1–7. IEEE (2019). https://doi.org/10.1109/CLEI47609.2019.235097
23. Sabahi, S., Parast, M.M.: The impact of entrepreneurship orientation on project performance: a machine learning approach. Int. J. Prod. Econ. **226**, 107621 (2020). https://doi.org/10.1016/j.ijpe.2020.107621
24. Chattapadhyay, D.B., Putta, J.: Risk identification, assessments, and prediction for mega construction projects: a risk prediction paradigm based on cross analytical-machine learning model. Buildings **11**(4), 172 (2021). https://doi.org/10.3390/buildings11040172
25. Sousa A., Faria J.P., Mendes-Moreira J., Gomes D., Henriques P.C., Graça R.: Applying machine learning to risk assessment in software projects. In: Kamp, M., et al. (eds) Machine Learning and Principles and Practice of Knowledge Discovery in Databases. ECML PKDD 2021. Communications in Computer and Information Science, **1525**. Springer, Cham (2021). https://doi.org/10.1007/978-3-030-93733-1_7
26. Đumić, M., Šišejković, D., Čorić, R., Jakobović, D.: Evolving priority rules for resource constrained project scheduling problem with genetic programming. Futur. Gener. Comput. Syst. **86**, 211–221 (2018). https://doi.org/10.1016/j.future.2018.04.029
27. Bourhnane, S., Abid, M.R., Lghoul, R., Zine-Dine, K., Elkamoun, N., Benhaddou, D.: Machine learning for energy consumption prediction and scheduling in smart buildings. SN Applied Sci. **2**(2), 1-10 (2020). https://doi.org/10.1007/s42452-020-2024-9
28. Adamu, P.I., Aromolaran, O.: Machine Learning Priority Rule (MLPR) for Solving Resource-Constrained Project Scheduling Problems (2018). http://eprints.covenantuniversity.edu.ng/id/eprint/11059
29. Zohrehvandi, S., Khalilzadeh, M.: APRT-FMEA buffer sizing method in scheduling of a wind farm construction project. Engineering, Construction and Architectural Manage. (2019). https://doi.org/10.1108/ECAM-04-2018-0161
30. Öhman, M., Hiltunen, M., Virtanen, K., Holmström, J.: Frontlog scheduling in aircraft line maintenance: from explorative solution design to theoretical insight into buffer management. J. Oper. Manag. **67**(2), 120–151 (2021). https://doi.org/10.1002/joom.1108

31. Zohrehvandi, S.: A project-scheduling and resource management heuristic algorithm in the construction of combined cycle power plant projects. Computers **11**(2), 23 (2022). https://doi.org/10.3390/computers11020023
32. Zohrehvandi, S.: Modeling in project planning & scheduling in construction management and project time optimization. Academia Letters, Article 4765 (2022). https://doi.org/10.20935/AL4765
33. Takami Narita, V., Ikeziri, L.M., Bernardi De Souza, F.: Evaluation of dynamic buffer management for adjusting stock level: a simulation-based approach. J. Ind. Prod. Eng. **38**(6), 452–465 (2021). https://doi.org/10.1080/21681015.2021.1931493
34. Zohrehvandi, S., Vanhoucke, M., Khalilzadeh, M., Amiri, M., Shadrokh, S.: A fuzzy project buffer management algorithm: a case study in the construction of a renewable project. International Journal of Construction Management, 1-10 (2022). https://doi.org/10.1080/15623599.2022.2045860
35. She, B., Chen, B., Hall, N.G.: Buffer sizing in critical chain project management by network decomposition. Omega **102**, 102382 (2021). https://doi.org/10.1016/j.omega.2020.102382
36. Zohrehvandi, S., Honarmand Shahzileh, Z.: A heuristic algorithm in project scheduling and project time optimization: through managing the size of the project buffer, feeding buffers, and resource buffers. Procedia Computer Science (2022)
37. Rachidi, S., Leclercq, E., Pigné, Y., Lefebvre, D.: Pn modeling of discrete event systems with temporal constraints. In: 2017 21st International Conference on System Theory, Control and Computing (ICSTCC), pp. 70–75. IEEE (2017). https://doi.org/10.1109/ICSTCC.2017.8107013
38. Raz, T., Barnes, R., Dvir, D.: A critical look at critical chain project management. Project Manage. J. **34**(4), 24–32 (2003). https://doi.org/10.1177/2F875697280303400404

Advances of Engineering Technology and Artificial Intelligence in Application Management

Measuring the Efficiency of Turkish Energy Distribution Companies Using Data Envelopment Analysis

Leyla Polat[1(✉)], Babek Erdebilli[2], and Abdullah Yıldızbaşı[2]

[1] Aviation Management Department, Necmettin Erbakan University, Konya, Turkey
lpolat@erbakan.edu.tr

[2] Industrial Engineering Department, Ankara Yıldırım Beyazıt University, Ankara, Turkey

Abstract. The digitalization of everyday items and our presence in the virtual world increase our reliance on electrical energy. Our dwindling energy resources exacerbate existing issues. There are numerous studies on circular economies and sustainability in the manufacturing and service sectors. Energy distribution enterprises are critical in this area since both supply energy and meet user demand. Academics evaluate the effectiveness of energy distribution corporations in a variety of locales and countries using a variety of methods. Turkey has been privatizing since 1994. This circumstance necessitates a review of the performance of local enterprises in this sector. Turkey's energy distribution system is divided into 21 areas, each of which has its own private energy provider. The performance of the 21 energy distribution enterprises evaluated is quantified using data envelopment analysis (DEA). The aim is to implement interregional comparisons based on published input and output numbers as well as firm efficiency. Additionally, the characteristics of inefficient companies are extracted. As a result, our research contributes to these firms' growth and success. Besides contributing to the academic literature, this study contributes useful data to the sector.

Keywords: Electrical Energy · Energy Distribution · Data Envelopment Analysis (DEA)

1 Introduction

The digitalization of everyday devices and the fact that our presence in the virtual environment spans such a vast and uninterrupted region naturally raises the need for electrical energy. Our energy resources are depleting at a rapid rate in response to rising demand, posing serious issues. As a result, the ideas of circular economy [1], sustainability [2], and green economy [3] are introduced into the literature for use in the manufacturing and service sectors. These concepts address issues such as resource efficiency, waste evaluation, and transfer to future generations. As a result, our energy needs are addressed with minimizing the damage we inflict to the earth as a species.

Energy distribution companies that provide energy access also play a critical role in supplying energy and meeting the user's energy demand. In this context, one of the

A. Mirzazadeh et al. (Eds.): SEMIT 2022, CCIS 1808, pp. 97–110, 2023.
https://doi.org/10.1007/978-3-031-40395-8_7

first measures that may be taken is to evaluate the energy distribution of an entire city or country in order to maximize energy efficiency. Distribution firms' performance is measured differently in different nations. In addition to this internationally recognized topic, this paper discusses private energy distribution companies in Turkey.

Since 1994, Turkey's energy distribution has been privatized [4]. This condition necessitates monitoring the performance of firms functioning in this sector in our country. In terms of energy distribution, our country is divided into 21 regions, and each region's energy need is met by a variety of private firms. The efficiency with which the country consumes and distributes energy is critical. The data envelopment analysis method is used to quantify the performance of businesses in this study. The input and output are calculated using data from the companies' yearly activity reports. 14 private electricity distribution companies are handled in order to obtain reliable data and achieve effective results.

The study is often divided into five sections. Following the introduction section in which the subject is defined, the literature on our study subject is examined. This worldwide research is summarized in the literature review section. The methodology section then discusses the data envelopment analysis approach and model. Following that, we present the content and results of the case study in which we utilized the method. The conclusion section makes decisions regarding the energy distribution based on the method's findings.

2 Literature Review

Data envelopment analysis is used to evaluate a company's performance and efficiency. Tschaffon and Meza [5] also utilize this approach to evaluate the efficiency of twenty different Brazilian energy distribution companies. In this instance, however, a different strategy was taken, and undesirable outcomes were classified as choice variables. In this study, which has twenty Decision-Making Units, the BCC Model and the Inverted Frontier approach are utilized to rank the decision makers. Among these, Coelba, an energy distribution company, is regarded as the most efficient.

As energy demand continues to grow, the usage of fossil fuels has become prevalent, resulting in environmental degradation. On the other hand, sustainability and green energy principles promote the use of renewable energy sources. San Cristóbal [6] addressed this issue in his study by analyzing the efficiency of thirteen renewable energy sources that are being used in Spain. It makes independent use of each objective function and three unique criteria developed using Multiple Criteria Data Envelopment Analysis. The model form created in this part is based on three efficiency criteria: minimizing d0, minimizing the total deviations, and minimizing the largest deviation. As a result, the results are believed to be more effective than those produced using conventional data envelopment analysis. Windpower 10 P 50 MW is a non-dominant outcome in a field of 13 renewable technologies.

Energy studies that are comprehensive and allow for the independent or simultaneous application of a number of approaches are relatively common in the literature. The data envelopment analysis approach is commonly used in the energy sector to evaluate the efficiency of energy distribution businesses. Additionally, Sadjadi and Omrani [7] conduct an examination of commercial energy distribution firms operating in Iran since 1992. Additionally, to the usual data envelopment approach, a novel method is described here that accounts for the uncertainty associated with the output variables. The authors discuss 38 power distribution companies using 2004 data using parametric Stochastic Frontier Analysis (SFA), a technique that improves the robustness of the traditional data Envelopment Technique. SFA and conventional data envelopment analysis are used to examine companies. As a result, it is stated that applying SFA generates more effective and accessible outcomes in terms of ranking.

On behalf of Iran, Azadeh et al. [8] conducted similar research. Between 2001 and 2011, seventeen energy distribution companies were designated as Decision Making units. These organizations' network length, carrying capacity, and personnel count are determined as inputs, while their customer base and total power sales are determined as outputs. An SDEA model is constructed for each input variable. Consequently, the most critical and effective input is determined to be the Network Length.

Miliotis [9], on the other hand, conducts a data envelopment analysis on behalf of the Greek Public Electricity Authority's energy distribution regions. When applied to 45 distribution zones, it is established that data envelopment analysis generates more dependable findings than straightforward econometric analysis. The research identifies places with low levels of output and makes recommendations for raising productivity. Similarly, the objective of creating positive regional rivalry is mentioned.

Sadjadi et al. [10] introduce the data envelopment analysis approach and propose a novel model for parameter uncertainty elimination. However, as long as this model is symmetric, it is possible to handle variable uncertainties. The study's inputs include operating expenses, personnel count, transformer capacity, and network length, while the study's outputs include total power sales, customer count, and service area size. If companies are efficient, as this research of 37 energy distributors found, they may develop their own preferences and objectives. We combine robust DEA and STEM approaches in this work to analyze the envelope boundary and calculate target values in an uncertain environment. As a consequence, the researchers have argued that using their developed model, it is reasonable to develop goals based on uncertain data and corporate preferences.

Turkey began privatized electricity distribution in 1994 [4]. Due to widespread usage of this strategy, it promotes competition but also results in the creation of efficient or inefficient distribution. As a result, assessing energy distribution firms' efficiency becomes critical. The approach of Data Envelopment Analysis is used to quantify various inputs and outputs, as well as their productivity. Along with research undertaken for other nations, one may come across studies conducted in Turkey that make use of data envelopment analysis. Petridis et al. [11] take a fresh approach to the topic by utilizing Directional Distance Function (DDF) Network DEA. Profitability is achieved in this new model by accounting for undesirable outputs and monitoring efficiency. This section will examine the cost of growth for an energy distribution company that is currently unable to meet its energy delivery obligations. As a result, twenty enterprises around Turkey are evaluated, and one is chosen to run the locomotives. Simultaneously, it is discovered that firm efficiency are lower in the south of the country than in the west. Along with electricity distribution companies, the literature includes research on the efficiency of gas distribution companies in Turkey using the data envelopment approach. Ertürk and Aşk [12] perform DEA analyses on the performance of 38 gas distribution firms. Their objective is to identify common features of companies with low levels of inefficiency and to identify parameters that impact a business's efficiency. Companies are evaluated according to their ownership structure (public versus private), maturity level (new versus established), licensing method (tender versus non-tender), scale (small versus huge), and SDI (Socio-economic Development Index). As a consequence, public firms outperform private organizations in terms of productivity, non-tender firms outperform tender firms in terms of efficiency, and big firms outperform small enterprises in terms of efficiency. It is argued that companies with poor efficiency levels operate in limited geographic areas yet have large investment costs and design flaws in their distribution networks.

Yardımcı and Karan [13] explore gas distribution firms in a similar manner to their analysis. However, in this case, both the service quality and efficiency of the businesses are evaluated. Efficiency is assessed in terms of rates set by the Energy Market Regulatory Authority (EMRA). As a consequence, the relationship between improved productivity and service quality is established, and conclusions about the efficacy of laws are drawn (Table 1).

Table 1. Studies that are related to Data Envelopment Analysis and Energy Distribution

Reference	Year	Country	DAE Method	Inputs	Outputs
Tschaffon & Meza [5]	2014	Brazil	• BCC Model Inverted Frontier method	Equivalent Duration of Interruption per Consumer Unit (DEC) Equivalent Frequency of Interruption per Consumer Unit (FEC) OPEX	Number of Consumers Served (NCONS) Consumption in TWh (CONS) Network Extension (NETWORK) Aneel Consumer Satisfaction Index (IASC)
Cristóbal [6]	2011	Spain	Multiple Criteria Data Envelopment Analysis (MCDEA) Model	Investment ratio Implement period Operating and maintenance costs	Power Operating hours Useful life. Tons of CO2 avoided
Sadjadi & Omrani [7]	2008	Iran	Parametric Stochastic Frontier Analysis (SFA)	Operating CostsNumber Of Employees Transformer Capacity Network Length	Units Of Energy Delivered Number Of Customers Size Of Service Area

(*continued*)

Table 1. (*continued*)

Reference	Year	Country	DAE Method	Inputs	Outputs
Azadeh et al. [8]	2015	Iran	Stochastic Data Envelopment Analysis (SDEA)	The network length Transformers capacity The number of employees	The number of customers. Total electricity sales
Miliotis [9]	1992	Greece	Data Envelopment Analysis (DEA)	Network total length Capacity of installed transformation points General expenses monetary units Administrative labour Technical labour	Number of customers Energy supplied Total Area
Sadjadi et al. [10]	2011	Iran	Interactive Robust Data Envelopment Analysis (IRDEA) Model Step Method (STEM)	Network length Transformers capacity Number of employees	Number of Customers Total electricity sales
Petridis et al. [11]	2019	Turkey	Network DEA	Number of StaffNet Consumption Number of transformators Length of Cables Installed Capacity	Energy supply
Ertürk & Türüt-Aşık [12]	2011	Turkey	Data Envelopment Analysis (DEA)	Total length of network. Length of steel pipeline. Length of PE pipeline Number of employees Total costs. Operating costs Capital costs	Total consumptionResidential consumption. Industrial consumption Total number of customers Peak demand
Yardımcı & Karan [13]	2015	Turkey	Data Envelopment Analysis (DEA) Stochastic Frontier Analysis (SFA)	OPEX of the ordinary consumers	Total consumption of the ordinary consumers. Number of ordinary consumers Total length of network

(*continued*)

Table 1. (*continued*)

Reference	Year	Country	DAE Method	Inputs	Outputs
Santos et al. [14]	2011	Portugal	Data Envelopment Analysis (DEA)	Operating costs Total network length Transformers capacity	Number of units of electricity delivered 1000–Total Interruption Time
Pahwa et al. [15]	2003	U.S.A	Data Envelopment Analysis (DEA)	Distribution systems losses (DLosses). Distribution operation and maintenance expenses (DO&M); Distribution capital additions expenses (DCapEx) Distribution line transformers (DTrans). Distribution lines (DLines)	Distribution system peak load (SysPeak) Retail sales (RSales) Retail customers (RCust)
Medeiros et al. [16]	2022	Brazil	Data Envelopment Analysis (DEA) Cross-Efficiency Analysis (CEA) Ratio-based Efficiency Analysis (REA)	Operational Expenditure (OPEX)	Underground network length High Voltage network length Overhead distribution network length Delivered energy weighted by voltage level Number of consumers
Düzgün [17]	2018	Turkey	Data Envelopment Analysis (DEA) BCC Model	The amount of energy consumed in the pure distribution region Total transformer capacity. Ratio of line length to population density	Amount of energy accrued A parameter aimed at minimizing downtime
Hess & Cullmann [18]	2007	Germany	Data Envelopment Analysis (DEA) Parametric Stochastic Frontier Analysis (SFA)	Labor Length of the grid in Km (aerial, cable lines)	Total amount of electricity delivered to end users The total number of customers

(*continued*)

Table 1. (*continued*)

Reference	Year	Country	DAE Method	Inputs	Outputs
Gouveia et al. [19]	2014	Portugal	Value-Based DEA Multiple Criteria Decision Analysis (MCDA)	Maintenance and outage repairing costs Supply interruptions (minutes of lost load) Complaints per customer. Number of incidents (LV and clients' installations)	Clients Network lines length
Mirza et al. [20]	2017	Pakistan	Stochastic Frontier Analysis Malmquist Index	Distribution losses (energy losses of electric utilities) Peak load as proxy for transformer capacity Network length	Average electricity consumption Growth in the number of customers
Arcos-Vargas et al. [21]	2017	Spain	Data Envelopment Analysis (DEA)	The level of remuneration The network segment The energy not supplied (undesirable output)	Electricity consumption Points of supply
Pombo & Taborda [22]	2006	Colombia	Data Envelopment Analysis (DEA) Malmquist Productivity Index	Employees in power distribution + commercialization Number of transformers + substations Power lines network Regional GDP per capita National installed capacity in electricity generation	Total sales Total customers Urban area served
Førsund & Kittelsen [23]	1998	Norway	Data Envelopment Analysis (DEA) Malmquist Index	Labour Energy loss Materials Capital	Distance index Number of customers Total energy delivered

(*continued*)

Table 1. *(continued)*

Reference	Year	Country	DAE Method	Inputs	Outputs
Edvardsen & Førsund [24]	2003	Denmark Finland Norway Sweden Netherlands	Malmquist Productivity Index Data Envelopment Analysis (DEA)	Replacement Value (RV) Energy loss. Total Operating Maintenance Costs (TOM)	The energy delivered Total Lines Number of Customers
Zhang & Bartels [25]	1998	Australia Sweden New Zealand	Data Envelopment Analysis (DEA)	The number of employees Total kilometres of distribution lines Total transformer capacity	Total number of customers served
Cullmann et al. [26]	2006	Poland Czech Republic Slovakia Hungary	SFA (Stochastic Frontier Analysis) COLS (Corrected Ordinary Least Squares)	The number of employees (labor), Estimated by the number of workers The length of the electricity grid (capital)	Total sales The number of customers
Ervural et al. [27]	2016	Turkey	Data Envelopment Analysis (DEA)	Total Renewable Energy Potential Network Length Total Installed Power of Renewable Energy Transformer Capacity	Energy Generation from Renewable Sources Number of Consumer

3 Methodology

It is required to develop a model to evaluate decision-making processes in greater depth and to compare current and anticipated consequences. It is anticipated that a mathematical model would develop that does quantitative analysis rather than qualitative. On the other hand, under this model, it is vital to know how much the decision-making units influence the outcome and which units should be considered for efficiency. As a result, Data Envelopment Analysis is utilized [28], the foundations of which were set by Cooper and Rhodes in 1978.

Data envelopment analysis, a type of linear programming, is a non-parametric technique for determining the efficiency of decision-making units. It assures that inputs collected using various scales produce different outputs [29, 30]. The definition refers to the decision-making units whose relative actions are quantified, such as enterprises and institutions that create comparable outputs from comparable inputs [31, 32].

There are instances of data envelopment analysis methodologies in every unit of production, service, and financial sector in the literature. However, the approach, which was developed for non-profit public organizations, is being used to analyze productivity in private enterprises as well [33]. Numerous advantages exist for data envelopment analysis. As a result, it gives several advantages for research by allowing it to be used for a variety of objectives in a variety of areas. These benefits are detailed below [30].

- Unlike parametric approaches, it does not require a functional correlation between the input and output.
- Units that are homogeneous are compared to one another.
- Decision-making units can be compared directly to one another or to other combinations of these components.
- Efficiency measurements may be performed on decision-making units with various inputs and outputs;
- It provides critical information on how to awaken inactive decision-making units.
- Input and output values can have a different unit system.

The variables and symbols necessary for data envelopment analysis, as well as the model to be constructed using these variables and symbols, are listed below [34]. The following symbols are used for the case study:

e_k: Efficiency score for $\mathrm{DMU_k}$,
y_{rk}: Amount of output r for $\mathrm{DMU_k}$,
x_{ik}: Amount of input i for $\mathrm{DMU_k}$,
u_r: Weight attached to output r,
v_i: Weight attached to input i,

$$e_k = \max \sum_{r=1}^{s} u_r y_{rk} \tag{1}$$

$s.t.$

$$\sum_{i=1}^{m} v_i x_{ik} = 1 \tag{2}$$

$$\max \sum_{r=1}^{S} u_r y_{rk} - \sum_{i=1}^{m} v_i x_{ik} \leq 0 \quad k = 1, \ldots, n \tag{3}$$

$$y_i \geq 0 \quad i = 1, \ldots, m \tag{4}$$

$$u_r \geq 0 \quad r = 1, \ldots, s \tag{5}$$

4 Case Study

In this study, which uses data envelopment analysis, primarily data collection and classification stages are applied. Annual reports obtained from companies are used for data collection. However, at the end of this stage, data on 21 companies that need to be evaluated cannot be accessed. Therefore, 14 companies were determined in terms of the consistency and efficiency of the work, and they were named as DMUs in accordance with the analysis. The data in the reports are classified as input and output to be used in analysis. Accordingly, Subscriber Count, Installed Power (MVA), Number of Transformers and Line Length (km) are determined as input. The output resulting from these input values is obtained as Distributed Energy (KWh). These values are shown in Fig. 1.

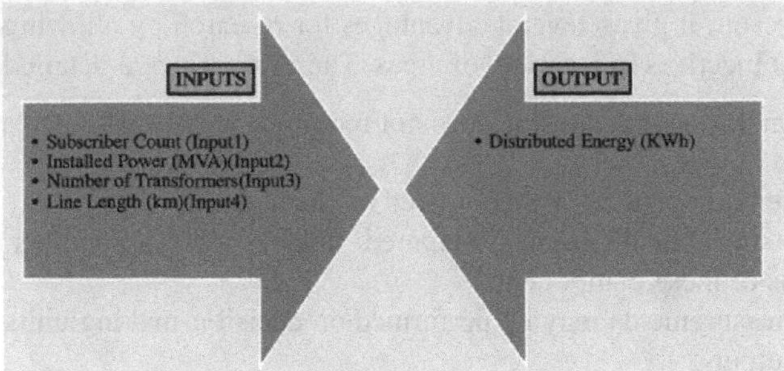

Fig. 1. Inputs and Output of the Analysis

The companies examined within the scope of the study are listed in Table 2. Amon them, BEDAŞ that supplies energy to the largest population comes first, followed by BAŞKENT EDAŞ, which also supplies the energy of the capital city of Turkey. KCETAŞ, which operates in the smallest area, comes last in this ranking.

Table 2. Decision Maker Units of the Analysis

DMU	Name of the DMU
DMU-1	BEDAŞ
DMU-2	TOROSLAR
DMU-3	BAŞKENT
DMU-4	AYEDAŞ
DMU-5	ULUDAĞ
DMU-6	SEDAŞ
DMU-7	AKDENİZ
DMU-8	OEDAŞ
DMU-9	ARAS
DMU-10	ÇORUH
DMU-11	FIRAT
DMU-12	ÇAMLIBEL
DMU-13	TREDAŞ
DMU-14	KCETAŞ

After determining the input and output values to be used in the method for DMUs, data envelopment analysis is started to be applied. In the analysis carried out, it is desired to reach the result of how efficient the output values we have according to the inputs. For this, the model is established for each DMU according to the method. The model created for the DMU-1 is given below.

for DMU-1;

$$Max\ 26920411943U_1 \tag{6}$$

s.t.

$$5134980V_1 + 15956V_2 + 14365V_3 + 47367V_4 = 1 \tag{7}$$

$$26920411943U_1 - 5134980V_1 - 15956V_2 - 14365V_3 - 47367V_4 \leq 0 \tag{8}$$

$$U_1 \geq 0, V_1 \geq 0, V_2 \geq 0, V_3 \geq 0, V_4 \geq 0 \tag{9}$$

The efficiency analysis results of DMUs are given in Table 3, and they are also classified according to their efficiency values. According to the classification, Those with DEA efficiency value 1 are called efficient, and those with a value less than 1 are called less efficient (Ganley and Cubbin). Accordingly, according to the inputs determined for DMU-1, DMU-7 and DMU-13, it is seen that the energy distribution efficiencies are 100%. The rest DMU-2, DMU-3, DMU-4, DMU-5, DMU-6, DMU-8, DMU-9, DMU-10, DMU-11, DMU-12,DMU-14 are followed as less efficient.

Table 3. Results of the DEA Model

DMU	DEA Efficiency Value	Type
DMU-1	1	Efficient
DMU-2	0,381	Less Efficient
DMU-3	0,429	Less Efficient
DMU-4	0,836	Less Efficient
DMU-5	0,518	Less Efficient
DMU-6	0,9	Less Efficient
DMU-7	1	Efficient
DMU-8	0,414	Less Efficient
DMU-9	0,108	Less Efficient
DMU-10	0,473	Less Efficient
DMU-11	0,368	Less Efficient
DMU-12	0,763	Less Efficient
DMU-13	1	Efficient
DMU-14	0,635	Less Efficient

5 Conclusion

In terms of energy saving, it is of great importance to examine energy distribution companies and therefore to consider the use of cities and countries. From this point of view, eliminating the deficiencies or mistakes in energy is a guide. In this study, companies in Turkey are examined. The efficiency of these companies in energy distribution is calculated by creating a CCR model thanks to the data envelopment analysis. A comparison is made with the determined input and output values by creating related models for 14 different institutions.

As a result of the analysis, it is seen that the institutions named BEDAŞ, Akdeniz, TREDAŞ are effective in energy distribution. The efficiencies of these companies were found to be as 100%, therefore, 3 of 14 different energy distribution companies in Turkey are effective in this regard. On the other hand, ARAS EDAŞ company called DMU-9, serving the east of the country, comes in last in this ranking.

When the results are examined in general, it is seen that the institutions with the lowest effective value in energy distribution are located in the east of the country. The reason for this may be the weather conditions or geographical features of the region. On the other hand, it can be said that companies in the west have higher productivity levels.

Our other aim in the study is to reveal the common characteristics of companies with low efficiency levels, to raise their awareness on this issue and to improve their activities in energy distribution. In this context, it is reached that the input values called subscriber count and installed power should be reconsidered. As a result, the number of subscribers is not as high as those in the west, but despite this, the formation of excess energy distribution poses a problem.

In future studies, it is aimed primarily to raise awareness of companies with low efficiency in energy distribution and to improve energy use. At the same time, the use of new technologies will be explored for those who cannot go further in the current situation or who want to increase their efficiency with less cost. Subsequently, qualitative and quantitative research is going to be made to ensure a large-scale energy saving on behalf of the country and to use all energy resources in a sustainable way.

References

1. WR Stahel 2016 The circular economy Nature 531 7595 435 438
2. H ten Have B Gordijn 2020 Sustainability Med. Health Care Philos. 23 2 153 154 https://doi.org/10.1007/s11019-020-09946-3
3. Krugman, P.: Building a Green Economy. New York Times, 5 (2010). Wikipedia. https://tr.wikipedia.org/wiki/Turkiye_Elektrik_Dagitim. Accessed 27 Nov 2021
4. P Tschaffon LA Meza 2014 Assessing the efficiency of the electric energy distribution using data envelopment analysis with undesirable outputs IEEE Lat. Am. Trans. 12 6 1027 1035
5. JR San Cristóbal 2011 A multi criteria data envelopment analysis model to evaluate the efficiency of the renewable energy technologies Renewable Energy 36 10 2742 2746
6. SJ Sadjadi H Omrani 2008 Data envelopment analysis with uncertain data: an application for Iranian electricity distribution companies Energy Policy 36 11 4247 4254
7. A Azadeh SM Haghighi M Zarrin S Khaefi 2015 Performance evaluation of Iranian electricity distribution units by using stochastic data envelopment analysis Int. J. Electr. Power Energy Syst. 73 919 931

8. PA Miliotis 1992 Data envelopment analysis applied to electricity distribution districts J. Oper. Res. Soc. 43 5 549 555
9. SJ Sadjadi H Omrani A Makui K Shahanaghi 2011 An interactive robust data envelopment analysis model for determining alternative targets in Iranian electricity distribution companies Expert Syst. Appl. 38 8 9830 9839
10. K Petridis MG Ünsal PK Dey HH Örkcü 2019 A novel network data envelopment analysis model for performance measurement of Turkish electric distribution companies Energy 174 985 998
11. M Ertürk S Türüt-Aşık 2011 Efficiency analysis of Turkish natural gas distribution companies by using data envelopment analysis method Energy Policy 39 3 1426 1438
12. Yardımcı, O., Karan, M.B.: Efficiency and service quality analyses of the natural gas distribution companies: a case study of Turkey. In: Energy Technology and Valuation Issues, pp. 165–198 (2015). https://doi.org/10.1007/978-3-319-13746-9_9
13. SP Santos CA Amado JR Rosado 2011 Formative evaluation of electricity distribution utilities using data envelopment analysis J. Oper. Res. Soc. 62 7 1298 1319
14. A Pahwa X Feng D Lubkeman 2003 Performance evaluation of electric distribution utilities based on data envelopment analysis IEEE Trans. Power Syst. 18 1 400 405
15. GO Medeiros 2022 Efficiency analysis for performance evaluation of electric distribution companies Int. J. Electr. Power Energy Syst. 134 107430
16. B Düzgün 2018 Türkiye elektrik iletim ve dağıtım şebekesinin enerji verimliliğinin değerlendirilmesi ve 2023 projeksiyonları Politeknik Dergisi 21 3 621 632
17. B Hess A Cullmann 2007 Efficiency analysis of East and West German electricity distribution companies–do the "Ossis" really beat the "Wessis"? Utilities Policy 15 3 206 214
18. MC Gouveia LC Dias CH Antunes J Boucinha CF Inácio 2015 Benchmarking of maintenance and outage repair in an electricity distribution company using the value-based DEA method Omega 53 104 114
19. FM Mirza I Mushtaq K Ullah 2017 Assessing the efficiency dynamics of post reforms electric distribution utilities in Pakistan Utilities Policy 47 18 28
20. A Arcos-Vargas F Núñez-Hernández G Villa-Caro 2017 A DEA analysis of electricity distribution in Spain: an industrial policy recommendation Energy Policy 102 583 592
21. C Pombo R Taborda 2006 Performance and efficiency in Colombia's power distribution system: effects of the 1994 reform Energy Econ. 28 3 339 369
22. FR Førsund SA Kittelsen 1998 Productivity development of Norwegian electricity distribution utilities Resour. Energy Econ. 20 3 207 224
23. DF Edvardsen FR Førsund 2003 International benchmarking of electricity distribution utilities Resour. Energy Econ. 25 4 353 371
24. Y Zhang R Bartels 1998 The effect of sample size on the mean efficiency in DEA with an application to electricity distribution in Australia, Sweden and New Zealand J. Prod. Anal. 9 3 187 204
25. A Cullmann C Hirschhausen von 2008 Efficiency analysis of East European electricity distribution in transition: legacy of the past? J. Prod. Anal. 29 2 155 167
26. BC Ervural B Ervural S Zaim 2016 Energy efficiency evaluation of provinces in Turkey using data envelopment analysis Procedia Soc. Behav. Sci. 235 139 148
27. F Phillips 2005 25 years of data envelopment analysis Int. J. Inf. Technol. Decis. Mak. 4 03 317 323
28. Ü Özden 2008 Veri zarflama analizi (VZA) ile Türkiye'deki vakıf üniversitelerinin etkinliğinin ölçülmesi İstanbul Üniversitesi İşletme Fakültesi Dergisi 37 2 167 185
29. Depren, Ö.: Veri zarflama analizi ve bir uygulama (2008)
30. Ö Akgöbek İ Nişancı S Kaya T Eren 2015 Veri Zarflama Analizi Yaklaşımını Kullanarak Bir Eğitim Kurumunun Şubelerinin Performanslarını Ölçme Sosyal Bilimler Araştırma Dergisi 4 3 43 54

31. Sarı, Z.: Veri zarflama analizi ve bir uygulama (2015)
32. Gülcü, A., Tutar, H., Yeşilyurt, C.: Sağlık sektöründe veri zarflama analizi yöntemi ile göreceli verimlilik analizi. Seçkin Yayıncılık, Ankara (2004)
33. BD Rouyendegh A Yildizbasi I Yilmaz 2020 Evaluation of retail ındustry performance ability through ıntegrated ıntuitionistic fuzzy TOPSIS and data envelopment analysis approach Soft. Comput. 24 16 12255 12266 https://doi.org/10.1007/s00500-020-04669-2
34. Ganley, J.A., Cubbin, J.S.: Public sector efficiency measurement: applications of data envelopment analysis. Elsevier Science Inc. (1992)

Monocular Vision-Based Prediction of Cut-In Manoeuvres with LSTM Networks

Yagiz Nalcakan[1,2](✉) and Yalin Bastanlar[1]

[1] Izmir Institute of Technology, Urla, Izmir, Turkey
{Yagiznalcakan,yalinbastanlar}@iyte.edu.tr
[2] TTTech Auto Turkey Software, Izmir, Turkey

Abstract. Advanced driver assistance and automated driving systems should be capable of predicting and avoiding dangerous situations. In this paper, we first discuss the importance of predicting dangerous lane changes and provide its description as a machine learning problem. After summarizing the previous work, we propose a method to predict potentially dangerous lane changes (cut-ins) of the vehicles in front. We follow a computer vision-based approach that only employs a single in-vehicle RGB camera, and we classify the target vehicle's maneuver based on the recent video frames. Our algorithm consists of a CNN-based vehicle detection and tracking step and an LSTM-based maneuver classification step. It is computationally efficient compared to other vision-based methods since it exploits a small number of features for the classification step rather than feeding CNNs with RGB frames. We evaluated our approach on a publicly available driving dataset and a lane change detection dataset. We obtained 0.9585 accuracy with the side-aware two-class (cut-in vs. lane-pass) classification model. Experiment results also reveal that our approach outperforms state-of-the-art approaches when used for lane change detection.

Keywords: Vehicle Behavior Prediction · Vision-based Maneuver Classification · Maneuver Prediction · Driver Assistance Systems

1 Introduction

Prediction of intended maneuvers of surrounding vehicles is an important research area that supports the development of Advanced Driver Assistance Systems (ADAS). Also, it is one of the challenging problems to reach fully driverless vehicles. Moreover, statistical data show that unexpected maneuvers of drivers on highways may lead to deadly accidents. According to the U.S. Department of Transportation, National Highway Traffic Safety Administration's (NHTSA) 2018 report on "Driving Behaviors Reported for Drivers and Motorcycle Operators Involved In Fatal Crashes" [12], one of the top-3 reasons for fatal crashes is failure to keep the vehicle in the proper lane. Therefore, early prediction of risky lane-change maneuvers of surrounding vehicles can help drivers to avoid fatal crashes on the road.

Detection and distance measurements for surrounding vehicles can be obtained via different sensors, including radar, camera, and LiDAR. Each of these sensors has pros

A. Mirzazadeh et al. (Eds.): SEMIT 2022, CCIS 1808, pp. 111–123, 2023.
https://doi.org/10.1007/978-3-031-40395-8_8

and cons compared to each other. For example, although LiDAR can detect much smaller objects and generate more detailed images compared to the others, it is still an expensive sensor. Radar has advantages in extreme illumination and weather conditions, but its field of view is generally narrow, and its noisy output requires cleaning [14]. A camera, which is the sensor we use in this study, is cheap and easily accessible. It enables us to obtain various information (such as color, speed, distance, depth, etc.) simultaneously if accompanied by powerful computer vision techniques.

In our study, we focus on vehicles in front and only employ a single in-vehicle forward-looking RGB camera. This brings simplicity to our approach compared to other studies in the literature that use a camera, radar, and LiDAR sensors ([4, 6, 9]). Since there is no benchmark dataset for the classification of potentially dangerous cut-in maneuvers in traffic, we have prepared a classification dataset with the videos of the publicly available Berkeley Deep Drive dataset [17], which consists of videos that are collected via the front camera of the vehicles on highways of various cities. We have cut and labeled 875 video clips containing vehicle maneuvers belonging to cut-in or lane-pass classes. These video clips cover two seconds of action. In our experiments, we represented this duration with various frames (15, 30, 45, or 60). As the number of frames increases, it becomes a dense representation and requires more computation. We made labeled clips and the source code of our methods publicly available[1]. Apart from the dataset we prepared, we evaluated our method on a cut-in and lane-pass maneuver subset extracted from a lane change detection benchmark dataset [8].

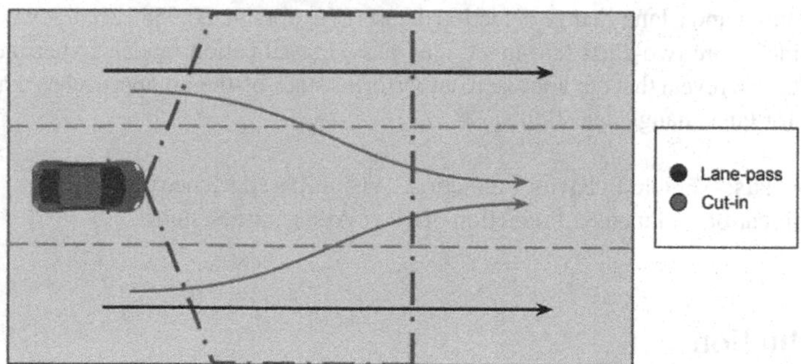

Fig. 1. Lane-pass and cut-in maneuvers (green area indicates considered safety field for ego vehicle.)

We classify the maneuver of the vehicles in front, whether they are cutting into the ego vehicle's lane or keeping their lane (Fig. 1). In our experiments, we evaluated several models for two-class classification of cut-in and lane-pass maneuvers, as well as 3-class models to discriminate left-hand side and right-hand side cut-ins. There is no doubt that the proposition of classifying maneuvers into two or three is an oversimplification of real-life cases. However, this scheme is enough to predict risky cut-in maneuvers and enables us to compare our results with the state-of-the-art lane-change detection methods ([2, 5, 7]).

1 https://github.com/ynalcakan/cut-in-maneuver-prediction.

Our approach consists of three steps (Fig. 2). The first step is CNN-based vehicle detection, where we employ YOLOv4 [3] to detect vehicles in each frame of the sequence. The second step is tracking the detected vehicles using DeepSort [16]. In the third step, extracted features from the detected and tracked bounding boxes of vehicles in front are fed into an LSTM network to be classified.

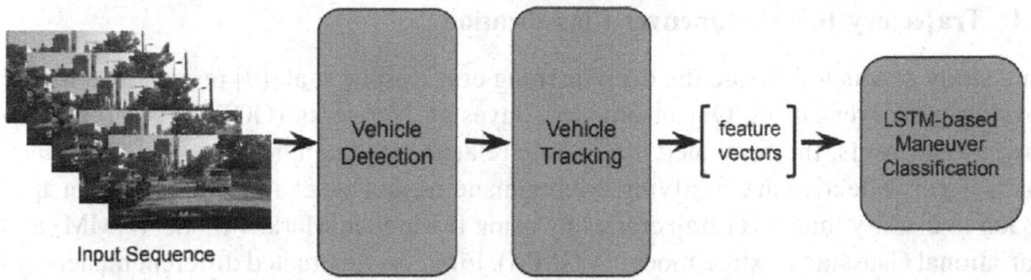

Fig. 2. Overview of the proposed approach.

The main contribution of our work is that the proposed approach is computationally cheaper than the previous work that feeds CNNs with video frames and uses complex architectures [2, 5, 7, 18]. Instead, a small number of features are extracted from the input sequence and fed into an LSTM in our work. Despite its simplicity, it exceeds the classification accuracies reported in the compared studies (cf. Section 5.3). A second important advantage is that the proposed approach employs simple equipment (a standard field-of-view RGB camera) and does not require a calibration procedure or any other specific adjustment depending on the ego-vehicle.

The remainder of this paper is structured as follows: the related works are reviewed in Sect. 2. Section 3 has detailed information about our method for maneuver prediction task, and Sect. 4 provides information about datasets. Finally, experimental results are discussed in Sect. 5, which is followed by the conclusion in Sect. 6.

2 Related Work

In the literature, different classifications have been made on modeling vehicle motions. LeFévre et al. [11] divided motion modeling approaches into physics-based, maneuver-based, and interaction-aware models by their targets' motion. As our approach considers the target vehicle's maneuvers to classify its motion, it is among the maneuver-based models.

Most of the work done in maneuver classification is on lane change prediction. They try to classify right lane change, left lane change, and no lane change maneuvers. There are few studies on detecting risky cut-in maneuvers, which we focus on.

We would like to discuss the recent studies by dividing them into two according to their methodologies: trajectory-based and vision-based maneuver classifications.

Trajectory-based maneuver classification is about projecting the trajectory of each surrounding vehicle on the ground plane using an on-vehicle camera, radar, or external sensors (i.e., surveillance cameras) and classifying the maneuver with this trajectory information. Vision-based classification is about extracting features from an image sequence and classifying the maneuver using these features.

2.1 Trajectory-Based Maneuver Classification

In a study conducted before the deep learning era, Kasper et al. [9] proposed to model driving maneuvers using Object-oriented Bayesian Networks (OOBN). According to their experiments, the combined use of lane-related coordinate features and occupancy grids is very effective in classifying driving maneuvers. Deo et al. [4] proposed an approach to classify maneuver trajectories by using the hidden Markov model (HMM) and variational Gaussian mixture model (VGMM). First, they extracted different maneuvers like lane-pass, overtake, cut-in, and drift-into-ego-lane from highway recorded videos, radar, and LiDAR data. Then they classified all trajectories using VGMM. Their method reached 0.842 accuracy on all maneuvers and 0.559 accuracy on overtaking and cut-in maneuvers. Scheel et al. [13] used the trajectories of the right lane change, left lane change, and follow maneuvers as input to an attention-based LSTM network. They reported the prediction accuracies of maneuvers as 0.784 for left lane change, 0.962 for follow, and 0.679 for right lane change. Altché et al. [1] proposed an LSTM-based method to predict future vehicle trajectories on the NGSIM dataset [15], in which two-layer LSTM achieved better RMSE results compared to other similar approaches in two and three seconds prediction horizons.

2.2 Vision-Based Maneuver Classification

With the increasing popularity of deep learning methods in vision, recent studies of vision-based maneuver classification generally use convolutional neural networks (CNNs) to get visual information regarding the scene. The usual practice is using a CNN as a feature extractor by feeding video frames into CNN and using an RNN or an LSTM as a classifier. In [7], features are extracted by a CNN on region-of-interest (ROI), width, height, and center coordinate values are added to the feature vector. Then, classification of the lane change maneuvers is performed by an LSTM. Their best model achieved 0.745 accuracy. Another approach in the same study [7] was converting movements of objects into contours in an RGB image and feeding CNNs with this motion history image. However, the performance was worse.

Another study that first crops ROIs from the original frames [5] exploited two modes of input video: high frame rate video and its optical flows. They compared two-stream CNNs and spatio-temporal multiplier networks. In a follow-up study [2], the authors also included a slow-fast network (the one that uses videos of high and low frame rates), which achieved 0.908 accuracy and performed slightly better than other alternatives.

The studies discussed above have used the Prevention dataset [8] to test their methods. Among other studies that perform vision-based maneuver classification on different datasets, Lee et al. [10] proposed a method that can be used for adaptive cruise control, which uses a front-faced radar and camera outputs to infer the lane change maneuvers.

In their method, they convert the traffic scenes to a simplified bird's eye view (SBV), and those SBVs are given as input to a CNN network to predict lane keeping, right cut-in, and left cut-in intentions. Yurtsever et al. [18] proposed a deep learning-based action recognition framework for classifying dangerous lane change behavior in video captured by an in-car camera. They used a pre-trained Mask R-CNN model to segment vehicles in the scene and a CNN + LSTM model to classify the behaviors as dangerous or safe. In our work, we extract bounding boxes of surrounding vehicles with well-performing computer vision techniques. This step exists in previous vision-based methods as well. However, unlike them ([2, 5, 7, 10, 18]), we do not feed a feature extractor CNN with RGB frames of the sequence. Instead, we feed an LSTM with a feature vector consisting of bounding box data, which is very fast. With a 15-frame model, we can make an estimate every two seconds.

To the best of our knowledge, no vision-based cut-in/lane-pass classification accuracy is reported in the literature. However, we can compare our method's performance with previously reported lane-change classification methods (that do not differ if a vehicle is entering or exiting ego-lane). Thus, in addition to the cut-in detection performances, we share our method's performance on the lane change prediction task on the publicly available Prevention dataset (cf. Section 5.3). Results indicate that with the proposed LSTM approach, a 3-class (left lane-change, right lane-change, no lane-change) classification accuracy of over 94% can be obtained, whereas previously reported lane-change classification accuracies ([2, 5, 7]) do not reach 92% on the same dataset even with complex models.

3 Methodology

3.1 Vehicle Detection

As we extract our features using the bounding box of the target vehicle, it is crucial to detect the surrounding vehicles with high accuracy. Therefore, as a vehicle detection network, we used YOLOv4 [3], which is widely used in similar methods. Each frame of the image sequence is fed into the pre-trained YOLOv4, and bounding boxes of the target vehicles are sent to the vehicle tracking step together with the same input image (Fig. 3).

3.2 Vehicle Tracking

Detected vehicles per frame (bounding boxes) can have position errors caused by YOLOv4. We added a vehicle tracking step to the pipeline to minimize those errors. Tracking is done via DeepSort [16], known for its ease of implementation with YOLO. Corrected bounding boxes of the target vehicle are given as input to the feature extraction step.

3.3 Feature Extraction and Network Architecture

Many visual cues may allow us to predict whether any of the surrounding vehicles make a cut-in maneuver or not. In our work, we obtain cues from the detected bounding boxes

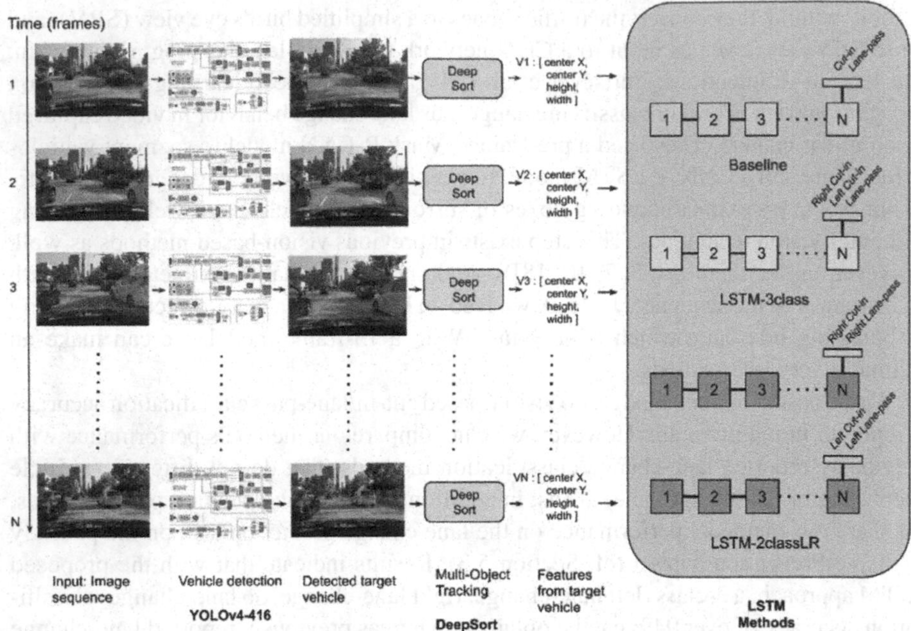

Fig. 3. Pipeline of the proposed approach. Following the steps for extracting the bounding boxes of target vehicles (TVs), the baseline LSTM method uses feature vectors of TVs and classifies maneuvers as cut-in or lane-pass. LSTM-3class method classifies into 3: right cut-in, left cut-in or lane-pass classes. As a third alternative, LSTM-2classLR has two separate LSTMs for left-hand side and right-hand side TVs. We conducted experiments with varying sequence lengths (15, 30, 45, and 60 frames) all representing two seconds of the video.

of surrounding vehicles. Specifically, we extract the center (x, y) coordinates, width, and height values of the bounding box. Collected features are given to a single-layer LSTM to obtain the classification result. We tried four different sequence lengths (15, 30, 45, and 60). A shorter sequence length means more sparse representation (3 out of 4 frames are neglected in 15-frame sequences) of the action but faster maneuver prediction due to decreased processing time. As hyperparameters of the LSTM, various hidden unit sizes, batch sizes, optimizer types, activation function types, and dropout amounts are evaluated to find the best performing LSTM architecture. Evaluated hyperparameters are given in Table 1, and the proposed framework can be seen in Fig. 3.

Table 1. Evaluated LSTM hyperparameters.

Hidden Units	Batch Sizes	Optimizer	Activation	Dropout
60 128 256 512	5 10 50 100	Adam RMSProp AdaDelta	ReLU Sigmoid Tanh	0 0.25 0.5

4 Dataset

4.1 BDD-100K Dataset and Labeling

A subset of the Berkeley Deep Drive Dataset [17] was used in this study. This dataset consists of 100K driving videos labeled for ten tasks (road object detection, instance segmentation, drive-able area, etc.). The videos were captured by the front camera of the vehicles at various times of the day in New York, Berkeley, San Francisco, and Tel Aviv. We focused on lane change actions that happened on highways. 875 video sequences containing vehicle maneuvers belonging to cut-in and lane-pass classes (Fig. 1) were cut from approximately 20K videos. The final distribution contains 405 cut-in and 470 lane-pass samples, divided into train-validation-test datasets using a 60%–20%–20% split ratio.

Figure 4 shows the principle while labeling cut-in samples in our dataset. At the starting frame of the sequence, the target vehicle is on the other lane, and there is no indication whether a cut-in will occur or not. The lane change event occurs as the target vehicle enters the safety field (the polygon indicated with green lines in Fig. 4). The sequence is cut when the vehicle enters the ego-lane with its whole body (no need to be aligned in the center). For the lane-pass class, the vehicles that pass by the ego vehicle from the right or left side are labeled during their stay in the safety field.

4.2 Prevention Dataset and Labeling

In 2019, Izquierdo et al. [7] published a benchmark dataset called "The PREVENTION dataset: a novel benchmark for PREdiction of VEhicles iNTentIONs" for lane change detection problem. The dataset has 356 h of driving video, mostly on highways. They provide detections, trajectories, and labels in addition to the raw data. They continuously improve the dataset, but the current version has only three labels for vehicle maneuvers: left lane change, right lane change, and no lane change.

Since recent studies have used the Prevention Dataset [2, 5, 7], we also included it in our evaluation. We generated two separate subsets, one is a cut-in/lane-pass subset, and the other is a lane change detection subset. The number of samples used for lane change prediction and cut-in prediction tasks is shown in Table 2. Since the number of samples of no lane change and lane change categories are unbalanced in the original dataset, the same skewness also occurs in the prepared subsets.

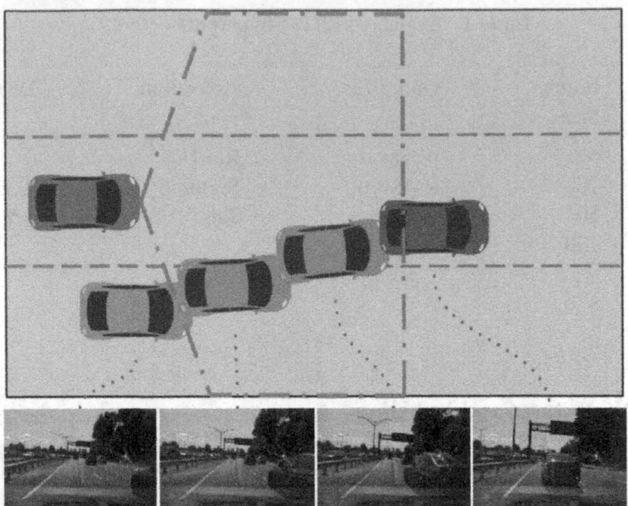

Fig. 4. Start and end points of maneuvers that are labeled as cut-in.

Cut-in/lane-pass subset sequences were created to have at least 60 frames to make them comparable with our BDD-100K cut-in/lane-pass dataset. Sequences were labeled in the manner shown in Fig. 4. For the lane change detection subset, to keep as many samples as possible, we have included sequences that have at least 50 frames.

Table 2. Distribution of samples extracted from the Prevention Dataset both for lane change prediction task and cut-in/lane-pass classification task.

Task Class	Lane Change Prediction	Cut-in/Lane-pass Prediction
No Lane Change	4827	-
Left Lane Change	267	-
Right Lane Change	200	-
Lane-pass	-	1132
Cut-in	-	114

For the train-validation-test split, the same split ratio of 60%–20%–20% was used as in the BDD-100K subset. In addition, hyperparameter selection was made by selecting from the same hyperparameter pool (Table 1) with the grid search method as in the BDD-100K subset.

5 Experimental Results

5.1 Cut-In/Lane-Pass Classification Results on BDD-100K Dataset

We evaluated our approach with different methods where classification strategy varies. As a baseline method, a single-layer LSTM model is trained with four features (center (x, y) coordinates, width, and height of the target vehicle's bounding box) for a side-agnostic 2-class classification, i.e., each sample is a cut-in or a lane-pass. In the LSTM-3class method, samples are classified as left-hand side cut-in, right-hand side cut-in, and lane-pass. This second strategy is closer to several lane-change prediction studies in the literature, where maneuvers were classified as left lane-change, right lane-change, and no lane-change. Examining the target vehicle's center coordinates makes it straightforward to extract if it is on the left or right of the ego vehicle. Thus, as a third method (LSTM-2classLR), we train two networks; one is responsible for left-hand side maneuvers and the other for the right-hand side. Each performs a 2-class classification (cut-in/lane-pass). Test performances of these three methods are presented in Table 3.

Table 3. Cut-in/Lane-pass classification results of different methods for varying sequence lengths on BDD-100K dataset.

Method	Sequence Length	Accuracy	Precision (Cut-in)	Recall (Cut-in)	Precision (Lane-pass)	Recall (Lane-pass)
Baseline	15	0.8851	0.8551	0.8939	0.9114	0.8780
	30	**0.9256**	0.8841	**0.9531**	**0.9620**	0.9048
	45	0.9189	**0.9275**	0.9014	0.9114	0.9351
	60	**0.9256**	**0.9275**	0.9143	0.9241	**0.9359**
LSTM-3Class	15	**0.9324**	**0.8960**	0.9230	**0.9620**	**0.9383**
	30	0.9121	0.8667	0.9077	0.9494	0.9146
	45	**0.9324**	0.8769	**0.9245**	0.9494	0.9146
	60	0.9256	0.8829	0.9077	**0.9620**	**0.9383**
LSTM-2ClassLR	15	0.9311	0.9321	0.9021	0.9302	0.9524
	30	**0.9585**	**0.9494**	0.9500	0.9651	**0.9648**
	45	0.9452	0.9171	0.9483	0.9651	0.9434
	60	0.9519	0.9160	**0.9648**	**0.9767**	0.9439

For all models mentioned above, hyperparameters (Table 1) were optimized by grid search, and the model with the highest accuracy on the validation set was evaluated on the test set.

Our baseline method, which classifies the sequences without separating if the maneuver is on the right or the left, reached an accuracy of 0.9256 with 30-frame and 60-frame sequences and slightly lower accuracy for other sequence lengths. Increasing the number of classes to three (right cut-in, left cut-in, lane-pass) resulted in a slight improvement, achieving 0.9324 accuracy. When we trained two separate networks for the right-hand side and left-hand side (LSTM-2classLR), the classification accuracy increased to

0.9585. The best values were obtained with 30-frame sequences, but for other lengths as well the accuracies were increased compared to the baseline and LSTM-3class methods.

5.2 Cut-In/Lane-Pass Classification Results on Prevention Dataset

Each method tested on the BDD-100K dataset is also evaluated on the Prevention cut-in/lane-pass subset (cf. Section 4.2). Accuracy, precision, and recall results with different sequence lengths are shown in Table 4. While all three models are highly successful, LSTM-2ClassLR is slightly better than the others, which is consistent with the results of the BDD-100K dataset. These results indicate that the success of the proposed approach is not specific to a dataset and works well on a benchmark dataset as well.

We observe occasional drops in precision and recall values of cut-in compared to those of lane-pass class. This is due to the skewness in the dataset. Since the number of lane-pass samples is much higher, the model is inclined to prefer lane-pass more. In the lane-change study with this dataset [2] as well, reported lane-change precision and recall are much lower than those of no lane-change class.

Table 4. Cut-in/Lane-pass classification results of different methods for varying sequence lengths on Prevention dataset.

Method	Sequence Length	Accuracy	Precision (Cut-in)	Recall (Cut-in)	Precision (Lane-pass)	Recall (Lane-pass)
Baseline	15	0.9718	0.9259	0.8333	0.9775	0.9909
	30	**0.9799**	**0.9630**	**0.8667**	**0.9820**	**0.9954**
	45	0.9638	0.8519	0.8214	0.9775	0.9819
	60	0.9759	0.8889	0.8276	0.9777	0.9865
LSTM-3Class	15	0.9638	0.6786	**0.9286**	**0.9865**	0.9733
	30	**0.9719**	**0.9524**	0.8958	0.9775	**0.9909**
	45	0.9558	0.7976	0.7976	0.9730	0.9730
	60	0.9598	0.6786	0.7500	0.9820	0.9732
LSTM-2ClassLR	15	0.9788	0.9285	**0.8903**	**0.9845**	0.9920
	30	0.9740	0.9286	0.8452	0.9791	0.9919
	45	0.9665	0.9286	0.7917	0.9710	0.9918
	60	**0.9789**	**0.9524**	0.8690	0.9818	**0.9946**

5.3 Lane Change Prediction Results on Prevention Dataset

To compare with the studies in the literature, we trained our LSTM-3Class model for lane change detection using the Prevention Dataset which [2, 5], and [7] used in their studies. As we explained above, the LSTM-3Class model runs with 15, 30, 45, and 60-frame inputs. Since we allowed 50-frame sequences in the lane change detection subset (to

Table 5. Comparison with the previous lane change maneuver classification studies.

	Method	Accuracy
Biparva *et al.* [2]	Spatiotemporal Multiplier Network	0.9190
Izquierdo *et al.* [7]	GoogleNet + LSTM	0.7440
Fernandez-Llorca *et al.* [5]	Spatiotemporal Multiplier Network	0.9194
Ours (15-frame)	LSTM-3Class	**0.9270**
Ours (30-frame)	LSTM-3Class	**0.9371**
Ours (45-frame)	LSTM-3Class	**0.9484**

keep more samples), we compare only the results of 15-frame, 30-frame, and 45-frame LSTM-3Class models with other studies. That comparison can be seen in Table 5.

Even though the focus of our study is cut-in prediction, we see that if the proposed LSTM-based approach is trained for lane change prediction, its performance exceeds the previously reported performances which are 3-class lane-change prediction accuracies of 0.7440 in [7], 0.9190 in [2], and 0.9194 in [5].

5.4 Computational Efficiency

Execution times[2] of our LSTM models for 30-frame input sequences can be seen in Table 6. As shown, the vehicle detection and tracking steps of our pipeline take much more time than the classification step, which is not more than 2 ms. Since the vehicle detection step also exists in previous works before the classification step, our approach has the advantage of having just one layer and fewer parameters in the classification step.

Computation times are directly proportional to the number of frames. Thus, the total time is 2 s for 15-frame sequences and 8 s for 60-frame sequences. Please note that, in the proposed approach, we process two seconds of video regardless of the number of frames in the sequence (15, 30, 45, or 60).

Table 6. Execution times of compared methods for a 30-frame input sequence.

Method	Vehicle Detection and Tracking (sec/seq)	Classification (msec/seq)	Total (sec/seq)
Baseline		2.11	4.0041
LSTM-3class	4.002	1.29	4.0032
LSTM-2classLR		1.95	4.0039

[2] All evaluations are done on a PC with Ubuntu 16.04, i7-7700K CPU, 16 GB RAM and an Nvidia GeForce GTX 1080 GPU.

Vehicle detection and tracking modules can be executed as frames arrive. Thus, if we use 15-frame sequences, we are able to produce a classification result (cut-in/lane-pass) for the scene every two seconds. As can be seen in Tables 3 and 4, results of 15-frame sequences are either the best or very close to the best results. From this point of view, we can argue that the proposed approach can be considered for actual implementations to detect cut-in maneuvers.

6 Conclusions

The approaches developed for ADAS and autonomous vehicles should be as simple and affordable as possible. Therefore, methods that work with monocular vision, as in our study, may be preferable. In this work, we proposed a simple approach to predict possible dangerous cut-in maneuvers. Side-aware method, LSTM-2classLR, achieved a promising result (0.9585 accuracy) using just the center coordinates, width, and height of the target vehicle's bounding box on the BDD-100K cut-in/lane-pass subset. Furthermore, our approach exceeds the current lane-change detection methods in the literature by %3 on the accuracy metric.

Another advantage of our approach is that we obtain features directly from the target vehicle bounding box and feed them into an LSTM. This is computationally cheaper than feeding a complex CNN with video frames to extract features ([2, 5, 7, 18]). Thus, the classification times are shorter than the methods in the literature.

Future work regarding this task of computer vision can be planned to increase the number of maneuver classes (e.g., a vehicle drifting in ego-lane and braking), to involve a higher number of features that can be extracted from the camera frames (i.e., without the need of extra equipment) or to investigate more generalized training procedures (e.g., semi-supervised techniques). These efforts would lead to more robust maneuver detection methods for driver assistance systems.

Acknowledgments. This work was supported by the Scientific and Technological Research Council of Turkey (TÜBİTAK), Grant No: 2244-118C079.

References

1. Altché, F., de La Fortelle, A.: An LSTM network for highway trajectory prediction. In: 2017 IEEE 20th International Conference on Intelligent Transportation Systems (ITSC), pp. 353–359. IEEE (2017)
2. Biparva, M., Fernández-Llorca, D., Izquierdo-Gonzalo, R., Tsotsos, J.K.: Video action recognition for lane-change classification and prediction of surrounding vehicles. arXiv preprint arXiv:2101.05043 (2021)
3. Bochkovskiy, A., Wang, C.Y., Liao, H.Y.M.: Yolov4: Optimal speed and accuracy of object detection. arXiv preprint arXiv:2004.10934 (2020)
4. Deo, N., Rangesh, A., Trivedi, M.M.: How would surround vehicles move? A unified framework for maneuver classification and motion prediction. IEEE Trans. Intell. Veh. **3**(2), 129–140 (2018). https://doi.org/10.1109/TIV.2018.2804159

5. Fernández-Llorca, D., Biparva, M., Izquierdo-Gonzalo, R., Tsotsos, J.K.: Two-stream networks for lane-change prediction of surrounding vehicles. In: 2020 IEEE 23rd International Conference on Intelligent Transportation Systems (ITSC), pp. 1–6. IEEE (2020)
6. Garcia, F., Cerri, P., Broggi, A., de la Escalera, A., Armingol, J.M.: Data fusion for overtaking vehicle detection based on radar and optical flow. In: 2012 IEEE Intelligent Vehicles Symposium, pp. 494–499. IEEE (2012)
7. Izquierdo, R., Quintanar, A., Parra, I., Fernández-Llorca, D., Sotelo, M.: Experimental validation of lane-change intention prediction methodologies based on CNN and LSTM. In: 2019 IEEE Intelligent Transportation Systems Conference (ITSC), pp. 3657–3662. IEEE (2019)
8. Izquierdo, R., Quintanar, A., Parra, I., Fernández-Llorca, D., Sotelo, M.: The prevention dataset: a novel benchmark for prediction of vehicles intentions. In: 2019 IEEE Intelligent Transportation Systems Conference (ITSC), pp. 3114–3121. IEEE (2019)
9. Kasper, D., et al.: Object-oriented Bayesian networks for detection of lane change maneuvers. IEEE Intell. Transp. Syst. Mag. **4**(3), 19–31 (2012). https://doi.org/10.1109/MITS.2012.2203229
10. Lee, D., Kwon, Y.P., McMains, S., Hedrick, J.K.: Convolution neural network- based lane change intention prediction of surrounding vehicles for acc. In: 2017 IEEE 20th International Conference on Intelligent Transportation Systems (ITSC), pp. 1–6. IEEE (2017)
11. Lefèvre, S., Vasquez, D., Laugier, C.: A survey on motion prediction and risk assessment for intelligent vehicles. ROBOMECH J. **1**(1), 1–14 (2014)
12. Insurance Information Institute, Facts + Statistics: Highway safety. https://www.iii.org/fact-statistic/facts-statistics-highway-safety. Accessed 10 Oct 2022
13. Scheel, O., Nagaraja, N.S., Schwarz, L., Navab, N., Tombari, F.: Attention-based lane change prediction. In: 2019 International Conference on Robotics and Automation (ICRA), pp. 8655–8661. IEEE (2019)
14. Sivaraman, S., Trivedi, M.M.: Looking at vehicles on the road: a survey of vision-based vehicle detection, tracking, and behavior analysis **14**, 1773–1795 (2013). IEEE
15. U.S. Federal Highway Administration - US Highway 101 dataset. https://ops.fhwa.dot.gov/trafficanalysistools/ngsim.htm. Accessed 10 Oct 2022
16. Wojke, N., Bewley, A., Paulus, D.: Simple online and realtime tracking with a deep association metric. In: 2017 IEEE international conference on image processing (ICIP), pp. 3645–3649. IEEE (2017)
17. Yu, F., et al.: Bdd100k: a diverse driving dataset for heterogeneous multitask learning. In: Proceedings of the IEEE/CVF conference on computer vision and pattern recognition, pp. 2636–2645 (2020)
18. Yurtsever, E., et al.: Risky action recognition in lane change video clips using deep spatiotemporal networks with segmentation mask transfer. In: 2019 IEEE Intelligent Transportation Systems Conference (ITSC), pp. 3100–3107. IEEE (2019)

Randomized Low-Rank Nonlinear RX Detector

Selçuk Yapıcı and Fatih Nar(✉)

Ankara Yıldırım Beyazıt University, Ankara, Turkey
fatih.nar@aybu.edu.tr

Abstract. Anomaly Detection is an important topic in various application areas, including image analysis and network intrusion detection. The Reed–Xiaoli (RX) detector is an efficient and accurate anomaly detector that can be used if analyzed data is Gaussian distributed. However, in the real-world, data is rarely Gaussian distributed. For nonlinear data, kernel RX (KRX) method is proposed and widely employed. The biggest issue with the KRX method is its high computational complexity, which prevents using it for big data or in real-time scenarios. As a remedy, in the literature, Random Fourier Features approximation of the KRX method is proposed, namely RRX. Another weakness of the KRX is numerical issues, basically kernel matrix being bad-conditioned, which can be solved by regularization. This situation also applies to the RRX method. In this study, we extend the RRX method with randomized Singular Value Decomposition (SVD) as an efficient solution owing to SVD being the best low-rank approximation. Our proposed method, randomized low-rank RX (RLR-RX), provides better computational complexity and better detection performance than both RRX and KRX methods. Experiments on the Airport-Beach-urban (ABU) Dataset shows that proposed RLR-RX method provides better detection performance as its Area Under the Curve (AUC) is 0.9707 where AUC is 0.9660 for RRX and 0.8842 for KRX while RLR-RX is 30% faster than RRX and 44 times faster than KRX.

Keywords: Anomaly Detection · RX · Kernel RX · Random Fourier Features · Low-Rank · Randomized SVD

1 Introduction

Anomaly detection (AD) is an important approach to detect outliers as desired targets or to clean the outliers in the data for further machine learning tasks. Thus, AD is used in various application areas, such as remote sensing, finance, and network intrusion detection. Basically, AD assumes that anomalies/outliers are rare in the data and tries to discover the data that differs from most of the data [1, 2]. A similar concept to AD is target detection, where the fundamental difference is AD not assuming known target spectra, while target detection uses the known spectra of targets in interest [3].

AD methods employ various approaches. In one popular approach, background is modeled using a probability distribution, such as Gaussian distribution. All data is used to find probability distribution parameters since occurrence of anomalies is assumed to be rare. Finally, data points with low probability or distant from the distribution center

A. Mirzazadeh et al. (Eds.): SEMIT 2022, CCIS 1808, pp. 124–141, 2023.
https://doi.org/10.1007/978-3-031-40395-8_9

are marked as anomalies. Note that some methods propose censoring the outlier data to eliminate corruption of background statistics [3]. As a popular AD approach, the Reed-Xiaoli (RX) detector assumes that background is multivariate Gaussian distributed and anomalies are distant from the data center based on the Mahalanobis metric [4]. Thus, RX can find target pixels that have different spectral signature from the background. However, Gaussian distribution assumption fails in data with complex feature relations, especially at the tails of the distribution. As a remedy, a nonlinear version of RX has been introduced using kernelization approach, namely kernel RX (KRX) [5]. Downside of the KRX method is its huge space and time complexity for large data where space complexity is quadratic and time complexity is cubic regarding the amount of data. This situation limits the practical use of the KRX method in real-world scenarios. In the literature, randomized RX (RRX) method which uses random Fourier Features (RFF), is proposed to reduce to space and time complexity of the KRX method while keeping its detection performance [6].

Besides improvements proposed for the KRX method, researchers also proposed improvements to standard RX method. Basically, they try to preserve computational efficiency of RX while improving its detection performance. First and second order statistic estimation are used by [7] while the kurtosis-based test is used by [8] to refine RX detection mechanism. Acito et al., analyzes the CFAR property of the RX method, considering the signal-dependent noise in hyperspectral images [9]. In [10], authors estimate the background probability density function using a kernel density estimator, where bandwidth selection process is obtained via extracted locally adaptive information. As an improvement to RX, in [11], authors use median-mean line metric to handle degrading effects of anomalous outliers.

Researchers also proposed several approaches and methods to improve computational efficiency of the RX and KRX methods to obtain fast versions or implementations. In the first approach, researchers propose algorithmic or mathematical ways of improving the computational efficiency such as using rank-1 update using Woodbury matrix identity of covariance matrix as sliding window moves to next pixel [12–18]. Second group of studies is focused on efficient parallel implementations using multicore CPUs, massively parallel GPUs, specific hardware such as FPGAs, or even heterogeneous computing environments [19–22]. Also, in [6, 23], randomization-based approaches are proposed to ease the huge computational load of the KRX method.

Besides RX and its variants, in the literature, anomaly detection approaches based on different ideas are also proposed. In [24], authors used Gauss–Markov random field to find small regions in the scene which they assumed as anomalies in a homogeneous background. Some researchers also investigate the use of clustering for anomaly detection [25, 26]. In [27], authors use maximum entropy and developed a nonparametric estimation for detecting anomalies in hyperspectral images. In [28], a projection pursuit-based method is proposed for anomaly detection in hyperspectral images. Later, local-sparsity-divergence is used by [29] for anomaly detection in hyperspectral images. In the literature, some subspace and sparsity-based anomaly detection methods are also proposed [30–32]. In some studies, spatial information is also incorporated for anomaly detection since neighboring pixels may share common characteristics [33, 34]. In [35], authors investigate the importance of band selection on the performance of the anomaly detectors. As Deep Learning becomes popular in many research areas, it is also applied to anomaly detection where Deep Belief Network (DBN) is used [36]. In this method, unsupervised auto-encoder is used to learn the high-level features as a way of modeling the background / clutter.

In the literature, several low-rank approximations are also proposed for the anomaly detection. In [37], authors propose to decompose the model matrix into a low-rank matrix, a sparse matrix, and a noise matrix where background is represented by low-rank matrix and anomalies are assumed to be represented by the sparse matrix. Similarly, in [38], authors assume that a low-rank matrix represents the background and sparse matrix represents the anomalies where they used low-rank representation and a learned dictionary. Finally, in [23], authors propose use of RFF [39] and Nyström approximations [40] of KRX as low-rank approximations. Such randomization techniques to speed-up kernel methods are also applied for different kernelized approaches [41]. In [23], authors stated that these low-rank approximations also act as regularizer, but our experiments show that they cannot provide strong regularization in all cases.

All the efforts in the literature show that an anomaly detection method which can provide high detection accuracy for homogeneous and heterogeneous data in a robust and computationally efficient manner is in great demand. However, these requirements are contradicting to each other since accurate anomaly detection requires more computational resources. Also, anomaly detection methods should be simple and adaptation to data must be easily done with a few parameters if possible. Instead of developing a completely new anomaly detection with such characteristics, some researchers tried to increase the computational efficiency of an existing detector that already provides satisfactory detection accuracy [23]. More detailed comparison and review of anomaly detection for hyperspectral Images are given in [1–3].

In this study, the RRX method [23] is extended using the randomized Singular Value Decomposition (SVD) [42] as an efficient and accurate approximation of the KRX method. Owing to this approximation, proposed RLR-RX method can detect anomalies for Gaussian and non-Gaussian distributed data. The RLR-RX method first uses RFF [39] to map original data to high dimensional space where data becomes linear and thereby covariance matrix is constructed using the mapped data. Instead of inverting this covariance matrix for detecting anomalies as done in RRX, the covariance matrix is decomposed using a randomized SVD method [42] and eigenvectors with low or zero eigenvalues are eliminated, and this smaller low-rank approximated covariance matrix is efficiently inverted. Therefore, RLR-RX method becomes faster than RRX while an implicit regularization being enforced. Consequently, RLR-RX is also significantly faster than KRX since RRX is already significantly faster than KRX.

2 RX Detectors

RX detector is easy to understand and easy to implement, hence become one of the most popular anomaly detection methods in the literature [1–3].

2.1 RX Anomaly Detector

Let $\mathbf{X} \in \mathbb{R}^{n \times d}$ be a data in the matrix form, where n is the number of data and d is the data dimension, while **X** being centered. In RX method, background is characterized by the covariance matrix $\mathbf{\Sigma}$ where RX simply calculates the distance of test data x_* towards the distribution mean using the squared Mahalanobis distance as [4]:

$$D_{RX}(x_*) = x_*^{\mathsf{T}}(\mathbf{X})^{-1}x_* \text{where} \mathbf{X} = \frac{1}{n}x^{\mathsf{T}}x \tag{1}$$

For moderate data dimensions (i.e., $d < 250$), inverse of covariance matrix ($\mathbf{\Sigma}^{-1}$) can be efficiently computed. Note that the dimensionality of the data is much lower than the number of data ($d \ll n$) [23].

2.2 Kernel RX (KRX) Anomaly Detector

Computational efficiency and accuracy of the RX is perfect if anomalies are rare, and X is Gaussian distributed. However, more flexible models are required since real-life data is rarely obeying these assumptions. KRX is an elegant solution which kernelize the RX method by mapping nonlinear features $\mathrm{X} \in \mathbb{R}^{n \times d}$ into linear features $\Phi \in \mathbb{R}^{n \times \mathfrak{H}}$ in a high dimensional Hilbert space $\mathfrak{H}$ via mapping $\varnothing$: $\mathrm{x} \in \mathbb{R}^{d} \rightarrow \varnothing(\mathrm{x}) \in \mathbb{R}^{d \times \mathfrak{H}}$. Note that, now a linear solution can be applied in $\Phi \in \mathbb{R}^{n \times \mathfrak{H}}$ [5]. Finally, test data $\mathrm{x}_* \in \mathbb{R}^{d}$ is mapped with $\varnothing(\mathrm{x}_*)$ and anomalousness is measured by the RX formula in (1):

$$D_{KRX}(x_*) = \varnothing(x_*)^{\mathsf{T}}(\Phi^{\mathsf{T}}\Phi)^{-1}\varnothing(x_*) \tag{2}$$

Using the Riesz theorem, the dot product between samples in $\mathfrak{H}$ becomes $K(\mathrm{x}, \mathrm{x}') = \langle\varnothing(\mathrm{x}), \varnothing(\mathrm{x}')\rangle \in \mathbb{R}$ which can be expressed in terms of kernel matrices [43]. By help of linear algebra, RX formulation in infinite space $\mathfrak{H}$ defined in the Eq. (2) can be transformed into the formulation given in Eq. (3):

$$D_{KRX}(x_*) = k_*^{\mathsf{T}}(\mathbf{KK})^{-1}k_* \tag{3}$$

where $\mathrm{k}_* = [K(\mathrm{x}_*, \mathrm{x}_1), \ldots, \mathrm{K}(\mathrm{x}_*, \mathrm{x}_n)]^{\mathrm{T}} \in \mathbb{R}^{n}$ contains the similarities between x_* and all points in X using kernel function K, and $\mathrm{K} \in \mathbb{R}^{n \times n}$ stands for the kernel matrix containing all data similarities [5]. Note that, KRX also requires centering the data (now in $\mathfrak{H}$) as in the linear RX method [4, 43].

2.3 Randomized RX (RRX) Anomaly Detector

KRX can handle nonlinear data, but it does not scale well for the large data as the inversion of kernel matrix K has cubic time complexity, where K is an $\boldsymbol{n} \times \boldsymbol{n}$ matrix as $\boldsymbol{n}$ is the size of data. In [6] and [4], RRX method is proposed which uses Random Fourier Features (RFF) to approximate KRX efficiently using the Bochner's theorem (see [39] and [4] for details on Bochner's theorem).

Following the Bochner's theorem and RFF approach, the kernel matrix $\mathrm{K} \in \mathbb{R}^{n \times n}$ can be approximated with the explicitly mapped data, $\mathrm{Z} = [\mathrm{z}_1 \cdots \mathrm{z}_n]^{\mathrm{T}} \in \mathbb{R}^{n \times 2D}$ for the given n data points. Approximation of the kernel matrix K becomes $\hat{K} \approx ZZ^T$. However, in RRX [4], the linear RX in Eq. (1) is executed with explicitly mapped points onto RFF instead of using $\hat{K}$ for computational efficiency, which is defined as [23]:

$$D_{RRX}(x_*) = z_*^\mathsf{T}(\mathbf{G})^{-1}z_* \tag{4}$$

where $\mathbf{G} = \frac{1}{n}\mathbf{Z}^\mathsf{T}\mathbf{Z}$ and $z(x) = \frac{1}{\sqrt{2D}}$ [cos($w_1{}^T$ x), sin($w_1{}^T$ x),..., cos(sin $w_D{}^T$x), sin($w_D{}^T$x)]^T which approximates the Radial Basis Function (RBF) kernel. Here, a $2D$-dimensional randomized feature map z: $\mathbb{R}^d \rightarrow \mathbb{R}^{2D}$ is explicitly constructed and the data x_i is mapped into a nonlinear space through the explicit mapping $z(x_i)$ [39]. Finally, linear RX formula is used on the mapped data matrix Z where this data matrix now has size of $n \times 2D$. As in RX and KRX, data matrix Z is also centered as well. Final covariance matrix will be in the size of $2D \times 2D$. Therefore, space and time complexity of the RRX becomes in the order D of instead of n. Typically, $d < D \ll n$ so RRX method becomes much faster than KRX method while RX method being the fastest [4].

3 Proposed Method

The RRX method provides significant execution efficiency compared to the KRX method. However, both methods may fail at providing good detection accuracy if the covariance matrix in the RRX method or the kernel matrix in the KRX method becomes ill-conditioned, i.e., having high condition number. This happens if the largest eigenvalue is much larger than the smallest eigenvalue (ill-conditioned) or if there is a zero eigenvalue (not invertible). In such cases, inversion of these matrices is not possible or any operation with this matrix becomes numerically unstable. One common solution is to regularize the RRX and the KRX methods, as shown below [23, 37]:

$$D_{RRX}(x_*) = z_*^\mathsf{T}(\mathbf{G} + \lambda\mathbf{I})^{-1}z_* \text{and} D_{KRX}(x_*) = k_*^\mathsf{T}(\mathbf{KK} + \lambda\mathbf{I})^{-1}k_* \tag{5}$$

where $\mathbf{I}$ is the identity matrix and λ is a positive scalar. This regularization approach is simple and improves the condition number of the matrix, but it also causes a change in the modeled background statistics. One way to handle this problem is using low-rank approximation of the covariance matrix or kernel matrix to be inverted. SVD known as the best low-rank approximation, where r is the rank of the approximation. Here, r is chosen such that low or zero eigenvalues are removed [37, 42].

Let decompose the covariance matrix as $\mathbf{G} = \mathbf{V}\mathbf{S}\mathbf{V}^\mathsf{T}$ using randomized SVD since $\mathbf{G}$ is symmetric and positive definite [42]. Here, $\mathbf{V}$ is a square matrix that contains eigenvectors and $\mathbf{S}$ is a diagonal matrix with eigenvalues on the diagonal (largest to smallest, largest being at top left cell). All the matrices ($\mathbf{G}$, $\mathbf{V}$, and $\mathbf{S}$) are size of $2D \times 2D$ as shown below:

$$\mathbf{G} = \begin{bmatrix} \\ \\ \end{bmatrix}_{2D\times 2D} = \begin{bmatrix} \mathbf{V} \\ \\ \end{bmatrix}_{2D\times 2D} \begin{bmatrix} \mathbf{S} \\ \\ \end{bmatrix}_{2D\times 2D} \begin{bmatrix} \mathbf{V}^\mathsf{T} \\ \\ \end{bmatrix}_{2D\times 2D} \tag{6}$$

Using low-rank approximation of $\widehat{\mathbf{G}} = \widehat{\mathbf{V}}\widehat{\mathbf{S}}\widehat{\mathbf{V}}^{\mathsf{T}}$ with rank r is defined as:

$$\widehat{\mathbf{G}} = \Big[\quad\Big]_{2D\times 2D} \approx \Big[\widehat{\mathbf{V}}\Big]_{2D\times r}\Big[\widehat{\mathbf{S}}\Big]_{r\times r}\Big[\widehat{\mathbf{V}}^{\mathsf{T}}\Big]_{r\times 2D} = \widehat{\mathbf{V}}\widehat{\mathbf{S}}\widehat{\mathbf{V}}^{\mathsf{T}} \tag{7}$$

Here $\widehat{\mathbf{S}}$ is the top-left $r \times r$ part of the $\mathbf{S}$ matrix and $\widehat{\mathbf{V}}$ is the left r column of the $\mathbf{V}$. Thus, in $\widehat{\mathbf{S}}$, largest r eigenvalues are stored while r eigenvectors corresponding to these largest r eigenvalues are placed in $\widehat{\mathbf{V}}$. Therefore, most of the information in $\mathbf{G}$ matrix is preserved in $\widehat{\mathbf{G}}$ while low and zero eigenvalues are eliminated which leads to better conditioned $\widehat{\mathbf{G}}$ matrix. Consequently, using the low-rank definition $\mathbf{G} \approx \widehat{\mathbf{G}} = \widehat{\mathbf{V}}\widehat{\mathbf{S}}\widehat{\mathbf{V}}^{\mathsf{T}}$, $D_{RRX}(x_*)$ becomes $D_{RLR-RX}(x_*)$ as below:

$$D_{RLR-RX}(x_*) = z_*^{\mathsf{T}}\left(\widehat{\mathbf{G}}\right)^{-1} z_* \tag{8}$$

Then using the low-rank definition Eq. (8) as below:

$$D_{RLR-RX}(x_*) = z_*^{\mathsf{T}}\left(\widehat{\mathbf{V}}\widehat{\mathbf{S}}\widehat{\mathbf{V}}^{\mathsf{T}}\right)^{-1} z_* \tag{9}$$

Using the inverse of low-rank definition $\widehat{\mathbf{G}}^{-1} = \widehat{\mathbf{V}}\widehat{\mathbf{S}}^{-1}\widehat{\mathbf{V}}^{\mathsf{T}}$

$$D_{RLR-RX}(x_*) = z_*^{\mathsf{T}}\left(\widehat{\mathbf{V}}\widehat{\mathbf{S}}^{-1}\widehat{\mathbf{V}}^{\mathsf{T}}\right) z_* = z_*^{\mathsf{T}}\widehat{\mathbf{V}}\left(\widehat{\mathbf{S}}\right)^{-1}\widehat{\mathbf{V}}^{\mathsf{T}} z_* \tag{10}$$

Which finally becomes

$$D_{RLR-RX}(x_*) = v_*^{\mathsf{T}}\left(\widehat{\mathbf{S}}\right)^{-1} v_* \tag{11}$$

Here $\mathrm{v}_* = \widehat{\mathbf{V}}^{\mathsf{T}} z_*$ is $r \times 1$ vector, which is mapped from d dimensional space (x_*) to $2D$ dimensional space (z_*) and finally r dimensional space (v_*). Since $\widehat{\mathbf{S}}$ is a diagonal matrix, its inverse is just the inverse of the eigenvalues (scalars) in the diagonal. Thus, there is no extra computation for the matrix inverse operation in RLR-RX. The most computational part in RLR-RX is decomposition of $\mathbf{G}$ using SVD which is done in a much faster way using the randomized SVD algorithm [42]. Computation of $v_* = \widehat{\mathbf{V}}^{\mathsf{T}} z_*$ is also fast, so proposed RLR-RX detector becomes faster than KRX detector.

Once randomized SVD is used to decompose the matrix $\mathbf{S}$, inverse of $\mathbf{S}$ become computationally efficient since randomized SVD has computational complexity lower than $O(n^3)$ and computational complexity of $\mathbf{S}^{-1}$ is just $O(n)$. Resulting algorithm of the proposed RLR-RX detector is given in the Algorithm 1 where $\mathbf{X}$ is input data, D is number of bases in random Fourier Features, r is the rank for low-approximation using randomized SVD, and τ is distance threshold such that pixels with distances larger than the τ are marked as target. In the RLR-RX algorithm, $\mathbf{X}$ is mapped to a higher dimension as $\mathbf{Z}$ using RFF which approximates the KRX method. Then, linear RX method is used with the covariance matrix $\mathbf{G}$ that is obtained using the mapped data $\mathbf{Z}$. Finally, low-rank approximation of $\mathbf{G}$ is obtained using randomized SVD then Eq. (11) is used for applying RLR-RX anomaly detection.

Algorithm 1: Randomized Low-Rank RX (RLR-RX) Detector

Inputs: A, r ▹ A: input matrix, r: desired rank

$[h,w] \leftarrow$ size(A) ▹ h: rowCount(A), w: columnCount(A)

$p \leftarrow min(2r, w)$ ▹ p is at most twice of rank r

$\mathbf{X} \leftarrow randn(w, p)$ ▹ X matrix is $w \times p$ with random values

$\mathbf{Y} \leftarrow \mathbf{AX}$ ▹ Y marix is $w \times p$ with random values

$\mathbf{W}_1 \leftarrow orth(\mathbf{Y})$ ▹ Orthogonalized Y is assigned to W_1

$B \leftarrow \mathbf{W}_1^T\mathbf{A}$ ▹ B is formed by the inverse of W_1

$[\mathbf{W}_2, \mathbf{S}, \mathbf{V}] \leftarrow svd(\mathbf{B}$, 'econ') ▹ economy-size decomposition of $\mathbf{B}^{-1}$

$\mathbf{U} \leftarrow \mathbf{W}_1\mathbf{W}_2$ ▹ U is matrix with size $w \times p$

$r \leftarrow min(r$, column count of U)

$\mathbf{U} \leftarrow \mathbf{U}_{*,1:r}$ ▹ Left r-columns of U

$\mathbf{S} \leftarrow \mathbf{S}_{1:r,1:r}$ ▹ Top-left $r \times r$ part of S

$\mathbf{V} \leftarrow \mathbf{V}_{*,1:r}$ ▹ Left r-columns of V

Return U, S, V

Computational complexity of the proposed RLR-RX method compared to RX, KRX, and RRX methods is given in Table 1. As seen in Table 1, proposed RLR-RX method provides the same space complexity with RRX method while having better time complexity compared to RRX method. Note that execution time of the RLR-RX method can be further reduced using efficient code optimization techniques, especially in memory allocations.

Table 1. Space and time complexity for RX, RRX, RLR-RX, and KRX methods.

	Space Complexity		**Time Complexity**			
Method	T	$\mathbf{C}^{-1}$	T	$\mathbf{C}$	$\mathbf{C}^{-1}$	**AD**
RX	-	d^2	-	nd^2	d^3	nd^2
RLR-RX	nD	D^2	ndD	nr^2	r^3	nr^2
RRX	nD	D^2	ndD	nD^2	D^3	nD^2
KRX	n^2	n^2	n^2d	n^3	n^3	n^3

T is the mapping operation of the data into another space. **C** is the covariance/kernel matrix.

4 Results

This section compares the detection performance and the execution time efficiency of the RX, KRX, RRX, and proposed RLR-RX methods in both synthetically generated data and real-world Airport-Beach-Urban (ABU) dataset [44]. All the experiments are executed on Intel i7 4700HQ 2.4 GHz PC with 16 GB memory.

4.1 Synthetic Dataset

Synthetic image with a size of 100 × 100 and 2 spectral channels (Fig. 1a) with 2.72% of fused anomalies (Fig. 1b) is randomly generated (green and blue channels). Distribution of data (non-Gaussian) and the data points are shown in Fig. 1c [6].

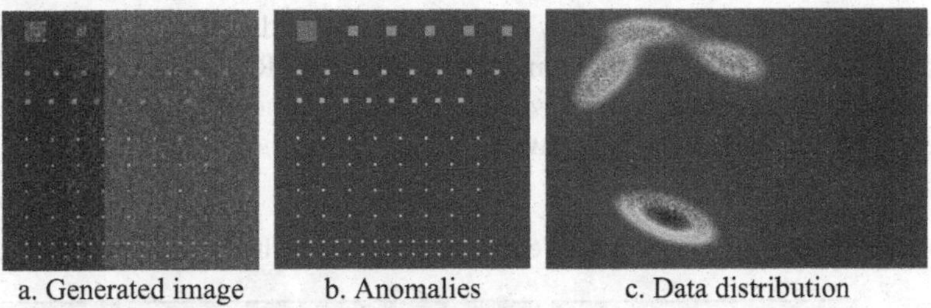

a. Generated image b. Anomalies c. Data distribution

Fig. 1. Synthetic dataset with non-Gaussian distribution.

In Fig. 2, execution times of the RX, KRX, RRX, and proposed RLR-RX anomaly detectors are shown with respect to data size. In Fig. 2a, execution time of the KRX detector is measured up to 2500 data points where it is shown in log-scale because of the cubic complexity of the KRX. RX, RRX, and RLR-RX are fast detectors since RX is linear and RRX method and RLR-RX method are efficient approximations of the KRX method since they use RX on mapped space. In Fig. 2b, KRX is excluded, and execution times are shown in linear scale to compare the execution time of the fast detectors. Although RX method is fast, it can only handle Gaussian distributed data, which is a strong limitation for the real-world scenarios. Also, use of KRX becomes impractical as data size gets larger, i.e., for $n > 5000$. As seen in Fig. 2, RRX and RLR-RX detectors are fast, while they can handle non-Gaussian data as KRX does.

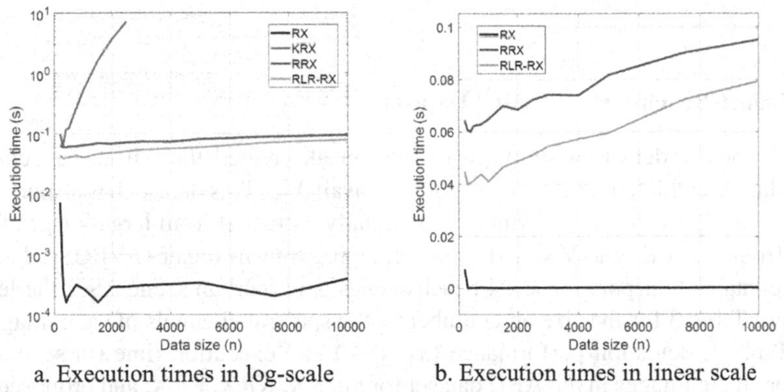

a. Execution times in log-scale b. Execution times in linear scale

Fig. 2. Execution time with respect to data size on synthetic data

In Table 2, detection accuracy and execution time of the RX, KRX, RRX, and RLR-RX detectors are shown with respect to data size on synthetic data. Detection accuracy is presented as Area Under Curve (AUC) value as a summary of the ROC curve, where higher the AUC value better the performance of the detector. As AUC value gets closer to 1, detection accuracy increases such that detection rate increases and false alarm rate decreases. As seen in Table 2, execution time of proposed RLR-RX method is always faster than RRX method and detection performance is better or similar. The KRX method is slowest one because of its cubic complexity on data size, where RX method is the faster one as it has cubic complexity on the number of data dimensions. Note that, RX method becomes much faster compared to RRX and RLR-RX methods since the dimension of synthetic data is only 2 whereas execution time difference becomes lower for hyperspectral data because they have hundreds of channels.

Table 2. Execution time and detection performance with respect to data size.

n (Data Size)	Detection Performance (AUC)				Execution Time (Seconds)				RLR-RX is x times faster than KRX	RLR-RX is % times faster than RRX
	RX	KRX	RRX	RLR-RX	RX	KRX	RRX	RLR-RX		
200	0.6963	**0.9921**	0.9907	0.9864	0.0007	0.0500	0.0867	**0.0480**	1.04	80.64%
300	0.7246	**0.9859**	0.9856	0.9838	0.0004	0.0824	0.0827	**0.0495**	1.66	67.05%
400	0.7052	**0.9797**	0.9782	0.9775	0.0004	0.1267	0.0861	**0.0510**	2.48	68.71%
500	0.7265	0.9895	**0.9898**	0.9893	0.0004	0.1804	0.0857	**0.0508**	3.55	68.73%
750	0.7145	**0.9884**	0.9850	0.9875	0.0004	0.3744	0.0847	**0.0525**	7.14	61.41%
1000	0.7410	**0.9907**	0.9902	0.9896	0.0004	0.6449	0.0877	**0.0534**	12.09	64.38%
1500	0.7194	**0.9879**	0.9857	0.9857	0.0004	1.5920	0.0901	**0.0569**	27.98	58.41%
2000	0.7273	**0.9877**	0.9859	0.9861	0.0004	3.8498	0.0939	**0.0589**	65.39	59.54%
2500	0.7148	**0.9898**	0.9874	0.9880	0.0004	7.6288	0.0984	**0.0619**	123.27	59.00%
3000	0.7200		0.9881	**0.9881**	0.0004		0.0984	**0.0659**		49.27%
4000	0.7207		0.9878	**0.9885**	0.0004		0.1032	**0.0702**		46.94%
5000	0.7183		0.9884	**0.9893**	0.0004		0.1107	**0.0747**		48.09%
7500	0.7267		**0.9889**	0.9882	0.0004		0.1224	**0.0865**		41.60%
10000	0.7254		**0.9895**	0.9889	0.0005		0.1317	**0.1019**		29.25%

4.2 Airport-Beach-Urban (ABU) Dataset

In their anomaly detection study [44], Kang et al. created the Airport-Beach-Urban (ABU) dataset, which they also made publicly available. This dataset has airport, beach, and urban images (see Fig. 3) which are manually extracted from large images that are gained from the Airborne Visible/Infrared Imaging Spectrometer (AVIRIS). The ABU dataset contains 5 airport scenes, 4 beach scenes, and 6 urban scenes. See the leftmost column of Table 3 for the size and number of the spectral channels of each image.

In Table 3, detection performance (as AUC) and execution time (in seconds) are given for all the images in the ABU dataset for the RX, KRX, RRX, and proposed RLR-RX methods. As Seen in Table 3, RLR-RX always gives the best execution efficiency as it has the lowest execution time. Also, RLR-RX provides the best detection accuracy, as it provides the highest AUC values for most of the images, and for each background class (airport, beach, urban).

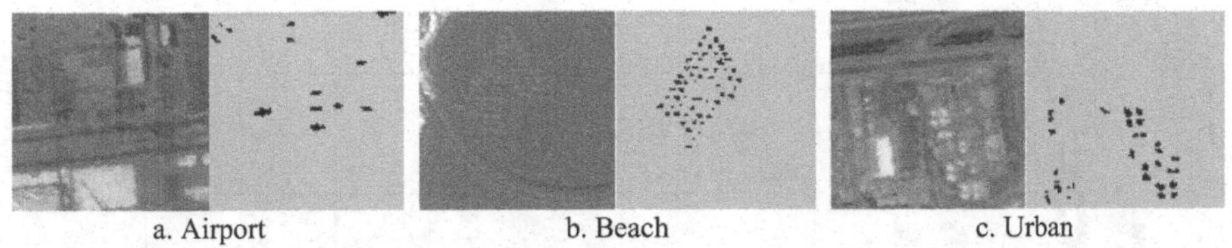

a. Airport b. Beach c. Urban

Fig. 3. Example scenes from ABU dataset

Table 3. Detection performance comparison for the ABU dataset.

	RX d=2		KRX r=3000		RRX D=256		RLR-RX D=256, r=128	
	AUC	Time (secs)	AUC	Time (secs)	AUC	Time (secs)	AUC	Time (secs)
Airport-1, 100x100x205	0.8221	0.063150	0.9311	12.045569	0.9224	0.358812	0.9265	0.277196
Airport-2, 100x100x205	0.8404	0.064029	0.9732	12.109578	0.9628	0.358880	0.9716	0.278251
Airport-3, 100x100x205	0.9288	0.062950	0.9456	12.622220	0.9537	0.350079	0.9529	0.285013
Airport-4, 100x100x191	0.9526	0.059603	0.9857	12.240329	0.9743	0.347297	0.9850	0.284930
All Airport Images	**0.8860**	**0.062433**	**0.9589**	**12.254424**	**0.9533**	**0.353767**	**0.9590**	**0.281348**
Beach-1, 150x150x188	0.9807	0.102275	0.5074	15.237153	0.9843	0.574739	0.9755	0.416774
Beach-2, 100x100x193	0.9106	0.055894	0.5532	16.299159	0.9229	0.363845	0.9296	0.289537
Beach-3, 100x100x188	0.9998	0.055936	0.9985	11.864610	0.9882	0.347647	0.9986	0.267836
Beach-4, 150x150x102	0.9538	0.040958	0.7847	16.463607	0.9623	0.517094	0.9664	0.378158
All Beach Images	**0.9612**	**0.063766**	**0.7110**	**14.966132**	**0.9644**	**0.450831**	**0.9675**	**0.338076**
Urban-1, 100x100x204	0.9907	0.063172	0.9889	12.374027	0.9846	0.352361	0.9945	0.267262
Urban-2, 100x100x207	0.9946	0.066138	0.9491	11.881633	0.9921	0.341110	0.9968	0.270310
Urban-3, 100x100x191	0.9513	0.056752	0.9634	11.863191	0.9560	0.338222	0.9634	0.266350
Urban-4, 100x100x205	0.9887	0.061322	0.9376	12.299675	0.9810	0.345810	0.9853	0.267964
Urban-5, 100x100x205	0.9692	0.061324	0.9761	12.131038	0.9731	0.346614	0.9734	0.270846
All Urban Images	**0.9789**	**0.061742**	**0.9630**	**12.109913**	**0.9774**	**0.344823**	**0.9827**	**0.268546**
All ABU Dataset	***0.9449***	***0.062577***	***0.8842***	***13.033215***	***0.9660***	***0.380193***	***0.9707***	***0.293879***

As seen in Fig. 4, RLR-RX and KRX methods provide the best performance for airport-4 scene where RX method performs worse. Since the background of the airport-4 scene is not perfectly Gaussian distributed, the RX method gives relatively lower performance compared to nonlinear methods, namely KRX and its approximations RRX and RLR-RX. Both RRX and RLR-RX use Random Fourier Features (RFF), but RLR-RX performs better since it excludes eigenvectors corresponding to low or zero eigenvalues. By doing this, condition matrix of covariance matrix become better and numerical stability is increased. This acts as a regularization and thus RLR-RX method improves the performance of the RRX method. Note that, for the airport-4 scene, RLR-RX method is almost 2 orders of magnitude faster than the KRX method while providing the same performance.

As seen in Fig. 5, RLR-RX and RRX methods provide best performance for beach-4 scene where KRX method performs worse. RX method gives relatively lower performance since background of the beach-4 scene is not perfectly Gaussian distributed.

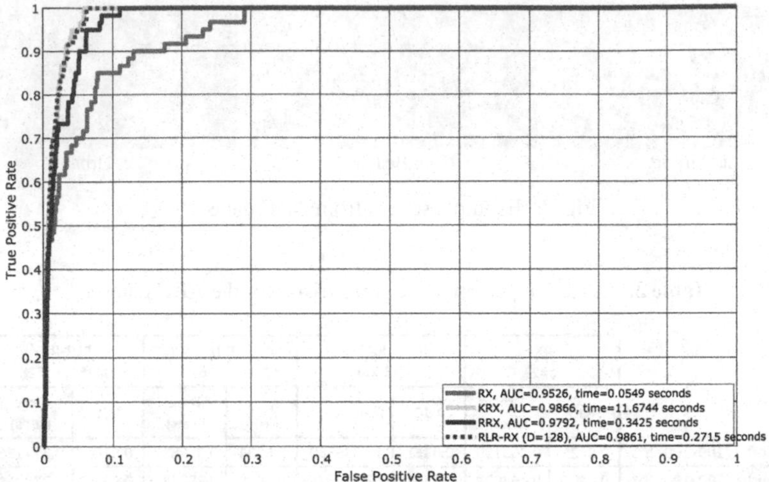

Fig. 4. ROC curve of airport-4 scene from ABU dataset

Although RLR-RX and RRX approximate the KRX, in beach-4 scene KRX performs worse than them, even worse than linear RX method. Main reason for this low performance is the bad conditioning of the kernel matrix in KRX, which causes numerical instability. Since RRX uses a lower number of bases, this acts as regularization and RRX indeed approximates regularized version of KRX. Same applies for the RLR-RX since it has regularization of RRX. In addition, RLR-RX removes eigenvectors corresponding to low eigenvalues, which provides a good estimation for best low-rank approximation known to be achieved by SVD.

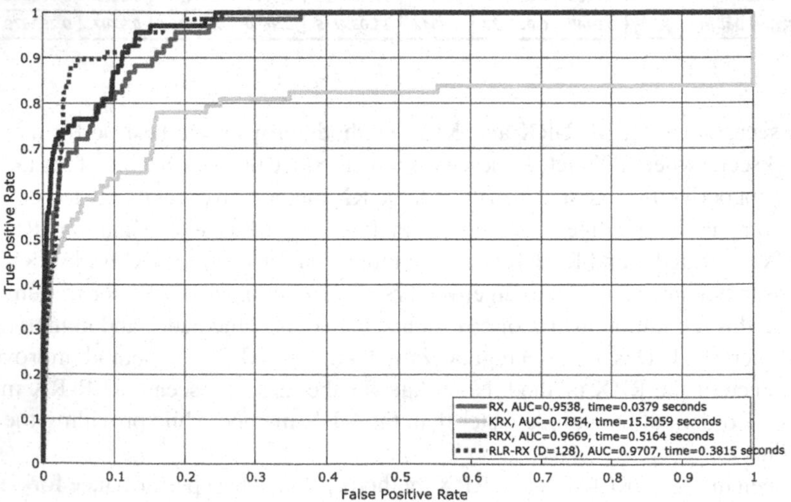

Fig. 5. ROC curve of beach-4 scene from ABU dataset

As seen in Fig. 6, RLR-RX and RX methods provide the best performance for urban-2 scene where KRX method performs worse. Since the background of the urban-4 scene is close to Gaussian distribution, the RX method gives good performance compared to nonlinear methods, namely KRX and its approximations RRX. Although RLR-RX is also an approximation of KRX, it still achieves the performance of RX since it provides better regularization compared to RRX, and inherently compared to KRX.

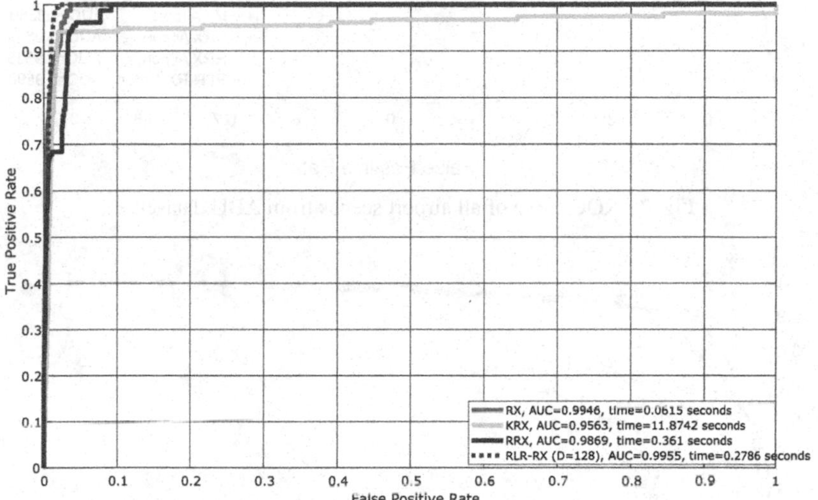

Fig. 6. ROC curve of urban-2 scene from ABU dataset.

Overall performances of the RX, KRX, RRX, and RLR-RX detectors for airport scenes in ABU dataset are given in the Fig. 7 where all nonlinear detectors have similar detection performances (see Table 3). For the airport scenes, the RX detector provides the lowest performance since Gaussian background assumption is not satisfied.

Overall detector performances for beach scenes are given in the Fig. 8 where RRX and RLR-RX detectors have similar detection performances while KRX detector has lowest performance (see Table 3). In beach scenes, the KRX detector performs even worse than RX detector. The RX detector provides good detection performance since Gaussian background assumption is sufficiently valid. The KRX detector has worse detection performance in some beach scenes since the condition number of kernel matrix in KRX is high, which causes numerical problems (see Fig. 5). One can claim that for relatively simple backgrounds, higher dimensional representation of KRX may cause low or zero eigenvalues, as internal dimension of the data is much lower.

Overall performances of the RX, KRX, RRX, and RLR-RX detectors for urban scenes are given in the Fig. 9 where all nonlinear detectors have similar detection performances (see Table 3) while RLR-RX detector provides the highest performance. In urban dataset, KRX performs slightly worse compared to other nonlinear detectors since in some urban scenes condition number of the kernel matrix in KRX is high causing numerical problems (see Fig. 6).

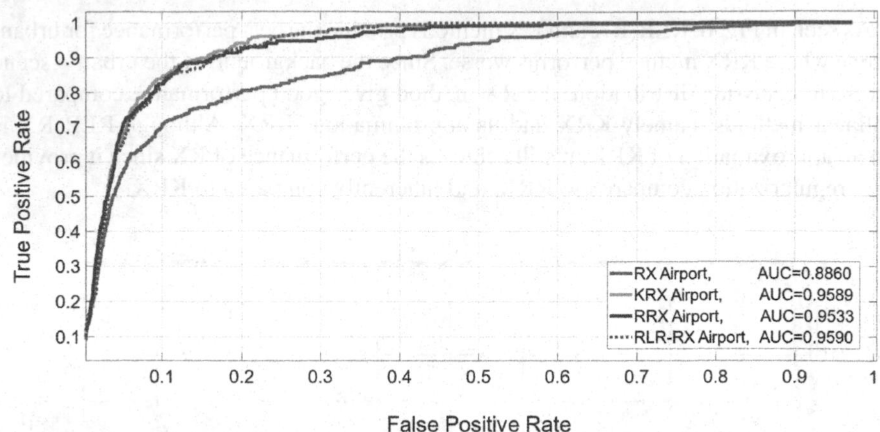

Fig. 7. ROC curve of all airport scenes from ABU dataset.

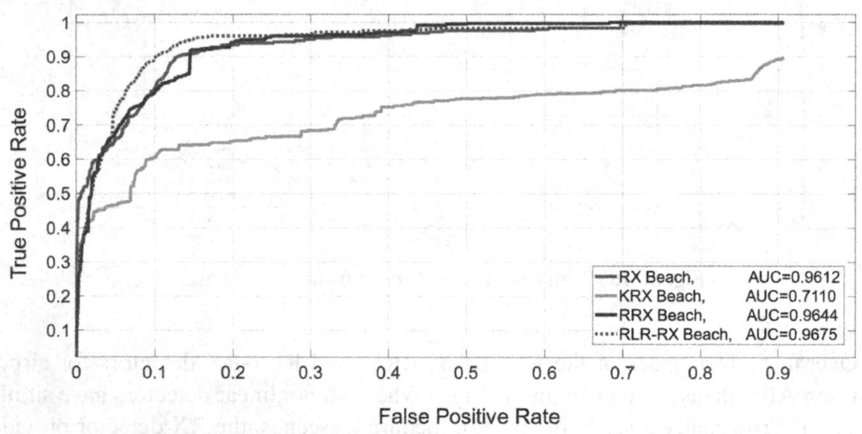

Fig. 8. ROC curve of all beach scenes from ABU dataset.

Overall performances of the RX, KRX, RRX, and RLR-RX detectors for all scenes are given in the Fig. 10, where all nonlinear detectors have similar detection performances (see Table 3) where RLR-RX provides the highest performance.

Condition Numbers of each matrix to be inverted in RX, KRX, RRX, and LRL-RX methods versus the obtained detection accuracy is shown in Fig. 11 on ABU dataset. In this figure, detection accuracy is presented using AUC value and numerical stability of the detector is presented using condition number. Here condition number shows how stable the numerical system in the detector where lower value means higher numerical stability. Note that, best condition number is 1 since eigenvalues are same and data is distributed equally in all principal axes, i.e., data has circular distribution. If condition number is infinity, that means there is at least one zero eigenvalue, and such matrix is indeed not invertible.

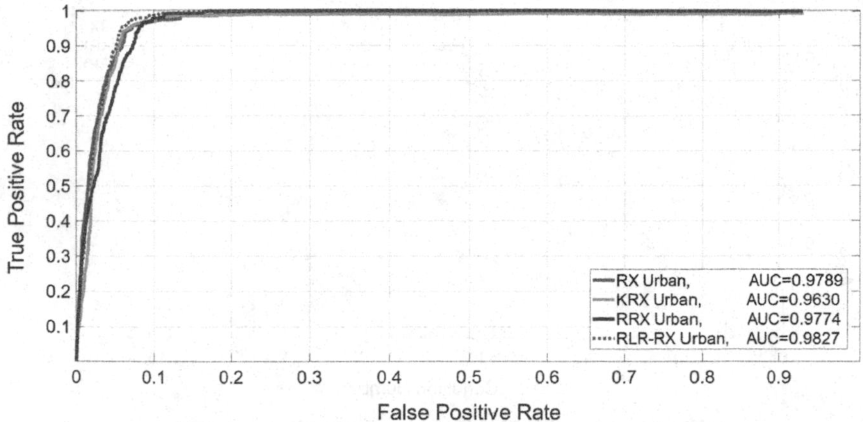

Fig. 9. ROC curve of all urban scenes from ABU dataset.

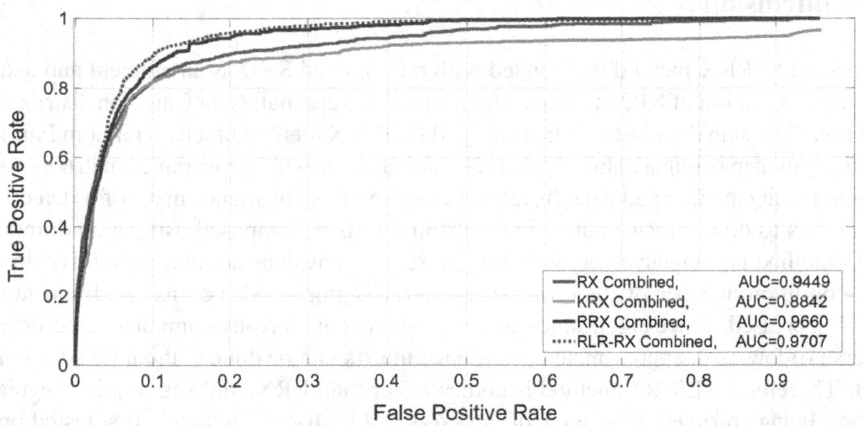

Fig. 10. ROC curve of all 13 scenes from ABU dataset.

As seen in Fig. 11, KRX has unexpectedly low detection performances for 2 cases. One can see that the condition number of KRX is worse compared to the other detectors. Proposed RLR-RX detector has the best condition number versus detection accuracy characteristics, which is followed by the RRX method. This is expected since RLR-RX is an extended version of RRX and both methods use RFF to approximate KRX detector where RLR-RX has stronger regularization because of applied low-rank approximation. RRX is followed by RX regarding to condition number, but detection accuracy of RX is lower for the scenes violating Gaussian background assumption, i.e., for nonlinear data. So, Fig. 11 demonstrates superiority of proposed RLR-RX method compared to other methods regarding to numerical stability and detection accuracy.

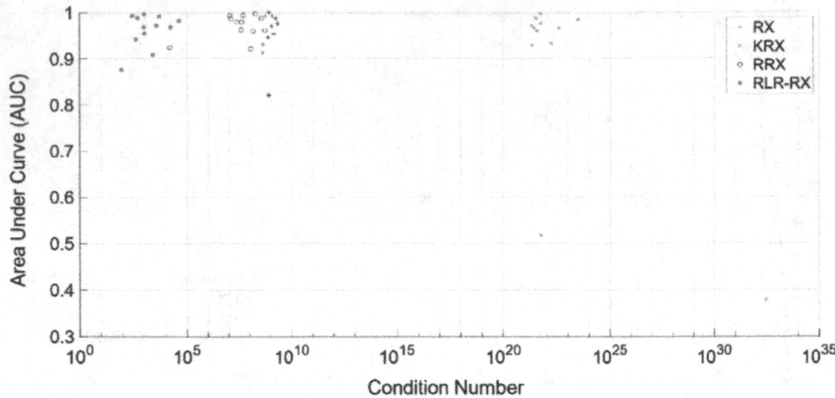

Fig. 11. Condition Number versus Detection Accuracy.

5 Conclusions

In this study, RRX method is extended with randomized SVD as an efficient and accurate approximation of KRX method, which can detect anomalies for Gaussian distributed and non-Gaussian distributed data. Proposed RLR-RX method first uses random Fourier Features to map original data to high dimensional space where covariance matrix is constructed using the mapped data. Instead of inverting this covariance matrix for detecting anomalies as done in RRX, the covariance matrix is decomposed using a randomized SVD method and eigenvectors with low or zero eigenvalues are eliminated. By doing this condition number of the covariance matrix is improved, i.e., its condition number is decreased. Since eigenvalues and eigenvectors are already computed, an efficient inverse of low-rank approximated covariance matrix can be done without no additional cost. Therefore, RLR-RX method becomes faster than RRX while an implicit regularization being enforced. Efficiency of the proposed RLR-RX method is first tested on a synthetic data, which confirms that RLR-RX is always faster than RRX and much faster than KRX. Proposed RLR-RX is also tested on real-world dataset, Airport-Beach-Urban (ABU) dataset with 13 hyperspectral images. These experiments also confirms that the proposed method performs better compared to RX, KRX, and RRX methods for most of the images.

One advantage of the proposed RLR-RX method is its simplicity and efficient resource usage. It maps original data to higher dimension first where it applies RX method in combination with randomized SVD. Therefore, efficiency and accuracy improvement techniques that are proposed for the RX method is also applicable to RLR-RX method. Mapping data to a higher dimension, applying RX method with randomized SVD are all parallelizable which facilitates even more efficient implementations. In this study, proposed RLR-RX method is tested within global detection scenarios, but it can be easily adapted as local anomaly detector as well. Thereby, improvement techniques proposed for local RX are also applicable to proposed RLR-RX method.

References

1. Borghys, D., Achard, V., Rotman, S.R., Gorelik, N., Perneel, C., Schweicher, E.: Hyperspectral anomaly detection: a comparative evaluation of methods. In: 2011 XXXth URSI General Assembly and Scientific Symposium (2011)
2. Guo, Q., Pu, R., Cheng, J.: Anomaly detection from hyperspectral remote sensing imagery. Geosciences **6**, 56 (2016)
3. Matteoli, S., Diani, M., Corsini, G.: A tutorial overview of anomaly detection in hyper-spectral images. IEEE Aerosp. Electron. Syst. Mag. **25**, 5–28 (2010)
4. Irving, R.S., Yu, X.: Adaptive multiple-band CFAR detection of an optical pattern with unknown spectral distribution. IEEE Trans. Acoustics, Speech Signal Process. **38**, 1760–1770 (1990)
5. Kwon, H., Nasrabadi, N.M.: Kernel RX-algorithm: a nonlinear anomaly detector for hyperspectral imagery. IEEE Trans. Geosci. Remote Sens. **43**, 388–397 (2005)
6. Nar, F., Pérez-Suay, A., Padrón, J.A., Camps-Valls, G.: Randomized RX for target detection. In: IGARSS 2018–2018 IEEE International Geoscience and Remote Sensing Symposium (2018)
7. Taitano, Y.P., Geier, B.A., Bauer, K.W.: A locally adaptable iterative RX detector. EURASIP J. Advances Signal Process. **2010**, 1–10 (2010)
8. Matteoli, S., Diani, M., Corsini, G.: A kurtosis-based test to efficiently detect targets placed in close proximity by means of local covariance-based hyperspectral anomaly detectors. In: 2011 3rd Workshop on Hyperspectral Image and Signal Processing: Evolution in Remote Sensing (WHISPERS) (2011)
9. Acito, N., Diani, M., Corsini, G.: On the CFAR property of the RX algorithm in the presence of signal-dependent noise in hyperspectral images. IEEE Trans. Geoscience Remote Sensing **51**, 3475–3491 (2012)
10. Matteoli, S., Veracini, T., Diani, M., Corsini, G.: A locally adaptive background density estimator: an evolution for RX-based anomaly detectors. IEEE Geosci. Remote Sens. Lett. **11**, 323–327 (2013)
11. Imani, M.: RX anomaly detector with rectified background. IEEE Geosci. Remote Sens. Lett. **14**, 1313–1317(2017)
12. Rossi, A., Acito, N., Diani, M., Corsini, G.: RX architectures for real-time anomaly detection in hyperspectral images. J. Real-Time Image Proc. **9**, 503–517 (2014)
13. Chang, C.-I., Wang, Y., Chen, S.-Y.: Anomaly detection using causal sliding windows. IEEE J.of Selected Topics in Applied Earth Observations and Remote Sensing **8**, 3260–3270 (2015)
14. Zhao, C., Wang, Y., Qi, B., Wang, J.: Global and local real-time anomaly detectors for hyperspectral remote sensing imagery. Remote sensing **7**, 3966–3985 (2015)
15. Zhao, C., Yao, X., Huang, B.: Real-time anomaly detection based on a fast recursive kernel RX algorithm. Remote Sensing **8**, 1011 (2016)
16. Zhao, R., Du, B., Zhang, L., Zhang, L.: A robust background regression based score estimation algorithm for hyperspectral anomaly detection. ISPRS J. Photogrammetry Remote Sensing **122**, 126–144 (2016)
17. Zhao, C., Deng, W., Yan, Y., Yao, X.: Progressive line processing of kernel RX anomaly detection algorithm for hyperspectral imagery. Sensors **17**, 1815 (2017)
18. Zhao, L., Lin, W., Wang, Y., Li, X.: Recursive local summation of RX detection for hyperspectral image using sliding windows. Remote Sensing **10**, 103 (2018)
19. Molero, J.M., Paz, A., Garzón, E.M., Martínez, J.A., Plaza, A., García, I.: Fast anomaly detection in hyperspectral images with RX method on heterogeneous clusters. The Journal of Supercomputing **58**, 411–419 (20110

20. Molero, J.M., Garzon, E.M., Garcia, I., Plaza, A.: Analysis and optimizations of global and local versions of the RX algorithm for anomaly detection in hyperspectral data. IEEE J. Selected Topics in Applied Earth Observations and Remote Sensing **6**, 801–814 (2013)
21. Molero, J.M., Garzon, E.M., García, I., Quintana-Orti, E.S., Plaza, A.: Efficient implementation of hyperspectral anomaly detection techniques on GPUs and multicore processors. IEEE J. Selected Topics in Applied Earth Observations and Remote Sensing **7**, 2256–2266 (2014)
22. Yang, B., Yang, M., Plaza, A., Gao, L., Zhang, B.: Dual-mode FPGA implementation of target and anomaly detection algorithms for real-time hyperspectral imaging. IEEE J. Selected Topics in Applied Earth Observations and Remote Sensing **8**, 2950–2961 (2015)
23. Hidalgo, J.A.P., Pérez-Suay, A., Nar, F., Camps-Valls, G.: Efficient nonlinear RX anomaly detectors. IEEE Geosci. Remote Sens. Lett. **18**, 231–235 (2020)
24. Schweizer, S.M., Moura, J.M.F.: Hyperspectral imagery: clutter adaptation in anomaly detection. IEEE Trans. Inf. Theory **46**, 1855–1871 (2000)
25. Zhou, J., Kwan, C., Ayhan, B., Eismann, M.T.: A novel cluster kernel RX algorithm for anomaly and change detection using hyperspectral images. IEEE Trans. Geo-science Remote Sensing **54**, 6497–6504 (2016)
26. Duran, O., Petrou, M.: A time-efficient method for anomaly detection in hyperspectral images. IEEE Trans. Geosci. Remote Sens. **45**, 3894–3904 (2007)
27. He, L., Pan, Q., Di, W., Li, Y.: Anomaly detection in hyperspectral imagery based on maximum entropy and nonparametric estimation. Pattern Recogn. Lett. **29**, 1392–1403 (2008)
28. Malpica, J.A., Rejas, J.G., Alonso, M.C.: A projection pursuit algorithm for anomaly detection in hyperspectral imagery. Pattern Recogn. **41**, 3313–3327 (2008)
29. Yuan, Z., Sun, H., Ji, K., Li, Z., Zou, H.: Local sparsity divergence for hyperspectral anomaly detection. IEEE Geosci. Remote Sens. Lett. **11**, 1697–1701 (2014)
30. Sun, W., Tian, L., Xu, Y., Du, B., Du, Q.: A randomized subspace learning based anomaly detector for hyperspectral imagery. Remote Sensing **10**, 417 (2018)
31. Zhu, L., Wen, G.: Hyperspectral anomaly detection via background estimation and adaptive weighted sparse representation. Remote Sensing **10**, 272 (2018)
32. Soofbaf, S.R., Sahebi, M.R., Mojaradi, B.: A sliding window-based joint sparse representation (SWJSR) method for hyperspectral anomaly detection. Remote Sensing **10**, 434 (2018)
33. Du, B., Zhao, R., Zhang, L., Zhang, L.: A spectral-spatial based local summation anomaly detection method for hyperspectral images. Signal Process. **124**, 115–131 (2016)
34. Wang, L., Zhao, C.: Anomaly detection technique of HIS. In: Hyperspectral Image Processing. Springer, pp. 217–256 (2016)
35. Huber-Lerner, M., Hadar, O., Rotman, S.R., Huber-Shalem, R.: Hyperspectral band selection for anomaly detection: the role of data Gaussianity. IEEE J. Selected Topics in Applied Earth Observations and Remote Sensing **9**, 732–743 (2015)
36. Ma, N., Peng, Y., Wang, S., Leong, P.H.W.: An unsupervised deep hyperspectral anomaly detector. Sensors **18**, 693 (2018)
37. Zhang, Y., Du, B., Zhang, L., Wang, S.: A low-rank and sparse matrix decomposition-based Mahalanobis distance method for hyperspectral anomaly detection. IEEE Trans. Geoscience and Remote Sensing **54**, 1376–1389 (2015)
38. Niu, Y., Wang, B.: Hyperspectral anomaly detection based on low-rank representation and learned dictionary. Remote Sensing **8**, 289 (2016)
39. Rahimi, A., Recht, B.: Random features for large-scale kernel machines. In: Advances in Neural Information Processing Systems (NIPS) 2007
40. Drineas, P., Mahoney, M.W.: Approximating a gram matrix for improved kernel-based learning. In: International Conference on Computational Learning Theory (2005)
41. Scholkopf, D.A.F.M.B., Achlioptas, F., Bernhard, M.: Sampling techniques for kernel methods. Adv. Neural. Inf. Process. Syst. **14**, 335 (2002)

42. Halko, N., Martinsson, P.-G., Tropp, J.A.: Finding structure with randomness: probabilistic algorithms for constructing approximate matrix decompositions. SIAM Rev. **53**(2), 217–288 (2011)
43. Camps-Valls, G., Bruzzone, L.: Kernel Methods for Remote Sensing Data Analysis. Wiley (2009)
44. Kang, X., Zhang, X., Li, S., Li, K., Li, J., Benediktsson, J.A.: Hyperspectral anomaly detection with attribute and edge-preserving filters. IEEE Trans. Geosci. Remote Sens. **55**(10), 5600–5611 (2017)

Where is Risk Going and Roles of Using Internet Data – A Case Study of Weighted Beta CAPM in Vietnam Listed Banks Under Macro Context

Dinh Tran Ngoc Huy[1(✉)], Nguyen Dinh Trung[2], Le Ngoc Nuong[3(✉)], Phan Anh[4], Ly Lan Yen[5], and Tran Duc Thang[6]

[1] Banking University HCMC, Ho Chi Minh City, Vietnam
dtnhuy2010@gmail.com
[2] National Economics University (NEU), Hanoi, Vietnam
[3] Thai Nguyen University of Economics and Business Administration, Thai Nguyen, Vietnam
[4] Banking Academy, Hanoi, Vietnam
[5] Academy of Finance, Hanoi, Vietnam
[6] National Economics University, Hanoi, Vietnam

Abstract. In recent years we recognize the importance of internet data from reliable websites of banks and Bureau statistics that can help us to build risk models for banks. During past years with lots of achievements in banking sector, we could classify listed banks on Vietnam stock exchange into 2 groups: Previous SOEs banks (including Vietcombank and Vietinbank) and Private banks (including Saigon Hanoi Bank - SHB, Eximbank- EIB, Navibank -NVB or NCB, Sacombank-STB and Asia Commercial Bank-ACB). Banks in Vietnam play a major roles in providing loans and financial services to socio-economy during pre-low (L) inflation stage 2011–2015, where there is low CPI of 0.6% in year 2015. This is historical period of economy since global crisis 2008. The research findings tell us that CPI, GDP growth ad Rf have positive correlation with weighted beta CAPM while lending rate has positive relationship with weighted beta. Hence, bank system will control lending rate and Treasury bond rate at proper levels, not increasing too much. Also it is in the paper we introduce the formula of calculating weighted beta CAPM for bank sector, an improvement from traditional beta formula. Besides, this study also give out recommendations for enhancing risk management function and risk management information system (RMIS) of Vietnam banks in future.

Keywords: internet data · RMIS · socio-economic roles · Vietnam banks · weighted beta CAPM

1 Introduction

First, we recognize the importance of socio-economic roles in banking also increase to a new level in recent years.

Next, We emphasize that the role of reliable internet data increasing in recent years. There is evidence in banking sector showing that internet data serving better for building

A. Mirzazadeh et al. (Eds.): SEMIT 2022, CCIS 1808, pp. 142–162, 2023.
https://doi.org/10.1007/978-3-031-40395-8_10

information system for better bank management. In order to prevent systematic risk prevention for commercial banks, The authors propose some recommendations in the near future as follows:

First, the perception of regulatory agencies management as well as commercial banks need to be improved about systemic risks as well as its negative effects, leading to financial instability main on a large scale.

Second, agencies and regulators It is necessary to properly appreciate the importance of the measurement of systemic risk in the banking sector row. To do so, the first step is to develop a synchronous information base system and is centralized and unified at the State Bank.

Next, we need to build a set of warning indicators early systematic risk for early detection risk signs. At the same time, increase strengthen measuring tools systemic risk in the region-Vietnam commercial banks; consider to choose methodsin accordan ce with the banking sector in Vietnam, using a combination of methods to make predictions (Do Thu Hang, Ta Thanh Huyen, 2021).

In fact, there are many challenges in bank operation I the country, for instance, the level of diversification of service types is not high, mainly focusing on providing traditional banking services such as capital mobilization, lending and payment, other types of services, especially new services. In addition to the technical and technological factors, it is the inadequacies in the quality of human resources of commercial banks. Because banking business is a business on the basis of risk-taking, but in the end, all risks stem from human factors, so in order to minimize risks, the quality of human resources in the banking system must be maintained.

Last but not least, we conduct this study to improve what we called Risk management information system (RMIS) for Vietnam bank sector from internet data, as a reliable source of risk information. Under advantages of internet of things application, everything can be connected in internet, therefore, in this paper we mainly focus on using reliable internet data in comparing and evaluating 2 key factors: stock price and beta CAPM under macro factors effects, for 2 big banks in Vietnam: Group 1: Vietinbank -CTG and Vietcombank - VCB (previously, SOE) and Group2 including: Asia commercial bank -ACB, Eximbank -EIB, Navibank -NVB or NCB, Sacombank-STB and Saigon Hanoi Bank -SHB (previously, private banks).

Look at below chart we see:

- For group 1: beta VCB and beta CTG has the same trend over years, while stock price of VCB has increased in 2015 compared to beta CTG. (Figs. 1 and 2)
- For group 2: beta ACB and beta STB and beta EIB have moved in the same trend in past years. Only in the exceptional case of NVB, beta NVB has gone down in 2014 (Figs. 3, 4, 5, 6 and 7)..

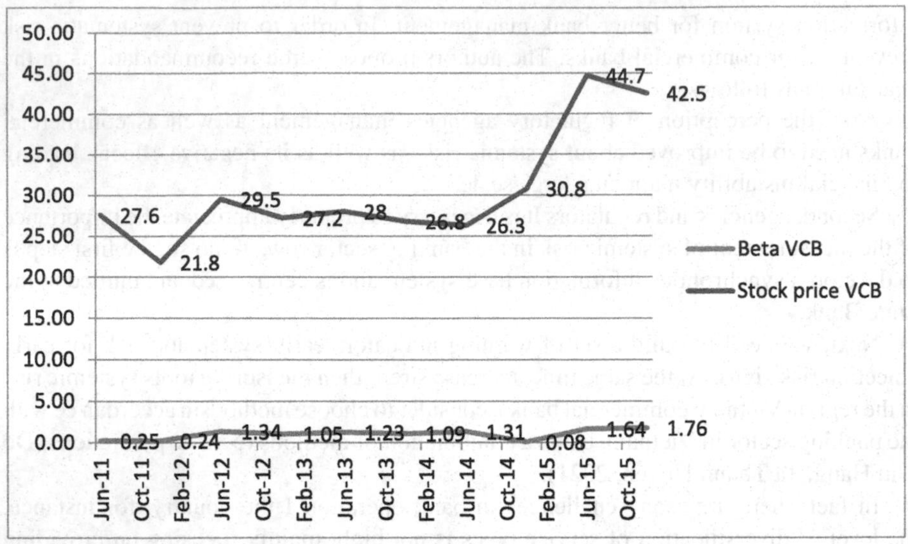

(source : author calculation and stock exchange)

Fig. 1. Variation of beta and stock price VCB.

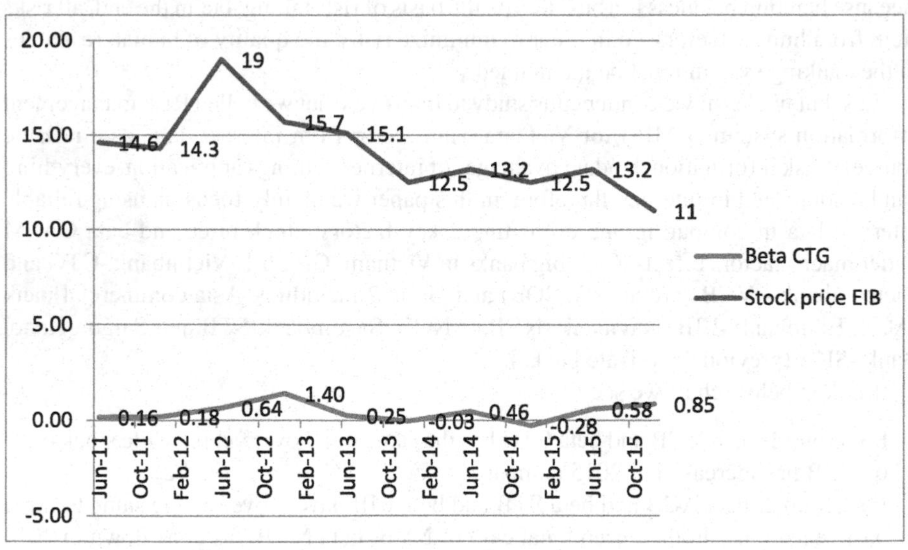

(source : author calculation and stock exchange)

Fig. 2. Variation of beta and stock price CTG.

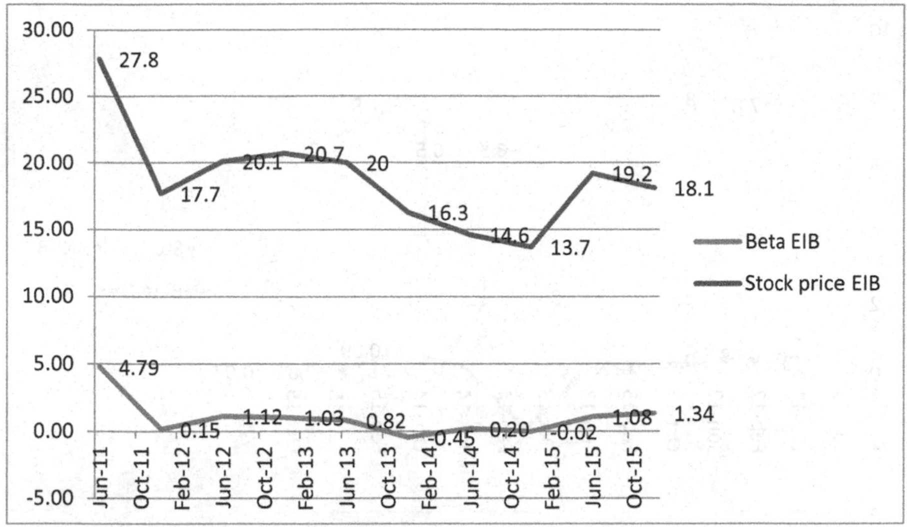

(source : author calculation and stock exchange)

Fig. 3. Variation of beta and stock price EIB.

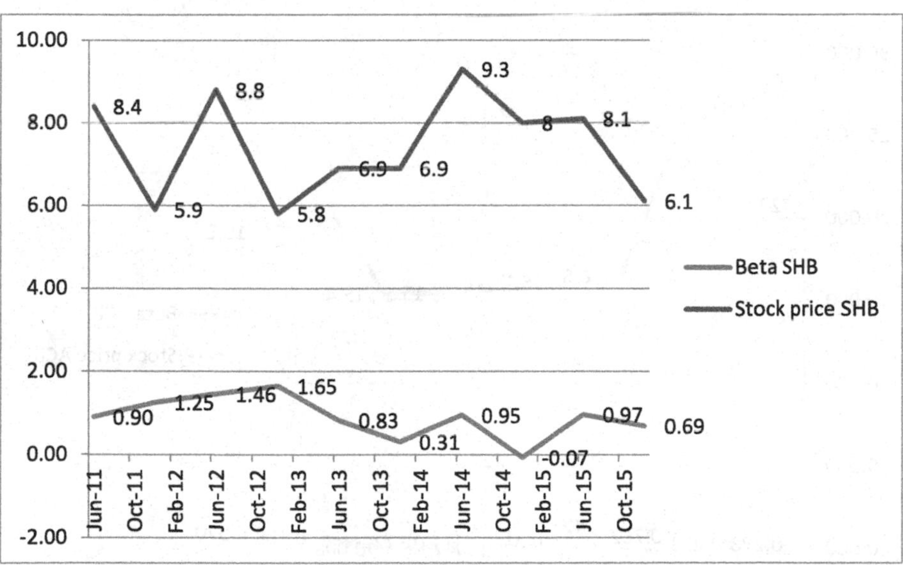

(source : author calculation and stock exchange)

Fig. 4. Variation of beta and stock price SHB.

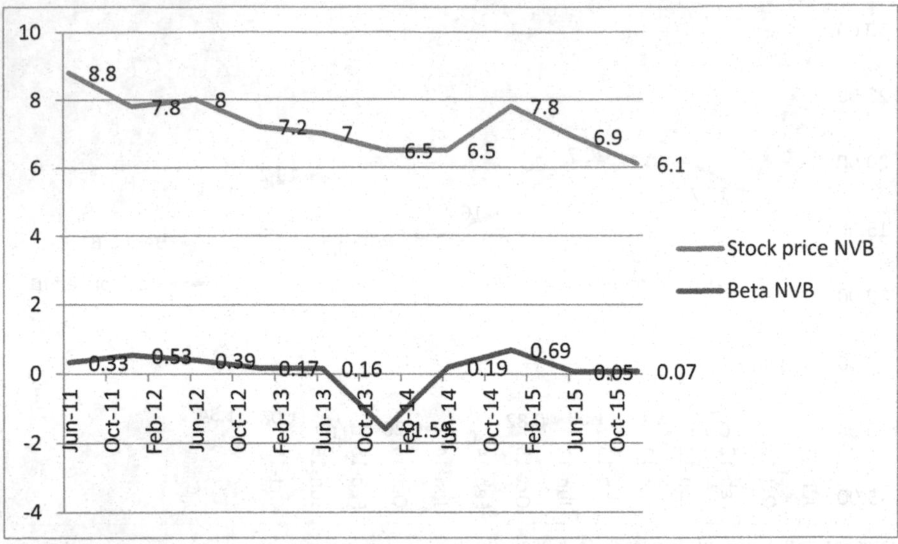

(source : author calculation and stock exchange)

Fig. 5. Variation of beta and stock price NVB.

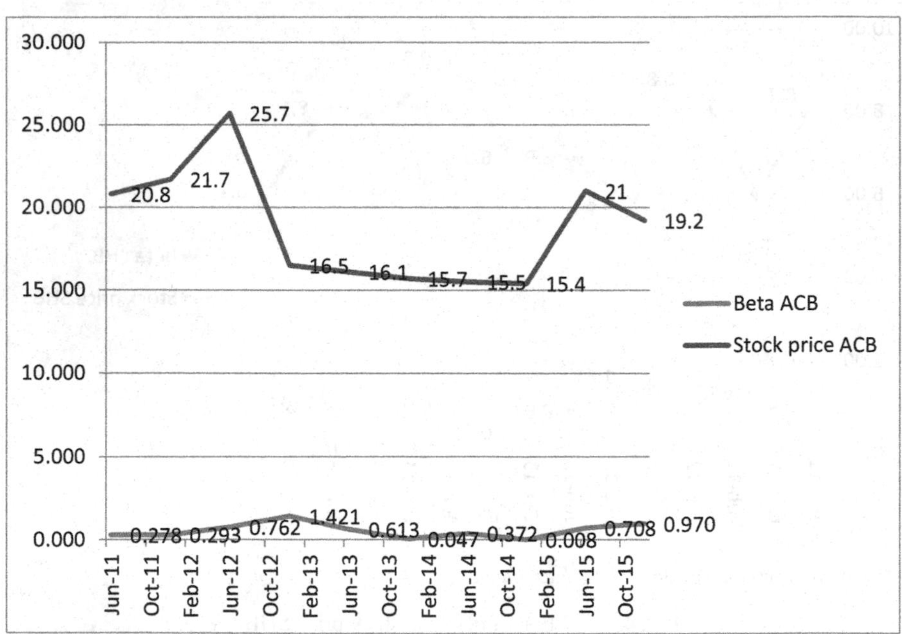

(source : author calculation and stock exchange)

Fig. 6. Variation of beta and stock price ACB.

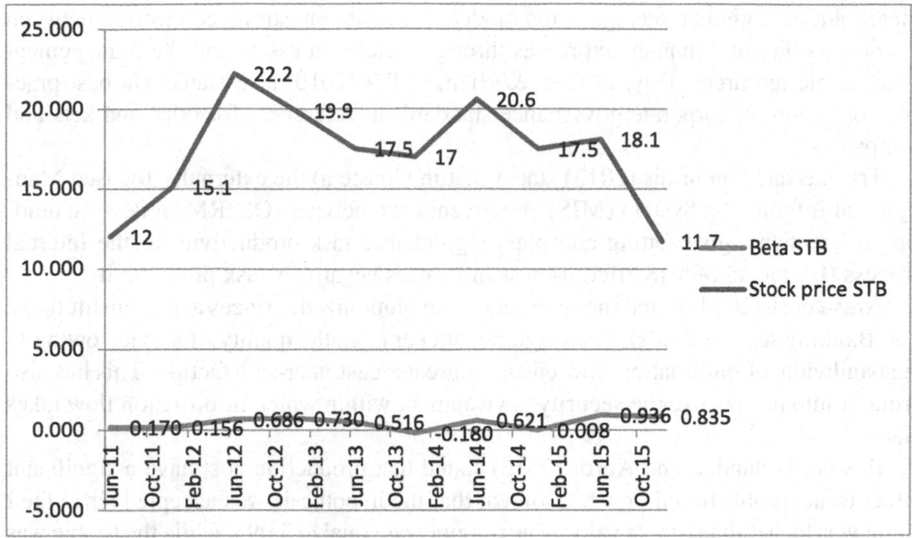

(source : author calculation and stock exchange)

Fig. 7. Variation of beta and stock price STB.

All internet data such as stock price, exchange rate, inflation, GDP growth, risk free rate we take from reliable internet data sources, esp. From website of State Bank of Vietnam, Bureau of Statistics, Ministry of Finance, banks, etc.

Research Questions:

Question 1: What are internal and extern effects on Weighted beta CAPM of total banks and for each bank beta?
Question 2: What are risk management implications and solutions?
Question 3: What are Weighted beta CAPM formula that paper suggest?

We organize the study with introduction, literature review, methodology, main results, discussion and conclusion.

This paper will use two formulas or equations: weighted beta index will be expressed in a formula of market value times (x) beta of each listed bank according to average weighted formula (see methodology section below).

First formula: beta CAPM -weighted index formula.

Second, OLS regression equation for weighted beta, in which Y (weighted beta) = function f (x1,x2,…x9): 9 independent macro variables such as GDP CPI, Rf, SP500, VNIndex,…

2 Literature Review

First, Burja (2011) stated firm performance information for instance, firm profitability, is useful in substantiating managerial decisions. This objective aims achieving superior economic results that will increase the company's competitiveness and will satisfy shareholders. Authors used regression model, and figure out strong connection between the profitability of company expresses through Return on assets and the management of available resources. Huy, D.T.N., & Hien, D.T.N (2010) also stated via best practices of European corporate governance standards as references for other markets and companies.

Trivelas and Satouridis (2013) stated that in Greece a) the externally focused Management Information System (MIS) effectiveness archetypes (OS, RM) reflecting innovation, creativity, goal setting and planning enhance task productivity b) the Internal process (IP) model of MIS effectiveness influences negatively task productivity.

Arasu et al. (2014) found the Internet has revolutionized services across institutions. The Banking sector has registered significant change in the quality of service owing to the bandwidth of information flow ensuring greater customer-satisfaction. This has also brought into perspective the security environment within which information flow takes place.

Beside, Wulandari and Abror (2016) stated that production cost have a significant effect to net profit. Based on t-test known that the hypothesis was accepted since the t count was higher than t-table value. The t-count was equal to 3,095, while the t-table was 2,776, with a significant value of 0.036 smaller than 0.05, which means that production costs significantly affect net income at PT Indorama Synthetics Tbk.

And Huy. D.T.N et al. (2020) estimated effects of extern factors on stock price of a listed bank in Vietnam in an econometric model.

Then, Madhdi and Khadafi (2020) stated that a positive and significant influence from net profit margin, operating profit margin, and gross profit margin on stock prices in Good Consumer Industry Company listed on the Indonesia Stock Exchange, while partially net profit margin and gross profit margin were not there is a positive and insignificant influence on stock prices on Good Consumer Industry Company listed on the Indonesia Stock Exchange, while operating profit margin, partially there is a positive and significant effect on stock prices on Good Consumer Industry Company listed on the Indonesia Stock Exchange on 2012–2014.

Dinh Tran Ngoc Huy (2015) mentioned better risk management and corporate governance standards is needed in a limited South Asian corporate governance standards after financial crisis.

Last but not least, Huy, D.T.N et al. (2020) measure effects of external factors on bank stock price in case of a big listed bank in Vietnam - Vietcombank which left the direction for further researches on internal factors effects measuring. Whereas Do Thu Hang 7 TA Thanh Huyen (2021) pointed that Shocks include internal shock born (from the fall/difficulty of an institution) or exogenous (side shock outside). The shock is then transferred to the interrelated transmission channels, including: bilateral linkages; market (information); structure: similarity in structure asset/liability structure (risk of shocks) symmetry), products, payment systems.

It is also important to note, when considering the concept of risk, systematic risk in Vietnam, it is necessary to distinguish between Two concepts Systematic risk and Systemic risk. Both these terms are translated is systematic risk but has different implications.

Systematic risk - is the term for total risk case (macroeconomics) cannot be mitigated by hedging or diversifying (Aghion et al. 2010). This is the risk related to securities risk factors undiversified, determined by Market trend. This systemic risk considered as speculative risk due to volatility prices of financial instruments. On the other hand, Systemic risk is a term that refers to having can be understood as an organization's risk financial spread to institutions/institutions other mechanism or the entire system and muscle breakdown or major dysfunction of financial markets (Mishkin 1995).

Table 1. Summary of previous studies. Source: Search data.

AUTHORS	YEAR	CONTENTS, RESULTS
Arasu et al. (2014)	2008	the Internet has revolutionized services across institutions. The Banking sector has registered significant change in the quality of service owing to the bandwidth of information flow ensuring greater customer-satisfaction. This has also brought into perspective the security environment within which information flow takes place
Endri E. et al.	2020	the variables of Non-Performing Loans (NPL), Loan to Deposit Ratio (LDR), Return on Assets (ROA), Interest Rate (SBI), and Exchange Rate (FOREX) affect NIM. The exchange rate variable has a predominant effect, while the NPL factor has a less strong influence on NIM. The empirical evidence from this research is important for commercial banks in Indonesia to improve operational efficiency through NIM performance. Internal and external factors of a bank should be subject of attention of bank managers
Huy, D.T.N et al.	2019	specified stock price (and later, net profit) of listed Vietnam firms such as Vietcombank can be affected by external and internal macro factors
Hang, T.T.B., Nhung, D.T.H., Huy, D.T.N et al.	2020	Information on Vietnam stock exchange can support to calculate firm risk measures or asset/equity beta

In case the market goes down, this contributes deterioration of the financial position of the organizations operating in that market.

And Dinh Tran Ngoc Huy, Phan Ngoc Quynh Nhu, Tran Thi Thanh Nga, Ta Van Thanh (2022) stated Risk free rate reduce in short term will reduce beta and Fluctuation in exchange rate will influence beta. Hoang Van Long et al. (2022) also mentioned economic development policies, in a construction sector case, to limit the negative effects of exchange rate, and inflation, i.e. not increasing much. Then Hoang Xuan Que et al. (2022) pointed roles of digital data and transformation to help us to build better risk model and management information system at banks (Table 1).

Therefore we identify the research gap: In previous studies, many scientists analyze internal factors effects on net profit and business results, and macro effects as well, however they do not classify internal and external macro effects, so this is the research gap for this paper to explore, and also authors will suggest a weighted beta CAPM formula.

Also we make comparative analysis: Compared to other previous studies, they done with traditional CAPM formula, however here authors present an innovative (new) weighted beta CAPM formula, that is adjusted beta (wegited formula applied) in banking sector, therefore it can be expanded for future studies in other countries and markets and industries as well.

3 Methodology

3.1 Method and Data

This study mainly use combination of quantitative methods and qualitative methods including synthesis, inductive and explanatory methods. And it emphasizes again important roles of internet data in sustainable modern bank management.

For quantitative analysis, the study is supported with OLS regression.

Data is collected from reliable internet sources and websites.

Formula to calculate Weighted beta CAPM from a pool data of many banks as follow:

$$\text{Weighted Beta CAPM(time t) average} = (\text{Beta of (Commercial bank i at time 0)}$$
$$+ \ldots + \text{Beta of bank i at time t}) \times \text{market value of stock of (Commercial bank i at time t)}$$
$$/\text{Total (Market value of stocks of banks)}$$

Beta (Commercial bank i at time t) is calculated in traditional formula of Beta CAPM with weekly data (Figs. 8, 9, 10, 11, 12, 13, 14 and 15).

Looking at Descriptive Statistics Below, We See that:

- In Group 1: standard deviation of SP500 and exchange rate are highest values.
- In Group 2: standard deviation of SP500 and exchange rate are highest values.(but with lower values than those of group 1)

	BETACTG	CPI	EXRATE	G	IM	R	RF	SP500	TRADEBA...	VNINDEX
Mean	0.656675	0.028008	22809.67	0.057983	166.6833	0.095217	0.039517	2670.148	4.483333	822.8833
Median	0.491700	0.030200	22923.00	0.065200	150.4000	0.095000	0.037000	2590.230	-100.0000	858.8200
Maximum	2.533700	0.047400	23230.00	0.070800	267.2000	0.110000	0.061800	3703.060	410.0000	1067.500
Minimum	-0.275800	0.006300	21780.00	0.018100	127.3000	0.080000	0.012200	2043.940	-500.0000	579.0300
Std. Dev.	0.701284	0.012080	427.6367	0.017170	42.17356	0.010451	0.016243	513.0916	313.6589	172.2477
Skewness	1.607032	-0.262708	-1.235511	-1.467570	1.446639	-0.011162	-0.030322	0.526233	0.289823	-0.244276
Kurtosis	5.507438	2.206974	3.825801	3.807463	3.903326	1.815576	1.919779	2.340080	1.781900	1.596927
Jarque-Bera	8.308726	0.452476	3.393948	4.633522	4.593525	0.701679	0.585278	0.771590	0.909879	1.103648
Probability	0.015696	0.797528	0.183237	0.098592	0.100584	0.704097	0.746292	0.679910	0.634486	0.575898
Sum	7.880100	0.336100	273716.0	0.695800	2000.200	1.142600	0.474200	32041.77	53.80000	9874.600
Sum Sq. Dev.	5.409784	0.001605	2011605.	0.003243	19564.70	0.001201	0.002902	2895893.	1082201.	326362.0

Fig. 8. CTG factors statistics

	BETAVCB	CPI	EXRATE	G	IM	R	RF	SP500	TRADEBA...	VNINDEX
Mean	1.192525	0.028008	22809.67	0.057983	166.6833	0.095217	0.039517	2670.148	4.483333	822.8833
Median	1.084800	0.030200	22923.00	0.065200	150.4000	0.095000	0.037000	2590.230	-100.0000	858.8200
Maximum	2.099400	0.047400	23230.00	0.070800	267.2000	0.110000	0.061800	3703.060	410.0000	1067.500
Minimum	0.590600	0.006300	21780.00	0.018100	127.3000	0.080000	0.012200	2043.940	-500.0000	579.0300
Std. Dev.	0.471423	0.012080	427.6367	0.017170	42.17356	0.010451	0.016243	513.0916	313.6589	172.2477
Skewness	0.455134	-0.262708	-1.235511	-1.467570	1.446639	-0.011162	-0.030322	0.526233	0.289823	-0.244276
Kurtosis	2.252966	2.206974	3.825801	3.807463	3.903326	1.815576	1.919779	2.340080	1.781900	1.596927
Jarque-Bera	0.693324	0.452476	3.393948	4.633522	4.593525	0.701679	0.585278	0.771590	0.909879	1.103648
Probability	0.707044	0.797528	0.183237	0.098592	0.100584	0.704097	0.746292	0.679910	0.634486	0.575898
Sum	14.31030	0.336100	273716.0	0.695800	2000.200	1.142600	0.474200	32041.77	53.80000	9874.600
Sum Sq. Dev.	2.444631	0.001605	2011605.	0.003243	19564.70	0.001201	0.002902	2895893.	1082201.	326362.0

Fig. 9. VCB factors statistics

	BETAEIB	CPI	EXRATE	G	IM	R	RF	SP500	TRADEBA...	VNINDEX
Mean	1.388333	0.028008	22809.67	0.057983	166.6833	0.095217	0.039517	2670.148	4.483333	822.8833
Median	1.425000	0.030200	22923.00	0.065200	150.4000	0.095000	0.037000	2590.230	-100.0000	858.8200
Maximum	2.500000	0.047400	23230.00	0.070800	267.2000	0.110000	0.061800	3703.060	410.0000	1067.500
Minimum	0.390000	0.006300	21780.00	0.018100	127.3000	0.000000	0.012200	2043.940	-500.0000	579.0300
Std. Dev.	0.569399	0.012080	427.6367	0.017170	42.17356	0.010461	0.016243	513.0916	313.6589	172.2477
Skewness	0.036050	-0.262708	-1.235511	-1.467570	1.446639	-0.011162	-0.030322	0.526233	0.289823	-0.244276
Kurtosis	2.933702	2.206974	3.825801	3.807463	3.903326	1.815576	1.919779	2.340080	1.781900	1.596927
Jarque-Bera	0.004797	0.452476	3.393948	4.633522	4.593525	0.701679	0.585278	0.771590	0.909879	1.103648
Probability	0.997604	0.797528	0.183237	0.098592	0.100584	0.704097	0.746292	0.679910	0.634486	0.575898
Sum	16.66000	0.336100	273716.0	0.695800	2000.200	1.142600	0.474200	32041.77	53.80000	9874.600
Sum Sq. Dev.	3.566367	0.001605	2011605.	0.003243	19564.70	0.001201	0.002902	2895893.	1082201.	326362.0

Fig. 10. EIB factors statistics

	BETASHB	CPI	EXRATE	G	IM	R	RF	SP500	TRADEBA...	VNINDEX
Mean	0.635833	0.028008	22809.67	0.057983	166.6833	0.095217	0.039517	2670.148	4.483333	822.8833
Median	0.865000	0.030200	22923.00	0.065200	150.4000	0.095000	0.037000	2590.230	-100.0000	858.8200
Maximum	1.130000	0.047400	23230.00	0.070800	267.2000	0.110000	0.061800	3703.060	410.0000	1067.500
Minimum	-1.460000	0.006300	21780.00	0.018100	127.3000	0.080000	0.012200	2043.940	-500.0000	579.0300
Std. Dev.	0.707267	0.012080	427.6367	0.017170	42.17356	0.010451	0.016243	513.0916	313.6589	172.2477
Skewness	-2.401782	-0.262708	-1.235511	-1.467570	1.446639	-0.011162	-0.030322	0.526233	0.289823	-0.244276
Kurtosis	7.721237	2.206974	3.825801	3.807463	3.903326	1.815576	1.919779	2.340080	1.781900	1.596927
Jarque-Bera	22.68216	0.452476	3.393948	4.633522	4.593525	0.701679	0.585278	0.771590	0.909879	1.103648
Probability	0.000012	0.797528	0.183237	0.098592	0.100584	0.704097	0.746292	0.679910	0.634486	0.575898
Sum	7.630000	0.336100	273716.0	0.695800	2000.200	1.142600	0.474200	32041.77	53.80000	9874.600
Sum Sq. Dev.	5.502492	0.001605	2011605.	0.003243	19564.70	0.001201	0.002902	2895893.	1082201.	326362.0

Fig. 11. SHB factors statistics

4 Main Results

4.1 Overall Results

We see in below figure (Figs. 16, 17, 18, 19, 20, 21, 22 and 23):

	BETAACB	CPI	EXRATE	G	IM	R	RF	SP500	TRADEBA...	VNINDEX
Mean	0.990000	0.028008	22809.67	0.057983	166.6833	0.095217	0.039517	2670.148	4.483333	822.8833
Median	0.805000	0.030200	22923.00	0.065200	150.4000	0.095000	0.037000	2590.230	-100.0000	858.8200
Maximum	3.370000	0.047400	23230.00	0.070800	267.2000	0.110000	0.061800	3703.060	410.0000	1067.500
Minimum	0.400000	0.006300	21780.00	0.018100	127.3000	0.080000	0.012200	2043.940	-500.0000	579.0300
Std. Dev.	0.786789	0.012080	427.6367	0.017170	42.17356	0.010461	0.016243	513.0916	313.6589	172.2477
Skewness	2.524943	-0.262708	-1.235511	-1.467570	1.446639	-0.011162	-0.030322	0.526233	0.289823	-0.244276
Kurtosis	8.372413	2.206974	3.825801	3.807463	3.903326	1.815576	1.919779	2.340080	1.781900	1.596927
Jarque-Bera	27.18209	0.452476	3.393948	4.633522	4.593525	0.701679	0.585278	0.771590	0.909879	1.103648
Probability	0.000001	0.797528	0.183237	0.098592	0.100584	0.704097	0.746292	0.679910	0.634486	0.575898
Sum	11.88000	0.336100	273716.0	0.695800	2000.200	1.142600	0.474200	32041.77	53.80000	9874.600
Sum Sq. Dev.	6.809400	0.001605	2011605.	0.003243	19564.70	0.001201	0.002902	2895893.	1082201.	326362.0

Fig. 12. ACB factors statistics

	BETANVB	EX_RATE	SP500	TRADEBA...	CPI	G	IM	R	RF	VNINDEX
Mean	0.099000	21864.80	1701.587	-232.2000	0.068270	0.056730	154.4800	0.132500	0.073505	490.1750
Median	0.180000	21780.00	1734.160	-162.5000	0.063850	0.056500	153.9500	0.125000	0.065275	492.8800
Maximum	0.690000	23230.00	2103.840	498.0000	0.181300	0.066800	194.8000	0.190000	0.132000	593.0500
Minimum	-1.590000	20618.00	1292.280	-1162.000	0.006300	0.043800	117.4000	0.100000	0.046000	351.5500
Std. Dev.	0.627702	876.1553	327.3917	465.6620	0.059925	0.007141	25.76659	0.031380	0.024419	83.37681
Skewness	-2.127988	0.108851	-0.061715	-0.405459	0.921046	-0.361761	0.145331	0.844274	1.469319	-0.196155
Kurtosis	6.604228	1.708458	1.360020	2.975371	2.637092	2.181881	1.849123	2.335049	4.388549	1.735476
Jarque-Bera	12.95991	0.714782	1.126987	0.274248	1.468753	0.497001	0.587084	1.372230	4.401524	0.730387
Probability	0.001534	0.699499	0.569217	0.871862	0.479805	0.779970	0.745618	0.503528	0.110719	0.694062
Sum	0.990000	218648.0	17015.87	-2322.000	0.682700	0.567300	1544.800	1.325000	0.735050	4901.750
Sum Sq. Dev.	3.546090	6908834.	964668.1	1951570.	0.032319	0.000459	5975.256	0.008862	0.005367	62565.23

Fig. 13. NVB factors statistics

	BETASTB	CPI	EX_RATE	G	IM	R	RF	SP500	TRADEBA...	VNINDEX
Mean	0.447800	0.068270	21864.80	0.056730	154.4800	0.132500	0.073505	1701.587	-232.2000	490.1750
Median	0.568500	0.063850	21780.00	0.056500	153.9500	0.125000	0.065275	1734.160	-162.5000	492.8800
Maximum	0.936000	0.181300	23230.00	0.066800	194.8000	0.190000	0.132000	2103.840	498.0000	593.0500
Minimum	-0.180000	0.006300	20618.00	0.043800	117.4000	0.100000	0.046000	1292.280	-1162.000	351.5500
Std. Dev.	0.381396	0.059925	876.1553	0.007141	25.76659	0.031380	0.024419	327.3917	465.6620	83.37681
Skewness	-0.343855	0.921046	0.108851	-0.361761	0.145331	0.844274	1.469319	-0.061715	-0.405459	-0.196155
Kurtosis	1.725435	2.637092	1.708458	2.181881	1.849123	2.335049	4.388549	1.360020	2.975371	1.735476
Jarque-Bera	0.873941	1.468753	0.714782	0.497001	0.587084	1.372230	4.401524	1.126987	0.274248	0.730387
Probability	0.645990	0.479805	0.699499	0.779970	0.745618	0.503528	0.110719	0.569217	0.871862	0.694062
Sum	4.478000	0.682700	218648.0	0.567300	1544.800	1.325000	0.735050	17015.87	-2322.000	4901.750
Sum Sq. Dev.	1.309166	0.032319	6908834.	0.000459	5975.256	0.008862	0.005367	964668.1	1951570.	62565.23

Fig. 14. STB factors statistics

	WEIGHTE...	CPI	EX_RATE	G	IM	R	RF	SP500	TRADEBA...	VNINDEX
Mean	0.579000	0.068270	21864.80	0.056730	154.4800	0.132500	0.073505	1701.587	-232.2000	490.1750
Median	0.775000	0.063850	21780.00	0.056500	153.9500	0.125000	0.065275	1734.160	-162.5000	492.8800
Maximum	1.360000	0.181300	23230.00	0.066800	194.8000	0.190000	0.132000	2103.840	498.0000	593.0500
Minimum	-0.970000	0.006300	20618.00	0.043800	117.4000	0.100000	0.046000	1292.280	-1162.000	351.5500
Std. Dev.	0.707993	0.059925	876.1553	0.007141	25.76659	0.031380	0.024419	327.3917	465.6620	83.37681
Skewness	-0.999279	0.921046	0.108851	-0.361761	0.145331	0.844274	1.469319	-0.061715	-0.405459	-0.196155
Kurtosis	3.223575	2.637092	1.708458	2.181881	1.849123	2.335049	4.388549	1.360020	2.975371	1.735476
Jarque-Bera	1.685090	1.468753	0.714782	0.497001	0.587084	1.372230	4.401524	1.126987	0.274248	0.730387
Probability	0.430613	0.479805	0.699499	0.779970	0.745618	0.503528	0.110719	0.569217	0.871862	0.694062
Sum	5.790000	0.682700	218648.0	0.567300	1544.800	1.325000	0.735050	17015.87	-2322.000	4901.750
Sum Sq. Dev.	4.511290	0.032319	6908834.	0.000459	5975.256	0.008862	0.005367	964668.1	1951570.	62565.23

Fig. 15. Weighted beta factors statistics. *Source: author calculation and stock exchange*

Correlation Matrix										
	BETACTG	CPI	EXRATE	G	IM	R	RF	SP500	TRADEBA...	VNINDEX
BETACTG	1.000000	0.336933	-0.208220	0.148388	0.764773	0.138517	0.258014	-0.279036	-0.421643	-0.150356
CPI	0.336933	1.000000	0.355839	0.084484	0.413563	-0.414518	-0.181729	0.255209	-0.220207	0.414535
EXRATE	-0.208220	0.355839	1.000000	-0.085689	-0.083666	-0.775791	-0.724295	0.686922	0.531029	0.767832
G	0.148388	0.084484	-0.085689	1.000000	0.183953	-0.269621	0.461428	-0.451641	-0.519267	-0.057490
IM	0.764773	0.413563	-0.083666	0.183953	1.000000	0.092188	0.151470	-0.215029	-0.381218	0.008190
R	0.138517	-0.414518	-0.775791	-0.269621	0.092188	1.000000	0.639799	-0.670855	-0.392501	-0.877965
RF	0.258014	-0.181729	-0.724295	0.461428	0.151470	0.639799	1.000000	-0.834478	-0.664628	-0.821145
SP500	-0.279036	0.255209	0.686922	-0.451641	-0.215029	-0.670855	-0.834478	1.000000	0.841299	0.865637
TRADEBA...	-0.421643	-0.220207	0.531029	-0.519267	-0.381218	-0.392501	-0.664628	0.841299	1.000000	0.604803
VNINDEX	-0.150356	0.414535	0.767832	-0.057490	0.008190	-0.877965	-0.821145	0.865637	0.604803	1.000000

(source : author calculation and stock exchange)

Fig. 16. CTG macro elements correlation.

Correlation Matrix										
	BETAVCB	CPI	EXRATE	G	IM	R	RF	SP500	TRADEBA...	VNINDEX
BETAVCB	1.000000	0.010098	-0.383907	0.400397	-0.010006	0.128686	0.447294	-0.454337	-0.602414	-0.447930
CPI	0.010098	1.000000	0.355839	0.084484	0.413563	-0.414518	-0.181729	0.255209	-0.220207	0.414535
EXRATE	-0.383907	0.355839	1.000000	-0.085689	-0.083666	-0.775791	-0.724295	0.686922	0.531029	0.767832
G	0.400397	0.084484	-0.085689	1.000000	0.183953	-0.269621	0.461428	-0.451641	-0.519267	-0.057490
IM	-0.010006	0.413563	-0.083666	0.183953	1.000000	0.092188	0.151470	-0.215029	-0.381218	0.008190
R	0.128686	-0.414518	-0.775791	-0.269621	0.092188	1.000000	0.639799	-0.670855	-0.392501	-0.877965
RF	0.447294	-0.181729	-0.724295	0.461428	0.151470	0.639799	1.000000	-0.834478	-0.664628	-0.821145
SP500	-0.454337	0.255209	0.686922	-0.451641	-0.215029	-0.670855	-0.834478	1.000000	0.841299	0.865637
TRADEBA...	-0.602414	-0.220207	0.531029	-0.519267	-0.381218	-0.392501	-0.664628	0.841299	1.000000	0.604803
VNINDEX	-0.447930	0.414535	0.767832	-0.057490	0.008190	-0.877965	-0.821145	0.865637	0.604803	1.000000

(source : author calculation and stock exchange)

Fig. 17. VCB macro elements correlation.

Correlation Matrix										
	BETAEIB	CPI	EXRATE	G	IM	R	RF	SP500	TRADEBA...	VNINDE
BETAEIB	1.000000	0.155218	0.159855	0.394881	0.508124	-0.320816	-0.086799	0.056751	-0.054052	0.36428
CPI	0.155218	1.000000	0.366830	0.004404	0.413563	-0.414518	-0.181729	0.255209	-0.220207	0.41453
EXRATE	0.159855	0.355039	1.000000	-0.085689	-0.083666	-0.775791	-0.724295	0.686922	0.531029	0.76783
G	0.394881	0.084484	-0.085689	1.000000	0.183953	-0.269621	0.461428	-0.451641	-0.519267	-0.05749
IM	0.508124	0.413563	-0.083666	0.183953	1.000000	0.092188	0.151470	-0.215029	-0.381218	0.00819
R	-0.320816	-0.414518	-0.775791	-0.269621	0.092188	1.000000	0.639799	-0.670855	-0.392501	-0.87796
RF	-0.086799	-0.181729	-0.724295	0.461428	0.151470	0.639799	1.000000	-0.834478	-0.664628	-0.82114
SP500	0.056751	0.255209	0.686922	-0.451641	-0.215029	-0.670855	-0.834478	1.000000	0.841299	0.86563
TRADEBA...	-0.054852	-0.220207	0.531029	-0.519267	-0.381218	-0.392501	-0.664628	0.841299	1.000000	0.60480
VNINDEX	0.364282	0.414535	0.767832	-0.057490	0.008190	-0.877965	-0.821145	0.865637	0.604803	1.00000

Fig. 18. EIB macro elements correlation

Correlation Matrix										
	BETASHB	CPI	EXRATE	G	IM	R	RF	SP500	TRADEBA...	VNINDEX
BETASHB	1.000000	-0.228581	-0.011854	0.244650	-0.480409	-0.208929	-0.055766	0.037226	0.014026	0.066297
CPI	-0.228581	1.000000	0.355839	0.084484	0.413563	-0.414518	-0.181729	0.255209	-0.220207	0.414535
EXRATE	-0.011854	0.355839	1.000000	-0.085689	-0.083666	-0.775791	-0.724295	0.686922	0.531029	0.767832
G	0.244650	0.084484	-0.085689	1.000000	0.183953	-0.269621	0.461428	-0.451641	-0.519267	-0.057490
IM	-0.480409	0.413563	-0.083666	0.183953	1.000000	0.092188	0.151470	-0.215029	-0.381218	0.008190
R	-0.208929	-0.414518	-0.775791	-0.269621	0.092188	1.000000	0.639799	-0.670855	-0.392501	-0.877965
RF	-0.055766	-0.181729	-0.724295	0.461428	0.151470	0.639799	1.000000	-0.834478	-0.664628	-0.821145
SP500	0.037226	0.255209	0.686922	-0.451641	-0.215029	-0.670855	-0.834478	1.000000	0.841299	0.865637
TRADEBA...	0.014026	-0.220207	0.531029	-0.519267	-0.381218	-0.392501	-0.664628	0.841299	1.000000	0.604803
VNINDEX	0.066297	0.414535	0.767832	-0.057490	0.008190	-0.877965	-0.821145	0.865637	0.604803	1.000000

(source : author calculation and stock exchange)

Fig. 19. SHB macro elements correlation.

As We Analyze from the Above Figures:

- Group 1: in both case VCB and CTG, correlation between beta and Rf is higher than that between beta and lending rate R (0.4 > 0.1 and 0.2 > 0.1, respectively)

Correlation Matrix										
	BETAACB	CPI	EXRATE	G	IM	R	RF	SP500	TRADEBA...	VNINDEX
BETAACB	1.000000	0.301399	0.012415	0.015720	0.399435	0.010349	0.040732	-0.040497	-0.163941	0.051257
CPI	0.301399	1.000000	0.355839	0.084484	0.413563	-0.414518	-0.181729	0.255209	-0.220207	0.414535
EXRATE	0.012415	0.355839	1.000000	-0.085689	-0.083666	-0.775791	-0.724295	0.686922	0.531029	0.767832
G	0.015720	0.084484	-0.085689	1.000000	0.183953	-0.269621	0.461428	-0.451641	-0.519267	-0.057490
IM	0.399435	0.413563	-0.083666	0.183953	1.000000	0.092188	0.151470	-0.215029	-0.381218	0.008190
R	0.010349	-0.414518	-0.775791	-0.269621	0.092188	1.000000	0.639799	-0.670855	-0.392501	-0.877965
RF	0.040732	-0.181729	-0.724295	0.461428	0.151470	0.639799	1.000000	-0.834478	-0.664628	-0.821145
SP500	-0.040497	0.255209	0.686922	-0.451641	-0.215029	-0.670855	-0.834478	1.000000	0.841299	0.865637
TRADEBA...	-0.163941	-0.220207	0.531029	-0.519267	-0.381218	-0.392501	-0.664628	0.841299	1.000000	0.604803
VNINDEX	0.051257	0.414535	0.767832	-0.057490	0.008190	-0.877965	-0.821145	0.865637	0.604803	1.000000

(source : author calculation and stock exchange)

Fig. 20. ACB macro elements correlation.

Correlation Matrix										
	BETANVB	EX_RATE	SP500	TRADEBA...	CPI	G	IM	R	RF	VNINDEX
BETANVB	1.000000	-0.495650	-0.168160	0.044034	0.198754	0.095546	0.356647	0.058524	0.226459	-0.191149
EX_RATE	-0.495650	1.000000	0.476195	-0.491811	-0.382440	0.519076	0.038528	0.006143	-0.772931	0.295409
SP500	-0.168160	0.476195	1.000000	-0.485719	-0.844053	0.136776	-0.613771	-0.664122	-0.652624	0.950618
TRADEBA...	0.044034	-0.491811	-0.485719	1.000000	0.156409	-0.107369	0.161388	0.553061	0.264192	-0.375438
CPI	0.198754	-0.382440	-0.844053	0.156409	1.000000	0.090566	0.500206	0.428665	0.580486	-0.861426
G	0.095546	0.519076	0.136776	-0.107369	0.090566	1.000000	0.440105	0.223263	-0.421402	-0.016434
IM	0.356647	0.038528	-0.613771	0.161388	0.500206	0.440105	1.000000	0.663798	0.117679	-0.664368
R	0.058524	0.006143	-0.664122	0.553061	0.428665	0.223263	0.663798	1.000000	-0.045403	-0.746263
RF	0.226459	-0.772931	-0.652624	0.264192	0.580486	-0.421402	0.117679	-0.045403	1.000000	-0.444136
VNINDEX	-0.191149	0.295409	0.950618	-0.375438	-0.861426	-0.016434	-0.664368	-0.746263	-0.444136	1.000000

(source : author calculation and stock exchange)

Fig. 21. NVB macro elements correlation.

Correlation Matrix										
	BETASTB	CPI	EX_RATE	G	IM	R	RF	SP500	TRADEBA...	VNINDEX
BETASTB	1.000000	-0.498235	-0.255636	-0.053913	0.106345	0.053196	-0.181280	0.206729	0.488269	0.295357
CPI	-0.498235	1.000000	-0.382440	0.090566	0.500206	0.428665	0.580486	-0.844053	0.156409	-0.861426
EX_RATE	-0.255636	-0.382440	1.000000	0.519076	0.038528	0.006143	-0.772931	0.476195	-0.491811	0.295409
G	-0.053913	0.090566	0.519076	1.000000	0.440105	0.223263	-0.421402	0.136776	-0.107369	-0.016434
IM	0.106345	0.500206	0.038528	0.440105	1.000000	0.663798	0.117679	-0.613771	0.161388	-0.664368
R	0.053196	0.428665	0.006143	0.223263	0.663798	1.000000	-0.045403	-0.664122	0.553061	-0.746263
RF	-0.181280	0.580486	-0.772931	-0.421402	0.117679	-0.045403	1.000000	-0.652624	0.264192	-0.444136
SP500	0.206729	-0.844053	0.476195	0.136776	-0.613771	-0.664122	-0.652624	1.000000	-0.485719	0.950618
TRADEBA...	0.488269	0.156409	-0.491811	-0.107369	0.161388	0.553061	0.264192	-0.485719	1.000000	-0.375438
VNINDEX	0.295357	-0.861426	0.295409	-0.016434	-0.664368	-0.746263	-0.444136	0.950618	-0.375438	1.000000

(source : author calculation and stock exchange)

Fig. 22. STB macro elements correlation.

Correlation Matrix										
	WEIGHTE...	CPI	EX_RATE	G	IM	R	RF	SP500	TRADEBA...	VNINDEX
WEIGHTE...	1.000000	-0.675692	0.242682	-0.033510	-0.022178	0.198671	-0.654256	0.380817	0.298337	0.329958
CPI	-0.675692	1.000000	-0.382440	0.090566	0.500206	0.428665	0.580486	-0.844053	0.156409	-0.861426
EX_RATE	0.242682	-0.382440	1.000000	0.519076	0.038528	0.006143	-0.772931	0.476195	-0.491811	0.295409
G	-0.033510	0.090566	0.519076	1.000000	0.440105	0.223263	-0.421402	0.136776	-0.107369	-0.016434
IM	-0.022178	0.500206	0.038528	0.440105	1.000000	0.663798	0.117679	-0.613771	0.161388	-0.664368
R	0.198671	0.428665	0.006143	0.223263	0.663798	1.000000	-0.045403	-0.664122	0.553061	-0.746263
RF	-0.654256	0.580486	-0.772931	-0.421402	0.117679	-0.045403	1.000000	-0.652624	0.264192	-0.444136
SP500	0.380817	-0.844053	0.476195	0.136776	-0.613771	-0.664122	-0.652624	1.000000	-0.485719	0.950618
TRADEBA...	0.298337	0.156409	-0.491811	-0.107369	0.161388	0.553061	0.264192	-0.485719	1.000000	-0.375438
VNINDEX	0.329958	-0.861426	0.295409	-0.016434	-0.664368	-0.746263	-0.444136	0.950618	-0.375438	1.000000

Fig. 23. Weighted Beta macro elements correlation. Source: author calculation and stock exchange

– Group 2: Correlation of macro factors is changing for each bank case. For instance: in case STB, correlation between trade balance and beta is higher than that between VNIndex and beta (0.4 > 0.2), or in case NVB, correlation between IM and beta is higher than that between lending rate and beta, or trade balance (0.3 0.05 > 0.04). (see figure and)

4.2 OLS Regression Results

Run OLS regression with Eviews gives below results (Tables 2, 3 and 4):

Table 2. Regression for bank group 1. Source: author calculation and stock exchange

Bank group 1 – Previous SOEs banks		
	Coefficient - VCB	Coefficient – CTG
Internal factors		
CPI	−3.1	−6.75
G	−46.2	0.6
IM (Industrial manufacturing)	0.006	0.01
R	9.93	10.3
Rf	−2.3	8.2
VNIndex	0.005	0.001
External factors		
Exchange rate	4.19E	0.0002
SP500	0.0013	0.0001
Trade balance	0.0009	0.0009
R-squared	0.53	0.74
SER	0.5	0.41
Akaike info criterion	1.74	1.28

Analysis:
2011–2015 is the historical and special period, from the global crisis time 2008–2009 until the year with low CPI of 0.6% in the country (Figs. 24, 25 and 26).

We can infer from the above chart 8 and 9 that weighted beta is lower than beta VCB and higher than beta CTG. And weighted beta in year 2015 is higher than those of joint stock banks (previously private banks).

5 Discussion

During Pre – L Inflation:
In groups of banks (SOEs previously) VCB and CTG we find out: GDP growth and Risk free rate (Rf) have higher impacts on beta CAPM, for internal factors. While for external factors, Exfchange rate and Sp500 have higher impacts on market risk.

Table 3. Regression for bank group 1. Source: author calculation and stock exchange

Bank group 2 – Previous private banks					
	Coefficient - ACB	Coefficient - NVB	Coefficient - SHB	Coefficient - STB	Coefficient - EIB
Internal factors					
CPI	−9.6	−1.2	−0.1	−3.1	1.27
G	9.2	1.5	−18.2	−13.4	29.5
IM (Industrial manufacturing)	0.008	0.01	0.008	0.009	0.02
R	2.3	−5.7	18.1	6.4	−14.5
Rf	5.8	5.04	10.03	4.8	53.7
VNIndex	−0.003	−0.0004	0.004	0.003	0.006
External factors					
Exchange rate	0.00016	−0.0004	6.21E	−9.75E	−0.0009
SP500	0.00017	4.45E	−0.0004	0.0007	−0.001
Trade balance	0.0008	−0.0003	0.0007	0.0005	−0.0004
R-squared	0.65	0.2	0.78	0.53	0.85
SER	0.44	0.96	0.4	0.45	0.95
Akaike info criterion	1.42	2.96	1.24	1.43	2.94

In groups of joint stock banks (5 private banks) we figure out: trade balance and SP500 have higher impacts on beta CAPM, for external factors. For internal factors, Rf, GDP growth and lending rate have higher impacts on market risk. Thts happen during post –L inflation stage.

Suggestions for a Better Management Information System:
Sanusi and Johl (2020) stated that Information System (IS) risk management implementation is a program that enables an organizations capture, manage and analyses the risks that are peculiar to IS adoption in a secure system. By implementing IS risk management organizations can improve operation efficiencies and save cost of risk investment. Meanwhile, bank is an institution that relies heavily on information technology for the network of business activities therefore; there is need to be aware of various risks associated with the usage of information system.

Pursuant to the provisions of Clause 4, Article 3 of Circular 13/2018/TT-NHNN, risk management is the identification, measurement, monitoring and control of risks in the operation of commercial banks and bank branches. Foreign goods.

Accordingly, for the internal control system of commercial banks, it is required by law to have internal regulations to ensure that the requirements in Clause 2, Article 5 of Circular 13/2018/TT-NHNN are met as follows:

Table 4. Regression for Weighted beta CAPM (total 7 banks). Source: author calculation and stock exchange

	Coefficient
Internal factors	
CPI	−8.4
G	−34.6
IM (Industrial manufacturing)	0.007
R	8.3
Rf	−11.7
VNIndex	−1.78E
External factors	
Exchange rate	0.0002
SP500	0.0012
Trade balance	0.0011
R-squared	0.82
SER	0.51
Akaike info criterion	1.69

No.2. Commercial banks and foreign bank branches must have internal regulations in compliance with the provisions of Article 93 of the Law on Credit Institutions, which must ensure the following requirements:

a) Conform to the provisions of this Circular and relevant laws;
b) Authority to issue:
   (i) For commercial banks: The Board of Directors and the Members' Council shall issue regulations on the organization, administration and operation of the commercial bank, except for matters falling within the competence of the General Meeting of Shareholders. East, owner; The Supervisory Board promulgates the internal regulations of the Supervisory Board; The General Director (Director) promulgates the regulations, processes and operating procedures (hereinafter referred to as internal processes);
   (ii) For foreign bank branches: The General Director (Director) shall issue the internal regulations of the foreign bank branch according to the regulations of the parent bank or use the internal regulations of the parent bank. Promulgate;
c) Satisfy the requirements and contents of control activities specified in Article 14, Clause 1 and 2, Article 15 of this Circular;

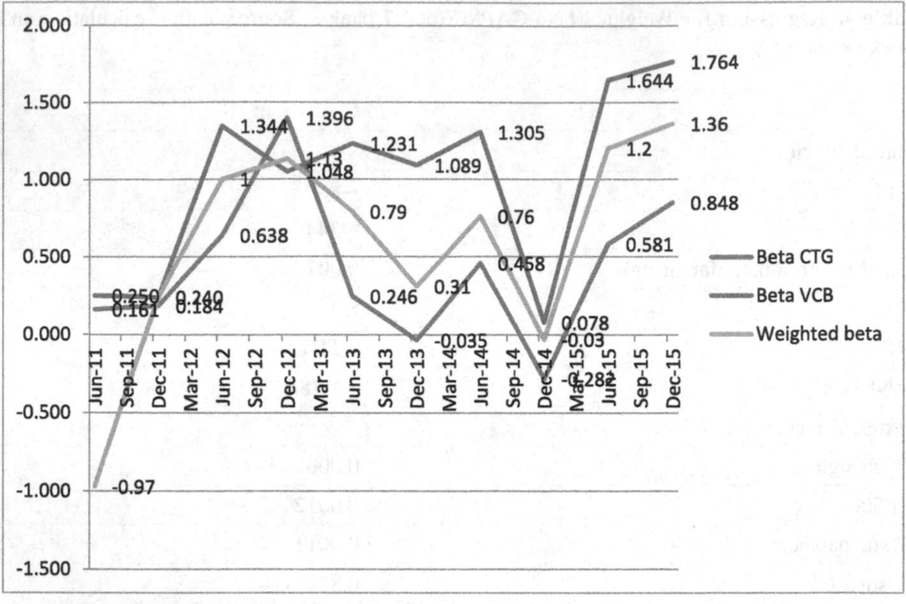

(source : author calculation and stock exchange)

Fig. 24. Group 1 SOE banks (previously) beta comparison.

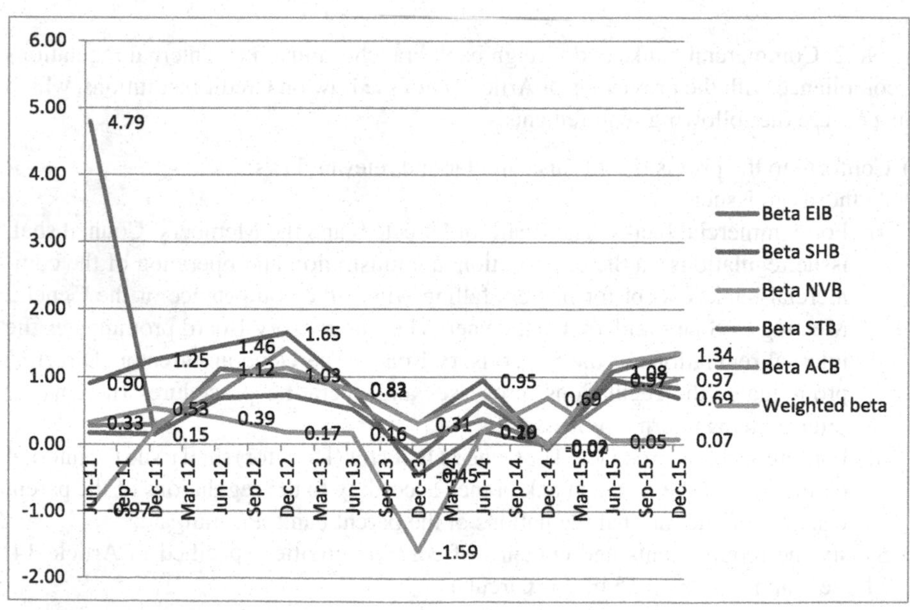

(source : author calculation and stock exchange)

Fig. 25. Group 2 private banks (previously) beta comparison.

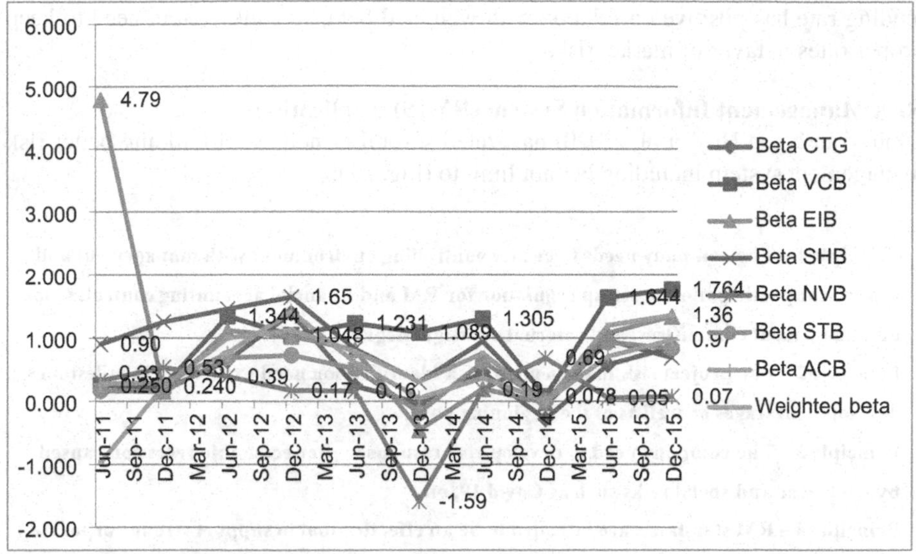

Fig. 26. Total 7 listed banks (previously) beta and weighted beta comparison. Source: author calculation and stock exchange

d) To be periodically evaluated according to the provisions of this Circular and regulations of commercial banks, foreign bank branches for suitability, compliance with the provisions of law and amendments and supplements (if necessary). Set).

In the internal regulations on the internal control system of this commercial bank, there must be internal regulations on risk management, including at least the contents specified in Clause 1, Article 23 of Circular 13/2018. /TT-NHNN the following:

- Developing, promulgating and implementing risk management policies;
- The formulation, issuance and implementation of risk limits for each type of material risk (including methods for establishing risk limits, individuals and departments implementing risk limit development, allocating risk limits and handling violations for cases of risk limit violations);
- Identify, measure, monitor and control risks for each type of material risk (including risk measurement and control methods and models);
- Endurance test;
- Internal reporting mechanism on risk management;
- Risk management for new products, operating in new markets;
- Other necessary contents as required by management for each type of material risk.

6 Conclusion

Because GDP growth, CPI and Risk free rate have negative correlation with weighted beta CAPM, a representative measure of bank market risk, Ministry of Finance, State bank of Vietnam and relevant agencies need to control GDP growth as well as rates of Treasury bonds toward benefits for managing risk (not increasing Rf too much). Also lending rate has positive correlation with weighted beta, so bank system need to keep proper rates in favor of market risk.

Risk Management Information System (RMIS) Implications

Dinh Tran Ngoc Huy et al. (2020) has stated several principles of building better risk management system including but not limit to (Fig. 27):

Principle 1 – The company needs to ensure controlling environment with management and supervisor participation to set up regulation for RM and financial accounting control, scope of management committees, and external oversight degree.

Principle 2 – For project risk management, risk identification need to be done in milestones development stages as well as at the beginning phase.

Principle 3 – The company need to develop risk responses after economic recession caused by trade war and social risks such as Covid 19, etc.

Principle 4 – RM standards are intended to be an effective tool to support strong corporate governance as well as Quality management system ISO 9001.

Principle 5 – The company ensures strong corporate governance structure because it has positive correlation with effective risk management system.

Principle 6 – RM reports need to be connected with good ERP system and effective management information system.

Principle 7 – The corporation understands it is important to build good infrastructure and information security to avoid and mitigate IT risks

Principle 8 – The internal control system should be coordinated with RM function to analyze risks both from internal and external environments.

Principle 9 – Corporation needs to use and apply good models such as PDCA or DMAIC or combination of SWOT and 7S into business operation, management and esp. Risk management functions.

Principle 10 – Corporate management pay attention to environmental and social risks for CSR and sustainable development

(source: Huy, D.T.N et al, 2020)

Fig. 27. Suggested Several Risk management principles for banks and companies.

If this research was done in other countries, we could use same research model for other countries and what we need to do is to recognize features of their economic cycle, their macro policies, strengths and weaknesses, then we could estimate beta CAPM for industires such as banking sector, etc….and recommend policies.

Limitation of Research

We can expand our research model for other industries and other markets. In future we can expand our model with more varibales such as public debt, market capitalization on stock exchange, etc… This will help to improve our model.

References

Arasu, B.S.: Information systems success in the context of internet banking: scale development. J. Internet Bank. Commer. **19**(3), 1–15 (2014)

Aghion, P., Angeletos, G.M., Banerjee, A., Manova, K.: Volatility and growth: credit constraints and the composition of investment. J. Monet. Econ. **57**(3), 246–265 (2010)

Burja, C.: Factors influencing the companies' profitability. Annales Universitatis Apulensis Series Oeconomica **13**(2), 215 (2011). https://doi.org/10.29302/oeconomica.2011.13.2.3

Huy, D.T.N.: The critical analysis of limited south Asian corporate governance standards after financial crisis. Int. J. Quality Res. **15**(1), 741 (2015)

Huy, D.T.N., Nhu, P.N.Q., Nga, T.T.T., Van Thanh, T.: Using new model approach for enhancing risk management mechanism in a case of Vietnam listed bank. Int. J. Ecosystems Ecology Sci. **12**(4) (2022)

Dat, P.M., Mau, N.D., Loan, B.T.T., Huy, D.T.N.: Comparative China corproate goevrnance standards after financial crisis, corporate scandals and manipulation. J. Security and Sustainability Issues **9**(3) (2020). https://doi.org/10.9770/jssi.2020.9.3(18)

Hang, D.T., Huyen, T.T.: Systematic risk status at Vietnam banks system and some recommendations. Journal of Banking Science & Training, No. 227 (2021)

Endri, E., Marlina, A., Hurriyaturroman: Impact of internal and external factors on the net interest margin of banks in Indonesia, Banks and Bank Syst. **15**(4), 99107 (2020). https://doi.org/10.21511/bbs.15(4).2020.09

Hang, T.T.B., Nhung, D.T.H., Nhung, D.H., Huy, D.T.N., Hung, N.M., Dat, P.M.: Where beta is going - case of Vietnam hotel, airlines and tourism company groups after the low inflation period. Entrepreneurship and Sustainability Issues **7**(3) (2020). https://doi.org/10.9770/jesi.2020.7.3(55)

Huy, D.T.N.: Estimating Beta of Viet Nam listed construction companies groups during the crisis. J. Integration and Dev. (2012)

Hac, L.D., et al.: Enhancing risk management culture for sustainable growth of Asia commercial bank -ACB in Vietnam under mixed effects of macro factors. Entrepreneurship and Sustainability Issues **8**(3) (2021)

Huy, D.T.N.: Beta of Viet Nam listed computer and electrical company groups during and after the financial crisis 2007–2011. Asian Journal of Finance & Accounting **5**(1) (2013)

Huy, D.T.N., Dat, P.M., và Anh, P.T.: Building and econometric model of selected factors' impact on stock price: a case study. J. Security and Sustainability Issues **9**(M), 77–93 (2020). https://doi.org/10.9770/jssi.2020.9.M(7)

Huy, D.T.N., Loan, B.T., Anh, P.T.: Impact of selected factors on stock price: a case study of Vietcombank in Vietnam. Entrepreneurship and Sustainability Issues **7**(4), 2715–2730 (2020). https://doi.org/10.9770/jesi.2020.7.4(10)

Huy, D.T.N., Hien, D.T.N.:The backbone of European corporate governance standards after financial crisis, corporate scandals and manipulation. Economic and Business Rev. **12**(4) (2010)

Huy D.T.N., Nhan V.K., Bich N.T.N., Hong N.T.P., Chung N.T., Huy P.Q.: Impacts of internal and external macroeconomic factors on firm stock price in an expansion econometric model—a case in Vietnam Real Estate Industry, Data Science for Financial Econometrics-Studies in Computational Intelligence, **898**, Springer (2021). http://doi-org-443.webvpn.fjmu.edu.cn/ https://doi.org/10.1007/978-3-030-48853-6_14

Hoang, N.T., et al.: Determining factors for educating students for choosing to work for foreign units: absence of self-efficacy. J. Teachers, Educators and Trainers **12**(2), 11–19 (2021). https://jett.labosfor.com/index.php/jett/article/view/531. Access 28 July 2021

Hong, T.V., et al.: Developing a smart library model in vietnam public library system. Revista Geintec-Gestao Inovacao e Tecnologias **11**(3), 1320–1329 (2021). https://www.google.com/search?q=Hong. Access 17 May 2021

Van Long, H., Cong, L.T., Huy, D.T.N.: Management implications with risk management from regression model approach - a case in Vietnam construction sector. International Journal of Ecosystems and Ecology Science **12**(4) (2022)

Que, H.X., Huy, D.T.N., Thang, T.D., Van Thanh, T., Van Long, H.: Estimating weighted bank beta index under macro effects in vietnam in industry 4.0 and roles of digital transformation for better risk management information system. International Journal of Ecosystems and Ecology Science **12**(4) (2022)

Huy, D.T.N., An, T.T.B., Anh, T.T.K., Nhung, P.T.H.: Banking sustainability for economic growth and socio-economic development – case in Vietnam. Turkish J. Comput. Mathematics Educ. **12**(2), 2544–2553 (2021)

Hang, N.T., Huy, D.T.N.: Better risk management of banks and sustainability-a case study in Vietnam. Revista geintec Inovacao E Tecnologias **11**(2) (2021)

Mahdi, M., Khaddafi, M.: The influence of gross profit margin, operating profit margin and net profit margin on the stock price of consumer good industry in the indonesia stock exchange on 2012–2014. International J. Business Economics and Social Dev. **1**(3) (2020). https://doi.org/10.46336/ijbesd.v1i3.53

Mishkin, F.: Comment on systemic risk. In: Kaufman, G., (ed.) Research in Financial Services: Banking, Financial Markets, and Systemic Risk, JAI Press, Greenwich, CT, **7**, 31–45 (1995)

Hang, N.T., et al.: Educating and training labor force Under Covid 19; Impacts to Meet Market Demand in Vietnam during Globalization and Integration Era. Journal for Educators, Teachers and Trainers **12**(1), 179–184 (2021)

Thach, N.N., et al.: Measuring the volatility of market risk of vietnam banking industry after the low inflation period 2015–2017. Review of Pacific Basin Financial Markets and Policies **23**(04) (2020)

Tram, P.N., Huy, D.T.N.: Educational, political and socio-economic development of Vietnam based on Ho Chi Minh's Ideology. Elementary education Online **20**(1) (2021)

Tangjitprom, N.: Macroeconomic factors of emerging stock market: the evidence from Thailand. International Journal of Financial Research (2012)

Ting, C.C.: Market value of the firm, market value of equity, return rate on capital and the optimal capital structure. International Journal of Financial Research (2012)

Vu, T.D.T., Huy, D.T.N., Trang, N.T.H., Thach, N.N.: Human education and educational issues for society and economy-case in emerging markets including Vietnam. Elementary education Online **20**(2) (2021)

Nam, V.Q., Tinh, D.T., Huy, D.T.N., Le, T.-H., Huong, L.T.T.: Internet of things (IoT), artificial intelligence (AI) applications for various sectors in emerging markets-and risk management information system (RMIS) issues. Design Engineering, Issue **6**, 609–618 (2021)

Wulandari, M., Abror, A.: The effect of production cost to net profit: a case study of PT. indorama synthetics TBK. Emerging Markets: Business And Management Studies Journal **4**(1) (2016). https://www.amazon.com/Management-Perspectives-Corporate-Governance-Economic/dp/1952046645

The Role of Digital Transformation in the Vietnamese Banking Sector

Khanh-Duy Pham(✉)

University of Economics Ho Chi Minh City (UEH), Ho Chi Minh City, Vietnam
duy.pham@ueh.edu.vn

Abstract. The fourth Industrial Revolution is based on digital technology. It integrates intelligent technologies related to physics and biology to optimize processes and production methods that can completely change the way people live and profoundly affect the economy and society of countries worldwide, including Vietnam. As a leading sector in the economy, the banking industry is one of the pioneers in applying Information and Communication Technology (ICT) to business activities. For that reason, banks have many opportunities and face significant challenges in this digital transformation trend in all aspects from state regulations, security, and privacy issues. Using ICT and its ability to increase the growth of the banking system is an issue that needs further study. This study employs a quantitative method to investigate the role of ICT on banks' stability in Vietnam, one of the fastest-growing digital transformations globally, from 2009 to 2020. The research results indicate that applying ICT to the bank's operations is necessary and helps increase the bank's operational stability. However, digital transformation in the banking and financial sectors involve enormous costs yet yield low profit in the short term.

Keywords: ICT · Digital Transformation · Information Technology · Bank Stability · Bank Performance

1 Introduction

The influence of globalization, fiercely competitive environment, and constant innovation in the banking industry and non-banking financial institutions on customers' consumption behavior is evident. Digital transformation opens up opportunities for banks to approach and serve a wide range of customers, promoting comprehensive financial development. Optimizing customer convenience is a measure of the effectiveness of this transformation, in which high technology is a decisive factor in helping banks detect customer needs and satisfy them quickly. Thereby achieving competitive advantages, reducing manual human resources, product distribution costs and improving profits. However, this digital transformation trend has not shown precise economic efficiency. At the same time, the level of investment capital in technology is very high, which causes significant obstacles in applying high technology to banks, increasing risks for the bank when not finding a proper direction. What are the highlights of the application

A. Mirzazadeh et al. (Eds.): SEMIT 2022, CCIS 1808, pp. 163–175, 2023.
https://doi.org/10.1007/978-3-031-40395-8_11

of ICT in banks in the last decade (2009–2020) and in general? What stage is the bank in this trend? How are the ICT Index and financial indicators correlated to the bank's performance? This study uses ICT Index to measure the current situation of IT development and application accurately and at the same time evaluate and rank the units that the Institute of Technology recognizes. In Viet Nam, for the banking industry, the ICT index is measured by four groups of indicators, including technical infrastructure, human infrastructure, application ICT, and organizational environment and policy. Assess the readiness of banks for IT development and application through ICT Index combined with financial factors including bank size, equity to total assets ratio, bad debt, and customer's deposit-to-loan ratio impact the bank's performance (D. K. Pham et al. 2021).

In order to promote the achieved results and accompany the national digital transformation work, on May 11, 2021, the Governor of the State Bank of Vietnam signed Decision No. 810/QD-NHNN promulgating the Plan to transform the banking sector to 2025, with orientation to 2030. Currently, the SBV has submitted to the government a proposal to develop a Decree on a Mechanism for Controlled Testing of Fintech (Fintech) activities in the banking sector. According to a survey by the State Bank of Vietnam's Strategy Institute, 96% of the surveyed banks are building development strategies based on 4.0 technologies, of which 92% are developing strategies and developing application services on the Internet and Mobile, 48% have an automation strategy, 16% have an IoT strategy. In addition, 100% of banks also plan to expand cooperation with Fintech companies to provide banking products and services related to the following areas: Payment (92%); digital banking services (76%); big data (68%); Blockchain technology (16%). Nevertheless, difficulties in digital transformation about the legal mechanism, shortage of high-quality personnel in specialized fields associated with banking and technology, ensuring network security, and fiercely competitive environment (H. C. Pham et al. 2021).

2 Literature Review

Sahut (2000) qualitative research on the impact of ICT on the French banking system has taken evidence of the current state of banks in France and compared with Europe to conclude that the NICT changes the basic structure of the banking system competition between banks, but also provides the possibility for nonbank financial institutions to compete with them. The advantage will go to those who understand the change potential associated with new technologies, and those who rely on a good understanding of the financial business will know how to implement these technologies to create a competitive advantage. A large number of studies (Alfredo Martin-Oliver, 2008; Costas Lapavitsas, 2008; Shu, 2005) have found that IT is beneficial in reducing the transaction costs of banks, improving service quality, optimizing business structure, and driving business transformation and upgrade. However, IT is stated can bring significant challenges to commercial banks (Dr. Christopher P. Holland, 1997). Other authors assessed the response of Nigerian banks to digital transformation trends and examined the extent to which they have adopted advanced technologies in their operations and the resulting efficiencies (Agboola, 2010). The three types of variables involved in the adoption and deployment of IT equipment used for the study are: Nature and extent of application of advanced technologies; Level of use of identified technologies; Impact of the application of IT equipment on bank operations (Le and Pham 2022).

From all indications, ICT presents enormous potential for business process restructuring of Nigerian banks. Investment in ICT should be a key component of bank executives' overall strategy to ensure operational efficiency. The bank's management must increase investment in ICT to facilitate fast, convenient, and accurate services, or else it will lose to its competitors. Muhammad et al. (2013), using annual bank data for the period 2001–2011, found that ICT in the banking industry in Nigeria increased return on equity. An inverse relationship was also found between the additional sustainable investment in ICT and the efficiency that the study recommends, along with a shift in focus towards policies that would promote efficient use of efficient and reasonable ICT equipment instead of additional investment. By researching primary data collected by questionnaires for bank staff and customers, secondary data was collected from the Rastra Bank Nepal website, ICT-related journals, banking articles, and other published sources. The author of the research paper "Role of Information Communication Technology (ICT) in Nepalese Banking Industry"[1] has affirmed the role of IT application in banking, saying that "ICT is central to banking", the author said thanks to In ICT, the bank satisfies customers based on their expectations, reduces operational costs and effectively manages the competition. Research by Chinonso.V. Agu (2020) used the data of 35 African banks for the period 2013–2015 of the GMM (generalized method of the time), showing that ICT has primarily influenced the operations of the country banks in the short term. In the long term, these investments turn out to be very profitable to improve the bank's performance.

In Vietnam, there are also many studies on bank performance. Research by Long (2019) on the operation of 20 Vietnamese banks in the period 2008–2017, using the regression method using FEM (firm estimate) shows that the size of the bank, the ratio of Cost-to-revenue, equity-to-total assets ratio, and deposit-to-debt ratio all have an impact on operating performance. Research by Jonathan A. Batten (2019) on 35 Vietnamese banks in the period 2006–2012 by FEM, REM methods show that the size, level of capital adequacy risk, productivity, and operating costs have a positive impact positive while the manager's ownership ratio negatively affects the bank's performance. Thuy (2021) conducted a study on the topic "ICT and Bank Performance: Empirical Evidence from Vietnam" to examine how readiness for IT development and application (ICT Index) affects operations bank action. The author said that investment in IT would fundamentally change the bank's business model and promote the bank to operate more efficiently. Vietnamese commercial banks tend to rapidly shift to retail banking and payment services on digital platforms. The bank's operation no longer depends mainly on the activities of the credit department.

[1] April 2018-American Scientific Research Journal for Engineering, Technology, and Sciences 42(1).

3 Research Methods

3.1 Research Models

To analyze the impact of the ICT application on bank performance, following Nguyen Van Thuy, the author builds a research model as follows:

$$Performance_{it} = \beta_0 + \beta_1 ICT_{it} + \beta_2 Size_{it} + \beta_3 ETA_{it} + \beta_4 DLR_{it} + \beta_5 LLP_{it} + \beta_6 GDP_{it} + \beta_7 INF_{it} + \varepsilon_{it} \quad (1)$$

In Eq. (1), the dependent variable is the performance of the bank shown through three indicators ROA (return on total assets), ROE (return on equity), and Zscore (an indicator of risk assessment or bank insolvency) (Table 1).

Table 1. Variable list, description, and prediction

Type variable	Name	Definition	Expected sign
Dependent variables	ROA	Profit after tax/total assets	
	ROE	Profit after tax/equity	
	Z-Score	(ROA + ETA)/ROA Standard Deviation	
Independent variables	ICT Index	Collected from the Ministry of Information and Communication	(+)
	Size	On the log value of a bank's total assets	(+)
	ETA	Equity/total assets	(–)
	DLR	Customer's deposits/loans	(+)
	LLP	Provision of loss loans/total loans	(–)
Macroeconomic variables	GDP	Collected from Government reports	(+)
	INF		(–)

3.2 Data

Research data is collected from the annual financial statements of 39 commercial banks, State-owned banks operating in the 2009–2020 period. ICT Index is taken from the Ministry of Information and Communication data for commercial banks at the same period. Thus, this research has 203 observations, synthesized, processed, and designed using STATA 15 software. Descriptions of the data are shown in Table 2.

4 Empirical Analysis

Observing the matrix of correlation coefficients between variables, the ICT Index variable has a strong positive correlation with ROA and ROE, showing the significant influence of ICT investment on banks' efficiency and operations. The independent variables

Table 2. Descriptive statistics table of variables

Variable	Obs	Mean	Std. Dev	Min	Max
ROA	203	0.0065282	0.001334	0.00319	0.00965
ROE	203	0.0772109	0.02355	0.0353286	0.2104348
Z-Score	203	18.07235	12.25461	4.095624	95.99393
ICTIndex	203	0.6294008	0.0647954	0.3728	0.8114
Size	203	19.00689	1.139808	16.20776	21.17315
ETA	203	0.0814434	0.0333803	0.0262139	0.2553888
DLR	203	1.144274	0.2003171	0.7185942	1.73678
LLP	203	0.0134893	0.005399	0.005125	0.0397882
GDP	203	0.0219522	0.0127827	0.0025	0.0354
INF	203	0.0599453	0.0129618	0.0291	0.0708

Table 3. Correlation matrix of variables

	ROA	ROE	ZScore	ICTIndex	SIZE	ETA	DLR	LLP	GDP	INF
ROA	1.0000									
ROE	0.7532	1.0000								
ZScore	−0.0544	−0.0230	1.0000							
ICTIndex	0.4096	0.6181	−0.0029	1.0000						
SIZE	0.4599	0.5035	−0.1046	0.6989	1.0000					
ETA	−0.2435	−0.3085	0.2970	−0.3731	−0.5778	1.0000				
DLR	0.0801	−0.0988	0.2416	−0.2033	−0.1363	−0.0303	1.0000			
LLP	0.0207	0.0793	0.0806	0.2242	0.3230	−0.1896	0.1049	1.0000		
GDP	0.1298	0.0413	−0.1023	−0.0215	0.1163	−0.2200	−0.1559	−0.2137	1.0000	
INF	−0.1946	−0.1564	−0.0104	−0.0571	−0.0723	−0.0540	0.0085	−0.0388	0.0337	1.0000

have a relatively low correlation with each other, so we can predict that there is no multicollinearity in the regression model (Table 3 and 4).

Test for multicollinearity: The result is VIF $<$ 3. Therefore, the variables in the model do not have multicollinearity.

The study continues to perform a regression analysis to measure the trend and impact of the independent variables on the dependent variable with Pooled OLS pooled least-squares methods, fixed effects models FEM, and the REM random-effects model. The regression results of the Pooled OLS method are as follows (Table 5).

Observing this result, we can see that the variable ICT Index is statistically significant with all 3 models, 1% level in model 1 and 2 (p-value $<$ 0.01), 5% level in model 3 (p-value $<$ 0.05). In model 1 with the dependent variable ROA, most of the independent variables are statistically significant except the ETA variable.

Next, the regression results according to the FEM method (Table 6).

Table 4. Multicollinearity test

Variable	VIF	1/VIF
ICTIndex	2.74	0.365458
SIZE	2.06	0.484893
ETA	1.62	0.615889
DLR	1.22	0.816740
LLP	1.19	0.840061
GDP	1.12	0.894474
INF	1.02	0.980275
Mean VIF	1.57	

Table 5. Pooled least-squares method

	(1)	(2)	(3)
	ROA	ROE	Z-Score
ICTIndex	0.005***	0.194***	35.204**
	(0.002)	(0.029)	(17.472)
SIZE	0.000***	0.003	0.064
	(0.000)	(0.002)	(1.144)
ETA	0.002	−0.042	150.854***
	(0.003)	(0.049)	(30.093)
DLR	0.001***	0.004	17.812***
	(0.000)	(0.007)	(4.161)
LLP	−0.037**	−0.421	220.973
	(0.016)	(0.264)	(161.568)
GDP	0.012*	0.028	54.576
	(0.007)	(0.110)	(67.287)
INF	−0.017***	−0.227**	20.989
	(0.006)	(0.100)	(61.428)
_cons	−0.006***	−0.076**	−43.408**
	(0.002)	(0.034)	(20.787)
N	203	203	203
adj. R^2	0.294	0.397	0.164
BIC	−2147.647	−1014.272	1591.450

(*continued*)

Table 5. (*continued*)

	(1)	(2)	(3)
	ROA	ROE	Z-Score
Rss	0.000	0.065	24479.638

Standard errors in parentheses
$* p < 0.10$, $** p < 0.05$, $*** p < 0.01$

Table 6. Fixed Effects Modeling Method

	(1)	(2)	(3)
	ROA	ROE	Z-Score
ICTIndex	0.010***	0.160***	−2.792
	(0.002)	(0.019)	(4.024)
SIZE	0.002***	0.017***	−0.656
	(0.000)	(0.004)	(1.075)
ETA	−0.000	−0.004	167.469***
	(0.004)	(0.047)	(34.016)
DLR	0.002**	0.026**	−3.576*
	(0.001)	(0.010)	(1.874)
LLP	−0.008	−0.219	−62.049
	(0.023)	(0.234)	(48.787)
GDP	−0.011	−0.082	−3.646
	(0.012)	(0.143)	(36.195)
INF	−0.010**	−0.160**	1.262
	(0.005)	(0.061)	(19.414)
_cons	−0.032***	−0.362***	23.602
	(0.006)	(0.077)	(20.351)
N	203	203	203
adj. R^2	0.548	0.544	0.593
BIC	−2309.062	−1277.638	1089.600
Rss	0.000	0.018	2120.914

Standard errors in parentheses
$* p < 0.10$, $** p < 0.05$, $*** p < 0.01$

Like the OLS Synthesis method, the ICT Index variable has statistical significance in models 1 and 2. However, in model 3, it has no statistical significance and impact of ICT Index for Z-score the opposite indicates that more investment in technology increases the risk of bankruptcy. This result is not consistent with the expected hypothesis of the author.

Finally, the regression results according to the REM method (Table 7).

Table 7. Random Effects Modeling Method

	(1)	(2)	(3)
	ROA	ROE	Z-Score
ICTIndex	0.008***	0.167***	−2.795
	(0.001)	(0.033)	(3.825)
SIZE	0.001***	0.010***	−0.201
	(0.000)	(0.002)	(0.931)
ETA	−0.001	−0.023	168.592***
	(0.006)	(0.048)	(33.850)
DLR	0.002***	0.024***	−2.854
	(0.001)	(0.009)	(1.999)
LLP	−0.037	−0.380	−39.829
	(0.025)	(0.269)	(51.895)
GDP	0.014	0.066	−11.978
	(0.010)	(0.125)	(31.321)
INF	−0.016***	−0.196***	3.844
	(0.004)	(0.055)	(18.574)
_cons	−0.010**	−0.228***	13.709
	(0.004)	(0.060)	(16.705)
N	203	203	203

Standard errors in parentheses
* $p < 0.10$, ** $p < 0.05$, *** $p < 0.01$

With REM, the ICT Index variable is also strongly statistically significant, has a positive effect on ROA and ROE, and is not statistically significant for Z-Score. The variables SIZE, DLR, and INF have strong statistical significance in models 1 and 2. In model 3, only the variable ETA is statistically significant (significant 1% level) and has the same effect dimension with Z-Score.

According to FEM regression results, F-test results of 3 models: Prob > F =

0.0000 < α (α = 1%): Hypothesis H0 is rejected: FEM will be more suitable than Pooled OLS.

Next, perform the Hausman test for three models to get the following results (Table 8):

Hypothesis H0 is accepted: REM will be more suitable than FEM.

After finding a suitable method as REM, the author checks the model's defects, such as variable variance and autocorrelation (Table 9).

Table 8. Hausman test results

Ho: difference in coefficients not systematic					
Model (1): ROA		Model (2): ROE		Model (3): Z-Score	
Chi2 (11)	11.26	Chi2 (7)	7.32	Chi2 (13)	15.59
Prob > chi2	0.4568	Prob > chi2	0.3962	Prob > chi2	0.5415

Table 9. Results of LM – Breusch and pagan Lagrangian Multiplier Test

Model (1): ROA		Model (2): ROE		Model (3): Z-Score	
chibar2(01)	69.90	chibar2(01)	422.68	chibar2(01)	317.44
Prob > chibar2	0.0000	Prob > chibar2	0.0000	Prob > chibar2	0.0000

Hypothesis H0 was rejected. All three models have variable variance phenomena (Table 10).

Table 10. Wooldridge test results for autocorrelation in panel data

H0: no first-order autocorrelation					
Model (1): ROA		Model (2): ROE		Model (3): Z-Score	
F (1,25)	0.751	F (1,25)	1.028	F (1,25)	23.393
Prob > F	0.3944	Prob > F	0.3204	Prob > F	0.4135

In all three models: Hypothesis H0 is accepted (p-value > 5%), there is no autocorrelation in all three models.

Since model 3 has no defects, it is only necessary to fix models 1 and 2. After fixing the above two models together with model 3 are as follows (Table 11).

According to the results of REM regression after fixing the defects of the three models as follows:

Firstly, the regression coefficient of the variable ICT Index with two models 1 and 2 is 0.005 and 0.104, respectively, with 99% confidence, showing that readiness for IT development and application has a positive impact on the performance of banks. But the impact of the ICT Index variable on Z-Score is not consistent with the author's expectation, increasing the application of IT in operations increases the risk of bank bankruptcy.

Second, the regression coefficient of the SIZE variable with two models (1 and 2) is 0.001 and 0.005, respectively, with 99% confidence, showing that bank size has a positive impact on bank performance. This result is consistent with the research expectations of ("The Determinants of Banking Performance in Front of Financial Changes: Case of Trade Banks in Tunisia," 2015) but contrary to the results of (Thuy 2021). In model 3,

Table 11. Results of regression analysis of the models after fixing

	(1)	(2)	(3)
	ROA	ROE	ZScore
ICTIndex	0.005***	0.104***	−2.754
	(0.001)	(0.034)	(10.085)
SIZE	0.001***	0.005***	−0.216
	(0.000)	(0.001)	(1.022)
ETA	0.006**	−0.010	168.593***
	(0.002)	(0.029)	(13.273)
DLR	0.002***	0.012***	−2.927
	(0.000)	(0.004)	(2.066)
LLP	−0.044***	−0.494***	−40.566
	(0.013)	(0.183)	(77.072)
GDP	0.014***	0.057	−11.417
	(0.005)	(0.071)	(32.554)
INF	−0.012***	−0.178***	4.015
	(0.004)	(0.055)	(20.382)
_cons	−0.010***	−0.088***	14.049
	(0.002)	(0.020)	(18.337)
N	203	203	203

Standard errors in parentheses
* $p < 0.10$, ** $p < 0.05$, *** $p < 0.01$

the variable SIZE harms the Z-Score, indicating that the larger the bank, the higher the probability of bankruptcy. This does not match the author's expectations. However, in Viet Nam, the number of banks' bad debts is increasing. On a large scale, if credit risk management is not adequate, it will cause the bank to lose money and not regulate the cash flow.

Third, the variable ETA is only statistically significant at 5% for model 1. A regression coefficient of 0.006 shows that capital structure (the ratio of equity to total assets) has a positive impact on the ROA of banks. When equity is high, the bank will be proactive in all activities, which will increase operational efficiency. This result is consistent with the expectations of (Rahman 2015). In model 3, the ETA variable positively affects the Z-Score variable with a regression coefficient of 168,593 with a confidence level of up to 99%, showing that this effect is powerful. The result is consistent with capital structure theory. The higher the equity to total assets ratio, the lower the risk of using debt, leading to a lower risk of bankruptcy.

Fourthly, in models 1 and 2, the regression coefficients of the DLR variable are 0.002 and 0.012, respectively, along with the 99% confidence level, showing that the ratio of capital mobilization to total credit balance has a positive impact on the efficiency of banking operations. When the bank has abundant customer deposits, it will open an investment channel that brings high profits. Although the operation of commercial banks has now seen a significant shift from credit to technology-based payment services, in Vietnam, this trend is still in the early stages and not completely strong. However, in model 3, the high ratio of customer deposits to credit balance increases the risk of bank failure (regression coefficient is −2.927), which is inconsistent with the author's prediction. However, the banks will face high risk if they use customers' deposits to invest in non-interest activities such as securities or foreign exchange.

5 Conclusion

The research results are consistent with all previous studies that applying technology to the bank's operations is necessary and helps increase the bank's operational efficiency. Because of the legal mechanism and the health of the Vietnamese economy, the banking system and credit institutions are bound to the government, contributing to minimizing the number of banks going bankrupt. Therefore, it helps reduce some of the burdens in effectively managing the bank's operations. Research shows that although digital transformation in banking requires huge costs and these investments are not profitable in the short term, there have been specific achievements. This success is since banks have had a particular digital product - positioned themselves in the new competitive environment and have had a few banks switch to flexible, modular, enabling infrastructure platforms new technology synchronization. When a bank has mastered the application of technology, it will earn significant profits and profoundly change its organizational structure, thereby expanding its market share and developing stronger.

Recommendations to the Vietnamese commercial banking system in the application of ICT:

Regarding the legal mechanism, there is no regulation on standards for data connection and sharing between banks and no common standards and guidelines for other organizations to follow uniformly set and efficient.

The national database system on citizen identification is incomplete, and there is no mechanism for banks to compare and verify customers online (e-KYC). Therefore, the SBV needs to issue specific and detailed guiding laws suitable to our country's economic health, creating opportunities for Vietnamese banks to approach and develop ICT comprehensively. In parallel with the development of modern technology, network security also exists many gaps. Nowadays, in the world, even developed countries with the most advanced technology have not found a perfect solution to ensure network safety and security. Therefore, the Vietnamese banking system needs to make efforts to update advanced security software suitable for the infrastructure and at the same time regularly warn customers about acts of impersonating a bank appropriating customers' assets. Its human resources are also an essential factor to support the bank's internal network security and IT development. IT department staff is the core in the investment process for IT, it is necessary to open training courses to improve expertise, ability to operate technology and handle problems. At the same time, sales staff also need attention and support, the bank's products and services when IT applications will become diverse and complex for customers. Therefore, employees need to understand products, electronic documents, and operating procedures to support customers promptly and give them a sense of security. Banks must focus on investing in IT infrastructure with their potential. A regular increase in total assets will help the bank strengthen its capacity, create a strong potential for IT development, modernize banking operations, cut costs, and help bank profits grow day by day. In developing the digital economy, payment intermediaries are banks and Fintech companies, and telecommunications, electronics, and IT firms. Therefore, the cooperation between the banking system and Fintech companies will bring high efficiency to the parties. This enriches products and services that are safe and convenient for users and solves the problem of overinvestment in the technology of the banking system. Social networks such as Facebook, Instagram, Zalo are platforms with high traffic volume and indirect access to a wide range of customers at low cost. Therefore, banks should strengthen propaganda through these platforms, encouraging customers to access more electronic products and services of the bank (Vu Le and Pham, 2022).

Acknowledgment. This paper was presented at International Conference on Science, Engineering Management and Information Technology 2022, and benefited from conference participants and discussants. We appreciate the constructive comments and valuable suggestions from the anonymous referees. Special thanks to Le Vu Linh Toan for excellent research assistance. Any remaining errors or shortcomings are the authors' responsibility. Financial supports from University of Economics Ho Chi Minh City (UEH) are acknowledged to conduct this research.

References

Agboola, A.: Information and Communication Technology (ICT) in Banking Operations: An Evaluation of Recent Experiences in Nigeria. LAP LAMBERT Academic Publishing (October 19, 2010) (2010)

Alfredo Martin-Oliver, V.S.-F.: The output and profit contribution of information technology and advertising investments in banks. J. Financial Intermediation **17**(2), 229–255 (2008)

Agu, C., Aguegboh, E.: ICT and Bank Performance in Sub-Saharan Africa: A Dynamic Panel Analysis. Retrieved from MPRA (2020)

Costas Lapavitsas, P.L.: Globalization and contemporary banking: on the impact of new technology. Contributions to Political Economy **27**(1), 31–56 (2008)

Christopher, P., Holland, P.A.: The impact of globalisation and information technology on the strategy andprofitability of the banking industry. In: Proceedings of the Thirtieth Hawaii International Conference, **3** (1997)

Batten, J.A., Vo, X.: Determinants of bank profitability—evidence from Vietnam. Emerging Markets Finance and Trade, **55**(1), 112 (2019)

Long, V.M.: Nhân tố ảnh hưởng đến hiệu quả hoạt động của các ngân hàng thương mại cổ phần. *Tạp chí Tài chính kỳ 2 tháng 5/2019* (2019)

Nouaili, M.A., Abaoub, E., Anis, O.: The determinants of banking performance in front of financial changes: case of trade banks in Tunisia. Int. J. Economics and Financial Issues **5**(2), 410417 (2015)

Muhammad, A., Gatawa, D.N., Birnin, H.S.: Impact of information and communication technology on bank performance: a study of selected commercial banks in Nigeria (2001–2011). European Scientific Journal (2013)

Rahman, H.: Determinants of bank profitability: empirical evidence from. Int. J. Business Manage. **10**(8) (2015)
Sahut, J.-M.: The impact of ICT and the internet in banking. Les Cahiers du Numérique, 3 (2000)
Shu, W.: Does information technology provide banks with profit? Information and Management, 781–787 (2005)
Thuy, N.V.: ICT and bank performance: empirical evidence from Vietnam. J. Contemporary Issues in Business and Government, **27**(2) (2021)

The Digital Roles of Technology Management Applications in Digital Economy

Esra Sipahi Döngül[1(✉)], Dinh Tran Ngoc Huy[2], Tran Duc Thang[3], and Le Ngoc Nuong[4]

[1] Faculty of Health Sciences, Department of Social Work, Aksaray University, Aksaray, Turkey
[2] Banking University HCMC, Vietnam - International University of Japan, Ho Chi Minh City, Japan
[3] National Economics University, Hanoi, Vietnam
[4] Thai Nguyen University of Economics and Business Administration, Thai Nguyen, Vietnam

Abstract. The development that has emerged with the spread of technology in production life has reached a point where companies will increase their ability to analyze by increasing their speed significantly. This newly formed ecosystem creates a performance system based on dynamic processes and continuous increase with a highly dynamic technology. Cloud systems computer technologies, systems that control processes within the supply chain such as ERP and SAP, vehicles used in the production process and logistics process and that can be managed online, driverless vehicle technologies, unmanned deliveries, wearable technologies, nano technologies, use of robots in production processes have taken their place in our lives as technologies that have developed at an incredible rate in the last 10–15 years and no longer surprise us. In this article, the advantages of Industry 4.0 are mentioned in the literature industry 4.0 and the studies related to supply chain management are discussed and risk management processes are explained by emphasizing the general structure of the digital supply chain that makes supply chain activities efficient.

Keywords: industry 4.0 · risk management · the digital supply chain

1 Introduction

Today, internet use has become the backbone of commercial life. With this transformation, new business understanding, and business values also take place in our lives.

The concept of Industry 4.0, which was mentioned for the first time at the Hannover fair in 2011, was included in the "Recommendations for the Implementation of the Industry 4.0 Strategic Initiative" report, which introduced this concept in 2013 and outlined strategies that will be needed in the future (Kagermann, Wahlster ve Helbig, 2013).

The concept of industry 4.0, mentioned at the World Economic Forum in Davos in 2016, has become heard in many countries as well as the United States and Korea.

A. Mirzazadeh et al. (Eds.): SEMIT 2022, CCIS 1808, pp. 176–189, 2023.
https://doi.org/10.1007/978-3-031-40395-8_12

Industry 4.0 is, in the most general words, the integration of innovative information and communication technology with industrial activities. The main objective here is to make sure that we're not going to provide more effective organizational processes by integrating the processes and products in the value chain with the smart network system, which will allow the creation of different, new products and services to meet customer expectations (Barreto et al. 2017:1246).

Thanks to technological advances such as artificial intelligence, 3D printers, space, robotics, bio, nano technologies, each object interacts with other objects over the Internet and is constantly renewed and thus smarted by this interaction in Industry 4.0 (Aksoy 2017:37), the main goal is the implementation of smart factories with self-managed production processes. (Wan and Zhou, 2015:136).

According to the World Bank report published in October 2016, G-20 member Turkey is the 17th largest economy in the world and the 7th largest in Europe. 800 billion GDP (gross domestic product) exceeds 800 billion USD. Between 2000 and 2014, per capita income in Turkey almost tripled and exceeded USD 9,000 according to the October 2016 report. Turkey is a member of the Organisation for Economic Co-operation and Development (OECD) and the G20 and has become an increasingly important donor of Official Development Assistance (ODA). Turkey Logistics Sector has a share of approximately 13% in GDP. The monetary equivalent is over $100 billion. At the end of 2016, Turkey's exports decreased by 0.84% compared to the previous year and amounted to 142 billion 610 million dollars, according to the joint data of the Ministry of Customs and TURKSTAT. Imports decreased by 4.17% compared to the previous year to 198 billion 577 million dollars.

According to the 2016 report, which consists of statistics of the answers of over 1,000 professionals prepared by the World Bank and reveals our inadequacies in logistics, Turkey has fallen from 30th to 34th place in the logistics index. Germany again ranked first in the rankings. Turkey's average score in the logistics performance index for 2016 was 3.42 points, with customs with the lowest score of 3.18, while the highest score was 3.75. Turkey ranked 31st in the quality of trade and transportation infrastructure from the report criteria, while industry ranked 43rd in the field of tracking and traceability of shipments, which reflects 4.0 in the field of logistics. It scored 3.39 in the field of tracking and traceability of shipments as a score While the logistics sector experienced them in economic life in Turkey, industry 4.0 developments in the world began to affect life.

The logistics industry has made technology part of its business. Industry, information technology for a long time, Radio Frequency Identification Systems (RFID), Warehouse Management Systems (WMS), Transport Management Systems (TMS), Enterprise Resource Planning (ERP), Container Management Unit (CMC), Container Management Systems (CMS), vehicle tracking systems, geographic information systems, Advanced Planning Systems (APS) have been using such systems for a long time. The platforms that integrate them and analyze the information from this program have also become a part of our lives. However, it is a great task for the owners and employees of the company to move these integrations forward with business projects and to make the bridge between manufacturers and consumers easier to use. The way to make this change successful is through collaborations.

The fact that the vehicle, which sold for $20,000 after its first discovery at the end of the 19th Century, fell to $850 and then to $360 after its initial discovery can be seen as an indication of the extent to which consumption increased with the commissioning of the assembly line. This mass production has been the driving force of the industrial revolution in the UNITED States. When examining the 2nd Industrial Revolution, it is necessary to mention the studies to increase industrial efficiency, which was called Taylorism and theorized by Frederick Winslow Taylor. Taylor has formed the basis of business management through his work. One of the most prominent features of this period is the widespread use of road transportation, especially due to developments in the automotive sector. Today's world giants, such as UPS, which was founded during this period, are good examples for the logistics sector.

In this article, the advantages of Industry 4.0 are mentioned in the literature industry 4.0 and the studies related to supply chain management are discussed and risk management processes are explained by emphasizing the general structure of the digital supply chain that makes supply chain activities efficient.

2 Methodology

In order to achieve the set objectives, the following contents will be researched and implemented, in which will focus on some main contents, authors also analyze relevant previous studies. Specifically: - Researching and synthesizing techniques for feature extraction and recognition applied to the collected data set. Several techniques for feature extraction or filtering and data smoothing can be used to optimize the analyzing. Authors also use experience and perform literature review to analyze related studies and get theories relating to studies.

3 Literature

After the first industrial revolution, which was produced with steam power machines, which was the first of the industrial revolutions in the industry, the second industrial revolution was started, which was mass produced with electric power. Then the third industrial revolution was started, in which production was further automated by the use of information technologies and electronics.

In 2011, Industry 4.0, the fourth industrial revolution, first appeared in Germany (Aksoy 2017). Industry 4.0 is based on the Internet of Things, cyber-physical systems and the internet of services. In short, the Internet of Things (IoT) is based on the ability of objects to communicate with other objects over the Internet and to be controlled over the Internet.

Some advantages of Industry 4.0 over other industrial revolutions include; it is especially important to reduce costs, increase the flexibility of production, gain self-awareness of objects and systems and facilitate the observation and control of the system, achieving high efficiency.

Decision-making problems are frequently encountered wherever there is a person. The decision-making process is the process of selecting the ones that best suit the purposes or objectives among all existing alternatives (Evren & Ülengin, 1992b). These decision-making problems can be personal, company and environmental. Apart from the fact that the decisions of the organizations are suitable only for one person, there should be decisions that can be seen as appropriate by everyone for the purposes of the enterprise. Being intuitive when making these decisions can lead to the wrong decision-making.

Scientific solution methods are preferred for a decision taken for the specified purposes. When we look at the studies on Industry 4.0 and supply chain management in the literature, it is often seen that the integration process is analyzed observationally. Yan and Huang (2009), Atzori et al. (2010), Miorandi et al. (2012), Gubbi et al. (2013) focused on what an internet-of-things supply chain should look like.

For this purpose, they went to applications such as testing new technologies and conducting surveys. Mukhopadhyay and Suryadevara (2014) talked about the advantages of the Internet of Things and the difficulties experienced in the process of adoption. By drawing attention to the potential technological benefits on enterprises, they mentioned important points that will contribute to the development of enterprises.

Hofmann and Rüsch (2017), Bär et al. (2018) studies have examined the internal activities of small and medium-sized enterprises integrated with Industry 4.0. By examining IOT usage, they aim to develop strategies for supply chain management between businesses and Industry 4.0.

Yildiz et al. (2018), Toker (2018) explained the evolution of Industry 4.0, talked about their paradigms and examined the Industry 4.0-based digital supply chain. They also talked about the overall structure of the digital supply chain, which makes supply chain activities efficient.

Industry 4.0 refers to a way of working in the supply chain in which the processes will be connected to a common network and all processes will be integrated together. The concept of Industry 4.0, announced in Germany in 2011, was seen as an important factor in making Germany a manufacturing center. Born in Germany, this concept emphasizes the place of information technologies in production and aims to make production completely based on automation.

Trung-Hieu Le, Nguyen Thuy Dung, Dinh Tran Ngoc Huy, Nguyen Thi Phuong Thanh, Dinh Tran Ngoc Hien, Nguyen Thi Hang (2021) mentioned solutions such as: applications for smart house and solutions for office building with IoTs uses such as warning system and cameras, as well as initial principles to set up IoT design.

Beside, Nguyen Dinh Trung, Dinh Tran Ngoc Huy, Trung Hieu Le, Dao Thi Huong, Nguyen Thi Hoa (2021) showed. Internet of things and AI also affect smart ways of connection between educators and learners via internet and discussion forum for case solving. Moreover, the beneficial impact on quality of teaching can be derived from such technology applications as those application helping us to identify human or learners activities via accelerometer and wearable sensor.

The main features of Industry 4.0 are horizontal integration created through the supply chain, end-to-end engineered digital integration, vertical integration and network production systems throughout the supply chain. All this is connected using cyber physical systems and perfected with virtual reality and then adapted to the service of users. All these integrations combine to create the internet of things. In this context, it is possible to say that the Internet of Things consists of connecting smart devices and generating value.

4 Problems Likely to Occur in Industry 4.0

Since Industry 4.0 is based on autonomous communication between devices in the value chain, large amounts of data are generated and monitored interconnectedly in a more automated way. In this context, cyber-physical systems and the Internet of Things will form the backbone of the smart factory. Therefore, a cyberattack will quickly spread to units that are the nervous system of smart companies and will be effective not only in part of the company, but in all areas of the company. Therefore, the workability of Industry 4.0 depends on how robust the safety standards are.

Dinh Tran Ngoc Huy, Nguyen Thi Phuong Thanh, Trung-Hieu Le, Nguyen Thuy Dung, Hoang Van Thuc, Sylwia Gwoździewicz, Esrasipahi. (2021) pointed ICT and AI and IoTs application will affect considerably on electrical engineering sector and electric industry. For instance, AI and robots can contribute to enhance productivity while IoTs can help to record and resolve Big Data for these industries together with data protection and security solutions.

While the robustness of data security standards is critical, it's also important to simplify and simplify them. Data security is not just a technological challenge. At the same time, people play an important role in data security. The way to prevent this is through education and awareness raising. The virus is produced on the Internet every two seconds.

Hundreds of malicious software are released into the system on a daily basis. According to December 2015 data, there are currently 350 million computer viruses. These viruses are intended for attack involving information theft. A third of these attacks are carried out on businesses employing up to 250 people.

For example, the damage of virus attacks to the German economy amounts to 50 billion euros. It is also stated that data theft costs an average of 3 million euros per business *(*http://www.dw.com/tr/dijital-devrimin-d%C3%BC%C5%9Fman%C4%B1-sibersald%C4%B1r%C4%B1lar*/a-18322334)*.

Turkey ranks in the top 10 for countries that have been cyber-attacked. In the third quarter of 2015, users were found to have downloaded harmful and highly dangerous mobile apps to their phones 160,717 times. 2,681 viruses were discovered in these applications downloaded by TrendLabs. However, TrendLabs says that in the future, the internet of things will be safer. For this, he develops the premise that you will not be able to sell the unsafe product *(*http://blog.trendmicro.com/*)*.

According to Trend Micro, the number of mobile malware is projected to increase to 20 million by the end of 2016. In the first 3 months of the year, 450 million viruses developed for android-based phones were detected worldwide.

As devices become more connected through the Internet of Things, security and privacy have become the primary concern between consumers and businesses. Cyberattacks are a growing threat as more devices connect around the world. Hackers can damage systems, critical infrastructure, and even people's homes. As a result, many technology companies are working on cybersecurity to ensure the privacy and security of this information.

In 2016, 67.8% of people who responded to a Vormetric survey of cyberattacks and threats - people working in countries such as Japan, Germany, Canada and the United States as senior it managers - said their systems were hacked at some point and that these attacks increased by 7% in 2016. Again, 88% of respondents have sensitively defended their data (Thales 2016 Global Data Report by Garrett Parker).

The same report stated that the data was lost not only to insiders, but rather to externally funded attacks. In addition, the report highlights the security weaknesses of both internal factors and external factors consisting of suppliers in the supply chain in data usage. The report also stated that according to the most conservative estimates, the number of internet-connected devices will be approximately 20 billion in the next 3 years.

In order to prevent this data security problem, measures should be taken to protect intellectual property rights. Intellectual Property data determines the manufacturing process of a product and is as valuable as design plans. These contain specific and unique information about the product and its manufacture. Those with this knowledge need the right equipment to develop the counterfeit product. Endüstri 4.0 kapsamında veri işleme zorunlu olarak gerçekleşmektedir. Therefore, data protection, data protection principles must be redefined and supported by protocols so that the information of customers and employees is not compromised by a cyberattack. If customer information cannot be protected as a result of the data breach, this may result in reduced customer trust and loss. Necessary measures should also be taken against the virus. Data security will become more difficult as the system used grows and the computers etc. in the system increase. Sometimes shutting down the system can be seen as the solution. But first of all in a factory, stopping a transaction in less than an hour will have very serious financial and logistical consequences. It has also been determined that the cause of some attacks is aimed at stopping production in factories.

In the event of any virus attack, there is a risk of infection on all machines. This can sabotage the production process in smart factories. Therefore, data security is important not only for the protection of privacy or intellectual property rights, but also for the sustainability of the company's activities.

Data security, environmental protection, health and safety are also important in companies. If networks and computers experience data security issues, machines can cause problems that do not fit their original program.

For example, from a smart home project, the system can reveal the entire profile of the person living in the house. This includes all habits of the person living in the house. Thieves or attackers in a house with a data security issue may be able to know about the condition of the home from the information about the landlord. The house could be vulnerable to attack. In the same way, they can be connected to refrigerators etc. remotely, causing consequences that will cause distress to the safety of the person. In the same way, there will be problems in the health sector within the scope of Industry 4.0. In particular, the personal information of patients can be obtained and security problems may arise for these individuals. Especially in the pharmaceutical sector, these losses are thought to be very large (European Parliament Economic and Scientific Policy Industry).

Therefore, when investigating issues such as productivity increase within the scope of industry 4.0, the effects of such losses on productivity should be investigated. Insurance companies are seen to pay attention to the following issues in the policies within the scope of coverage regarding the direct loss of customers after the cyberattack. Costs for replacing lost/stolen data, Information Technology forensic examination costs, costs related to notification to customers, costs related to the establishment of a call center support unit. Responsibilities arising from negligence, virus transmission, liability arising from blocking access to the System, responsibility arising from hacker attacks or destruction of third-party digital assets. The work stoppage in the company is also covered within the scope of the policy conditions as a profit loss guarantee.

5 Industry 4.0 Studies in the World and the European Union

On the fact that the software bubble does not collapse on the Internet, on the contrary, the area covered by new applications expands; Following this technological development, studies on industrialization and information technology relations were initiated by the German government in 2006. The definition of industry 4.0, which was first used at the Hannover Fair in Germany in 2011, was put into the government program by the German Government in 2012.

In April 2013, the German government published its report "Guaranteeing the future of the German manufacturing industry: strategic initiative industry 4.0 - Recommendations for the implementation of the final report of the Industry 4.0 Working Group". Initially, the conditions that made the fourth industrial revolution or industrial 4.0 possible developed uniquely in Germany.

Germany has developed industry 4.0 as a long-term strategy to maintain the country's technological leadership in industrial production research and development with its competitive and innovative manufacturing sector.

Following these developments in the field of industrialization in Germany, a series of studies were launched in 2012 by the European Union to restore Europe's relatively deteriorating economy for a sustainable Europe. Within the scope of this study;

1. Technical arrangements have been made to improve resource efficiency. In order to encourage these regulations and accelerate the adoption of new technologies, it was decided to provide incentives in areas that support infrastructure and R&D/innovation projects. In this context, advanced manufacturing technology basic technology markets, bio product markets, raw materials market, clean vehicles market for sustainability and smart grid systems were included in the incentive scope.
2. On the one hand, it was decided to make improvements to stimulate trade in the domestic market, while strengthening the SMEs that form the backbone of the European economy and to make agreements to liberalize trade for fast-growing economies to increase exports.
3. Providing sufficient financial resources to support investment and innovation in the public and private sectors was set as the main goal.
4. Efforts have been launched to organize trainings to provide the necessary trained manpower for the new industry.

By 2020, around 30 billion devices are expected to be connected, according to some sources, and around 24 billion, according to some sources. Ten billion of them will be phones, tablets and wearable systems.

Billions of dollars will be transferred to Internet of Things (IOT) solutions such as development of this system, preparation of applications, device hardware, system integrations, creation of data storage systems, security and connectivity. The recycling of these resources is calculated as $13 trillion by 2025. Gartner believes that interconnected objects increased by 30% in 2016 compared to 2015 and reached 6.4 billion.

It estimates that 5.5 million objects are connected every day in 2016, reaching 20.8 billion units by 2020. In addition, investments in this area are projected to increase by 22% in 2016 compared to 2015.

http://www.gartner.com/newsroom/id/3165317.

Conditions of Success of Industry 4.0 in the World and European Economy

According to the researches carried out, industry 4.0 will be possible by meeting certain basic requirements. The main requirements are listed as follows:

- Standardization of systems, platforms and protocols;
- Making changes to the business organization that reflect new business models
- Ensuring digital security and information protection
- Providing the necessary training to find suitable skilled workers
- To be able to carry out the necessary research for investment
- Regulation of legal infrastructure

Smart Factories and the Future of Automated Manufacturing

The combination of virtual, physical worlds through cyber-physical systems and the combination of technical processes and business processes leads to a new industrial age in manufacturing, the smart factory concept of industry 4.0.

Smart factories are created by placing cyber-physical systems in production systems. Smart factories provide significant quality, time, resource and cost advantages compared to classical production systems.

Smart factories are designed according to sustainable and service-oriented business practices. In addition, there may be a trend towards adaptable, self-adaptable and learnable systems with fault tolerance and risk management. According to the International Robot Federation, the number of robotic units that will form the foundations of smart factories in the world is increasing day by day.

In the smart factory, the high level of automation comes standard: production processes are automatically controlled with a virtual network of physical system-based production systems, flexible production systems that can respond in real time ensure the optimizing of on-premises production processes. Production advantages are not limited to one-time production conditions; is also optimized for the global network. This represents a production revolution in terms of creating a production value model that creates different market opportunities while saving costs and time with innovation.

After 2020 in Turkey, there will be mainstream, internet of things and connected issues in the health sector. There will be areas where the Internet of Things will be used in particular, patient follow-ups that are maintained at home, and analyses of whether products harmful to health are used.

In the field of health, especially in the field of health, the development of passive sensors that can be glued to clothes or skin, buried or even swallowed, and systems that can integrate technology with the human body have already begun, especially in the field of health, monitoring patients who are over a certain age or at risk of falling directly, detecting complications remotely, checking whether rules such as diet are observed.

After the advent of 3D printers, it became possible to meet individual boutique needs more easily in addition to mass production. Now you will be able to produce the product in your home by making a specially designed copy of the product you want with your 3D printer in your home. This will eliminate the logistics processes and lead you to meet your own needs with communication in a completely digital environment.

Warehouse and Field Management

Warehouses, distribution centers and areas are a fundamental part of supply chains and supply chain companies. As a result, the efficiency achieved in these facilities directly affects the entire company. It will be useful to mention RFID systems again in warehouse management. As is known, active and passive tags are used in RFID systems.

While active tags sometimes contain additional sensors while having their own battery power, passive tags have an RFID antenna and a microchip for storing information. RFID tags and sensors can minimize human use and scaner use in warehouses.

Packages, pallets and containers labeled with RFID that share between infrastructure and machinery, and warehouses, will be monitored through the cloud. Platforms and programs can automate asset and location tracking by translating physical location into digital data. In addition, it can reduce the risks to workplace health and safety by taking people from these physical areas.

Trailer movements, fuel usage and wasted time can be reduced by taking images of the facilities with camera systems. The personnel working there can be monitored to leave their field of duty by determining their duty areas.

Customers use long-range networks or Low Power Wide Area Networks (LPWAN's) that allow them to track specific items to track their shipments. Likewise, satellite trackers provide approximate location data on an item almost anywhere on the planet, even in areas without cellular coverage.

In contrast, Bluetooth tags and markers offer tracking data in narrower and more limited areas. These tags can be used in retail stores to track customer traffic and provide marketing messages to those customers.

Business Models of the Future

Platform Technologies the Internet of Things is about the use of technology. Companies that use technology at the highest level, from data analysis to automation and platform solutions, will stand out in this race. Those who cannot use the technology properly risk extinction. However, digital strategy definitions integrated into business strategy are critical in technology use.

While the business model was created in logistics companies, optimization between costs and service levels was important. By eliminating this equation, automation helps companies reduce their costs and enable them to provide better service. That's why many companies are looking for ways to improve their operations, from storage to final consumer delivery. All processes from automatic loading and unloading to fast delivery, which increases the speed of loading and unloading operations in warehouses, become measurable.

Especially with platform technology, new companies are building their business models on sharing. These technologies will have a lot of impact on the industry in the future. The biggest example of these companies is virtual shipping companies. These companies create a shipping pool in their business models and compare freight prices, enabling consumers to receive the lowest cost offers while reducing the profitability of logistics companies.

One of the most important reasons for the success of these companies is to use technology and the other is that they can make fast pricing. In addition to these companies, UBER is an example of creating shared logistics for transportation companies. Offering a solution that matches existing capacity with distribution needs, UBER wants to continue its success among transit passengers in food distribution and e-commerce products distribution.

In addition, the UBERCARGO service it has established in Hong Kong provides express delivery. In addition, in a recent trend, large retail and e-commerce sites that receive external services have established companies that will carry out their own logistics operations.

To that end, Amazon is making several investments. Also in Ali baba, one of the world's giants, he is trying to improve delivery services for his sellers with Cainiao, which he established to manage port logistics operations (Industry 4.0: Building the digital enterprise PWC 2016).

Professions of the Future

One of the most feared consequences of industrial 4.0 change is the problem of unemployment. Can this result be lived. The answer to that question is about the education system. While industry 4.0 change is happening, it is very important that we adapt our education system to change.

The most important result of Industry 4.0 in employment is that the work to be done with body strength will become brain power through automation and smart factories. From this point of view, we can say that the job descriptions we are looking at may change. There will be employment growth, especially in it technologies and innovation-oriented business areas. Moreover, even today, the shortage in these areas is significantly greater.

The UK will be short of 800,000 jobs in technology by 2020, according to a study by the UK Digital Economy Coalition (Coadec).

In Germany, where Industry 4.0 began, job descriptions are already changing.

Business names will change. Professions such as industrial data science, robotics, IT solution architecture, Industrial solution architecture, cloud computing expertise, data security expertise, network engineering, 3D printer engineering, Wearable technology design will start to take place in our lives.8 Today's professions such as software and analyst will also increase recruitment. It is thought that serious jobs will be created in these areas as nanotechnology will develop. At the same time, work accidents will be prevented due to the reset of arm strength in production.

6 Results

It should be noted that one of the most important issues when using all these technologies is to analyze the data correctly. Perhaps one of the most important denominators of the Internet of Things is big data. However, it is important for us to know what data is healthy and how healthy it is in the big data.

Specialization in the digital field is still a problem for the sector. Although data analytics can be used to improve performance, plan routes and optimize operations by levers of scale economy, dynamic routings can be troubled, systems such as TMS and WMS have been used in the industry for years. What these programs have in common is that they are programs that combine supply chain solutions. Some companies prefer to use only some features of these programs. Like a financial module or just an operating module.

However, the biggest feature of the programs is that when you use all the modules together, you can achieve all the advantages of the program. Especially if all modules are used together, the benefit of the ports of the modules to each other can reach an incredible size. With skilled users, this benefit is even greater. Orders can be optimised with options such as the lowest shipping fee and fastest delivery.

Platforms that will enable the integration of management systems such as TMS, YMS and WMS can organize all events. The purpose of the integration platforms will be to ensure that the supply chain is carried out with complete synchronization. This synchronization can be moved to advanced stages and transformed from the private sector, for example, to the creation of inter-port planning models. Thus, all time losses can be avoided with a process to be prepared from warehouse to ship taking into account the unloading and loading times of the ships docking at Ambarlı Port.

References

Aksoy, S.: Değişen Teknolojiler ve Endüstri 4.0: Endüstri 4.0'ı Anlamaya Dair Bir Giriş. SAV Katkı, [Changing Technologies and Industry 4.0: An Introduction to Understanding Industry 4.0. SAV Contribution], **4**, 34–41 (2017)

Atzori, L., Lera, A., Morabito, G.: The internet of things: a survey. Comput. Netw. **54**(15), 2787–2805 (2010). https://doi.org/10.1016/j.comnet.2010.05.010

Bär, K., Herbert-Hansen, Z.N.L., Khalid, W.: Considering Industry 4.0 aspects in the supply chain for an SME. Prod. Eng. Res. Devel. **12**(6), 747–758 (2018). https://doi.org/10.1007/s11740-018-0851-y

Barreto, L., Amaral, A., Pereira, T.: Industry 4.0 implications in logistics: an overview. Procedia Manufacturing, **13**, 1245–1252 (2017). https://doi.org/10.1016/j.promfg.2017.09.045

Huy, D.T.N.: The critical analysis of limited south asian corporate governance standards after financial crisis. Int. Journal for Quality Res. **15**(1) (2015)

Dat, P.M., Mau, N.D., Loan, B.T.T., Huy, D.T.N.: Comparative China corproate goevrnance standards after financial crisis, corporate scandals and manipulation. J. Security and Sustainability Issues, **9**(3) (2020). https://doi.org/10.9770/jssi.2020.9.3(18)

Huy, D.T.N.: The critical analysis of limited south asian corporate governance standards after financial crisis. Int. Journal for Quality Res. **9**(4) (2015)

Huy, D.T.N., Le, T.H., Hang, N.T., Gwoździewicz, S., Trung, N.D., Van Tuan, P.: Further researches and discussion on machine learning meanings-and methods of classifying and recognizing users gender on internet. Advances in Mechanics **9**(3), 1190–1204 (2021)

DT Ngu, DTN Huy, PT Thanh, ES Döngül. : Language teaching application to english students at master's grade levels on history and macroeconomic-banking management courses in universities and colleges, J. Language Linguistic Studies **17**(3) (2021)

Tinh, D.T., Thuy, N.T., Huy, D.T.N.: Doing business research and teaching methodology for undergraduate, postgraduate and doctoral students-case in various markets including Vietnam. Elementary education Online **20**(1) (2021)

Huy, D.T.N.: Digital transformation, IoTs and AI Applications in electric and electrical engineering sector in vietnam in industry 4.0 – and cyber zecurity risk solutions. Design Engineering, pp. 589–601 (2021). http://www.thedesignengineering.com/index.php/DE/article/view/2015

Evren, R., Ülengin, F.: Yönetimde Karar Verme, ITÜ Yayını, No.1478, [Management Decision Making, ITU Publication, No.1478], İstanbul (1992)

Gubbi, J., Buyya, R., Marusiz, S., Palanizwami, M.: Internet of things (IoT): a vision, architectural elements, and future directions. Futur. Gener. Comput. Syst. **29**(7), 1645–1660 (2013). https://doi.org/10.1016/j.future.2013.01.010

Hofmann, E., Rüsch, M.: Industry 4.0 and the current status as well as future prospects on logistics. Computers in Industry, **89**, 23–34 (2017). https://isiarticles.com/bundles/Article/pre/pdf/83979.pdf

Huy, D.T.N., Hien, D.T.N.: The backbone of European corporate governance standards after financial crisis, corporate scandals and manipulation. Economic and Business Rev. **12**(4) (2010)

Hoang, N.T., et al.: Determining factors for educating students for choosing to work for foreign units: Absence of self-efficacy. J. teachers, Educators and Trainers **12**(2), 11–19 (2021). https://jett.labosfor.com/index.php/jett/article/view/531. Access 28 July 2021

Hang, T.T.B., Nhung, D.T.H., Nhung, D.H., Huy, D.T.N., Hung, N.M., Dat, P.M.: Where beta is going - case of vietnam hotel, airlines and tourism company groups after the low inflation period. Entrepreneurship and Sustainability Issues **7**(3) (2020). http://doi.org/https://doi.org/10.9770/jesi.2020.7.3(55)

Hanh, H.T., Chuyen, B.M., Huy, D.T.N., Phuong, N.T.T., Phuong, H.T.L., Nuong, L.N.: Challenges and opportunities from impacts of fdi and income on environment pollution: role of financial accounting transparency in FDI firms. J. Security & Sustainability Issues **10**(2) (2020)

Huy, D.T.N.: Estimating Beta of Viet Nam listed construction companies groups during the crisis. Journal of Integration and Dev. **15** (2012)

Hanh, H.T., Huy, D.T.N., Phuong, N.T.T., Nga, L.T.V., Anh, P.T.: Impact of macro economic factors and financial development on energy projects-case in ASEAN countries. Management **24**(2) (2020)

Hac, L.D., et al.: Enhancing risk management culture for sustainable growth of Asia commercial bank -ACB in Vietnam under mixed effects of macro factors. Entrepreneurship and Sustainability Issues **8**(3) (2021)

Huy, D.T.N. : Beta of Viet Nam listed computer and electrical company groups during and after the financial crisis 2007–2011. Asian Journal of Finance & Accounting **5**(1) (2013)

Van Thuc, H., Thao, D.T.T., Thach, N.N., Huy, D.T.N., Thanh, N.T.P.: Desining data transmission system with infrared rays. Psychology Educ. J. **57**(8), 658–663 (2020)

Kagermann, H.: Recommendations for implementing the strategic initiative Industrie 4.0. Munchen: national Academy of Science Engineering (2013). https://www.din.de/blob/76902/e8cac883f42bf28536e7e8165993f1fd/recommendations-for-implementing-industry-4-0-data.pdf

Miorandi, D., Sicari, S., Pellegrini, F., Chlamtac, I.: Internet of things: vision, applications and research challenges. Ad Hoc Netw. **10**(7), 1497–1516 (2012). https://doi.org/10.1016/j.adhoc.2012.02.016

Mukhopadhyay, S.C., Suryadevara, N.K.: Internet of things: challenges and opportunities. In: Mukhopadhyay, S.C. (ed.) Internet of Things. SSMI, vol. 9, pp. 1–17. Springer, Cham (2014). https://doi.org/10.1007/978-3-319-04223-7_1

Trung, N.D., Huy, D.T.N., Van Tuan, P., Huong, D.T.: Ict and digital tech effects on marketing strategies and choosing competitor affecting on business operation-a case in hotel and entertainment sector. Design Engineering 6 (2021)

Lan, N.T.N., Yen, L.L., Ha, N.T.T., Van, P.T.N., Huy, D.T.N.: Enhancing roles of management accounting and issues of applying ifrs for sustainable business growth: a case study. J. Security & Sustainability Issues **10**(2) (2020)

Trung, N.D., Huy, D.T.N., Le, T.H., Huong, D.T., Hoa, N.T.: ICT, AI, IOTs and technology applications in education-a case with accelerometer and internet learner gender prediction. Advances in Mechanics **9**(3), 1288–1296 (2021)

Thach, N.N., Hanh, H.T., Huy, D.T.N., Vu, Q.N.: Technology quality management of the industry 4.0 and cybersecurity risk management on current banking activities in emerging markets-the case in Vietnam. Int. J.for Quality Res. **15**(3), 845 (2021)

Hang, N.T., et al. : Educating and training labor force under Covid 19; impacts to meet market demand in vietnam during globalization and integration Era. Journal for Educators, Teachers and Trainers **12**(1), 179–184 (2021)

Thach, N.N., et al.: Measuring the volatility of market risk of vietnam banking industry after the low inflation period 2015–2017. Review of Pacific Basin Financial Markets and Policies **23**(04) (2020)

Thales : Global Data Report by Garrett Parker (2016)

Toker, K.: Endüstri 4.0 ve Sürdürülebilirliğe Etkileri . İstanbul Üniversitesi İşletme Fakültesi İşletme İktisadı Enstitüsü Yönetim Dergisi ,[4.0 and Its Effects on Sustainability . Istanbul University Business School Business Economics Institute Management Journal] **29**(84), 51–64 (2018). https://dergipark.org.tr/tr/pub/iuiieyd/issue/38206/441403

Le, T.H., et al.: Internet of Things (IOT) uses and applications -solutions in emerging markets and Vietnam. Turkish Journal of Computer and Mathematics Educ. **12**(11) (2021)

Van Tuan, P., Huy, D.T.N., Trung, N.D., Hoa, N.T.: Marketing strategies for tourism and digital tech applications in tourism industry-a case of och tourism corporation in Vietnam. Design Engineering, 7 (2021)

Tram, P.N., Ngoc Huy, D.T.: Educational, political and socio-economic development of Vietnam based on Ho Chi Minh's Ideology. Elementary education Online **20**(1) (2021)

Van Tuan, P., Huy, D.T.N., Hoa, M.B.A.N.T., Huong, D.T.: Technology applications, it effects on marketing and role of digital marketing. In: Stock Investment Industry-And Industrial Competitors Impacts On Business Risk Level, Design Engineering, pp. 1828–1843 (2021)

Dat, P.M., Mau, N.D., Loan, B.T.T., Huy, D.T.N.: Comparative china corporate governance standards after financial crisis, corporate scandals and manipulation. J. Security & Sustainability Issues **9**(3) (2020)

Hang, T.T.B., Nhung, D.T.H., Huy, D.T.N., Hung, N.M., Pham, M.D.: Where Beta is going–case of Viet Nam hotel, airlines and tourism company groups after the low inflation period. Entrepreneurship and Sustainability Issues **7**(3), 2282 (2020)

Ha, T.T.H., et al.: Modern corporate governance standards and role of auditing-cases in some Western european countries after financial crisis, corporate scandals and manipulation. International Journal of Entrepreneurship **23**(1S) (2019)

Nam, V.Q., Tinh, D.T., Huy, D.T.N., Le, T.H., Huong, L.T.T.: Internet of things (IoT), artificial intelligence (AI) applications for various sectors in emerging markets-and risk management information system (RMIS) issues. Design Engineering, Issue **6**, 609–618 (2021)

Wan, J.; Zhou, C., Hu, K.: Industrie 4.0: enabling technologies. In: Intelligent Computing and Internet of Things (ICIT). In: 2014 International Conference on. IEEE, pp. 135–140 (2015). https://doi.org/10.1109/ICAIOT.2015.7111555

Yan, B., Huang, G.: Supply chain information transmission based on RFID and internet of things, 2009 ISECS International Colloquium on Computing, Communication. Control, and Management (2009). https://doi.org/10.1109/CCCM.2009.5267755

Yıldız, A., Karakoyun, F., Parlak, I.E.: Endüstri 4.0 Temelli Dijital Tedarik Zinciri", Mühendislik Alanında Akademik Araştırmalar. Salman, S. (ed.), Gece Kitaplığı, [Industry 4.0 Based Digital Supply Chain, Academic Research in Engineering, Editor: Salman, S., Night Library] Ankara, pp. 416–426 (2018). https://doi.org/10.15295/bmij.v6i4.322

https://www.dw.com/tr/dijital-devrimin-d%C3%BC%C5%9Fman%C4%B1-siber-sald%C4%B1r%C4%B1lar/a-18322334. Accessed 20 Dec 2021

http://blog.trendmicro.com/. Accessed 23 Dec 2021

European Parliament Economic and Scientific Policy Industry) https://www.europarl.europa.eu/RegData/etudes/STUD/2016/570007/IPOL_STU(2016)570007_EN.pdf. Accessed 01 Jan 2022

http://www.gartner.com/newsroom/id/3165317. Accessed 19 Dec 2021

Industry 4.0: Building the digital enterprise PWC 2016. https://www.pwc.com/gx/en/industries/industries-4.0/landing-page/industry-4.0-building-your-digital-enterprise-april-2016.pdf. Accessed 21 Dec 2021

Emphasizing the Relationship between Scans and Exploits Events' Data: An Exploratory Data Analysis Over Time

Abdellah Houmz[1,2](✉), Othmane Cherqi[1,2], Karim Zkik[3], and Houda Benbrahim[2]

[1] TICLab, International University of Rabat, Rabat, Morocco
{abdellah.houmz,othmane.cherqi}@uir.ac.ma
[2] ENSIAS, Mohammed V University of Rabat, Rabat, Morocco
houda.benbrahim@um5.ac.ma
[3] ESAIP Ecole d'Ingénieur, CERADE, Angers, France
karim.zkik@uir.ac.ma, Kzkik@esaip.org

Abstract. As web services have gone mainstream, incident diagnosis has become a vital tool in reducing service downtime and guaranteeing high service reliability. Telemetry data can be collected in many forms including time series and incident sequence data. Correlation analysis techniques are significant tools that cyber security experts utilize for incident diagnosis. Despite their importance, little research has been done on the correlation of two forms of data streams for incident diagnosis: continuous time series data and temporal event data. In this study, we propose an approach for evaluating the correlation between scanning campaigns and exploits publication events data. Using an events' effect detection method, we investigate the relationship between network scans and exploits publication. We refer to exploits dataset that contains information about cyber events and the items that are affected. We also use a dataset of network scans taken from two telescope networks. We found that the ratio of exploits related to an increase in network scans can go up to 25% and changes depending on various factors, such as the platform and the type of the exploited service.

Keywords: Cyber Intelligence · Cybersecurity · Network Telescope · Time series · Exploit · Nmap · Network Scan

1 Introduction

The rise in the use of internet services helped businesses to prosper and thrive. At the same time, they opened their systems to various critical threats that can result in huge losses. As a result, and according to Konceptanalytics [1], the security market is expected to reach US$276.1 billion in 2025. The main types of threats are networkbased. They exploit vulnerable products and systems after scanning and identifying them.

The publication of a new exploit can impact network scans. Jumratjaroenvanit and Teng-Amnuay [2] found, by analyzing 439 vulnerabilities, that various factors such as the availability of patches and exploit codes contribute to the probability of an attack. In

A. Mirzazadeh et al. (Eds.): SEMIT 2022, CCIS 1808, pp. 190–201, 2023.
https://doi.org/10.1007/978-3-031-40395-8_13

addition, Allodi and Massacci [3] found that the existence of proof-of-concept exploits is a significantly better risk factor. An exploit is a set of commands or data used to take advantage of a vulnerability or a flaw in a program or a system to grant the intruder unauthorized access or help him launch attacks. Attackers run scans on the target network to identify exposed services, then target vulnerable ones using available exploits. Thus, scans on networks can be an indication of a coming attack. In addition, the publication of new exploits may incite attackers to look for vulnerable devices to try the newly published exploit, which leads to an increase in the volume of scans targeting a service.

Little is known in the literature about the impact of an exploit publication on the network's scans. Raftopoulos et al.[4] found that exploitation activity followed towards hosts that replied to scans and they estimated that 8% of hosts were compromised. Therefore, understanding the relation between exploits' publication and the other aspects of cyber security can help security administrators to better manage and secure their systems, and prepare for attacks following network scans.

In this perspective, we conducted this study to develop an approach that is capable of assessing the impact generated by the publication of new exploits. We gathered data about network scans on two different countries, in addition to a list of exploits published during the same period of time. Afterward, we applied an impact detection method to study the impact of exploits on network scans' time series.

The goal of this study is to validate the existence of a relationship between exploits and network scans. We seek to understand the type of the relationship, and whether all exploits have an impact on network scans.

The rest of the paper is organized as follows: we begin with related work to this study in Section II, then we present the proposed model and data used in Section III. In Section IV we present the found results, and finally, we conclude in Section V.

2 Related Work

We present in this section the work related to our study. We are studying the relationship between two concepts: network scans and software vulnerability exploits. We present work related to each of them.

Network scans were used as a tool to find vulnerable victims over the internet. They can be categorized following their nature into active and passive scans, or following their targets into single or distributed scans [5]. The goal of network scans can be: fingerprinting applications and operating systems [6], measurements, checking the quality of service, penetration testing, etc. To mitigate the risk of scans, several methods have been developed. They are based on packets' information to classify them as belonging to a scan campaign or not. Packets' information used include source and destination addresses, protocols, and port numbers [7]. Packets and flow information can be processed by algorithms based on multiple techniques, such as graphs [8], artificial neural networks, anomaly detection [9], fuzzy logic [10], thresholds, and rules.

Exploits of software vulnerability were of huge importance, especially for system administrators, because a vulnerability with an exploit developed and published is riskier and needs to be patched in a timely manner. The question that most papers try to answer is: how to predict that a vulnerability will be exploited? Householder et al. [11] analyzed a dataset of all identified vulnerabilities and found that 4.1% of CVE-IDs have public exploit code associated with them within the first year. The vulnerability CWE category, the vendor, and the CVSS score are among the good predictors of the exploit development. Allodi and Massacci [3] followed a case-control methodology to study and evaluate the effectiveness of the CVSS score for prioritizing vulnerabilities to fix. They found that choosing vulnerabilities with a high CVSS score is equivalent to random selection.

Instead of only analyzing historical data about exploits' development, other studies went further and created models to predict the exploitability of a vulnerability based on available data. Yin et al. [12] proposed a framework named ExBERT that analyses vulnerability text descriptions to predict its exploitability. Bhatt et al. [13] used machine learning classifiers trained with previous vulnerability exploit-history and achieved an accuracy around 85%. They also found that vulnerability severity, type, and software configurations are important features. Edkrantz and Said [14] also used a machine learning-based classifier based on linear SVM and achieved 83% accuracy. Other similar studies for exploitability prediction are done by Almukaynizi et al. [15] and Bozorgi et al. [16].

Studies that were found about network traffic and exploits [17, 18] were about the detection of polymorphism and metamorphism of exploits used by malware in network traffic. The study [19] that we found to be close to ours was done about vulnerabilities instead of exploits.

3 Model and Dataset

3.1 Data Collection

For the study of the correlation of exploits and network scans, we collected two data sets. The first is about scans received in a network telescope. The second contains information about vulnerability exploits published each day.

1) *Darknet data:* A network telescope (darknet, black hole) is a sensor that records traffic received in a group of passive and unassigned network addresses. Network telescopes are used to intercept port scans, worm activity, traffic from replayed DoS activities on spoofed IP addresses, etc. The data we use is collected from two /20 network telescopes in different countries. The traffic was recorded from November 11, 2014 to December 1, 2019, and contains information about each packet such as the source and destination IP addresses, the source and destination ports - if applicable, and the transport protocol.

   The telescope network data gives an idea about cyber events overall on the internet, particularly about attacks and misconfiguration traffic. It is usually hosted in many places such as research laboratories, universities,and internet service providers (ISPs). The traffic received in the darknet is representative of the overall internet traffic, especially the malicious one, as attackers do not have reliable techniques to detect network telescopes.
2) *Exploits:* The vulnerability exploits database [20] is a non-profit project maintained by Offensive Security [21]. It contains CVE compliant public exploits and vulnerability proofs-of-concept published by security researchers and system penetration testers. The data contain the date of the publication of the exploits, the affected platform

(Windows, Linux, PHP, etc.), a text description of the exploit, the type of the exploit: Web applications, DoS, etc., and the port of the product that is exploited in the case of a network service.

3.2 Proposed Model

For the analysis of scans and exploits datasets, Fig. 1 shows the important steps: we clean and extract the publication of exploits as events, we extract time series of scans from the network telescope data logs, and we execute the algorithm to detect the impact of exploits publication on scans time series.

3.3 Data Processing

We process traffic logs to transform them into scans time series. For each packet received in the telescope network, basic information is saved, such as the source and destination addresses, the transport protocol, and the source and destination port numbers. To extract time series that represent the volume of scans targeting a specific port, we select packets related to scans, such as TCP packets with SYN flag, then we aggregate them by destination TCP port.

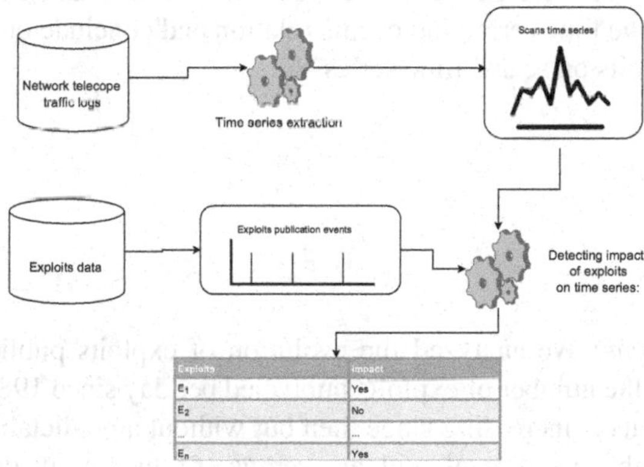

Fig. 1. Pipeline

We use two methods to aggregate the packets received each day. The first focuses on the overall volume regardless of its source, thus we count the number of packets received in that day as the scans' volume. The second measures the intensity of the scan by the number of scanners targeting the port on that day, thus we count the number of distinct IP addresses as the scans' volume.

The exploits are transformed into a series of events, where the date of event occurrence is the day of the exploit publication. We filtered them to include only exploits related to a port number, then we fed them with scans to the impact detection algorithm.

We filtered out all exploits that are not related to a port number, then we transform exploits into a series of events.

3.4 Impact Detection Method

Having scans' time series and exploits publication's time processed, we proceed to detect the events that were followed by an increase in the scans' volume using the method proposed by Luo et al. [22].

Luo et al. [22] proposed an approach for discovering the aspects of time series and timed events dependency. It assesses three aspects of the dependency: *(i)* the existence of the dependency, *(ii)* the temporal order of the dependency: to check whether the events are triggering the time series changes or the inverse, and *(iii)* the effect type: whether it results in a decrease or an increase of the series values.

The time series of scans' traffic and exploits publications events are processed for each port number. For a scan time series $S = (s_1,..,s_m)$ of a port p and a sequence $E = \{e_1,...,e_n\}$ of exploits (events) occurring in timestamps $T_e = (t_1,..,t_n)$, we extract sub-time series of length k, which is the window size, from the scans time series S before and after each exploit's publication event. We create a set of sub-series of length k before events denoted as: $L^{front}{}_k = \{l_k{}^{front}(S,e_i), i = 1,...,n\}$, and a similar set for sub-series of length k after the event denoted as: $L^{rear}{}_k = \{l_k{}^{rear}(S,e_i), i = 1,...,n\}$, as well as a third set composed of randomly sampled sub-series of length k from the scans time series.

For each TCP port, we extract the three sets of subseries of scans related to the published exploits, we then use a multivariate two-sample test to compare the distributions from which the two sets are derived. The results of the test statistic help us to study the tree aspects of the time series and events relation and conclude on the impact of the publication of exploits on scans' time series.

4 Results

4.1 EDA

1) *Exploits data:*

a) *Exploits over time:* We analyzed the evolution of exploits publication over time. Figure 2 shows the number of exploits published per day since 1988. The number of published exploits is increasing since then but without a predictable pattern. 43,789 exploits were published in total, with an average of four exploits published each day during the last 5 years.

b) *Exploits distribution:* Exploits have different types and affect multiple platforms and ports. In the exploits data, only 7.44% of vulnerabilities are labeled with the affected port. Figures 3, 4, and 5 show the distribution of types, platforms, and ports of exploits respectively. More than half of the exploits are for web applications, and 16.3% of exploits can grant remote access. The distribution of the affected platforms shows that almost half of the exploits are for PHP only. Microsoft Windows is the second targeted platform with 22.7%, followed by Linux with 6.8%, then other platforms with 22% combined. In terms of network ports used by the affected services, 75% of the exploits labeled with ports are related to web services including HTTP (80/TCP), HTTPS (443/TCP), FTP (21/TCP), and HTTP alternative (8080/TCP).

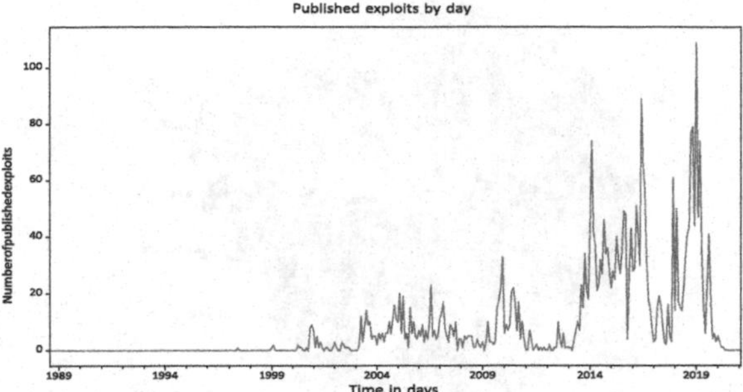

Fig. 2. Exploits publication time series

2) *Scan data:* Scans' time series were extracted from network traffic. Figures 6 and 7 show scans' traffic time series extracted using different methods. In both methods, the time series does not follow a regular and easily predictable pattern of evolution over time. Both figures show that time series extracted from different geographical locations have values close to each other. We can conclude that the traffic caught by network telescopes is generally location agnostic. In addition, the time series extracted with different methods have different shapes. It shows that the mean number of packets sent by each scanner changes over time.

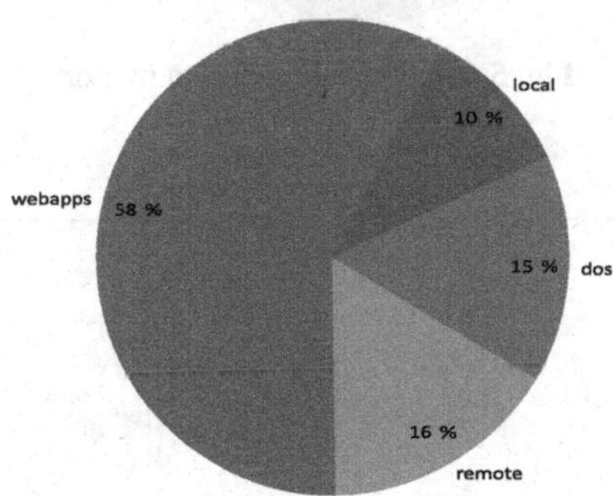

Fig. 3. Exploits distribution by type

Port numbers are used to link exploits and scans. Figure 8 shows top targeted services' port numbers. Almost half the traffic targeted the Telnet (23/TCP) service, followed other remote access services such as SSH 22/TCP, an alternative to telnet port (2323/TCP), then SAMBA (445/TCP) service and web services such as HTTP (80/TCP), HTTPs(443/TCP), FTP(21/TCP) and HTTP alternative (8080/TCP). Finally, all remaining ports count for roughly 30% of traffic.

Comparing services targeted by exploit versus services targeted by scans, we notice that scans are mostly targeting remote access services such as SSH, Telnet, etc., while exploits are published for web services. In the following, we investigate the correlation between the publication of an exploit and the increase in the volume of scans.

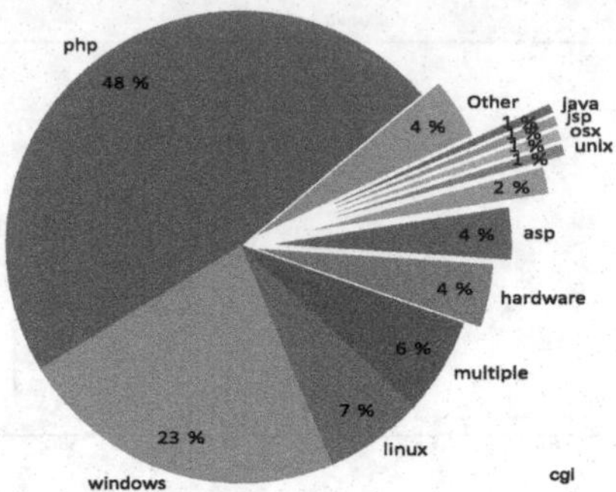

Fig. 4. Exploits distribution by platform

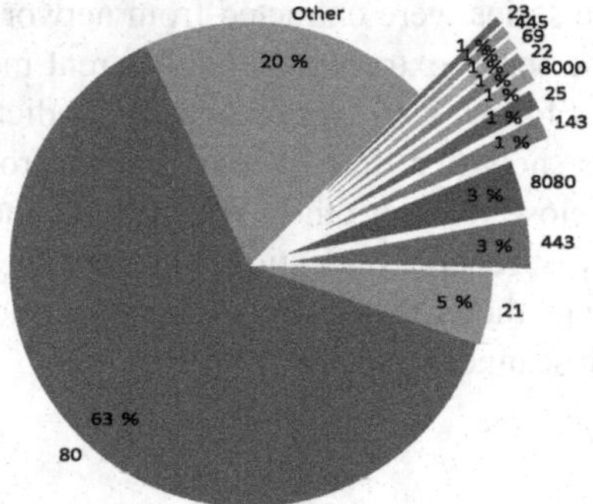

Fig. 5. Exploits distribution by port

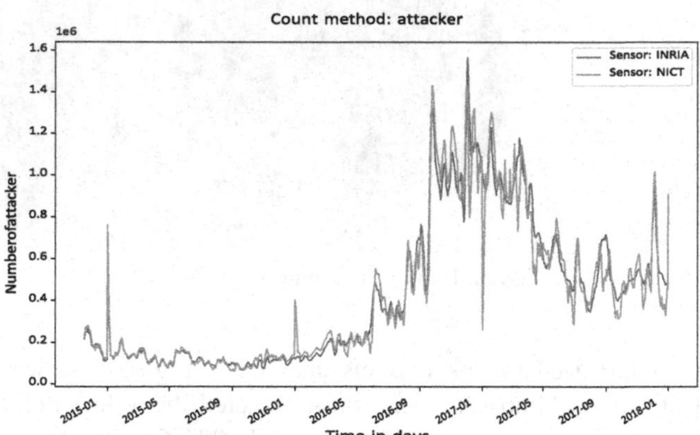

Fig. 6. Scans time series counted by numbers of attackers

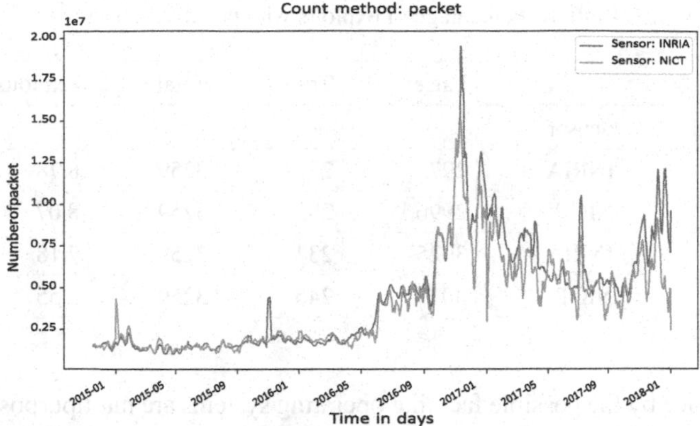

Fig. 7. Scans time series counted by numbers of packets

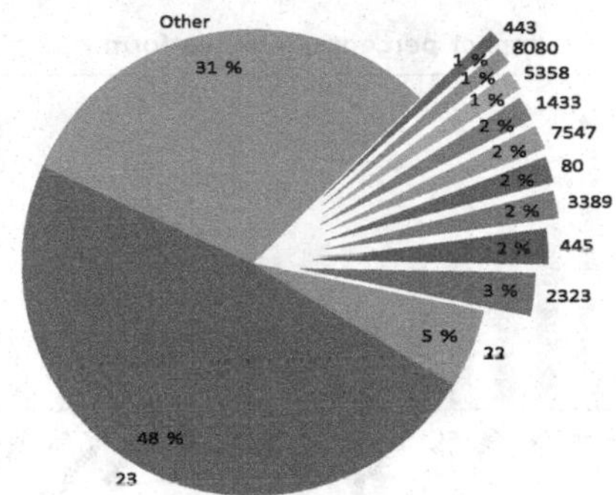

Fig. 8. Top scanned ports

4.2 Exploits Impact Analysis

1) *Detected impact ratios:* We applied the algorithm for detecting the impact of exploits publication on scans received on the two target network telescopes.
   a) *statistics of impact on all ports:* We found that 7.18% to 8.78% of published exploits were followed by an increase in the scan rate for target ports. Table 1 shows the ratio of exploits publications having an impact depending on the target network telescope and the count method used. The use of a different scans count method and the application on a different network telescope did not show a significant impact on the ratio of exploits with impact on scans.

   b) *Effect of the Properties of exploits on their impacton scans:* In addition to the overall ratio of exploits with a positive impact on scans, we explored in detail the impact ratios related to each attribute of the published exploit. Figure 9 shows the different ratios obtained for each platform. We observe that the ratios for operating systems such as Linux, UNIX, Windows, and iOS are low compared to the other platforms. On the other hand, web platforms such as PHP, JSP, CGI are around 15%i, which makes them higher than the average ratio of 7%. We could explain that

Table 1. Percentage of exploits with positive impact

Impact		False	True	Total	Exploits Ratio
Count method	Sensor				
Attacker	INRIA	2973	286	3259	8.78
	NICT	2996	263	3259	8.07
Packet	INRIA	3025	234	3259	7.18
	NICT	3013	246	3259	7.55

difference by the possible fact that operating systems are multipurpose platforms, therefore, the publication of an exploit is not related to a specific service and does not generate scans.

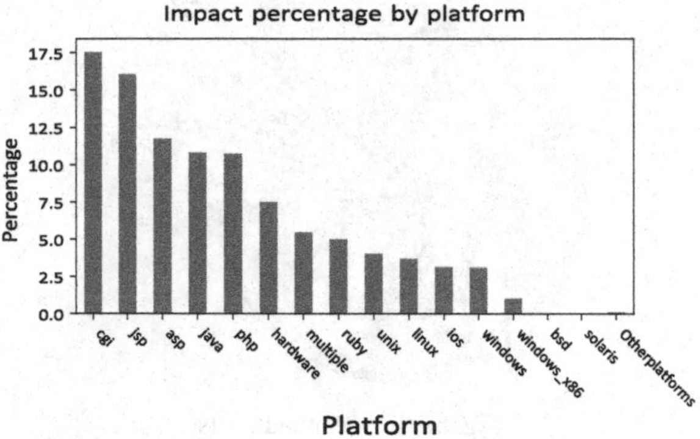

Fig. 9. Ratios of impact by platform

Figure 10 shows ratios of the top 15 ports with the highest numbers of related exploits. That emphasizes the relationship between target ports and impact ratios. It shows that exploits have different impact ratios depending on the affected port. The two ports that were found to have a higher impact ratio are those of HTTP (80/TCP) and HTTPS(443/TCP).

The *type* attribute of an exploit, as defined in the dataset, shows in Fig. 11 that the exploits of type "local" have the highest impact ratio on scans, they are followed by exploits related web applications, then DoS attacks with an impact ratio of 5.17%, and finally the exploits related to remote access with a ratio of 4.60%.

We conclude that the impact of exploits on networks' scans depends on factors such as the type of the exploits, the platform, and the target service or port, with impact ratios ranging from 0% to roughly 25%.

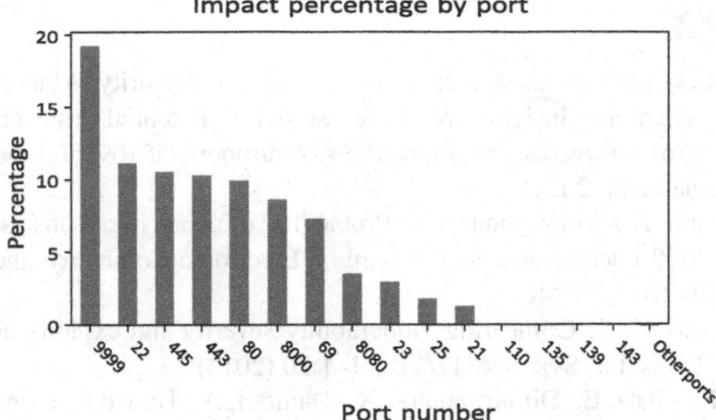

Fig. 10. The percentage of exploits with positive impact by port number

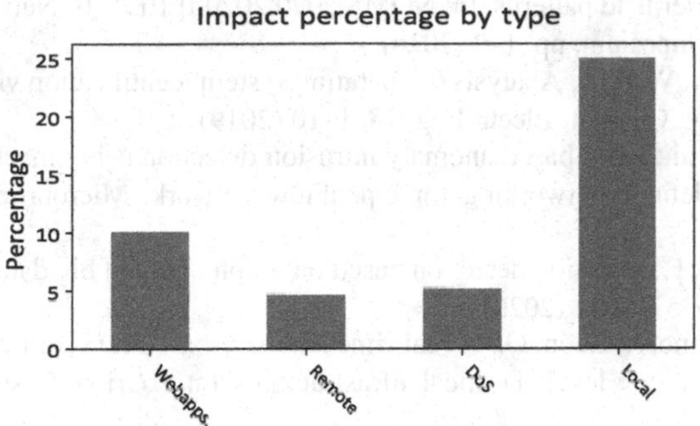

Fig. 11. The percentage of exploits with positive impact by exploit type

5 Conclusion

Our study examined the relation between network scans and exploits publication using an event's impact detection method. We used an exploits dataset containing information about daily published exploits with the affected products. In addition, we used a network scans dataset extracted from two telescope networks. The impact of each published exploit is studied on the scans time series for the same port. We found that around 8% of exploits publication is related to an increase in network scans. This ratio changes depending on the type, the target port, and the platform of the exploit. The presented approach can help security practitioners gain more insight on the relation between scans and exploits, as well as build security systems leveraging the approach. This work is subject to some limitations, such as the small size of the network telescope and the use of open ports search engines by attackers. Some future work includes the integration of other datasets about exploits or integrating this approach in a security system that needs to assess the impact of exploits when published.

References

1. Konceptanalytics and R. a. M. ltd.: Global Cyber Security Market (By Segment, EndUsers & Region): Insights & Forecast with Potential Impact of COVID-19 (2021–2025). https://www.researchandmarkets.com/reports/5510975/global-cyber-security-market-by-segmentend (2021)
2. Jumratjaroenvanit, A., Teng-Amnuay, Y.: Probability of attack based on system vulnerability life cycle. In: 2008 International Symposium on Electronic Commerce and Security. IEEE, pp. 531–535 (2008)
3. Allodi, L., Massacci, F.: Comparing vulnerability severity and exploits using case-control studies. ACM Trans. Inf. Syst.Sec. **17**(1), 1:1–1:20 (2014)
4. Raftopoulos, E., Glatz, E., Dimitropoulos, X., Dainotti, A.: How dangerous is internet scanning? In: Steiner, M., Barlet-Ros, P., Bonaventure, O. (eds.) TMA 2015. LNCS, vol. 9053, pp. 158–172. Springer, Cham (2015). https://doi.org/10.1007/978-3-319-17172-2_11
5. Griffioen, H., Doerr, C.: Discovering collaboration: unveiling slow, distributed scanners based on common header field patterns. In: NOMS 2020 2020 IEEE/IFIP Network Operations and Management Symposium, pp. 1–9 (2020)
6. Song, J., Cho, C., Won, Y.: Analysis of operating system identification via fingerprinting and machine learning. Comput. Electr. Eng. **78**, 1–10 (2019)
7. Satheesh, N., et al.: Flow-based anomaly intrusion detection using machine learning model with software defined networking for OpenFlow network. Microprocess. Microsyst. **79**, 103285 (2020)
8. Abid, A., Jemili, F.: Intrusion detection based on graph oriented big data analytics. Procedia Comp.r Sci. **176**, 572–581 (2020)
9. Clotet, X., Moyano, J., León, G.: A real-time anomaly-based IDS for cyber-attack detection at the industrial process level of critical infrastructures. Int. J. Crit. Infrastruct. Prot. **23**, 11–20 (2018)
10. Saidi, F., Trabelsi, Z., Ghazela, H.B.: Fuzzy IDS as a service on the cloud for malicious TCP port scanning traffic detection. Intelligent Decision Technol. **14**(2), 171–180 (2020)
11. Householder, A.D., Chrabaszcz, J., Novelly, T., Warren, D., Spring, J.M.: Historical analysis of exploit availability timelines. In: 13th ${$USENIX$}$ Workshop on Cyber Security Experimentation and Test (${$CSET$}$ 20) (2020)
12. Yin, J., Tang, M., Cao, J., Wang, H.: Apply transfer learning to cybersecurity: predicting exploitability of vulnerabilities by description. Knowl.-Based Syst. **210**, 106529 (2020)
13. Bhatt, N., Anand, A., Yadavalli, V.S.S.: Exploitability prediction of software vulnerabilities. Qual. Reliab. Eng. Int. **37**(2), 648–663 (2021)
14. Edkrantz, M., Said, A.: Predicting Cyber Vulnerability Exploits with Machine Learning. In: SCAI, pp. 48–57 (2015)
15. Almukaynizi, M., Nunes, E., Dharaiya, K., Senguttuvan, M., Shakarian, J., Shakarian, P.: Proactive identification of exploits in the wild through vulnerability mentions online. In: 2017 International Conference on Cyber Conflict (CyCon US). IEEE, pp. 82–88 (2017)
16. Bozorgi, M., Saul, L.K., Savage, S., Voelker, G.M.: Beyond heuristics: Learning to classify vulnerabilities and predict exploits. In: Proceedings of the 16th ACM SIGKDD International Conference on Knowledge Discovery and Data Mining, pp. 105–114 (2010)
17. Chinchani, R., van den Berg, E.: A fast static analysis approach to detect exploit code inside network flows. In: Valdes, A., Zamboni, D. (eds.) RAID 2005. LNCS, vol. 3858, pp. 284–308. Springer, Heidelberg (2006). https://doi.org/10.1007/11663812_15
18. Zhang, Q., Reeves, D.S., Ning, P., Iyer, S.P.: Analyzing network traffic to detect self-decrypting exploit code. In: Proceedings of the 2nd ACM Symposium on Information, Computer and Communications Security, ser. ASIACCS'07. Association for Computing Machinery, New York, NY, USA, pp. 4–12 (2007)

19. Houmz, A., Mezzour, G., Zkik, K., Ghogho. M., Benbrahim, H.: Detecting the impact of software vulnerability on attacks: a case study of network telescope scans. J. Network Comp. Appl. 103230 (2021)
20. Offensive Security's Exploit Database Archive. https://www.exploit-db.com/
21. Offensive Security Community Projects | Offensive Security. https://www.offensivesecurity.com/community-projects/
22. Luo, C., et al.: Correlating events with time series for incident diagnosis. In: Proceedings of the 20th ACM SIGKDD International Conference on Knowledge Discovery and Data Mining – KDD'14. ACM Press, New York, New York, USA, pp. 1583–1592 (2014)

Fire Resistance Analysis Through Synthetic Fire Tests

Aybike Özyüksel Çiftçioğlu[1(✉)] and M. Z. Naser[2]

[1] Department of Civil Engineering, Faculty of Engineering, Manisa Celal Bayar University, Manisa, Turkey
aybike.ozyuksel@cbu.edu.tr

[2] School of Civil and Environmental Engineering & Earth Sciences, AI Research Institute for Science and Engineering (AIRISE), Clemson, USA

Abstract. Fire resistance analysis is a complex procedure. In this pursuit, engineers design experiments. However, fire tests are expensive and complex and require specialized equipment that is not accessible to many engineers. This further constrains the ability to test and advance fire research. In order to overcome the above challenges, this paper adopts novel machine learning to generate synthetic fire test data via Generative Adversarial Networks (GANs) from real fire tests to expand our knowledge database. Thus, with the addition of new tests, engineers will have access to a much larger pool of data that can help us to better analyze and design structures for fire. In addition, the availability of more data allows us to seriously integrate machine learning into the fire domain. Thus, this paper presents a new approach to expanding fire test data and applying regression and classification machine learning to predict the fire response of reinforced concrete columns. GANs provide an efficient way to generate synthetic data from real fire tests. Moreover, new data additions contribute to improving predictions of classification-based machine learning in comparison with regression-based machine learning.

Keywords: Classification · Columns · Concrete · Fire · GANs · Regression · Synthetic Data

1 Introduction

The construction of fire-resistant reinforced concrete columns is an important advancement in the field of structural engineering [14]. Columns subjected to fire exhibit a wide range of behaviors, ranging from cracking to collapse to remain intact. As such, it is important to understand the effect of fire on concrete columns during the design and analysis. Fire-resistant reinforced concrete columns are designed to withstand the high-temperature environment to which they are subjected when exposed to fire. These columns are used in areas that require high levels of resistance to fire, such as high-rise buildings. Although these columns have been considered a step forward, there are still some questions about their effectiveness and durability. Few studies have been conducted on this type of column when they are exposed to fire and making a decision

A. Mirzazadeh et al. (Eds.): SEMIT 2022, CCIS 1808, pp. 202–210, 2023.
https://doi.org/10.1007/978-3-031-40395-8_14

about their safety is difficult. The only way to find out whether these columns are strong enough is by testing them in practice. However, testing is time-consuming and costly. In this research, the behavior of columns in fire-resistance reinforced concrete is studied by generating a large amount of synthetic data with GANs to achieve a better understanding of the effects of fire on structural integrity. We implement regression and classification analyses on these types of columns to better understand their limitations and to evaluate the level of fire resistance provided by different types of columns.

In regression and classification analyses, the accuracy of models depends on the type of data being analyzed. Regression models often focus on the relationship between variables, while classification models focus on predicting an outcome variable [5, 10, 22]. The outcomes of the analysis can vary depending on the type of data used [9, 11]. In this study, we conduct regression and classification analyses on two separate datasets: one with real data and one with synthetic data.

In the literature, there is research on fire-resistant reinforced concrete constructions. Balaji et. al. [1] investigated the axial capacity of reinforced columns of different sections exposed to fire. Finite element software ANSYS was used to perform the thermal analysis. The fire ratings based on various failure criteria were determined, and the minimum rating was accepted as the design fire rating. Yang et. al. [27] examined the shear behavior of fire-damaged reinforced concrete beams. They proposed prestressed steel strips for the refurbishment of fire-exposed beams. Qiao et. al. [21] proposed an innovative reinforced concrete-filled stainless steel tube column. According to the test findings, the proposed tube columns have a higher ultimate bearing capacity and superior ductility than standard tube columns. Wang et. al. [25] present a numerical investigation of the fire performance of eight two-way reinforced concrete slabs subjected to different restrictions on the plane. In terms of the fire behavior of the tested slabs, the influences of geometric linearity and thermal stress were investigated. They contended that in-plane restriction type, restriction level, aspect ratio, and slab thickness had a substantial impact on fire resistance. Kodur et. al. [15] investigated the fire resistance of concrete structural elements reinforced with fiber-reinforced polymers. They contended that fiber-reinforced polymers and fire insulation had a substantial influence on fire resistance.

2 Database

However, when it comes to regression and classification analyses, data scientists can often become overwhelmed with the magnitude of options available. This is where we conduct regression and classification analyses on two separate datasets: one with real data and one with synthetic data.

2.1 Real Data

In this paper, we study the effects of fires on reinforced concrete columns using data collected from 144 columns [2, 7, 8, 12, 13, 16, 17, 20, 23, 24]. The real data were collected from literature through extensive works. Dataset statistics are listed in Table 1. This table shows the minimum, mean, maximum, and standard deviation of some values (width (W), steel reinforcement ratio (r), length (L), concrete strength (fc), the restraint situations (K), the concrete cover (C), and the magnitude of applied load (P) of the column) of the columns.

Table 1. Statistics of real data.

	W (mm)	r (%)	L (m)	fc (MPa)	K	C (mm)	P (kN)	FR (min)
Minimum	200.00	0.89	2.10	24.00	0.50	25.00	20.00	31.00
Maximum	869.00	4.39	5.76	138.00	1.00	61.00	5373.00	636.00
Average	312.55	2.09	3.88	47.08	0.77	38.83	1207.69	168.21
Std	61.08	0.49	0.71	27.58	0.23	6.48	1069.53	113.78

2.2 Synthetic Data

One of the most challenging information technologies to develop is the creation of machine learning models. There are many datasets that are not available to the public, and this makes it difficult for a machine to make predictions based on these datasets. One solution has been proposed: Utilize Generative Adversarial Nets (GANs) [6] to produce synthetic data with the same qualities as actual data and use them as a training set for automated machine learning [19]. A GAN is a deep neural network that consists of two nets. One net creates fake data samples with given parameters, and another net is trained to distinguish between fake and real samples. We create Continuous Time Generative Adversarial Networks (CTGAN) [26] and CopulaGan [4] models that we successfully use to produce synthetic data with properties similar to those of real-world data. The CTGAN model uses a normal distribution to model latent variables or multidimensional random vector parameters. The CopulaGan model is a Gaussian copula that can be used as a multivariate normal distribution with a covariance matrix and correlation matrix.

3 Methodology

This paper focuses on regression and classification analyses of fire-resistant reinforced concrete columns through eXtreme Gradient Boosting (Xgboost) regression and Xgboost classification algorithms [3]. The algorithm is a machine learning algorithm that combines several algorithms to perform many tasks. It is capable of regression analysis, classification, and even clustering. It can be used for both large and small-scale problems. The disadvantage is that it does not perform very well in limited and non-structured data.

Based on their fire resistance time, we perform classification analysis to establish which types of columns are most resistant to fires and which are least resistant, and we employ regression analysis to forecast the fire resistance behavior of reinforced concrete columns with varying components.

3.1 Xgboost Regression Model

Xgboost [3] is a machine learning algorithm that can be used for regression problems. It includes an efficient implementation of gradient boosting machines. The algorithm has been developed for high-performance computing and is scalable to parallel processing on very large datasets without significant speed penalties. The algorithm is based on gradient boosting machines, a variant of the stochastic gradient descent algorithm of deep neural networks that also use decision trees to build models.

3.2 Xgboost Classification Model

Xgboost [3] is a powerful supervised learning algorithm that can be used to perform classification tasks. It is extremely fast and efficient with high accuracy rates. It also has great flexibility in terms of parameters such as boosting parameters and the number of iterations. It uses the Gradient Boosting Machine and Gradient Descent to classify input variables in an iterative process. This means that it doesn't stop once it has found a single best decision tree, but rather continues to update the decision tree based on new information. The algorithm is not only able to find the best classification tree, but it also generates accurate predictions on how well one classifier will perform when compared to another.

4 Results and Discussion

Current deep learning methods have been shown to be able to learn from small datasets. However, this approach is limited by the scarcity of natural data. In order to overcome the data shortage, we use a set of (GANs) for modeling synthetic data. GANs are neural networks that generate new data points with the same properties as real data points. We implement GANs using the most prevalent approaches, CTGAN and CopulaGan to generate 10000 synthetic data from the real dataset for training purposes. Using real-world data, we demonstrate how different methods compare in terms of accuracy. Tables 2 and 3 present statistical information on synthetic data collected using both methodologies. Table 4 also offers synthetic data reports for both techniques. As a consequence, the synthetic data to be utilized in the study continuation were chosen as CopulaGan data, since synthetic data developed using the CopulaGan technique are more consistent with real data than CTGAN. Figure 1 also shows the FR distribution of actual and synthetic data from CopulaGan.

The Xgboost regression model [3] is a popular machine learning algorithm that has gained momentum in recent years. We use this model to analyze two datasets: one is based on a real-world dataset, and the other is synthetic data generated by CopulaGan. In both datasets, 20% of the dataset is used for train data, while the remaining 80% is set aside for test data.

Following the regression analysis, the R2 values obtained with these two data sets, which demonstrate how similar their estimations are to the real data, are provided in Table 5. The dataset obtained with the real dataset is 87%, whereas the dataset obtained with the synthetic dataset is 65%. In addition, Fig. 2 and Fig. 3 demonstrate how the

Table 2. Statistics of the CTGAN synthetic data

	W (mm)	*r* (%)	*L* (m)	*fc* (MPa)	*K*	*C* (mm)	*P* (kN)	*FR* (min)
Minimum	108.00	-0.13	1.14	-21.00	0.34	11.00	-1645.00	-232.00
Maximum	699.00	5.88	7.19	183.00	1.14	53.00	7425.00	826.00
Average	313.76	2.37	3.84	39.35	0.69	34.54	1106.90	139.81
Std	44.20	0.60	0.65	28.04	0.23	8.08	1260.46	139.46

Table 3. Statistics of the CopulaGAN synthetic data

	W (mm)	*r* (%)	*L* (m)	*fc* (MPa)	*K*	*C* (mm)	*P* (kN)	*FR* (min)
Minimum	200.00	0.89	2.10	24.00	0.50	25.00	20.00	31.00
Maximum	869.00	4.39	5.76	138.00	1.00	61.00	5373.00	636.00
Average	312.55	2.09	3.88	47.08	0.77	38.83	1207.69	168.21
Std	61.08	0.49	0.71	27.58	0.23	6.48	1069.53	113.78

Table 4. Synthetic Data Report

	CopulaGAN	CTGAN
Column correlations:	0. 951	0.143
Mean correlation between synthetic and real columns:	0. 970	0.878

values predicted by the Xgboost regressor relate to the values in the dataset for the real and synthetic datasets, respectively.

Machine learning is an effective tool for evaluating data and making predictions. In this paper, we explore how the Xgboost classification machine learning model can be used to identify patterns between datasets and make classification decisions on them. RC columns are classified based on how long they can withstand fire. Class 1 fire resistance time is defined as being less than one minute, class 2 fire resistance time as being between one minute and two minutes, class 3 fire resistance time as being between two minutes and three minutes, class 4 fire resistance time as being between three minutes and four minutes, and class 5 fire resistance time as being greater than four minutes. To show the efficacy of the Xgboost machine learning classification approach, we employ real-world data and synthetic data with CopulaGan. To that end, 75% of both real and synthetic datasets were designated as train data and 25% as test data. The train and test data were then subjected to standard scaling.

Figure 4 and Fig. 5 show the confusion matrix images obtained following Xgboost analysis for real and synthetic datasets, respectively. Figure 4 illustrates that over the real dataset, there is only one incorrect prediction for class 3, and there are no incorrect predictions for classes 1, 2, 4, and 5. Moreover, Fig. 5 indicates that all predictions

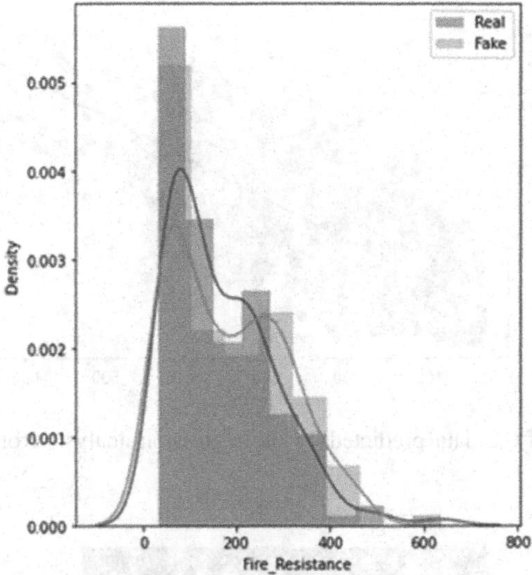

Fig. 1. FR distribution of real and synthetic data from CopulaGan

Table 5. R2 Results of Xgboost Machine Learning Models

	Real Data	Synthetic Data
Regression	0.87	0.65
Classification	0.99	1

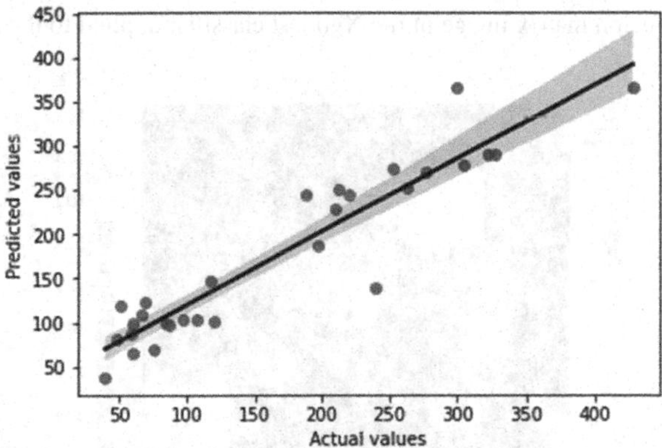

Fig. 2. Comparison of the data predicted by regression analysis from real data with real data

obtained for all classes using the synthetic dataset are correct. Furthermore, as shown in Table 5, the performance indicators by means of the classification R2 values are 99.99% for actual and 100% for synthetic data [18].

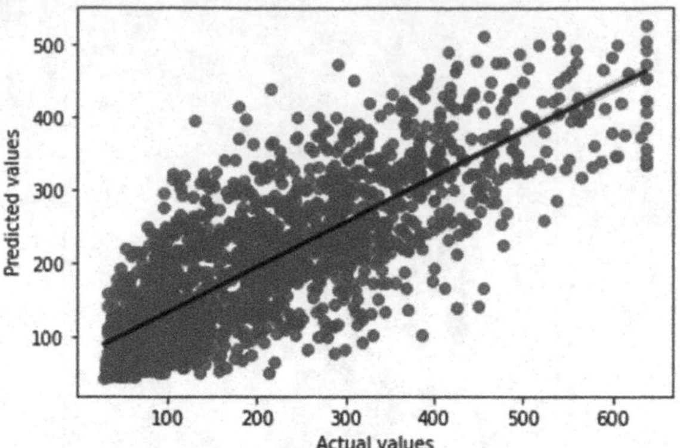

Fig. 3. Comparison of the data predicted by the regression analysis from synthetic data with synthetic data

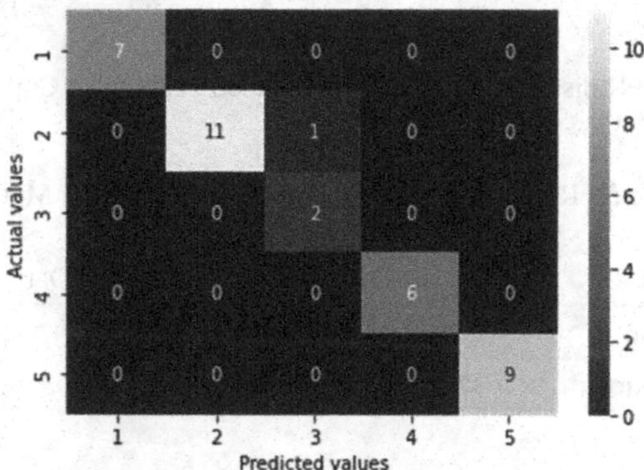

Fig. 4. Confusion matrix image of the Xgboost classifier applied to the real dataset

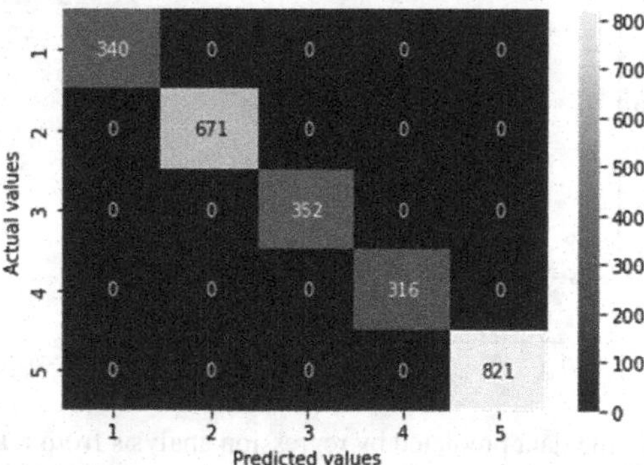

Fig. 5. Confusion matrix image of the Xgboost classifier applied to the synthetic dataset

5 Conclusions

This paper presents an approach to expanding real fire test databases by means of synthetic and validated data. This newly generated data is obtained from Generative Adversarial Networks. Based on the findings of this work, the following conclusions can be made:

1. GANs present a robust method to generate synthetic data from real fire tests.
2. The CopulaGan method creates synthetic data which is more consistent with real fire-resistant RC column data than CTGAN.
3. It seems that the addition of new data can aid in improving predictions from classification-based machine learning as opposed to regression-based machine learning, and hence future testing is required to further explore this front.
4. Machine learning, with the addition of GANs, since it overcomes the limitations in data, could help open a new frontier for fire research.

The main limitation of the study can be attributed to the use of only two techniques (CopulaGAN and CTGAN) to generate tabular synthetic data. For the next studies, the classification and regression outcomes of synthetic data generated by several alternative GAN techniques, such as TVAE and GaussianCopula, can be compared.

References

1. Balaji, A., Luquman K.M., Nagarajan, P., Madhavan Pillai, T.M.: Studies on the behavior of reinforced concrete short column subjected to fire. Alexandria Eng. J. **55**(1), 475–486 (2016)
2. Bažant, Z.P., Kaplan, M.F., Bazant, Z.P.: Concrete at High Temperatures Material Properties and Mathematical Models (1996)
3. Chen, T., Guestrin, C.: XGBoost a scalable tree boosting system. In: Proceedings of the 22nd ACM SIGKDD International Conference on Knowledge Discovery and Data Mining, pp. 785–794. Association for Computing Machinery, New York, NY, USA (2016)
4. CopulaGan Model (2021). httpssdv.devSDVuser_guidessingle_tablecopulagan.html
5. Ghoreishi, M., Mirzazadeh, A., Weber, G.-W.: Optimal pricing and ordering policy for non-instantaneous deteriorating items under inflation and customer returns. Optimization **63**(12), 1785–1804 (2014)
6. Goodfellow, I.J., et al.: Generative Adversarial Networks (2014)
7. Harmathy, T.Z.: Effect of Mositure on the Fire Endurance of Building Elements. ASTM Spec. Tech. Publ. (1965)
8. Hertz, K.D.D.: Limits of spalling of fire-exposed concrete. Fire Saf. J. **38**(2), 103–116 (2003)
9. Khalilpourazari, S., Khalilpourazary, S., Özyüksel Çiftçioğlu, A., Weber, G.-W.: Designing energy-efficient high-precision multi-pass turning processes via robust optimization and artificial intelligence. J. Intell. Manuf. **32**(6), 1621–1647 (2020)
10. Khalilpourazari, S., Mirzazadeh, A., Weber, G.-W., Pasandideh, S.H.R.: A robust fuzzy approach for constrained multi-product economic production quantity with imperfect items and rework process. Optimization **69**(1), 63–90 (2020)
11. Khalilpourazari, S., Pasandideh, S.H.R.: Modeling and optimization of multi-item multi-constrained EOQ model for growing items. Knowledge-Based Syst. **164**, 150–162 (2019)
12. Klingsch, E.W.H.: Explosive spalling of concrete in fire. Tese doutorado (2014)
13. Kodur, V., Cheng, F., Wang, T., Latour, J., Leroux, P.: Fire Resistance of High-Performance Concrete Columns (2001)

14. Kodur, V.K., Naser, M.Z.: Structural Fire Engineering. McGraw Hill Professional (2022)
15. Kodur, V.K.R., Bhatt, P.P., Naser, M.Z.: High temperature properties of fiber reinforced polymers and fire insulation for fire resistance modeling of strengthened concrete structures. Compos. Part B Eng. **175**, 107104 (2019)
16. Kodur, V.R., Mcgrath, R.C., Latour, J.C., Maclaurin, J.W.: Experimental Studies for Evaluating the Fire Endurance of High- Strength Concrete Columns (2000)
17. Naser, M.Z.: Heuristic machine cognition to predict fire-induced spalling and fire resistance of concrete structures. Autom. Constr. **106**, 102916 (2019)
18. Naser, M.Z., Alavi, A.H.: Error metrics and performance fitness indicators for artificial intelligence and machine learning in engineering and sciences. Archit. Struct. Constr. (2021)
19. Patki, N., Wedge, R., Veeramachaneni, K.: The synthetic data vault. In: 2016 IEEE International Conference on Data Science and Advanced Analytics (DSAA), pp. 399–410 (2016)
20. Phan, L.T., Carino, N.J.: Fire performance of high strength concrete research needs. In Advanced Technology in Structural Engineering, pp. 1–8. American Society of Civil Engineers, Reston, VA (2000)
21. Qiao, Q., Li, J., Mou, B., Cao, W.: Axial compressive behavior of reinforced concrete-filled stainless steel tube (RCFSST) stub columns experimental research. J. Build. Eng. **44**, 103431 (2021)
22. Rather, S.A., Bala, P.S.: Analysis of Gravitation-Based Optimization Algorithms for Clustering and Classification. IGI Global (2020)
23. Raut, N., Kodur, V.: Response of Reinforced Concrete Columns Under Fire-Induced Biaxial Bending (2011)
24. Ulm, F.-J., Coussy, O., Bažant, Z.P.: The "chunnel" fire. i chemoplastic softening in rapidly heated concrete. J. Eng. Mech. **125**(3), 272–282 (1999)
25. Wang, Y., et al.: Numerical modelling of in-plane restrained concrete two-way slabs subjected to fire. Fire Saf. J. **121**, 103307 (2021)
26. Xu, L., Skoularidou, M., Cuesta-Infante, A., Veeramachaneni, K.: Modeling tabular data using conditional GAN. In: Advances in Neural Information Processing Systems (2019)
27. Yang, Y., Feng, S., Xue, Y., Yu, Y., Wang, H., Chen, Y.: Experimental study on shear behavior of fire-damaged reinforced concrete T-beams retrofitted with prestressed steel straps. Constr. Build. Mater. **209**, 644–654 (2019)

Unsupervised Machine Learning for Fire Resistance Analysis

Aybike Özyüksel Çiftçioğlu[1](✉) and M. Z. Naser[2]

[1] Department of Civil Engineering, Faculty of Engineering, Manisa Celal Bayar University, Manisa, Turkey
aybike.ozyuksel@cbu.edu.tr

[2] School of Civil and Environmental Engineering & Earth Sciences, AI Research Institute for Science and Engineering (AIRISE), Clemson, USA

Abstract. Due to its inert nature, concrete has good fire resistance properties. As such, concrete has often been favored for construction – especially where fire hazard is expected. However, this does not mean that reinforced concrete cannot catch fire. It can still be affected by heat and, if exposed to high temperatures, can eventually break down. Therefore, the fire resistance of the reinforced concrete (RC) columns is a critical concern. There are many ways for assessing the fire resistance of structures, but it is difficult to quantify the fire resistance in quantitative terms. The purpose of this work is to investigate the use of unsupervised machine learning by means of clustering to examine the fire resistance of RC columns. A database of over 144 RC columns subjected to standard fire conditions has been collected and then examined via the interpretable Fuzzy C-Means algorithm (FCM) and the Classification and Regression Tree (CART) model. Our results indicate that this clustering technique groups RC columns into four natural groups – each with specific properties and characteristics. Moreover, the CART model is used to analyze the variables used as the basis for the clustering of RC columns. Accordingly, when RC columns are separated into four natural clusters, the first split occurs due to restrictions, and the second separation is controlled by the compressive strength and reinforcement ratios of the columns. This research might be the first to attempt to leverage clustering analysis to investigate the fire response of RC columns. The findings of the study clearly show that unsupervised machine learning can provide valuable insights to fire engineers often missing from traditional supervised learning.

Keywords: Clustering · Columns · Concrete · Fire · Machine Learning

1 Introduction

The fire resistance analysis of RC columns is of great significance in the field of fire engineering. The behavior of RC columns in a fire is complicated and is difficult to be analyzed in the traditional way [19]. The goal of this study is to research the fire resistance of RC columns which can be affected by many parameters. In the present study, FCM clustering which is a powerful data mining technique is employed to analyze RC columns

A. Mirzazadeh et al. (Eds.): SEMIT 2022, CCIS 1808, pp. 211–221, 2023.
https://doi.org/10.1007/978-3-031-40395-8_15

exposed to fire. The technique is capable of grouping objects into categories by assigning each object a membership score that indicates the level of membership in a group. The model is built using data collected from the literature [8, 14, 18, 22, 23, 33, 34].

The database was examined using FCM algorithms. Our results show that this clustering technique divides the RC column into four natural groups each with its own characteristics. Furthermore, the CART model is used to analyze variables used as a base for clustering RC columns. Therefore, when the RC column is separated into four natural groups, the first separation is caused by restrictions and the second by compressive strength and reinforcement ratios of the columns.

Several studies have been published in the literature on the use of artificial intelligence and machine learning technologies to solve engineering challenges [4, 6, 10, 13, 15, 21, 29, 35]. Noman et al. [24] conducted two fire tests to investigate the experimental findings of the change in design variables of a two-story RC building. Jihong and Wenwen [37] investigated the damage that steel components caused during the fire test as well as the failure mechanisms of steel. For various fire conditions, they proposed a scientific method. Pressure experiments on fire-resistant steel columns were conducted by Wu et al. [38] to study several characteristics, including buckling. Qin et al. [28] summarized the damage to reinforced concrete structures caused by a major fire. They also discussed firefighting deficiencies and corrective measures taken to eliminate fire damage in buildings. To evaluate the bending bearing capacity of RC beams, Gedam [7] proposed a performance-based fire resistance design technique to evaluate the bending bearing capability of RC beams. This researcher validated the approach to fire resistance design using experimentally obtained and compiled data. Packialakshmi et al. [25] added polypropylene fiber to the concrete mix to increase thermal resistance. The thermal resistance gain was reported to be around 5% based on the 28-day test results. Buttignol et al. [3] study simple analytical approaches to forecast the structural response of RC columns subjected to fire. They computed the total deflections and failures (in time and type) of RC columns with various properties. In front of machine learning and RC columns under fire, a series of works were also recently published by the authors [23, 32].

The outcomes of this study illustrate that unsupervised machine learning can provide useful insights to fire engineers that are typically missing from traditional supervised learning.

2 Database

The database collected utilized in this study includes information on 144 RC columns that have been exposed to fire [1, 9, 11, 16–18, 20, 22, 23, 27, 30, 33, 34, 36]. The variables in the dataset are *W*: column width, *r*: steel reinforcement ratio, *L*: length, *fc*: concrete compressive strength, *K*: restraint situations (fixed-fixed = 0.5, fixed-pinned = 0.7, and pinned-pinned = 1), *C*: concrete cover to reinforcement, *P*: magnitude of applied load, and *FR*: fire resistance. The statistics of the dataset are listed in Table 1. The variable correlations are examined in order to understand more about the relationships between variables in the data set. Figure 1 depicts the colormap correlation matrix of the dataset's characteristics. A strong positive connection is represented by yellow, whereas a strong negative correlation is represented by dark purple. The variables with the strongest positive correlation with *FR*, as shown in the figure, are *C* and *W*, respectively. The variable with the largest negative connection to *FR*, on the other side, is *K*.

Table 1. Statistics of the dataset.

	W (mm)	*r* (%)	*L* (m)	*fc* (MPa)	*K*	*C* (mm)	*P* (kN)	*FR* (min)
Minimum	200.0	0.9	2.1	24.0	0.5	25.0	0.0	60.0
Maximum	406.0	4.4	5.8	138.0	1.0	64.0	5373.0	300.0
Average	317.3	2.1	3.8	53.3	0.8	39.0	1417.5	158.7
Std	44.1	0.7	0.6	32.6	0.2	7.6	1236.5	72.0
Skewness	0.8	0.5	-0.2	1.3	0.0	-0.3	1.6	0.3

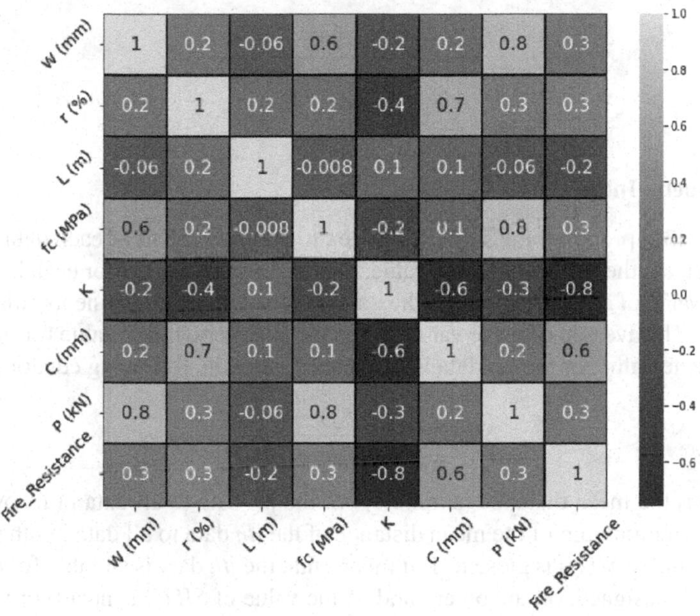

Fig. 1. Statistical insights to the collected database (top: frequency, bottom: correlation matrix)

3 Methodology

3.1 Fuzzy C Means Clustering Algorithm

Dunn [5] presented and Bezdek [2] developed the Fuzzy C-Means algorithm (FCM), which is one of the most widely used fuzzy clustering approaches. FCM is employed in this study because of its accuracy, high performance, and ease of implementation. Objects can belong to two or more clusters, according to the algorithm concept. According to the fuzzy logic principle, each data belongs to one of the clusters with a membership value ranging from 0 to 1. The total of all data membership values in all classes must equal 1. Whichever cluster the object is close to, its membership in that cluster grows bigger than its membership in other clusters. In contrast to solid clustering, the possibility of each data belonging to more than one cluster in FCM is the main distinguishing feature that sets it apart from other clustering approaches.

The objective function in Eq. 1 is minimized using the FCM.

$$J = \sum_{i=1}^{N} \sum_{j=1}^{C} u_{ij}^{m} d_{ij}^{2} \tag{1}$$

where C is the number of clusters (chosen by the user), N is the number of data, *uij* is the *ith* data's membership in the *jth* cluster, m is the fuzziness constant, and *dij* is the distance between the *ith* data and the *jth* cluster center. Distance measurement is commonly calculated as the Euclidean distance. The membership degree *uij* is calculated as in Eq. 2.

$$u_{ij} = \frac{1}{\sum_{j=1}^{C} \left(\frac{d_{ij}}{d_{ik}}\right)^{2/(m-1)}} \tag{2}$$

3.2 Silhouette Index

Rousseeuw [31] proposed the silhouette index to describe the fit of each data to its own set. To calculate the silhouette index value, the dataset is clustered for each k value. The silhouette value of each data point in the dataset is calculated to define its suitability for its own set. The average of these values gives the silhouette index value for the k value. The silhouette value for the *jth* data is calculated using the following equation.

$$SIL(j) = \frac{b(j) - a(j)}{max(a((j), b(j)))} \tag{3}$$

where *a(j)* is the mean distance (similarity) of the *jth* data to all data in its own cluster and *b(j)* is the minimum of the mean distance of the *jth* data to all data in other clusters.

If the value of *SIL(j)* is close to 1, it means that the *jth* data is suitable for the cluster to which it is assigned, on the other hand, if the value of *SIL(j)* is near 0 or negative, it indicates that the data is not appropriate for the cluster to which it has been allocated.

3.3 Principal Component Analysis (PCA)

In several areas, large data sets are becoming more prevalent. Working with large data sets may be time-consuming and expensive. Hence, it is vital to minimize the size of such datasets while keeping the data information. One of the oldest and most extensively used approaches for this purpose is principal component analysis (PCA). Pearson [26] proposed and Hotelling [12] refined the notion of decreasing the size of data while maintaining information. PCA changes the original variables with fewer correlations into new variables based on the relationship between variables in a multivariate dataset.

3.4 Decision Tree as an Interpretable Model

One of the most extensively used approaches for trustworthy inference is the decision tree, which is a procedure that uses a tree to describe the learned function. A decision tree is composed of roots, branches, and leaves. The initial cells of decision trees are referred to as roots. According to the root condition, each observation is categorized as "Yes" or "No". Below the root are the nodes. The nodes are used to classify each observation. As the number of nodes rises, so does the model's complexity. The leaves of the decision tree are at the bottom. Non-dividing nodes are leaves.

The degree of homogeneity of the nodes determines the accuracy of the classification. Entropy is a prominent statistic for determining the homogeneity of nodes. Entropy is a measure of the uncertainty of the data. For example, if a node has only one class, its entropy will be lower. Consequently, the data should be partitioned in such a way that the entropy is minimized. The better the quality of the divides, the better the outcome.

4 Results and Discussion

The nine-variable dataset was scaled with a standard scaler for data processing. PCA was applied to the dataset to decrease the size of the dataset and make the clustering more interpretable. As observed in Fig. 2, the number of variables most compatible with the dataset for PCA was determined as three components by plotting the cumulative values of the explained variance corresponding to the components. Therefore, the dataset was split into three components for further analysis.

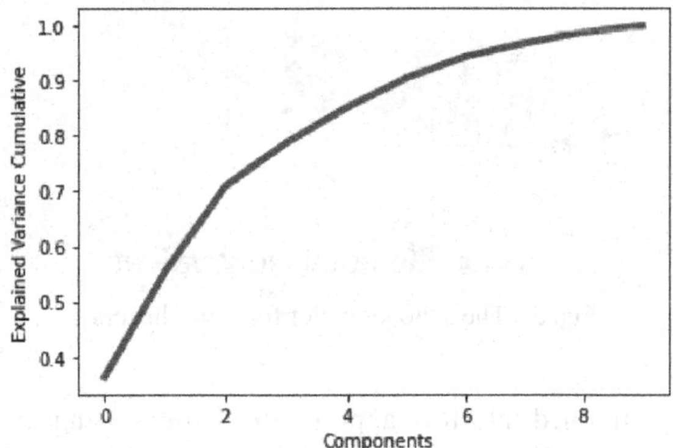

Fig. 2. PCA model statistic

On the preprocessed data, an appropriate number of clusters were sought for proper clustering using the FCM approach. As a result, as shown in Table 2, silhouette values ranging from 1 to 10 were assigned to each cluster. The cluster with the highest silhouette rating was determined to be "most appropriate". Table 2 reveals that the number of clusters with the highest silhouette score was four. This leads to the determination that there are four RC column clusters. Figure 3 also depicts the silhouette plot for four clusters.

Table 2. Average Silhouette scores of clusters

Number of clusters	Average Silhouette score
2	0.39
3	0.41
4	0.48
5	0.39
6	0.40
7	0.39
8	0.41
9	0.38
10	0.38

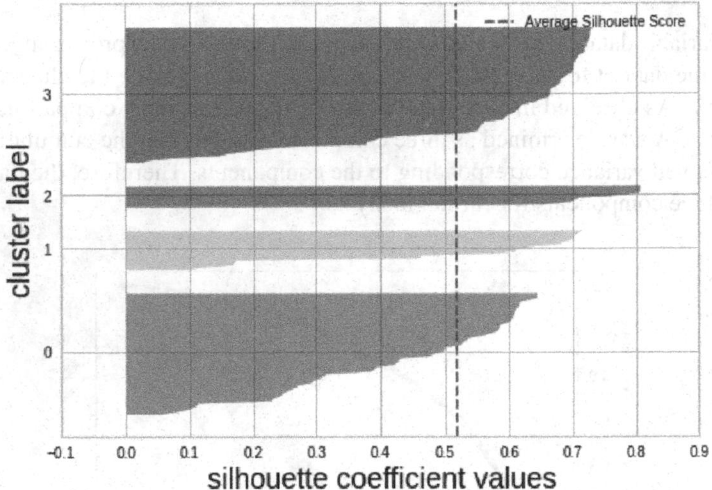

Fig. 3. The silhouette plot for four clusters

The data was partitioned into four appropriate clusters using the FCM clustering approach. Figure 4 depicts clustering plots based on the relationship between the three PCA components of the data.

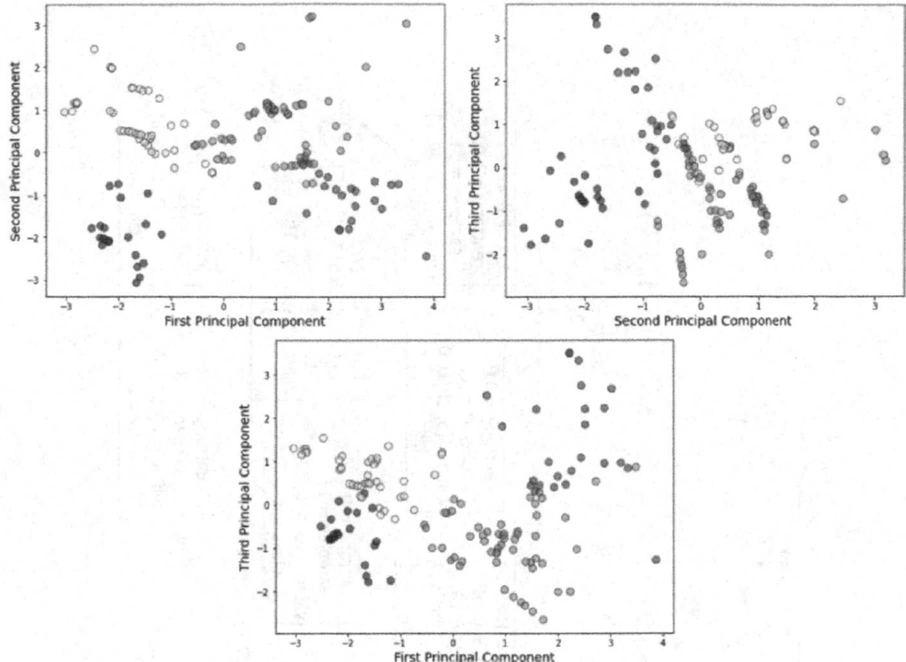

Fig. 4. Visualization of clustering in the dataset

The decision tree of the classification and regression tree model (CART) is also shown in Fig. 5. The initial split occurred in terms of restrictions, as seen in the figure. The CART model identified the fixed-fixed or fixed-pinned support forms of the columns independently from the pinned-pinned support form in this initial division. The second split was based on the compressive strength and reinforcement ratios of the columns. Moreover, Table 3 contains information about the splits of the algorithm. Knowing the information on the splits as listed in Table 4 will help designers to predict the performance of RC columns without fire testing. Then it is possible that designers can alter the properties of RC columns that belong to clusters of low fire resistance.

Figure 6 depicts the distribution of columns related to fire resistance according to the FCM method. Cluster 3 has the largest fire resistance, as indicated in the figure, whereas Cluster 1 has the lowest fire resistance and is followed by Clusters 4 and 2, respectively.

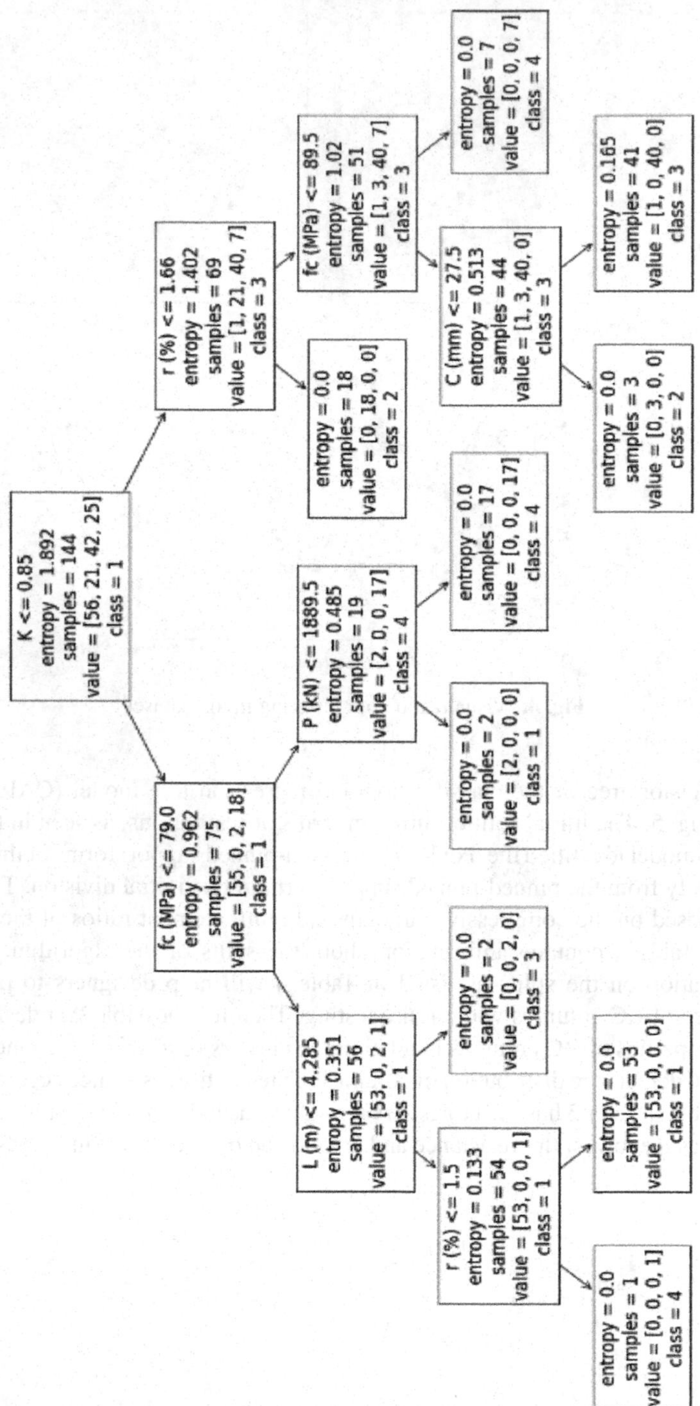

Fig. 5. Decision tree by CART model

Table 3. Splits of algorithm

Split	FCM
First split	K
Second split	f_c, r
Number of split node	8
Number of leaf node	8

Table 4. Feature range for all columns

Algorithms	Cluster 1	Cluster 2	Cluster 3	Cluster 4
FCM	$K \leq 0.85 \& f_c \leq 79 \& L \leq 4.285 \& r > 1.5$	$K > 0.85 \& r \leq 1.66$	$K > 0.85 \& r > 1.66 \& f_c \leq 89.5 \& C > 27.5$	$K > 0.85 \& r > 1.66 \& f_c > 89.5$
	$K \leq 0.85 \& f_c > 79 \& P \leq 1889.5$	$K > 0.85 \& r > 1.66 \& f_c \leq 89.5 \& C \leq 27.5$	$K \leq 0.85 \& f_c \leq 79 \& L > 4.285$	$K \leq 0.85 \& f_c > 79 \& P > 1889.5$
	-	-	-	$K \leq 0.85 \& f_c \leq 79 \& L \leq 4.285 \& r \leq 1.5$

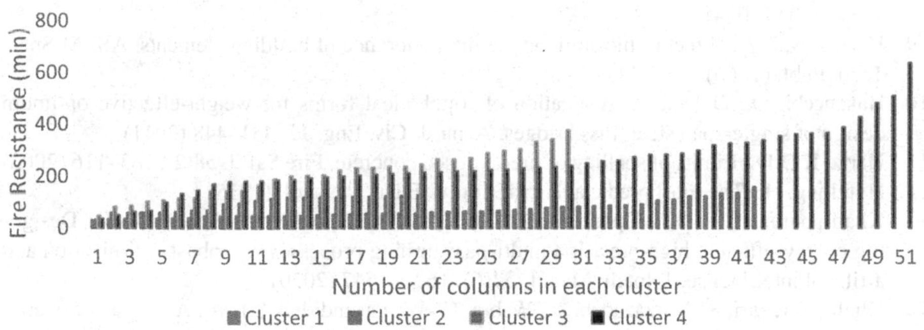

Fig. 6. Distribution of clusters

5 Conclusions

This paper on the application of unsupervised machine learning to study the fire resistance of RC columns is one of the first attempts presented in this research. The findings of this paper clearly show how unsupervised machine learning can provide fire engineers with valuable insights that are often missing from more traditional supervised learning. In addition,

1. There appear to be four natural clusters for fire-exposed RC columns.
2. Integration of interoperability techniques improves our insights into unsupervised machine learning analysis.
3. Additional works on the frontier of fire and unsupervised machine learning are warranted to improve our understanding of the fire response of RC columns.

References

1. Bažant, Z.P., Kaplan, M.F., Bazant, Z.P.: Concrete at High Temperatures: Material Properties and Mathematical Models (1996)
2. Bezdek, J.: Pattern Recognition With Fuzzy Objective Function Algorithms (1981)
3. Buttignol, T.E.T., Bittencourt, T.N.: Simplified design procedures for the structural analysis of reinforced concrete columns in fire. Eng. Struct. **246**, 113076 (2021)
4. Dogan, E.: Solving design optimization problems via hunting search algorithm with levy flights. Struct. Eng. Mech. **52**(2) (2014)
5. Dunn, J.C.: A Fuzzy Relative of the ISODATA Process and Its Use in Detecting Compact Well-Separated Clusters (1973)
6. Erdal, F., Dogan, E., Saka, M.P.: Optimum design of cellular beams using harmony search and particle swarm optimizers. J. Constr. Steel Res. **67**(2), 237–247 (2011)
7. Gedam, B.A.: Fire resistance design method for reinforced concrete beams to evaluate fire-resistance rating. Structures. **33**, 855–877 (2021)
8. Ghoreishi, M., Mirzazadeh, A., Weber, G.-W.: Optimal pricing and ordering policy for non-instantaneous deteriorating items under inflation and customer returns. Optimization **63**(12), 1785–1804 (2014)
9. Harmathy, T.Z.: Effect of mositure on the fire endurance of building elements. ASTM Spec. Tech. Publ. (1965)
10. Hasançebi, O., Dogan, E.: Evaluation of topological forms for weight-effective optimum design of single-span steel truss bridges. Asian J. Civ. Eng. **12**, 431–448 (2011)
11. Hertz, K.D.D.: Limits of spalling of fire-exposed concrete. Fire Saf. J. **38**(2), 103–116 (2003)
12. Hotelling, H.: The most predictable criterion. J. Educ. Psychol. (1935)
13. Khalilpourazari, S., Khalilpourazary, S., Özyüksel Çiftçioğlu, A., Weber, G.-W.: Designing energy-efficient high-precision multi-pass turning processes via robust optimization and artificial intelligence. J. Intell. Manuf. **32**(6), 1621–1647 (2020)
14. Khalilpourazari, S., Mirzazadeh, A., Weber, G.-W., Pasandideh, S.H.R.: A robust fuzzy approach for constrained multi-product economic production quantity with imperfect items and rework process. Optimization **69**(1), 63–90 (2020)
15. Khalilpourazari, S., Pasandideh, S.H.R.: Modeling and optimization of multi-item multi-constrained EOQ model for growing items. Knowledge-Based Syst. **164**, 150–162 (2019)
16. Klingsch, E.W.H.: Explosive spalling of concrete in fire. Tese doutorado (2014)
17. Kodur, V., Cheng, F., Wang, T., Latour, J., Leroux, P.: Fire Resistance of High-Performance Concrete Columns (2001)
18. Kodur, V., McGrath, R., Leroux, P., Latour, J.: Experimental Studies for Evaluating the Fire Endurance of High-Strength Concrete Columns (2005)
19. Kodur, V.K., Naser, M.Z.: Structural Fire Engineering. McGraw Hill Professional (2022)
20. Kodur, V.R., Mcgrath, R.C., Latour, J.C., Maclaurin, J.W.: Experimental Studies for Evaluating the Fire Endurance of High- Strength Concrete Columns (2000)

21. Kouka, N., Fdhila, R., Hussain, A., Alimi, A.M.: Dynamic multi objective particle swarm optimization with cooperative agents. In: 2020 IEEE Congress on Evolutionary Computation (CEC), pp. 1–8 (2020)
22. Liu, J.-C.C., Tan, K.H., Yao, Y.: A new perspective on nature of fire-induced spalling in concrete. Constr. Build. Mater. **184**, 581–590 (2018)
23. Naser, M.Z.: Heuristic machine cognition to predict fire-induced spalling and fire resistance of concrete structures. Autom. Constr. **106**, 102916 (2019)
24. Noman, M., Yaqub, M., Fahad, M., Butt, F., Khalid, B.: Dynamic characteristics of RC structures in short and long duration real fires. Case Stud. Constr. Mater. **16**, e01058 (2022)
25. Packialakshmi, S., Krishnakumar, Erskine, S., Anuradha, B.: Performance evaluation of fire resistant characteristics in polypropylene fiber concrete. Mater. Today Proc. (2021)
26. Pearson, K.: On lines and planes of closest fit to systems of points in space. London, Edinburgh, Dublin Philos. Mag. J. Sci. **2**(11), 559–572 (1901)
27. Phan, L.T., Carino, N.J.: Fire performance of high strength concrete: research needs. In: Advanced Technology in Structural Engineering, pp. 1–8. American Society of Civil Engineers, Reston, VA (2000)
28. Qin, D., Gao, P., Aslam, F., Sufian, M., Alabduljabbar, H.: A comprehensive review on fire damage assessment of reinforced concrete structures. Case Stud. Constr. Mater. e00843 (2021)
29. Rather, S.A., Bala, P.S.: Analysis of gravitation-based optimization algorithms for clustering and classification. IGI Global (2020)
30. Raut, N., Kodur, V.: Response of Reinforced Concrete Columns Under Fire-Induced Biaxial Bending (2011)
31. Rousseeuw, P.J.: Silhouettes: A graphical aid to the interpretation and validation of cluster analysis. J. Comput. Appl. Math. (1987)
32. Seitlllari, A., Naser, M.Z.: Leveraging artificial intelligence to assess explosive spalling in fire-exposed RC columns. Comput. Concr. (2019)
33. Shah, A.H., Sharma, U.K.: Fire resistance and spalling performance of confined concrete columns. Constr. Build. Mater. **156**, 161–174 (2017)
34. Song, T.-Y., Han, L.-H., Tao, Z.: Structural behavior of SRC beam-to-column joints subjected to simulated fire including cooling phase. J. Struct. Eng. (2015)
35. Tirkolaee, E.B., Mardani, A., Dashtian, Z., Soltani, M., Weber, G.W.: A novel hybrid method using fuzzy decision making and multi-objective programming for sustainable-reliable supplier selection in two-echelon supply chain design. J. Clean. Prod. **250**, 119517 (2020)
36. Ulm, F.-J., Coussy, O., Bažant, Z.P.: The "Chunnel" Fire. I: Chemoplastic softening in rapidly heated concrete. J. Eng. Mech. **125**(3), 272–282 (1999)
37. Wenwen, C., Jihong, Y.: The most adverse fire scenario research of steel frame structure fire-resistant design based on structural vulnerability analysis. Structures **34**, 2861–2875 (2021)
38. Wu, Y., Xu, Y., Shi, Y., Ban, H.: Overall buckling behavior of fire-resistant steel welded I-section columns under ambient temperature. J. Constr. Steel Res. **157**, 32–45 (2019)

Apriori Algorithm in Market Basket Analysis: A Retailer Example in Turkey

Anıl Aksoy[1], Burcin Kaplan[1](✉), and Vildan Gülpınar Demirci[2]

[1] Istanbul Aydin University, Istanbul, Turkey
burcinkaplan@aydin.edu.tr
[2] Aksaray University, Aksaray, Turkey

Abstract. In recent years, along with the technological improvements and data volume increase, data mining in CRM and marketing's common strategical issues became more popular. There is an increasing trend that data mining can help customer relations and the research of these analyses' is directly related to consumers. In this study, the management of customer relations and the timeline of customer's life cycle research models were explained along with the theory of togetherness apriori algorithm. The authors collected the data via a Turkish company's retail sales verification in the Istanbul airport. The sales data for two months of this company has been analyzed. From the total number of 1650 transactions, 1550 customer transactions were found who pick more than one product. In this two-month dataset, 42 groups of product associations were examined using SPSS 15.0 module program. The research showed that the products displayed together and which one can display separately from other products have emerged. This study also provided a general insight into the efficient demand number of the goods to be evaluated for the customers' needs and demands.

Keywords: Data Mining · Apriori Algorithm · Customer Relationship Management

1 Introduction

Airport stores emerged as a new and important distribution channel for retailers (Ünder and Atalık 2016; Lin and Chen 2013), which required the application of different marketing strategies due to the potential of customers from different customer segments and different nations. Commercialization of airports increased the importance of airport store customers motivating researchers for making attempts to understand the buying behaviors of customers that are becoming different (Graham et al. 2014). Considering that the customer group for airport stores is not limited to passengers, but includes airport employees, passengers' relatives and local residents (Freathy and O'Connell 2012), it is seen that the customer potential further increases.

Customers of airport stores have different characters than those of other retailers. Products sold at an airport sport could be interesting in particular for those customers from a different country or culture. This may reduce the stress of international passengers,

A. Mirzazadeh et al. (Eds.): SEMIT 2022, CCIS 1808, pp. 222–235, 2023.
https://doi.org/10.1007/978-3-031-40395-8_16

the number of whom is quickly increasing, while waiting for their flights and, the volume of their commercial activities may increase due to the interesting products and interior layouts of stores (Sadıkoğlu 2017; Han et al. 2014).

Shopping at airports is now considered an important aspect of not only tourism research but also the customer relations management for airport business management and marketing. Airport retail business has become a more important source of income for airport business enterprises. Among the main sources of income for airport business enterprises are the shopping and food courts, which have a potential to minimize the concerns and distresses of passengers (Sadıkoğlu 2017). Security checks and passport checks for passengers and distances between the gates as well as complicated and unfamiliar environments are among those factors that could cause a time pressure at an airport (Lin and Chen 2013). The time pressure that may occurs due to the flight procedures within an airport may negatively affect the amount of potential purchases at that airport (Han et al. 2014; Sadıkoğlu 2017). Therefore, the time pressure could be considered a significant disadvantage for airport store customers. Due to all these factors, many passengers arrive at the airport long before the scheduled flight time and the idle time, which is the waiting period while passengers spend at the airport before the flight could turn into "*happy hours*". This plays a role to increase the traffic at the airport stores (Lin and Chen 2013). When directed properly, the time pressure at an airport may encourage customers to shop more. At this point, it is critical to develop a series of retail sales strategies in order to trigger the buying behaviors of passengers (Sadıkoğlu 2017). Airports provides an environment that could trigger the instant buying behaviors of passengers and, those who shop impulsively become open to instant, unexpected ideas to purchase (Lin and Chen 2013; Omar and Kent 2001). The main reason is that the attempt to keep the shopping time shorter due to the time pressure has a higher effect on making instant decisions. From this point of view, a customers in an airport environment should be considered a consumer who makes instant decisions (Sharma and Nanda 2012). Therefore, airport store customers differ from other store customers in this respect.

The positive effect of the different and interesting environment of an airport store as well as the both negative and positive effect of the time pressure and, the instant buying behavior pattern as a result thereof increase the importance of product placement at the store. Knowing which products are purchased together by customers and a proper placement of these products at the store using this information as well as advanced customer relation practices would contribute to the increase of sales and profitability. From this point of view, the purpose of the research is identify the buying behaviors of airport store customers that are different from other store customers since they tend to make instant decisions and be affected by different physical environments. The fact that customer profile diversity and time constraints affect the purchasing behavior at the airports distinguishes airport retailing from retail activities in different locations. This article aimed to contribute to the literature using market basket analysis for airport management and marketing as one of the few studies in the field that focuses on this aspect of the subject.

For this purpose, we applied the market basket analysis method, which is frequently used in literature to understand the buying behaviors of customers (Unvan 2021) and, which is made use of to place products at a store and identify those products purchased together. It is expected that an application of this research on airport store customers with different buying behaviors would contribute to further research in this field.

2 Literature Review

This section is intended to provide a brief explanation of a series of research conducted about the market basket analysis and association rules, which have an important place in the field of data mining for marketing.

Pradhan et al. (2022) performed product groupings for "efficient" and "inefficient" customers, using the assumption that customers with higher average CLV (customer lifetime value) for retailers have a more meaningful purchasing pattern. Association rule mining was used for market basket analysis using a genetic algorithm. The study found that the product options of more productive customers were better mapped compared to less efficient customers. The potential of the results to assist retailers in category management for better commercialization and improved profitability was highlighted.

Çiçek and Kabasakal (2021), in their study using monthly basket data from an e-retailer in Turkey, used market basket analysis to extract segment-specific rules that associate product-level purchasing decisions with gender, location, and age group.

Musalem et al. (2018) used the market basket analysis method to determine the interrelationships between product categories, using data from a supermarket store. The study aims to provide segmentation of shopping trips based on the composition of each shopping cart. The research results show that retailers can potentially benefit if they shift from the traditional category management approach, where retailers single-handedly manage product categories, to a customer management approach where retailers define, acknowledge, and strengthen the relationships between product categories.

Alan (2016) analyzed the voucher transactions of a supermarket for 7 days by means of using a packaged software of SPSS Clementine 11.1 and Microsoft SQL Server 2005 for the database. Based on the association rules described according to this analysis, it was suggested that the supermarket could change the buying behaviors of customers with a more efficient shelf arrangement.

Kaur and Kang (2016) analyzed the customers' behaviors by means of applying the association rules with the aim of increasing the sales rates. The resulting threshold values significantly affected the research and thus it was concluded that the values should be automatized for better threshold values. Secondly, it was suggested that the recognition of outliers would result in options for another research on the market.

Doğan et al. (2014) analyzed the customer data of a leading insurance company operating in Turkey by means of using the Apriori algorithm and, attempted to identify the product groups purchased together by the customers. Accordingly, 64% of the customers purchasing comprehensive insurance had also traffic insurance and, 55% of those with fire insurance had also compulsory earthquake insurance, which consists of 9% of the total number.

Timor et al. (2017) analyzed the shopping records of a company that operates in the field of ready-made clothing. This study during which a packaged software of SPSS Clementine was used was intended to identify the customers' shopping habits by means of using the association rules. Accordingly, it was suggested that a business should arrange its production based on its sales based on an efficient marketing strategy, sales, advertising and promotional activities.

2.1 Customer Relationship Management for Marketing

Considering its approach intended to "provide people with opportunities to live better", the concept of marketing includes all the individual activities of creating, presenting and changing goods, services and ideas of great importance to meet desires and needs of individuals and groups in the right combinations thereof. And the Customer Relationship Management (CRM) is a way of management that is designed to understand customers, establish tight bonds with customers, retain potential customers and gain new and more profitable customers during the activities of marketing.

Today, marketing mentality changes as the technology advances. The globalizing world economy centers around customers by means of defocusing manufacturers in trade. Since there is a limited number of manufacturers and a lot of markets, customers have the right to choose any alternative they may wish (Bergeron 2002). CRM is known as a stage of processing customer focused projects during the phases of marketing and sales. Another important issue is that it must be remembered that CRM should be understood only as software and automation, CRM is not a whole of technologies, but based on a process instead. CRM is a recurring process as created to continuously improve facts that are relevant to one another and accomplish results that are compatible with one another based on these facts (Taşpınar 2005).

CRM is a technology based action of sales for businesses to combine marketing with information technologies. Therefore, computer software and technological applications are important for CRM. CRM has some certain functional characteristics such as data storage, customer loyalty, management of potential customers and winning new customers (Kalakota and Robinson 2001). In terms of information, CRM is a whole of customer focused decisions and strategies in which all customer information is gathered in a certain center, and there is an aim to use the conclusions from this information to protect their existing customers, increase the possibility of trading with them, and offer them value added and compatible services in all aspects of trade and, gather together all business processes and information management system for these purposes (Taşpınar 2005).

Among the purposes of CRM are also those intended to create the measurements of customer satisfaction, speed up the process for customer feedbacks, increase the profitability in relation with operational business activities, minimize the operation costs at each step and level, and improve and increase the frequency of the portfolio of goods and customers customized for customers (Karadeniz 2008).

In parallel with the advanced technology and increased use of internet applications, one of the biggest opportunity offered by E-CRM is to enhance the level of customer satisfaction and monitor the customer behaviors by means of making use of the opportunities for wider markets offered by e-trade.

2.2 Data Mining

Data are the information that is needed to get results during a research or process operation. Information is the processed and interpreted version of data. Data are in general considering the undefined, raw facts (Barutçugil 2002). Information is maintained as processed data that affects the possible alternatives. Data are sometimes renewed, updated or summarized. Data are gathered to test hypotheses and thus depending on unprocessed and non-analyzed numbers. When tested, data are calculated based on information that covers everyone and everything.

Data warehouse is a storage that is used during the process of data mining to solve problems, create queries and conduct analyses. It is the version of such databases with the same direction used for more than one purpose gathered under a single roof. Data warehouses are created when data from multi sources are gathered.

As the amount of data is gradually increased every passing day in today's world of information, it becomes harder to properly and accurately interpret such data. It is very important to analyze and interpret the data in order to get accurate and useful information therefrom. Data mining is used to reveal hidden correlations on data that are kept in data warehouses. Data mining is the process of discovering information as an attempt to make raw data meaningful in every environment and every situation where there are data.

Process is a concept of great importance for data mining. This classic standard process was identified by the consortium of *Cross-Industry Standard Process for Data Mining (CRISP-DM)* about at the end of the 1996's. This consortium was led by Daimler Chrysler, and the data mining platform of Clementine was created by SPSS and NCR. The most important breakthrough was made by SPSS in this consortium. Under the leadership of SPSS, it has become a method used by many companies (Şimşek 2006).

As the cost of information processing reduces, the way to get and store raw information becomes easier, great advancements are achieved and, the number of analytical tools gets increased in the field of database management system, the interest in data mining is soaring up day by day (Park et al. 2001).

It is possible to apply data mining, which is improving during the recent years, into all types of businesses with data warehouses where data are gathered and stored, irrespective of the industry they operate. Applications of data mining are used in many fields such as marketing, retailing, financing, insurance, astronomy, biology, medicine, genetics, security, logistics, supply chains, meteorology, banking and telecommunication etc. (Rygielski et al. 2002: 488). There are two main reason of this flexibility that it is used in so many different areas: the first one is that it is possible to use data mining algorithms in all the industries where data are available, and the second one is that it makes it possible for businesses to know their customers and satisfy them by means of meeting their requirements and needs in an optimum manner.

It is very hard to group customers with different preferences and tastes. One could mention the importance of the application of data mining techniques in order to divide customers into homogenous groups by individual packages for marketing strategies. Data mining applications are in general used to reveal and identify customer profiles.

During the application of marketing activities such as sales campaigns and promotions, customer groups with similar demographics and previous buying attitudes are turned into such customer groups with homogenous or similar characteristics for qualifications by means of clustering and classification analyses of data mining. This makes it possible to create different strategies for these groups.

For the retail industry, many data that are obtained from store shopping membership cards and credit cards such as sales details, customer profiles, product transfer details and service information are monitored by data mining. And e-trade applications, the number of which is increasing during the recent years, form a comprehensive database for the retail industry. It is critical for many companies to use properly these databases in terms of corporate competition and business achievements.

There are many different techniques used for the data mining. All of these techniques have their own advantages and disadvantages during the process of solving a problem. Among the most frequent used ones are decision trees, neural networks, clustering analyses, k-nearest neighbor algorithms, fuzzy logic and market basket analyses & association rules. The main distinction between classification and regression models, which are used to predict the future based on the data available in the database and which are the most preferred one among the data mining techniques is that the predicted dependent variable has a categorical or continuing characteristic in its structure.

2.3 Market Basket Analysis and Association Rule Mining

In order to identify the decision making behaviors of customers when purchasing a product, an attempt was made to conduct an analysis through different applications. For these analyses, data pools and superimposing correlations. These types of methods that are used to identify which products and services are more preferable among those specified by customers are called market basket analyses. A market basket analysis may be used as a starting point for such positions, which are in general consisting of data with commercial meanings, but for which there is no information to identify correlations on the dataset. This makes it possible to make use of different campaigns in order to increase the profit on sale thanks to certain patterns in the dataset (Karagöz 2007).

The association analysis is used to identify and measure which customer purchases more than one products put up for sale during the shopping. The association rules significantly shed light on consumers' behaviors. These rules make it possible for managers to develop more efficient sales.

The market basket analysis is the most popular type of analysis for which the association rules are applied. This analysis is used to analyze the customers' buying habits and consumption tendencies by means of identifying the associations or correlations between the products. In addition, the basket analysis technique is simply used to identify which products are purchased together and which products should be included into which campaigns, and analyze the basket data in order to identify the closeness among the product combinations. Based on the result of this analysis, managers are able to make and execute a plan in order to apply a more efficient sales strategy and develop promotions for customers (Alan 2016).

An analysis where the association rules are applied identifies the consumer behaviors to understand which products are purchased together and, the information obtained therefrom contributes to the sales and marketing departments. This makes it possible to identify categorizations by means of analyzing consumption groups and products preferred by customers during all these procedures.

Apriori Algorithm. Agrawal et al. (1993) and Agrawal and Srikant (1994) developed the Apriori algorithm to overcome the difficulty of processing possible association rules for the wide range of merchandise in shopping analysis. Ting et al. (2010) explained the basic premise of association rules among products, i.e. the frequency with which a customer buys an item BB (Consequent) is observed on the condition that he has also bought an item AA (antecedent). Pradhan et al. proposed that the important thing was the ability of the algorithms to limit the search space and check for only a subset of all these rules (Pradhan et al. 2022).

It has become the most used algorithm for the deduction of association rules. This algorithm is named this way because it uses a priori knowledge of common objects, i.e. it gets the information from the preceding step. This technique is used on the rule that all the subsets of a set of common objects must be of common. Another important issue is that it is assumed that the objects within a set of objects are of lexicographic order. Unlike other algorithms, it is different in the way of producing candidate object sets and, the way of choosing candidate object sets to be counted. Apriori creates candidate object sets by means of combining the sets of common objects created in the previous transition. It deletes small ones out of those subsets formed in the previous transition irrespective of the transactions in the data pool (Döşlü 2008). The solution way of an apriori cycle is to offer a recurring solution proposal. The baseline object sets grow by means of embedding its subsets. As the first step, the inclusion criteria are defined to create one-layer object sets and, the items that are frequently used for the transitions in the subset are preferred to cluster by means of creating the candidate of the object it transited into. The inclusion criteria are defined by means of conducting significant analysis on the dataset and, the procedures are repeated respectively until it reduces (Agrawal and Srikant 1994). $A \rightarrow B$ is the base presentation of an association rule. The left side symbolizes the object/product/theme on the left, and the one on the right is called the right side. More than one product may appear on the left side of the rule. In the structure of the $A \rightarrow B$, $A \subset I$, $B \subset I$, and $A \cap B = \emptyset$ and a rule must provide minimum support and minimum confidence. Each rule has two values support and trust. The support value (s) is the ratio of $A \cup B$ receipts among the sales receipts in the D database, which corresponds to the receipt ratio containing both A and B to all receipts. The support value, therefore, indicates the frequency of the correlation between the respective products. Another value, confidence (c), shows how many of the chips containing A also contain B. This value is a conditional probability value. The confidence value indicates the strength of the rule (Bilgic 2019).

3 Method

The dataset used in this research consists of shopping transactions of one of the foreign bag and clothing companies that operate in the retail industry at the New Istanbul Airport for 61 days in May and June, 2019. After the eliminations among 1650 vouchers collected during this period, the number of vouchers reduced to 1550. There are 78 product groups observed on these 1550 vouchers. Thereafter, these product groups were combined and, 42 product categories were created to better define the associations.

A "market basket analysis", an association rule technique, was used to identify the association among the products consisting of the dataset. For this technique, the apriori algorithm was preferred since it is prior to other algorithms and it is commonly used, as described in the previous section in a detailed manner. The method is to find the sets of products in close associations with one another inside the data groups. This research aimed to reveal the buying habits of customers based on these close associations and, thus enhance the subsequent campaigns and marketing strategies by means of identifying the products that are purchased together the most and the products that are not preferred.

4 Findings of the Research

This research first analyzed the gender and age distributions of the airport store customers. Table 1 shows the gender distribution and, Table 2 shows the age distribution.

Table 1. Gender distribution.

Gender	Frequency	Percent	Cumulative Percent
Male	787	50,8	50,8
Female	763	49,2	100,00
Total	1550	100,00	

Age distribution is shown on the Table 2.

Table 2. Age distribution.

Age	Frequency	Percent	Cumulative Percent
18–25	472	30,5	30,5
26–34	444	28,6	59,1
35–46	192	12,4	71,5
47–56	177	11,4	82,9
57–65	165	10,6	93,5
65+	100	6,5	100,0
Total	1550	100,0	

As shown in Table 2, the shopping was mostly made by the gender groups of 18–28 (30.5%) and 26–34 (28.6%). These results that the store products are addressing young people.

The data under this research were analyzed by a packaged software of SPSS Clementine. The research used the Apriori algorithm. Accordingly, as a first step, the distribution of 42 product groups were identified in the shopping transactions and then the purchase rates were calculated for each product group.

In order to see the general association, the support value was maintained at a level of 3% and the confidence value at a level of 25% and all the products and product groups in association with one another were observed. As a result of the analysis, 12 association rules were shown in the following schedule.

Table 3. Association rules obtained from data section.

Rule	Consequent	Antecedent	Support %	Confidence %
1	Wallet	Small passport holder	7,871	99,18
2	Sleeping set	Neck Pillow	7,097	98,182
3	Waterproof money bag	Waterproof wallet	8,903	97,826
4	34 Lt of suitcase	13″ Laptop Bag	3,935	96,721
5	17 Lt of back-pack	Small size belt pack	5,484	96,471
6	40 Lt of Suitcase	15″ Laptop Bag	4,516	95,714
7	18 Lt of back-pack	Big size belt pack	15,161	94,043
8	25 Lt of back-pack	Medium size belt pack	20,71	91,589
9	Leather wallet	Leather credit card holder	8,194	77,165
10	Wallet	Credit card holder	7,935	75,61
11	Sleeping set	Foldable big backpack	4,968	55,844
12	Leather credit card holder	40 Lt of suitcase	11,29	43,429

According to Table 3:

For the rule Wallet - Small Passport Holder: The possibility that a Wallet and a Small Passport Holder are seen together on the total voucher transactions is 7.81%. It is possible to say that a customer who purchases a Wallet is likely to purchase a Small Passport Holder by probability of 99.18%.

For the rule Sleeping Set - Neck Pillow: The possibility that a Sleeping Set and a Neck Pillow are seen together on the total voucher transactions is 7.097%. It is possible to say that a customer who purchases a Sleeping Set is likely to purchase a Neck Pillow holder by probability of 99,182%.

For the rule Waterproof Money Bag - Water Proof Wallet: The possibility that a Waterproof Money Bag and a Water Proof Wallet are seen together on the total voucher transactions is 8.903%. It is possible to say that a customer who purchases a Waterproof Money Bag is likely to purchase a Water Proof Wallet holder by probability of 97.826%.

For the rule 34 Lt of Suitcase - 13″ Laptop Bag: The possibility that a 34 Lt of Suitcase and a 13″ Laptop Bag are seen together on the total voucher transactions is 3.935%. It is possible to say that a customer who purchases a 34 Lt of Suitcase is likely to purchase a 13″ Laptop Bag by probability of 96,721%.

For the rule 17 Lt of Backpack - Small Size Belt Pack: The possibility that a 17 Lt of Backpack and a Small Size Belt Pack are seen together on the total voucher transactions is 5.484%. It is possible to say that a customer who purchases a 17 Lt of Backpack is likely to purchase a Small Size Belt Pack by probability of 96.471%.

For the rule 40 Lt of Suitcase - 15″ Laptop Bag: The possibility that a 40 Lt of Suitcase and a 15″ Laptop Bag are seen together on the total voucher transactions is 4.516%. It is possible to say that a customer who purchases a 40 Lt of Suitcase is likely to purchase a 15″ Laptop Bag by probability of 95.714%.

For the rule 18 Lt of Backpack - Big Size Belt Pack: The possibility that a 18 Lt of Backpack and a Big Size Belt Pack are seen together on the total voucher transactions is 15.161%. It is possible to say that a customer who purchases a 18 Lt of Backpack is likely to purchase a Big Size Belt Pack by probability of 94.043%.

For the rule 25 Lt of Backpack - Medium Size Belt Pack: The possibility that a 25 Lt of Backpack and a Medium Size Belt Pack are seen together on the total voucher transactions is 20.71%. It is possible to say that a customer who purchases a 25 Lt of Backpack is likely to purchase a Medium Size Belt Pack by probability of 91.589%.

For the rule Leather Wallet - Leather Credit Card Holder: The possibility that a Leather Wallet and a Leather Credit Card Holder are seen together on the total voucher transactions is 8.194%. It is possible to say that a customer who purchases a Leather Wallet is likely to purchase a Leather Credit Card Holder by probability of 77.165%.

For the rule Wallet - Credit Card Holder: The possibility that a Wallet and a Credit Card Holder are seen together on the total voucher transactions is 7.935%. It is possible to say that a customer who purchases a Wallet is likely to purchase a Credit Card Holder by probability of 75.61%.

For the rule Sleeping Set - Foldable Big Backpack: The possibility that a Sleeping Set and a Foldable Big Backpack are seen together on the total voucher transactions is 4.968%. It is possible to say that a customer who purchases a Sleeping Set is likely to purchase a Foldable Big Backpack by probability of 55.844%.

For the rule Leather Credit Card Holder - 40 Lt of Suitcase: The possibility that a Leather Credit Card Holder and a 40 Lt of Suitcase are seen together on the total voucher transactions is 11.29%. It is possible to say that a customer who purchases a Leather Credit Card Holder is likely to purchase a 40 Lt of Suitcase by probability of 43.429%.

Figure 1 shows the associations of the products frequently purchased.

According to Fig. 1, medium size belt packs are frequent purchased together with 25 Lt of backpacks. In addition, the power of purchasing bags and belt packs together is high. The association rules for the products are as follows.

The new minimum support value was identified as 5% and the minimum confidence value as 50% and the products with the most intense associations with one another are listed in the market basket analysis. Accordingly, the product groups with the highest associations are identified as follows: wallet-small passport holder, sleeping set-neck pillow, waterproof money bag-waterproof wallet, 17 LT of backpack-small size belt pack, 18 LT of backpack-big size belt pack, 25 LT of backpack-medium size belt pack, wallet-credit card holder, leather wallet-leather credit card holder and leather credit card holder- 40 LT of suitcase.

Table 4 shows the association rules for some products by gender.

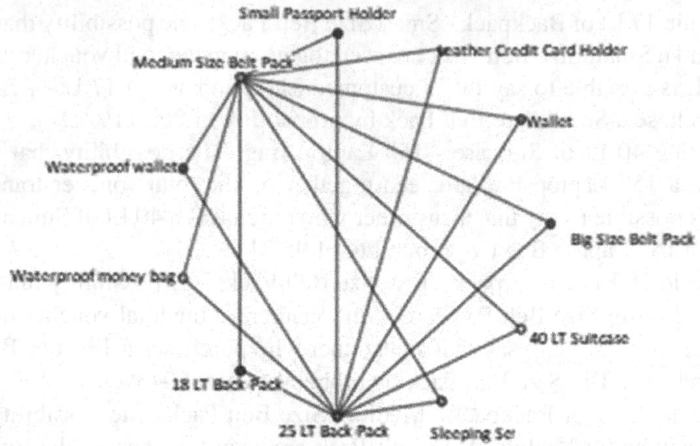

Fig. 1. Associations with high frequency.

Table 4. Association rules for bags by gender.

Distribution	Consequent	Antecedent	Support %	Confidence %
Distribution by Male	25 Lt of backpack	Medium size belt pack	10,323	94,043
Distribution by Female	Medium size belt pack	25 Lt of backpack	10,129	93,750
Distribution by Male	Leather credit card holder	Leather wallet	4,065	73,016
Distribution by Female	Leather credit card holder	Leather wallet	4,129	81,250
Distribution by Male	Wallet	Credit card holder	4,194	78,462
Distribution by Female	Wallet	Credit card holder	3,742	72,414

According to Table 4, for the rule 25 Lt of bag and medium size bag created depending on the gender factor:

The support rate for the backpack and belt pack among the males making the transactions is 10.32%. The rate of the females are so close, which is 10.12%.

According to Table 4, the support rates for both females and males within the rule wallet-credit card holder and the rule leather wallet-leather credit card holder is very close and, the confidence rate thereof is significantly high. The important point is that the female customers have a higher confidence rate than the male customers for the rule leather credit holder-leather wallet. This rate is 81.25%.

Considering the confidence rate, it is seen that female customers take these products in the same basket more than male customers. According to this result, product images prepared for male customers may be rearranged for female customers. This would make it possible to significantly increase the sale rate for female customers.

5 Conclusion and Discussion

This study mentions the association rules, one of the data mining techniques that are frequently used these days. The study is intended to find meaningful correlations among the products and identify the buying habits of customers by means of using the association rules. Based on these results, it is also intended to develop marketing strategies for the future shelf arrangements and sales campaigns.

After the product distributions were analyzed, the dataset was reviewed using an apriori algorithm to find the association rules. The same procedure was repeated for the products and then the product groups, and the rules obtained therefrom were presented in tables providing explanations thereon.

An analysis on the results suggests that the sales of bags and belt packs are higher than those of other products. Of course, the restrictions of our research should be taken into consideration. These are the facts that many products available at these stores are not available at other stores and, the most preferred ones that are not available in the domestic market are put up for sale only in this place.

The associations between backpacks and belt packs, wallets and credit card holders, laptop bags and suitcases with the highest level of confidence may indicate that that the customers visiting the store in this period have a better-than average income, and thus their buying habits and needs are shaped accordingly.

Further studies may be conducted on different datasets with algorithms that include different working conditions and methods. Other association rules may be deducted using actual data and, the results thereof may be compared. New and stronger algorithms may be created by means of combining the good characteristics of the algorithms.

Although the local activities of customers are not known due to security reasons, association rules may be created for customers shopping at the website of the store and grouped according to the customer profile, and it may be possible to ensure that customers purchase different products by means of developing different campaigns. Or it is possible to create new customer groups thanks to an advertising campaign to be organized aiming for customer groups from different countries.

In addition, it was observed based on the results that some female customers purchase the products for male customers and, some male customers purchase the products for female products. Among these criteria, the product ranges and color scales available at the store in that period were taken into consideration. In addition, it may be assumed that both genders purchase these products as gifts. Accordingly, during the future marketing strategies, it is possible to make decisions that would affect both female and male customers.

The information obtained as a result of the study may be used to make a more efficient shelf arrangement or organize different product campaigns. Shelf arrangement and visual expression may be taken into consideration to increase in particular the sales of the products with lower sales figures. It is recommended that a shelf arrangement intended for male and female customers are turned into a more functional shelf arrangement.

Accordingly, it is expected that a change to the visual arrangement and, the exhibition of certain products together would result in change to the buying behaviors of customers.

References

Agrawal, R., Srikant, R.: Fast algorithms for mining association rules. In: Proceedings of the 20th VLDB Conference, Santiago, pp. 487–499 (1994)

Alan, B.: Veri madenciliği ve market veritabaninda birliktelik kurallarinin belirlenmesi. Yüksek Lisans Tezi, Recep Tayyip Üniversitesi Sosyal Bilimler Enstitüsü (2016)

Barutçugil, İ.: Bilgi yönetimi. Kariyer Yayıncılık, İstanbul (2002)

Bergeron, B.: Essentials of CRM. Wiley, New York (2002)

Bilgiç, E.: R programlama dili ile pazar sepet analizi: Muş il merkezindeki bir süpermarkette tüketicilerin satın alma davranışlarının tespiti üzerine bir uygulama. Anemon Muş Alparslan Üniversitesi Sosyal Bilimler Dergisi **7**(3), 89–97 (2019)

Çiçekli, U.G., Kabasakal, İ: Market basket analysis of basket data with demographics: a case study in e-retailing. Alphanumer. J. **9**(1), 1–12 (2021)

Doğan, B., Erol, B., Buldu, A.: Sigortacılık sektöründe müşteri ilişkileri yönetimi için birliktelik kuralı kullanılması. Marmara Fen Bilimleri Dergisi **3**, 105–114 (2014)

Döşlü, A.: Veri madenciliğinde market sepet analizi ve birliktelik kurallarının belirlenmesi. Yüksek Lisans Tezi, Yıldız Teknik Üniversitesi Fen Bilimleri Enstitüsü (2008)

Freathy, P., O'Connell, F.: Spending time, spending money: passenger segmentation in an international airport. Int. Rev. Retail Distrib. Consum. Res. **22**(4), 397–416 (2012)

Graham, A., Saito, S., Nomura, M.: Airport management in Japan: any lessons learnt from the UK? J. Airpt. Manag. **8**(3), 244–263 (2014)

Han, H., Kim, W., Hyun, S.S.: Overseas travelers' decision formation for airport-shopping behavior. J. Travel Tour. Mark. **31**(8), 985–1003 (2014)

Kalakota, R., Robinson, M.: E-Business 2.0: Roadmap for Success, 2nd edn. Addison Wesley, Hoboken (2001)

Karadeniz, N.: Müşteri ilişkileri yönetimi açısından veri madenciliği yönetimi ve hizmet sektörü üzerine bir uygulama. Yüksek Lisans Tezi, Marmara Üniversitesi Sosyal Bilimler Enstitüsü (2008)

Karagöz, N.E.: Market veri tabanında veri madenciliği uygulaması. Yüksek Lisans Tezi, İstanbul Ticaret Üniversitesi Sosyal Bilimler Enstitüsü (2007)

Kaur, M., Kang, S.: Market basket analysis: Identify the changing trends of market data using association rule mining. Procedia Comput. Sci. **85**, 78–85 (2016)

Moldenhauer, C., Zwirnmann, H.: Basket analysis in practice: mathematical models and applications in offline retail. In: Buttkus, M., Eberenz, R. (eds.) Performance Management in Retail and the Consumer Goods Industry, pp. 369–384. Springer, Cham (2019). https://doi.org/10.1007/978-3-030-12730-5_24

Musalem, A., Aburto, L., Bosch, M.: Market basket analysis insights to support category management. Eur. J. Mark. **52**(7/8), 1550–1573 (2018)

Lin, Y.H., Chen, C.-F.: Passengers' shopping motivations and commercial activities at airports – the moderating effects of time pressure and impulse buying tendency. Tour. Manag. **36**, 426–434 (2013)

Omar, O., Kent, A.: International airport influences on impulsive shopping: trait and normative approach. Int. J. Retail Distrib. Manag. **29**(5), 226–235 (2001)

Park, S.C., Piramuthu, S., Shaw, M.J.P.: Dynamic rule refinement in knowledge-based data mining systems. Decis. Support Syst. **31**, 205–206 (2001)

Pradhan, S., Priya, P., Patel, G.: Product bundling for 'Efficient' vs 'Non-Efficient' customers: market basket analysis employing genetic algorithm. Int. Rev. Retail Distrib. Consum. Res. **32**, 293–310 (2022)

Rygielski, C., Wang, J.C., Ten, D.C.: Data mining techniques for customer relationship management. Technol. Soc. **24**(4), 483–502 (2002)

Sadikoglu, G.: Modeling of the travelers' shopping motivation and their buying behavior using fuzzy logic. Procedia Comput. Sci. **120**, 805–811 (2017)

Sharma, A., Nanda, A.: Impulse buying at airport terminals: a case of Indian consumers. Asian J. Manag. Res. **3**(1), 68–82 (2012)

Şimşek, U.T.: Veri madenciliği ve müşteri ilişkileri yönetiminde bir uygulama. Doktora Tezi, İstanbul Üniversitesi Sosyal Bilimler Enstitüsü (2006)

Taşpınar, H.: Bilişim altyapısında CRM teknik altyapısı ve işlevsellikleri. Seçkin Yayınevi, Ankara (2005)

Timor, M., Ezerçe, A., Gürsoy, U.T.: Müşteri profili ve alışveriş davranışlarını belirlemede kümeleme ve birliktelik kuralları analizi: Perakende sektöründe bir uygulama. İstanbul Üniversitesi İşletme Fakültesi İşletme İktisadı Enstitüsü Yönetim Dergisi **22**(68) (2017)

Ting, P.H., Pan, S., Chou, S.S.: Finding ideal menu items assortments: an empirical application of market basket analysis. Cornell Hosp. Q. **51**(4), 492–501 (2010)

Under, U., Atalik, O.: An importance-performance analysis for airport duty free shops: a crosscultural comparison of airport shoppers. J. Manag. Mark. Logist. **3**(4), 318–328 (2016)

Ünvan, Y.A.: Impacts of Bitcoin on USA, Japan, China and Turkey stock market indexes: causality analysis with value at risk method (VAR), communications in statistics. Theory Methods **50**(7), 1599–1614 (2021)

Human Factors Management Systems Based on Information Technology

A Machine Learning Approach to Detect Infected People to Coronavirus Based on Raman Spectroscopy Data

Omid Aligholipour[1(✉)] and Safa Sadaghiyanfam[2]

[1] Electrical and Electronics Engineering, Gazi University, Ankara, Turkey
omid.aligholipour@gmail.com

[2] Biomedical Engineering, Katip Celebi University, Izmir, Turkey

Abstract. With the onset of coronavirus disease, many people lost their lives and were subsequently recognized as a pandemic by the World Health Organization. In this study, we present a machine learning-based method to diagnose patients infected to Covid-19 with a higher accuracy rate. Although there has been an impressive focus on the evaluation of chest Computed Tomography (CT) images, the Raman spectroscopy dataset has been considered in this study. The dataset contains 3 groups involving: healthy individuals, people with Covid-19 and flu diagnosis. In pre-processing step, a combination of two popular methods, ant colony and Cuckoo Search with genetic algorithm optimization, is used to select more critical features and consequently decrease the dimension. Obtained feature space were examined through two approaches; first unsupervised classification methods used to examine the correlation of data. In the next, neural networks are employed to distinguish groups and detect infected patients. Based on achieved results, the proposed hybrid feature selection model outperforms the existing approach in terms of sensitivity and accuracy.

Keywords: Covid 19 · Ant Colony · Genetic Algorithm · Neural Networks · Unsupervised Classification

1 Introduction

The application of machine learning and neural networks in the field of biomedical data analysis has been considerably increased during the last decades, such as biomedical signal and image processing and gene expression. New Severe Acute Respiratory Syndrome Coronavirus (SARS-CoV-2) is an RNA-type virus that causes the Covid-19 disease has contributed to severe life-threatening and even death. According to WHO, approximately 202 million people have been affected, and more than 4 million deaths were reported [1] Since the first reported case of SARS-CoV-2 in December 2019, researchers worldwide have considerably focused on the behavior and structure of the virus to analyze the structure of that and do actions to prevent and treat it. Although proper treatment and effective drugs have not been recognized, some vaccines have positively affected the human body's autoimmune system against the virus. Owing to the admissible results of

A. Mirzazadeh et al. (Eds.): SEMIT 2022, CCIS 1808, pp. 239–248, 2023.
https://doi.org/10.1007/978-3-031-40395-8_17

machine learning and artificial intelligence approaches in disease diagnosis, prediction, prevention, treatment and management, there is great interest in using such algorithms to help current clinical procedures in the fight against Covid-19.

According to the information obtained from patients infected with coronavirus, the virus mainly affects the lungs and the structure of proteins [2] Owing to the relation between deaths and lung failures in Covid-19 patients, there has been immense focus in this field. Some studies have been supposed to analyze and evaluate generally the chest MR images of patients and impact of the coronavirus on the structure of the proteins [3–5]. Raman spectroscopy has been utilized to determine the vibrational modes of molecules with ultrahigh sensitivity at near-physiological conditions and is used in several areas [6].

In this study, analysis of a dataset containing Raman spectroscopy data of healthy and infected people are presented. First feature selection methods are utilized to extract more important features and eliminate others from dataset. Once feature set is obtained, a simple feedforward neural network is used to determine people who infected by coronaviruses. In addition, clustering algorithms are employed to discover patterns in dataset. This survey is involved into three primary sections. The recent studies in the field of application of machine learning and artificial intelligence approaches in the topic of Covid-19 is given in Sect. 2. Section 3 contains the main objective of this study, where details of employed algorithms are explained. This section also provides an overview of Covid-19 dataset. In the last section, the result and discussion of the obtained results have been presented.

2 Related Works

Several topics in Covid-19 have been considered during pandemic. The main objective of proposed studies includes classification, detection, diagnosis and other issues like processing of social media information. Onur Dogan et al. [7] represented a detailed review of application of artificial intelligence and machine learning approaches in Covid-19 outbreak. According to this study, since analysis of CT images is the most effective technique for detect and diagnosis for Covid-19, CNN has the most widely used algorithm. A mathematical model of mask designed by [8] aimed to assessing the status of the mask and the local extent of the pandemic based on various parameters using machine learning algorithms.

The effect of the virus on lungs and processing the Xray images of chest and lungs have been exceedingly studied since the epidemic started. Although the true accuracy rate of diagnosis of such approaches are acceptable, high costs in the devices for image acquisition and processing and the inadequacy of the number of devices are the disadvantageous aspects of the detection mechanisms with this method. Convolutional Neural Network has been exceedingly employed for visual imagery and is a type of multilayer perceptron. To extract features from CXR images, CNN was applied followed by SVM classifier to achieve higher accuracy in classification [9]. A self-supervised artificial intelligence method has been proposed by Yan et al. [10] which aims to diagnose Covid-19 virus based on CT images. Segmentation and quantification of the CT images of the lungs associated with the virus are evaluated by Shan et al. [11].

The study of cognition, classification and processing of social media information is another important issue because firstly there is a flood of fake and unreal information in the virtual world that can affect people's thoughts. One approach is introduced by Nguyen et al. [12] to categorize the twitter information about Covid-19 as recovered, suspected, confirmed, and death cases, location or travel history of the cases. Muller et al. [13] offered a self-supervised language modeling to analysis tweets by the key-words "wuhan", "ncov", "coronavirus", "covid", "sars-cov-2" from a defined time. A comprehensive study presented by [14] which focuses on the comparison of several articles and application of machine learning and deep learning methods in determining the Covid-19 which covers a wide range of references associated with this issue. Several topics such as Precision Diagnostics, Protein Structure Prediction, Drug Repurposing and Spread Forecasting for Epidemiology were covered.

In addition, influence of the virus on blood cells and detection of the virus based upon the influence of the virus on the structure of proteins and blood cell analysis has been studied in several articles. Brinati et al. [15] showed a machine learning approach to distinguish Covid positive patients according to blood tests. Several ML algorithms such as Random Forest (RF), Support Vector Machines (SVM), Native Bayes (NB) and K-nearest neighbors (KNN) have been considered as classifiers. Obtained results present the best accuracy rate by the modification of RF. Also, the study highlights the dominance influence of the Aspartate Aminotransferase (AST) in detection. A combination of PCR and Blood analysis to effectively reduce the false negative rate was introduced by [16]. The article suggests that in case that AST and LDH hematological levels were used synergistically with the genetic test, the accuracy would be higher. Yin et al. [17] stated the identification of Covid-19 based on Raman spectroscopy. After extracting features by analyzing variance of the groups (ANOVA analysis), SVM algorithm was used as classifier which achieves 90% accuracy in determining. Garip Ustaoğlu et al. [18] presented a review on novel diagnostic and treatment methods for covid 19. For diagnostic purposes, multivariate analysis methods including PCA, SVM, LDA and hierarchical cluster analysis on different sources (Infrared, Raman and Vibrational spectroscopy) were explained. Goulart et al. [19] evaluated the immunoglobulins IgM and IgG of Raman features in serum samples by multivariate technique PCA and Partial Least Squares (PLS). Authors declared rapid evaluation of diagnosis with regards to immunoglobulins affected by corona virus.

3 Proposed Approach

3.1 Dataset

This study aims to determine infected people according to Raman spectroscopy data [17] Totally data of 112 people are investigated for whose 63 were initially identified as Covid-19 patients, including 58 symptomatic and five asymptomatic patients. All of the Covid-19 patients were positive based on the PCR test. Computed tomography (CT) scans were performed, which showed 76.5 abnormal results. In addition, there are 59 patients with flu diagnosis and suspected to Covid-19 diseases with negative PCR test results. The healthy control group consisted of 55 healthy individuals recruited at the

Sichuan Cancer Hospital and Chengdu Public Health Clinical Medical Center. Totally, 465 attributes with 891 spectra were considered for further processing (see Table 1).

Table 1. Dataset description

Dataset	Number of individuals
Healthy	55
Suspected	59
Infected with Covid-19	63

3.2 Feature Selection

Especially in dealing with a large dataset, the performance of machine learning algorithms has been directly affected by many attributes. Dimension reduction is the transformation of high dimensional data into a meaningful representation of the original data in lower dimensions which contributes to facilitating the visualization and data understanding, reducing the measurements and storage, and reducing the training and utilization time [20]. To the success of many learning algorithms in their attempts to construct models of data, feature selection can play a critical role. Instead of using one dimension reduction algorithm, a combination or mixture of several algorithms could result in successfully selecting appropriate features [21, 22]. Although a combination may lead to a better classification rate, different algorithms are used independently in this study, and the obtained matrix contains the results of both approaches. This perspective helps to benefit the strong side of each algorithm, which may successfully contribute to creating the final matrix with the most influential features. Santana et al. [23] evaluated the performance of feature selection methods GA and ACO with respect to various situations including examination individually and with increasing the number of classifiers. Ant colony and cuckoo search algorithm based on genetic algorithm are chosen in this study owing to their powerful performance in feature selection [24]. In the next, two feature extraction methods used in this study are given.

Ant Colony Optimization. Inspired by the behavior of natural ants, Ant Colony Optimization was introduced By Marco Dorigo in 1996 [25]. Initially, it was used to solve Travelling Salesman Problems. However, today it can be used in different NP-hard problems. In this technique, in every iteration, each ant, after finding the food, spreads a specific material called pheromone along the path between colony and food to assist other ants in finding a better path to the food. The possibility of choosing the path with a high level of pheromone is much higher than other paths. As a result, the amount of pheromone will increase on the path. The flow chart of this method is illustrated in Fig. 1.

CSO-GA. Genetic algorithms (GA) is a meta-heuristic optimization algorithm founded upon the principles of natural evolution and it benefits the principles of population genetics that artificially evolve solutions to a given problem by using a stochastic, directed and highly parallel search. Since the problem of feature selection is well suited as an optimization problem, GAs as stochastic optimization procedures have been successfully applied in many dimension reduction tasks. Given a set of d-dimensional input dataset, the objective of the GA is to find a transformed set of patterns in an m-dimensional space (where m < d) that maximizes a set of optimization criteria [26, 27]. Siedlecki and Sklansky [28] introduced GAs as an approach for feature selection. In GA, there are five important issues including chromosome encoding, fitness evaluation, selection, genetic operators and stop criteria. There has been several optimizations of GA. In this study, a combination of Cuckoo search (CS) algorithm and GA is used for feature selection. Cuckoo search (CS) algorithm is a meta-heuristic algorithm developed by Yang and Deb in 2009 [29]. This algorithm is designed based on the behavior of some cuckoo species which have benefited from some special abilities such as selecting the recently spawned nests and removing existing eggs. They lay their eggs in the other bird's nests so they feed their nestlings. However, it is possible that the host identifies the alien egg. In this case, the host bird can either abandon the nest to build new nest or throw the egg away.

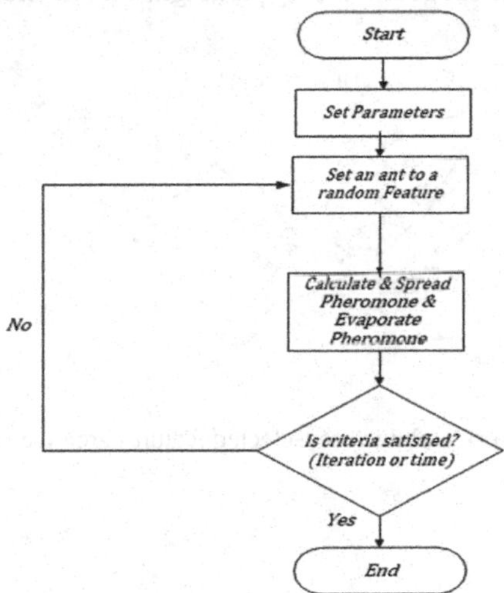

Fig. 1. Ant Colony optimization scheme

The behavior of these birds has been presented in four steps:

1. Each cuckoo lays one egg in a randomly chosen nest.
2. The nests with high quality of eggs will survive by the next generation.
3. The number of available host nests is fixed,
4. An alien egg with a probability $p_a = [0, 1]$ could be discovered.

Several hybrid applications of GA and Cuckoo algorithms were introduced. Abdel-Baset and Hezam [30] presented two different hybrid schemes that use both algorithms in different phases. In the first phase, GA or CSA explores the search space to identify the most promising regions of the search space. In the second phase, either GA or CSA, which did not operate in the first phase, is implemented to improve the solution.

A combination of Cuckoo search optimization and GA is considered in this study in which mutation and breed steps of GA are replaced with the update step of Cuckoo search algorithm.

3.3 Neural Networks

Neural networks are among the most commonly used machine learning and artificial intelligence methods to approximate some functions. Feedforward neural network is probably the most straightforward kind which doesn't contain any feedback or cycle in the network, which means that each neuron has one connection(see Fig. 2). Feedforward neural network consists of 3 layers: input, hidden, and output layers. In this regard, the activation function is defined to transform a linear regression model to a non-leaner model by making the input capable of learning and performing more complicated tasks. Choosing proper transfer function and learning algorithm is tricky way that affects the result of classification. In this study LM algorithm and Hyperbolic tangent transfer function (TANSIG) are chosen for learning paradigm and transfer function, respectively.

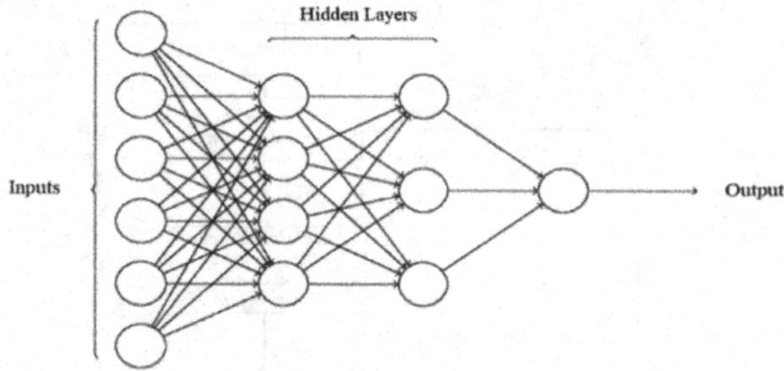

Fig. 2. Simple neural network architecture; selected features are given as input, one hidden layer and output

3.4 Cross-Validation

Overfitting is a critical issue in data science where the statistical model exactly fits against the training data. When in the training phase, it takes so long to perform training, or if there are insufficient features to train, the performance on unseen data becomes worse. The objective of the cross-validation technique is to determine the model's performance to predict new data that was not used to estimate it. In this study, the 5-fold cross-validation is implemented, which means that the original dataset is divided into five equal-sized partitions. One partition is selected as validation data to test the model's performance, while the remaining partition is used as training data. This process repeats five times, with each of the five partitions used exactly once as the validation data. The average of these estimations will represent the performance of the model.

4 Results

The dataset in this study encompasses three different groups. In the first experiment, the statistical pattern of the two groups is investigated. Because the symptoms of patients with positive Covid tests are similar to a patient with flu diagnosis, an unsupervised classification method is used to determine the separation rate of these two groups. K-means and Fuzzy C-means (FCM) algorithms are probably the best-known algorithms for analyzing the structure of the dataset. The output of a clustering algorithm strongly depends on the pattern and structure of the dataset. Therefore, choosing the best method to correctly group data is a challenging aspect. Accuracy, Sensitivity, Specificity and F1-Score are the parameters that selected in this study to examine the performance of the clustering algorithms. Table 2 represents the results of the k-means and FCM algorithms on these groups. Each algorithm is run 20 times, and the average of obtained results is presented. With respect to the acquired results, it can be seen that there is a considerable overlapping between the distributions of data in the two groups. Therefore, distinguishing the two groups in the dataset is not possible by just clustering them. In addition, if K-means is applied for all groups (Covid, Suspected, Healthy), the accuracy of clustering is 50.85%, which again indicates the complicated structure of the dataset.

Table 2. Unsupervised classification results

Methods	Accuracy	Sensitivity	Specificity	F1-Score
K-means	50.37	51.6	49.07	51.55
Fuzzy C-means	50.44	51.6	49.2	51.59

In the second experiment, the proposed model distinguishes infected patients to Covid-19 with healthy people. In this perspective, firstly, feature selection methods are applied to the data. Ant colony and cuckoo search algorithm with GA optimization approach are considered in this study. The extracted features with both methods are gathered into a matrix. 5-fold cross-validation and simple feedforward neural networks are exploited to evaluate the dataset. Obtained results evaluated based on several methods including Accuracy, True Positive Rate, False Negative Rate, Positive Prediction Value and False Discovery Rate, which are given in Table 3. Although Yin et al. [17] utilized SVM algorithm as a classifier and achieved approximately 90% accuracy in classification, with combination of feature selection and neural network, our proposed model acquires about 96%. Goulart et al. [19] employed PCA and PLS algorithms and achieved 84%, of 95%, and 90.3% for sensitivity, specificity and accuracy, respectively. Based on results obtained, proposed approach achieves better classification and sensitivity rates.

Table 3. Result of proposed model

	Accuracy	TPR	FNR	PPV	FDR
Proposed model	96.12	93.31	3.99	96.03	4.08
Yin et al. [17]	87	93	–	–	–
Goulart et al. [19]	90.3	84	–	–	–

5 Conclusion

During the last two years, there has been a considerable focus on discovering new methods to diagnose, treat and manage coronavirus. Although X-ray image processing, PCR, and Antigen tests are generally used for diagnosis and prediction, Raman spectroscopy could also be used for these purposes. In this study, a machine learning-based technique is exploited to analyze the structure of data in order to get better solution than previous study. In this regard, Raman spectroscopy data of 3 groups of people has been used. In this first step, well-known feature selection methods are utilized to reduce the dimension of the data. Obtained results are given to unsupervised classification methods and feedforward neural networks and to evaluate the structure of data and determine the Covid patients. Results represent the high overlapping distribution and overlapping rate between groups that means complex structure of data. On the other hand, a simple feedforward neural networks successfully identify the Covid patients with a high rate of accuracy.

Although proposed model achieves acceptable results in detecting Covid-19 patients, for widespread usage of Raman Spectroscopy in diagnostic purposes, more data and analysis are needed in order to get more reliable results. For further studies, more evolution of the Raman in diagnostic Covid-19, and analysis the differences and comparison the performance of two most popular methods PCR and Raman could be considered. In addition, more reliable results can be obtained by conducting more laboratory experiments for industrial use.

References

1. WHO Coronavirus (COVID-19) Dashboard, August 2021. https://covid19.who.int/
2. Verdecchia, P., Cavallini, C., Spanevello, A., Angeli, F.: The pivotal link between ACE2 deficiency and SARS-CoV-2 infection. Eur. J. Intern. Med. **76**, 14–20 (2020)
3. Rahaman, M.M., et al.: Identification of COVID-19 samples from chest X-ray images using deep learning: a comparison of transfer learning approaches. J. X-Ray Sci. Technol. **28**, 821–839 (2020)
4. Liu, F., et al.: Prognostic value of interleukin-6, C-reactive protein, and procalcitonin in patients with COVID-19. J. Clin. Virol. **127**, 104370 (2020)
5. Lanjanian, H., et al.: High-throughput analysis of the interactions between viral proteins and host cell RNAs. Comput. Biol. Med. **135**, 104611 (2021)
6. Tanwar, S., Paidi, S.K., Prasad, R., Pandey, R., Barman, I.: Advancing Raman spectroscopy from research to clinic: translational potential and challenges. Spectrochim. Acta Part A Mol. Biomol. Spectrosc. **260**, 119957 (2021)

7. Dogan, O., Tiwari, S., Jabbar, M.A., Guggari, S.: A systematic review on AI/ML approaches against COVID-19 outbreak. Complex Intell. Syst. **7**(5), 2655–2678 (2021)
8. Tirkolaee, E.B., Goli, A., Ghasemi, P., Goodarzian, F.: Designing a sustainable closed-loop supply chain network of face masks during the COVID-19 pandemic: pareto-based algorithms. J. Clea. Prod. **333**, 130056 (2022)
9. Sethy, P.K., Behera, S.K.: Detection of coronavirus disease (covid-19) based on deep features (2020)
10. Yan, Q., et al.: COVID-19 Chest CT image segmentation-a deep convolutional neural network solution. arXiv:2004.10987 (2020)
11. Shan F., et al.: Lung infection quantification of COVID-19 in CT images with deep learning. arXiv:2003.04655 (2020)
12. Nguyen, D.Q., Vu, T., Rahimi, A., Dao, M.H., Nguyen, L.T., Doan, L: WNUT-2020 task 2: identification of informative COVID-19 English tweets. arXiv preprint arXiv:2010.08232 (2020)
13. Müller, M., Salathé, M., Kummervold, P. E.: COVID-Twitter-BERT: a natural language processing model to analyse covid-19 content on Twitter. arXiv preprint arXiv:2005.07503 (2020)
14. Shorten, C., Khoshgoftaar, T.M., Furht, B.: Deep Learning applications for COVID-19. J. Big Data **8**(1), 1–54 (2021)
15. Brinati, D., Campagner, A., Ferrari, D., Locatelli, M., Banfi, G., Cabitza, F.: Detection of COVID-19 infection from routine blood exams with machine learning: a feasibility study. J. Med. Syst. **44**(8), 1–12 (2020)
16. Ferrari, D., et al.: Routine blood analysis greatly reduces the false-negative rate of RT-PCR testing for COVID-19. Acta Bio Medica: Atenei Parmensis **91**(3), e2020003 (2020)
17. Yin, G., et al.: An efficient primary screening of COVID-19 by serum Raman spectroscopy. J. Raman Spectrosc. **52**(5), 949–958 (2021)
18. Garip Ustaoğlu, Ş, Kaygusuz, H., Bilgin, M.D., Severcan, F.: Novel approaches for COVID-19 diagnosis and treatment: a nonsystematic review. Turk J Biol. **45**(4), 358–371 (2021)
19. Goulart, A.C.C., Zângaro, R.A., Carvalho, H.C., Silveira, L., Jr.: Diagnosing COVID-19 in human sera with detected immunoglobulins IgM and IgG by means of Raman spectroscopy. J. Raman Spectrosc. **52**(12), 2671–2682 (2021)
20. Guyon, I., Elisseeff, A.: An introduction to variable and feature selection. J. Mach. Learn. Res. **3**, 1157–1182 (2003)
21. Nemati, S., Basiri, M.E., Ghasem-Aghaee, N., Aghdam, M.H.: A novel ACO–GA hybrid algorithm for feature selection in protein function prediction. Expert Syst. Appl. **36**(10), 12086–12094 (2009)
22. Sadeghzadeh, M., Teshnehlab, M., Badie, K.: Feature selection using combine of genetic algorithm and ant colony optimization. In: Gao, X.Z., Gaspar-Cunha, A., Köppen, M., Schaefer, G., Wang, J. (eds.) Soft Computing in Industrial Applications, pp. 127–135. Springer, Heidelberg (2010). https://doi.org/10.1007/978-3-642-11282-9_14
23. Santana, L.E., Silva, L., Canuto, A.M., Pintro, F., Vale, K.O.: A comparative analysis of genetic algorithm and ant colony optimization to select attributes for an heterogeneous ensemble of classifiers. In: IEEE Congress on Evolutionary Computation, pp. 1–8 (2010)
24. Jothi Prakash, V., Karthikeyan, N.K.: Enhanced evolutionary feature selection and ensemble method for cardiovascular disease prediction. Interdiscip. Sci. Comput. Life Sci. **13**(3), 389–412 (2021). https://doi.org/10.1007/s12539-021-00430-x
25. Dorigo, M., Maniezzo, V., Colorni, A.: Ant system: optimization by a colony of cooperating agents. IEEE Trans. Syst. Man Cybern. Part B **26**(1), 29–41 (1996)
26. Goldberg, D.E., Holland, J.H.: Genetic algorithms and machine learning (1988)
27. Raymer, M.L., Punch, W.F., Goodman, E.D., Kuhn, L.A., Jain, A.K.: Dimensionality reduction using genetic algorithms. IEEE Trans. Evol. Comput. **4**(2), 164–171 (2000)

28. Siedlecki, W., Sklansky, J.: A note on genetic algorithms for large-scale feature selection. In Handbook of Pattern Recognition and Computer Vision, pp. 88–107 (1993)
29. Yang, X.S., Deb, S.: Cuckoo search via Lévy flights. In 2009 World Congress on Nature and Biologically Inspired Computing (NaBIC), pp. 210–214 (2009)
30. Abdel-Baset, M., Hezam, I.: Cuckoo search and genetic algorithm hybrid schemes for optimization problems. Appl. Math. **10**(3), 1185–1192 (2016)

Exploring the Behavioural Factors of Cervical Cancer Using ANOVA and Machine Learning Techniques

Maide Çakır[1(✉)], Ali Degirmenci[2], and Omer Karal[2]

[1] Istanbul Nisantasi University, 34398 Istanbul, Turkey
maidecakrr@gmail.com
[2] Ankara Yıldırım Beyazıt University, 06010 Ankara, Turkey
karal@ybu.edu.tr

Abstract. Cervical cancer is the fourth most common and one of the deadliest types of cancer in the female population. However, it does not show any symptoms in the first stage. Therefore, early diagnosis is very difficult. On the other hand, there are some risk factors directly or indirectly associated with it. The effect of these risk factors on predicting the diagnosis of cervical cancer was investigated with machine learning-based algorithms and promising results were obtained. However, studies on which risk factors are more effective than others are scarce. This study focuses on investigating how the selection of promising factors associated with cervical cancer will affect the predictive ability of machine learning-based classification algorithms such as Gaussian Naive Bayes (GNB), k Nearest Neighbor and Decision Tree. ANOVA F-test is applied to evaluate each risk factor independently according to the desired class. In order to ensure the reliability of the results, K-fold cross validation technique is used at different K values. In the selected cervical cancer behavioral risk dataset, the GNB algorithm showed the highest performance (%94) with eight risk factors for all K values.

Keywords: Cancer Prediction · *k*NN Classification · Navie Bayes · Decision Tree · ANOVA F-Test

1 Introduction

Cervical cancer is a serious disease that can result in death if not treated in its initial stages [1]. The difficulties encountered in the diagnosis of the disease and the absence of symptoms in the early stages make cervical cancer even more dangerous [2]. Early diagnosis is extremely important since the treatment of the disease can only be achieved by applying treatment in the initial stages [3]. Responses to the behavior and habits of people with cervical cancer showed that they had certain behaviors and habits.

The fact that machine learning based methods give more successful results with each passing day has paved the way for their applications in different fields such as economy [4], medicine [5], accent recognition [6], meteorology [7], outlier detection [8–10]. Recently, significant progress has been made in the detection of cervical cancer. For

A. Mirzazadeh et al. (Eds.): SEMIT 2022, CCIS 1808, pp. 249–260, 2023.
https://doi.org/10.1007/978-3-031-40395-8_18

the first time, Sobar et al. proposed Naive Bayes (NB) and Logistic Regression (LR) to determine cervical risk based on behavior and its determinant [11]. 91.67% and 87.5% accuracy and 0.96 and 0.97 AUC scores are obtained from the NB and LR methods, respectively. Oyelakin et al. used Gaussian NB (GNB) and LR to diagnose cervical cancer [12]. The experimental results showed that the GNB-based model (0.98 accuracy) outperformed its LR counterpart (0.90 accuracy). Midyanti et al. proposed the ADALINE Neural Network (ADALINE-NN) method to predict cervical cancer risk and compared it with NB and LR methods [13]. The data set, consisting of 21 cervical cancers and 51 patients without cervical cancer, was divided into 70% training and 30% testing. Compared to the NB and LR approaches, ADALINE-NN has been observed to have better accuracy with a value of 97.2%. Gamara et al. presented a Neural Network-based model for early cervical cancer risk detection based on behavior information [14]. The NN trained using scaled conjugate gradient backpropagation achieved an overall accuracy of 98% in early cervical cancer risk estimation. Nilnumpetch et al. applied four different NN-based approaches (standard NN, Dual output NN (DONN), Cascade Generalization-NN (CGNN), Cascade generalization using duo output NN(CG-DONN)) for cervical cancer diagnosis [15]. The best accuracy obtained from NN, CG-NN, DONN, and CG-DONN are 83.33, 87.50, 100, and 95.83, respectively. DONN has been found to provide the highest accuracy. From the overall mean correct percentage, CG-DONN provides the maximum overall mean for the breast cancer Coimbra and cervical cancer behavioral risk datasets of 71.39 and 87.88, respectively. Curia presented an ensemble model for the classification of cervical cancer development that combines the Decision Tree (DT), LR, and NN models with soft voting as part of a clinical decision support system [16]. With the developed ensemble-based classifier model, 94.5% accuracy and 0.98 AUC values were obtained. Alpan analyzed the performances of eight different machine learning algorithms: Bayesian Net, NB, J48, Random Tree, Random Forest (RF), *k* Nearest Neighbor (*k*NN), LR, and Support Vector Machine (SVM) for early detection of cervical cancer based on behavior determinants [17]. Experimental results demonstrated that all algorithms work successfully with minimum accuracy of 85% and SVM achieves the highest accuracy of 91,67%. Ratul et al. used 11 different supervised machine learning models such as DT, NN, RF, *k*NN, SVM, CatBoost (CatB), GNB, Gradient Boosting Classifier (GradB), AdaBoost (AdaB), XG Boost (XGB), XG Boost with RF (XGBRF) to predict early jeopardies of cervical cancer [18]. They obtained 93.33% accuracy by tuning the hyperparameters of *k*NN, DT, SVM, RF, and Multi-Layer Detector algorithms with grid search cross validation method. Çiçek et al. developed a user-friendly web-based software using Python sklearn and Dash libraries, which contain 8 different machine learning algorithms (LR, DT, SVM, RF, LightGBM, GNB, AdaBoost, and XGBoost) for cervical cancer classification analysis [19]. Machine learning models were evaluated with different performance metrics, and the accuracy, sensitivity, specificity, negative predictive value, Matthews correlation coefficient and F1-score values obtained from a RF classification model were 94.44%, 100%, 93.33%, 100%, 83.67%, and 94.44 respectively. Unlike the existing studies, Akter et al. determined the important features in the data set and predicted cervical cancer with three different machine learning models: DT, RF, and XGBoost [20]. An accuracy of 93.33% was obtained with all three machine learning models used.

As can be seen from the detailed literature review for early cervical cancer risk detection based on behavioral information, various machine learning-based methods have been used and promising results have been obtained. However, studies on which risk factors are more effective than others are quite limited. This study focuses on the selection of the most prominent behavioral factors associated with cervical cancer. Thus, it is analyzed how the selected risk factors will affect the prediction ability of machine learning-based classification algorithms such as NB, *k*NN, and DT. Analysis of variance (ANOVA) F-test is applied to evaluate each risk factor independently according to the desired class. The success of the methods is determined by the performance criteria. The *K*-fold cross validation technique is used at different *K* values to ensure the reliability of the results.

This study is organized as follows. In Sect. 2, details of the data set are provided. In Sect. 3, NB, kNN, DT machine learning methods, ANOVA feature selection technique, and K-fold cross validation algorithm are described. In Sect. 4, performance metrics are explained, and experimental results are discussed. In Sect. 5, conclusions and future aspects of this study is given.

2 Data Set

The "Cervical Cancer Behavior Risk" dataset available on the UCI (University of California, Irvine) Machine Learning Repository website was used in the study [21]. There are 72 records of cervical cancer in the dataset, and each case contains 19 different behavioral risks that may affect cervical cancer. These behavioral risks are detailed in Table 1. Data with and without cervical cancer are labeled +1 and −1, respectively. The attribute properties of this dataset are integers. There is no missing value in the data set.

Table 1. Details of Features in The Data Set.

Name of Attributes	
Behavior sexual risk	Behavior eating
Intention aggregation	Intention commitment
Attitude spontaneity	Norm significant person
Perception vulnerability	Perception severity
Motivation willingness	Social support emotionality
Social support instrumental	Empowerment knowledge
Empowerment desires	Behavior personal hygine
Attitude consistency	Norm fulfillment
Motivation strength	Social support appreciation
Empowerment abilities	

3 Research Algorithms and Concepts

3.1 *k* Nearest Neighbors Classification

The k Nearest Neighbor algorithm is an easy-to-implement supervised machine learning algorithm that can be used to solve both classification and regression problems. A user-defined k value is determined for the algorithm to work. This k value means the nearest neighbors (number of elements) to look at in the dataset to determine the class of the query instance. The kNN algorithm computes the distance between the query sample and other samples in the dataset, and then determines the k closest samples. Although the Euclidean metric is generally used for distance, it can also be used for other metrics such as Chebyshev, Mahalanobis, Manhattan. However, in the study, Manhattan distance was preferred because of its better performance in high-dimensional data [22]. Query sample is assigned to which class the majority belongs to in the k samples closest to the query sample.

3.2 Decision Tree Classification

Decision tree algorithm is one of the machine learning methods with a tree-like structure used to solve regression and classification problems [23]. Two terminologies are used in the DT classification algorithm: entropy and information gain. These help to progressively develop a relevant decision tree while at the same time breaking down a dataset into increasingly smaller subsets. The aim here is to maximize the information gain by making choices that reduce the entropy value. For this purpose, the error function at each node is recalculated and the nodes with the lowest error are selected. The root node, which is the beginning of the decision tree, represents the independent variable that affects the dependent variable. This node is divided into multiple branches. When you start from the root node and continue to other nodes, the influence of the independent variable on the dependent variable decreases. Parameters such as the maximum tree depth to be used in the nodes, the minimum number of elements decide the branching of the decision tree. Branches that cannot form nodes under them are designated as terminal nodes and the decision tree structure is completed. When predicting a data point, True/False questions are asked until the last leaf node is reached. The predictive value is then produced by averaging the samples at the leaf node. Because decision tree classification is non-parametric and resembles a tree-like structure, it is easy to understand and interpret.

3.3 Naive Bayes Theorem

Bayes' theorem is widely used in calculating conditional probability is a theorem. Naive Bayes is a classification method based on Bayes' theorem [24]. This method decides the classes after performing conditional probability calculations on the samples. It is expressed as

$$\mathrm{P(A|B) = P(B|A)\ * P(A)\ /P(B)} \tag{1}$$

- P (A|B) is the posterior probability of A given B

- P (B|A) is the likelihood which is the probability of B event given A event
- P (A) is the prior probability of A event
- P (B) is the prior probability of B event

The NB classifier greatly simplify learning by assuming that features are independent given class. It can give more successful results with far fewer samples in the training sets than other methods when the features of the data set are uncorrelated.

3.4 ANOVA

One of the most important issues in machine learning is the application of various preprocessing techniques to improve the prediction performance of the model. Choosing the most suitable feature for model training affects the calculation speed as well as the prediction performance. There are three categories of feature selection methods described in the literature: filter, wrapper, and embedded [25]. Within the scope of the study, the features were selected by a filter-based selection technique called ANOVA F-test [12]. It is a univariate filter selection technique used to evaluate each feature independently according to that target class. It is based on the law of total variance, in which the observed variance in a given variable is divided into components attributable to different sources of variation [26]. It is also a tool used to measure whether there is a statistically significant difference between the means of independent groups. Features that show statistical significance for model training are preserved.

A statistical F-test compare two variances, s_1 and s_2, by dividing them. The result is always a positive number. The basic equation for comparing two variances with the f-test could be shown as follows:

$$F = S_1^2/S_2^2 \quad (2)$$

To conduct the one-way ANOVA test, the f-value obtained after performing an f-test is used.

3.5 *K*-Fold Cross Validation Technique

The K-fold cross validation is used to evaluate the performance of the applied methods independently of the samples in the data set. The data set is randomly divided into K equal parts. Then, one of K pieces is used as test data and the remaining K – 1 pieces are used as training data to validate the method. The model created from the training data and the test data are classified. The accuracy of the model is determined in this way. It is run K times and a different piece of test data is used in each run. The performance of the algorithm is then measured more precisely by averaging the results obtained. In this study, K values are chosen as 2, 3, 4, and 5.

4 Experiments and Results

4.1 Performance Criteria

Different performance measures have been proposed to compare the performance of machine learning methods. The frequently utilized performance metrics for the classification methods are accuracy, recall, precision, and F1-score. They are defined as

$$\text{Accuracy} = (\text{TP} + \text{TN}) / (\text{TP} + \text{FP} + \text{FN} + \text{TN}) \quad (3)$$

$$\text{Recall} = \text{TP} / (\text{TP} + \text{FP}) \quad (4)$$

$$\text{Precision} = \text{TP} / (\text{TP} + \text{FP}) \quad (5)$$

$$\text{F1} - \text{score} = \left(\left(\text{Precision}^{-1} + \text{Recall}\right)/2\right)^{-1} \quad (6)$$

In these equations, TP indicates true positive, FP is true negative, FN represents false negatives and TN is true negative.

4.2 Experimental Results

Three different machine learning methods (GNB, kNN, and DT) are used in the estimation of the Cervical Cancer Behavior Risk data set. Hyperparameters have a significant impact on the performance of machine learning-based methods. Therefore, the hyperparameters must be set properly before training the method. Comprehensive grid search method, which is a simple and widely used technique in hyperparameter optimization, was preferred in the study. Along with the hyperparameter setting of each method, the effect of each behavior causing cervical cancer on performance and the selection of the K parameter in the K-fold cross-validation method was also examined. The effect of each behavioral risk causing cervical cancer was determined by the ANOVA F-test method and was shown graphically in Fig. 1.

As seen in Fig. 1, according to the ANOVA F-test results, the 5 most effective features are empowerment of abilities (29.17), perception severity (24.37), empowerment of knowledge (21,16), motivation of strength (19.55) and empowerment of desires (18.66), respectively, while the least effective 5 features are attitude spontaneity (0.50), attitude consistency (1.11), Social support instrumental (1.29), behavior sexual risk (2.92) and intention commitment (4.16), respectively.

The visuals of the performances of the grid search obtained for the GNB, *k*NN, and DT classification models in the study are shown in Figs. 2, 3 and 4, respectively. Analysis is done by adding features to the dataset in order of importance from highest to lowest.

The accuracy result of GNB is shown in Fig. 2. As can be seen from Fig. 2a, for $K = 2$, GNB yields an accuracy of 79.72 with the most effective first feature (empowerment of abilities), 83.19 with the two most effective features (empowerment of abilities and perception severity), and 88.33 with the three most effective features (empowerment of

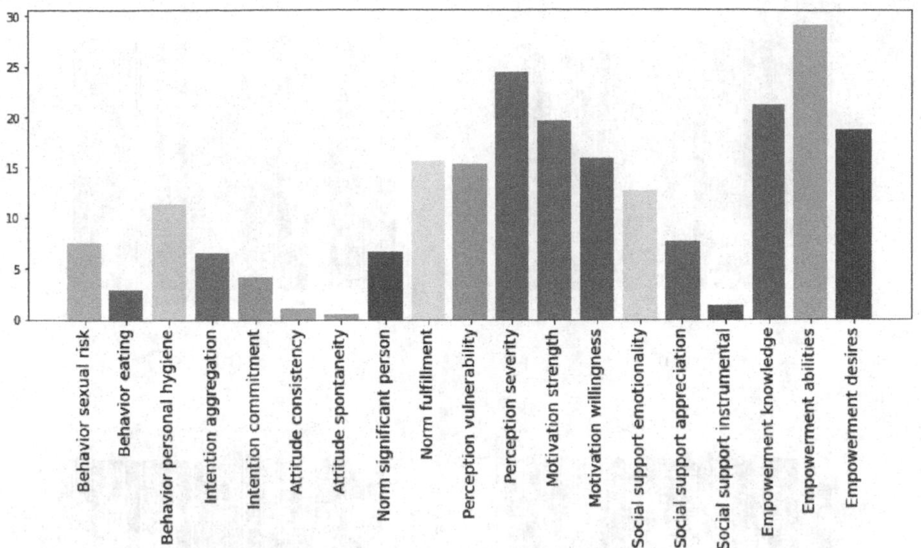

Fig. 1. Feature importance with an ANOVA F-test method

abilities, perception severity and empowerment of knowledge), while it has showed the highest accuracy (89.16) using the most effective eight features together (empowerment abilities, perception severity, empowerment knowledge, motivation strength, empowerment desires, motivation willingness, norm fulfillment, and perception vulnerability). In the experiments performed by taking $K = 3$ in the K-fold cross validation technique (Fig. 3b), the highest accuracy (92.36) with GNB was obtained by using the 9 most effective features together. Similarly, for $K = 4$ and 5, the highest accuracies with GNB were measured as (92.08) and (92.71), respectively (see Fig. 3c and 3d). The fact that the GNB algorithm gives close results even at different K values in the K-fold cross validation technique shows that it is a useful algorithm in the diagnosis of cervical cancer.

The accuracy performance metric results for the kNN classification algorithm are demonstrated for different K values in Fig. 3. In the kNN algorithm, the Manhattan distance metric is used to determine the closest samples and the effect of the nearest neighbor number (k) is analyzed. The hyperparameter k is investigated from 1 to 25 with an increment.

For K = 2, as seen in Fig. 3a, the highest accuracy (60.64) with kNN (k = 7) was obtained by using the first four most effective features together. In Fig. 3b, for K = 3, the highest accuracy (67.70) with kNN (k = 4) was found by using the 17 most effective features together. In Fig. 3c, for K = 4, the highest accuracy (72.22) with kNN (k = 9) was measured by using the most effective first feature. Finally, for K = 5, the highest accuracy (74.60) with kNN (k = 9) was obtained by using the five most effective features together (Fig. 3d). As can be understood from the results, the performance of the kNN classification algorithm varies with the number of features changing at different k and K values.

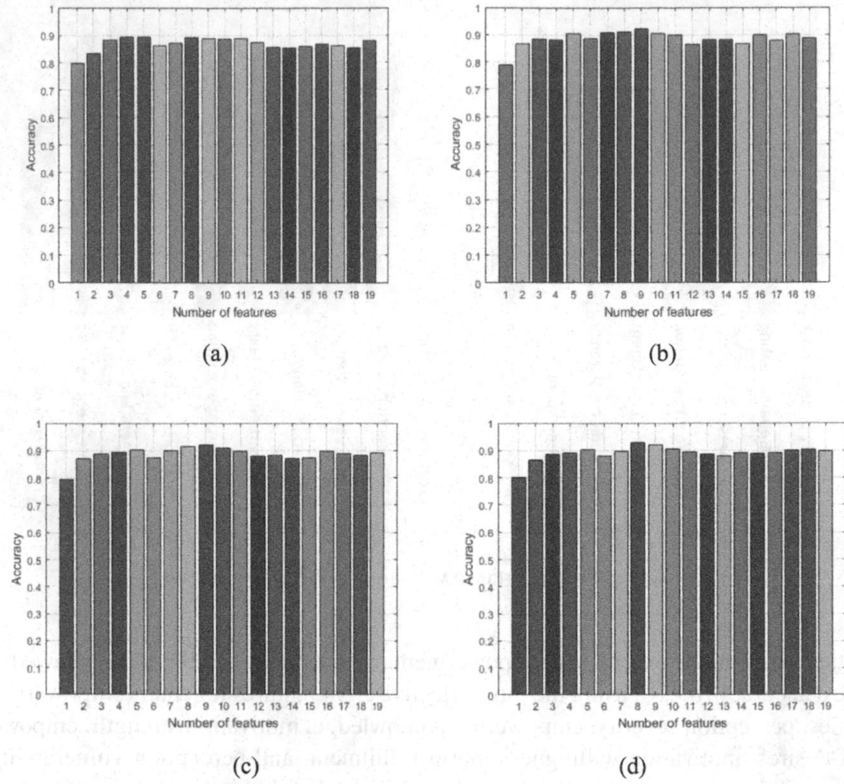

Fig. 2. Accuracy scores of GNB for different K values in k-fold cross validation (a) $K = 2$, (b) $K = 3$, (c) $K = 4$, (d) $K = 5$

The performance of the DT classification algorithm in K-fold cross validation for different K values is presented in Fig. 4. In the DT algorithm, the effect of the maximum depth hyperparameter (dh) is analyzed along with the number of features. The maximum dh is searched in the range 1–20 with one increment.

For K = 2, as seen in Fig. 4a, the highest accuracy (60.64) with DT (dh = 2) was obtained by using the 10 most effective features together. In Fig. 4b, for K = 3, the highest accuracy (68.75) with DT (dh = 2) was found by using the 15 most effective features together. In Fig. 4c, for K = 4, the highest accuracy (73.05) with DT (dh = 2) was measured using the four most effective features. Finally, for K = 5, the highest accuracy (75.76) with DT (dh = 2) was obtained by using the eight most effective features together (Fig. 4d). As can be seen from the results, for dh = 2, the performance of the DT classification algorithm changes with the number of features changing at different K values. In other words, as the K value in the K-fold cross validation technique increases, the performance of the DT classification algorithm also rises.

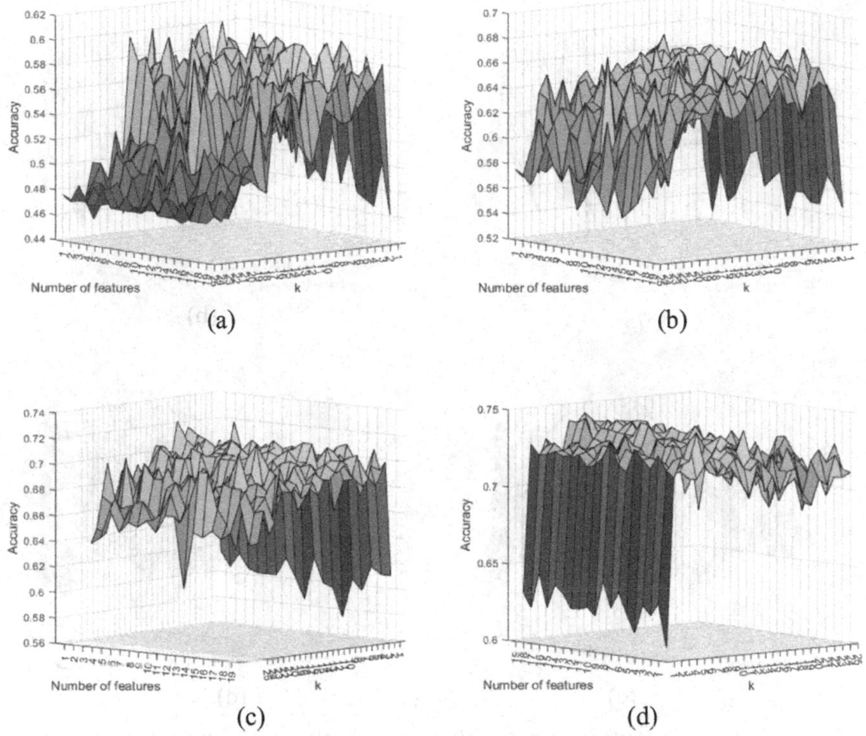

Fig. 3. Accuracy scores of kNN for different K values in K-fold cross validation (a) $K = 2$, (b) $K = 3$, (c) $K = 4$, (d) $K = 5$

Table 2 shows the highest results obtained with each method for K values ranging from 2 to 5 in K-fold cross validation. The number of features with the highest result and the method-specific hyperparameters of this result are given together. The highest results in the methods compared in four different performance metrics are highlighted in bold.

As can be seen from Table 2, the most accurate classification is provided by the GNB technique with 92.71% accuracy, 8 features, and K = 5. The kNN technique, on the other hand, showed the lowest classification performance with 60.65% accuracy, 4 features, k = 7 and K = 2. The DT technique also performed very close to the kNN technique.

The effect of the number of features and other parameters on the verification of the performance of kNN and DT techniques is quite high compared to GNB. The performance of the GNB technique did not change at all, especially at 3, 4, and 5 values of K, according to the number of features determined (8 or 9). This shows that the GNB technique gives more realistic results in estimating cervical cancer. Therefore, GNB technique can be used for early diagnosis of cervical cancer.

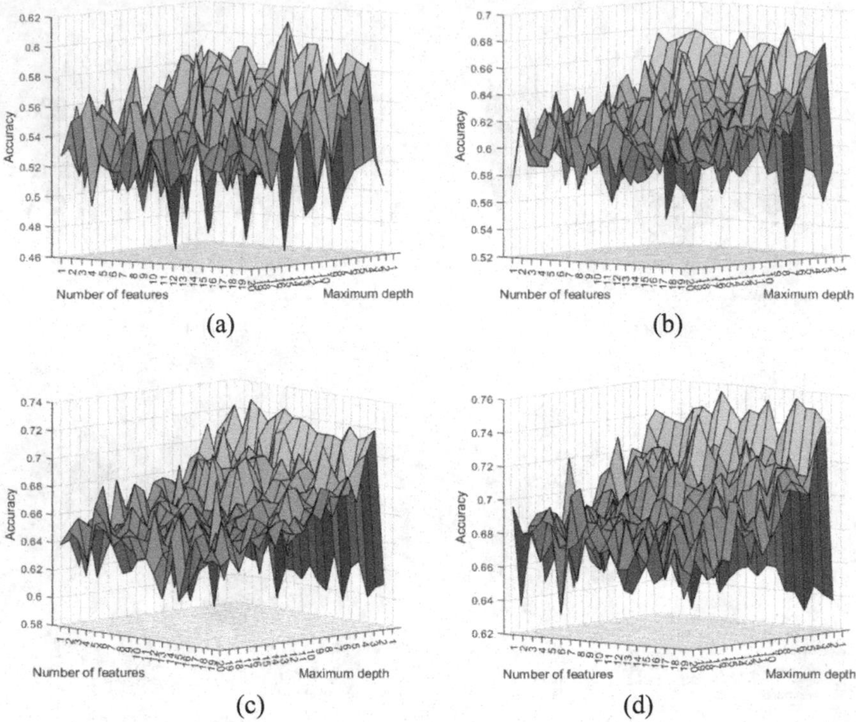

Fig. 4. Accuracy scores of DT for different K values in K-fold cross validation (a) K = 2, (b) K = 3, (c) K = 4, (d) K = 5

Table 2. Results of the compared methods in all performance metrics

Method		Accuracy	Recall	Precision	F1-score
GNB	$K = 2$, 8 features	0.8917	0.7944	0.8570	0.8087
	$K = 3$, 9 features	0.9236	0.8568	**0.9000**	**0.8681**
	$K = 4$, 9 features	0.9208	0.8534	0.8953	0.8534
	$K = 5$, 8 features	**0.9271**	**0.8700**	0.8944	0.8653
*k*NN	$K = 2$, 4 features, $k = 7$	0.6065	0.4777	0.6515	0.5458
	$K = 3$, 17 features, $k = 4$	0.6771	0.6048	0.6448	0.6173
	$K = 4$, 1 feature, $k = 9$	0.7222	**0.6150**	0.7075	0.6388
	$K = 5$, 5 features, $k = 9$	**0.7460**	0.5988	**0.7700**	**0.6597**
DT	$K = 2$, 10 features, max_depth = 2	0.6111	0.4984	0.6167	0.5486
	$K = 3$, 15 features, max_depth = 2	0.6875	0.5721	0.7110	0.6295
	$K = 4$, 4 features, max_depth = 2	0.7306	**0.6025**	0.7458	**0.6599**
	$K = 5$, 8 features, max_depth = 2	**0.7576**	0.5879	**0.7867**	0.6572

5 Conclusion

In the study, the effect of each risk factor directly or indirectly related to cervical cancer was evaluated independently with the ANOVA F-test. With ANOVA analysis, risk factors were ranked in order of importance, and then machine learning-based classifier algorithms (GNB, kNN, and DT) were trained on these factors incrementally in order of importance from highest to lowest. K-fold cross-validation technique was used at different K values to ensure the reliability of the results. In the selected cervical cancer behavioral risk dataset, the GNB algorithm showed the highest performance (94%) across eight risk factors for all K values. In other words, it is concluded that GNB has a superior performance compared to kNN and DT.

References

1. Alam, T.M., Khan, M.M.A., Iqbal, M.A., Abdul, W., Mushtaq, M.: Cervical cancer prediction through different screening methods using data mining. (IJACSA) Int. J. Adv. Comput. Sci. Appl. **10**(2), 388–396 (2019)
2. Deng, X., Luo, Y., Wang, C.: Analysis of risk factors for cervical cancer based on machine learning methods. In: 5th IEEE International Conference on Cloud Computing and Intelligence Systems (CCIS), pp. 631–635. IEEE (2018)
3. Shetty, A., Shah, V.: Survey of cervical cancer prediction using machine learning: a comparative approach. In: 9th International Conference on Computing, Communication and Networking Technologies (ICCCNT), pp. 1–6. IEEE (2018)
4. Ozaslan, I.N., Degirmenci, A., Karal, O.: Tourism demand forecasting for Turkey by using Adaboost algorithm. In: Innovations in Intelligent Systems and Applications Conference (ASYU), pp. 1–5. IEEE (2022)
5. Apaydin, M., Yumus, M., Degirmenci, A., Kesikburun, S., Karal, O.: Deep convolutional neural networks using U-net for automatic intervertebral disc segmentation in axial MRI. In: Innovations in Intelligent Systems and Applications Conference (ASYU), pp. 1–6. IEEE (2022)
6. Muttaqi, M., Degirmenci, A., Karal, O.: US accent recognition using machine learning methods. In: Innovations in Intelligent Systems and Applications Conference (ASYU), pp. 1–6. IEEE (2022)
7. Apaydin, M., Yumuş, M., Değirmenci, A., Karal, Ö.: Evaluation of air temperature with machine learning regression methods using Seoul City meteorological data. Pamukkale Üniversitesi Mühendislik Bilimleri Dergisi **28**(5), 737–747 (2022)
8. Degirmenci, A., Karal, O.: Robust incremental outlier detection approach based on a new metric in data streams. IEEE Access **9**, 160347–160360 (2021)
9. Degirmenci, A., Karal, O.: Efficient density and cluster based incremental outlier detection in data streams. Inf. Sci. **607**, 901–920 (2022)
10. Degirmenci, A., Karal, O.: iMCOD: Incremental multi-class outlier detection model in data streams. Knowl. Based Syst. **258**, 109950 (2022)
11. Machmud, R., Wijaya, A.: Behavior determinant based cervical cancer early detection with machine learning algorithm. Adv. Sci. Lett. **22**(10), 3120–3123 (2016)
12. Oyelakin, A.M., Muhammed-Thani, S., Salau-Ibrahim, T.T., Rilwan, D.M.: Performance analysis of selected machine learning algorithms for the detection of cervical cancer based on behavioral risk dataset. Int. J. Inf. Secur. Priv. Digit. Forensics **5**(1), 15–21 (2021)
13. Midyanti, D.M., Bahri, S., Midyanti, H.I.: ADALINE neural network for early detection of cervical cancer based on behaviour determinant. Sci. J. Inform. **8**(2), 283–288 (2021)

14. Gamara, R.P.C., Neyra, R.Q., Recto, K.H.A.: Behavior-based early cervical cancer risk detection using artificial neural networks. In: 13th International Conference on Humanoid, Nanotechnology, Information Technology, Communication and Control, Environment, and Management (HNICEM), pp. 1–6. IEEE (2021)
15. Nilnumpetch, C., Amornsamankul, S., Kraipeerapun, P.: Cancer prediction using cascade generalization and duo output neural network. In: Proceedings of the Sixth International Conference on Research in Intelligent and Computing, pp. 65–70 (2021)
16. Curia, F.: Cervical cancer risk prediction with robust ensemble and explainable black boxes method. Heal. Technol. **11**(4), 875–885 (2021)
17. Alpan, K.: Performance evaluation of classification algorithms for early detection of behavior determinant based cervical cancer. In: 5th International Symposium on Multidisciplinary Studies and Innovative Technologies (ISMSIT), pp. 706–710. IEEE (2021)
18. Ratul, I.J., Al-Monsur, A., Tabassum, B., Ar-Rafi, A.M., Nishat, M.M., Faisal, F.: Early risk prediction of cervical cancer: A machine learning approach. In: 19th International Conference on Electrical Engineering/Electronics, Computer, Telecommunications and Information Technology (ECTI-CON), pp. 1–4. IEEE (2022)
19. Cicek, İB., İlhami, S.E.L., Yağin, F.H., Colak, C.: Development of a Python-based classification web interface for independent datasets. Balkan J. Electr. Comput. Eng. **10**(1), 91–96 (2022)
20. Akter, L., Islam, M., Al-Rakhami, M.S., Haque, M.: Prediction of cervical cancer from behavior risk using machine learning techniques. SN Comput. Sci. **2**(3), 1–10 (2021)
21. UCI Machine Learning Repository: Cervical Cancer Behavior Risk Data Set. https://archive.ics.uci.edu/ml/datasets/Cervical+Cancer+Behavior+Risk. Accessed 21 Jan 2022
22. Aggarwal, C. C., Hinneburg, A., Keim, D. A.: On the surprising behavior of distance metrics in high dimensional space. In: Van den Bussche, J., Vianu, V. (eds.) ICDT 2001. LNCS, vol. 1973, pp. 420–434. Springer, Heidelberg (2001). https://doi.org/10.1007/3-540-44503-X_27
23. Onder, Z., Degirmenci, A., Karal, O.: Estimating breakpoints in piecewise linear regression using machine learning methods. In: Innovations in Intelligent Systems and Applications Conference (ASYU), pp. 1–6. IEEE (2022)
24. Saritas, M.M., Yasar, A.: Performance analysis of ANN and Naive Bayes classification algorithm for data classification. Int. J. Intell. Syst. Appl. Eng. **7**(2), 88–91 (2019)
25. Pintas, J.T., Fernandes, L.A.F., Garcia, A.C.B.: Feature selection methods for text classification: a systematic literature review. Artif. Intell. Rev. **54**(8), 6149–6200 (2021)
26. St, L., Wold, S.: Analysis of variance (ANOVA). Chemom. Intell. Lab. Syst. **6**(4), 259–272 (1989)

Mutual Effect Between Language Use and Media Technology via Digital Communication

Mau Vu Nguyen(✉) and Huong Hoa Le

People's Police University, Ho Chi Minh City, Vietnam
nguyenmauvu.dhcsnd@gmail.com

Abstract. Over the years, technology has revolutionized our globe and daily lives. Additionally, it has created amazing tools and resources, putting useful information at our fingertips so much that we have had new quicker ways to communicate, especially through social networking or digital platforms. And this study aims to investigate ways of English used in some famous American universities' Facebook pages to find out several newly developed linguistic features based on theoretical viewpoints of Bodomo (2010) and Crystal (2006, 2011) with the support of a qualitative approach. The results show that innovative linguistic features are developed into some trends of styles, grammar use, pragmatics, and vocabulary due to two groups of factors, namely face-to-face communication habits and socio-technical affordances. Moreover, this research makes an effortful contribution to reflecting the mutual effect in the rapid development of English and media technology that are becoming more and more dominant and attract large numbers of new users every day.

Keywords: Computer-mediated communication · Facebook · Linguistic features · Language change · Media technology

1 Introduction

Nowadays, we can claim that technology changes so fast that "new elements" quickly become "ex-elements" in digital media. However, this does not prevent us from recording and updating what is happening day by day, then many helpful results come with us, especially in the research field. Therefore, every modern scholar keeps in mind that reflecting every change, even small ones, as well as absorbing new technologies are responsibilities of enthusiastic researchers who will find out new trends in/for digital discourse in the age of digital media.

In fact, our mankind is staying at a new period when research subjects should be put together into a certain relationship, and their results must be taken into more comprehensive, practical and easily seen considerations. This direction is true with the situation of computer-mediated communication (CMC) studies because of two main reasons, including the fast pace of communicative technology development and much more users' engagement in CMC.

A. Mirzazadeh et al. (Eds.): SEMIT 2022, CCIS 1808, pp. 261–278, 2023.
https://doi.org/10.1007/978-3-031-40395-8_19

Concerning the language, many researchers also penetrate and explore this fruitful practical resource for various purposes. Particularly, it is not difficult for us to see most of this research divided into two major directions. Many linguists [1–3] concerned with linguistic features or practices collected from social networking exchange, while other scholars [4–7] considered web-based social networks as a motivative tool for foreign language education.

As the two renowned linguists in this area, Bodomo [8] and Crystal [9] state in their research, language used in CMC has a lot of potentials to make up numerous innovative forms and usages than ever in any mode of communication. Consequently, Bodomo proposes a model (Fig. 1) which is called the Technology-conditioned approach to Language Change and Use (TeLCU). It is the theoretical basis for himself and many researchers in the investigation of the development of language variation through CMC.

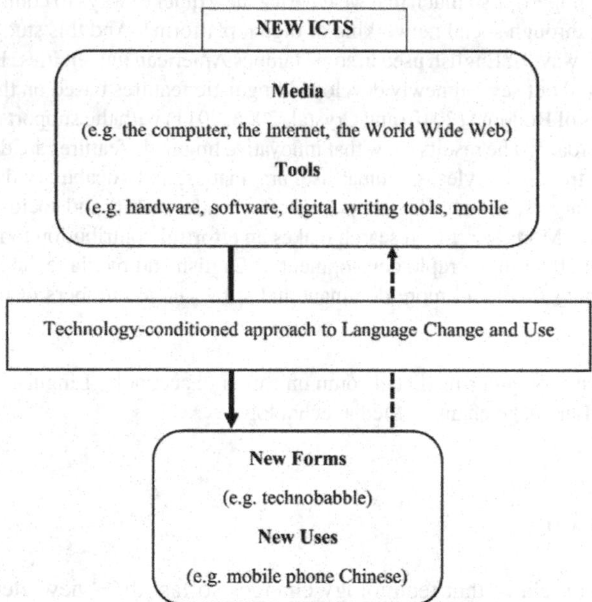

Fig. 1. TeLCU – the relationship between new ICTs (information and communication technologies) and new forms of language and literacy (Adapted from Bodomo [8, p. 42])

He suggests that there is a causal relationship between the emergence of new tools and media of communication in our society and the use of language. In other words, new tools and media of communication demand the creation of new forms and ways of communication, leading to changes in the way we use language in its various forms, including both the spoken language and the written language. However, Bodomo does not exclude the possibility of a "reverse" process, i.e. the ability where new forms of language and literacy reinforce changes in new technologies for communication. For instance, the rapid development of the Facebook platform is apart from language practices changed and innovated by Facebook users. Indeed, this study also aims to provide some evidence for further discussing the incompletion of Bodomo's model.

In the meantime, Crystal [9] addresses the online linguistic issues that affect us on daily basis, as well as he provides new linguistic analyses on some online communicative cases to explore the evolving multilingual characters of the Internet, especially language changes. The effect of the Internet on the characters of individual language has been very limited, for example, individual words, orthographic patterns which seem to be little different from the language used outside the electronic medium. However, Crystal believes that "little difference" is not the same as "no difference" (p. 57), he, therefore, claims an important task of Internet linguistics is to describe the way that vocabulary, grammar, graphology, and pragmatics are being used in novel ways within the various outputs.

It will be a shortcoming if we do not observe and record what changes in language in the Facebook platform because this online social network attracts the most populated users around the world. Facebook, created by Mark Zuckerberg in 2004 is the most widely used social networking site to date, with 1.79 billion monthly active users in 2016 [10] and roughly 2.89 billion monthly active users as of the second quarter of 2021 [11]. If Facebook were a country, it would be substantially bigger than China whose population was estimated to be 1.37 billion in the same year [12]. There is no doubt that Facebook has a powerful connection for the global community, and it may be considered as a zoomed-out society for both virtual and real communication through the internet. With its outstanding functions, Facebook provides users with several types of communication, including posts and comments in status updates (asynchronous mode) and conversations between two users or among users in a group in Facebook Messenger (synchronous mode).

For these reasons, the researchers carried out a synthesis, complementary and up-to-date research in ICTs (information and communication technologies) in order to reflect what and how the language has been used in one of the most popular social networks. At the same time, the study made a contribution to highlighting the mutual relationship between language use and ICTs through the data analysis collected from some American universities' Facebook pages.

2 Research Method

2.1 Research Design

This study follows a qualitative approach with the support of the quantitative one that employs the combination of several methods. According to Wray and Bloomer [13], one of the key features of linguistic variables is that they can often be counted or quantified while qualitative methods, by definition, involve description and analysis rather than the counting of features. A qualitative method is hence used to analyze and describe linguistic data, while employing quantification, we can look for non-standard orthography from the data and give statistics in terms of frequencies of occurrence in percentage.

2.2 Data Collection and Description

Data collected was all posts and comments in the year 2016 from the five official American universities' Facebook sites, including Princeton University, Harvard University,

Yale University, Colombia University and Massachusetts Institute of Technology (MIT). The rationale for this selection includes: firstly, these sites are public, authentic and open-access without any member registration; secondly, the language for communication and interaction on these sites is mostly English; thirdly, they are five prominent American universities where are recognized (according to US. News and World Report [14]) and received a great deal of interest (the number of posts and comments shown in Table 1); and finally, the data collected in the entire year of 2016 are sufficient to show outstanding annual events to ensure various topics in social life, not just learning and teaching activities.

Table 1. Statistics of selected data

No	University	No. of Post	No. of Live Post	No. of Post (<10 comments)	No. of Post (≥10 comments)	No. of Selected Comment
1	Princeton	635	533	407	126	2,907
2	Harvard	555	555	54	501	23,578
3	Yale	652	504	380	124	3,165
4	Columbia	619	555	485	70	1,685
5	MIT	630	610	432	178	4,792
TOTAL		3091	2757	**1,758**	**999**	**36,127**

Note: A post that has at least one comment is a "live post".

The data contains a large number of posts and comments. Each university had over 600 posts, except for Harvard University (555 posts) received the biggest number of comments. As seen from Table 1, a lot of posts achieved little attention from the Facebook community. Particularly 1,758 posts contain at least one comment but under ten comments, accounting for 63.7%. That is the reason why 999 posts, which bear at least 10 comments, have a total of 36,127 comments were chosen to research. It also means that these posts are about outstanding topics which get much attraction from network users – representatives for a zoomed-out society.

As a result, the data analysis took place on the size of 999 posts and 36,127 comments. They must conform to some criteria as follows: each message had to be a product of one-to-one or one-to-many exchange; each message had to be written in English, or a mixture of English and other languages. Even though the social and language background of posters and commentators are very diverse from various cultures, more non-native speakers are using English than native speakers nowadays. As Crystal [15] said, roughly five non-native English speakers to every one native speaker in the world contribute to changes in English, as a lingua franca, because numbers always count when it comes to language change.

2.3 Data Analysis and Tools

The data (posts and comments) was firstly analysed in terms of non-standard orthography after being fully transmitted into Microsoft Word with the support of checking spelling and grammar. Secondly, the results contributed to showing new forms and uses of language compared with Bodomo's view. After that, some newly developed ways of using English were found from the posts and comments in terms of vocabulary, grammar, pragmatics, and styles based on Crystal's classified main types of linguistic features and the support of technical tools.

3 Results

3.1 Newly Developed Styles

In linguistics, style "refers to ways of speaking – how speakers use the resource of language variation to make meaning in social encounters" [16, p. 32]. Also, contemporary approaches to style in sociolinguistics understand style as a repertoire of linguistic features associated with personae and identities that are linked to particular contexts [17, 18]. In this sense, style is perceived to be an additional mechanism that prompts people to exhibit a language variation according to the circumstances (Table 2).

Eleven linguistic styles were found and classified with various frequencies in a total of 37,126 posts and comments. The statistics showed that 21.3% of posts and comments utilised these linguistic styles. Especially, ***the use of literary quotes*** (6.9%) would refer to a catchphrase or 'saying' which a user could post within a message. With the support of technological functions, it has been so easy to do some activities. It is simply to copy and paste what you want to quote regardless of how long the saying is. Even we could paste some 'links' referring to any story or event in your message. That is the most outstanding function which made Facebook users feel very convenient and useful, is suitable for those who have a high spirit of showing proof, especially intellectual people. Next, ***the use of capital letters*** (2.2%) adds emphasis to highlight an essential idea, name or word, etc. Message postings written only with capital letters are usually considered as a strongly marked form of communication, such as shouting. Here are some instances of capital letters used as a form of emphasis found in the data.

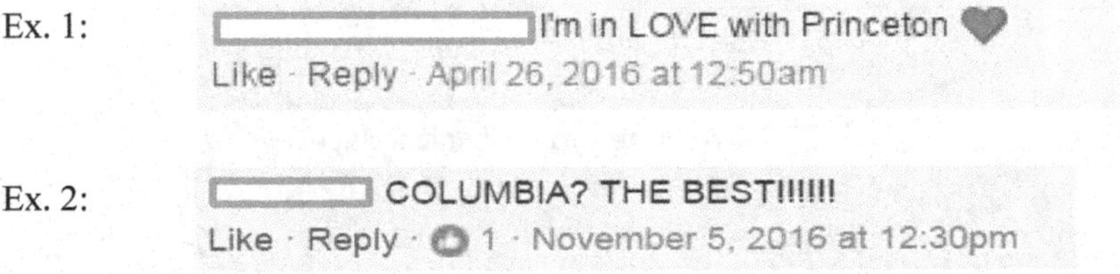

Ex. 1:
I'm in LOVE with Princeton
Like · Reply · April 26, 2016 at 12:50am
Ex. 2:
COLUMBIA? THE BEST!!!!!!
Like · Reply · 1 · November 5, 2016 at 12:30pm

Inversely, ***the omission of capital letters*** (3.1%) is also a linguistic practice by online users. In general, the Internet is not case-sensitive; interlocutors have the tendency to use lower-case letters, referred to as a keystroke principal (Crystal, 2006), even in the case of the first letter in the sentence, or proper names.

Table 2. Innovative linguistic features in styles in American universities' Facebook

<table>
<tr><th>No</th><th>Linguistic styles</th><th>Examples</th><th>No. of post (P)/comment (C)</th><th>Percentage (in total of P + C)</th></tr>
<tr><td>1</td><td>Literary quotes</td><td>- "Life is a fairy tale"
- <link></td><td>2553</td><td>6.9%</td></tr>
<tr><td>2</td><td>The omission of capital letters</td><td>turkish, i, new york</td><td>1142</td><td>3.1%</td></tr>
<tr><td>3</td><td>Capital letters</td><td>LOVE, THE BEST</td><td>810</td><td>2.2%</td></tr>
<tr><td>4</td><td>Use of interjections</td><td>yikes, hmm, shh, aww, whoops, wow, ohh, ahh, waoo, uh, eh, uhm, whao, hey, ek, aeh, whaa hoo</td><td>614</td><td>1.7%</td></tr>
<tr><td>5</td><td>Spelling mistakes</td><td>intresting, inovation, developlmentally paradaise</td><td>584</td><td>1.6%</td></tr>
<tr><td>6</td><td>Use of laughter</td><td>kkkk, kaka, haha, eheheh, hehe, lol, lmao</td><td>556</td><td>1.5%</td></tr>
<tr><td>7</td><td>Repetition of letters and words</td><td>Nooo, uhhh, wayyyyy, oooooh</td><td>421</td><td>1.1%</td></tr>
<tr><td>8</td><td>Creative spelling</td><td>thru, plz, coz, cnt</td><td>410</td><td>1.1%</td></tr>
<tr><td>9</td><td>Phonetic spelling</td><td>u, r, n, yr, m, h, b, ur</td><td>346</td><td>0.9%</td></tr>
<tr><td>10</td><td>Informal language use</td><td>tho, congrats, wanna, gotta, kinda, gimme, ma'am, ain't, y'all, brava</td><td>260</td><td>0.7%</td></tr>
<tr><td>11</td><td>Keyboard symbols</td><td>:0, @,:))), xD, XO,:-D, *…*,):,:((,;(, ^or,:'D,:c,:'), -[^; ~, o(^-^)o,:|, = D, /-_-\,:S, TnT,;-;,:0), $</td><td>193</td><td>0.5%</td></tr>
<tr><td>Total</td><td></td><td></td><td>7889</td><td>21.3%</td></tr>
</table>

Ex. 3:

Ex. 4:

Wow newyork city nice place
Like · Reply · 1 · July 19, 2016 at 10:27am
How i wish i could work my ideas with MIT.
Like · Reply · 1 · May 10, 2016 at 10:57pm

The statistics also show that a little use of ***symbols*** (0.5%) which are visual cues made up of computer keyboard characters to display emotion. However, facial expressions, gestures, and conventions of body posture and distance, the kinesics and proxemics of spoken language are essential in physically articulating opinions and attitudes, and visually displaying the overall tone of everyday conversations and of moderating social relationships [19]. With the lowest percentage of linguistic styles, the use of keyboard symbols tends to reduce in users' communicative process partly due to the increasing invention of 'emoticons' and 'stickers' on the Facebook platform.

In addition, Crystal [19] claims that ***spelling mistakes*** (which appeared in 584 posts and comments on these sites) found within the online written exchange or internet-using situations do not indicate the lack of education, but purely a function of typing inaccuracy. In other words, not all interlocutors spend time on revising before sending. Because of the nature of language use and linguistic variations that appeared in posts and comments, analytical study of spelling mistakes might be very difficult and seemly irrelevant in the context of technological affordances. However, nowadays this feature can be easily solved in line with the development of written-based communicative technology when the function of detecting and correcting spelling mistakes has been built and integrated into technological devices and the media platforms themselves. It also means that the language standards have been considered to maintain by improving the technology of spell checker for more convenience in online communication.

As ***laughter*** is a big part of face-to-face communication, it is also part of online communication as shown in 556 posts and comments. According to statistics, users opted to invent orthographic representations of laughter to enhance their intended meaning. For instance, there were hundreds of uses of "haha" and its variants. "Haha" was the most productive laughter created by interlocutors. Another marker of laughter was "kkkk", "kaka", "hehe", "eheheh", "lol" *(laugh out loud)* and "lmao" *(laugh my ass off)*.

However, the basic difference between spoken communication and written communication is the lack of real auditory sounds or interlocutors' tones. The latter is filled with many communicative strategies such as repetition of letters/ words, use of various punctuations and interjections, but the former still relies on users' imagination, or sometimes interlocutors accept to forget this element which is perhaps determined quite small during the "conversation". It does not mean that no one pays attention to this vivid detail which probably makes any far-spaced language-based exchange more directly and perfectly. For example:

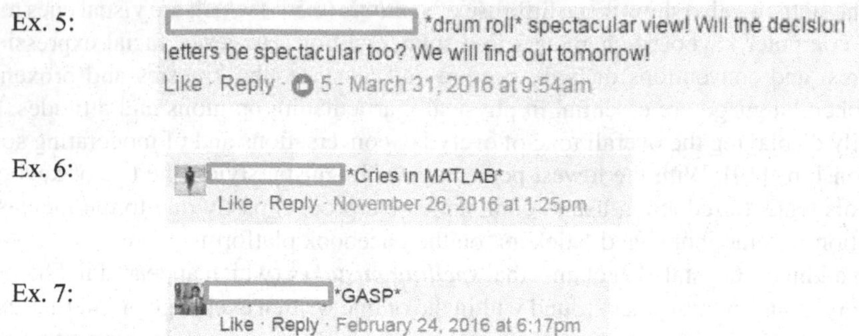

Ex. 5:
drum roll spectacular view! Will the decision letters be spectacular too? We will find out tomorrow!
Like · Reply · 5 · March 31, 2016 at 9:54am
Ex. 6:
Cries in MATLAB
Like · Reply · November 26, 2016 at 1:25pm
Ex. 7:
GASP
Like · Reply · February 24, 2016 at 6:17pm

Here is the popular way some Facebook users like to show the sound which they make at the same time of "speaking" online because they have sensible reasons to want readers to know what is happening with them, as well as how they feel by expression of acoustics. They have the same idea of putting "words for sounds" between two asterisks (Ex. 5, 6, and 7) and describe these sounds by using a noun phrase "drum roll", action verb "cries", or by a noun in capitals "GASP" which is used to describe the sound of strong breath and exhaustion after trying to decode the writing of his friend.

3.2 Changes in Grammatical Use

Grammatical features represent many possibilities of syntax and morphology, defined in terms of such factors as the distinctive use of sentence structure, word order, and word inflections [19]. The communicative types which take place on these sites include one-to-one (but others can read conversation contents) and one-to-many. Therefore, the use of first person pronouns reflects that the main topics in Facebook are those related to common interesting issues which any interlocutor wants to express his/ her opinions or emotions. Thus, it is not surprising to see a higher presence of 'I/my/me' or 'we/our/us' in the comments than in the posts. On the contrary, in terms of syntactically reduced form and subject pronoun, a sentence that is reduced in this way, subsequently, refers to the fact that the subject or a pronoun is omitted. Also, there are some other ways to save time (if necessary) on Facebook discussion, namely contraction. It is not difficult to see some reduced forms, like: "ain't" represents the standard informal contractions "isn't, aren't, hasn't, haven't and 'm not"; "y'all" is the contracted reduced form of "you all"; as well as the use of "-in" instead of "-ing" found in gerunds and verb suffixes.

Next, based on the data collected from Facebook comments of famous universities, some mistakes in the use of articles and grammatical structures are also found, as follows:

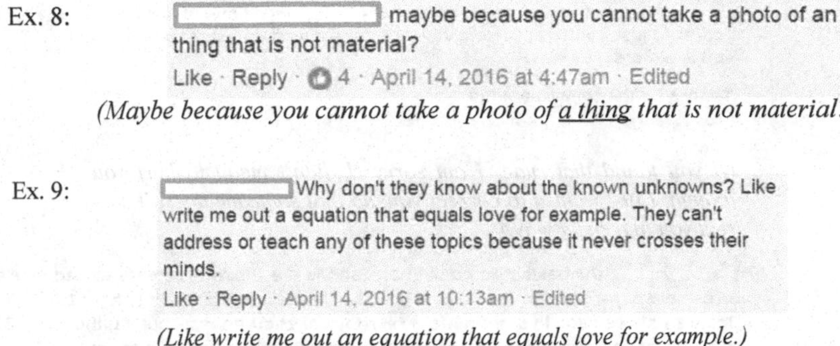

Ex. 8: maybe because you cannot take a photo of an thing that is not material?
Like · Reply · 4 · April 14, 2016 at 4:47am · Edited

(Maybe because you cannot take a photo of a thing that is not material?)

Ex. 9: Why don't they know about the known unknowns? Like write me out a equation that equals love for example. They can't address or teach any of these topics because it never crosses their minds.
Like · Reply · April 14, 2016 at 10:13am · Edited

(Like write me out an equation that equals love for example.)

Relating to ***articles***, many languages do not use articles at all, including Vietnamese and Japanese. Since the intricacies of the definite and indefinite articles in English are notoriously complex, even advanced students can struggle with getting these uses right. However, it is sure that using the right articles in English is a part of how English works. The articles perform a discourse function, by indicating new and old information. They often evolve from demonstratives (e.g. "this" and "that"). They evolve independently in unrelated languages. Normally, once an article system becomes a part of a language, it is an all-or-nothing thing. This is unlike a verbal inflection system, a gender system, or a case system. Once the system is in place, it is not optional. So do two indefinite articles "a, an", with one thing mentioned the first time, English users must put article "an" before if the word begins with a vowel or "mute h", and "a" in front of consonant-initial word. Fortunately, making mistakes with articles rarely affects meaning, thus in electronic informal communication as Facebook, users tend to ignore these grammatical rules regarding English articles and pay more attention to meaningful words or phrases. Even more seriously, ***the lack of obeying tense in use and verb forms*** is increasingly seen on these sites shown in Ex. 10–14.

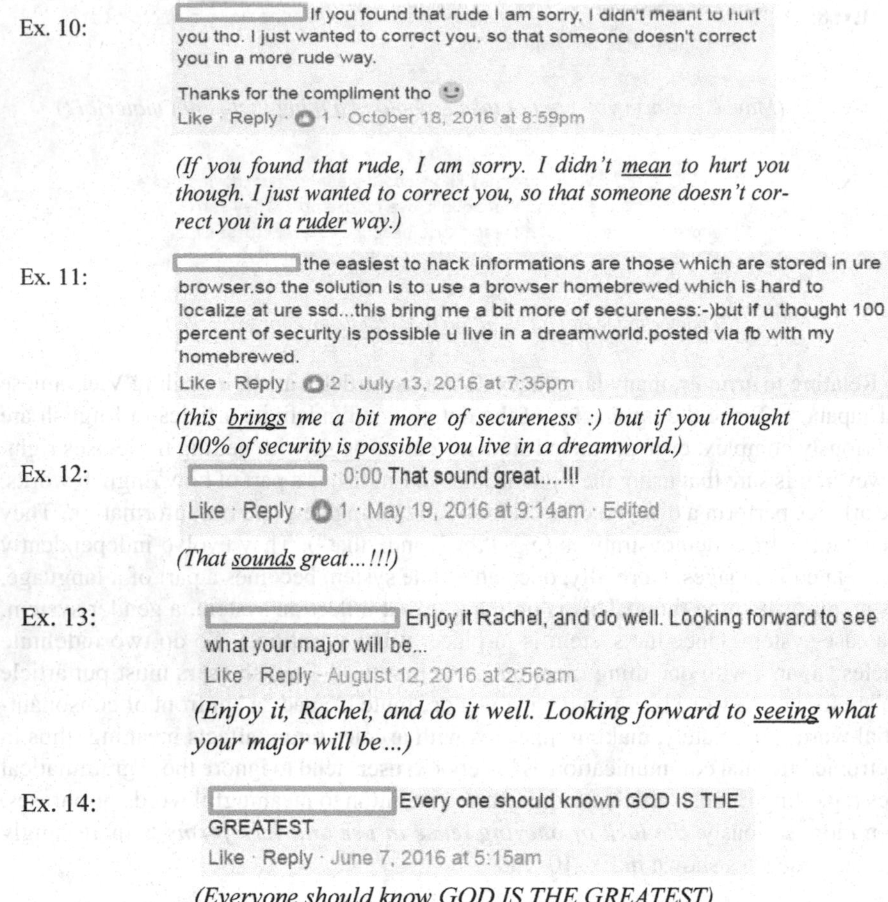

Ex. 10:

If you found that rude I am sorry. I didn't meant to hurt you tho. I just wanted to correct you. so that someone doesn't correct you in a more rude way.
Thanks for the compliment tho
Like · Reply · 1 · October 18, 2016 at 8:59pm

(If you found that rude, I am sorry. I didn't <u>mean</u> to hurt you though. I just wanted to correct you, so that someone doesn't correct you in a <u>ruder</u> way.)

Ex. 11:

(this <u>brings</u> me a bit more of secureness :) but if you thought 100% of security is possible you live in a dreamworld.)

Ex. 12:

0:00 That sound great....!!!
Like · Reply · 1 · May 19, 2016 at 9:14am · Edited

(That <u>sounds</u> great...!!!)

Ex. 13:

Enjoy it Rachel, and do well. Looking forward to see what your major will be...
Like · Reply · August 12, 2016 at 2:56am

(Enjoy it, Rachel, and do it well. Looking forward to <u>seeing</u> what your major will be...)

Ex. 14:

Every one should known GOD IS THE GREATEST
Like · Reply · June 7, 2016 at 5:15am

(Everyone should know GOD IS THE GREATEST)

Some mistakes in the use of verb forms without 's' preceded with a singular noun in the simple present tense (Ex. 11–12), as well as the past auxiliary 'did' and the modal auxiliary 'should' follow by past participles (Ex. 11 and 14) can be seen very often in comments by Facebook users. In addition, interlocutors do not also write the right forms of verbs and adjectives in some cases relating to syntactic structures "look forward to + V-ing" (Ex. 13) and comparatives of the short adjective 'rude' (Ex. 10).

3.3 New Trends of Pragmatics

Pragmatics studies and explains the choice available to people when they speak or write, and it also points out the factors which govern their choice. So, in terms of pragmatics, it is necessary to analyze the intentions of site-owners and users to evaluate the effects of their linguistic decisions on Facebook's posts and comments. ***Run-on sentences*** instantiate sentence constructions without any kind of punctuation. In the context of Facebook comments, these might be motivated because their purpose is to imitate speech where pauses are made whenever needed, without the need for any punctuation sign.

Break sentences happen because of the influence of commentary turns where some sentences are sent quickly in order to achieve quicker communication. An additional meaning for them is that they are another strategy for emphasis and for simplifying sentence structures. Besides, posting another new comment aims to supplement previous opinions with different expressions. Brevity is mainly shown by the use of abbreviations. The special network vocabulary often takes abbreviations to simplify the article, save printing space and reading time, thus meeting the requirements of computer science and high-speed development of network technology.

Today's online communication environment is more and more visually oriented. Thus, using ***symbicons*** [20] to convey messages – the most visible part of pragmatics – is a crucial type of communication by Facebook interlocutors in particular and by online users in general. According to Smallman et al., symbicons are "hybrids that combine the best aspects of symbols and icons" which are found in the analysis of the conversations on Facebook in this current paper. They consist of emoticons, asterisks, and symbols replacing words. By replacing a word with a symbol that stands for the word, several keystrokes may be saved. In example 15, a user utilizes the symbol "$" for "money" to add an idea relating to the issue of money in this case that it is not easy to be expressed directly. This last symbol does not seem to pose any difficulties in interpretation. People get to know the discourse and use their experience as well as pragmatic knowledge to achieve the most likely and relevant interpretation. By using the symbol "$" instead of the word with five keystrokes were saved in terms of message length and even more in implicit contextual meaning. Additionally, this strategy was used to save space.

Ex. 15:

Colombia still has hundreds of girls messed up by this vaccine and the company just washed their hands and moved on. Several countries banned it, in Europe politicians still can afford ethics. Developing countries are just sweeping cases under the rug. $
Like · Reply · 2 · January 31, 2016 at 9:29am

Emoticons are used to enhance alphabetic writing by conveying moods or emotions that are normally expressed with extralinguistic cues such as facial expressions and tone of voice in spoken interaction. Symbols in imitation of facial expressions in a monomodal written means of expression may help to make it easier to interpret text-only communication. The experienced communicator seems to know that some messages might need additional information to disambiguate text-only communication. The economic principle does not always hold, as has been shown, and people seem willing to spend a little bit of time and effort to insert emoticons to enhance their messages. Examples below were typed on a mobile phone that did not have any preformatted emoticons.

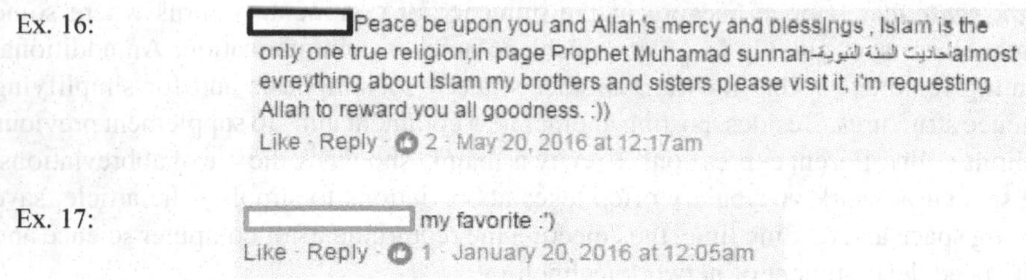

Ex. 16:
Peace be upon you and Allah's mercy and blessings , Islam is the only one true religion,in page Prophet Muhamad sunnah-أحاديث السنة النبويةalmost evreything about Islam my brothers and sisters please visit it, i'm requesting Allah to reward you all goodness. :))
Like · Reply · 2 · May 20, 2016 at 12:17am
Ex. 17:
my favorite :')
Like · Reply · 1 · January 20, 2016 at 12:05am

Because online communication is different from face-to-face situations, Facebookers also invent some ways to express their facial expressions through combinations of letters and strokes on the keyboard, and now there are even images incorporated into CMC gadgets. This is where ***Emoji***, also called, emoticons or smiley faces, comes in. Although emoticons represent an aspect of visual language or non-verbal language, this study aims to find out new ways of using language on Facebook communication, so it needs to pay attention to one of the most used pragmatic features with their meanings, as well as to see how Facebookers express their emotions online. Emoji can be used on Facebook statuses, comments and messages.

Nowadays emoticons are used worldwide and are developed into a quite standardized symbol system to express some common facial expressions or emotions, for example,:) represents *happy* and:(represents *unhappy*. Facebook version 2.0 (release date: Feb. 21, 2017) natively supports 2074 emojis, including choices such as smileys and people, animals and nature, food and drink, activity, travels and places, objects, symbols, flags. In CMC, the non-alphabetic symbols such as:),:(and;) are sometimes converted into emoticons (😊 smiley face, ☹ frowny face, 😉 winking) because they have already been pre-formatted and integrated into some applications for computers or mobile phones (Table 3).

Table 3. Frequencies of emoticon and sticker use on Facebook pages

University	Emoticonymy		Total
	Emoticons	Stickers	
Princeton	495	35	530
Harvard	2850	540	3390
Yale	705	40	745
Columbia	288	36	324
MIT	1040	40	1080
TOTAL	**5378**	**691**	**6069**

With the figures collected from the data, *emoticons or emojis* were employed with a high frequency, 14.5% total of posts and comments contain this feature with various types. Besides, we notice another kind of conveying users' emotions, that is *Sticker*, accounting for 11.4% of emoticonymy. What is the real difference between the two?

While emoticons/ emojis rest in-line with your text and can sometimes be typed in by using the right combination of characters, e.g.:) will turn into a smiley emoticon. 'Stickers' cannot be invoked via text and are sent as a separate line to text. Facebook users can send stickers on their comments by clicking the smiley face icon in the bottom-right corner of the comments field, or on their post by using *Sticker button.* As the result, we cannot exactly know the number of stickers at a particular period, as well as the meaning of these stickers also depends on different cognitions.

For these reasons, 'sticker' was not chosen for data analysis. But there is a concern about the introduction of Stickers on electronic communication and functional differences between emojis and stickers. We should put ourselves into the role of Facebook administrators, and consider why we need to create them, stickers. It can be seen that this issue relates to technological aspects which are increasingly developing to supply high demands from Facebook users. For those who want to have multiple options in showing their mind and emotions in what ways they satisfy most. It means that technology must change with the pace of modern life. The birth of new media tools is to keep pace with human progress; in other words, it helps to maintain stable development of social life and from that, to make a contribution to improving the living standards, especially promoting effective communications between humans and humans. Thus, we can infer that the appearance of 'Stickers' on the Facebook platform is a part of new communicative technology due to the change in what way people would like to communicate online. Further understandingly, to an extent what people require a new communicative tool to convey their mind through new language both online and offline. It depends on the speed of human and technological development, but we are sure about one thing, the development of social life in which communicative languages exist and technology is always going ahead. Therefore, we can conclude that if one language changes in some aspect leading to change in communicative ways, a new means of communication will have a chance to be invented for this changing demand.

Asterisks to frame words or phrases often serve the same purpose as emoticons. By adding explicit words, the message is rendered even more unambiguous. Actions described explicitly in words, such as the one illustrated in the example below, may also be marked to resemble additional prosodic features by repetition of letters.

Ex. 18:

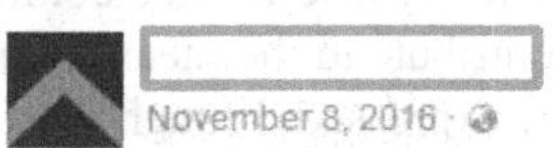

"Hey *Princeton U*, what do you say? The Cubs are gonna win today!"

3.4 Lexical Features

Facebook posts and comments, a kind of online communication, make great use of abbreviated forms. The fast pace of no-stop-point conversations requires brevity, both more and less informal nature of many communicative situations allows for a less elaborate discourse, typing is demand, the vast amount of information and possibilities available on the platform will not let anyone linger in one place longer than necessary. Therefore, the less text there is to write, the better it is. Frequently used abbreviations of conversational phrases are as follows: "tbf" for "to be fair", "brb" for "be right back", etc.

Acronyms are often written in lower case, again as the consequence of simplification and quickening of the typing process. Capitals are used for adding emphasis and for most two-letter abbreviations (IT - information technology, HU – Harvard University, NY – New York) since those are easier recognizable as acronyms if written in upper case and will not be confused with a misspelled word. Conventional abbreviations continue appearing in these communication forums. It means that these words or phrases refer to abbreviations that are agreed or generally accepted, in Standard English. For example, AI = Artificial Intelligence, PhD = Doctor of Philosophy.

As regards the use of unconventional abbreviations, these are used for the same reason as conventional ones. Yet, unconventional abbreviations also have another function. Unlike most conventional abbreviations, unconventional abbreviations are fairly innovative. Consequently, showing that one can use and think up innovative abbreviations helps to establish his or her social and linguistic identity and thus status on the chat.

3.5 Some Factors Leading to These Newly Developed Ways of Language Use

Effects of Face-to-Face (F2F) Communication Habits. Transference of spoken language into written-based communicative situations is a clear example to prove the influence of face-to-face (F2F) method on CMC. This phenomenon is analyzed and mentioned above. They are intentional cases of punctuation-free in order to show the fast pace of "speaking" without any pause, like exchanging face to face. This way is used a lot in run-on sentences from a pragmatic view. Other examples related to the reduction of personal pronouns or auxiliaries to achieve brevity in writing, even using much more slang or informal words while writing for academic issues. In addition, interlocutors tend to use a lot of interjections to reveal diversified emotions, such as from enthusiastic (whoop, whaa hoo), cheerful (hey) to surprised (yikes, wow, ohh, uh), even angry (graooo)… that is the same as communicating face to face with other users directly.

With the development of the CMC, human communication rapidly changes into interaction via the Internet, in which the messages are mainly transmitted by written words. However, a word is just an indirect part of the whole message because it only carries the literal meaning of the utterances in face-to-face communication. Other linguistic or paralinguistic elements that contribute to the meaning of a message like tone, gestures and facial expressions cannot be expressed through written words. Thus, there may be deficiencies in the meaning of a written message, leading the receiver to a misunderstanding of the sender's intended message on the part of the receiver. As a result, online users have to compensate for the missing parts of the message by fully employing the device for delivering the message: the keyboard.

In the CMC of later period, users started trying to use non-alphabet buttons such as numbers, punctuations and other symbols that can be found in a keyboard to represent the non-literal meanings; for example, moods and attitudes. The representation is mostly a simple icon combining two to three non-alphabet symbols. As the icons usually represent the emotions of the users and the smiley face is the most common icon in the conversations, people named these types of expressions as "emoticons" or "smileys".

That is the reason why a new form of language, emoticons, comes in. CMC in this generation has developed to a multi-functional social networking interface such as Facebook, allowing the users to interact with a group of people in several ways apart from chatting; for example, sharing photos and videos and setting up open discussions. The increase of the interaction methods in Facebook can help to move the CMC to the face-to-face end by sharing visual and audio information. As for coordinating with the change of the communication mode, the users tend to shift their conversation to the face-to-face end as well. As a result, the use of emoticons in today's Facebook communication is not only due to the compensation of missing meaning of the message but aims to deliver a more accurate and finer non-literal meaning that is expressed in the spoken F2F communication. One of the possible ways is to decorate the emotions with English letters in order to show a more delicate facial expression. In fact, using symbicons sometimes result in a better visual effect than its English counterparts, for example, the use of the symbol "$" to replace "money" in meaning and far-reaching is implicature for those who are afraid to say about the issue of money as their private opinion. There is also evidence supporting the effects of perfect F2F interaction in Facebook communication. That users utilize capital letters, repetition of letters/ words, repetition of punctuations, asterisks and words for laughter to highlight their emotion, tone and impression also indicates users' stylistic habits.

Socio-Technical Affordances. With the rapid development of technology which contributes to improving online communication for mankind, the way people communicate has changed in multiple dimensions with fruitful innovations around the world. Regarding the most favourite social networking site at present, Facebook has a huge number of users worldwide. The statistics show that more and more people prefer Facebook to do online work, and of course, communication is one of the indispensable activities. Thus, the close relationship between mankind and technology has created a system, namely the socio-technical system [21] in which people and technology are the constituents. This term was originally utilized to describe systems that involve a complex interaction between humans, machines, and context. As, in our perspective, the influence runs in both directions, between the social and technical dimensions of the system, it can be said that the social and the technical components co-evolve. Therefore, the socio-technical aspects of web-based social networks involve the coordination of technology, social network sites and users who shall cooperate and adjust to optimize the performance of the complete system. Because users pursue a certain goal and must, therefore, interact with others through technology, particularly on Facebook. As social interaction takes place through technology, the technical dimension mediates the social dimension. The social dimension also influences the technical dimension, as the interactions between the users of the social network create numerous social needs which the technical dimension must meet. For example, the invention of Sticker is to help Facebookers show their mind and emotions easier and more conveniently. Thus, factors leading to new trends in using language on Facebook may also be controlled by two main constituents.

Concerning factors caused by Facebook users, in the situation of fast real life, most people spend time using technological facilities for varied living purposes, such as work, study, entertainment, etc. As a result, Facebook takes up 22% of the internet time and users spend an average of 20 min per day on the site [22]. Facebook CEO Mark Zuckerberg said people spent 50 million fewer hours per day on the site last quarter after 2017. He posted "our focus in 2018 is making sure Facebook is not just fun, but also good for people's well-being and for society" [23]. Facebook intends to do this by encouraging meaningful connections between people rather than passive consumption of content. Although in recent times many people recognize that the balance is tilted toward social networks, they are striving to decline the time for non-technological activities, such as homework, learning, sports, playing with children… Unfortunately, in our society at this time, we have to be concerned with technology, especially the social network which is the main subject of this study, enabling us to contact and interact with other people for work or study. Therefore, the only thing to do on the social network Facebook exchange is to manipulate as fast as possible, for example, from making text by keyboards to using symbols for keystroke reduction or employing emoticons and stickers with 1–2 finger movements, even without using punctuations to pause a long piece of writing. All these strategies just fight against the constraints of time-consuming, which can be the main reason leading to many abbreviations and contractions. On contrary, some Facebook users do not care about the time saving on this site, they pay more attention to creative ways of expression, aiming to show their meaningful message as well as to contain private communicative styles. Moreover, from social network exchange, language acquisition takes place in the direction of inheriting developed features to create innovative trends. This process is described by the socio-technical system mentioned above.

As for factors caused by technology, some factors come from technical infrastructure, technological devices, and outstanding Facebook functions. Technology has a lot of powers which are proved by the fact that its efficiency is improved in not only qualitative usage but also quantitative large-scale extension. Firstly, that upgrading the infrastructure guarantees networks to connect thoroughly and globally is a necessary condition for attracting a huge number of active users more and more. Besides, the development and competition among technological devices diversifying tools for Facebook login and information exchange (such as personal computers, tablets, smartphones, smart TV which prices are decreasing), this is the sufficient condition for users to possess a device and keep communication in social networks. Last but not least, the Facebook platform is unceasingly developed and integrated some more technical functions effective for fast communication and users' styles.

4 Conclusions and Discussions

This study was carried out based on some viewpoints of Crystal (2011) and Bodomo (2010) about digital communication on the Internet. Linguistic analysis of Facebook posts and comments in American universities' official pages in 2016 shows some results, as follows.

Firstly, some linguistic features which have been gradually developed in new means of CMC are becoming familiar to Facebookers with high occurrences. In addition, we also see that some new technological functions which have been integrated to further serve for human communication, are explored to better show users' minds and emotions. Thus, online human language is increasingly fruitful and perfect thanks to the fast progress of technology. The evolution of new communicative technology creating a new form of language is presented in Bodomo's model, however, it is not completed. But at this time, because communication among people is developed at a new level, a new kind of technology is required, for example, the spelling checker and the invention of Sticker are likely considered as ways of language use, from linguistic to non-linguistic. From that, the inverse process which Bodomo has just forecasted since 2010, is timely formulated along with technological development and social demand at this study's period.

Secondly, four groups of features carry many creative traces by Facebook users at this moment. They are four trends of styles, grammar, pragmatics, and vocabulary. Among them, the most preeminent tendency is users' styles, including graphic features and orthographic features, covering eleven linguistic features interpreted above. While the repertoire is quite difficult to be added more creatively, the word is the meaningful constituent in conversations, especially in online communication. It is not easy for Facebookers to create new words, except for some ways of shortenings in clear context between writer and reader.

Finally, these trends of using English on Facebook at this time can be explained by two groups of factors. Because, the first and foremost reason, Facebook users are affected by some habits of face-to-face communication. They want to employ all features of written language along with integrated technological functions to show their minds in a comprehensive way including both linguistic and non-linguistic forms. Besides, the socio-technical theory can be used to describe the mutual relationship between society and technology. In this case, human in society plays an important role to determine the choice of technology as a communicative tool as well as highlighting their linguistic styles, even they set up the higher requirement for a functional technological upgrade. On contrary, the promotion of technology, from infrastructure to integrated functions in technological devices, is supplying the incessant demand of human beings. So, the close-knit relationship between people and technology makes the human language on CMC favourable to develop in various creative and plentiful ways.

The advancement of technology has made communication unbelievably fast and convenient. It's incredible to look back and see how much easier communication has gotten over the years. Communication tools offer one of the most significant examples of how quickly technology has evolved. These impacts are often unpredictable as technologies are adopted in new contexts and come to be used in ways that sometimes diverge significantly from the use cases envisioned by their designers. Our mankind knows how to apply these developments effectively and creatively, even with the inter-disciplinary approach to explore further application for human life and work. Therefore, the survival purpose of any ICT should derive from human demands in the time of real situations with the majority of people.

References

1. Pérez-Sabater, C.: The linguistics of social networking: a study of writing conventions on Facebook. Linguistik Online **56**(6), 81–93 (2013)
2. Halim, N.S., Maros, M.: The functions of code-switching in Facebook interactions. Procedia Soc. Behav. Sci. **118**, 126–133 (2014)

3. Androutsopoulos, J.: Networked multilingualism: some language practices on Facebook and their implications. Int. J. Biling. **19**(2), 185–205 (2015)
4. Clark, C., Gruba, P.: The use of social networking sites for foreign language learning: an auto-ethnographic study of Livemocha. In: Curriculum, Technology & Transformation for an Unknown Future. Proceedings Ascilite Sydney, vol. 164–173 (2010)
5. Liu, M., et al.: An analysis of social network websites for language learning: implications for teaching and learning English as a Second Language. CALICO J. **32**(1), 114–152 (2015)
6. Bailey, D., Park, I., Haji, S.A.: An investigation of Facebook for language learning: better understanding perceptions and participation. CALL-EJ **18**(02), 14–30 (2017)
7. Yu, L.T.: Incorporating Facebook into an EFL writing course: student perception and participation in online discussion. CALL-EJ **19**(01), 1–22 (2018)
8. Bodomo, A.B.: Computer-Mediated Communication for Linguistics and Literacy: Technology and Natural Language Education. Information Science Reference, New York (2010)
9. Crystal, D.: Internet Linguistics: A Student Guide. Routledge, London and New York (2011)
10. Number of monthly active Facebook users worldwide as of 3rd quarter 2016 (in millions). https://www.statista.com/statistics/264810/number-of-monthly-active-facebook-users-worldwide. Accessed 07 Jan 2017
11. Number of monthly active Facebook users worldwide as of 2nd quarter 2021(in millions). https://www.statista.com/statistics/264810/number-of-monthly-active-facebook-users-worldwide. Accessed 26 Dec 2021
12. If social networks were countries, which would they be? https://www.weforum.org/agenda/2016/04/facebook-is-bigger-than-the-worlds-largest-country. Accessed 07 Jan 2017
13. Wray, A., Bloomer, A.: Projects in Linguistics: A Practical Guide to Researching Language, 2nd edn. Hodder Arnold, London (2006)
14. National University Rankings. https://www.usnews.com/best-colleges/rankings/national-universities/data. Accessed 11 May 2017
15. Crystal, D.: English – is it still one language? Spotlight **8**, 36–38 (2016)
16. Coupland, N.: Style: Language Variation and Identity. Cambridge University Press, Cambridge (2007)
17. Bucholtz, M., Hall, K.: Locating identity in language. In: Llamas, C., Watt, D. (eds.) Language and Identities, pp. 18–28. Edinburgh University Press, UK (2010)
18. Johnstone, B.: Locating language in identity. In: Llamas, C., Watt, D. (eds.) Language and Identities, pp. 29–36. Edinburgh University Press, Edinburgh (2010)
19. Crystal, D.: Language and the Internet, 2nd edn. Cambridge University Press, Cambridge (2006)
20. Smallman, H.S., Oonk, H.M., St. John, M., Cowen, M.B.: Symbicons: advanced symbology for two-dimensional and three-dimensional displays. Technical report 1850, SPAWAR System Center San Diego, San Diego, CA (2001)
21. Baxter, G., Sommerville, I.: Socio-technical systems: from design methods to systems engineering. Interact. Comput. **23**(1), 4–17 (2011)
22. Incredible Facebook Statistics and Facts. https://www.brandwatch.com/blog/47-facebook-statistics. Accessed 11 Aug 2018
23. Facebook Users Spent 50 Million Fewer Hours Per Day on the Site Last Quarter. http://time.com/5127913/facebook-daily-usage-drop-earnings. Accessed 11 Aug 2018

Factors Determining Customers' Intention to Use Digital Banking - The Case of Vietnam

Khanh-Duy Pham(✉)

University of Economics Ho Chi Minh City (UEH), Ho Chi Minh City, Vietnam
duy.pham@ueh.edu.vn

Abstract. In the context of the industrial revolution 4.0, the influence of new digital technology inventions and achievements has brought many valuable products to serve the global economy. For the banking and finance industry, in particular, digital banking is one of the typical products representing the impact of this revolution on the whole sector. This paper examines the factors affecting Generations Z and Y consumers' intention to use digital banking in Vietnam. Using the technology acceptance research model (TAM), the study has built a research scale including six factors and 18 observed variables. Empirical results show that trust and risk levels do not impact customers' attitudes towards digital banking. Meanwhile, ease of use and usefulness is proven to affect customers' attitudes towards digital banking services significantly. At the same time, customers' attitude towards digital banking positively influences customers' intention to use digital banking. The empirical research contributes to the current literature as a reference for policy-makers, bank managers, and researchers concerning how to improve the intention of customers to use their new services.

Keywords: Digital banking · Intention to use · Behavioral finance · Technology acceptance model (TAM) · Industry 4.0 · Usage intention behaviour

1 Introduction

In the current age of modernization, the new smartphones technologies development and the emergence of new information technology systems have increased customer demand for advanced technology (Alkhowaiter 2020). For the financial market, commercial banks are constantly taking steps to convert traditional banking services to digital banking applications to satisfy and meet customers' expectations (Korir 2020). Digital banking plays a core and essential role in the existence and competition among commercial banks and contributes to the economic growth of each country. In particular, in the context of the global pandemic Covid-19 causing severe impacts and financial crisis worldwide, digital banking can be said to be a development opportunity capable of recovering this severe downturn in financial markets.

Due to the significant influence of new digital technology inventions, digital banking soon became an attractive topic for researchers worldwide. Although there is much

A. Mirzazadeh et al. (Eds.): SEMIT 2022, CCIS 1808, pp. 279–286, 2023.
https://doi.org/10.1007/978-3-031-40395-8_20

research worldwide, Vietnamese consumers' differences in culture and behavior compared to other countries, so the intention to use digital banking in Vietnam may vary. Moreover, existing research papers mainly focus on diverse research subjects in many generations. However, there will be other effects on customers' behavior and intention to use at different ages. Therefore, this study will inherit some previous research results and build a suitable model specifically for the factors affecting the choice to use customers' digital banking in Generation Y and Z in Vietnam, Vietnam.

2 Literature Review

2.1 Digital Banking

Digital banking is a product of digital technology and results from the Industrial Revolution 4.0 (Chen and Lam 2014). With the continuous development of globalization and modernization, digital banking is now an extensive system covering most traditional banking services such as withdrawals, money transfers, deposits, savings, and bank account management (Kamble and Afza 2018). All these services are integrated into a unique application on mobile devices or in social networking sites on the Internet. Customers can easily manage their accounts and perform complex online procedures with just a few simple steps, saving considerable effort and time compared to transactions in traditional banking. With the above advantages, the appearance and development of digital banking have been making a significant contribution to the economic growth of each country.

The advent of digital banking has created many opportunities for commercial banks to upgrade service quality and break down many cost barriers to get closer to customer needs (Khanboubi and Boulmakoul 2019). Digital banks have created favorable conditions for Vietnamese commercial banks to increase profits in the retail segment by up to 45% compared to the previous years (SBV 2019). In addition, digital banking is also considered a current development trend, creating a boom for the banking sector and the national economy (Lipton et al. 2016). This new technology has shortened transaction execution time, reduced customers' costs, and increased commercial banks' business efficiency many times. Therefore, digital banking plays a considerable role in commercial banks' development and helps the domestic banking market reach out and catch up with the world's trends. It also promotes the significant growth and development of the Vietnamese economy.

2.2 Literature Review

By reviewing the literature resource, we found the research paper of Ruangkanjanases and Wongprasopchai (2017), which has a similar research object for the same customer group in Generations Y and Z in Thailand. The authors examined factors affecting customer satisfaction with digital banking services by inheriting Davis (1989)'s TAM model. The paper investigates the following key elements: (1) Perceived usefulness; (2) Perceived ease of use; (3) Price perception; (4) Perceived risk; (5) Perception of likeability; and (6) Perceiving experientiality. After surveying 400 students of Generation

Y and Z in the Thai digital banking market, the final research results showed perceived usefulness, ease of use, and compatibility positively impact customer satisfaction with digital banking services in both age generations. In addition to the three factors above, generation Z, in particular, is also most dependent on the perceived risk factor in using digital banking services.

For related studies in Vietnam, the paper with the most similar topic and approach is the study by Dương and Nguyệt (2021). Aiming to investigate the external and internal factors of the banking environment that affect the success and development of digital banking, the authors have inherited the UTAUT2 research model designed by Venkatesh, Thong, and Xu (2012). This model uses a research scale to survey the target customer group about the factors affecting their intention to use digital banking. The six main factors used by the authors to make the observed variable include: (1) Expected efficiency; (2) Expected effort; (3) Social influence; (4) Hedonic mechanism; (5) Usage conditions; (6) Price value. The research results show that Usage conditions, expected efficiency, and price value are the three most impacted customers' intention to use mobile banking.

3 Research Hypothesis

Perceived ease of use (SD) is defined as the degree to which a customer believes that using a product will be effortless (Davis et al. 1989). Thanks to the modernity and advanced system of digitization technology, digital banks have more straightforward and less complicated operation procedures for customers than products with similar functions launched before. In addition, customers can easily find user manuals and conveniently receive help and support if they encounter difficulties during use (Chang and Polonsky 2012). So, the hypothesis put forward is:

H1: Perceived ease of use (SD) positively affects customer attitudes towards digital banking (TD).

Perceived usefulness (HI) represents the extent to which customers believe that using a product will bring about better results and effectiveness in many respects (Davis et al. 1989). Customers will consider choosing between various businesses in the current saturated commercial banking market. They will often prefer the digital banking services that are the most valuable and practical to their lives (Chang and Polonsky 2012). Therefore, the usefulness of digital banking will change customers' attitudes, thereby hypothesizing:

H2: Perceived usefulness (HI) positively impacts customers' attitudes towards digital banking (TD).

Perceived reliability (TC) is expressed through the level of trust of customers for the product (Davis et al. 1989). The commercial bank will positively affect customers' attitudes if its digital banking services bring about a quality customer experience similar to what the bank has advertised in the past. At the same time, a digital banking service with high credibility will also contribute to reducing the risks for customers, so it is possible to hypothesize:

H3: Perceived trust (TC) positively impacts customers' attitudes towards digital banking (TD).

Contrary to trust, customer attitudes (TD) are also influenced by perceived risks of a product (RR) due to the uncertainty to assess the negative consequences of a product for customers before using (Davis et al. 1989). The perception of the risk of digital banking is reflected in the insecurity of customers when having to provide account information or personal information during their use. If customers have perceived potential risks, they will have a skeptical attitude towards that product, leading to the customer's behavioral decision to go to another brand with a lower level of risk.

H4: Perceived risk (RR) hurts customer attitudes towards digital banking (TD).

The customer's attitude (TD) will be built to lead to this customer's intention to use the product (Davis et al. 1989). Customers will feel that using digital banking that meets all four of the above criteria is wise and right. A positive attitude will make customers want to continue using that digital banking product in the future and recommend to relatives and friends to use.

H5: Customer's attitude towards digital banking (TD) positively affects customers' intention to use digital banking (YD).

Proposed research model

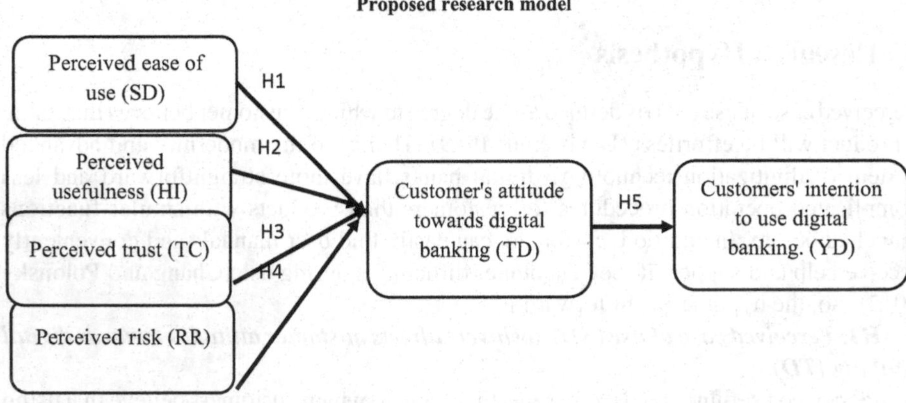

From the above research model, we establish the following two equations. The first regression equation examines the factors impacting customer's attitudes towards digital banking:

$$\mathrm{TD} = \alpha_0 + \alpha_1\mathrm{SD} + \alpha_2\mathrm{HI} + \alpha_3\mathrm{TC} + \alpha_4\mathrm{RR} \tag{1}$$

The second equation examines the relationship between customer's attitude towards digital banking to customers' intention to use digital banking:

$$\mathrm{YD} = \beta_0 + \beta_1\mathrm{TD} \tag{2}$$

4 Research Results

Due to many limitations in the context of the Covid-19 pandemic in Vietnam, we collected a total of 102 valid survey questionnaires.

4.1 Descriptive Statistics

Through the statistical frequency method, the research results were determined to be the most relevant and objective for the following customers: male or female, at the age of Generation Y (birth year from 1981 to 1995) and generation Z (birth year from 1996 to 2010), and have a monthly income of 5 to 15 million Vietnam Dong.

4.2 Reliability Test

The value of Variable Correlation – Total adjustment is higher than 0.3. The Cronbach's Alpha value of all observed variables is higher than 0.6. These tests prove a close correlation between the variables and that the survey questionnaire is built with high reliability, appropriate for research.

4.3 Exploratory Factor Analysis (EFA)

The KMO value (0.766) is more significant than 0.7, showing that the factor analysis is suitable with the research data set. Meanwhile, the Sig. Value is 0.000, reporting that the observed variables in the factor are correlated with each other and have statistical significance. In addition, the total variance extracted has a value of 74.096%, proving that the research model is appropriate. Finally, all factor loading coefficients have approximately 0.7 or higher values, so all measurement variables will remain.

4.4 Correlation Coefficient Analysis

The results show all Sig. Values are all 0, suggesting a statistically significant correlation between the variables and the correlation coefficient. The strongest correlation belongs to the relationship of H5, including two variables, Customer attitude (TD) and the variable Intention to use digital banking (YD), with the value at 0.7.

4.5 Linear Regression Analysis

The results in Table 1 suggest no impact of the variable RR and TC on the dependent variable TD (both sig. values are more significant than 0.05), so two hypotheses H3 and H4 are rejected. Moreover, both Beta values of SD and HI are more significant than 0, showing that the independent variables SD and HI positively affect the dependent variable TD. Thereby, we accept H1 and H2. In addition, all VIF values are less than 2, reporting no multicollinearity phenomenon.

The results of linear regression analysis in Table 2, with Sig. Value at 0.000 and VIF value at 1 suggest a positive effect of Customer Attitude (TD) on customers' intention to use digital banking (YD). Thereby, hypothesis H5 is accepted.

Table 1. Regression results of Eq. (1)

	Unstandardized Coefficients		Standardized Coefficients	t	Sig	Collinearity Statistics	
	B	Std. Error	Beta			Tolerance	VIF
	1.124	0.421		2.668	0.009		
SD	0.25	0.073	0.324	3.412	0.001	0.652	1.533
HI	0.276	0.082	0.342	3.384	0.001	0.578	1.731
TC	0.144	0.084	0.145	1.709	0.091	0.819	1.222
RR	0.042	0.048	0.068	0.868	0.388	0.971	1.030

With dependent variable Customer Attitude (TD); independent variables include Perceived ease of use (SD); Perceived usefulness (HI); Perceived trust (TC); Perceived risk (RR)

Table 2. Regression results of Eq. (2)

	Unstandardized Coefficients		Standardized Coefficients	t	Sig	Collinearity Statistics	
	B	Std. Error	Beta			Tolerance	VIF
	1.313	0.293		4.481	0		
TD	0.707	0.072	0.7	9.791	0	1	1

With dependent variable is customers' intention to use digital banking (YD), the independent variable is Customer Attitude (TD)

5 Conclusion

Inheriting the TAM research model, the study has concluded commercial banks in Vietnam about the factors affecting customers' intention to use digital banking. First, perceived trust and risk have no impact on customer attitudes towards digital banking services. This finding is in line with the research results conducted by Dương and Nguyệt (2021).

In addition, perceived ease of use and usefulness positively impact customers' attitudes towards services. At the same time, customers' attitudes towards digital banking services also positively correlate with customers' intention to use digital banking. Among two factors, the perceived usefulness of digital banking services more affects customer attitude. These findings suggest that opinions and the influence from surrounding relationships such as relatives, friends, etc., can impact customers' attitudes toward digital banking.

Moreover, we find that perceived ease of use affects customers' attitudes towards banking services, different from Ruangkanjanases and Wongprasopchai (2017)'s study. This divergence can be explained by the growth of digital technology in Thailand being faster and higher than in Vietnam. Thailand customers in generations Y and Z can access technology earlier than those in Vietnam. Therefore, more proficiency and familiarity in smart devices and electronic applications soon became an advantage for the Thailand customers. That is why the perceived ease of use no longer influences their usage behavior. Meanwhile, Vietnamese consumers are still struggling in digital banking operations, especially those who do not have many opportunities to interact with current digital technologies. So, the ease of use can affect Vietnamese customers' attitudes toward this application.

Based on the above research results, we first imply that commercial banks should focus on improving the usefulness of digital banking services, in particular, by saving costs and time for transactions. To replace traditional digital banking services, digital banking services must also show their usefulness through more attractive discounting and preferential policies for customers.

Second, banks can improve customers' attitudes towards digital banking services thanks to the product's ease of use. Therefore, commercial banks need to develop digital banking products to ensure straightforward usage. In other words, the operations used on electronic devices need to be streamlined and simplified to support customers to learn how to use them efficiently. Besides, banks also need detailed user manuals to try to do it by themselves.

Finally, commercial banks also need to improve and enhance the efficiency of digital banking services. In particular, they need to build and train a team of quality employees with both professional knowledge and specialized skills. Besides, building the trustworthiness of the brand image in the market is also essential so that customers can feel confident in their digital banking services. This confidence can eliminate customers' sense of risk while using these products.

When commercial banks fully ensure the above factors, customers' attitudes can favor their digital banking services. Then, customers will tend to maintain their usage behavior, even recommending to their surroundings as relatives and friends.

During the research process, in the context of social distancing in Vietnam caused by the Covid-19 pandemic, our study encountered many limitations in terms of time and space, with only 102 answers. At the same time, the study has been conducted with two specific age groups, namely the Y generation and the Z generation. Therefore, future research articles will inherit the scale and research model to conduct surveys for other customers of different age groups. We can also further compare the difference in research results between customers in age X and customers in generations Y and Z and customers in different regions in Vietnam.

Acknowledgment. This paper was presented at International Conference on Science, Engineering Management and Information Technology 2022, and benefited from conference participants and discussants. We acknowledge the constructive comments and valuable suggestions from the anonymous referees. Special thanks to Nguyen Thanh Le for excellent research assistance. Any remaining errors or shortcomings are the authors' responsibility. Financial grants from University of Economics Ho Chi Minh City (UEH) are acknowledged to conduct this research.

References

WA Alkhowaiter 2020 Digital payment and banking adoption research in Gulf countries: a systematic literature review Int. J. Inf. Manage. 53 102102

Y-W Chang MJ Polonsky 2012 The influence of multiple types of service convenience on behavioral intentions: the mediating role of consumer satisfaction in a Taiwanese leisure setting Int. J. Hosp. Manag. 31 1 107 118

J Chen K Lam 2014 How to Prepare for Asia's Digital-Banking Boom McKinsey and Company New York

FD Davis 1989 Perceived usefulness, perceived ease of use, and user acceptance of information technology MIS Q. 13 319 340

FD Davis RP Bagozzi PR Warshaw 1989 User acceptance of computer technology: a comparison of two theoretical models Manag. Sci. 35 8 982 1003

Dương, L.T.T.Y., Nguyệt, N.N.T.M.: Các yếu tố tác động tới ý định sử dụng mobile banking tại Việt Nam: mô hình UTAUT2 mở rộng. Paper presented at the Hội thảo quốc tê các nhà khoa học trẻ 2020 (ICYREB 2020) (2020)

PR Kamble N Afza 2018 Emerging trends in banking Int. J. Manag. Res. Rev. 8 5 1 7

F Khanboubi A Boulmakoul 2019 Digital transformation in the banking sector: surveys exploration and analytics Int. J. Inf. Syst. Change Manag. 11 2 93 127

Korir, V.: Factors Affecting the Adoption of Digital Banking in Kenya: A Case Study of Commercial Banks. United States International University-Africa (2020)

Lipton, A., Shrier, D., Pentland, A.: Digital banking manifesto: the end of banks?: Massachusetts Institute of Technology USA (2016)

A Ruangkanjanases S Wongprasopchai 2017 Factors influencing customer adoption of mobile banking services: empirical examination between generation Y and generation Z in Thailand Adv. Sci. Lett. 23 1 628 633

SBV: Phát triển ngân hàng số: Lấy khách hàng là trung tâm - Ứng dụng công nghệ 4.0 là nền tảng (2019). https://sbv.gov.vn/webcenter/portal/m/menu/trangchu/ddnhnn/nctd/nctd_chitiet?leftWidth=0%25&showFooter=false&showHeader=false&dDocName=SBV399897&rightWidth=0%25¢erWidth=100%25&_afrLoop=22101104429769311#%40%3F_afrLoop%3D22101104429769311%26centerWidth%3D100%2525%26dDocName%3DSBV399897%26leftWidth%3D0%2525%26rightWidth%3D0%2525%26showFooter%3Dfalse%26showHeader%3Dfalse%26_adf.ctrl-state%3D10w3n0c2ou_51

V Venkatesh JY Thong X Xu 2012 Consumer acceptance and use of information technology: extending the unified theory of acceptance and use of technology MIS Q. 36 157 178

The Breach is Dead, Long Live the Breach: A Spatial Temporal Study of Healthcare Data Breaches

Narjisse Nejjari[1,2(✉)], Karim Zkik[3], and Houda Benbrahim[2]

[1] College of Engineering and Architecture, TICLab, International University of Rabat, Rabat, Morocco
v-narjisse.nejjari@uir.ac.ma

[2] IRDA, Rabat IT Center, ENSIAS, Mohammed V University, Rabat, Morocco

[3] ESAIP Ecole d'Ingénieur, CERADE, Angers, France

Abstract. In recent years, a growing number of healthcare organizations have been affected by data breaches. In healthcare entities, preventing data security incidents mainly requires a comprehensive understanding of the context and the factors contributing to such threats. Utilizing publicly available federal data, we examine, from a spatio-temporal perspective, the factors and the context associated to data breaches targeting healthcare sector in the United States (US) between 2009 and 2021. We shed light on healthcare data breaches that occurred during the Covid19 Pandemic era to gain a better understanding of the impact of the global context on data breach incidents. In our findings, the hacking and IT incidents are the most common types of breaches targeting specifically Healthcare providers entities. Victim healthcare organizations are more frequent in Texas, California and Florida. Over the course of years, Emails and Network servers have become the main targeted breach locations. By understanding and identifying factors related to data breach incidents, healthcare IT security professionals can mitigate the risk of leaks.

Keywords: Healthcare data breaches · data security · data analysis · time series analysis

1 Introduction

Nowadays, digital healthcare services provide more convenient and accessible treatment, improving our lives significantly. The use of Electronic Health Record (EHR) [1] systems has enabled the healthcare industry to provide more efficient, cost-effective services. No one can deny that the adoption of electronic health records (EHRs) helped improve the quality of healthcare industry services for both the patient and the services provider, especially by making patient health information widely accessible. Hence, healthcare data has become increasingly digitized, distributed, and easily accessible. In this context, concerns about privacy and data security have increased.

A. Mirzazadeh et al. (Eds.): SEMIT 2022, CCIS 1808, pp. 287–303, 2023.
https://doi.org/10.1007/978-3-031-40395-8_21

In fact, the data collected by healthcare entities are customers' and employees' sensitive information, such as protected health information (PHI), including medical and payment records, payer and provider employee data, etc. Storing this data on network servers, making it accessible from smartphones and other intelligent devices has led to major privacy violations. Software vulnerabilities, security breaches, and human error cause unauthorized users to access these databases. Consequently, sensitive data is breached, resulting in data leakage.

Actually, and specifically in a pandemic era context, the modern healthcare industry is suffering both external and internal attacks. Security breaches impact not only security professionals but also clients, stakeholders, organizations, and businesses. The impact of data breaches is almost always the same regardless its type.

According to the Ponemon Institute's (IDX) Sixth Annual Benchmark Study on Privacy and Security of Healthcare Data [2], the healthcare industry is the most targeted industry for cybercrime. In the past two years, 89% of healthcare organizations experienced a data breach. Healthcare has the highest expense of any industry for cybersecurity breaches, with an average cost of $7.13 million. (IBM) [3] resulting in a devastating financial impact on the healthcare sector. US breaches cost the most, compared with other countries. For instance, 2021 has been a particularly dire year for healthcare data breaches [4]. So many large data breaches have occurred, causing networks to go down for weeks and disrupting healthcare services across the country. So far this year, exposures reported to the federal government have affected the records of 40,099,751 individuals [5]. In January 2021, Florida Healthy Kids Corporation reported a data breach that compromised the personal information (Social Security numbers, dates of birth, names, addresses, and financial data) of 3,500,000 individuals[6].

In the last few years, many studies dealt with the problem of data breach related to the healthcare sector [7–11]. In the context of healthcare, security breaches can be defined as "illegitimate access or disclosure of the protected health information that compromises the privacy and security of it" [7]. However, and to the best of our knowledge, only few of them focus their research on digging deeper on the context in which the breach occurred [12]. In [13], authors concentrate their studies on the use of IT in the healthcare sector while studying health data breaches. Other works give insights to the various categories of data breaches on healthcare organizations [7]. In this study, our main concern was to investigate the healthcare data breaches reported by federal agencies in the United States over the last 11 years (2009–2021). We aimed at examining the type of the targeted healthcare entities, the type of these breaches, and other data breach related factors. The goal is to statistically explore, using a time series analysis-based approach, the variation of healthcare data breach incidents during the last 11 years. In light of confirmed incidents, our study shed light on healthcare data security incidents.

The rest of the paper is organized as follows. In Sect. 2, we review the current literature realized to study healthcare data breaches. Section 3 provides information about the data source used to conduct this study. In Sect. 4 we analyze healthcare data breaches over data breaches over the last eleven years, with a focus on the COVID-19 era. In Sect. 5, we discuss our empirical results, in Sect. 6, we present limitations of our study and in Sect. 7, we conclude.

2 Related Work

Healthcare data breaches are increasingly being investigated by security researchers and experts in order to improve data privacy and security in healthcare organizations. Some previously published survey papers discussed data security issues in general, while others focused specifically on systems intended for use in healthcare entities.

Many recent studies have focused on analyzing the occurrence of data breach incidents and the size of the breaches over the years [3, 12, 14–17, 77]. Other studies proposed methods to study factors related to healthcare data breaches [9, 18, 19]. A related field of research examines the privacy and security of healthcare data in the wake of the Covid-19 pandemic [20–28].

2.1 Healthcare Data Breaches

An extensive literature review and analysis of work done to maintain security and privacy in the Healthcare sector is presented in [29]. E-Healthcare has become more accessible thanks to recent technological advances. Still, there are some unresolved data privacy issues, that get bigger with the context of global pandemic. Healthcare systems that hold, store, share and manage extremely private medical data face significant challenges. These systems must ensure the cyber security conditions of confidentiality, integrity, availability, accountability, and non-repudiation.

In general, data breach studies on healthcare entities follows one of two lines of research: Studying the security posture of the healthcare entity or understanding the breach pattern and its characteristics.

The first line of research tries to identify weaknesses in healthcare entity infrastructure and enhance its security level. The second line of research focuses on the attackers' behavior, including their intention and motivation.

Other studies proposed the analysis of data breach likelihood [12, 30, 31]. Seh et al. [7] use several data sources such as HIPAA journal, the Office for Civil Rights (OCR) report and Privacy Rights Clearinghouse (PRC) Database to give insights about the various categories of data breaches in different organizations and focusing mainly on the healthcare system.

So far, a considerable amount of studies have focused on assessing the risk of data breach by defining their underlying causes and triggers [8, 9, 18, 19]. The author in [9] presents a model of factors associated with healthcare data breaches. The authors explored the relationships between level of organizational factors, level of exposure, level of security and the likelihood of the occurrence of a data breach. Another body of related work presents studies on reputational risk of data breach and their impact on patient welfare [10, 32, 33]. Securing healthcare data has been the focus of many important healthcare regulations. As an example, we can cite the commission on Enhancing National Cybersecurity established in 2016 [34]. The commission role is to provide recommendations for raising security awareness for electronically stored data including healthcare data and mandating data breach reporting. A study of Electronic Health Record (EHR) Adoption in US hospitals was conducted by Adler-Milstein et al. [35] to examine hospital EHR trends.

Several survey papers on data privacy and security in healthcare organizations have been published [68–70]. The authors of [68] present a survey of network technologies related to data security and piracy in the healthcare industry. An other work [69] highlites data privacy and access control issues in healthcare systems that manage patient-related information, but focus only on authorized access. In [70], authors examine security and privacy issues associated with WSN-based healthcare systems. Hence, they fully focus on anonymity.

A review of the previous research work in the field of data privacy in healthcare sector revealed that there is a lack of works that deal specifically with security breaches in hospitals.

2.2 Data Breaches' Impacting Factors

A recent review of literature on this topic found that studying factors associated to data breaches would help to address organizations' vulnerability.

Considering previous works, the causes of data breaches were summarized into two categories: Intentional data breaches caused by a malicious act where the intent is to cause harm to an organization [36] and unintentional data breaches caused by accidental actions and without malicious intent [36].

In their work, Khan et al. [37] identified five items of intentional data breach: hackers, unauthorized access, malicious insiders, state-sponsored actors and terrorists [38–43]. Five items were also identified for unintentional data breach: Malicious software [43], vulnerable network infrastructure [38, 40]}, unauthorized logical access [44, 45], stolen intellectual property [46, 47], flawed authorization checks [48–50] and flawed software [48, 51].

The location of breached information is also an important factor to highlight when studying data breaches. Identifying exactly where the data leak started could help security specialists to target their efforts on specific locations. Many works have been conducted in this field [38, 48, 49, 52, 76].

Khan et al. [37] divided data breach location into two major categories: Physical data breach and Logical data breach. Some of the items related to Physical data breaches are Lost paper files, Stolen hardware, Unauthorized physical access, and Unauthorized personal computer [37]. Logical data breaches are related to malicious software, Vulnerable network infrastructure, Unauthorized logical access, etc. [37].

A data breach can also be studied according to its aspects. By technical aspect, we refer to organizations' IT security measures, specifically technics used to detect data breach threats such as monitoring network traffic and emails logs, intrusion detection systems (IDS), access control systems, etc. [53–56].

However, non-technical aspects cover security awareness for employees, customers and stakeholders, security policy implementation and legal perspectives that target data privacy in the organizations. This aspect is related to a major part to human factors that may contribute to data breach incidents [56–59, 72–75]. As an example of legal perspective, Westland [59] investigated whether the information provided in Sarbanes-Oxley reporting can be used as a statistical "predictor" for future security breaches in a company. The primary contribution of this research consists of providing several valid models to construct a link between actual security breaches and SOX audits assessed the strength of internal control in companies.

The most similar work to ours is [9], in which authors developed a model of factors associated with breaches of health data. They looked at the relationship between the level of organizational factors, level of exposure and level of security and the likelihood of the occurrence of a data breach in healthcare organizations. The data used in this work was obtained from the Health and Human Services database of health facilities reporting breaches of data and from a large national database of technical and organizational infrastructure information. To examine a representative data breach model binary logistic regression was utilized. According to their analysis, the occurrence of accidents is due to a series or chain of events rather than to a single cause of failure. These factors may be categorized by examining the following: information systems (technological factors), business process factors and organizational factors. The Swiss cheese model is used to explore the data breach causation chain.

2.3 Healthcare Data Security Issues During COVID-19

Throughout the COVID-19 pandemic, healthcare data breaches increased exponentially [20]. Over the last two years, healthcare entities are facing heightened cybersecurity threats, especially data breach incidents. In March 2020 alone, the World Health Organization (WHO) and the US Health Agency have been threatened by security breach incidents.

With the widespread use of the internet and intelligent devices to access healthcare services, as well as an increase in the number of patients for hospitals and healthcare entities, the healthcare sector has emerged as a key target for data security breaches.

Cyber criminals targeting healthcare industry are also taking advantage of individuals seeking healthcare information or using healthcare pandemic-related mobile applications by launching the phishing, scamming, and malware attacks. Prior surveys related to COVID-19 privacy issues covered a wide range of data security related topics, including ethical and privacy issues in digital solutions (such as contact-tracing applications), private versus public safety issues and personal data sharing frameworks in healthcare sector [20–28, 71].

Despite the fact that privacy protection is required for healthcare organizations, it remains a challenge due to the variety of factors that influence the level of control that a subject has over their personal health data. A recent study published by Shuja et al. [22] authors reviewed the privacy issues related to COVID-19 open source data. Authors pointed out the importance of federated data in fighting the pandemic, as well as maintaining user privacy through anonymity. Moreover, other surveys discussed the quantification of privacy risks and its impact on digital solutions [60] and on emerging technologies related to healthcare services privacy issues in COVID-19 context [37].

According to [67], the main cybersecurity challenges of the health sector could be emphasized in the following: remote work security assurance, endpoint device management, human errors, the lack of security awareness, inadequate senior-level security risk assessment, inadequate business continuity plans, the lack of coordinated incident response, constraints on budget and resources, and vulnerability of medical systems [67].

In the context of the COVID-19 pandemic, these challenges grow larger and become more difficult to manage.

3 Dataset

3.1 The Office of Civil Rights (OCR) Data

This research endeavor was based on the The Office of Civil Rights (OCR) [61] data source. The Office of Civil Rights breach data in the U.S. Department of Health and Human Services (HHS) provides Breach report [62], which is a list of breaches of unsecured protected health information. It also provides a comprehensive information report about healthcare data breaches, titled “Report to Congress on Breaches of Unsecured Protected Health Information”. Two pathways for reporting data are used: Healtcare entities may report directly to HHS through TeleTracking or to state health departments or state hospital associations, which then share data with HHS [62].

3.2 Dataset Description

The dataset covers about 4440 data breach incidents between 2009 and 2021; and it is composed of the following attributes: Name of Covered Entity, State, Covered Entity Type, Individuals Affected, Breach Submission Date, Type of Breach, Location of Breached Information and Business Associate Presence status.

In this analysis, we focus on studying Covered Entity Type, Individuals Affected, Type of Breach and Location of Breached Information, all from a time series perspective. A breach may involve any of the following types of incidents: theft, loss, hacking/IT incident, improper disposal, unauthorized access/disclosure, other, or unknown (not reported or data missing). Breach incidents may involve any of the following information, information technology, or devices: paper/films, network server, laptop, desktop computer, e-mail, electronic medical record, other portable electronic device, or other.

4 Healthcare Data Breach Analysis in US between 2009 and 2021

In this section, we provide insights into healthcare data breaches faced by healthcare entities in United States over the last 11 years (2009–2021). The main goal is to present an in-depth analysis of healthcare data breaches, as well as shed light on the impact of the Covid-19 Pandemic on the nature of breaches and the victim organizations.

4.1 Breach Occurrence

According to The Office for Civil Rights (OCR) Department of Health and Human Services (HSS.Gov.) [62], Healthcare data breaches can be defined as an impermissible use or disclosure under the Privacy Rule that compromises the security or privacy of the protected health information [61]. Figure 1 illustrates the occurrence of data breach incidents reported in HHS portal, over the last 11 years. The figure shows that the slope of the graph increased significantly in the fourth quarter of 2019. This prominent increase in data breach incidents was due to the American Medical Collection Agency (AMCA) healthcare data breach which is a professional debt collection service that specializes in collecting medical data [63]. This data breach created a "cascade of events" and went undetected for more than eight months, resulting in the theft of information of more than 20 million patients and healthcare professionals, making it one of the biggest data breaches in the healthcare sector. Due to unauthorized access, this massive data breach exposed consumer personal data and payment information. The last quarter of 2019 also marked the start of Covid-19 era around the world.

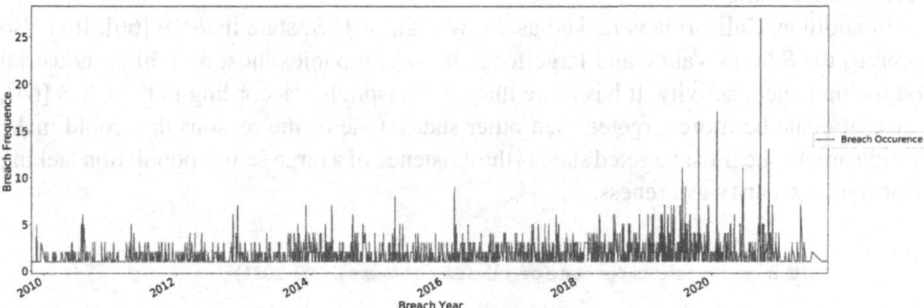

Fig. 1. Representation of Data breach incidents between 2009 and 2021.

4.2 Breach Occurrence by Healthcare Entity Type

According to Fig. 2, the majority of targeted healthcare entities are Healthcare providers such as, but not limited to, doctors, clinics, psychologists, dentists, chiropractors, nursing homes, pharmacies. The second most targeted entities are Health Plans. Health Plans include Health insurance companies, or health maintenance organizations, Employer-sponsored health plans, Government programs that pay for health care, like Medicare, Medicaid, and military and veterans' health programs.

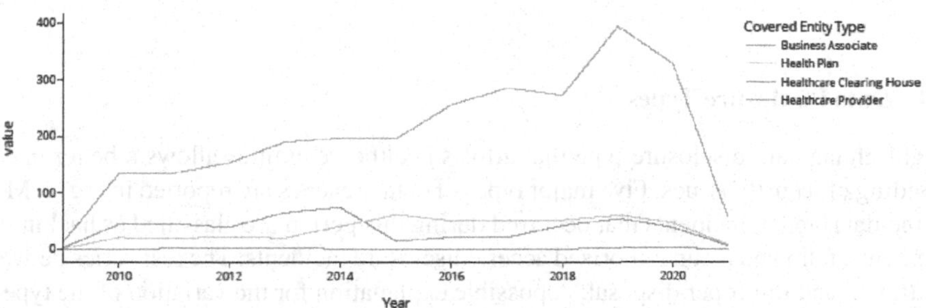

Fig. 2. Breach Occurrence by Healthcare Entity Type.

4.3 Breach per States

Figure 3 presents the distribution of healthcare data breaches in the US states. It reports the frequency of data breaches in states where victim healthcare entities are located.

The data indicate that data breaches are more frequent in Texas(TX), California(CA), and Florida(FL). Texas, for example contains more than 8% of hospitals in the US. Texas has 407 hospitals, which is the highest number of hospitals in the country, according to the CMS [64]. Being the second most populous U.S. state [65], Texas faces challenges related to protecting all of its 254 counties, which enhances its likelihood to be the most affected state in the US.

In addition, California is ranked as the wealthiest U.S. state in 2019 [66]. It is also home to the Silicon Valley and large technology companies, hosting a high industrial and technological activity. It has more than 341 hospitals - according to the CMS [64], hence, it could be more targeted than other states. One of the reasons that could make Florida among the most targeted state is the existence of a large senior population lacking information security awareness.

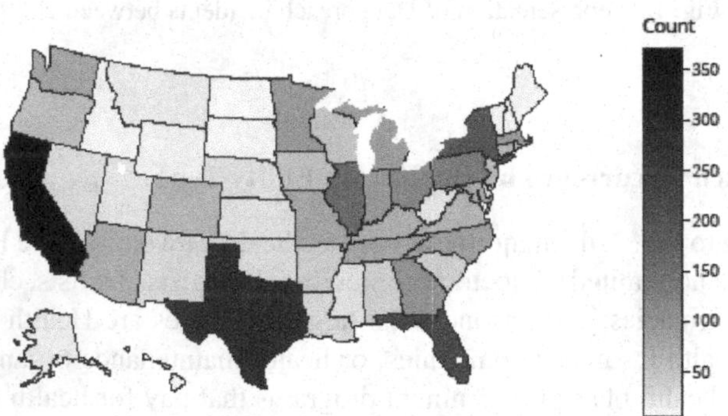

Fig. 3. Data Breach frequency per States.

4.4 Data Disclosure Types

Highlighting data disclosure type that affects healthcare entities allows a better understanding of security issues. Five major types of data breaches are reported in Fig. 4. Most of the data breach incidents that occurred during this period are classified as hacking/IT incidents, followed by unauthorized access/disclosure incidents. The rest varies between theft, loss and improper disposal. A possible explanation for the variation of the type of data breach over time is that hacking /IT incidents get more attackers' attention due to the variety and creativity of its security software.

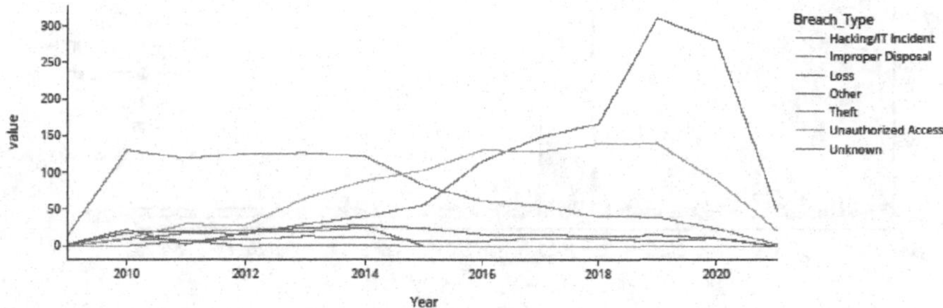

Fig. 4. Distribution of Data Disclosure Types over Years.

4.5 Breached Locations

Figure 5 illustrates locations of the data breach, which are: Email, Network servers, Paper/Films, Electronic medical records, laptop and another portable electronic device.

According to our findings, over the last years, Email and network servers have proven to be the most vulnerable places for personal health information. In fact, more than 46% are located on email and more than 15% on network servers.

The breakdown of data breaches by the location of breaches highlights the importance of increasing email security and providing further training to healthcare employees. The crucial pathway for attackers looking to infiltrate healthcare sensitive systems is the deficient security practices in this sector.

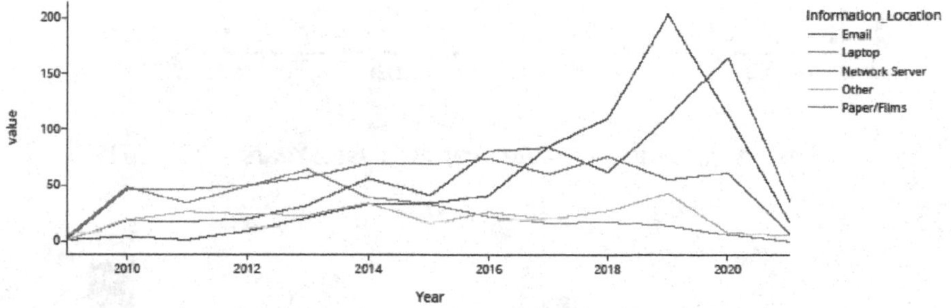

Fig. 5. Distribution of Breached Locations over Years.

4.6 Healthcare Data Breach Analysis: A Focus on COVID-19 Era

In this sub-section, we focus on studying data breach incidents during the COVID-19 pandemic (2020–2021). We investigate the type and geographical distribution of victim healthcare entities, the targeted location of breached data, and the type of data disclosure used. During this period, healthcare organizations face the challenge of ensuring the safety of highly personal and sensitive medical data. Healthcare entities should use these data to control outbreaks and spreads of Coronavirus while protecting the privacy of their clients.

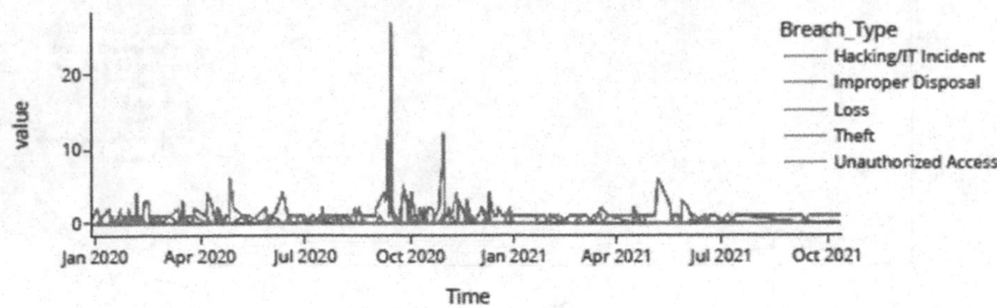

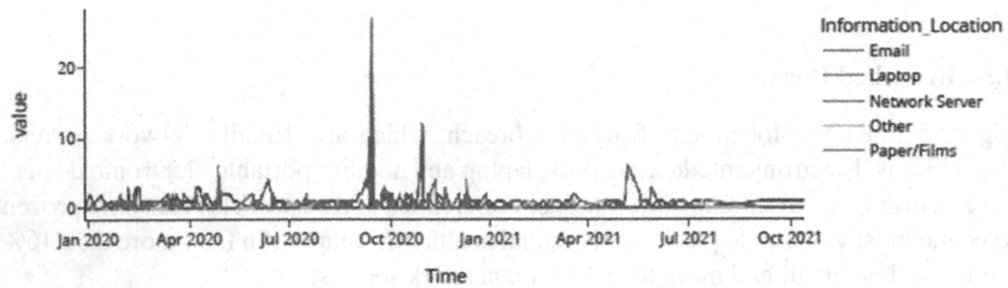

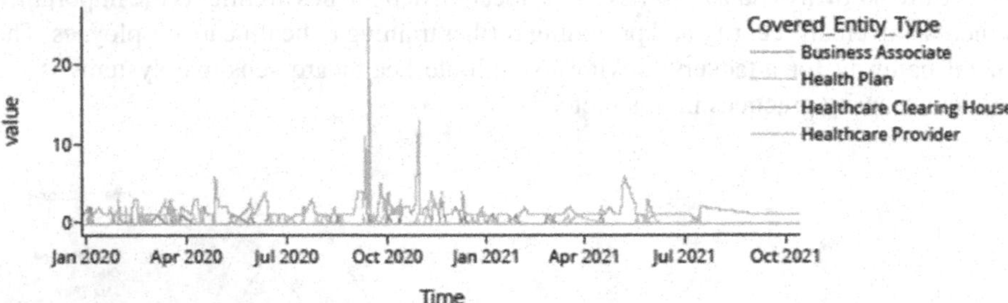

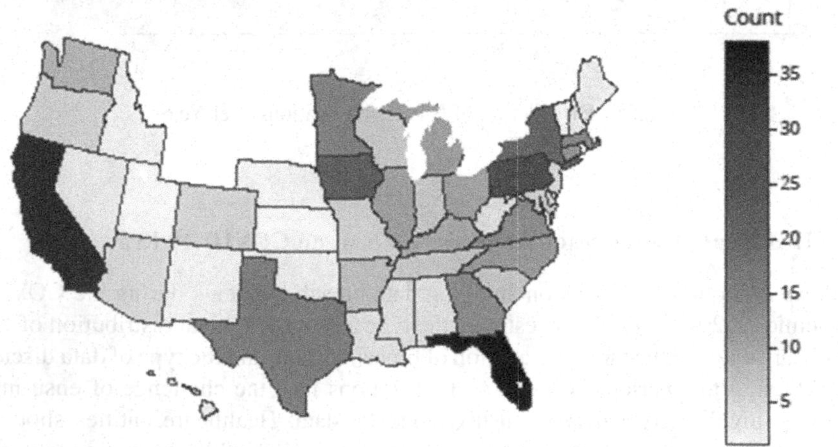

Fig. 6. Data breach incidents during the COVID-19 pandemic (2020–2021).

The graphs below depict some of the changes that occurred during this time period. Healthcare providers remain the most frequently targeted healthcare entities. These two last years, Florida has the most breaches (43), followed by California (42) and New York (32). Hacking/IT incidents continue to dominate and are more likely to target network servers than emails (Fig. 6).

In 2020, a well-known healthcare business associate in Florida, in charge of several administrative and financial services, was the victim of a phishing attack [16]. About 1,670 individuals were affected and data such as Social Security numbers, driver's license numbers, health insurance and financial information were leaked. Also a big dental support organization [16], based in Florida with more than 320 affiliated dental practices across 20 states, has been affected by a security breach. More than 1 million protected health information and payment card numbers were potentially stolen.

The increased use of cloud services and encryption has had both positive and negative effects on data security and privacy over the years. On the bright side, it reduced the number of loss/theft incidents. On the negative side, data breaches targeting network servers and emails have increased. Many network servers store large volumes of patient data, making them ideal targets for hackers.

5 Results and Findings Discussion

Understanding the context of data breaches targeting hospitals could help reduce the incidence of data security breaches over time or help assess the risk in terms of data breaches. Healthcare entities in the United States, particularly healthcare providers, are a potential target for data security breaches, making them a fertile ground for security researchers and experts. On the one hand, HIPPA regulations impose a basic level of IT security on those types of entities, and on the other hand, the frequency of data breaches targeting healthcare providers has recently increased.

Our results show that hacking and IT incidents are the most prevalent types of breaches targeting healthcare providers. Emails and network servers are the locations of most breaches. The implications of these findings are significant for policy and practice: This could help them target their efforts towards a specific type of breach that could be more damaging for a specific type of healthcare organization that maybe at bigger risk. The following conclusions can be drawn from highlighting data breaches during the Covid-19 era:

- The number of incidents involving data breaches increased significantly in the fourth quarter of 2019.
- Healthcare providers in Florida and California continue to be the most frequently targeted healthcare entities.
- Hacking/IT incidents on network servers continue to be more common than those on email servers.

Compared to an analysis covering the periode from 2009 to 2016 by Gabriel et al. [31], 185 hospitals were breached during the study period, while according to our findings, from 2018 to 2019, 155 hospitals were victims of data breach incidents. We can say that data breaches on hospitals are becoming more commonplace in the US; especially with healthcare systems digitalization.

Findings about the location of data breaches have shifted over time. Prior to 2016, the most common location of breached information was paper records and films, which occurred mostly due to theft, improper disposal and unauthorized access. This finding changes over years, during our study period, Network servers and email proved to be the most targeted and vulnerable locations. These could be due to the data storage methods used before the Electronic Health Records Incentive Program in 2016 in US; data was largely collected on paper and stored in filing cabinets rather than in digital form.

Weak password protection, the lack of intrusion detection or prevention and insider errors like the 'inevitable click', might contribute to the surge in hacking breaches. As the way attackers exploit healthcare organizations becomes progressively more creative, we believe it is necessary to get ahead of the education and training of medical staff. Enforcing strong credentials and multi-factor authentication, encryption for sensitive data, scanning of all devices, checking for all kinds of vulnerabilities and scanning for network security misconfigurations would have contributed to data protection.

6 Limitations and Future Work

It is plausible that a number of limitations could have influenced the obtained results. The first major limitation of this work is data availability; we have conducted the analysis based on data available on the Centers for Medicare Medicaid Services database and the U.S. Department of Health and Human Services, assuming that is a centralized reporting database for all data breaches in the healthcare sector.

Although analyzing data breaches in hospitals helps identify several factors of breach incidents in US hospitals; other types of healthcare entities, such as physician practices and clearinghouses, suffer also from breaches and might be an area of study for future work, in order to get a global view of data breaches impact on all healthcare facilities.

Our knowledge of data breaches victim hospitals is largely based on available data at a given duration of time. Besides this, we aim at future work to use this data to construct a predictive machine learning model, in order to predict the risk of targetability of hospitals by data breach incidents. This could help healthcare organizations to shift from a reactive,' wait-and-see' approach to a proactive approach, preventing a data breach from happening or at least reducing its impact. Hunting for malicious threats in order to ensure that patient data remains safe and secure, so becomes an obligation for healthcare organizations. However, healthcare work environments are usually complex. However, introducing new changes in health IT systems, like remediation activities, IT upgrades and updates may disrupt care processes and lead to reduced quality.

Future research could look into a variety of aspects of healthcare data breaches that target hospitals, including:

- Add more factors that may help to better understand hospital security breaches, such as hospital rating or meaningful use of EHRs criteria.
- Investigate the security posture of victim hospitals in depth using a review of their usable security measures.
- Propose a well-defined data security protocol that is appropriate for each type of hospital.

7 Conclusion

In this study, we have analyzed healthcare data breaches in US over the last 11 years (2009–2021). Our research aims at identifying which types of healthcare entities are most frequently targeted by data breaches, as well as what types of breaches are most common for those entities. Additionally, this study presents the geographical distribution of data breach incidents and highlights its variations over pandemic time. In light of confirmed incidents, our study sheds light on healthcare data security incidents.

Aiming at improving health care processes through health information technology, the US government has promulgated requirements for "meaningful use" (MU) of electronic health records (EHRs) as a condition for providers receiving financial incentives for the adoption and use of these systems. Increasing regulatory requirements like Health Insurance Portability and Accountability Act (HIPAA), Payment Card Industry Data Security Standard, etc. may put IT security at the forefront of many hospitals' strategic agendas. As personal medical information becomes increasingly 'digitalized', and medical devices more connected to cyberspace; hospitals should establish a 'security culture' alongside their technical security measures (encryption, virtual private network, antivirus, etc.). This could lead to a fairly consistent increase in IT security expenditures across almost all types of hospitals.

Both individuals and organizations encounter a variety of damages after a data breach incident. In addition to the significant financial losses that organizations sustain due to data breaches, the incidents continue to severely harm the organizations' image, damaging their reputation and brand value. Healthcare entities should be aware that the disclosure of personal medical information may affect their reputation, the quality of the service, and sometimes may be an attempt on patients' life. Thus, in order to ensure patient safety, cybersecurity must be incorporated into patient care.

The onslaught of COVID-19 security breaches has left a plethora of victims. The global spread of COVID-19 has generated a large amount of health data as well as a wide range of privacy, data protection, security and compliance issues for hospitals and healthcare organizations. Post-COVID era forced healthcare industries to prioritize data integrity and protection. These challenges drive the need for healthcare providers and organizations to take serious concerns about data breaches.

References

1. de Groot, A.C., Toonstra, J.: 10. In: Casuïstiek in de dermatologie deel 2, pp. 33–36. Bohn Stafleu van Loghum, Houten (2010). https://doi.org/10.1007/978-90-313-8458-7_10
2. Sixth Annual Ponemon Benchmark Study on Privacy and Security of…, IDX. https://www.idx.us/knowledge-center/sixth-annual-benchmark-study-on-privacy-and-security-of-health care-data (consulté le janv. 12, 2022)
3. Cost of a Data Breach Report 2021 | IBM. https://www.ibm.com/security/data-breach (consulté le janv. 12, 2022)
4. Labrecque, L.I., Markos, E., Swani, K., Peña, P.: When data security goes wrong: Examining the impact of stress, social contract violation, and data type on consumer coping responses following a data breach. J. Bus. Res. **135**, 559–571 (2021). https://doi.org/10.1016/j.jbusres.2021.06.054

5. The biggest healthcare data breaches of 2021, Healthcare IT News, 16 novembre 2021. https://www.healthcareitnews.com/news/biggest-healthcare-data-breaches-2021 (consulté le janv. 12, 2022)
6. Florida Healthy Kids, Florida Healthy Kids. https://www.healthykids.org/incident/ (consulté le janv. 12, 2022)
7. Seh, A.H., et al.: Healthcare data breaches: insights and implications. Healthcare **8**(2), 133 (2020). https://doi.org/10.3390/healthcare8020133
8. Collins, J.D., Sainato, V.A., Khey, D.N.: Organizational Data Breaches 2005–2010: Applying SCP to the Healthcare and Education Sectors, vol. 5, no 1, p. 17 (2011)
9. McLeod, A., Dolezel, D.: Cyber-analytics: Modeling factors associated with healthcare data breaches. Decision Support Syst. **108**, 57–68 (2018). https://doi.org/10.1016/j.dss.2018.02.007
10. Confente, I., Siciliano, G.G., Gaudenzi, B., Eickhoff, M.: Effects of data breaches from user-generated content: a corporate reputation analysis. Eur. Manage. J. **37**(4), 492–504 (2019). https://doi.org/10.1016/j.emj.2019.01.007
11. Wikina, S.B.: What caused the breach? an examination of use of information technology and health data breaches. Perspect. Health Inf. Manag. **11**, no Fall, 1h (2014)
12. Benchmark study on patient privacy and data security. 27(1), 69–81, Journal of healthcare protection management: publication of the International Association for Hospital Security
13. 2021 Data Breach Investigations Report | Verizon. https://www.verizon.com/business/resources/reports/dbir/ (consulté le janv. 12, 2022)
14. December 2019 Healthcare Data Breach Report, HIPAA Journal, 21 janvier 2020. https://www.hipaajournal.com/december-2019-healthcare-data-breach-report/ (consulté le janv. 12, 2022)
15. 2019 Cost of A Data Breach Study Reveals Increase in U.S. Healthcare Data Breach Costs. https://www.hipaajournal.com/2019-cost-of-a-data-breach-study-healthcare-data-breach-costs/ (consulté le janv. 12, 2022)
16. Ayatollahi, H., Shagerdi, G.: Information security risk assessment in hospitals. Open Med. Inform. J. **11**(1), 37–43 (2017). https://doi.org/10.2174/1874431101711010037
17. Bai, G., (Xuefeng) Jiang, J., Flasher, R.: Hospital risk of data breaches. JAMA Intern. Med. **177**(6), 878 (2017). https://doi.org/10.1001/jamainternmed.2017.0336
18. Sowmiya, B., Abhijith, V.S., Sudersan, S., Sakthi Jaya Sundar, R., Thangavel, M., Varalakshmi, P.: A survey on security and privacy issues in contact tracing application of covid-19. SN Comput. Sci. **2**(3), 1–11 (2021). https://doi.org/10.1007/s42979-021-00520-z
19. Vadrevu, P.K., Adusumalli, S.K., Mangalapalli, V.K., Swain, S.K.: A review on privacy preservation techniques in surveillance and health care data publication. Int. J. Eng. Res. Technol. **9**(5) (2021). Consulté le: 12 janvier 2022. [En ligne]
20. Shuja, J., Alanazi, E., Alasmary, W., Alashaikh, A.: COVID-19 open source data sets: a comprehensive survey. Appl. Intell. **51**(3), 1296–1325 (2020). https://doi.org/10.1007/s10489-020-01862-6
21. Motivations and Limits for COVID-19 Policy Compliance in Germany and Switzerland. https://www.ijhpm.com/article_4035.html (consulté le janv. 12, 2022)
22. Kim, J., Kwan, M.-P.: An examination of people's privacy concerns, perceptions of social benefits, and acceptance of COVID-19 mitigation measures that harness location information: a comparative study of the U.S. and South Korea. ISPRS Int. J. Geo-Inform. **10**(1), 25 (2021). https://doi.org/10.3390/ijgi10010025
23. Ferrag, M.A., Shu, L., Choo, K.-K.R.: Fighting COVID-19 and future pandemics with the internet of things: security and privacy perspectives. IEEE/CAA J. Automatica Sinica **8**(9), 1477–1499 (2021). https://doi.org/10.1109/JAS.2021.1004087

24. Health Care Cybersecurity Challenges and Solutions Under the Climate of COVID-19: Scoping Review. https://www.ncbi.nlm.nih.gov/pmc/articles/PMC8059789/ (consulté le janv. 12, 2022)
25. Hathaliya, J.J., Tanwar, S.: An exhaustive survey on security and privacy issues in Healthcare 4.0. Comput. Commun. **153**, 311–335 (2020). https://doi.org/10.1016/j.comcom.2020.02.018
26. Angst, C.M., Block, E.S., D'Arcy, J., Kelley, K.: When do IT security investments matter? accounting for the influence of institutional factors in the context of healthcare data breaches. MIS Quar. **41**(3), 893–916 (2017). https://doi.org/10.25300/MISQ/2017/41.3.10
27. Gabriel, M.H., Noblin, A., Rutherford, A., Walden, A., Cortelyou-Ward, K.: Data breach locations, types, and associated characteristics among US hospitals. Am. J. Manag. Care **24**(2), 78–84 (2018)
28. Johnson, K.: The Link Between Patient Experience and Hospital Reputation, no 1, p. 8 (2019)
29. Choi, S.J., Johnson, M.E., Lehmann, C.U.: Data breach remediation efforts and their implications for hospital quality. Health Serv. Res. **54**(5), 971–980 (2019). https://doi.org/10.1111/1475-6773.13203
30. Commission on Enhancing National Cybersecurity, NIST, 30 mai 2016. https://www.nist.gov/cybercommission (consulté le juill. 07, 2021)
31. Adler-Milstein, J., et al.: Electronic health record adoption in us hospitals: progress continues, but challenges persist. Health Aff (Millwood) **34**(12), 2174–2180 (2015)
32. Jan, M., Buchalcevova, A.: Introducing OSSF: a framework for online service cybersecurity risk management. Comput. Secur. **65**, 300–313 (2017)
33. Freeha, K., et al.: Data breach management: an integrated risk model. Inform. Manage. **58.1**, 103392 (2021)
34. Kylie, B., Bennett, A.J., Griffiths, K.M.: Security considerations for e-mental health interventions. J. Med. Internet Res. **12.5**, e1468 (2010)
35. Cook, I., Pfleeger, S.: Security decision support challenges in data collection and use. IEEE Secur. Priv. **8**(3), 28–35 (2010)
36. Chirag, M., et al.: A survey on security issues and solutions at different layers of Cloud computing. J. Supercomput. **63.2**, 561–592 (2013)
37. Ahmed, S.Z., Shah, M.H., Ahmed, J.: Information security management needs more holistic approach: a literature review. Int. J. Inform. Manage. **36.2**, 215–225 (2016)
38. Vance, A., Lowry, P.B., Eggett, D.: Using accountability to reduce access policy violations in information systems. J. Manage. Inform. Syst. **29**(4), 263–290 (2013). https://doi.org/10.2753/MIS0742-1222290410
39. Slee, P.: 6. In: Casuïstiek in de inwendige geneeskunde: medische vignetten, pp. 21–22. Bohn Stafleu van Loghum, Houten (2008). https://doi.org/10.1007/978-90-313-6596-8_6
40. Grobauer, B., Walloschek, T., Stocker, E.: Understanding cloud computing vulnerabilities. IEEE Secur. Priv. **9**(2), 50–57 (2010)
41. Yayla, A.A., Qing, H.: The impact of information security events on the stock value of firms: the effect of contingency factors. J. Inform. Technol. **26**(1), 60–77 (2011). https://doi.org/10.1057/jit.2010.4
42. Biener, C., Eling, M., Wirfs, J.H.: Insurability of cyber risk: an empirical analysis. Geneva Papers Risk Insuran. Issues Pract. **40**(1), 131–158 (2015). https://doi.org/10.1057/gpp.2014.19
43. Andrijcic, E., Horowitz, B.: A macro-economic framework for evaluation of cyber security risks related to protection of intellectual property. Risk Anal. **26**(4), 907–923 (2006)
44. Hole, K., Netland, L.-H.: Toward risk assessment of large-impact and rare events. IEEE Secur. Priv. **8**(3), 21–27 (2010)
45. Paintsil, E.: Evaluation of privacy and security risks analysis construct for identity management systems. IEEE Syst. J. **7**(2), 189–198 (2012)

46. Nima, Z., et al.: BYOD security engineering: a framework and its analysis. Comput. Secur. **55**, 81–99 (2015)
47. Fu, K., Blum, J.: Controlling for cybersecurity risks of medical device software. Biomed. Instrum. Technol. **48**, 38 (2014)
48. Ogie, R.: Bring your own device: an overview of risk assessment. IEEE Consum. Electron. Magaz. **5**(1), 114–119 (2015)
49. Hart, M., Manadhata, P., Johnson, R.: Text classification for data loss prevention. In: Fischer-Hübner, S., Hopper, N. (eds.) Privacy Enhancing Technologies. PETS 2011. LNCS, vol. 6794. Springer, Berlin, Heidelberg (2011). https://doi.org/10.1007/978-3-642-22263-4_2
50. Fred, C.: Forensic methods for detecting insider turning behaviors. In: 2012 IEEE Symposium on Security and Privacy Workshops. IEEE (2012)
51. Elisa, C., et al.: A white-box anomaly-based framework for database leakage detection. J. Inform. Secur. Appl. **32**, 27–46 (2017)
52. Sherali, Z., et al.: Detecting insider threats: solutions and trends. Inform. Secur. J. Global Perspect. **21.4**, 183–192 (2012)
53. Bell, Alison J.C.., Brooke Rogers, M., Pearce, Julia M.: The insider threat: behavioral indicators and factors influencing likelihood of intervention. Int. J. Critic. Infrastruct. Protect. **24**, 166–176 (2019). https://doi.org/10.1016/j.ijcip.2018.12.001
54. Andrew, P.M., et al.: A preliminary model of insider theft of intellectual property. Carnegie-Mellon University Pittsburgh Pa Software Engineering Institute (2011)
55. Christopher, W.J.: The information content of Sarbanes-Oxley in predicting security breaches. Comput. Secur. **90**, 101687 (2020)
56. Jung, G., Lee, H., Kim, A., Lee, U.: Too much information: assessing privacy risks of contact trace data disclosure on people With COVID-19 in South Korea. Front. Public Health **8** (2020). https://doi.org/10.3389/fpubh.2020.00305
57. OCR Home | HHS.gov. https://www.hhs.gov/ocr/index.html (consulté le janv. 12, 2022)
58. U.S. Department of Health and Human Services (HHS), HHS.gov, 2019. https://www.hhs.gov/ (consulté le juill. 07, 2021)
59. Multistate Settlement Resolves 2019 American Medical Collection Agency Data Breach Investigation, HIPAA J. 12 mars 2021
60. The Centers for Medicare & Medicaid Services, CMS Data Navigator Glossary of Terms (2019). [En ligne]. Disponible sur: https://www.cms.gov/Research-Statistics-Data-and-Systems/Research/ResearchGenInfo/Downloads/DataNav_Glossary_Alpha.pdf
61. U. C. Bureau, Census.gov, Census.gov. https://www.census.gov/en.html (consulté le janv. 12, 2022)
62. Legislative Analyst's Office. https://lao.ca.gov/ (consulté le janv. 12, 2022)
63. He, Y., et al.: Health care cybersecurity challenges and solutions under the climate of COVID-19: Scoping review. J. Med. Internet Res. **23.4**, e21747 (2021)
64. Leon, M.D.L.A.C., Hipolito, J.I.N., Garcia, J.L.: a security and privacy survey for WSN in e-Health applications. In: Electronics, Robotics, Automotive Mechanics Conference 2009 (CERMA 2009), pp. 125–130 (2009)
65. Javadi, S.S., Razzaque, M.A.: Security and privacy in wireless body area networks for health care applications. In: Khan, S., Pathan, A.-S.K. (eds.) Wireless Networks and Security: Issues, Challenges and Research Trends, pp. 165–187. Springer Berlin Heidelberg, Berlin, Heidelberg (2013). https://doi.org/10.1007/978-3-642-36169-2_6
66. Wang, J., Zhang, Z., Xu, K., Yin, Y., Guo, P.: A research on security and privacy issues for patient related data in medical organization system. Int.l J. Secur. Appl. **7**(4), 287–298 (2013)
67. Babaee, T.E., et al.: Designing a sustainable closed-loop supply chain network of face masks during the COVID-19 pandemic: pareto-based algorithms. J. Clean. Product. **333**, 130056 (2022)

68. Goli, A., Mohammadi, H.: Developing a sustainable operational management system using hybrid Shapley value and Multimoora method: case study petrochemical supply chain. Environ. Dev. Sustain. 1–30 (2021). https://doi.org/10.1007/s10668-021-01844-9
69. Goli, A., Malmir, B.: A covering tour approach for disaster relief locating and routing with fuzzy demand. Int. J. Intell. Transp. Syst. Res. **18**(1), 140–152 (2020)
70. Goli, A., Keshavarz, T.: Just-in-time scheduling in identical parallel machine sequence-dependent group scheduling problem. J. Indust. Manage. Optimiz. **18**(6), 3807 (2022). https://doi.org/10.3934/jimo.2021124
71. Alireza, G., et al.: Hybrid artificial intelligence and robust optimization for a multi-objective product portfolio problem Case study: the dairy products industry. Comput. Indust. Eng. **137**, 106090 (2019)
72. Alinaghian, M., Goli, A.: Location, allocation and routing of temporary health centers in rural areas in crisis, solved by improved harmony search algorithm. Int. J. Comput. Intell. Syst. **10**(1), 894–913 (2017)
73. Narjisse, N., et al.: Conflict spectrum: An empirical study of geopolitical cyber threats from a social network perspective. In: 2021 Eighth International Conference on Social Network Analysis, Management and Security (SNAMS). IEEE (2021)
74. Hicham, H., et al.: STRisk: a socio-technical approach to assess hacking breaches risk. IEEE Trans. Depend. Secure Comput. (2022)
75. François, J., et al.: ThreatPredict: from global social and technical big data to cyber threat forecast. In: Palestini, C. (ed.) Advanced Technologies for Security Applications. NSPSSBPB, pp. 45–54. Springer, Dordrecht (2020). https://doi.org/10.1007/978-94-024-2021-0_5
76. Abdellah, H., et al.: Detecting the impact of software vulnerability on attacks: a case study of network telescope scans. J. Network Comput. Appl. **195**, 103230 (2021)
77. Sara, L., et al.: TD-RA policy-enforcement framework for an SDN-based IoT architecture. J. Network Comput. Appl. **204**,103390 (2022)

Technology-Aided Decision-Making: Systems, Applications, and Modern Solutions

A Bibliometric Analysis of the Last Ten Years of Fuzzy Min-Max Neural Networks

Ömer Nedim Kenger[1](✉), Zülal Diri Kenger[1], and Eren Özceylan[2]

[1] Department of Industrial Engineering, Hasan Kalyoncu University, Gaziantep, Turkey
omer.nedim@hku.edu.tr

[2] Department of Industrial Engineering, Gaziantep University, Gaziantep, Turkey

Abstract. Neural networks have been widely used in many application areas such as power systems, weather forecasting, face recognition, behaviour analysis, fingerprint identification, healthcare, fault detection, flood monitoring system, and surveillance system, and navigation. However, classic neural network methods are insufficient for real-life applications. To tackle with this problem, using the learning capability of neural networks and deduction capability of fuzzy systems, neural networks and fuzzy sets are incorporated called as NeuroFuzzy. The Fuzzy min-max neural network (FMNN) is a special type of NeuroFuzzy. In this paper, a bibliometric analysis is conducted on FMNN literature. We consider the studies that are published in the last decade due to there is a jump in this field in the last 10 years. Social network analysis results show that Chee Peng Lim, is the most influential researcher in the network. The Neurocomputing is found to be the most influential journal, publishing 12% of all publications in this field. In addition, the International Conference on Computing, Communication, and Networking Technologies is the most influential conference on FMNN. The findings of this paper can draw a road map for researchers in the FMNNs.

Keywords: Fuzzy Min-Max Neural Network · Hyperbox · Classification · Clustering

1 Introduction

Neural networks work similarly to nervous systems and the structure of neurons of the human brain [1, 2]. Human brains consist of millions of inter-connected neurons. Each neuron takes delivery of input from thousands of others. These neurons help us in finding out patterns, performing deductions, and making judgements [3, 4]. For years, research workers have investigated to development of intelligent machines that have the abilities of the human brain. To tackle this, neural networks and fuzzy sets are combined due to the computational efficiency of neural networks, the capability of fuzzy sets to present complicated class borders, and their complementary role in modelling the abilities of the human brain [4, 5]. This combination is titled as NeuroFuzzy and Fuzzy min-max neural network (FMNN) is a particular type of NeuroFuzzy.

FMNN models for classification and clustering are introduced by Simpson [6] and [7]. Inspired by the studies of Simpson [6] and [7], several modifications and overviews

A. Mirzazadeh et al. (Eds.): SEMIT 2022, CCIS 1808, pp. 307–323, 2023.
https://doi.org/10.1007/978-3-031-40395-8_22

related to FMNN have been explored. These modifications are General FMNN [8], adaptive resolution FMNN [9], weighted FMNN [10], inclusion/exclusion fuzzy hyperbox classifier [11], K-nearest hyperbox expansion rule [12]. Related studies and modifications of FMNN methods are reviewed in the studies of [1, 2, 4, 13–15]. The most detailed review is published by Khuat [15]. In this paper, we evaluate the existing literature from a different perspective. Considering the studies published in the last decade, a bibliometric and social network analysis is conducted on FMNN. Bibliometrics can be used to analyze the features of the publications in a specific research area or in a certain journal [17]. Bibliometric and social network analysis reveals the most productive authors, institutions, journals and the relationships between them. The purpose of this study is to evaluate the publications on FMNN in the last decade and to determine the most productive authors, journals, conferences, countries, and most frequently used keywords in this research field.

This work contributes to the literature by a few factors. Firstly, bibliometric and social network analysis has not been applied in FMNN. Secondly, bibliometric and social network analysis is a popular method used in the discovery and analysis of large-scale scientific data. Finally, this study provides significant information such as emerging research areas, trends, and gaps in FMNN literature.

This study investigates answers to the following questions:

i. Who is working on FMNN and who are working together?
ii. Which keywords are mostly used in publications?
iii. In which journals and conferences are papers published the most?
iv. In which country are studied on FMNN the most?
v. Which authors and papers are mostly cited?

The rest of the paper is organized as follows. Section 2 presents the data collection methodology. Results of the bibliometric analysis are discussed in Sect. 3. Gaps and future directions are discussed in Sect. 4. Finally, Sect. 5 presents the concluding remarks.

2 Data Source and Preprocessing

2.1 Data Collection

In order to conduct bibliometric and social network analysis, we collect the data from the WOS database. Since, WOS provides information that allows conducting bibliometric analysis easily. The title of ALL FIELDS ("fuzzy min-max") is searched in WOS databases between the years of 2012–2021. We reach the 126 studies in total. 15 of them are eliminated due to their spelling language and not related to FMNN. Figure 1 shows the number of publications including number of articles, and proceedings in the last ten years.

We use VOSviewer software in order to apply bibliometric and social network analysis due to the feature of practical for showing large bibliometric maps and interpreting them easily of it [16].

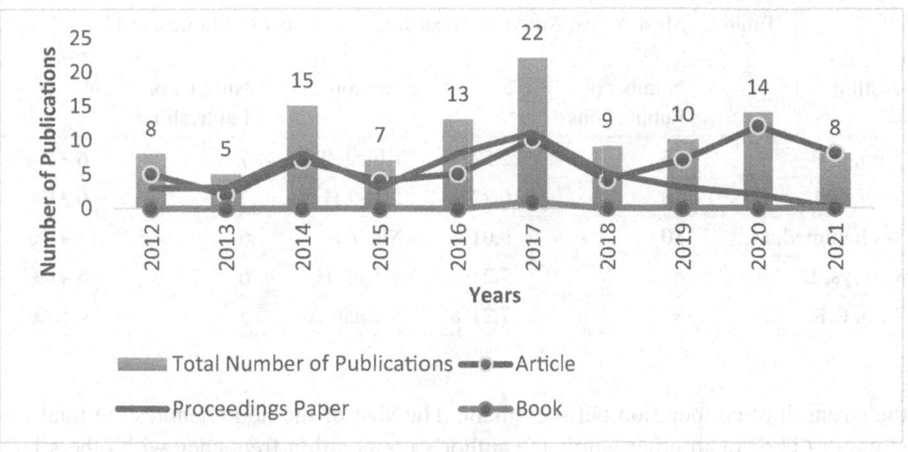

Fig. 1. Number of publications between the years of 2012–2021

3 Bibliometric Analysis Results

Bibliometrics is a science field predicated on quantitative analysis with the intersection and combination of fields such as mathematics, information science, and statistics [17]. Insights are obtained like network visualization and citation analysis as well as increasing the objectivity of the study through bibliometric tools [18].

In this section, we analyze the authors, keywords, publication sources and citations in the field of FMNN. Results of the analyses are given in the subsections of 3.1, 3.2, 3.3, 3.4, and 3.5 respectively.

3.1 The Analysis of Authors

Table 1 shows the top ten most influential authors who have at least 5 publications within the 183 different authors and the percentage of them in the total publication. Accordingly, Lim, C.P. has the maximum number of publications on FMNN between 2012 and 2021. Lim, C.P.'s publications make up almost a quarter of the total number of publications. Seera, M. and Mohammed, M.F. follows Lim, C.P. with 18 and 10 publications as seen in the Table 1.

Table 2 shows the top ten most influential authors according to the number of citations and the percentage of them in the total citations. As expected from Table 1's results Lim, C.P. is the author that has the maximum number of citations with the 628 citations. The authors who have more than 100 citations are: (i) Seera, M., (ii) Singh, H., (iii) Ishak, D., (iv) Loo, C.K. and (v) Mohammed, M.F.

In order to analyze the cooperation relationship, the cooperation network of authors is constructed by using VOSviewer. Figure 2 shows the visual presentation of the authors' cooperation relationship. There are 183 authors who have the publications about FMNN between 2012 and 2021. However, not all of them are connected to each other. The largest set of connected items consists of 36 authors. Links between nodes mean that there is a cooperation between them, and the link width between two nodes represents

Table 1. Most Active Authors (According to Number of Publication)

Author	Number of Publications	%	Author	Number of Publications	%
Lim, C.P	25	22,52%	Khuat, T.T	7	6,31%
Seera, M	18	16,22%	Liu, J.H	7	6,31%
Mohammed, M.F	10	9,01%	Ma Y.J	6	5,41%
Gabrys, B	8	7,21%	Singh, H	6	5,41%
Loo, C.K	8	7,21%	Kumar, A	5	4,50%

the strength of cooperation between them. The size of the node denotes the total link strength (TLS) or in other words the author's cooperation frequency with others [17]. 766 TLS exist in the network in total. The top 10 authors who have the highest TLS and link information are given in Table 3. Hereof, the author who has the highest cooperation frequency is Lim, C.P. with the 64 TLS.

Table 2. Most Active Authors (According to Number of Citations)

Author	Number of Citation	%	Author	Number of Citation	%
Lim, C.P	628	19,52%	Mohammed, M.F	119	3,70%
Seera, M	545	16,94%	Navahandi, S	83	2,58%
Singh, H	196	6,09%	Luo, Z.Z	45	1,40%
Ishak, D	156	4,85%	Miran, S.M	45	1,40%
Loo, C.K	140	4,35%	Tang, M.Y	45	1,40%

3.2 Keywords Analysis

The 244 keywords are connected to each other from 264 collected keywords. Figure 3 visualizes the network of these keywords. As expected, "fuzzy min-max neural network" is at the top of the list. The keywords that are used more than 35 times are as follows: (i) classification, (ii) pattern classification, (iii) hyperbox, (iv) neural network, and (v) clustering. Each node represents a keyword and each node's size is directly proportionate to its frequency of use. The biggest node is "fuzzy min-max neural network" with the degree of 73.

3.3 Analysis of Publication Sources

The distribution of journals and conferences are depicted in Figs. 4 and 5. While 64 of 111 papers are published in journals, 46 of them appeared in conference proceedings. There are 33 journals in total and the first six journals have published 33 articles, representing

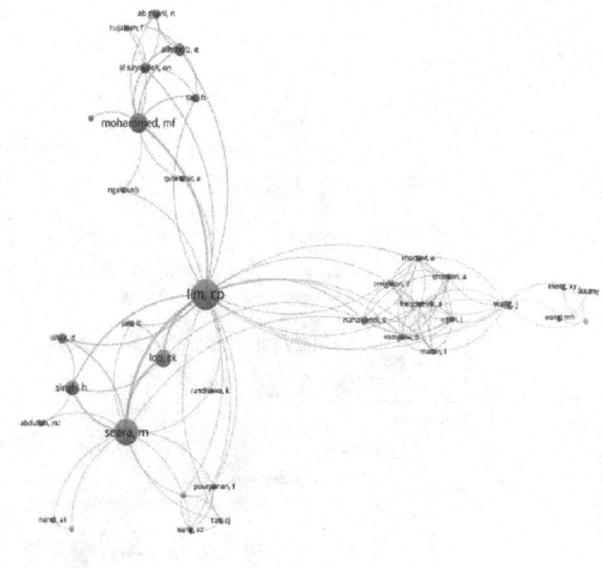

Fig. 2. The network of co-authorship

Table 3. The top 10 authors according to co-authorship total link strength

Rank	Author	Number of Publication	Link	Total Link Strength	Total Link Strength (%)
1	Lim, C.P	25	25	64	8,36%
2	Seera, M	18	14	43	5,61%
3	Mohammed, M.F	10	9	21	2,74%
4	Loo, C.K	8	5	20	2,61%
5	Liu, J.H	7	13	19	2,48%
6	Ma Y.J	6	14	17	2,22%
7	Singh, H	6	5	17	2,22%
8	Wang, J	2	13	13	1,70%
9	Alhroob, E	4	6	12	1,57%
10	Gabrys, B	8	5	12	1,57%

approximately 52% of all the published articles. The number of articles that have been published in Neurocomputing, the journal that publishes the most articles, constitutes 12% of the total number of articles.

36 conferences have contributed to the publications related with FMNN. According to Fig. 5, International Conference on Computing, Communication and Networking Technologies is the conference that has published the highest number of papers with four

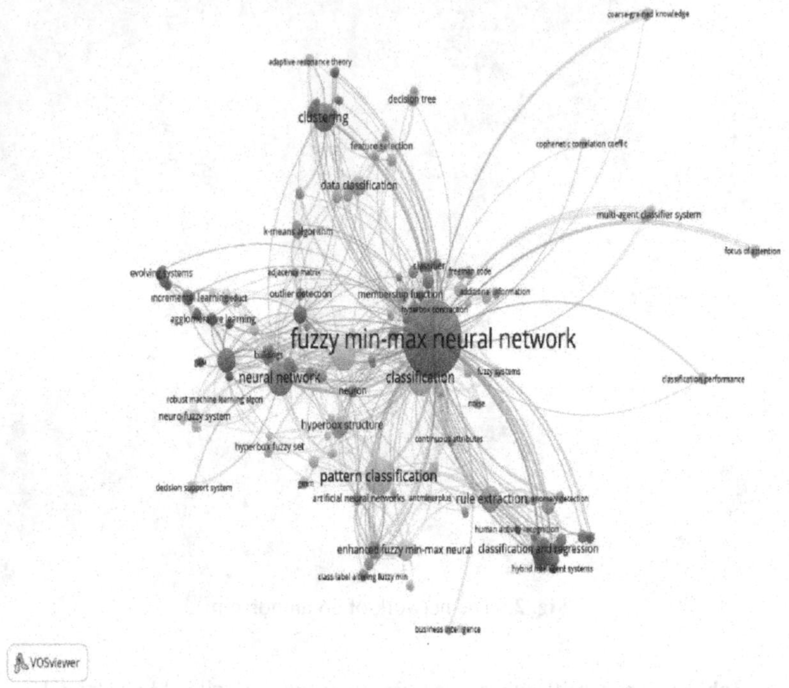

Fig. 3. The co-occurrence network of keywords

proceedings. The conferences that have published more than one proceeding International Conference on Neural Information Processing, International Joint Conference on Neural Networks, Conference of the North-American-Fuzzy-Information-Processing-Society, International Conference on Intelligent Computing and Control Systems and International Conference on Internet Technology and Secured Transactions. These conferences published 16 proceedings in total, representing approximately 35% of all the conference papers.

3.4 Country Analysis

At present, 15 countries have published at least one paper in the area. As shown in Fig. 6, the top ten productive countries are India, Australia, Malaysia, the People's Republic of China, Iran, Brazil, USA, England, Iraq, and Morocco. The most productive country is India contributes the 40 publications on FMNN. Australia, Malaysia, People's Republic of China follows the India by contributing 31, 29, and 18 publications, respectively.

3.5 Citation Analysis

The citation network of authors is shown in Fig. 7. In this area, 183 authors have published papers and 134 authors are cited 3218 times between 2012 and 2021. Top five cited authors, Lim, C.P., Seera, M., Singh, H., Ishak, D., Loo, C.K., with the citation number

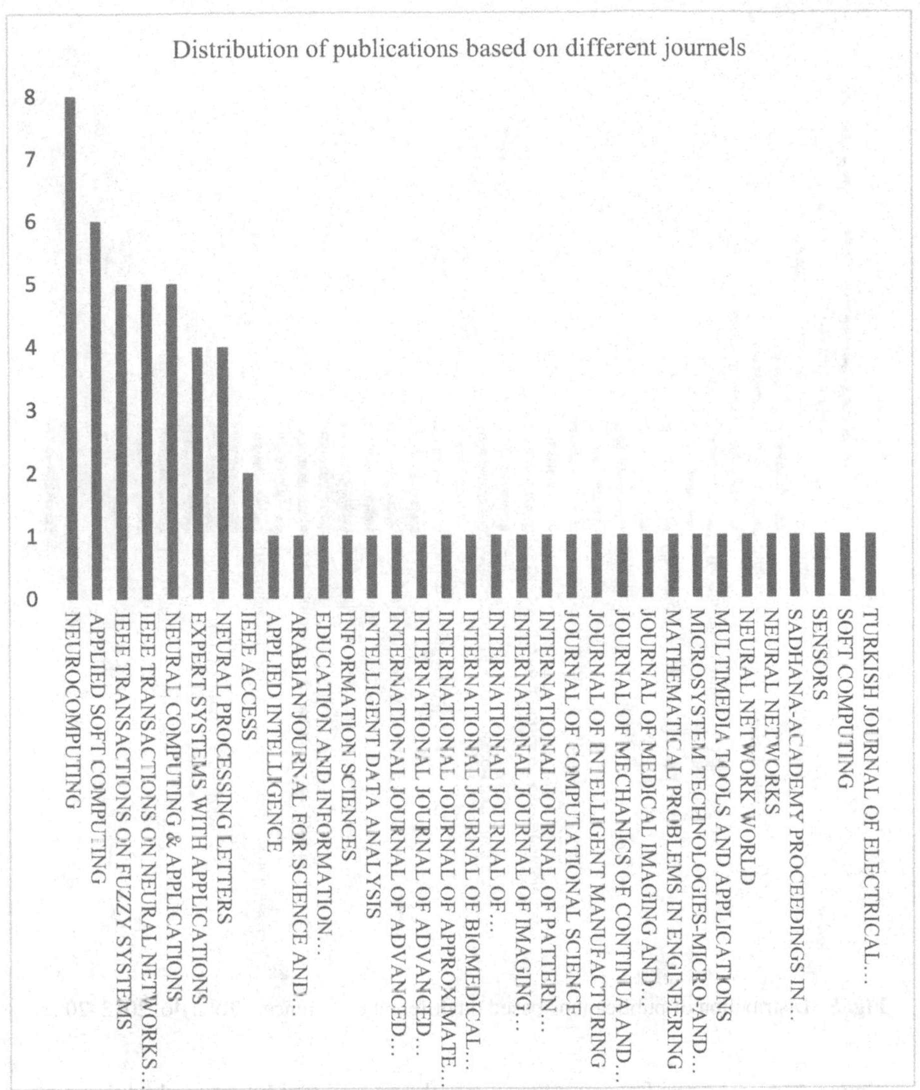

Fig. 4. Distribution of publications based on different journals (Total 64, 2012–2021)

of 628, 545, 196, 156, and 140, respectively. These authors have got 1665 citations, representing approximately 52% of total citations. The size of the nodes represents the strength of the author, cited from others.

The top 10 most influential papers with the highest citations, are given in Table 4. According to Table 4, the publication *"A hybrid intelligent system for medical data classification"* has the highest citations with 135. This paper is published by Seera, M. and Lim, C.P. in *Expert Systems with Applications.* Although the journal in which the most cited article is published is *Expert Systems with Applications, IEEE Transactions*

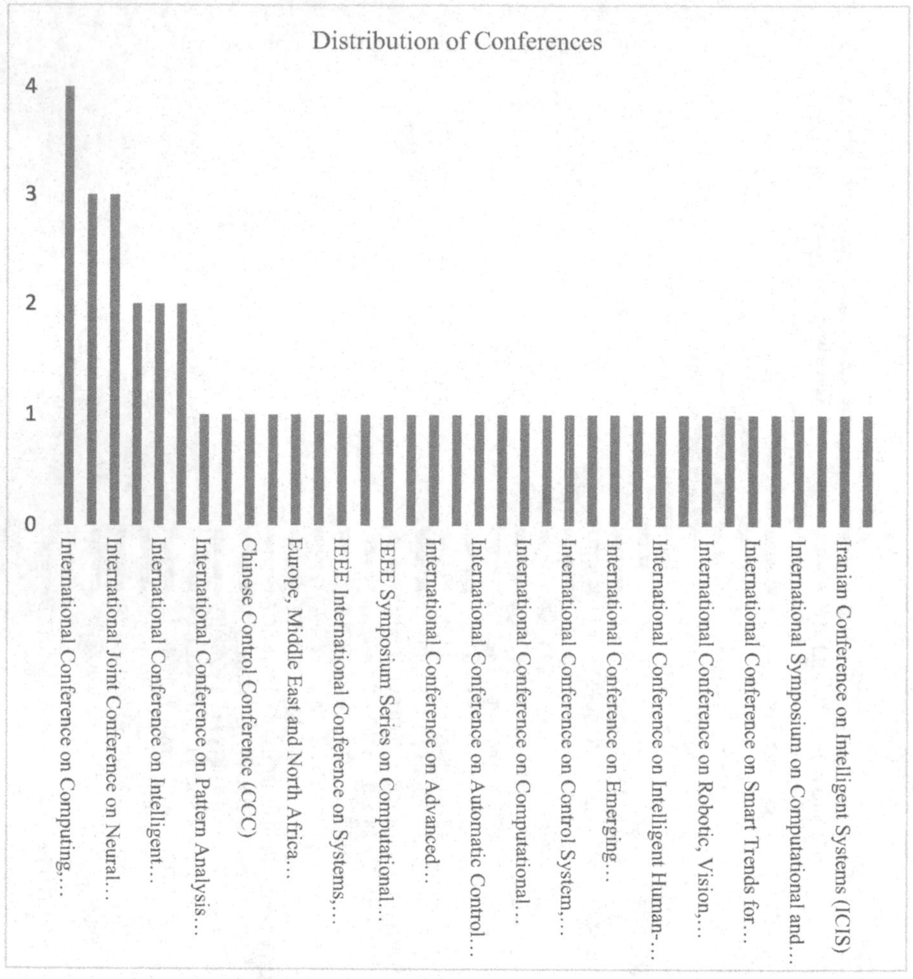

Fig. 5. Distribution of publications based on different conferences (Total 46, 2012–2021)

on Neural Networks and Learning Systems is the journal that has published the most of top 10 most influential publications.

4 Discussion and Future Directions

Neural networks are widely used in pattern recognition, extrapolation, classification, or prediction and have some advantages as adaptive learning, self-organization, real-time performance [18, 19]. In addition, FMNN has many important features such as nonlinear separability, ability of online learning, soft and hard decisions, etc. However, there are still open problems on the subject of misclassification, data presentation order, membership function, real-world big data, data editing, etc. Gaps and future research directions are discussed in this section.

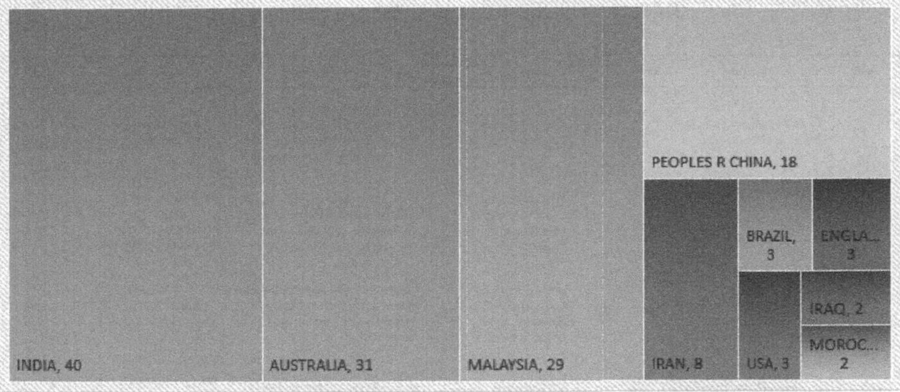

Fig. 6. The top 10 productive countries

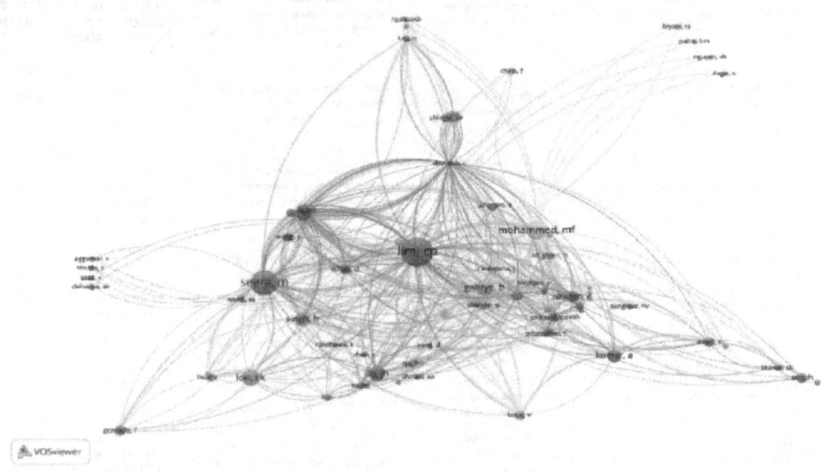

Fig. 7. The citation network of authors

Today, many sources produce data and therefore these data turn into big data. Feature selection algorithms can be used with FMNN to deal with big data. Besides data can come from more than one source in real life. However, in the literature, FMNN algorithms can learn only from a single source. Therefore, researchers should seek to build multi-source FMNN algorithms to tackle real-world problems.

The membership function improvement is another challenge. The decision whether the corresponding hyperbox is to be expanded, is mainly subject to the membership value. The membership function proposed by Simpson (1992) has a shortcoming such that it may lead to misclassification. Hence, new membership functions are proposed by Gabrys and Bargiela (2000) and Xue et al. (2020) in order to tackle this problem. However, a novel membership function has not yet been proposed considering features of data and noise.

Table 4. The top 10 most influential publications

Rank	Article Title	Types	Publication Year	Authors	Number of Citations	Author Keywords	Journal Title	Doi
1	A hybrid intelligent system for medical data classification	Article	2014	Seera, Manjeevan; Lim, Chee Peng	135	Fuzzy Min-Max neural network; Classification and regression tree; Random forest; Hybrid intelligent systems; Medical decision support	EXPERT SYSTEMS WITH APPLICATIONS	10.1016/j.eswa.2013.09.022
2	Fault Detection and Diagnosis of Induction Motors Using Motor Current Signature Analysis and a Hybrid FMM-CART Model	Article	2012	Seera, Manjeevan; Lim, Chee Peng; Ishak, Dahaman; Singh, Harapajan	108	Classification and regression tree; fault detection and diagnosis; fuzzy min-max neural network; induction motor; motor current signature analysis	IEEE TRANSACTIONS ON NEURAL NETWORKS AND LEARNING SYSTEMS	10.1109/TNNLS.2011.2178443
3	Condition monitoring of induction motors: A review and an application of an ensemble of hybrid intelligent models	Article	2014	Seera, Manjeevan; Lim, Chee Peng; Nahavandi, Saeid; Loo, Chu Kiong	75	Condition monitoring; Induction motor; Motor Current Signature Analysis; Fuzzy Min-Max neural network; Random Forest	EXPERT SYSTEMS WITH APPLICATIONS	10.1016/j.eswa.2014.02.028
4	An Enhanced Fuzzy Min-Max Neural Network for Pattern Classification	Article	2015	Mohammed, Mohammed Falah; Lim, Chee Peng	47	Fuzzy min-max (FMM) model; hyperbox structure; neural network learning; pattern classification	IEEE TRANSACTIONS ON NEURAL NETWORKS AND LEARNING SYSTEMS	10.1109/TNNLS.2014.2315214
5	Online Motor Fault Detection and Diagnosis Using a Hybrid FMM-CART Model	Article	2014	Seera, Manjeevan; Lim, Chee Peng	45	Classification and regression tree (CART); electrical motors; fuzzy min-max (FMM) neural network; online fault detection and diagnosis (FDD); rule extraction	IEEE TRANSACTIONS ON NEURAL NETWORKS AND LEARNING SYSTEMS	10.1109/TNNLS.2013.2280280
6	Evaluation of Feature Extraction and Recognition for Activity Monitoring and Fall Detection Based on Wearable sEMG Sensors	Article	2017	Xi, Xugang; Tang, Minyan; Miran, Seyed M.; Luo, Zhizeng	45	surface electromyography (sEMG); feature extraction; classifier; activity monitoring; fall detection	SENSORS	10.3390/s17061229
7	Multi-Level Fuzzy Min-Max Neural Network Classifier	Article	2014	Davtalab, Reza; Dezfoulian, Mir Hossein; Mansoorizadeh, Muharram	37	Classification; fuzzy min-max; hyperbox; machine learning; neural networks; neurofuzzy; neuron; supervised learning	IEEE TRANSACTIONS ON NEURAL NETWORKS AND LEARNING SYSTEMS	10.1109/TNNLS.2013.2275937
8	An intelligent temporal pattern classification system using fuzzy temporal rules and particle swarm optimization	Article	2014	Ganapathy, S.; Sethukkarasi, R.; Yogesh, P.; Vijayakumar, P.; Kannan, A.	33	Temporal fuzzy min-max (TFMM) neural network; particle swarm optimization algorithm (PSOA); pattern classification; rule extraction	SADHANA-ACADEMY PROCEEDINGS IN ENGINEERING SCIENCES	10.1007/s12046-014-0236-7
9	Offline and online fault detection and diagnosis of induction motors using a hybrid soft computing model	Article	2013	Seera, Manjeevan; Lim, Chee Peng; Ishak, Dahaman; Singh, Harapajan	32	Fault detection and diagnosis; Fuzzy Min-Max neural network; Classification and Regression Tree; Induction motor; Motor Current Signature Analysis	APPLIED SOFT COMPUTING	10.1016/j.asoc.2013.08.002
10	Classification of ball bearing faults using a hybrid intelligent model	Article	2017	Seera, Manjeevan; Wong, M. L. Dennis; Nandi, Asoke K.	30	Condition monitoring; Ball bearing; Electrical motor; Fuzzy min-max neural network; Random forest	APPLIED SOFT COMPUTING	10.1016/j.asoc.2017.04.034

Additively, streaming data, noisy data, missing or incomplete data, input data representation order, misclassification, and expansion coefficient value are other main issues that need to improve.

5 Conclusions

In this study, a bibliometric and social network analysis is conducted on FMNN literature. This paper differs from existing surveys in terms of evaluation of FMNN literature methodologically. The studies related to FMNN in the last decade are considered for this study and several analyses are done for these studies. We aim to reach such pieces of information as the most productive authors, publication trends, etc. We conduct the analysis on 111 papers published in the last decade. The analysis results show that the most active author is Lim C.P., the mostly used keyword is fuzzy min-max neural network, the publication source that publishes the highest number of studies in this field is Neurocomputing, and the author that has the maximum number of citations is Lim C.P. According to bibliometric analysis results the most influential conference is International Conference on Computing, Communication and Networking Technologies (ICCCNT). Finally, the most productive country is India.

For future research, gaps are discussed in the previous section. In addition, the scope of this study can be expanded by including all studies in the FMNN field. In addition, a survey can be conducted focusing on an area where FMNN is specifically applied.

References

1. Jain, B., Kolhe, V.: Survey on fuzzy min-max neural network classification. Int. J. Adv. Res. Comput. Commun. Eng. **4**, 30–34 (2015)
2. Jambhulkar, R.K.: A review on pattern classification using multilevel and other fuzzy min max neural network classifier. Int. J. Sci. Res. **3**, 898–900 (2014)
3. Hopfield, J.J.: Artificial neural networks. IEEE Circuits Devices Magaz. **4**, 3–10 (1988)
4. Alhroob, E., Mohammed, M.F., Lim, C.P., Tao, H.: A critical review on selected fuzzy min-max neural networks and their significance and challenges in pattern classification. IEEE Access **7**, 56129–56146 (2019)
5. Davtalab, R., Dezfoulian, M.H., Mansoorizadeh, M.: Multi-level fuzzy min-max neural network classifier. IEEE Trans. Neural Networks Learn. Syst. **25**, 470–482 (2014)
6. Simpson, P.K.: Fuzzy min-max neural networks—part 1: classification. IEEE Trans. Neural Networks **3**, 776–786 (1992)
7. Simpson, P.K.: Fuzzy min-max neural networks—part 2: clustering. IEEE Trans. Fuzzy Syst. **1**, 32–45 (1993)
8. Gabrys, B., Bargiela, A.: General fuzzy min-max neural network for clustering and classification. IEEE Trans. Neural Networks **11**, 769–783 (2000)
9. Rizzi, A., Panella, M., Frattale Mascioli, F.M.: Adaptive resolution min-max classifiers. IEEE Trans. Neural Networks **13**, 402–414 (2002)
10. Kim, H.J., Ryu, T.W., Nguyen, T.T., Lim, J.S., Gupta, S.: A weighted fuzzy min-max neural network for pattern classification and feature extraction. In: Laganá, A., Gavrilova, M.L., Kumar, V., Mun, Y., Tan, C.J.K., Gervasi, O. (eds.) ICCSA 2004. LNCS, vol. 3046, pp. 791–798. Springer, Heidelberg (2004). https://doi.org/10.1007/978-3-540-24768-5_85
11. Bargiela, A., Pedrycz, W., Tanaka, M.: An inclusion/exclusion fuzzy hyperbox classifier. Int. J. Knowl. Based Intell. Eng. Syst. **8**, 91–98 (2004)
12. Mohammed, M.F., Lim, C.P.: Improving the fuzzy min-max neural network with a k-nearest hyperbox expansion rule for pattern classification. Appl. Soft Comput. **52**, 135–145 (2017)
13. Kulkarni, S., Honwadkar, K.: Review on classification and clustering using fuzzy neural networks. Int. J. Comput. Appl. **136**, 18–23 (2016)
14. Al Sayaydeh, O.N., Mohammed, M.F., Lim, C.P.: Survey of fuzzy min–max neural network for pattern classification variants and applications. IEEE Trans. Fuzzy Syst. **27**, 635–645 (2019)
15. Khuat, T.T., Ruta, D., Gabrys, B.: Hyperbox-based machine learning algorithms: a comprehensive survey. Soft. Comput. **25**(2), 1325–1363 (2020). https://doi.org/10.1007/s00500-020-05226-7
16. Van Eck, N.J., Waltman, L.: Software survey: VOSviewer, a computer program for bibliometric mapping. Scientometrics **84**, 523–538 (2010)

17. Li, Y., Xu, Z., Wang, X., Wang, X.: A bibliometric analysis on deep learning during 2007–2019. Int. J. Mach. Learn. Cybern. **11**(12), 2807–2826 (2020). https://doi.org/10.1007/s13042-020-01152-0
18. Deniz, N., Ozcelik, F.: An extended review on disassembly line balancing with bibliometric and social network and future study realization analysis. J. Clean. Prod. **225**, 697–715 (2019)
19. Mostafaeipour, A., Goli, A., Qolipour, M.: Prediction of air travel demand using a hybrid artificial neural network (ANN) with Bat and Firefly algorithms:a case study. J. Supercomput. **74**, 5461–5484 (2018)
20. Goli, A., Tirkolaee, E.B., Weber, G.W.: An Integration of Neural Network and Shuffled Frog-Leaping Algorithm for CNC Machining Monitoring. Found. Comput. Dec. Sci. **46**, 27–42 (2021)
21. Goswami, B., Bhandari, G., Goswami, S.: Fuzzy min-max neural network for satellite infrared image clustering. In: 3rd International Conference on Emerging Applications of Information Technology, pp. 239–242 (2012)
22. Rey-del-Castillo, P., Cardeñosa, J.: Fuzzy min–max neural networks for categorical data: application to missing data imputation. Neural Comput. Appl. **21**, 1349–1362 (2012)
23. Susan, S., Khowal, S.K., Kumar, A., Kumar, A., Yadav, A.S.: Fuzzy min-max neural networks for business intelligence. In: International Symposium on Computational and Business Intelligence, pp. 115–118 (2013)
24. Shinde, S.V., Kulkarni, U.V.: Mining classification rules from fuzzy min-max neural network. In: 5th International Conference on Computing, Communications and Networking Technologies (ICCCNT), pp. 1–7 (2014)
25. Forghani, Y., Sadoghi Yazdi, H.: Fuzzy min–max neural network for learning a classifier with symmetric margin. Neural Process Lett **42**, 317–353 (2015)
26. Mohammed, M.F., Lim, C.P.: An enhanced fuzzy min–max neural network for pattern classification. IEEE Trans. Neural Networks Learn. Syst. **26**, 417–429 (2015)
27. Pawar, D.: Fuzzy min-max neural network with compensatory neuron architecture for invariant object recognition. In: International Conference on Computer, Communication and Control (IC4), pp. 1–5 (2015)
28. Upasani, N., Om, H.: Evolving fuzzy min-max neural network for outlier detection. Procedia Computer Science **45**, 753–761 (2015)
29. Landge, C.B., Shinde, S.V.: Pattern classification using modified enhanced fuzzy min-max neural network. In: International Conference on Computing Communication Control and automation (ICCUBEA), pp. 1–5 (2016)
30. Ma, Y., Liu, J., Zeng-guo, W.: Modified fuzzy min-max neural network for clustering and its application on the pipeline internal inspection data. In: 35th Chinese Control Conference (CCC), pp. 3509–3513 (2016)
31. Seera, M., Lim, C.P., Loo, C.K., Jain, L.C.: Data clustering using a modified fuzzy min-max neural network. In: Balas, V.E., Jain, L.C., Kovačević, B. (eds.) Soft Computing Applications. AISC, vol. 356, pp. 413–422. Springer, Cham (2016). https://doi.org/10.1007/978-3-319-18296-4_34
32. Shinde, S., Kulkarni, U.: Extracting classification rules from modified fuzzy min–max neural network for data with mixed attributes. Appl. Soft Comput. **40**, 364–378 (2016)
33. Arvindrao, V.A., Kolapwar, P.G.: Adaptive expansion algorithm for fuzzy min-max neural network in pattern classification. In: International Conference on Intelligent Computing and Control Systems (ICICCS), pp. 741–744 (2017)
34. Donglikar, N.V., Waghmare, J.M.: An enhanced general fuzzy min-max neural network for classification. In: International Conference on Intelligent Computing and Control Systems (ICICCS), pp. 757–764 (2017)

35. Liu, J., Ma, Y., Zhang, H., Su, H., Xiao, G.: A modified fuzzy min–max neural network for data clustering and its application on pipeline internal inspection data. Neurocomputing **238**, 56–66 (2017)
36. Sadeghian, P., Olmsted, A.: Assessment of fuzzy min-max neural networks for classification tasks. In: 12th International Conference for Internet Technology and Secured Transactions (ICITST), pp. 193–196 (2017)
37. Sadeghian, P., Wilson, C., Goeddel, S., Olmsted, A.: Classification of music by composer using fuzzy min-max neural networks. In: 12th International Conference for Internet Technology and Secured Transactions (ICITST), pp. 189–192 (2017)
38. Dinh Minh, V., Nguyen, V.H., Le, B.D.: Semi-supervised clustering in fuzzy min-max neural network. In: Akagi, M., Nguyen, T.-T., Duc-Thai, V., Phung, T.-N., Huynh, V.-N. (eds.) ICTA 2016. AISC, vol. 538, pp. 541–550. Springer, Cham (2016). https://doi.org/10.1007/978-3-319-49073-1_58
39. Alhroob, E., Ghani, N.A.: Fuzzy min-max classifier based on new membership function for pattern classification: a conceptual solution. In: 8th IEEE International Conference on Control System, Computing and Engineering (ICCSCE), pp. 131–135 (2018)
40. Seera, M., Randhawa, K., Lim, C.P.: Improving the fuzzy min–max neural network performance with an ensemble of clustering trees. Neurocomputing **275**, 1744–1751 (2018)
41. Waghmare, J.M., Kulkarni, U.V.: Unbounded recurrent fuzzy min-max neural network for pattern classification. In: Joint Conference on Neural Networks (IJCNN), Budapest, Hungary, pp. 1–8 (2019)
42. Alhroob, E., Mohammed, M.F., Sayaydeh, O.N.A., Hujainah, F., Ghani, N.A.: Analysis on misclassification in existing contraction of fuzzy min–max models. In: Saeed, F., Mohammed, F., Gazem, N. (eds.) IRICT 2019. AISC, vol. 1073, pp. 270–278. Springer, Cham (2019). https://doi.org/10.1007/978-3-030-33582-3_26
43. Khuat, T.T., Chen, F., Gabrys, B.: An improved online learning algorithm for general fuzzy min-max neural network. In: International Joint Conference on Neural Networks (IJCNN), pp. 1–9. Glasgow, United Kingdom (2020)
44. Khuat, T.T., Gabrys, B.: A comparative study of general fuzzy min-max neural networks for pattern classification problems. Neurocomputing **386**, 110–125 (2020)
45. Kumar, S.A., Kumar, A., Bajaj, V., Singh, G.K.: An improved fuzzy min–max neural network for data classification. IEEE Trans. Fuzzy Syst. **28**, 1910–1924 (2020)
46. Liu, J., Ma, Y., Qu, F., Zang, D.: Semi-supervised fuzzy min–max neural network for data classification. Neural Process Lett. **51**, 1445–1464 (2020)
47. Ma, Y., Liu, J., Zhao, Y.: Evolved fuzzy min-max neural network for unknown labeled data and its application on defect recognition in depth. Neural Process Lett. **53**, 85–105 (2021)
48. Porto, A., Gomide, F.: Granular evolving min-max fuzzy modeling. In: Proceedings of the 2019 Conference of the International Fuzzy Systems Association and the European Society for Fuzzy Logic and Technology (EUSFLAT 2019), pp. 14–21. Prague, Czech Republic (2019)
49. Mirzamomen, Z., Kangavari, M.: Fuzzy min-max neural network based decision trees. Intell. Data Anal. **20**, 767–782 (2016)
50. Arsene, C., Al-Dabass, D., Hartley, J.: Decision support system for water distribution systems based on neural networks and graphs. In: 14th International Conference on Computer Modelling and Simulation, pp. 315–323 (2012)
51. Arsene, C.T.C., Gabrys, B., Al-Dabass, D.: Decision support system for water distribution systems based on neural networks and graphs theory for leakage detection. Expert Syst. Appl. **39**, 13214–13224 (2012)
52. Futane, P.R., Dharaskar, R.V.: Video gestures identification and recognition using fourier descriptor and general fuzzy minmax neural network for subset of Indian sign language. In: 12th International Conference on Hybrid Intelligent Systems (HIS), pp. 525–530 (2012)

53. Liu, J., Yu, Z., Ma, D.: An adaptive fuzzy min-max neural network classifier based on principle component analysis and adaptive genetic algorithm. Math. Probl. Eng. 1–21 (2012)
54. Patil, M.E., Borole, M.V.: Signature recognition using krawtchouk moments. In: 3rd International Conference on Computing, Communication and Networking Technologies (ICCCNT'12), pp. 1–5 (2012)
55. Seera, M., Lim, C.P., Ishak, D., Singh, H.: Fault detection and diagnosis of induction motors using motor current signature analysis and a hybrid FMM–cart model. IEEE Trans. Neural Networks Learn. Syst. **23**, 97–108 (2012)
56. Yun, S.S., Choi, M.T., Kim, M., Song, J.B.: Intention reading from a fuzzy-based human engagement model and behavioural features. Int. J. Adv. Rob. Syst. **9**, 56 (2012)
57. Padam Priyal, S., Bora, P.K.: A robust static hand gesture recognition system using geometry based normalizations and krawtchouk moments. Pattern Recogn. **46**, 2202–2219 (2013)
58. Rajakumar, B.R., George, A.: On hybridizing fuzzy min max neural network and firefly algorithm for automated heart disease diagnosis. In: 4th International Conference on Computing, Communications and Networking Technologies (ICCCNT), pp. 1–5 (2013)
59. Seera, M., Lim, C.P., Ishak, D., Singh, H.: Application of the fuzzy min–max neural network to fault detection and diagnosis of induction motors. Neural Comput. Appl. **23**(1), 191–200 (2012). https://doi.org/10.1007/s00521-012-1310-x
60. Seera, M., Lim, C.P., Ishak, D., Singh, H.: Offline and online fault detection and diagnosis of induction motors using a hybrid soft computing model. Appl. Soft Comput. **13**, 4493–4507 (2013)
61. Singh, H., Seera, M., Abdullah, M.Z.: Detection and diagnosis of broken rotor bars and eccentricity faults in induction motors using the fuzzy min-max neural network. In: International Joint Conference on Neural Networks (IJCNN), pp. 1–5 (2013)
62. Ganapathy, S., Sethukkarasi, R., Yogesh, P., Vijayakumar, P., Kannan, A.: An intelligent temporal pattern classification system using fuzzy temporal rules and particle swarm optimization. Sadhana **39**(2), 283–302 (2014). https://doi.org/10.1007/s12046-014-0236-7
63. Jalesiyan, H., Yaghubi, M., Akbarzadeh, T.M.R.: Rule selection by guided elitism genetic algorithm in fuzzy min-max classifier. In: Iranian Conference on Intelligent Systems (ICIS), pp. 1–6 (2014)
64. Jawarkar, N.P., Holambe, R.S., Basu, T.K.: On the use of classifiers for text-independent speaker identification. In: 1st International Conference on Automation, Control, Energy and Systems (ACES), pp. 1–6 (2014)
65. Mohammed, M.F., Lim, C.P., Ngah, U.K.B.T.: Applying a multi-agent classifier system with a novel trust measurement method to classifying medical data. In: The 8th International Conference on Robotic, Vision, Signal Processing & Power Applications, vol. 291, pp. 355–362 (2014)
66. Mohammed, M.F., Lim, C.P., Quteishat, A.: A novel trust measurement method based on certified belief in strength for a multi-agent classifier system. Neural Comput. Appl. **24**(2), 421–429 (2012). https://doi.org/10.1007/s00521-012-1245-2
67. Seera, M., Lim, C.P.: A hybrid intelligent system for medical data classification. Expert Syst. Appl. **41**, 2239–2249 (2014)
68. Seera, M., Lim, C.P.: Online motor fault detection and diagnosis using a hybrid fmm-cart model. IEEE Trans. Neural Networks Learn. Syst. **25**, 806–812 (2014)
69. Seera, M., Lim, C.P., Nahavandi, S., Loo, C.K.: Condition monitoring of induction motors: a review and an application of an ensemble of hybrid intelligent models. Expert Syst. Appl. **41**, 4891–4903 (2014)
70. Seera, M., Lim, C.P., Loo, C.K.: Transfer learning using the online FMM model. Neural Inform. Process. 151–158 (2014)

71. Seera, M., Loo, C.K., Lim, C.P.: A hybrid FMM-CART model for human activity recognition. In: 2014 IEEE International Conference on Systems, Man, and Cybernetics (SMC), pp. 182–187 (2014)
72. Zhai, Z., Shi, D., Cheng, Y., Guo, H.: Computer-aided detection of lung nodules with fuzzy min-max neural network for false positive reduction. In: 2014 Sixth International Conference on Intelligent Human-Machine Systems and Cybernetics, vol. 1, pp. 66–69 (2014)
73. Lv, Y., Wei, X., Guo, S.: Research on fault isolation of rail vehicle suspension system. In: The 27th Chinese Control and Decision Conference (2015 CCDC), pp. 929–934 (2015)
74. Seera, M., Lim, C.P., Loo, C.K., Singh, H.: A modified fuzzy min–max neural network for data clustering and its application to power quality monitoring. Appl. Soft Comput. **28**, 19–29 (2015)
75. Wang, J., et al.: Patient admission prediction using a pruned fuzzy min–max neural network with rule extraction. Neural Comput. Appl. **26**(2), 277–289 (2014). https://doi.org/10.1007/s00521-014-1631-z
76. Anand, M., Kanth, R.R., Dhabu, M.: Efficient fuzzy min-max neural network for pattern classification. Smart Trends Inform. Technol. Comput. Commun. Commun. Comput. Inform. Sci. **628**, 840–846 (2016)
77. Azad, C., Jha, V.: A novel fuzzy min-max neural network and genetic algorithm-based intrusion detection system. In: Satapathy, S.C., et al. (eds.) Proceedings of the Second International Conference on Computer and Communication Technologies, Advances in Intelligent Systems and Computing, vol. 380, pp. 429–439 (2016)
78. Benchaou, S., Nasri, M., Melhaoui, O.E.: New approach of features extraction for numeral recognition. Int. J. Pattern Recogn. Artific. Intell. **30** (2016)
79. Deshmukh, S., Shinde, S.: Diagnosis of lung cancer using pruned fuzzy min-max neural network. In: 2016 International Conference on Automatic Control and Dynamic Optimization Techniques (ICACDOT), pp. 398–402 (2016)
80. Hu, J., Luo, Y.: A fuzzy min-max neural network with classification performance irrelevant to the input sequences of samples. In: 2016 3rd International Conference on Systems and Informatics (ICSAI), pp. 393–398 (2016)
81. Kaur, P.: Outlier detection using k-means and fuzzy min max neural network in network data. In: 2016 8th International Conference on Computational Intelligence and Communication Networks (CICN), pp. 693–696 (2016)
82. Seera, M., Lim, C.P., Loo, C.K.: Motor fault detection and diagnosis using a hybrid FMM-CART model with online learning. J. Intell. Manuf. **27**(6), 1273–1285 (2014). https://doi.org/10.1007/s10845-014-0950-3
83. Seera, M., Lim, C.P., Loo, C.K., Singh, H.: Power quality analysis using a hybrid model of the fuzzy min–max neural network and clustering tree. IEEE Trans. Neural Networks Learn. Syst. **27**, 2760–2767 (2016)
84. Aggarwal, S., Azad, V.: A hybrid system based on FMM and MLP to diagnose heart disease. Intell. Multidimension. Data Cluster. Anal. 293–325 (2017)
85. Azad, C., Jha, V.K.: Fuzzy min–max neural network and particle swarm optimization based intrusion detection system. Microsyst. Technol. **23**(4), 907–918 (2016). https://doi.org/10.1007/s00542-016-2873-8
86. Benchaou, S., Nasri, M., El Melhaoui, O.: Features extraction for offline handwritten character recognition. Europe MENA Cooper. Adv. Inform. Commun. Technol. Adv. Intell. Syst. Comput. **520**, 209–217 (2017)
87. Chandrashekhar, A., Vijay Kumar, J.: Fuzzy min-max neural network-based intrusion detection system. In: Proceedings of the International Conference on Nano-electronics, Circuits and Communication Systems, vol. 403, pp. 191–202 (2017)

88. Ilager, S., Prasad, P.S.V.S.S.: Scalable mapreduce-based fuzzy min-max neural network for pattern classification. In: Proceedings of the 18th International Conference on Distributed Computing and Networking ICDCN 2017, pp. 1–7 (2017)
89. Jahanjoo, A., Tahan, M.N., Rashti, M.J.: Accurate fall detection using 3-axis accelerometer sensor and MLF algorithm. In: 2017 3rd International Conference on Pattern Recognition and Image Analysis (IPRIA), pp. 90–95 (2017)
90. Kalaiselvi, C., Asokan, R.: A classification of chronic leukaemia using new extension of k-means clustering and EFMM based on digital microscopic blood images. Int. J. Biomed. Eng. Technol. **23**, 232–241 (2017)
91. Ma, Y., Liu, J., Li, T., Danyu, L.: Staged-adaptive data clustering in fuzzy min-max neural network. In: 2017 IEEE Symposium Series on Computational Intelligence (SSCI), pp. 1–5 (2017)
92. Mirzamomen, Z., Kangavari, M.R.: Evolving fuzzy min–max neural network based decision trees for data stream classification. Neural Process. Lett. **45**, 341–363 (2017)
93. Mohammed, M.F., Lim, C.P.: A new hyperbox selection rule and a pruning strategy for the enhanced fuzzy min–max neural network. Neural Netw. **86**, 69–79 (2017)
94. Seera, M., Wong, M.L.D., Nandi, A.K.: Classification of ball bearing faults using a hybrid intelligent model. Appl. Soft Comput. **57**, 427–435 (2017)
95. Shinde, S., Kulkarni, U.: Extended fuzzy hyperline-segment neural network with classification rule extraction. Neurocomputing **260**, 79–91 (2017)
96. Sonule, P.M., Shetty, B.S.: An enhanced fuzzy min–max neural network with ant colony optimization based-rule-extractor for decision making. Neurocomputing **239**, 204–213 (2017)
97. Xi, X., Tang, M., Miran, S.M., Luo, Z.: Evaluation of feature extraction and recognition for activity monitoring and fall detection based on wearable semg sensors. Sensors **17**, 1–20 (2017)
98. Zobeidi, S., Naderan, M., Alavi, S.E.: Effective text classification using multi-level fuzzy neural network. In: 2017 5th Iranian Joint Congress on Fuzzy and Intelligent Systems (CFIS), pp. 91–96 (2017)
99. Ahmed, A.A., Mohammed, M.F.: SAIRF: a similarity approach for attack intention recognition using fuzzy min-max neural network. J. Comput. Sci. **25**, 467–473 (2018)
100. Azad, C., Mehta, A.K., Jha, V.K.: Improved data classification using fuzzy euclidean hyperbox classifier. In: International Conference on Smart Computing and Electronic Enterprise (ICSCEE), pp. 1–6 (2018)
101. Hou, P., Yue, J., Deng, H., Liu, S., Sun, Q.: Contribution-factor based fuzzy min-max neural network: order-dependent clustering for fuzzy system identification. Int. J. Comput. Intell. Syst. **11**, 737–756 (2018)
102. Porto, A., Gomide, F.: Evolving granular fuzzy min-max regression. Fuzzy Logic Intell. Syst. Des. Theory Appl. **648**, 162–171 (2018)
103. Pourpanah, F., Zhang, B., Ma, R., Hao, Q.: Non-intrusive human motion recognition using distributed sparse sensors and the genetic algorithm based neural network. IEEE Sensors 1–4 (2018)
104. Upasani, N., Om, H.: Optimized fuzzy min-max neural network: an efficient approach for supervised outlier detection. Neural Network World **28**, 285–303 (2018)
105. Pourpanah, F., Lim, C.P., Wang, X., Tan, C.J., Seera, M., Shi, Y.: A hybrid model of fuzzy min–max and brain storm optimization for feature selection and data classification. Neurocomputing **333**, 440–451 (2019)
106. Khuat, T.T., Gabrys, B.: Accelerated training algorithms of general fuzzy min-max neural network using GPU for very high dimensional data neural information processing. Lect. Notes Comput. Sci. **11953**, 583–595 (2019)

107. Tran, T.N., Vu, D.M., Tran, M.T., Le, B.D.: The combination of fuzzy min–max neural network and semi-supervised learning in solving liver disease diagnosis support problem. Arab. J. Sci. Eng. **44**, 2933–2944 (2019)
108. Upasani, N., Om, H.: A modified neuro-fuzzy classifier and its parallel implementation on modern GPUs for real time intrusion detection. Appl. Soft Comput. **82**, 1–16 (2019)
109. Chavan, T.R., Nandedkar, A.V.: A convolutional fuzzy min-max neural network. Neurocomputing **405**, 62–71 (2020)
110. Dehariya, A.K., Shukla, P.: Medical data classification using fuzzy min max neural network preceded by feature selection through moth flame optimization. Int. J. Adv. Comput. Sci. Appl. **11**, 655–662 (2020)
111. Jerlin Rubini, L., Perumal, E.: Efficient classification of chronic kidney disease by using multi-kernel support vector machine and fruit fly optimization algorithm. Int. J. Imaging Syst. Technol. **30**, 660–673 (2020)
112. Kumar, A., Prasad, P.S.V.S.S.: Scalable fuzzy rough set reduct computation using fuzzy min–max neural network preprocessing. IEEE Trans. Fuzzy Syst. **28**, 953–964 (2020)
113. Meng, X., Liu, M., Wang, M., Wang, J., Wu, Q.: Fuzzy min-max neural network with fuzzy lattice inclusion measure for agricultural circular economy region division in heilongjiang province in China. IEEE Access **8**, 36120–36130 (2020)
114. Rubini, L.J., Perumal, E.: Hybrid kernel support vector machine classifier and grey wolf optimization algorithm based intelligent classification algorithm for chronic kidney disease. J. Med. Imag. Health Inform. **10**, 2297–2307 (2020)
115. Sayaydeh, O.N.A., Mohammed, M.F., Alhroob, E., Tao, H., Lim, C.P.: A refined fuzzy min–max neural network with new learning procedures for pattern classification. IEEE Trans. Fuzzy Syst. **28**, 2480–2494 (2020)
116. Boroumandzadeh, M., Parvinnia, E.: Automated classification of BI-RADS in textual mammography reports. Turk. J. Electr. Eng. Comput. Sci. **29**, 632–647 (2021)
117. Dutt, S., Ahuja, N.J., Kumar, M.: An intelligent tutoring system architecture based on fuzzy neural network (FNN) for special education of learning-disabled learners. Educ. Inf. Technol. **27**, 2613–2633 (2022)
118. Khuat, T.T., Chen, F., Gabrys, B.: An effective multiresolution hierarchical granular representation-based classifier using general fuzzy min-max neural network. IEEE Trans. Fuzzy Syst. **29**, 427–441 (2021)
119. Khuat, T.T., Gabrys, B.: An in-depth comparison of methods handling mixed-attribute data for general fuzzy min–max neural network. Neurocomputing **464**, 175–202 (2021)
120. Kumar, A., Sai Prasad, P.S.V.S.: Incremental fuzzy rough sets-based feature subset selection using fuzzy min-max neural network preprocessing. Int. J. Approx. Reason. **139**, 69–87 (2021)
121. Santhos Kumar, A., Kumar, A., Bajaj, V., Singh, G.K.: Class label altering fuzzy min-max network and its application to histopathology image database. Expert Syst. Appl. **176**, 1–9 (2021)
122. Meng, X., Li, R., Wang, K., Niu, B., Wang, X., Zhao, G. (eds.): WISA 2018. LNCS, vol. 11242. Springer, Cham (2018). https://doi.org/10.1007/978-3-030-02934-0

Selecting MCDM Criteria for Machining Center Ranking Decisions Using Design of Experiments and TOPSIS Approaches

Yusuf Tansel İç[1(✉)] and Mustafa Yurdakul[2]

[1] Baskent University, Ankara 06790, Turkey
yustanic@baskent.edu.tr
[2] Gazi University, Ankara 06570, Turkey

Abstract. Machining Centers (MC) is widely used in today's advanced machining industries such as aerospace and automotive. In the market, there is a huge number of MC models are sold. For a manufacturing firm, especially in the SMEs segment, the MC selection process is a difficult task for this reason. The main question arises from the MC selection problem "Which factor is crucial for the selection decision?" Multi-Criteria Decision Making models are widely used for MC selection problems. However, the correct determination of the criteria to be used in the selection process is very important for the ranking results. In this study, experiments are formed with experiments as rows and selection criteria as columns in a design of experiments structure. The TOPSIS approach provides machining centers' rating scores with different weight values for each experiment. With the application of the ANOVA approach, the statistically significant criteria on the ranking results are then determined to use in the machining center selection problems. We proposed a new procedure that is crucial to selecting the most suitable MC for identified machining tasks.

Keywords: Machining Center Selection · DoE-TOPSIS · Machining process

1 Introduction

Computer numerical control (CNC) Machining Centers (MC) are indispensable machine tools in manufacturing industries today. Machining centers can be sold in many brands, models, designs, and types in the market, and they come in different technical features (sizes, components, etc.). Instead of outcomes (specifications), it may be preferable to determine the sources (technical features) as selection criteria to make correct MC selection decisions. The differences in the technical features lead to different performance levels at the selection criteria. In this study, technical features are used as selection criteria to better representation of the MC selection decision process.

In the literature, there are various studies on machine tool selection. Multi-criteria decision-making (MCDM) methods are widely used in these studies [1–10]. For example, Lata et al. [1] proposed a fuzzy analytic hierarchy process (AHP) - a technique for order preferences to similarity by ideal solution (TOPSIS) model for CNC machine tool

A. Mirzazadeh et al. (Eds.): SEMIT 2022, CCIS 1808, pp. 324–343, 2023.
https://doi.org/10.1007/978-3-031-40395-8_23

selection. Li et al. [2] proposed a machine tool selection model based on a hybrid MCDM model. In the application of the model, a comprehensive weight technique integrates subjective weights, obtained using fuzzy decision-making trial and evaluation laboratory (FDEMATEL) with objective weights, obtained using entropy weighting (EW). Then, the VIKOR method is used to rank the alternative machine tools. Ding et al. [3] proposed an integrated MCDM approach that combines AHP and connection degree-based TOPSIS (CD-TOPSIS) method to select the optimal guide-way for machine tool remanufacturing. Chakraborty and Boral [4] developed a case-based reasoning (CBR) system for machine tool selection. Their study elucidated the development and application of a CBR system for machine tool selection while fulfilling varying user-defined requirements. It is based on some special process characteristics; past similar cases are retrieved to solve the machine tool selection problem. Sun [5] rated turning center alternatives with the data envelopment method. In another study, Sun [5] evaluated companies with production area capacity, product quality, delivery time, customer references, and sales support criteria. Cimren et al.'s [6] study evaluated the machining centers in four criteria sets named flexibility, efficiency, safety, and adaptability using the AHP method. On equipment selection, Georgakellos [7] developed a two-level hierarchical decision structure for the selection of the most appropriate hydraulic press in the metalworking industry.

In the literature, the selection criteria are generally taken from machine tool manufacturers' catalogs directly. It can be observed from the literature that there is not a unique set of criteria for the CNC machine tool selection problem, and the number of criteria changes from 5 to 20. As discussed in MCDM literature, the criteria must not only be independent, but the number of them must be approximately 7 ± 2 [8, 9]. Having a larger number of criteria in an MCDM selection model decreases the ability to discriminate among similar machines. Models with a lower number of criteria are expected to be more sensitive to the changes in criteria weights and be capable of producing rankings where alternative machine tools' ranking scores are more clearly separated from each other [9]. Various studies in the literature proposed a criteria determination procedure. Yurdakul and İç [9, 10] and İç and Yurdakul [11–13] aimed to determine the criteria to be used in the selection of machining centers. The selected criteria are applicable only in real-life specific situations [9–13]. Also, some studies investigated improving the criteria weighting procedure [14–16].

In the literature, there are some methodologies proposed to improve the robustness of the manufacturing systems [17, 18]. However, the authors' extensive literature survey shows that there is a need for more robust selected criteria set that can be used for a larger group of machine tool selection decisions to improve the manufacturing system performance, especially considering machining performance. This study aims to fill this area by developing a criteria selection methodology to obtain robust criteria set and achieve a clear separation among the alternative machine tools with the usage of TOPSIS and Design of Experiments (DoE) approaches.

2 Methodology

Each input factor for the DoE model corresponds to an MC selection criterion, and their low and high values are obtained through the MC machining centers' catalogs. The experimental design is also the decision matrix for the TOPSIS model. The TOPSIS approach model uses the factors' values in obtaining ranking scores. For the replications in the DoE, each randomly generated weight set provides a different ranking score (response values) for replication in the application of DoE. We used randomly generated five weight sets for criteria according to the 1–10 scale. The randomly generated weights are crucial to obtaining the randomness of the experiment. Therefore we can easily obtain five independent and randomly generated TOPSIS ranking scores by using the randomly assigned weights for each criterion. Once all ranking scores are obtained with the application of the TOPSIS approach, ANOVA analysis has conducted the determination of the statistically significant factors (selection criteria) on the ranking results (Fig. 1).

Since TOPSIS is a well-known and widely used MCDM methodology, its steps and applications are available in the literature. The interested readers can access the details of the TOPSIS method in ref. [9, 19, 20]. On the other hand, factorial design is a statistical method used in the design of experiments to determine important factors that contribute to the ranking scores selection decisions significantly. The basic and special application type of this method is the two-level ('low'; 'high') 2^k factorial design methodology

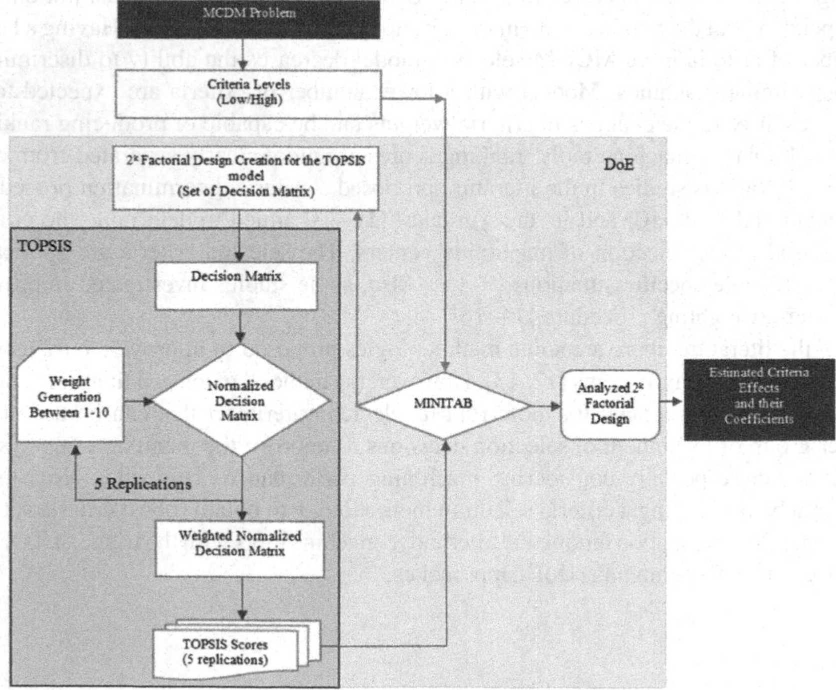

Fig. 1. The DoE -TOPSIS model.

[21]. We can examine significant factors, their relationships, and their impact levels in the application of the 2^k factorial design methodology. Today, various statistical package programs are used in performing the design of experiment steps, providing significant benefits in terms of time savings. Especially in DoE applications, when the number of factors increases, the user does not have to deal with the complexity of manual calculations and the mistakes that can be made. In the determination of the selection criteria in this study, the MINITAB R14 program is used for the design of experiments and calculations.

3 Application

In this section, the analysis of "which factors are more effective than each other" and "the level of interaction between them" in calculating the rating scores of 22 machining centers using the TOPSIS method and 15 factors (criteria) is performed with the MINITAB R14 statistical package program. Determination of the significance is made by calculating the "p" values of the factors. The "low" and "high" values taken for the criteria in the evaluations are presented in the Table 1.

Table 1. Low and high values of the criteria used in 2^{15} factorial design [6]

Symbol	Criteria/Specification	Unit	Low Level	High Level
I	Table Size	mm^2	140,000	3,750,000
II	Work piece weight	kg	300	5,000
III	X Axis Stroke	mm	497	3,200
IV	Y Axis Stroke	mm	405	1,400
V	Z Axis Stroke	mm	449	880
VI	Spindle speed	d/d	5,000	15,000
VII	Power	kW	11	37
VIII	Rapid traverse x,y,z	m/min	15	50
IX	Tool number	number	16	41
X	Tool change time	s	3	10
XI	Max. Tool diameter	mm	80	220
XII	Tool length	mm	130	567
XIII	Positioning	mm	0.001	0.005
XIV	Machine tool weight	kg	3,900	27,000
XV	Cost	€	33,123	485,143

In the analysis, the above values were entered into the program and as a result, the rating scores were found by entering the combinations created in line with the "Runs:128, Resolution: IV, Replicate:1, Fraction 1/256" options in MINITAB R14 to the TOPSIS program created in the Microsoft Excel program, analyzed and "p" values were calculated. While calculating the p values, randomly generated five different weight scores of 15 criteria were used. These criteria are widely used in MC selection studies and the most common ones employed in MC selection studies. The criterion weight scores and p values are given in Table 2. The details of TOPSIS decision matrix values, TOPSIS scores, and calculated p values used as factorial design outputs in MINITAB R14 are given in Appendix A. Table 3 shows the determination of the significant criteria.

Table 2. Randomly generated weighted scores and p values for 5 different TOPSIS result

Criteria	TOPSIS 1	[a]*p*	TOPSIS 2	p	TOPSIS 3	p	TOPSIS 4	p	TOPSIS 5	p
I	7	**0**	4	0	5	0	8	0	4	0
II	3	**0**	1	0.220	6	0	6	0	1	0.568
III	1	**0.016**	5	0	7	0	1	0.017	9	0
IV	6	**0**	0	0.721	9	0	2	0	9	0
V	5	**0**	1	0.363	5	0	1	0.147	6	0
VI	0	0.159	0	0.898	7	0	7	0	1	0.110
VII	6	**0**	10	0	6	0	10	0	10	0
VIII	8	**0**	5	0	8	0	7	0	2	0.202
IX	4	0.108	10	0	7	0	9	0	3	0.262
X	10	**0**	2	0.711	5	0	4	0	5	0
XI	9	**0**	10	0	6	0	6	0	0	0.842
XII	5	**0**	8	0	2	0.243	9	0	7	0
XIII	1	0.838	1	0.992	4	0	9	0	5	0
XIV	2	0.816	0	0.716	2	0.184	9	0	3	0.003
XV	9	**0**	1	0.224	9	0	1	0.782	3	0.046

[a] **See Appendix A3 for estimated effects and coefficients for TOPSIS 1 table. In the Appendix A3, bold items (factors) indicate that the effective factors for TOPSIS model. Their p values are smaller than 0.005**

4 Selection of Criteria to Be Used in MCDM Methods

Table 4 shows the criteria relations obtained as a result of 2^{15} experimental designs made with 7 alternative TOPSIS weights. Table 4 shows the alternative designs in which there is a strong relationship between the criteria. If the calculated p value is less than or equal to 0.05, the relationship is considered as statistically significant.

As a result of the analysis of Tables 3 and 4, the most significant factors (criteria) are determined as table size, y-axis stroke, power, rapid traverse, tool change time, maximum tool diameter, and tool length. The selected criteria are shown in Table 5 as a two-level hierarchical structure.

Table 3. Frequency of the significant criteria (p = 0.00 values)

	P = 0.00					
	TOPSIS 1	TOPSIS 2	TOPSIS 3	TOPSIS 4	TOPSIS 5	**Frequency**
Table Size	+	+	+	+	+	**5**
Work piece weight	+		+	+		3
X Axis Stroke		+	+		+	3
Y Axis Stroke	+		+	+	+	**4**
Z Axis Stroke	+		+		+	3
Spindle speed			+	+		2
Power	+	+	+	+	+	**5**
Rapid traverse x,y,z	+	+	+	+		**4**
Tool number		+	+	+		3
Tool change time	+		+	+	+	**4**
Max. Tool diameter	+	+	+	+		**4**
Tool length	+	+		+	+	**4**
Positioning			+	+	+	3
Machine tool weight				+		1
Cost	+		+			2

Table 4. Illustration of the statistically significant alternative TOPSIS weights (1–7) for each criteria pair

P<=0.05 repeated	I	II	III	IV	V	VI	VII	VIII	IX	X	XI	XII	XIII	XIV	XV
I		1,7	2,5,6,7	1,5,6,7	1	4	1,2,4,5,6,7	1,2,4,6,7	4,7	1,4,7	1,4,7	4,7	4,7	4,7	1,3,6,7
II			3	1,3,4,7		1,2,6,7	1,4,7	1,3,7	4	4	4,5	4	4	4	1,3,7
III				3,5,6,7		3	2,5,6,7	2,3,7	7		4,7	5,6,7	5,7	6	3
IV					1,4		5,6,7	1,3,7							1,3,7
V							1,4		4				4,5	1,4	
VI								4,7	4,5,7			4,5,6,7	6,7		3
VII								1,2,4,6,7			2,4,6,7	1,2,4,5,6,7			1,4
VIII										1,4,7	7	4	4	4,7	
IX											1,2,6,7				
X											1,4		3,4,7		1,6,7
XI														4,6,7	
XII													4	4,5,7	
XIII															2,3
XIV															
XV															

Table 5. Selected criteria

Main criteria	Sub-criteria (Selected criteria)
1. Productivity	1.1. Power
	1.2. Tool change time
	1.3. Rapid traverse
2. Flexibility	
2.1.Tool flexibility	2.1.1.Tool diameter
	2.1.2. Tool length
2.2.Work-piece flexibility	2.2.1. Table size
	2.2.2. Y-Axis stroke

5 Conclusions

This study was conducted to obtain the statistically significant selection criteria that contribute to the ranking results the most. The randomly generated weight sets make a selection of a robust and manageable (7 ± 2) set of criteria that can be applied even if MC user requirements and needs' similarities decline.

In this study, although the TOPSIS-based DoE model is successfully used in the MC selection problem, it should be noted that the ANOVA analysis in the DoE application offers the level of significance for only the factors' main and two-way effects.

Furthermore, in the DoE application, once the p values are obtained, one may obtain more than one list of independent 7 ± 2 criteria. Also, the inclusion of the three or four-way effects in the DoE model may lead to the selection of a set of different criteria.

For the future scope perspective, other DoE methodologies can combine with the TOPSIS or other MCDM methods such as VIKOR, GRA, and MOORA to select appropriate criteria for MC or other selection problems in manufacturing and industrial or financial models.

Apeendix A. An Example Appendix

A.1. MINITAB R14 Input and Output Values and Calculated P Values

M/C	Std Or.	R O	C. Pt	Bl.	table	w p	x	y	z	spe	pow	rtra	tnu	tcha	tdia	tlen	po	mtw	cost	Top. 5
1	6	1	1	1	3750000	300	3200	405	449	5000	11	15	16	3	80	130	1	3900	33123	42.4
2	103	2	1	1	140000	5000	3200	405	449	15000	37	15	16	3	220	130	1	3900	33123	50.8
3	16	3	1	1	3750000	5000	3200	1400	449	5000	11	50	41	10	220	567	5	3900	33123	53.1
4	10	4	1	1	3750000	300	497	1400	449	5000	11	15	16	3	220	130	1	3900	485143	36.5
5	3	5	1	1	140000	5000	497	405	449	5000	11	15	16	10	220	567	1	3900	33123	6.1
6	112	6	1	1	3750000	5000	3200	1400	449	15000	37	50	16	3	80	567	1	3900	33123	75.2
7	87	7	1	1	140000	5000	3200	405	880	5000	37	50	16	3	80	567	5	3900	33123	54.3
8	40	8	1	1	3750000	5000	3200	405	449	15000	11	15	41	3	220	567	1	27000	33123	47.6
9	24	9	1	1	3750000	5000	3200	405	880	5000	11	50	41	3	80	130	5	27000	33123	44
10	41	10	1	1	140000	300	497	1400	449	15000	11	15	16	10	80	567	5	27000	485143	33.3
11	21	11	1	1	140000	300	3200	405	880	5000	11	50	16	10	80	130	1	27000	33123	40.4
12	55	12	1	1	140000	5000	3200	405	880	15000	11	50	41	10	220	567	1	3900	33123	43.2
13	94	13	1	1	3750000	300	3200	1400	880	5000	37	50	16	10	80	130	5	3900	485143	59.5
14	85	14	1	1	140000	300	3200	405	880	5000	37	15	16	10	220	567	5	3900	485143	51.4
15	108	15	1	1	3750000	5000	497	1400	449	15000	37	50	41	3	220	130	5	3900	33123	48.2
16	97	16	1	1	140000	300	497	405	449	15000	37	50	41	10	220	567	5	3900	485143	35.7
17	19	17	1	1	140000	5000	497	405	880	5000	11	15	41	3	80	567	5	27000	485143	16.7
18	50	18	1	1	3750000	300	497	405	880	15000	11	50	41	3	80	130	1	3900	33123	26
19	31	19	1	1	140000	5000	3200	1400	880	5000	11	15	41	3	220	567	5	27000	33123	53.9
20	98	20	1	1	3750000	300	497	405	449	15000	37	15	16	10	80	567	1	3900	33123	41
21	128	21	1	1	3750000	5000	3200	1400	880	15000	37	50	41	10	220	567	5	27000	485143	69.1
22	51	22	1	1	140000	5000	497	405	880	15000	11	50	16	10	80	130	5	3900	33123	16.5
23	54	23	1	1	3750000	300	3200	405	880	15000	11	50	16	3	220	567	5	3900	33123	45.9

(*continued*)

(*continued*)

24	4	24	1	1	3750000	5000	497	405	449	5000	11	50	41	10	80	567	5	3900	485143	22.3
25	43	25	1	1	140000	5000	497	1400	449	15000	11	50	16	3	220	567	5	27000	33123	35.3
26	61	26	1	1	140000	300	3200	1400	880	15000	11	15	16	3	80	130	5	3900	33123	48.4
27	22	27	1	1	3750000	300	3200	405	880	5000	11	15	41	10	220	130	5	27000	485143	41.9
28	14	28	1	1	3750000	300	3200	1400	449	5000	11	15	41	3	80	567	5	3900	485143	53.5
29	121	29	1	1	140000	300	497	1400	880	15000	37	50	41	3	80	130	5	27000	485143	46.5
30	17	30	1	1	140000	300	497	405	880	5000	11	50	41	10	220	567	5	27000	33123	16.9
31	116	31	1	1	3750000	5000	497	405	880	15000	37	50	41	10	80	567	5	27000	33123	42.9
32	64	32	1	1	3750000	5000	3200	1400	880	15000	11	15	41	10	80	130	1	3900	33123	52.6
33	82	33	1	1	3750000	300	497	405	880	5000	37	50	16	10	220	130	5	3900	33123	38.8
34	2	34	1	1	3750000	300	497	405	449	5000	11	15	41	3	220	567	5	3900	33123	22.2
35	58	35	1	1	3750000	300	497	1400	880	15000	11	50	16	3	80	567	5	3900	485143	40
36	8	36	1	1	3750000	5000	3200	405	449	5000	11	50	16	10	220	130	1	3900	485143	41.2
37	100	37	1	1	3750000	5000	497	405	449	15000	37	50	16	3	220	567	1	3900	485143	42.2
38	63	38	1	1	140000	5000	3200	1400	880	15000	11	50	16	10	220	130	5	3900	485143	47
39	76	39	1	1	3750000	5000	497	1400	449	5000	37	15	16	10	220	567	5	27000	485143	49.7
40	71	40	1	1	140000	5000	3200	405	449	5000	37	50	41	10	220	567	1	27000	485143	54.3
41	37	41	1	1	140000	300	3200	405	449	15000	11	15	16	10	220	567	5	27000	33123	39.9
42	26	42	1	1	3750000	300	497	1400	880	5000	11	15	41	10	80	130	5	27000	33123	37.5
43	80	43	1	1	3750000	5000	3200	1400	449	5000	37	15	41	10	80	130	1	27000	485143	62.9
44	53	44	1	1	140000	300	3200	405	880	15000	11	15	41	3	80	567	1	3900	485143	43.3
45	111	45	1	1	140000	5000	3200	1400	449	15000	37	15	41	3	220	567	5	3900	485143	63
46	23	46	1	1	140000	5000	3200	405	880	5000	11	15	16	3	220	130	1	27000	485143	40.8
47	62	47	1	1	3750000	300	3200	1400	880	15000	11	50	41	3	220	130	1	3900	485143	53.5
48	57	48	1	1	140000	300	497	1400	880	15000	11	15	41	3	220	567	1	3900	33123	37.8
49	96	49	1	1	3750000	5000	3200	1400	880	5000	37	15	16	3	220	130	5	3900	33123	62.5
50	5	50	1	1	140000	300	3200	405	449	5000	11	50	41	3	220	130	5	3900	485143	37.5
51	29	51	1	1	140000	300	3200	1400	880	5000	11	50	41	10	80	567	5	27000	485143	51.4
52	27	52	1	1	140000	5000	497	1400	880	5000	11	15	16	3	80	130	1	27000	33123	35.5
53	125	53	1	1	140000	300	3200	1400	880	15000	37	50	16	3	220	567	1	27000	485143	71.9
54	104	54	1	1	3750000	5000	3200	405	449	15000	37	50	41	3	80	130	5	3900	485143	51.9
55	39	55	1	1	140000	5000	3200	405	449	15000	11	50	16	3	80	567	5	27000	485143	41
56	84	56	1	1	3750000	5000	497	405	880	5000	37	15	16	3	80	130	5	3900	485143	39.1
57	65	57	1	1	140000	300	497	405	449	5000	37	15	16	3	220	130	5	27000	33123	34.6
58	117	58	1	1	140000	300	3200	405	880	15000	37	50	41	3	220	130	5	27000	33123	51.8
59	48	59	1	1	3750000	5000	3200	1400	449	15000	11	15	16	3	220	130	5	27000	485143	50.5
60	72	60	1	1	3750000	5000	3200	405	449	5000	37	15	16	10	80	567	5	27000	33123	55.5
61	86	61	1	1	3750000	300	3200	405	880	5000	37	50	41	10	80	567	1	3900	33123	59.3
62	18	62	1	1	3750000	300	497	405	880	5000	11	15	16	10	80	567	1	27000	485143	26
63	1	63	1	1	140000	300	497	405	449	5000	11	50	16	3	80	567	1	3900	485143	8.1
64	32	64	1	1	3750000	5000	3200	1400	880	5000	11	50	16	3	80	567	1	27000	485143	59.4
65	35	65	1	1	140000	5000	497	405	449	15000	11	50	41	3	220	130	1	27000	485143	10.8

(*continued*)

(*continued*)

66	88	66	1	1	3750000	5000	3200	405	880	5000	37	15	41	3	220	567	1	3900	485143	60.3
67	105	67	1	1	140000	300	497	1400	449	15000	37	50	16	10	220	130	1	3900	33123	44.9
68	66	68	1	1	3750000	300	497	405	449	5000	37	50	41	3	80	130	1	27000	485143	40
69	67	69	1	1	140000	5000	497	405	449	5000	37	50	16	10	80	130	5	27000	485143	33.9
70	34	70	1	1	3750000	300	497	405	449	15000	11	50	16	10	220	130	5	27000	485143	21.3
71	124	71	1	1	3750000	5000	497	1400	880	15000	37	50	16	10	80	130	1	27000	485143	49.9
72	38	72	1	1	3750000	300	3200	405	449	15000	11	50	41	10	80	567	1	27000	485143	45.4
73	126	73	1	1	3750000	300	3200	1400	880	15000	37	15	41	3	80	567	5	27000	33123	75.5
74	114	74	1	1	3750000	300	497	405	880	15000	37	15	41	3	220	567	5	27000	485143	43
75	33	75	1	1	140000	300	497	405	449	15000	11	15	41	10	80	130	1	27000	33123	6.5
76	122	76	1	1	3750000	300	497	1400	880	15000	37	15	16	3	220	130	1	27000	33123	51.8
77	60	77	1	1	3750000	5000	497	1400	880	15000	11	15	16	10	220	567	5	3900	33123	39.4
78	91	78	1	1	140000	5000	497	1400	880	5000	37	50	16	3	220	567	5	3900	485143	48.5
79	127	79	1	1	140000	5000	3200	1400	880	15000	37	15	16	10	80	567	1	27000	33123	69.4
80	36	80	1	1	3750000	5000	497	405	449	15000	11	15	16	3	80	130	5	27000	33123	21.8
81	69	81	1	1	140000	300	3200	405	449	5000	37	15	41	3	80	567	1	27000	33123	57
82	59	82	1	1	140000	5000	497	1400	880	15000	11	50	41	10	80	567	1	3900	485143	36.8
83	110	83	1	1	3750000	300	3200	1400	449	15000	37	15	16	10	220	567	1	3900	485143	67.4
84	93	84	1	1	140000	300	3200	1400	880	5000	37	15	41	10	220	130	1	3900	33123	60.2
85	28	85	1	1	3750000	5000	497	1400	880	5000	11	50	41	3	220	130	5	27000	485143	38.4
86	78	86	1	1	3750000	300	3200	1400	449	5000	37	50	41	3	220	130	1	27000	33123	67.5
87	30	87	1	1	3750000	300	3200	1400	880	5000	11	15	16	10	220	567	1	27000	33123	57.7
88	102	88	1	1	3750000	300	3200	405	449	15000	37	15	41	10	220	130	5	3900	33123	50.8
89	79	89	1	1	140000	5000	3200	1400	449	5000	37	50	16	10	220	130	5	27000	33123	57.3
90	118	90	1	1	3750000	300	3200	405	880	15000	37	15	16	3	80	130	1	27000	485143	55.8
91	20	91	1	1	3750000	5000	497	405	880	5000	11	50	16	3	220	567	1	27000	33123	28.2
92	12	92	1	1	3750000	5000	497	1400	449	5000	11	50	16	10	80	130	1	3900	33123	36.6
93	52	93	1	1	3750000	5000	497	405	880	15000	11	15	41	10	220	130	1	3900	485143	24.7
94	11	94	1	1	140000	5000	497	1400	449	5000	11	15	41	10	220	130	5	3900	485143	30.9
95	46	95	1	1	3750000	300	3200	1400	449	15000	11	50	16	10	80	130	5	27000	33123	50
96	89	96	1	1	140000	300	497	1400	880	5000	37	15	16	10	80	567	5	3900	33123	47.4
97	83	97	1	1	140000	5000	497	405	880	5000	37	50	41	3	220	130	1	3900	33123	37.8
98	13	98	1	1	140000	300	3200	1400	449	5000	11	50	16	3	220	567	1	3900	33123	53
99	90	99	1	1	3750000	300	497	1400	880	5000	37	50	41	10	220	567	1	3900	485143	52.8
100	115	100	1	1	140000	5000	497	405	880	15000	37	15	16	10	220	567	1	27000	485143	39.2
101	99	101	1	1	140000	5000	497	405	449	15000	37	15	41	3	80	567	5	3900	33123	37
102	74	102	1	1	3750000	300	497	1400	449	5000	37	50	16	3	80	567	5	27000	33123	52.3
103	123	103	1	1	140000	5000	497	1400	880	15000	37	15	41	10	220	130	5	27000	33123	45.8
104	25	104	1	1	140000	300	497	1400	880	5000	11	50	16	10	220	130	1	27000	485143	34.3
105	109	105	1	1	140000	300	3200	1400	449	15000	37	50	41	10	80	567	5	3900	33123	61.8
106	70	106	1	1	3750000	300	3200	405	449	5000	37	50	16	3	220	567	5	27000	485143	56.6
107	44	107	1	1	3750000	5000	497	1400	449	15000	11	15	41	3	80	567	1	27000	485143	40.8

(*continued*)

(*continued*)

108	120	108	1	1	3750000	5000	3200	405	880	15000	37	50	16	10	220	130	1	27000	33123	55.3
109	119	109	1	1	140000	5000	3200	405	880	15000	37	15	41	10	80	130	5	27000	485143	49.6
110	68	110	1	1	3750000	5000	497	405	449	5000	37	15	41	10	220	130	1	27000	33123	39.3
111	107	111	1	1	140000	5000	497	1400	449	15000	37	15	16	3	80	130	1	3900	485143	45.4
112	42	112	1	1	3750000	300	497	1400	449	15000	11	50	41	10	220	567	1	27000	33123	40.3
113	7	113	1	1	140000	5000	3200	405	449	5000	11	15	41	10	80	130	5	3900	33123	37
114	73	114	1	1	140000	300	497	1400	449	5000	37	15	41	3	220	567	1	27000	485143	50.1
115	106	115	1	1	3750000	300	497	1400	449	15000	37	15	41	10	80	130	5	3900	485143	46
116	95	116	1	1	140000	5000	3200	1400	880	5000	37	50	41	3	80	130	1	3900	485143	61.8
117	77	117	1	1	140000	300	3200	1400	449	5000	37	15	16	3	80	130	5	27000	485143	57.8
118	101	118	1	1	140000	300	3200	405	449	15000	37	50	16	10	80	130	1	3900	485143	48.8
119	81	119	1	1	140000	300	497	405	880	5000	37	15	41	10	80	130	1	3900	485143	35.9
120	75	120	1	1	140000	5000	497	1400	449	5000	37	50	41	10	80	567	1	27000	33123	49.8
121	113	121	1	1	140000	300	497	405	880	15000	37	50	16	3	80	567	1	27000	33123	41.2
122	9	122	1	1	140000	300	497	1400	449	5000	11	50	41	3	80	130	5	3900	33123	32.2
123	49	123	1	1	140000	300	497	405	880	15000	11	15	16	3	220	130	5	3900	485143	15.2
124	47	124	1	1	140000	5000	3200	1400	449	15000	11	50	41	3	80	130	1	27000	33123	50.7
125	45	125	1	1	140000	300	3200	1400	449	15000	11	15	41	10	220	130	1	27000	485143	48.1
126	56	126	1	1	3750000	5000	3200	405	880	15000	11	15	16	10	80	567	5	3900	485143	43.9
127	15	127	1	1	140000	5000	3200	1400	449	5000	11	15	16	10	80	567	1	3900	485143	50.2
128	92	128	1	1	3750000	5000	497	1400	880	5000	37	15	41	3	80	567	1	3900	33123	55.6

A.2. Application Results

Rep: 128*1	5 different weight sets					Rep:128*1 Average (TOPSIS 1-5)	Rep:128*2=256 Average (TOPSIS 1-5)	
M/C	TOPSIS 1	TOPSIS 2	TOPSI S 3	TOPSIS 4	TOPSIS 5	topsis	topsis	
1	38.3	30.3	38	31.4	42.4	36.1	41.2	48.7
2	33.6	45.3	49.1	40.3	50.8	43.8	41.1	39.6
3	54.9	48.6	61.7	44	53.1	52.5	45.4	57.3
4	39.2	24.1	34.8	32.1	36.5	33.4	26.7	17.3
5	18.9	6.8	29.1	26.7	6.1	17.5	31.8	31.2
6	63.4	52.8	70.7	57.2	75.2	63.9	49	47.9
7	44.9	48.3	49.6	40	54.3	47.4	33.4	33.4
8	47.6	43.6	53.6	56.4	47.6	49.7	39.5	42.3
9	52.3	37.5	53.2	44.2	44	46.2	47.1	48.1
10	21	3.7	32.3	24.2	33.3	22.9	62.1	58.8
11	31.5	28.6	39.5	23.9	40.4	32.8	33.4	55.2
12	37.8	40.8	53.8	40.5	43.2	43.2	39.1	49.8
13	44.8	47.1	48.3	41	59.5	48.1	43.1	43.6
14	25	50.4	32.6	29.2	51.4	37.7	39.6	44.1
15	70.5	54.2	62.6	51.4	48.2	57.4	43.6	20.1
16	32.8	56.4	34.7	40.2	35.7	40	40	43.6
17	20.6	8.2	27.3	28.5	16.7	20.3	33.3	45.6
18	49.2	30.2	42.6	41.6	26	37.9	39.1	32.7
19	38.7	34.4	52.1	29.8	53.9	41.8	47.1	45.4
20	40	43.9	36.7	46.8	41	41.7	39.9	44
21	50.6	82.7	60.2	64.8	69.1	65.5	65.4	50.4
22	33.6	19.4	41.4	33.2	16.5	28.8	50.4	36.2
23	56.8	41.9	50.1	41.3	45.9	47.2	46.5	43.1
24	39.4	33.3	38.2	42.8	22.3	35.2	33.3	39.6
25	47.4	24.3	51.4	40.6	35.3	39.8	52.8	11.9
26	30.1	23.8	45.9	20.8	48.4	33.8	28.8	22.8
27	33.6	36.8	35.3	33.7	41.9	36.3	27.8	43
28	38.6	36.9	42.1	33	53.5	40.8	28.6	43.6
29	39.4	42.7	43.2	40.8	46.5	42.5	50.5	39.1
30	34.4	27.7	29.7	25.8	16.9	26.9	41.6	39.1
31	51.6	53.5	51.6	61.9	42.9	52.3	47.7	36.2
32	43.4	33.3	60	42.7	52.6	46.4	24.7	45.9
33	51.1	47.2	39.8	41.5	38.8	43.7	49.6	33.7
34	43.4	31.5	26.8	33.4	22.2	31.4	35.1	29.4
35	46	30.1	43.5	40.6	40	40	65.4	28.8
36	40.7	37.2	45.5	41.8	41.2	41.3	34	30.7
37	49.6	54	45.9	58.7	42.2	50.1	51.7	56.4
38	36	31.5	51	34	47	39.9	33.3	43.2

39	42.7	49.5	43.1	51.1	49.7	47.2	41.6	41.2
40	35.6	67.5	45.6	52.1	54.3	51	36.2	41.8
41	9.9	29	36.5	24.5	39.9	27.9	51.7	43
42	41.1	24.2	39.1	33.2	37.5	35	45.6	33.7
43	40.3	49.1	50.5	51.7	62.9	50.9	33.4	44
44	15.7	29.1	34.7	24.7	43.3	29.5	63.8	62.1
45	35.4	61.5	50.7	42.4	63	50.6	55.2	48.1
46	22.2	26.4	37.3	27.8	40.8	30.9	43.9	58.8
47	48.6	41.9	53.2	42.7	53.5	48	41.2	54.5
48	33.7	8.7	40.6	25.7	37.8	29.3	53.7	41.5
49	59.1	49.8	58.4	43.2	62.5	54.6	29	26.7
50	29.6	34.9	35.7	21.5	37.5	31.9	40.7	50.5
51	33.3	34.8	43.2	25.7	51.4	37.7	28.8	30.8
52	33.2	6.2	41.4	27.4	35.5	28.7	43.9	52.3
53	43	55.1	50.7	48.3	71.9	53.8	44.1	53.5
54	45.9	52.4	51.6	50.2	51.9	50.4	51.2	54.5
55	31.3	31.4	44.1	39.4	41	37.4	48.5	43.9
56	40.1	40.2	36.1	42.3	39.1	39.6	47.1	36.9
57	28.4	39.4	22	29.9	34.6	30.8	41.2	17.3
58	45.4	55.2	50.1	41.6	51.8	48.8	43.7	56.4
59	41.9	33.4	50.8	43.5	50.5	44	43.7	48.8
60	42.7	49.2	47.2	49.6	55.5	48.8	46.1	52.8
61	49.7	60.3	49.8	49	59.3	53.6	41.5	34.9
62	32	24	24.2	37.3	26	28.7	11.9	41
63	27.8	20.9	24.5	23.5	8.1	21	20.8	40.7
64	48.3	37.5	53	51.1	59.4	49.8	39.1	50
65	32.2	24.1	39.4	41.8	10.8	29.7	36.2	29.6
66	44.5	72.6	46.1	52.7	60.3	55.3	45.3	45.9
67	42.5	42.7	47.6	38.7	44.9	43.3	47.1	51
68	44.1	47.2	36.2	50.8	40	43.6	40.7	28.6
69	32.5	38.8	35.8	40	33.9	36.2	34	47.1
70	38.7	29.8	35.6	41.4	21.3	33.4	46.3	45.4
71	46.1	42.9	51.4	57.6	49.9	49.6	41	30.6
72	38.2	41.2	43.9	51	45.4	44	41.1	53.5
73	53.8	56.6	56.9	51.7	75.5	58.9	53.7	52.3
74	42.2	59.7	35.3	53	43	46.6	41.6	49.8
75	2.6	2.5	24.1	24.6	6.5	12.1	41.1	20.8
76	56.1	44.5	48.9	49.9	51.8	50.2	63.8	36.2
77	47.1	27.6	49.9	42.3	39.4	41.3	36	37.6

78	44.4	48.4	45	40.9	48.5	45.5	37.8	30.6
79	37	45	56.5	47.7	69.4	51.1	51	50.9
80	40.7	22.1	40.5	42.4	21.8	33.5	45.6	48.5
81	28.2	50.9	37.3	36.5	57	42	28.6	37.4
82	34.9	24.2	46	39.7	36.8	36.3	35.1	39.9
83	41.1	56	48.1	48.1	67.4	52.2	37.6	41.1
84	36	50.8	48	30.4	60.2	45.1	29.4	37.8
85	50.3	33.9	47.7	45.3	38.4	43.1	15.6	24.7
86	67.9	61.4	61.8	52.7	67.5	62.2	33.3	42.5
87	45.5	37.2	48.7	38.8	57.7	45.6	33.7	42.3
88	42.5	56.1	46.8	42.8	50.8	47.8	48.8	41.8
89	45.3	48.2	57.4	41.1	57.3	49.8	29.5	31.8
90	38.7	44.8	41.9	48.4	55.8	45.9	50.4	49
91	60	34.1	45.7	52.6	28.2	44.1	29.5	45
92	48.2	27.5	50.6	41.1	36.6	40.8	30	33.7
93	35.2	27.4	38.5	43.3	24.7	33.8	52.1	36.9
94	25.3	7.3	36.2	24.2	30.9	24.8	32.7	46.1
95	46.9	33.9	54.9	40.8	50	45.3	38.6	49.6
96	33.8	39.2	36	28.9	47.4	37	45.6	30.7
97	47.6	48.7	44.8	41.9	37.8	44.1	22.8	40
98	44.5	35.3	49.5	24.7	53	41.4	34.9	52.2
99	48.5	65.4	44.9	50.5	52.8	52.4	15.6	30.8
100	27.7	44.1	36.2	48.9	39.2	39.2	38.6	36.2
101	31.5	44.2	39.7	41.3	37	38.7	46.3	48.7
102	60.3	47.3	47.7	49.1	52.3	51.3	28.6	49.8
103	38.4	44.2	50	42.7	45.8	44.2	46.5	50.1
104	33.7	21.2	36.2	24.8	34.3	30.1	45.3	41.6
105	41.6	54.3	55.1	39.7	61.8	50.5	39.6	43.9
106	48.1	60.7	43	50.3	56.6	51.7	20.1	27.8
107	40.4	27.4	45.5	54.2	40.8	41.7	45	50
108	53.9	52.7	61.1	59.4	55.3	56.5	52.1	47.9
109	26.4	44.7	42.9	41.6	49.6	41	43.2	37.4
110	44.6	49.8	42	53.1	39.3	45.7	52.3	52.2
111	31.9	36	42.6	39.7	45.4	39.1	50.9	29
112	52.5	38.8	51.7	53.2	40.3	47.3	50.9	42.5
113	18.4	26	39.5	23.5	37	28.9	40.7	42.2
114	32.3	51.8	34	38	50.1	41.2	30	37.6
115	38.3	43.7	40.9	42.1	46	42.2	39.5	40.4
116	41.4	48.2	52.7	41.2	61.8	49.1	39.1	47.1

117	29.9	40.9	39.7	29.6	57.8	39.6	49.8	50.1
118	30.8	43.4	41.1	37.8	48.8	40.4	50.9	43.9
119	22.8	39.1	21.3	29.3	35.9	29.7	43.9	47.3
120	43.5	48	51.1	50.4	49.8	48.6	45.4	49.6
121	42	42.9	39.7	46.5	41.2	42.5	39.9	51.2
122	39.2	21	39.7	21.4	32.2	30.7	52.3	31.2
123	14.8	5	22.7	20.7	15.2	15.7	50.4	47.3
124	42.6	31.6	62.5	41.1	50.7	45.7	40.4	57.3
125	22.6	28.9	42.3	25.9	48.1	33.5	39.9	47.7
126	34.3	33.1	43.2	41.3	43.9	39.2	49.6	36
127	24.9	26	42.6	26.5	50.2	34	37.6	42.2
128	55.6	50.1	52	51.4	55.6	52.9	28.8	29.6

A.3. MINITAB Solution Result

Welcome to Minitab, press F1 for help.
Fractional Factorial Design
Factors: 15 Base Design: 15; 128 Resolution: IV
Runs: 128 Replicates: 1 Fraction: 1/256
Blocks: 1 Center pts (total): 0

Design Generators: H = ABFG; J = ACDEF; K = BEF; L = ABCEG; M = CDFG; N = ACDEG; O = EFG; P = ABDEFG
Factorial Fit: topsis1 versus table; w p; ...
Estimated Effects and Coefficients for topsis1 (coded units)

Term	Effect	Coef	SE Coef	T	P
Constant		39.493	0.1099	359.20	0.000
table	**14.192**	**7.096**	**0.1099**	**64.54**	**0.000**
wp	**2.920**	**1.460**	**0.1099**	**13.28**	**0.000**
x	**0.561**	**0.280**	**0.1099**	**2.55**	**0.016**
y	**6.292**	**3.146**	**0.1099**	**28.61**	**0.000**
z	**1.936**	**0.968**	**0.1099**	**8.80**	**0.000**
spe	-0.317	-0.159	0.1099	-1.44	0.159
pow	**5.995**	**2.998**	**0.1099**	**27.26**	**0.000**
rtra	**9.752**	**4.876**	**0.1099**	**44.35**	**0.000**
tnum	0.364	0.182	0.1099	1.66	0.108
tcha	**-4.902**	**-2.451**	**0.1099**	**-22.29**	**0.000**
tdia	**3.017**	**1.509**	**0.1099**	**13.72**	**0.000**
tlen	**1.105**	**0.552**	**0.1099**	**5.02**	**0.000**
pos	0.045	0.023	0.1099	0.21	0.838
mtw	-0.052	-0.026	0.1099	-0.23	0.816
cost	**-6.855**	**-3.427**	**0.1099**	**-31.17**	**0.000**
table*wp	-0.730	-0.365	0.1099	-3.32	0.002
table*x	-0.183	-0.091	0.1099	-0.83	0.412
table*y	-1.220	-0.610	0.1099	-5.55	0.000
table*z	-0.733	-0.366	0.1099	-3.33	0.002
table*spe	0.377	0.188	0.1099	1.71	0.096
table*pow	-1.148	-0.574	0.1099	-5.22	0.000
table*rtra	-1.861	-0.930	0.1099	-8.46	0.000
table*tnum	0.164	0.082	0.1099	0.75	0.461
table*tcha	-0.764	-0.382	0.1099	-3.47	0.001
table*tdia	0.617	0.309	0.1099	2.81	0.008
table*tlen	0.055	0.027	0.1099	0.25	0.805
table*pos	-0.080	-0.040	0.1099	-0.36	0.719
table*mtw	0.230	0.115	0.1099	1.04	0.304
table*cost	-1.886	-0.943	0.1099	-8.58	0.000
wp*x	-0.261	-0.130	0.1099	-1.19	0.244
w p*y	-0.505	-0.252	0.1099	-2.30	0.028
w p*z	-0.267	-0.134	0.1099	-1.22	0.233
w p*spe	0.905	0.452	0.1099	4.11	0.000

w p*pow	-0.508	-0.254	0.1099	-2.31	0.028
w p*rtra	-0.614	-0.307	0.1099	-2.79	0.009
w p*tnum	0.067	0.034	0.1099	0.31	0.762
w p*tch	-0.011	-0.005	0.1099	-0.05	0.961
w p*tdia	0.058	0.029	0.1099	0.26	0.794
w p*tlen	-0.061	-0.030	0.1099	-0.28	0.783
w p*pos	0.186	0.093	0.1099	0.85	0.404
w p*mtw	-0.067	-0.034	0.1099	-0.31	0.762
w p*cost	-0.489	-0.245	0.1099	-2.22	0.033
x*y	-0.127	-0.063	0.1099	-0.58	0.569
x*z	-0.089	-0.045	0.1099	-0.41	0.688
x*spe	-0.055	-0.027	0.1099	-0.25	0.805
x*pow	-0.136	-0.068	0.1099	-0.62	0.541
x*rtra	-0.198	-0.099	0.1099	-0.90	0.374
x*tnum	0.158	0.079	0.1099	0.72	0.478
x*tcha	0.055	0.027	0.1099	0.25	0.805
x*tdia	-0.195	-0.098	0.1099	-0.89	0.381
x*tlen	-0.345	-0.173	0.1099	-1.57	0.126
x*pos	-0.342	-0.171	0.1099	-1.56	0.130
x*mtw	0.080	0.040	0.1099	0.36	0.719
x*cost	-0.111	-0.055	0.1099	-0.50	0.617
y*z	-1.470	-0.735	0.1099	-6.69	0.000
y*spe	0.302	0.151	0.1099	1.37	0.180
y*pow	-0.342	-0.171	0.1099	-1.56	0.130
y*rtra	-1.248	-0.624	0.1099	-5.68	0.000
y*tnum	0.208	0.104	0.1099	0.95	0.352
y*tcha	-0.264	-0.132	0.1099	-1.20	0.239
y*tlen	-0.214	-0.107	0.1099	-0.97	0.338
y*mtw	0.148	0.074	0.1099	0.68	0.505
y*cost	-1.230	-0.615	0.1099	-5.59	0.000
z*pow	-0.567	-0.284	0.1099	-2.58	0.015
z*tnum	-0.242	-0.121	0.1099	-1.10	0.279
z*tdia	-0.070	-0.035	0.1099	-0.32	0.751
z*tlen	0.061	0.030	0.1099	0.28	0.783
z*pos	-0.092	-0.046	0.1099	-0.42	0.678
z*mtw	0.567	0.284	0.1099	2.58	0.015
spe*rtra	0.442	0.221	0.1099	2.01	0.053
spe*tnum	-0.064	-0.032	0.1099	-0.29	0.773
spe*tdia	0.070	0.035	0.1099	0.32	0.751
spe*tlen	0.095	0.048	0.1099	0.43	0.668
spe*pos	0.211	0.105	0.1099	0.96	0.345
spe*cost	0.167	0.084	0.1099	0.76	0.453
pow*rtra	-1.058	-0.529	0.1099	-4.81	0.000
pow*tdia	-0.098	-0.049	0.1099	-0.45	0.657
pow*tlen	-0.892	-0.446	0.1099	-4.06	0.000

pow*cost	-0.820	-0.410	0.1099	-3.73	0.001
rtra*tnum	-0.008	-0.004	0.1099	-0.04	0.972
rtra *tcha	-0.361	-0.180	0.1099	-1.64	0.111
rtra *tdia	0.427	0.213	0.1099	1.94	0.061
rtra *tlen	-0.023	-0.012	0.1099	-0.11	0.916
rtra *pos	-0.077	-0.038	0.1099	-0.35	0.730
rtra *mtw	0.245	0.123	0.1099	1.12	0.273
tnum*tdia	1.083	0.541	0.1099	4.92	0.000
tnum *cost	-0.058	-0.029	0.1099	-0.26	0.794
tnum *tdia	-0.533	-0.266	0.1099	-2.42	0.021
tnum *pos	0.120	0.060	0.1099	0.55	0.588
tnum *cost	2.133	1.066	0.1099	9.70	0.000
tdia*mtw	0.136	0.068	0.1099	0.62	0.541
tlen*pos	-0.230	-0.115	0.1099	-1.04	0.304
tlen*mtw	0.111	0.055	0.1099	0.50	0.617
pos*cost	-0.102	-0.051	0.1099	-0.46	0.647
mtw *cost	0.414	0.207	0.1099	1.88	0.069

S = 1.24391 R-Sq = 99.69% R-Sq(adj) = 98.77%

Analysis of Variance for topsis1 (coded units)

Source	DF	Seq SS	Adj SS	Adj MS	F	P
Main Effects	15	14918.8	14918.8	994.583	642.78	0.000
2-Way Interactions	80	978.0	978.0	12.224	7.90	0.000
Residual Error	32	49.5	49.5	1.547		
Total	127	15946.2				

References

1. Lata, S., Sachdeva, A.K., Paswan, M.K.: Selection of machine tool by using FUZZY TOPSIS method. In: AIP Conference Proceedings, vol. 2341, issue 1, p. 020015. AIP Publishing LLC (2021)
2. Li, H., Wang, W., Fan, L., Li, Q., Chen, X.: A novel hybrid MCDM model for machine tool selection using fuzzy DEMATEL, entropy weighting and later defuzzification VIKOR. Appl. Soft Comput. **91**, 106207 (2020)
3. Ding, Z., Jiang, Z., Zhang, H., Cai, W., Liu, Y.: An integrated decision-making method for selecting machine tool guideways considering remanufacturability. Int. J. Comput. Integr. Manuf. **33**(7), 686–700 (2020)
4. Chakraborty, S., Boral, S.: A developed case-based reasoning system for machine tool selection. Benchmark. Int. J. **24**(5), 1364–1385 (2017)
5. Sun, S.: Assessing computer numerical control machines using data envelopment analysis. Int. J. Prod. Res. **40**(9), 2011–2039 (2002)
6. Cimren, E., Budak, E., Catay, B.: Development of a machine tool selection system using analytic hierarchy process. Intell. Comput. Manufac. Eng. **4**, 1–4 (2004)
7. Georgakellos, D.A.: Technology selection from alternatives: a scoring model for screening candidates in equipment purchasing. Int. J. Innov. Technol. Manag. **2**(1), 1–18 (2005)

8. Ic, Y.T., Yurdakul, M., Eraslan, E.: Development of a component-based machining centre selection model using AHP. Int. J. Prod. Res. **50**(22), 6489–6498 (2012)
9. Yurdakul, M., Tansel İÇ, Y.: Application of correlation test to criteria selection for multi criteria decision making (MCDM) models. Int. J. Adv. Manufac. Technol. **40**(3–4), 403–412 (2007). https://doi.org/10.1007/s00170-007-1324-1
10. Yurdakul, M., Ic, Y.T.: Analysis of the benefit generated by using fuzzy numbers in a TOPSIS model developed for machine tool selection problems. J. Mater. Process. Technol. **209**, 310–317 (2009)
11. İç, Y.T., Yurdakul, M.: Analysis of the effect of the number of criteria and alternatives on the ranking results in applications of the multi criteria decision making approaches in machining center selection problems. J. Facul. Eng. Architect. Gazi Univ. **35**(2), 991–1001 (2020)
12. İç, Y.T., Yurdakul, M.: İşleme Merkezlerinin Yapısal Bileşenlerini Kullanan Bir Seçim Modelinin Geliştirilmesi. MATİM-Makina Tasarım ve İmalat Dergisi **18**(2), 53–62 (2020)
13. İç, Y.T., Yurdakul, M.: A component based model developed for machine tool selection decisions. In: Karwowski, W., Trzcielinski, S., Mrugalska, B. (eds.) AHFE 2019. AISC, vol. 971, pp. 279–288. Springer, Cham (2020). https://doi.org/10.1007/978-3-030-20494-5_26
14. Haseli, G., Sheikh, R., Wang, J., Tomaskova, H., Tirkolaee, E.B.: A novel approach for group decision making based on the best–worst method (G-bwm): application to supply chain management. Mathematics **9**(16), 1881 (2021)
15. Haseli, G., Sheikh, R., Sana, S.S.: Base-criterion on multi-criteria decision-making method and its applications. Int. J. Manage. Sci. Eng. Manage. **15**(2), 79–88 (2020)
16. Haseli, G., Sheikh, R.: Base Criterion Method (BCM). In: Kulkarni, A.J. (ed.) Multiple Criteria Decision Making: Techniques, Analysis and Applications, pp. 17–38. Springer Nature Singapore, Singapore (2022). https://doi.org/10.1007/978-981-16-7414-3_2
17. Tirkolaee, E.B., Mahmoodkhani, J., Bourani, M.R., Tavakkoli-Moghaddam, R.: A self-learning particle swarm optimization for robust multi-echelon capacitated location–allocation–inventory problem. J. Adv. Manuf. Syst. **18**(04), 677–694 (2019)
18. Tirkolaee, E.B., Dashtian, Z., Weber, G.W., Tomaskova, H., Soltani, M., Mousavi, N.S.: An integrated decision-making approach for green supplier selection in an agri-food supply chain: threshold of robustness worthiness. Mathematics **9**(11), 1304 (2021)
19. Shafipour-omran, B., Khalili-Damghani, K., Ghasemi, P.: Solving a supply chain problem using two approaches of fuzzy goal programming based on TOPSIS and fuzzy preference relations. J. Indust. Syst. Eng. **13**(2), 27–48 (2020)
20. Abdolazimi, O., Shishebori, D., Goodarzian, F., Ghasemi, P., Appolloni, A.: Designing a new mathematical model based on ABC analysis for inventory control problem: a real case study. RAIRO-Oper. Res. **55**(4), 2309–2335 (2021)
21. Montgomery, D.C.: Design and Analysis of Experiments. Wiley, New York, USA (1997)

Machine Learning and Fuzzy MCDM for Digital Advertising Effectiveness

Bilel Souissi[1(✉)] and Ahmed Ghorbel[2]

[1] MODLIS Laboratory, Faculty of Management and Economics of Sfax, University of Sfax, Airport Road, km 4, 3000 Sfax, Tunisia
bsuissi@gmail.com

[2] Faculty of Management and Economics of Sfax, University of Sfax, Airport Road, km 4, Sfax, Tunisia

Abstract. Today, digital advertising faces several serious challenges. As the advertising landscape expands daily, digital marketers and agencies struggle to keep up. Without planning to overcome these challenges, they will fight an uphill battle with little progress to show for it. To this end, we developed a combined approach based on Fuzzy Multi-Criteria Decision-Making (Fuzzy MCDM) methods and machine learning techniques to optimize display advertising campaign problems. Many criteria are combined, including technical, economic, and social. In the first phase, after applying the fuzzy VIKOR method, the proposed approach consisted of choosing a fraud problem as a top advertising problem. In the second phase, the fraud detection problem was solved using our UCB-LSTM-GA model. The results indicate that the combination of the fuzzy MCDM model and our UCB-LSTM-GA model provides effective linkages between fraud detection problems and the performance of online advertising objectives. Our approach achieves as high as 97.7% AUC, 97.5% precision, and 97.5% recall using real datasets from TalkingData by the popular python tools. The managerial implication of our work is that the advertisers can apply the proposed methodology to efficiently identify fraudulent clicks and impressions to protect customers' interests and reduce fraud losses and regulatory costs.

Keywords: Online advertising effectiveness · fraud detection · machine learning · UCB-LSTM-GA · Fuzzy MCDM

1 Introduction and Background

The dam bursts and the water of the online world flooded most of our lives. Inter-net has become a vital part of ordinary people's lives, so it is sometimes difficult to distinguish the offline world from the online world. Marketers and advertisers are also aware of the enormous impact of digital or online advertising on their brands. In addition, traditional advertising channels, such as print media and television, have steadily declined in the past few years. Advertisers spend less than half of what they used to five years ago on print media. In addition, internet-advertising revenue has increased by nearly 15% in the

A. Mirzazadeh et al. (Eds.): SEMIT 2022, CCIS 1808, pp. 344–356, 2023.
https://doi.org/10.1007/978-3-031-40395-8_24

past year. However, not everything is rosy in the world of online advertising. Traditional advertising focuses on the needs and requirements of customers. Nonetheless, online advertising needs to focus more on technology and speed of adoption, and with it comes a host of issues. The biggest hurdle for online advertisers right now is fraudulent traffic [1], Consumer–Brand Relationships [2], brand transparency signals [3], Social Media Policy Changes [4], and click fraud [5].

Although online advertising problems have a long history in quantitative programming models, MCDM methods have been implemented in the online advertising effectiveness but cannot determine the online advertising challenges selection. For example, [6] used fuzzy logic to increase the effectiveness of advertising campaigns. Furthermore, [7] used fuzzy-set qualitative comparative analysis to augment brand experience in native advertising on social media. In addition, [8] used fuzzy multi-criteria modeling of user effectiveness and experience in internet advertising. In this paper, we proposed the use of fuzzy MCDM approaches to identify the most common challenges that hinder the development of online advertising companies and then sought to solve the problem already selected by the first approach using hybrid machine learning models.

In an earlier work [9], we proposed a new methodology for online advertising effectiveness using supervised machine learning and metaheuristic methods. We implemented Long Short-Term Memory (LSTM) to predict the click-through rate (CTR) metric. We applied genetic algorithms (GAs) to find out on optimized sub-set of features, the optimum window size, and the number of units in the LSTM model. With this approach, we introduced a new advertisement ranking strategy that involves more ads factors and focused on a reinforcement learning technique to optimize the number of clicks on the ad.

Inspired by the working models of [1] and [10], our research was also based on real-life data. We used a dataset from TalkingData Kaggle.com (2018). The characteristics of this dataset are analyzed and presented in what follows.

To the best of the authors' knowledge, a combined approach based on concepts of Fuzzy MCDM methods and machine learning techniques to select the biggest hurdle for online advertisers' alternatives and detect ad click fraud to maximize the effectiveness of advertising has not been considered previously in that domain.

The main contributions of this paper are summarized as follows:

An optimization model of advertising effectiveness was proposed;

A hybrid Fuzzy MCDM approach related to the selection of the biggest challenges facing online advertising was used;

The UCB-LSTM-GA was used as machine learning algorithms and an optimization method for online advertising fraud detection systems;

The performance of these classifiers was validated using a 10-fold cross-validation technique to estimate the performance of the learned model and compare the performance of the different algorithms;

We built an algorithm that predicts whether a user will download an app after clicking a mobile app ad;

We tested how long it takes to perform the next click.

2 Materials and Methods

2.1 Study Area

Fraud risk is everywhere but for companies that advertise online, click fraud can happen at an overwhelming volume, resulting in misleading click data and wasted money. Ad channels can drive up costs by simply clicking on the ad on a large scale. With over 1 billion smart mobile devices in active use every month, China is the largest mobile market in the world and, therefore, suffers from massive volumes of fraudulent traffic. TalkingData offers the best-in-class Big Data products varying from highly scalable data mining, deep data analytics, Data Management Platform (DMP), analytical reports, industry benchmarking, and deep-dive market insight re-ports. Today, 80% of the Top 50 developers in China rely on them to track their app metrics, analyze user data points, and monetize. The dataset is huge, i.e., ~8 GB and 200 million observations (train + test).

2.2 Platform and Tools

We conducted the experiments using a computer with 8 GB RAM and an Intel Core i7 processor. In addition, we used a Kaggle platformer, which provides a host of features, 16 gigabytes of RAM, 6 h execution time, 5 Gigabytes of auto-saved disk space, and a Docker container with pre-installed python and R packages. To analyze and manipulate massive data and express the performance of our model, we used the popular tools R and Python.

2.3 Our Approach

Fuzzy VIKOR Method

To evaluate various alternatives, we applied the fuzzy VIKOR method, developed for multi-criteria optimization in complex systems. It identifies compromises and the best choice from a set of alternatives. Compromise solutions will be proposed by comparing how close they are to ideal alternatives, and each alternative can be evaluated by each criterion function. This section presents a systematic approach to the multi-criteria fuzzy VIKOR method in fuzzy environments. According to [11], it aims to find the best compromise solution among decision-makers to satisfy human cognitive goals. The purpose of this study was to use a new hybrid model of the MCDM approach to select challenges faced by the online advertising industry. To make informed comparison decisions in Fuzzy VIKOR, we sent a questionnaire to a group of four experts, who are senior executives of the company responsible for online marketing. Table 1 shows the five alternatives and three groups of criteria.

The VIKOR algorithm is stated as follows: the first one is the identification of the decision-making process objectives. Decision-makers were termed criteria and attributes alternatives, like multiple numbers.

$$\tilde{X}_k = \begin{array}{c} A/C \\ A_1 \\ A_2 \\ A_3 \\ A_4 \\ A_5 \end{array} \begin{array}{c} C_1\ C_2\ C_3 \\ \begin{bmatrix} x_{k11} & x_{k12} & x_{k13} \\ x_{k21} & x_{k22} & x_{k23} \\ x_{k31} & x_{k32} & x_{k33} \\ x_{k41} & x_{k42} & x_{k43} \\ x_{k51} & x_{k52} & x_{k53} \end{bmatrix} \end{array} \forall k = 1, \ldots, 4 \quad (1)$$

The second step is running the decision-making group and describing a set of relevant attributes. The design selection requires the identification of decision criteria, and then the evolution of scales is established in the order of the ranking of the concepts: ac-cording to their value, i.e., high or low values. Accordingly, we need to arrange the linguistic variables that have to be defined as the concept of fuzzy talks about linguistics.

Table 1. Marketing strategy alternatives and Criteria's

Marketing strategy alternatives	Criteria's
A1: fraudulent traffic	C1: Economical
A2: Consumer–Brand Relation-ship	C2: Social
A3: click fraud	C3: Technical
A4: brand transparence signal	
A5: Social Media Policy Changes	

In fact, weight importance criteria need to be assigned with regard to each criterion, and these linguistic variables can be expressed as positive trapezoidal fuzzy numbers: this is step 3.

$$\tilde{X} = \begin{array}{c} A/C \\ A_1 \\ A_2 \\ A_3 \\ A_4 \\ A_5 \end{array} \begin{array}{c} C_1\ C_2\ C_3 \\ \begin{bmatrix} x_{11} & x_{12} & x_{13} \\ x_{21} & x_{22} & x_{23} \\ x_{31} & x_{32} & x_{33} \\ x_{41} & x_{42} & x_{43} \\ x_{51} & x_{52} & x_{53} \end{bmatrix} \end{array}, \text{ where } \tilde{x}_{ij} \text{ is the rating of aggregated matrix} \quad (2)$$

The fuzzy weighted values for each criterion is determined based on the importance of each criterion:

$$\tilde{w}_j = \frac{\tilde{s}_j}{\sum_{i=1}^{5} \tilde{s}_j}, \forall j = 1, \ldots, 3 \quad (3)$$

where is the standard deviation value for the criterion. The standard deviation is given as follows:

$$\tilde{s}_j = \sqrt{\frac{1}{M} \sum_{i=1}^{5} (\widetilde{x}_{ij} - \widetilde{S}_{ij})}, \forall j = 1, \ldots, 3 \quad (4)$$

and is the total number of alternatives.

where,

$$\tilde{s}_{ij} = (\frac{1}{M}\sum_{i=1}^{5}\widetilde{\boldsymbol{x}}_{ij},\ \forall i = 1, \ldots, 5 \ and\ j = 1, \ldots, 3 \tag{5}$$

Step 4 and 5 describe the organized decision maker statement and getting aggregated fuzzy weight criteria. In addition, we estimate using some typical methods that exist in aggregate fuzzy weight and perform the procedures to calculate the weight.

Determine the fuzzy best value and fuzzy worst value

$$\tilde{x}_j^+ = \max_i \tilde{\boldsymbol{x}}_{ij} \text{ is the fuzzy best value} \tag{6}$$

$$\tilde{x}_j^- = \max_i \tilde{\boldsymbol{x}}_{ij} \text{ is the fuzzy worst value} \tag{7}$$

Therefore, using, we can calculate the fuzzy weights. Then the matrix is diversified. The sixth step is determining the best and worst two solutions and the seventh one-step is separation matrices and computing the final value.

Linear normalization formula indicated by score and is as follows:

$$\tilde{S}_i = \sum\nolimits_{j=1}^{3} \tilde{w}_j \left(\frac{\tilde{x}_j^+ - \widetilde{\boldsymbol{x}}_{ij}}{\tilde{x}_j^+ - \tilde{x}_j^-}\right) \tag{8}$$

$$\tilde{R}_i = \max_j \left[\tilde{w}_j \left(\frac{\tilde{x}_j^+ - \widetilde{\boldsymbol{x}}_{ij}}{\tilde{x}_j^+ - \tilde{x}_j^-}\right)\right] \tag{9}$$

The calculation of the VIKOR index is presented as follows:

$$\tilde{Q}_i = v \times \left(\frac{\widetilde{\boldsymbol{S}}_i - \tilde{S}_i^-}{\tilde{S}_i^+ - \tilde{S}_i^-}\right) + v \times \left(\frac{\widetilde{\boldsymbol{R}}_i - \tilde{R}_i^-}{\tilde{R}_i^+ - \tilde{R}_i^-}\right) \tag{10}$$

where;

$$\tilde{S}_i^+ = \max_i \widetilde{\boldsymbol{S}}_i \tag{11}$$

$$\tilde{S}_i^- = \max_i \widetilde{\boldsymbol{S}}_i \tag{12}$$

$$\tilde{Q}_i^+ = \max_i \widetilde{\boldsymbol{Q}}_i \tag{13}$$

$$\tilde{Q}_i^- = \max_i \widetilde{\boldsymbol{Q}}_i \tag{14}$$

UCB-lSTM-GA Model

In this work, our goal was to detect fraudulent clicks in mobile advertising and count the time of the next click. To this end, we used a 10-fold cross-validation technique that is used to estimate the skill of the models. A model for a given detective-modeling problem is often used to apply machine learning to compare and select models because it is easy to understand and implement. Furthermore, it creates some capabilities that are generally less inclined compared to other methods. With this in mind, LSTM-GA was implemented to develop a sequence classification model to handle the above situation. The goal is to identify suspicious events, i.e., fraudulent clicks, as quickly as possible by analyzing the data. In an earlier work [9], we used the UCB-LSTM-GA model to determine the best LSTM hyperparameters and the GA to select the best subset of features, window size, and the number of hidden units. We also tried to find out which parameters reduce the root mean square error (RMSE) model. Here, we investigated how to increase the flexibility of our approach to make it easier to adapt to new ad campaigns, analyze and compare different computational methods, and improve the performance of detecting fraudulent ads.

3 Results and Discussion

3.1 Fuzzy VIKOR Application for Online Advertising Problems Selection

The strategic choice challenge for sustainable manufacturing includes many factors. It is often incommensurable and contradictory and is often subject to uncertain-ty in real-world settings. Furthermore, in the group decision-making process, each decision maker has different information and opinions on the criteria weights and strategic performance ratings. This study provides a fuzzy VIKOR technique for choosing online advertising strategies.

In Table 2, we depicted the standard deviation value that were calculated using Eqs. (3) and (4). Thereafter, the fuzzy values were integrated to determine aggregated fuzzy weight criteria using Eqs. (5), (6) and (7). The results are shown in Table 3.

Table 2. Aggregated matrix

	A1	A2	A3	A4	A5
C1	1.00 1.19 1.19	2.21 3.22 3.41	1.41 2.45 3.00	2.21 3.22 3.41	1.00 2.00 2.71
C2	1.00 2.00 2.71	1.00 1.68 1.86	2.71 3.72 4.40	1.00 1.68 1.68	2.00 3.00 3.00
C3	1.00 2.00 2.71	1.00 2.00 2.00	1.68 2.71 3.00	1.00 1.68 1.86	1.68 2.71 3.00

The ranking of strategies following the VIKOR procedure and calculations is shown in Table 4. The closest compromise solution to the ideal solution is implemented as challenge A3. The difference between A3 and A5 VIKOR value (Qv = 0.5) (the challenge with the smallest value and the challenge next to it) is 0.32 >. There-fore, the compromise solution for challenge A3 is a stable solution because it satisfies the condition mentioned

Table 3. Values of basic variables in VIKOR method

	C1			C2			C3		
$\tilde{w}_j$	0.09	0.13	0.14	0.12	0.14	0.17	0.06	0.07	0.08
$\tilde{x}_j^{+}$	2.21	3.22	3.41	2.71	3.72	4.40	1.68	2.71	3.00
$\tilde{x}_j^{-}$	1.00	1.19	1.19	1.00	1.68	1.68	1.00	1.68	1.86
$\tilde{s}_{1j}$	0.09	0.13	0.14	0.12	0.12	0.10	0.06	0.05	0.02
$\tilde{s}_{2j}$	0.00	0.00	0.00	0.12	0.14	0.15	0.06	0.05	0.07
$\tilde{s}_{3j}$	0.06	0.05	0.03	0.00	0.00	0.00	0.00	0.00	0.00
$\tilde{s}_{4j}$	0.00	0.00	0.00	0.12	0.14	0.17	0.06	0.07	0.08
$\tilde{s}_{5j}$	0.09	0.08	0.04	0.05	0.05	0.09	0.00	0.00	0.00

in step 6. Based on these values, the first alternative Click fraud must be selected as the biggest challenge facing online advertising (Table 1). The order is as follows: Click fraud (A3) > Social Media Policy Changes (A5) > Consumer–Brand Relationship (A2) > fraudulent traffic (A1) > brand transparency signals (A4).

Table 4. Results of VIKOR method

	S	R	Q	Rank of alternative
A1	0.83	0.14	0.88	4
A2	0.59	0.15	0.45	3
A3	0.14	0.06	0.00	1
A4	0.64	0.17	1.13	5
A5	0.40	0.09	0.32	2

According to the results obtained using Fuzzy VIKOR methods, the click fraud problem is the biggest obstacle faced by online advertisers. In what follows, we will try to solve this problem using machine-learning techniques.

3.2 Sequence Classification Model For Ad Fraud Detection

According to Fig. 1, there are only 18717 attributed_time values, i.e., only 18,717 out of 10,000,000 clicks resulted in a download, which is less than 0.2%. This in-creases the severity of the problem and the need to find solutions that reduce this high rate of fraudulent clicks to avoid financial losses for companies and institutions that use mobile phones to display and market their products.

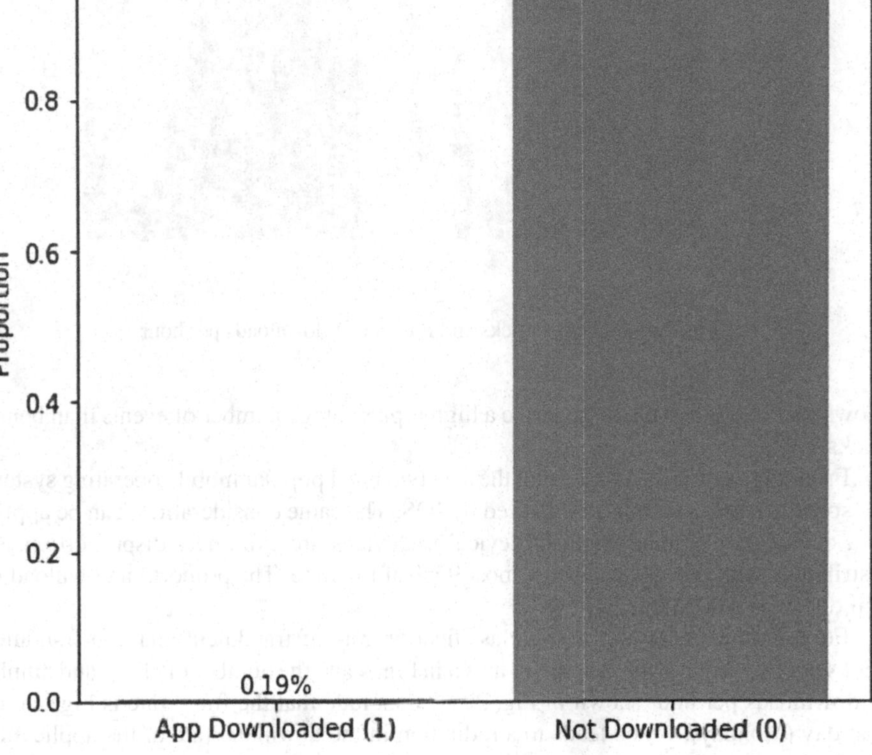

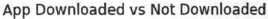

Fig. 1. Proportion of app downloaded

To find out the temporal distribution of OK and Fraud clicks, we calculated the number of clicks during each hour of the day. As can be seen from Fig. 5, there are very few valid clicks during the night hours and quite a high number of valid clicks during working hours of the day. However, it can be easily noticed that the fraudulent clicks are distributed uniformly throughout the day. This finding provides an idea about the targeted attempt of the fraud traffic generators (i.e., bot-nets and human-generated ones) to avoid raising suspicions.

Figure 2 shows that the minimal number of clicks occurs at about 20pm UTC time. The number of downloads, in general, follows the same pattern. Indeed, 20 here is effectively 4am in China, which makes sense for a traffic dip.

The ratio of the number of fraud clicks to total clicks on each device gives us in-sight into the behavior of fraud publishers. As can be seen from Fig. 3, devices with a lower number of clicks have a higher tendency to generate clicks through traffic generators. We can also conclude that invalid clicks generate more events than valid ones. Figure 4

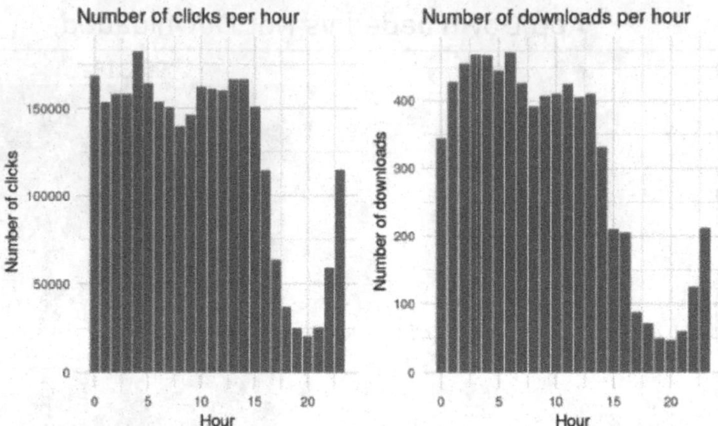

Fig. 2. Number of clicks and number of downloads per hour

shows that fraudulent clicks generate a higher percentage number of events than benign clicks.

From Fig. 3, we can assume that the first two most popular mobile operating systems are some versions of Android followed by IOS. The same considerations can be applied to a device (e.g., "some Android device"). Devices are extremely disproportionately distributed, with one device used almost 94% of the time. The proportion download for that device is 0.001326. (0.13%).

Furthermore, according to the classification rate of fraudulent and non-fraudulent clicks per Day-hour in the four days shown in Fig. 4 and the number of clicks and number of downloads per hour shown in Fig. 2, we conclude that the fraud rate is high on the first day (Monday), which leads to a reduction in the download rate of the application. Similarly, we can conclude that, in the case of fraud, the number of fraudulent clicks is high; consequently, the application is not downloaded. Moreover, we can see that the percentage of clicks increases from 2 am to 10 am (10 am to 6 pm in China) each day, i.e., working hours.

Figure 5 shows that going from clicking to purchasing takes as long as (almost) 20 h and as little as 4 s. The 4 s seem too low to make a decision. This person would have either seen the ad before or already been aware of the product some other way. Does that mean the ad was clicked on multiple times, but only one click was counted as a conversion? Alternatively, did the person click on the ad specifically with the intent to download it? (e.g., if the channel is something like a google search, the ad could be clicked during search results view and the app downloaded immediately because that's what the person intended to do right away). It is not in-stalled time (though that could be a factor too), but 20 h and even more between when a person clicks on an ad (and presumably arrives on the page of interest) to when they download it is reasonable. Marketing companies track people who arrive on their pages to view content and then come back later to download an app once decided. It is not known, though, how this particular advertiser tracks conversions from users who come by multiple times but download once after 4 s or less. Maybe they track a download as soon as it starts downloading. That still leaves

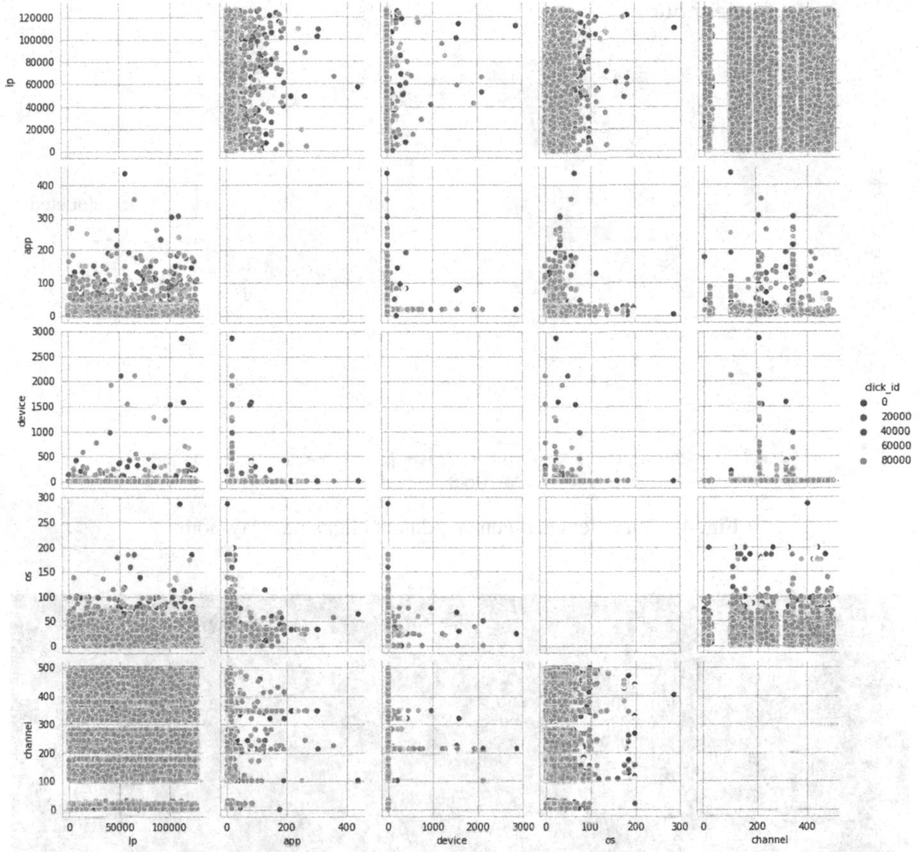

Fig. 3. The most frequent values of categorical features

too little time for decision-making: it is either a repeat visitor, a direct search visitor, or a robot. Furthermore, according to our analysis, we find that, on average, the user predates 5187.5 s to do the next click, and a user who previously or subsequently clicked on the same app-device-os-channel makes, on average, 26 clicks.

Figure 6 shows the sensitivity (true positive rate) as a function of the false positive rate. Moreover, the total area under the receiver operating characteristic curve (AUC-ROC curve) at different threshold settings is a performance measurement for the classification problem. Then, the receiver operating characteristic (ROC) is a probability curve, while the AUC is a degree or reparability measure. However, the AUC-ROC curve is simply the area below the ROC curve, which implies that our estimate is likely to be good. Figure 6 depicts a summary of the ROC curve of the applied feature selection technique and an optimization algorithm for the parameters.

As reported in Table 5 and Fig. 6, the integrated model of upper confidence bound (UCB), GA and LSTM network proves to be the most performant in fraud detection. Specifically, from the aspect of the Area under the ROC Curve (AUC) and F1-score, which measure the overall performance of models, the UCB-LSTM-GA achieves the

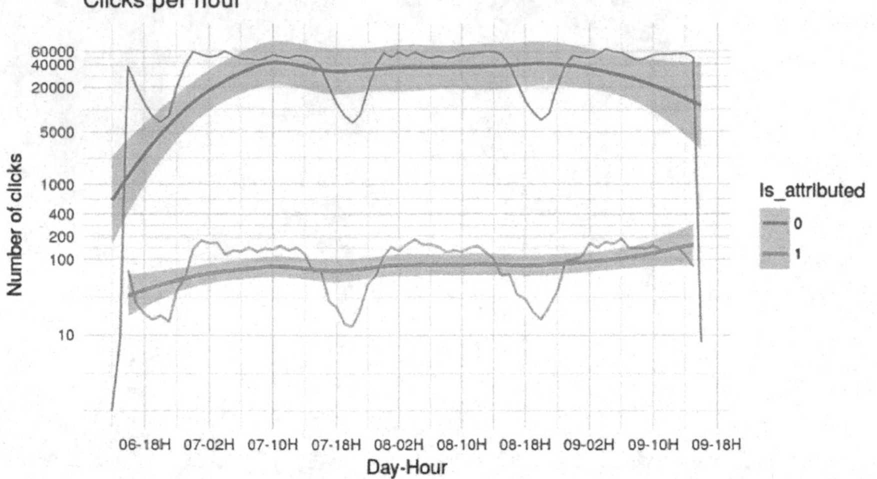

Fig. 4. Fraudulent and non-fraudulent clicks per Day-hour

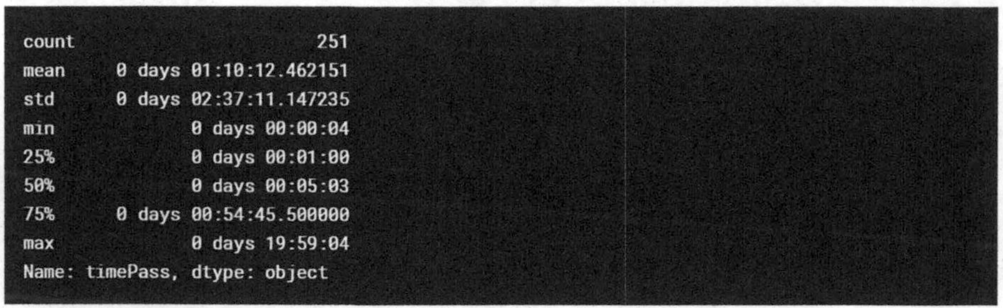

```
count                           251
mean      0 days 01:10:12.462151
std       0 days 02:37:11.147235
min                0 days 00:00:04
25%                0 days 00:01:00
50%                0 days 00:05:03
75%       0 days 00:54:45.500000
max                0 days 19:59:04
Name: timePass, dtype: object
```

Fig. 5. Time passed from clicking on the ad to downloading it.

highest AUC of 97.9% and the highest precision and recall value of 97.5%, followed by GFXGB, GBDT, and Support vector machine (SVM) models. Therefore, the UCB-LSTM-GA shows a better detection performance and statistical significance.

The proposed hybrid model learned to capture some aspects of the mobile advertising chaotic behavior and was able to maximize the fraud detection rate for mobile ads with outstanding performance compared to the other ad fraud detection models. In this research, we used GA and UCB technology and proved that it could effectively find the best solution for the model. The overall results indicate the advantage of UCB-LSTM-GA in detecting ad fraud. Experimental results show that using appropriately selected time windows and architectural factors in mobile advertising tasks can significantly improve the predictability of LSTM networks. The proposed UCB-LSTM-GA model can also overcome the limitations of commonly used methods, i.e., heuristic methods.

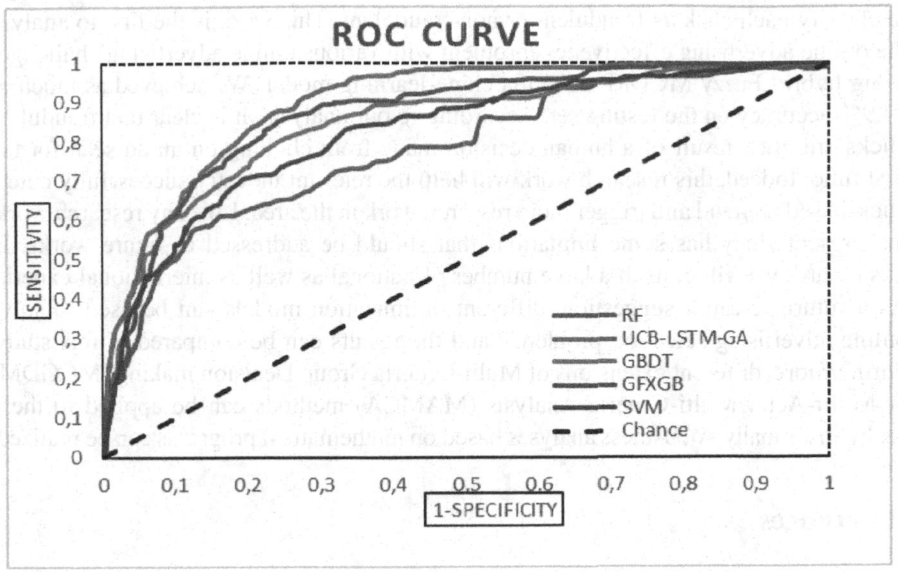

Fig. 6. This curve displays the sensitivity (true positive rate) as a function of the false positive rate.

Table 5. Comparison between our results and those of the literature

Model	AUC	Precision	*Recall*	*F1*
UCB-LSTM-GA	97.9	97.5	97.5	97.4
RF	90.4	87.8	84.6	84.2
GBDT	94.2	90.6	89.1	89.0
GFXGB	96.4	96.0	96.0	96.0
SVM	93.2	89.6	87.7	87.6

4 Conclusion

The present work proposed an optimization model of online advertising effective-ness using a hybrid Fuzzy MCDM approach related to selecting the biggest challenges facing online advertising. Here, we applied a machine learning technique for advertising fraud detection. In addition, methods, such as fuzzy VIKOR and LSTM, have been integrated into the proposed approach. This paper applies a fuzzy MCDM approach to evaluate and prioritize online advertising challenges based on technical, economic, and social criteria. In the first step, we constructed a judgment matrix for online advertising challenges for the group using a geometric mean of all individual judgments, and global priorities were calculated using the fuzzy VIKOR procedure. In the second step, the fuzzy VIKOR method was used to rank the challenges. Finally, we used our UCB-LSTM-GA model to study a new type of mobile advertising fraud detection based on real data that aims to classify each click as fraudulent or non-fraudulent. This work is the first to analyze the online advertising effectiveness problem with various online advertising challenges using hybrid Fuzzy MCDM and a ma-chine-learning model. We achieved as much as 97.9% accuracy on the testing set. According to our analysis, it is clear that fraudulent clicks are not a result of a human decision made from clicking on an ad seen for the first time. Indeed, this research work will help the relevant industry successfully detect click-based ad fraud and trigger more research work in the area. Like any research work, the present study has some limitations that should be addressed in future works. In this regard, we will consult a large number of national as well as international experts. As a future research suggestion, different optimization models can be used to solve online advertising selection problems, and the results can be compared to this study. Furthermore, different extensions of Multi-Criteria Group Decision making (MCGDM) or Multi-Actor Multi-Criteria Analysis (MAMCA) methods can be applied to these problems. Finally, robustness analyses based on mathematical programs can be realized.

References

1. Wu, Y., Xu, Y., Li, J.: Fraudulent traffic detection in online advertising with bipartite graph propagation algorithm. Expert Syst. Appl. **2021**(185), 115573 (2021)
2. Hayes, J.L., Brinson, N.H., Bott, G.J., Moeller, C.M.: The influence of consumer-brand relationship on the personalized advertising privacy calculus in social media. J. Interact. Mark. **2021**(55), 16–30 (2021)
3. Cambier, F., Poncin, I.: Inferring brand integrity from marketing communications: the effects of brand transparency signals in a consumer empowerment context. J. Bus. Res. **2020**(109), 260–270 (2020)
4. Luzon, Y., Pinchover, R., Khmelnitsky, E.: Dynamic budget allocation for social media advertising campaigns: optimization and learning. Eur. J. Oper. Res. Published online 2021 (2021)
5. Thejas, G.S., Dheeshjith, S., Iyengar, S.S., Sunitha, N.R., Badrinath, P.: A hybrid and effective learning approach for Click Fraud detection. Mach. Learn. Appl. **2021**(3), 100016 (2021)
6. Madera, Q., Castillo, O., García-Valdez, M., Mancilla, A.: A method based on interactive evolutionary computation and fuzzy logic for increasing the effectiveness of advertising campaigns. Inf. Sci. **2017**(414), 175–186 (2017)
7. Zhang, H.: Augmenting brand experience in native advertising on social medias using fuzzy-set qualitative comparative analysis. Microprocess. Microsyst. **2021**(82), 103991 (2021)
8. Jankowski, J., Kazienko, P., Wątróbski, J., Lewandowska, A., Ziemba, P., Zio\lo, M.: Fuzzy multi-objective modeling of effectiveness and user experience in online advertising. Expert Syst. Appl. **65**, 315–331 (2016)
9. Souissi, B., Ghorbel, A.: Upper confidence bound integrated genetic algorithm-optimized long short-term memory network for click-through rate prediction. Appl. Stochastic Models Bus. Ind. 1–22 (2022). https://doi.org/10.1002/asmb.2671
10. Thejas, G.S., Dheeshjith, S., Iyengar, S.S., Sunitha, N.R., Badrinath, P.: A hybrid and effective learning approach for Click Fraud detection. Mach. Learn. Appl. **3**, 10001 (2021)
11. Lu, M.T., Tzeng, G.H., Cheng, H., Hsu, C.C.: Exploring mobile banking services for user behavior in intention adoption: using new hybrid MADM model. Serv. Bus. **9**(3), 541–565 (2015)

Performance Measurement of Insurance Company Software Groups by Using Fuzzy-AHP and ELECTRE Method

Ezgi Ansen[1] and Yavuz Selim Özdemir[2(✉)]

[1] Istanbul Arel University, Istanbul, Türkiye
[2] Ankara Science University, Ankara, Türkiye
yavuz.selim.ozdemir@ankarabilim.edu.tr

Abstract. Measuring employee performance is critical to improving production and service processes in enterprises. However, as with all other abstract concepts, performance measurement has a complex process. Different approaches are used in the literature for performance measurement. One of these methods is Multi-Criteria Decision Making (MCDM). The MCDM aims to select the best alternatives by simultaneously evaluating the criteria. In addition, one or more decision-makers in the MCDM may be involved in the decision-making process at the same time. For these reasons, a Fuzzy-MCDM method is proposed for the performance evaluation of project groups operating in the software sector. The application part of the study aimed to determine the best-performing team among four software project groups working in an insurance company, combining the Fuzzy Analytic Hierarchy Process (F-AHP) and Elimination and Choice Translating Reality (ELECTRE) methods. Each group comprises five software engineers who are experts in their field. In the first stage, the main criteria and sub-criteria that impact performance most were determined. Then, the weights of the criteria were determined by the F-AHP method. Finally, with the ELECTRE method, the performance ranking of the software groups was made.

Keywords: Multi-Criteria Decision Making · Fuzzy-AHP · ELECTRE · Performance Measurement · Software Development

1 Introduction

Deciding between multiple alternatives has been a common problem humanity faces for centuries. It isn't easy to make the best decision with various alternatives for a single purpose. If the problem is based on selecting the best among the alternatives in terms of different criteria, these problems are called multi-criteria decision-making problems. In case more than one criterion-alternative and criteria have various priorities, multi-criteria decision-making methods are generally used. In the literature, different approaches are used for decision-making problems' solutions. With these methods, it is aimed to choose the best alternative according to the decision-maker.

A. Mirzazadeh et al. (Eds.): SEMIT 2022, CCIS 1808, pp. 357–365, 2023.
https://doi.org/10.1007/978-3-031-40395-8_25

In the literature, one of the most used methods is Analytical Hierarchy Method (AHP). The AHP method allows the decision-maker to model complex problems in a hierarchical structure that shows the connections between the problems' main goal, criteria, sub-criteria, and options [1]. The AHP method is based on pairwise comparisons. With these pairwise comparisons, the importance of alternatives and criteria relative to each other is evaluated [2]. In addition, it allows multiple decision-makers to assess at the same time [3].

Decision-making methods are mainly based on decision-makers' expressions. Fuzzy logic is one of the practical approaches used to digitize linguistic terms. The combination of fuzzy logic and AHP increases the effectiveness of the MCDM process.

Both subjective and objective analyses can be made by using MCDM methods. For that reason, these methods are also used for performance measurement. In recent decades, there has been an increase in performance analysis studies using MCDM techniques. MCDM techniques provide fast, consistent, and effective results in both performance measurement and performance comparisons between different workgroups.

This study aims to evaluate different software groups in an insurance company's performance evaluation. Thus, Fuzzy-AHP and ELECTRE methods are used together. First, F-AHP is used for the weight evaluation of criteria. Then the workgroups were ranked according to their performance using the ELECTRE method. The results are used to improve the software group performance of the company.

In the second part, literature research is briefly given. In the third part, F-AHP and ELECTRE methods are explained. In the fourth part, the results of the application will be shown. In the last part, the results are discussed.

2 Literature

There are different models in the literature for performance measurement. Deming Prize Model was implemented in 1951 [4]. EFQM excellence model was developed in 1988 by the European Quality Management Foundation and published in 1991 [5]. Kaplan and Norton developed the Balanced Scorecard Model in 1992 [6, 7]. Quantum Performance Measurement Model was developed by Hronec [8]. Performance Prism Model was developed by Neely and his colleagues [9, 10].

MCDM methods are frequently used in different areas, especially performance measurement. Wu et al. used fuzzy logic, MCDM, and Balanced Scorecard models together for performance measurement in the banking system [11]. Again, Wu et al. developed a similar MCDM and Balanced Scorecard model to measure the performance of universities [12]. A new MCDM method was developed by Gürbüz and Albayrak to measure the human resources performance [13]. Özdemir and Oktay measured the service quality for the aircraft maintenance process with the fuzzy MCDM method [14].

MCDM methods are widely used for decision-making process [15–17]. The most widely used MCDM method is the AHP approach. It was developed by Saaty in the 1980s to solve complex MCDM problems [18]. AHP is still very popular, and its different variations are frequently used [19].

AHP has some disadvantages arising from its algorithm and human nature [20]. In pairwise comparisons, as the number of alternatives increases, the inconsistency of the comparisons also increases. If there are more than seven alternatives to the problem, it is a better alternative to use the AHP method with other methods. One of the most common usages in the literature is the AHP-ELECTRE. AHP and ELECTRE methods are used together in many performance evaluation problems [21–23]. Also, it is used for selection and decision-making problems in the software industry [24].

The ELECTRE method was first developed by Benayoun and Sussman [25]. The algorithm of the method is based on binary superiority comparisons. It is mainly preferred in decision-making problems where the superiority of the alternatives over each other is essential [26].

To better implement linguistic uncertainty and decision makers' opinions in the decision-making process, MCDM methods and fuzzy logic are used together. As mentioned before, F-AHP is widely used for this purpose. Kahraman et al. used F-AHP to select the best supplier in the white goods industry in Turkey [27]. In the research, purchasing preferences of white goods manufacturers were evaluated. Göleç et al. used complex fuzzy methods to assess the performance of the manufacturing systems [28]. Here, fuzzy-based Approximate Reasoning and Fuzzy AHP methods were used to compare the results. According to the study, the F-AHP method has better results. Lee et al. used the F-AHP to evaluate the performance of the IT department in the manufacturing industry in the Taiwan [29]. Sun et al. assessed the performance of machines in the production process using the F-AHP method [30].

3 Methodology

In this study, there are two main stages. Firstly, criterion weights were determined by using the F-AHP method. Secondly, performance evaluations of the project groups were made with the ELECTRE method.

3.1 Fuzzy AHP

Fuzzy logic and numbers were firstly introduced by L. A. Zadeh [31]. In this study, fuzzy numbers and AHP methodology were used together. F-AHP is an extended version of the original method. This paper uses Buckley's methodology for fuzzy process' because of its computational advantages and consistent results [32]. Buckley's approach uses triangular fuzzy numbers. There are four steps in the F-AHP procedure.

Step1: Problem definition, decision-making group selection, and criteria definition are made. Here, criteria represent as C_m; $m = 1, 2, \ldots, M$, decision-makers described as D_k; $l = 1, 2, \ldots, K$.

Step2: The hieratical structure is constructed in this step, and pairwise comparisons are completed. Here, $\widetilde{d_{ij}^{k}}$ indicates the kth decision maker's preference of ith criterion over j^{th} criterion. In this paper, decision-makers (DMs) make pairwise comparisons using the given linguistic scale in Table 1 with consensus.

In this step of the initial matrix, the Consistency Index (CI) must be checked as Saaty proposed [33]. If the decision matrix is inconsistent, decision-makers must re-evaluate

Table 1. Fuzzy Numbers for Criteria Comparison.

Explanation	Importance Level	Inverse
Equally Important (EI)	(1,1,1)	(1,1,1)
Much Less Important (MLI)	(2,3,4)	(1/4, 1/3, 1/2)
Important (I)	(3,4,5)	(1/5, 1/4, 1/3)
Very Important (VI)	(6,7,8)	(1/8, 1/7, 1/6)
Absolutely Important (AI)	(8,9,9)	(1/9, 1/9, 1/8)

their decisions with consensus again. The pairwise group decision matrix is created, as shown in Eq. 1.

$$\tilde{A} = \begin{pmatrix} \tilde{a}_{11} & \cdots & \tilde{a}_{1n} \\ \vdots & \ddots & \vdots \\ \tilde{a}_{n1} & \cdots & \tilde{a}_{nn} \end{pmatrix} \tag{1}$$

Step-4 Defuzzified weights are calculated as shown in Eq. 2 and 3.

$$\mathrm{r}_i = \left(\prod_{j=1}^{n} \tilde{a}_{ij} \right)^{1/n} \tag{2}$$

$$\tilde{r}_i = \frac{\tilde{r}_i}{\sum_{r=1}^{n} \tilde{r}_n} \tag{3}$$

3.2 ELECTRE

ELECTRE is a well-known methodology in the literature [21, 34]. For that reason, the steps are given briefly. There are seven steps in the ELECTRE methodology.

Step1: The initial decision matrix is prepared and the matrix is represented as in Eq. 4 given below.

$$\begin{bmatrix} X_{11} & X_{12} & \cdots & X_{1n} \\ X_{21} & X_{22} & \cdots & X_{2n} \\ \vdots & \vdots & & \vdots \\ X_{m1} & X_{m2} & \cdots & X_{mn} \end{bmatrix} \tag{4}$$

Step2: Normalization of the initial matrix by using Eq. 5.

$$r_{ij} \frac{X_{ij}}{\sqrt{\sum_{k-1}^{m} X_{kj}^2}} \tag{5}$$

Step3: Weighted normalized matrix is created by using Eq. 6.

$$v_{ij} = r_{ij}.w_j \tag{6}$$

Step4: Formulation of concordance and discordance sets are given in Eqs. 7 and 8.

$$C_{kl} = \{j, \quad V_{kj} \geq V_{ij}\}, \; wherej = 1, 2, 3, \ldots, n \tag{7}$$

$$D_{kl} = \{j, \quad V_{kj} \geq V_{ij}\}, \; wherej = 1, 2, 3, \ldots, n \tag{8}$$

Step5: Create the concordance and discordance matrix are given in Eq. 9 and 10 respectively.

$$C_{kl} = \sum j \in C_{kl} W_j \tag{9}$$

$$d_{kl} = \frac{max_{j \in D_{kl}} |V_{kl} - V_{ij}|}{max_j |V_{kj} - V_{ij}|} \tag{10}$$

Step6: Calculation of concordance and discordance matrix average: This step calculates the average of concordance and discordance values. As a result;

a) In the concordance matrix; If C_{kl} is larger or equal to the C average, it states 1. Else 0.
b) In the discordance matrix; If D_{kl} is larger or equal to the D average, it states 0. Else 1.

Step 7: Calculate the net concordance and discordance matrix: This is the final step of the ELECTRE methodology. According to net matrixes, alternatives are compared. The calculation of concordance and dis-concordance matrix are given in Eq. 11 and Eq. 12.

$$C_p = \sum_{\substack{k-1 \\ k \neq p}}^{m} C_{pk} - \sum_{\substack{k-1 \\ k \neq p}}^{m} C_{kp} \tag{11}$$

$$D_p = \sum_{\substack{k-1 \\ k \neq p}}^{m} D_{pk} - \sum_{\substack{k-1 \\ k \neq p}}^{m} D_{kp} \tag{12}$$

4 Application

The application part is aimed to determine the best performing software group among the four software groups working in an insurance company. Criteria were selected by a group of managers and academics. As a result, three main criteria were determined.

The criteria are technical, managerial, and social. The sub-criteria of the technical main criterion consists of analysis, testing, and software development. The sub-criteria of the management main criterion are cost, time, scope, and risk. Social, our last main criterion, consists of four sub-criteria: communication within the team, communication with the customer, working environment, and interest in technological developments. F-AHP's hieratical tree structure is given in Fig. 1.

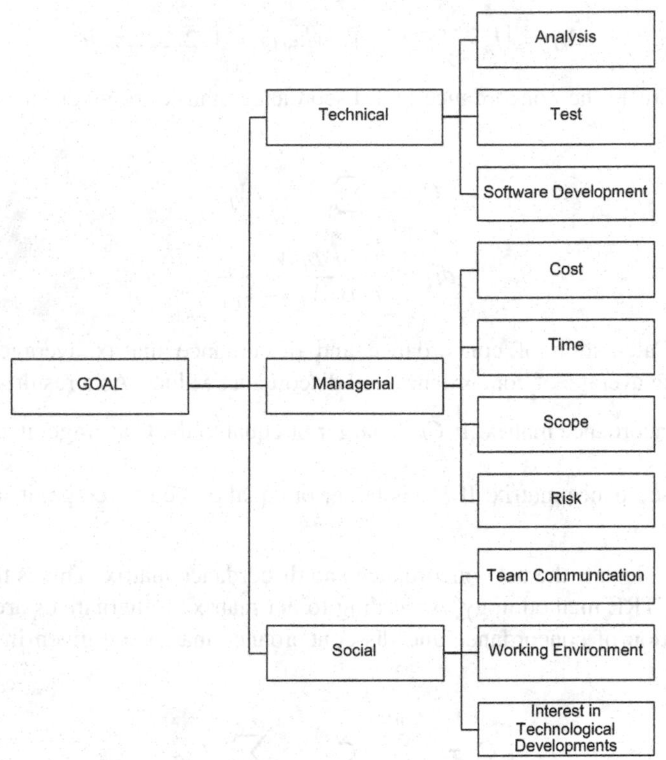

Fig. 1. Hieratical Structure of F-AHP.

Four software groups were selected from the insurance company. To prevent unfair competition between software groups, the software groups are named Group 1, Group 2, Group 3, and Group 4.

In the evaluation process, criteria weights were determined. The evaluation process details are given in the methodology part. The defuzzified weights are shown in Table 2. According to the table, the most crucial main criterion is Managerial. On the other hand, the most critical sub-criteria are Time, Scope, and Risk, respectively.

F-AHP weights were used in the first step of the ELECTRE method. After that, the initial matrix was conducted with the questionnaire results made to the people working on the software projects. Here, a 5-point Likert scale was used for evaluations. As stated before, seven steps of the ELECTRE were used. As a result, the best software group with the best performance was determined. According to the results, Group 2 is the best.

Table 2. Weights of Criteria

Main-Criteria	Weights	Sub-Criteria	Local weight	Global weight
Technical	0,2991	Analysis	0,3662	0,1095
		Test	0,3608	0,1079
		Software development	0,2729	0,0816
Managerial	0,5046	Cost	0,1605	0,0810
		Time	0,3283	0,1656
		Scope	0,2579	0,1301
		Risk	0,2533	0,1278
Social	0,1963	Team communication	0,2107	0,0414
		Customer Communication	0,3054	0,0600
		Working Environment	0,2477	0,0486
		Interest in Technological Developments	0,2361	0,0464

On the other hand, Groups 1, 3, and 4 do not have superiority over each other, and their performances are equal.

5 Conclusion

Performance measurement is a complicated process for companies. However, these measurements are essential for the progress of businesses and increasing their productivity. In the scope of this study, four software groups were evaluated using F-AHP and ELECTRE methods. After the problem definition and criteria selection part, weights were found with the F-AHP method, and the performance ranking of the software groups was made with the ELECTRE method. As a result, software development groups' performances were determined. The results could be used for performance improvement of the software development groups.

MCDM methods like TOPSIS, PROMETHE, VIKOR, and MABAC could be used for future work. On the other hand, there are new fuzzy approaches like intuitionistic fuzzy or hesitant fuzzy or different types of fuzzy sets like trapezoidal fuzzy or spherical fuzzy sets. These approaches could also be used for performance evaluation problems. Furthermore, linguistic assessments could be used for performance evaluation, and the performance score could be evaluated using a Fuzzy MCDM approach. The results could be used for comparison.

References

1. Eraslan, E., Algün, O.: İdeal performans değerlendirme formu tasarımında analitik hiyerarşi yöntemi yaklaşımı (2005)
2. Saaty, T.L., Sodenkamp, M.: The Analytic Hierarchy and Analytic Network Measurement Processes: The Measurement of Intangibles, vol. 1, pp. 91–166 (2010). https://doi.org/10.1007/978-3-540-92828-7_4
3. Özder, E.H., Özcan, E., Eren, T.: Staff task-based shift scheduling solution with an ANP and goal programming method in a natural gas combined cycle power plant. Mathematics **7** (2019). https://doi.org/10.3390/math7020192
4. Farrell, M.J.: The measurement of productive efficiency. J. R. Stat. Soc. Ser. A. (1957). https://doi.org/10.2307/2343100
5. Lynch, R., Cross, K.: Measure Up - the essential guide to measuring business performance. In: IEEE International Conference on Robotics and Automation (1991)
6. Kaplan, R.S., Norton, D.: The balanced score card measures that drive performance. Harv. Bus. Rev. **70**, 71–79 (1992). https://doi.org/10.1017/CBO9781107415324.004
7. Kaplan, R.S., Norton, D.P.: Linking the balanced scorecard to strategy. Calif. Manage. Rev. (1996). https://doi.org/10.2307/41165876
8. Hronec, S.M.: Vital signs: using quality, time, and cost performance measurements to chart your company's future. Amacom American Management Association (1993)
9. Neely, A., Adams, C., Crowe, P.: The performance prism in practice. Meas. Bus. Excell. (2001). https://doi.org/10.1108/13683040110385142
10. Neely, A., Adams, C., Kennerley, M.: The performance prism: the scorecard for measuring and managing business success. Cranf. Sch. Manag. (2002). https://doi.org/10.1108/eb016623
11. Wu, H.Y., Tzeng, G.H., Chen, Y.H.: A fuzzy MCDM approach for evaluating banking performance based on Balanced Scorecard. Expert Syst. Appl. (2009). https://doi.org/10.1016/j.eswa.2009.01.005
12. Wu, H.Y., Lin, Y.K., Chang, C.H.: Performance evaluation of extension education centers in universities based on the balanced scorecard. Eval. Program Plann. (2011). https://doi.org/10.1016/j.evalprogplan.2010.06.001
13. Gürbüz, T., Albayrak, Y.E.: An engineering approach to human resources performance evaluation: hybrid MCDM application with interactions. Appl. Soft Comput. J. (2014). https://doi.org/10.1016/j.asoc.2014.03.025
14. Ozdemir, Y.S., Oktay, T.: Evaluating service quality of an airline maintenance company by applying fuzzy-AHP. In: Calisir, F., Cevikcan, E., Camgoz Akdag, H. (eds.) Industrial Engineering in the Big Data Era. LNMIE, pp. 189–200. Springer, Cham (2019). https://doi.org/10.1007/978-3-030-03317-0_16
15. Haseli, G., Sheikh, R., Sana, S.S.: Base-criterion on multi-criteria decision-making method and its applications. Int. J. Manag. Sci. Eng. Manag. **15**, 79–88 (2020). https://doi.org/10.1080/17509653.2019.1633964
16. Rahmati, S., Mahdavi, M.H., Ghoushchi, S.J., Tomaskova, H., Haseli, G.: Assessment and prioritize risk factors of financial measurement of management control system for production companies using a hybrid Z-SWARA and Z-WASPAS with FMEA method: a meta-analysis. Mathematics. **10** (2022). https://doi.org/10.3390/math10020253
17. Goli, A., Mohammadi, H.: Developing a sustainable operational management system using hybrid Shapley value and Multimoora method: case study petrochemical supply chain. Environ. Dev. Sustain. 1–30 (2021). https://doi.org/10.1007/s10668-021-01844-9
18. Saaty, T.L.: The analytic hierarchy process. Education 1–11 (1980). https://doi.org/10.3414/ME10-01-0028

19. Piya, S., Shamsuzzoha, A., Azizuddin, M., Al-Hinai, N., Erdebilli, B.: Integrated fuzzy AHP-TOPSIS method to analyze green management practice in hospitality industry in the sultanate of Oman. Sustain. **14** (2022). https://doi.org/10.3390/su14031118
20. Ayyildiz, E., Taskin Gumus, A.: Pythagorean fuzzy AHP based risk assessment methodology for hazardous material transportation: an application in Istanbul. Environ. Sci. Pollut. Res. **28**(27), 35798–35810 (2021). https://doi.org/10.1007/s11356-021-13223-y
21. Soner, S., Önüt, S.: Multi-criteria supplier selection: an Electre-Ahp application. J. Eng. Nat. Sci. Sigma. (2006)
22. Chan, F.T.S.: Performance measurement in a supply chain. Int. J. Adv. Manuf. Technol. (2003). https://doi.org/10.1007/s001700300063
23. Shaik, M., Abdul-Kader, W.: Performance measurement of reverse logistics enterprise: a comprehensive and integrated approach. Meas. Bus. Excell. (2012). https://doi.org/10.1108/13683041211230294
24. Fernandes, J.M., Rodrigues, S.P., Costa, L.A.: Comparing AHP and ELECTRE i for prioritizing software requirements. In: 2015 IEEE/ACIS 16th International Conference on Software Engineering, Artificial Intelligence, Networking and Parallel/Distributed Computing, SNPD 2015 - Proceedings (2015)
25. Benayoun, R.B., Sussman, N.: Manual de Reference du Programme Electre. Note Synth. Format. (1966)
26. Daneshvar Rouyendegh, B., Erol, S.: Selecting the best project using the fuzzy ELECTRE method. Math. Probl. Eng. (2012). https://doi.org/10.1155/2012/790142
27. Kahraman, C., Cebeci, U., Ulukan, Z.: Multi-criteria supplier selection using fuzzy AHP. Logist. Inf. Manag. (2003). https://doi.org/10.1108/09576050310503367
28. Göleç, A., Taşkin, H.: Novel methodologies and a comparative study for manufacturing systems performance evaluations. Inf. Sci. (Ny). (2007). https://doi.org/10.1016/j.ins.2007.06.024
29. Lee, A.H.I., Chen, W.C., Chang, C.J.: A fuzzy AHP and BSC approach for evaluating performance of IT department in the manufacturing industry in Taiwan. Expert Syst. Appl. **34**, 96–107 (2008). https://doi.org/10.1016/j.eswa.2006.08.022
30. Sun, Q., Zhang, W.M., Li, P.Z.: A comprehensive evaluation approach for machining operation based on fuzzy AHP. In: Applied Mechanics and Materials (2014)
31. Zadeh, L.A.: Fuzzy sets. Inf. Control. **8**, 338–353 (1965). https://doi.org/10.1109/2.53
32. Buckley, J.J.: Fuzzy hierarchical analysis. Fuzzy Sets Syst. **17**, 233–247 (1985). https://doi.org/10.1016/0165-0114(85)90090-9
33. Saaty, T.L.: Decision making with the analytic hierarchy process. Int. J. Serv. Sci. (2008). https://doi.org/10.1504/IJSSCI.2008.017590
34. Beccali, M., Cellura, M., Mistretta, M.: Decision-making in energy planning. Application of the Electre method at regional level for the diffusion of renewable energy technology. Renew. Energy. (2003). https://doi.org/10.1016/S0960-1481(03)00102-2

A Combined Multi-objective and Multi Criteria Decision Making Approach for Wireless Sensors Location in Agriculture 4.0

Doha Haloui[1,2](✉), Kenza Oufaska[1], Mustapha Oudani[3], and Khalid El Yassini[2]

[1] LERMA Laboratory, International University of Rabat, Rabat, Morocco
doha.haloui@uir.ac.ma

[2] IA Laboratory, Faculty of Sciences, Moulay Ismail University, Meknes, Morocco

[3] TICLab Laboratory, International University of Rabat, Rabat, Morocco

Abstract. Today, the increasing adoption of digital and wireless sensor networks (WSN) in virtually every field has shifted the focus of research in an entirely new direction. This technology collects, monitors, and analyzes agricultural data. Furthermore, the use of wireless sensor networks in agriculture has resulted in numerous scientific advances. Global experience around the world demonstrates that remote monitoring, control, and sales of agricultural products via IoT, sensors, and modes of communication are carried out utilizing wireless sensors to ensure a high level of work quality. In this paper, we study the wireless sensor location problem for Agriculture 4.0. Overall, our framework can contribute to the development of more sustainable and smart agricultural production patterns, enhancing different strategies in the concept of Agriculture 4.0. The task of identifying an optimal agriculture strategy was mathematically formulated as a multi-objective linear programming model. We used the CPLEX solver to report solutions for the weighting method and epsilon constraint. To compare the obtained solutions by these solving methods, we have developed a systematic decision-support tool exploring the MARCOS method, a new MCDM method, to provide a ranking of such solutions over the various criteria.

Keywords: Wireless sensor networks · Agriculture 4.0 · Multi Objective Optimization · Multi criteria decision making

1 Introduction

Today, agriculture is one of the world's leading sectors. According to the United Nations (UN), the world's population will reach 8 billion by 2025 and 9.6 billion by 2050 [1]. This will give rise to a large boost in demand for a variety of human requirements, most notably food, both in terms of quality and quantity. Innovation and technology research play a big role in increasing agricultural production in an environmentally sustainable manner. It will be important for agriculture to use new digital technologies in the future because they will be able to boost the rate, efficiency, and effectiveness of farm production. When the Food and Agriculture Organization (FAO) of the United

A. Mirzazadeh et al. (Eds.): SEMIT 2022, CCIS 1808, pp. 366–382, 2023.
https://doi.org/10.1007/978-3-031-40395-8_26

Nations talks about this role, they call it "the Digital Agricultural Revolution" [2]. Other sources call this role "agriculture 4.0" [3]. This fourth agricultural revolution comes concurrent with "Industry 4.0," a new concept of smart manufacturing proposed by Germany in 2011. Its goal is to create a production model that is very flexible for a digital world and to make the industry smart and automated.

Many different types of data must be gathered to make good decisions in the agriculture system. Various factors affect data collection in agriculture monitoring, such as the geographic characteristics of the location from which data is taken, the weather and climate, the accessibility of markets, and transportation and storage facilities. Sensors are already used in agriculture to collect real-time data via wireless sensor networks (WSNs). The data collected in this manner shows current change, allowing the system to analyze agri-parameters in real-time [4]. In an agricultural environment, a wireless sensor network consists of interconnected sensors dispersed throughout the farmland. These sensors work together to identify and monitor real-time soil and weather information. The information is treated intelligently by an entrenched system. Furthermore, the information is sent to a diagnosis decision center by a wireless communication network. This allows farmers to remain focused on and manage their fields from afar.

Multi-objective optimization (MOO) enables the optimization of systems based on a variety of criteria, including environmental and economic factors [5]. Furthermore, environmental issues can be treated as objectives for decision-making rather than constraints required on the system, thanks to MOO [6]. MOO produces a set of non-dominated options (referred to as Pareto optimum solutions) which are alternatives (no conceivable solution may increase the value of any of the objectives in a Pareto optimum point without lowering the value of at least another objective.). The examination of these solutions gives insight into the trade-offs among objectives [7]. MOO has been effectively used in agriculture to manage resources in dry and semiarid areas. [8] used MOO to optimize reservoir operations and irrigation water allocation, whereas [9] employed MOO to achieve the optimal allocation of numerous reservoirs in a basin. MOO has also been used to analyze agricultural planning challenges, concentrating on either economic [10] or environmental [11].The aim of the paper is to develop a tool to optimize the agricultural planting strategy for a specified collection of crops on a specified number of parcels or geographical areas. In mathematical terms, we used a linear programming model (LP) with four sets of objective functions. A multi-objective LP model was solved using the scalarization method (epsilon-constraint and weighted sum). A fuzzy Measurement Alternatives and Ranking according to the Compromise Solution (fuzzy MARCOS) method was developed. The remainder of the paper is coordinated as follows: Sect. 2 outlines related works presented on wireless sensor networks-based smart agricultural systems. Section 3 discusses a background on agriculture 4.0 core technologies and the different types of agriculture sensors. A multi-objective linear programming problem was formulated in Sect. 4, while Sect. 5 discusses the different approaches used to solve the LP problem (weighted sum, epsilon constraint). Section 6 explains multi-criteria decision making using the MARCOS method. Finally, we present the numerical experiment in Sect. 7.

2 Related Works

A considerable number of studies have been published on the location of wireless sensors in smart agriculture in recent years. We summarize some of the research that has been conducted to date on wireless sensor networks-based smart agricultural systems: [12] invented a hybrid wireless sensor network design for agriculture. The above network eliminates the need for extensive human participation in agricultural production information collection systems and provides more precise data than current sensor networks. On the other hand, [13] presents an overview of brand-new research topics and technologies in the context of Agriculture 4.0. Several issues are explored, as well as future research opportunities. In [14], the authors modeled a wireless sensor network-based system design approach for a multiple-cropping scenario in smart agriculture. The primary issues the strategy targets are energy efficiency and cost benefits. The sensor architecture and MAC protocol are discussed, as well as the energy consumption of the overall system when using a fixed topology. [15] developed outdoor agricultural machinery using LSTM (Long Short-Term Memory); the system is capable of automatically watering and monitoring farm conditions, so fulfilling the aim of an intelligent machine. The study's approach can effectively accomplish the goal of green energy while minimizing water resource waste. Nevertheless [16] examines how sensors and sensor networks were integrated into the crop production process, as well as their added value and major bottlenecks from the users' viewpoint. The challenges are the development of sensor technology, data interoperability and management tools, as well as data and measurement services. However, [17] presents an approach comprised of a series of well-defined phases that span the whole life cycle of WSN-based agricultural monitoring applications. They examined a variety of existing real-world scenarios in which WSNs are used, and discovered numerous parallels but no framework defining the best practices that should be used in a broad, crop-independent context [18]. Suggested a new sensor network topology for real-time agricultural monitoring using autonomous robots in beacon mode. Additionally, the proposed scheme provides a secure connection to parent nodes and dynamically assigns network addresses. Numerous studies have been published on the topic of location problems: The paper [45] addresses a multi-echelon capacitated location–allocation–inventory issue under ambiguity by providing a robust mixed integer linear programming (MILP) model that takes into account production plants at level one, central warehouses at level two, and retailers at level three in order to design the optimal supply chain network. And [46] creates a bi-objective, multi-echelon, multi-supply mathematical model for locating, allocating, and distributing relief supplies in the face of uncertainty. For small and medium-scale problems, the model is solved using the epsilon-constraint method; for large-scale problems, the invasive weed optimization algorithm [48]. In this study, the suggested locations of crisis management throughout the region and the optimal points postulated by the Geographic Information System (GIS) were evaluated based on 18 criteria, both with and without the opinion of experts [47]. Proposed a model based on an actual case problem in agriculture that combines locating multiple depots and determining routing paths with a distance constraint. A problem-solving adaptive large neighborhood search (ALNS) algorithm exists. According to various studies, the location of urban farming has not been studied using a combination of multi-objective optimization and multi-criteria decision making methods while taking smart dimensions into account. This paper fills this gap in research by using both MOO and MCDM to find a smart urban farm.

3 Preliminaries

3.1 Agriculture 4.0 Core Technologies

The application of emerging industry 4.0 technologies presents an opportunity in the agricultural production system. As a result of developments in these technologies, massive amounts of data are generated and analyzed daily. So, the agriculture sector has evolved as an ideal prospect for the deployment of such technology, which can raise the efficiency of agricultural activities essentially because they require constant monitoring and control. This section highlights five core technologies in Agriculture 4.0.

Wireless Sensor Network (WSN): In recent years, WSNs have been commonly applied in diverse agricultural applications to enhance the efficiency of traditional farming methods [19, 49]. Sensor networks operate three essential functions: detecting; communication between the network's various components; and computation, through the use of hardware, software, and algorithms [20]. A wireless sensor and actuator network (WSAN) is a subset of a wireless sensor network (WSN) that includes an actuator. An actuator is a physical device (lamps, fans, pumps, valves, irrigation sprinklers, etc.) that interacts with the environment. These networks are composed of numerous sensors and actuator nodes that are connected via a wireless link. These nodes often include several components, each of which performs a specific purpose, such as detecting, controlling, computing, and communicating. In the context of Agriculture 4.0, WSNs and WSANs are being used in a diversity of ways to improve agricultural strategies [21]. These technologies have enabled the real-time monitoring of different parameters (such as water parameters, soil properties, and weather systems) and a timely response in the field.

Robotics has been generally adopted in industrial manufacturing to boost productivity, increase product authenticity, and eliminate the need for humans to perform repetitive activities. Meanwhile, agricultural production is undergoing a fundamental transformation as a result of the application of robotics to agriculture. Additionally, robotics is changing agricultural output, with significant applications including autonomous farming, aerial spraying, and monitoring. Collaboratively, smart tractors would develop operating paths and automatically avoid obstacles in the field, ensuring the safety of both farms and workers [22]. Computer vision lets robotic weeders tell the difference between weeds and crops. They can then spray herbicide directly on the weeds to kill them without hurting the crops [23].

Internet of Things refers to the connection among physical and digital "things" via standard and interoperable communication systems [24]. It has been used as a key technology in several domains, such as smart cities, smart homes, industrial production, and healthcare. Agriculture is no barring when it comes to the deployment of IoT solutions, as agricultural activities must be monitored and controlled continuously. Combining different Agriculture 4.0 technologies with IoT has shown that it has a lot of potential to make farming more efficient, with each technology having its own set of needs [25].To address them, agricultural literature on IoT has used a variety of communication protocols and technologies. Due to advancements in communication technology, many types of wireless networks (e.g., WiFi, RFID, Bluetooth, NFC, ZigBee, and Sigfox) can be selected to satisfy the different service needs of agricultural applications, such as high-throughput plant phenotyping, and real-time remote equipment control, for improved coverage, bandwidth, the density of connections, and end-to-end latency. Table 4 compares the most frequently used items in this domain [26]. Describes the development of an intelligent farming system using an Internet-of-Things-based Smart Agriculture System [27]. Investigated the challenges associated with IoT adoption in agriculture. Specifically, the IoT technology's development tendencies.

Big Data Analytics: The Internet of Things enables data collection at every stage of agricultural production and agri-food supply chain management. Thus, implementing big data analytics during marketing, processing, logistics, and food production will be significant. A data-driven agricultural industry would fundamentally alter agricultural production and consumption trends. For example, agricultural predictive analytics, mobile agricultural expert systems, and all rely on the power of big data to give farmers intelligent recommendations regarding precision farming. Accurate risk assessment may assist farmers in managing agricultural risks more effectively in terms of production, economics, and institutional, particularly personal and financial risk. In [28], a data-driven agriculture system for managing sustainability in the by-products supply chain was presented [29]. Gave a comprehensive assessment of the consequences of big data analytics on the agri-food supply chain from a variety of viewpoints, including functional, economic, environmental, social, and technological. Recent publications [29, 30, and [31] have provided in-depth assessments of the difficulties associated with using big data analytics in agriculture.

3.2 Types of Agricultural Sensors

The data obtained from sensors is usually required in order to uncover data-driven insights and patterns that assist farmers in maximizing yield and regulating their expenditure on irrigation, seeding, fertilizer use, water consumption, electricity consumption, and other factors. This section [32] presents the most widely used modern agricultural technologies and sensors.

Optical Sensors use light to determine soil properties. They can determine the moisture content, organic matter content, and clay content of the soil. Sensors of this type are used in drones, robotics, and satellites. Several optical sensors on the market work in different ways because of how they are built and what features they have [41].

Location Sensors: Using GPS, farms are accurately mapped using location or position sensors. Farmers use these tracking devices to determine when, where, and how many pesticides and fertilizers to employ. It can also identify irregular landscapes, uneven ground, and problems with leveling that result in waterlogging, among other things [42, 50, 51].

Acoustic sensors are used to detect sound. These sensors are frequently used in the field to identify pests. They have nodes that should be positioned in strategic areas around the field, so when a pest passes through, the sound can be easily recognized and recorded to the linked device along with its location. Pests are an impediment that inflicts damage on farms and introduces plant illnesses [32].

Electrochemical Sensors: The pH value and nutrient content of the soil are two of the most critical soil parameters that must be analyzed. Electrodes are used to measure the voltage between two sites to quantify the concentration of ions such as H+, K+, and NO3-. The electrode must be in touch with the soil sample for this approach to work. The conventional procedure is to conduct a chemical soil study, which is costly and time-consuming. Numerous electrode types are employed, including ISE-ion-selective electrodes, ISFET-ion-selective field-effect transistors, and chemically modified ion-selective field-effect transistors [43].

Airflow sensors are used to determine the soil's air permeability. The soil's air permeability is a property that indicates how well it resists air passage. This component is critical when determining the soil's type, structure, and moisture/humidity content. Temperature and heating are sensed by silicon chips in these sensors. They transmit information about the direction and speed of the circulation of air and gas through the soil [44].

Electromagnetic sensors: Use electric circuits to collect data on a variety of components, including level organic matter, water drainage, salinity, and soil texture. Electric circuits can be used to measure the charge's capacity to move through or build in the land. Electromagnetic sensors can sometimes be embedded directly in the soil (contact) or can be removed from the soil (Noncontact). The contact approach requires the sensor to be in direct touch with the soil, which is accomplished by the use of electrodes. These sensors can be put on tractors and other tracked vehicles. The electromagnetic induction (EMI) principle is used in the Non-contact method. Crop production is not directly influenced by electromagnetic characteristics (soil EC), however, this data is useful in determining the critical soil qualities for crop growth [32].

4 Problem Statement and Formulation

4.1 Problem Statement

The problem aims to build the optimal agricultural planting strategy of a set of crops on a set of parcels or land areas. Each crop is characterized by its specific yield, its water consumption, its ecological benefit and its required number of wireless sensors. The ecological benefit of a crop refers to its environmental value in the ecosystem. This value is proportional to many characteristics such as: soil protection, climate regulation and biodiversity maintenance.

Besides the maximization of the ecological benefits of the planted crops, one of the objectives of the problem is to maximize the food security by maximizing the overall produced yield of crops. In addition, the overall water consumed and the total wireless sensors used in all parcels should be minimize.

4.2 Problem Formulation

Let be the following parameters:

I: the set of crops indexed by i.

J: the set of land areas indexed by j.

W: The total available water quantity.

A_j: the surface of are j.

W_{ij}: the consumed water quantity when the crop j is planted in the area j.

S_{ij}: the number of sensors to be located when the crop j is planted in the area j.

E_i: the ecological benefit per unit area from planting the crop i.

Y_i: the yield per unit area of crop i.

Let be the following decision variables:

$$Xij = \begin{cases} 1 \text{ if the crop i is planted in the area j} \\ 0 \text{ Otherwize} \end{cases}$$

The following objective function should be optimized:

$$\text{Max}f_1 = \sum\nolimits_{iCI} \sum\nolimits_{jCJ} Y_I A_j X_{IJ} \tag{1}$$

The objective f_1 the sum of the produced yield from all parcels, represent the food security to be maximized

$$Maxf_2 = \sum_{iCI} \sum_{jCJ} E_i A_j X_{ij} \tag{2}$$

The objective f_2 the sum of the ecological benefits of all parcels, represent the overall ecological benefit to be maximized.

$$Minf_3 = \sum_{iCI} \sum_{jCJ} W_{ij} X_{ij} \tag{3}$$

The objective f_3 represents the total quantity of water consumed by the crops in all parcels.

$$Minf_4 = \sum\nolimits_{iCI} \sum\nolimits_{jCJ} S_{ij} X_{ij} \tag{4}$$

The objective f_4, the sum of wireless sensors deployed in all parcels, represents the total investment cost for sensors deployment.

These goals are restricted by the following constraints:

$$\sum\nolimits_{iCI} X_{ij} = 1, \quad \forall j \in J \tag{5}$$

The constraint 5 ensures to plant one crop i at each parcel j.

$$\sum\nolimits_{iCI} \sum\nolimits_{jCJ} W_{ij} X_{ij} \leq W, \quad \forall j \in J \tag{6}$$

The constraint 6 guarantees to respect the total available quantity of water.

The problem aims to build.

5 Solution Method: Multi-objective Optimization

Scalarization method converts the multi-objective function to a single solution and determines the weight prior to the optimization process. As shown in the following equation, the scalarization method incorporates multi-objective functions into the scalar weighting factor [33].

$$F(x) = w_1 f_1(x) + w_2 f_2(x) + \ldots . + w_n f_n(x) \tag{7}$$

The weight assigned to an objective function determines the fitness function's solution and indicates the performance priority [34]. A large weight assigned to an objective function indicates that it is more important than those with a lower weight. Scalarization weights can be determined in three ways: RS weights, ROC weights, and equal weights [35].

The overall problem can be expressed according to Equation number (7) in the following compact form as a multi-objective linear programming model.

$$\begin{cases} Max\ F(x) \\ Subject\ to\ Eqs\ 5-6 \end{cases} \tag{8}$$

5.1 Equal Weights

The following equation can be used to calculate equal weights [36].

$$w_i = \frac{1}{n} \text{ where i} = 1, 2, \ldots, \text{n and} \tag{9}$$

n is the number of objective functions

It follows from Eq. (9) that $w_1 = w_2 = w_3 = w_4 = \frac{1}{4}$

5.2 Rank Order Centroid (ROC) Weights

ROC weights can be used to rank criteria. The following equation can be used to determine the ROC weights [37].

$$w_i = \frac{1}{n} \sum_{k=i}^{n} \frac{1}{k} \tag{10}$$

So the weights computed by Eq. (10):

$$w_1 = \frac{25}{48}, w_2 = \frac{13}{48}, w_3 = \frac{7}{48}, w_4 = \frac{1}{16}$$

5.3 Rank Sum (RS) Weights

Each criterion is assigned a proportional weight through the use of RS weights. The following equation can be used to calculate RS weights [37].

$$w_i = \frac{2 * (n + 1 - i)}{n(n + 1)} \tag{11}$$

Now we can derive the weights according to Eq. (11):

$$w_1 = \frac{2}{5}, w_2 = \frac{3}{10}, w_3 = \frac{1}{5}, w_4 = \frac{1}{10}$$

5.4 Epsilon-Constraint Method

The e-constraint method optimizes one of the several objective functions while incorporating as constraints the other objective functions, as illustrated below [38]. There are several advantages to the e-constraint method over the weighting method.

For linear problems, the weighting method is used to determine the initial feasible region, resulting in a corner solution (extreme solution), resulting in only efficient extreme solutions. On the other hand, the e-constraint method modifies the initial feasible region and is capable of producing solutions that are not extremely efficient.

In multi-objective integer and mixed integer programming problems, the weighting technique cannot yield unsupported efficient solutions, whereas the e-constraint method does not suffer from this limitation [39].

Scaling the objective functions significantly affects the produced results when applying the weighting approach. Therefore, prior to computing the weighted total, we must scale the goal functions to a common scale. This is unnecessary for the e-constrained technique.

Additionally, the e-constraint method allows us to manage the number of efficiently created solutions by altering the number of grid points in each of the objective function ranges appropriately. With the weighting approach, this is not as simple.

The e-constraint method is used to solve the multi-objective LP. As a result, the auxiliary single-objective models are formulated in the following concise manner.

$$Maxf_1(x)$$
$$Subject\ to \begin{cases} f_2(x) \le \varepsilon_2 \\ f_3(x) \le \varepsilon_3 \\ f_4(x) \le \varepsilon_4 \\ Eqs\ 5 - 6 \end{cases} \tag{12}$$

6 Solution Method: Marcos Method

Agricultural decisions are frequently made using a variety of criteria, some of which are subjective. Economic, environmental, and cultural considerations all play a role in these decisions. Using conventional methods, it can be challenging to trade-off these characteristics. Multiple criteria decision making (MCDM) is a structured, quantitative method for analyzing agricultural decisions that include all of these elements. MCDM divided into two main categories of multi-criteria decision making: (1) multi-attribute utility theory with additional weight value function (SAW, WASPAS) and (2) similarity/dissimilarity to the best/worst options using distance measurements (MABAC, CODAS, MARCOS). In the first group, the linear transformation retains the normalized assessments' relative ranking. The utility of options in the second group is proportional to their distance from the ideal and negative-ideal solutions for each attribute.

Six steps comprise the algorithm for evaluating alternatives and ranking them according to the optimal compromise solution (MARCOS) [40].

Step 1: An effort to develop a decision matrix. There are N alternatives and M criteria for making decision. Individual experts' evaluation matrices are combined into a collective decision matrix in group decision-making. The extended matrix is constructed by combining the primary matrix with ideal and anti-ideal solutions in the following order:

$$X = \begin{array}{c} \\ AAI \\ A_1 \\ A_2 \\ \dots \\ A_m \\ A_I \end{array} \begin{array}{c} \begin{array}{cccc} C_1 & C_2 & \dots & C_n \end{array} \\ \begin{bmatrix} x_{aa1} & x_{aa2} & & x_{aan} \\ x_{11} & x_{12} & \dots & x_{1n} \\ x_{21} & x_{22} & & x_{2n} \\ & \vdots & \ddots & \vdots \\ x_{m1} & x_{m2} & \dots & x_{mn} \\ x_{ai1} & x_{ai2} & & x_{ain} \end{bmatrix} \end{array} \tag{13}$$

The ideal and anti-ideal solutions are represented by the abbreviations AI and AAI respectively. The optimal solution is the one that maximizes the value of all available alternatives in terms of beneficial criteria. When a cost criteria is used, the optimal solution is the lowest possible value. The method is quite the reverse for the anti-ideal solution:

$$AI = \begin{cases} max\ x_{ij}, j \in B \\ min\ x_{ij}, j \in C \end{cases} \text{ And } AAI = \begin{cases} min\ x_{ij}, j \in B \\ max\ x_{ij}, j \in C \end{cases} \tag{14}$$

where B is the set of maximization criteria and C is the collection of minimization criteria.

Step 2: Normalization. The normalized matrix $N = [n_{ij}]_{N*M}$ is calculated as:

$$n_{ij} = \begin{cases} \frac{x_{ij}}{A_{Ai}}, \ j \in B \\ \frac{x_{Ai}}{x_{ij}}, \ j \in C \end{cases} \tag{15}$$

Step 3: Weighted matrix. The weighted matrix $V = [v_{ij}]_{N*M}$ is calculated in relation to the relative weights to the criteria:

$$v_{ij} = w_j * n_{ij} \tag{16}$$

For the extended matrix, weighted values are calculated.

Step 4: Utility degrees. The formulas calculate utility degrees for all alternatives based on the ideal and anti-ideal solution values.

$$S_i = \sum\nolimits_{i=1}^{n} v_{ij}, K^- = \frac{S_i}{S_{AAI}} \ And\ K^+ = \frac{S_i}{S_{AI}} \tag{17}$$

Step 5: Different utility positive and negative functions are calculated. Each alternative's utility function includes the following utility values and functions:

$$f\left(K_I^-\right) = \frac{K_I^+}{K_I^+ + K_I^-}, f\left(K_I^+\right) = \frac{K_I^-}{K_I^+ + K_I^-} \; And \; f\left(K_I\right) = \frac{K_I^+ + K_I^-}{1 + \frac{1-f\left(K_I^+\right)}{f\left(K_I^+\right)} + \frac{1-f\left(K_I^-\right)}{f\left(K_I^-\right)}} \tag{18}$$

Step 6: Ranking. The alternative ranking is based on the algorithm's utility function as defined in Step 5.

7 Computational Experiment

Our proposed mathematical model is intended to support decision and policy making by providing a set of optimal alternatives that present the different solutions obtained using MOO techniques (weighted sum and epsilon constraint). The proposed model had different useful guidelines for making the right rules, which will lead to a smarter agriculture sector in the long run.

Based on different research, we can see that the location of urban farming has not been studied using combined multi-objective optimization and multi-criteria decision making methods while taking the smart dimensions into consideration. The current paper addresses this research gap by combining MOO and MCDM approaches to locate a smart urban farm. The proposed model aimed to maximize the ecological benefits of the planted crops and increase food security by maximizing the overall produced yield of crops. In addition, minimize the overall water consumed and the total wireless sensors used in all parcels. Specifically, the present paper contributes to the literature as follows:

- We introduce a multi-objective linear programming model for the location of an urban farm using wireless sensor networks.
- We use scalarization techniques (weighted sum, epsilon constraint) to solve the mathematical model proposed.
- We implement the different solutions obtained from MOO in the MCDM method (Marcos) to rank the efficient solutions.

The CPLEX 12.10.0 solver was used to implement the LP model. The model includes 8 continuous variables and 6 equations. The amount of time it took to solve a case depended on the case, but it was always between 0 and 0.5 CPU seconds on the computer.

Using historical data from agricultural statistics in a Moroccan farm, the current number of crops (n) and number of parcels (m) were estimated to be equal, while taking into account the total amount of water available (w).The different result solutions using scalarization methods for solving our linear programming model are presented in Table 1.

We first determined by calculating the individual optimum for every objective to generate the -constraint bounds imposed on the objective functions. The range within which each objective function must fall was defined. For each objective function, three-constraint limits are obtained. Finally, the LP model was successively solved for every possible epsilon-constraint value combination. In the first step, we search to maximize food security. In the second, we look to boost the ecological benefit. In the third, we minimize the quantity of water consumed, and in the fourth, we expect to decrease the total investment cost for sensors while incorporating the other objective functions as constraints. Table 2 summarizes the results of the epsilon-constraint method.

In our illustrative example, we utilize a dataset of solutions given by the four approaches used for solving the linear programming model, collected from CPLEX. The dataset consists of 20 different solutions (A1, A2, … A20). The alternatives are as follows: A1–A5 Equal Sum solution, A6-A10 Rank Sum solution, A11–A15 Rank Sum Centroid solution, and A15–A20 Epsilon constraint solution The assessment dimensions include four criteria groups (C1,… C4). These criteria groups are associated with the various objective functions: C1 food security, C2 ecological benefit, C3 quantity of water consumed, and C4 total investment cost for sensors. The results given by the MARCOS method are presented in Table 3.

Table 1. Solutions using weighted sum method

		n = m = 4 w = 100	n = m = 8 w = 200	n = m = 10 w = 250	n = m = 12 w = 300	n = m = 16 w = 400	n = m = 20 w = 500	n = m = 24 w = 600	n = m = 28 w = 700	n = m = 30 w = 750
ES	f_1	455	760	950	1140	1520	1900	3240	3780	4050
	f_2	405	1080	1350	1620	2160	2700	3240	3780	4050
	f_3	93	114	242	174	238	258	328	348	658
	f_4	81	130	130	222	247	298	444	464	453
	f_{opt}	171.5	399	482	591	798.75	1011	1427	1687	1747.25
RS	f_1	515	760	1310	1500	2240	2800	3240	3780	4050
	f_2	360	1080	870	1140	1200	1500	3240	3780	4050
	f_3	95	114	182	171	228	248	328	348	658
	f_4	101	130	195	195	262	313	444	464	453
	f_{opt}	284.9	592.2	729.2	888.3	1184.2	1489.1	2158	2530	2568.1
ROC	f_1	560	1030	1400	1680	2240	2800	3240	3780	4050
	f_2	300	720	750	900	1200	1500	3240	3780	4050
	f_3	96	178	182	171	228	248	328	348	658
	f_4	107	126	194	195	262	313	444	464	453
	f_{opt}	352.23	697.62	893.62	1081.62	1442.04	1808.85	2489.42	2912.75	3081.98

Table 2. Solutions using epsilon-constraint method

		f_1	f_2	f_3	f_4	f_{opt}
Max f_1	$\varepsilon_2 = 200, \varepsilon_3 = 100, \varepsilon_4 = 150$	400	200	58	74	400
	$\varepsilon_2 = 250, \varepsilon_3 = 100, \varepsilon_4 = 150$	480	250	63	92	480
	$\varepsilon_2 = 300, \varepsilon_3 = 100, \varepsilon_4 = 150$	560	300	96	107	560
	$\varepsilon_2 = 400, \varepsilon_3 = 100, \varepsilon_4 = 200$	560	300	96	107	560
	$\varepsilon_2 = 200, \varepsilon_3 = 100, \varepsilon_4 = 80$	400	200	58	74	400
Max f_2	$\varepsilon_1 = 560, \varepsilon_3 = 90, \varepsilon_4 = 100$	355	425	89	63	425
	$\varepsilon_1 = 560, \varepsilon_3 = 150, \varepsilon_4 = 80$	370	440	96	63	440
	$\varepsilon_1 = 560, \varepsilon_3 = 90, \varepsilon_4 = 200$	355	425	89	63	425
	$\varepsilon_1 = 560, \varepsilon_3 = 60, \varepsilon_4 = 100$	380	270	59	74	270
	$\varepsilon_1 = 560, \varepsilon_3 = 100, \varepsilon_4 = 150$	395	450	95	90	450
Min f_3	$\varepsilon_1 = 450, \varepsilon_2 = 300, \varepsilon_4 = 800$	440	225	57	65	57
	$\varepsilon 1 = 560, \varepsilon_2 = 300, \varepsilon_4 = 107$	440	225	57	65	57
	$\varepsilon 1 = 1030, \varepsilon_2 = 720, \varepsilon_4 = 130$	440	225	57	65	57
	$\varepsilon 1 = 350, \varepsilon_2 = 490, \varepsilon_4 = 90$	340	410	89	67	89
	$\varepsilon 1 = 400, \varepsilon_2 = 520, \varepsilon_4 = 80$	400	200	58	74	58
Min f_4	$\varepsilon_1 = 500, \varepsilon_2 = 300, \varepsilon_3 = 90$	420	295	67	61	61
	$\varepsilon_1 = 500, \varepsilon_2 = 300, \varepsilon_3 = 70$	420	295	67	61	61
	$\varepsilon_1 = 440, \varepsilon_2 = 220, \varepsilon_3 = 60$	400	200	58	74	74
	$\varepsilon_1 = 1000, \varepsilon_2 = 820, \varepsilon_3 = 180$	415	380	87	54	54
	$\varepsilon_1 = 1000, \varepsilon_2 = 820, \varepsilon_3 = 150$	415	380	87	54	54

Table 3. Result of MARCOS method.

Ai	Si	K-	K+	F(k-)	F(k +)	F(k)	Rank
AAI	0.582198						
A1	0.453544	4.7423916	0.7790197	0.141090	0.858909	0.1543085	8
A2	0.267960	2.8018753	0.4602564	0.141090	0.858909	0.1703649	6
A3	0.210292	2.1988801	0.3612040	0.141090	0.858909	0.1255502	16
A4	0.178123	1.8625132	0.3059499	0.141090	0.858909	0.2397623	3
A5	0.134029	1.4014516	0.2302126	0.141090	0.858909	0.2178508	4
A6	0.410236	4.2895553	0.7046336	0.141090	0.858909	0.1515926	9

(continued)

Table 3. (*continued*)

Ai	Si	K-	K+	F(k-)	F(k +)	F(k)	Rank
A7	0.267960	2.8018753	0.4602564	0.141090	0.858909	0.1471977	11
A8	0.165077	1.7260954	0.2835410	0.141090	0.858909	0.1500773	10
A9	0.144547	1.5114325	0.2482789	0.141090	0.858909	0.0919984	18
A10	0.101247	1.0586695	0.1739047	0.141090	0.858909	0.1448873	12
A11	0.389548	4.0732298	0.6690983	0.141090	0.858909	0.1758849	5
A12	0.207374	2.1683645	0.3561913	0.141090	0.858909	0.1667298	7
A13	0.158868	1.6611799	0.2728775	0.141090	0.858909	0.2995568	2
A14	0.194277	2.0314175	0.3336954	0.141090	0.858909	0.1377204	13
A15	0.101247	1.0586695	0.1739047	0.141090	0.858909	0.1164313	17
A16	0.554802	5.8011805	0.9529441	0.141090	0.858909	0.0744135	19
A17	0.402251	4.2060584	0.6909177	0.141090	0.858909	0.0616015	20
A18	0.559760	5.8530223	0.9614600	0.141090	0.858909	0.1299871	15
A19	0.508848	5.3206687	0.8740118	0.141090	0.858909	0.1305939	14
A20	0.498453	5.2119732	0.8561566	0.141090	0.858909	0.5678348	1
AI	0.095636						

8 Conclusion

WSNs are currently attracting considerable interest in agriculture. The analysis of data collected on the farm plays a critical part in agricultural cultivation. Sensor technology was primarily used to assist farmers in making decisions and scheduling production operations such as irrigation or plant protection, as well as assigning pesticides or nutrients based on sensor observed needs. Other sensors gathered data that could be used to determine the success of a production. An optimized strategy for planting a set of crops on a collection of land areas can certainly help in reducing the environmental impact of water consumption and the investment cost of sensors. The strategy contributes to the transformation towards a more sustainable agricultural system in the concept of Agriculture 4.0. The main purpose of this study is to develop a systematic decision-support tool exploring the MARCOS method. The task of identifying an optimal agriculture strategy was mathematically formulated as a multi-objective linear programming problem that seeks to reduce water consumption and the investment cost for sensors while simultaneously enhancing the food security and the ecological benefit of crops. However, it may also be noted that despite the use of wireless sensor networks in agricultural locations, many farms are unable to harness the power of smart technologies to generate useful information for their operations. The reasons are due to a lack of exploring the real data sources of farms and the use of erroneous data. This paper has a number of limitations. Like, the papers selected in this study were identified through a manual search in the digital databases, which is very sensitive to the input keywords. There is a possibility that publications with subtly different keywords would be missed, and also the difficulty in which different journals and academic papers can be accessed. Our future research will focus on the implementation of the specified solution and further incorporating mobility into sensors. Optimize cost and energy efficiency as a reduced number of sensors will be able to cover the same plot.

References

1. Food and Agriculture Organization. The Future of Food and Agriculture Trends and Challenges; Food and Agriculture Organization of the United Nations. Rome, Italy (2017)
2. Trendov, N.M., Varas, S., Zeng, M.: Digital Technologies in Agriculture and Rural Areas: Status Report. Rome, Italy (2019)
3. Rose, D.C., Chilvers, J.: Agriculture 4.0: broadening responsible innovation in an era of smart farming. Front. Sust. Food Syst. **2**, 87 (2018)
4. Davenport, T.H.: Analytics 3.0. Harvard Bus. Rev. **91**(12), 64–72 (2013)
5. Azapagic, A., Clift, R.: Life cycle assessment and multi objective optimization. J. Clean. Prod. **7**, 135–143 (1999)
6. García, N., Fernlandez-Torres, M.J., Caballero, J.A.: Simultaneous environmental and economic process synthesis of isobutane alkylation. J. Clean. Prod. **81**, 270–280 (2014)
7. Azapagic, A., Perdan, S.: An integrated sustainability decision-support framework Part II: problem analysis. Int. J. Sust. Dev. World **12**, 112–131 (2005)
8. Xevi, E., Khan, S.: A multi-objective optimisation approach to water management. J. Environ. Manage. **77**, 269–277 (2005)
9. Chen, Z.J., Cheng, Z.J., Yan, X.Q.: Multi objective optimization problem of multi reservoir system in semiarid areas. Math. Probl. Eng. (2013)
10. Dury, J., Schaller, N., Garcia, F., Reynaud, A., Bergez, J.E.: Models to support cropping plan and crop rotation decisions. A review. Agron. Sustain. Dev. **32**, 67–580 (2011)
11. Khoshnevisan, B., Bolandnazar, E., Shamshirband, S., Shariati, H.M., Anuar, N.B., Mat Kiah, M.L.: Decreasing environmental impacts of cropping systems using life cycle assessment (LCA) and multi-objective genetic algorithm. J. Clean. Prod. **86**, 67–77 (2015)
12. Prodanović, R., et al.: Wireless sensor network in agriculture: model of cyber security. Sensors **20**(23), 6747 (2020)
13. Araújo, S.O., Peres, R.S., Barata, J., Lidon, F., Ramalho, J.C.: Characterising the agriculture 4.0 landscape- emerging trends, challenges and opportunities. Agronomy **11**(4), 667 (2021)
14. Durga, P., Narayanan, G., Gayathri, B., Ramesh, M.V., Divya, P.: Modelling a smart agriculture system for multiple cropping using wireless sensor networks. In: 2017 Global Humanitarian Technology Conference (GHTC), pp.1–7. IEEE (2017)
15. Wu, C.H., Lu, C.Y., Zhan, J.W., Wu, H.T.: Using long short-term memory for building outdoor agricultural machinery. Front. Neurorobot. **14**, 27 (2020)
16. Thessler, S., Kooistra, L., Teye, F., Huitu, H., Bregt, A.K.: Geosensors to support crop production: Current applications and user requirements. Sensors **11**(7), 6656–6684 (2011)
17. Díaz, S.E., Pérez, J.C., Mateos, A.C., Marinescu, M.C., Guerra, B.B.: A novel methodology for the monitoring of the agricultural production process based on wireless sensor networks. Comput. Electron. Agric. **76**(2), 252–265 (2011)
18. Kim, Y.D., Yang, Y.M., Kang, W.S., Kim, D.K.: On the design of beacon based wireless sensor network for agricultural emergency monitoring systems. Comput. Stand. Interfaces **36**(2), 288–299 (2014)
19. Ojha, T., Misra, S., Raghuwanshi, N.S.: Wireless sensor networks for agriculture: the state-of-the-art in practice and future challenges. Comput. Electron. Agric. **118**, 66–84 (2015)

20. Abbasi, A.Z., Islam, N., Shaikh, Z.A.: A review of wireless sensors and networks' applications in agriculture. Comput. Stand. Interfaces **36**(2), 263–270 (2014)
21. Talavera, J.M., et al.: Review of IoT applications in agro-industrial and environmental fields. Comput. Electron. Agric. **142**, 283–297 (2017)
22. Fujimoto, Y., Murakami, S., Kaneko, N., Fuchikami, H., Hattori, T., Hayashi, Y.: Machine learning approach for graphical model-based analysis of energy-aware growth control in plant factories. IEEE Access **7**, 32183–32196 (2019)
23. Lottes, P., Behley, J., Milioto, A., Stachniss, C.: Fully convolutional networks with sequential information for robust crop and weed detection in precision farming. IEEE Robotics and Automation Letters **3**(4), 2870–2877 (2018)
24. Shi, X., et al.: State-of-the-art internet of things in protected agriculture. Sensors **19**(8), 1833 (2019)
25. Farooq, M.S., Riaz, S., Abid, A., Umer, T., Zikria, Y.B.: Role of IoT technology in agriculture: a systematic literature review. Electronics **9**(2), 319 (2020)
26. Sushanth, G., Sujatha, S.: IOT based smart agriculture system: In 2018 International Conference on Wireless Communications, Signal Processing and Networking (WiSPNET). pp. 1–4. IEEE (2018)
27. Dagar, R., Som, S., Khatri, S.K.: Smart farming–IoT in agriculture: In: 2018 International Conference on Inventive Research in Computing Applications (ICIRCA), pp. 1052–1056. IEEE (2018)
28. Belaud, J. P., Prioux, N., Vialle, C., Sablayrolles, C.: Big data for agri-food 4.0: application to sustainability management for by-products supply chain. Computers in Industry **111**, 41–50 (2019)
29. Lezoche, M., Hernandez, J. E., Díaz, M. D. M. E. A., Panetto, H., & Kacprzyk, J. : Agri-food 4.0: a survey of the supply chains and technologies for the future agriculture. Comput. Industry **117**, 103187 (2020)
30. Wolfert, S., Ge, L., Verdouw, C., Bogaardt, M.J.: Big data in smart farming–a review. Agric. Syst. **153**, 69–80 (2017)
31. Weersink, A., Fraser, E., Pannell, D., Duncan, E., Rotz, S.: Opportunities and challenges for big data in agricultural and environmental analysis. Ann. Rev. Resour. Econ. **10**, 19–37 (2018)
32. Ratnaparkhi, S., et al.: Smart agriculture sensors in IOT: a review. Materials Today: Proceedings (2020)
33. Murata, T., Ishibuchi, H., Tanaka, H.: Multi-objective genetic algorithm and its applications to flowshop scheduling. Comput. Ind. Eng. **30**(4), 957–968 (1996)
34. I. Dodgson, J.S., Spackman, M., Pearman, A., Phillips, L.D.: Multi-criteria analysis: a manual (2009)
35. Jia, J., Fischer, G.W., Dyer, J.S.: Attribute weighting methods and decision quality in the presence of response error: a simulation study. J. Behav. Decis. Mak. **11**(2), 85–105 (1998)
36. Linear models in decision making: Dawes, R. M., & dan Corrigan, B. Psychol. Bull. **81**, 95–106 (1974)
37. Einhorn, H.J., McCoach, W.: A simple multi attribute utility procedure for evaluation. Behav. Sci. **22**(4), 270–282 (1977)
38. Vira, C., Haimes, Y.Y.: Multiobjective decision making: theory and methodology. North-Holland Ser. Syst. Sci. Eng. 62–109 (1983)
39. Miettinen, K.M.: Nonlinear Multi objective Optimization. Kluwer Academic Publishers, Boston (1998)
40. Ilieva, G., Yankova, T., Radeva, I., Popchev, I.: Blockchain software selection as a fuzzy multi-criteria problem. Computers **10**(10), 120 (2021)
41. Ratnaparkhi, S., et al.: Smart agriculture sensors in IOT: A review. Materials Today: Proceedings (2020)

42. Xue, D., Huang, W.: Smart agriculture wireless sensor routing protocol and node location algorithm based on Internet of Things technology. IEEE Sens. J. **21**(22), 24967–24973 (2020)
43. Lin, J., Wang, M., Zhang, M., Zhang, Y., Chen, L.: Electrochemical sensors for soil nutrient detection: opportunity and challenge. In: Li, Daoliang (ed.) CCTA 2007. TIFIP, vol. 259, pp. 1349–1353. Springer, Boston, MA (2008). https://doi.org/10.1007/978-0-387-77253-0_77
44. Navulur, S., Prasad, M.G.: Agricultural management through wireless sensors and internet of things. Int. J. Electr. Comput. Eng. **7**(6), 3492 (2017)
45. Tirkolaee, E.B., Mahmoodkhani, J., Bourani, M.R., Tavakkoli-Moghaddam, R.: A self-learning particle swarm optimization for robust multi-echelon capacitated location–allocation–inventory problem. J. Adv. Manuf. Syst. **18**(04), 677–694 (2019)
46. Khalili-Damghani, K., Tavana, M., Ghasemi, P.: A stochastic bi-objective simulation–optimization model for cascade disaster location-allocation-distribution problems. Ann. Oper. Res. **309**(1), 103–141 (2021). https://doi.org/10.1007/s10479-021-04191-0
47. Theeraviriya, C., Sirirak, W., Praseeratasang, N.: Location and routing planning considering electric vehicles with restricted distance in agriculture. World Electric Vehicle J. **11**(4), 61(2020)
48. Ahmadi Choukolaei, H., Jahangoshai Rezaee, M., Ghasemi, P., Saberi, M.: Efficient crisis management by selection and analysis of relief centers in disaster integrating GIS and multicriteria decision methods: a case study of Tehran. Mathematical Problems in Engineering, (2021)
49. Oudani, M., Zkik, K.: Fuzzy Single-commodity model in Wireless Sensor Networks. Procedia Comput. Sci. **160**, 797–802 (2019)
50. El Hamdi, S., Abouabdellah, A., & Oudani, M.: Efficient Simulated Annealing Algorithm for Wireless Sensors Location in Logistics 4.0: In October 2020 5th International Conference on Logistics Operations Management (GOL), pp. 1–6, IEEE (2020)
51. El Hamdi, S., Oudani, M., Abouabdellah, A., Sebbar, A.: Fuzzy approach for locating sensors in industrial internet of things. Procedia Comput. Sci. **160**, 772–777 (2019)

Toward a Secure Industry 4.0: An SDN-Assisted Approach "SSI4"

Sara Lahlou[1(✉)], Mohammed Boulmalf[1], and Karim Zkik[2]

[1] TICLab, International University of Rabat, Rabat, Morocco
sara.lahlou@uir.ac.ma

[2] ESAIP Graduate School of Engineering, Angers, France

Abstract. Industry 4.0 is the technology trend that goes beyond the widespread of digital transformation in industries. It involves facilitating manufacturing through integrating Industrial Internet of Things (IIoT) to achieve higher manufacturing performance. Indeed, smart factories are equipped with sensors, actuators, and systems connected to Internet so that they can control their own manufacturing process. Moreover, the entire Industry 4.0 ecosystem is permeated by Artificial Intelligence (AI) to optimize the manufacturing operations to better interact with market changes. However, with the high connected systems using Internet, the manufacturing cyber security may be faced to significant threats with the emergence of IoT. In this paper, we propose a new approach to better manage cyberthreats related to highly connected systems in Industry 4.0. It is based on an efficient combination of the technologies of IoT, and SDN to improve the security and privacy of Industry 4.0 operations properly. Our proposed model namely "Secure-SDN-I4" (SSI4) incorporates a Machine Learning (ML) module that detects IIoT attacks. Then, SDN controller manages traffic through specific policy rules to block attacks and redirect benign flow packets to appropriate destinations.

Keywords: IIoT · SDN · ML · Security · Privacy · Industry 4.0

1 Introduction

Internet of Things (IoT) is the technology that turns common objects into connected devices through Internet. These objects are capable to detect inputs from the surrounding environment [1] and to produce outputs regarding specific purposes of sensing. As an extension of IoT, IIoT connects devices and sensors for a better production visibility and understanding of the manufacturing process [2]. Thus, enabling efficient and sustainable production. This smart manufacturing is known as Industry 4.0 [3] and is used interchangeably with the fourth industrial revolution. It represents a new concept in the industrial management chain as it makes use of digital technology, and data analysis techniques to create a highly connected ecosystem while ensuring flexibility and scalability. Also, to enhance the effectiveness of manufacturing operations, Artificial Intelligence (AI) [4] has been embedded to them for a better interaction while dealing with market changes. However, existing technologies are vulnerable to new forms of

A. Mirzazadeh et al. (Eds.): SEMIT 2022, CCIS 1808, pp. 383–396, 2023.
https://doi.org/10.1007/978-3-031-40395-8_27

security issues e.g.: Sinkhole attacks [5], False Routing Information attacks [6], and Transfer data from and to unauthorized devices [7], etc. [8]. IIoT can throttle the data collected from industrial environment but not securely and conveniently. This can badly affect Industrial Control Systems and sometimes the entire business model. Thus, companies are more likely to fall under the loss of competitiveness in the market. For that, adopters of Industry 4.0 technologies are in great need of new flexible management tools to better handle current security problems. Several studies [10] have investigated the importance of improving industry 4.0 security [11]. Some of them, have proposed the idea of integration of Software Defined Networking (SDN) to address the challenge of controlling and managing data securely [9]. SDN controls data traffic through multiple central controllers thanks to programmability. Indeed, it relies on managing automatically IIoT devices using specific applications for a better efficiency. Utilizing IIoT and SDN technologies all together contribute to reach a higher degree of performance and security in Industry 4.0.

In this vein, many works suggested security techniques to benefit from the fusion of SDN and Industry 4 such as physical and classical security methods [12]. However, those techniques remain very traditional and are usually tailored to address specific threats under specific network circumstances. Now, cyber attackers are adopting more sophisticated tools to success in their intrusion operations. Thus, they make the activity very dynamic and unpredictable. Therefore, more intelligent security techniques are needed to ensure a robust protection in the manufacturing system towards advanced cyber-attacks. Indeed, studies have proven that AI capabilities result in more safeguarded structures.

After analyzing previous studies, we propose in this paper a model namely "Secure-SDN-I4" based on Machine Learning (ML) techniques to ensure adequate security which is the primary concern in industry 4.0. This model combines data processing, analysis, security, and monitoring. The main contributions of this paper are following:

- This study proposes a framework namely "Secure-SDN-I4" focused on Industry 4.0 with the help of SDN and ML technologies to detect malicious behaviors in IIoT.
- We also address the issue of self-responsiveness to attacks as it can provide mitigation solution to secure in Industry 4.0 services.

The remaining sections of the paper are structured as follows. We present Background Study and Literature Review in Sect. 2. Section 3 highlights the proposed SDN-assisted approach (SSI4) for securing Industry 4.0. Finally, this work concludes with future ramifications in Sect. 4.

2 Background Study and Literature Review

2.1 Background Study

In this section, we discuss the background knowledge of Industry 4.0 concept and its security challenges. Then, we briefly outline main benefits of SDN technology in Industry 4.0 domain application.

Overview of Industry 4.0 Concept: The progression of Industry has gone through various stages over the past centuries. The First Industrial Revolution Namely Industry

1.0 has started at the end of the eighteenth century. It has introduced mechanical production facilities using steam power, weaving loom and mechanization. The powered machines have significantly increased human productivity and helped workers in the mass production of goods [13]. Industry 2.0 was the Second Industrial Revolution that began in the nineteenth century. The keys of this revolution were machines running on electrical energy. This allowed factories to develop modern and massive production lines. In the early twentieth century, Industry 3.0 was introduced through the development of new automated systems onto the assembly. It was a partial automation that made use of Programmable Logic Controllers (PLC), computers and electronics to perform human tasks. Even though automated systems were in use, they still relied on human input and intervention [14]. Lately, the Fourth Industrial Revolution known as Industry 4.0. Has integrated the application of information and communication technologies to industry. Internet connects all systems within multiple cyber-physical production systems that forms smart factories. Communication between machines and workers is implemented via IIoT to form networks with autonomous systems. Baheti and Gill in [15] defined cyber-physical system as "a new generation of systems with integrated computational and physical capabilities that can interact with humans through many new modalities."

Security challenges in Industry 4.0 With IIoT at the heart of this new movement, the control of manufacturing methods provides boundless opportunities in automation and optimization. Besides the numerous possibilities created by this revolution, a big challenge of security issues is faced. Indeed, cyber-threats are threatening many companies committing to Industry 4.0 paradigm. A recent survey by Lezzi et al. in [8] summarizes different types of cyber-threats that threaten IIoT (e.g., Transfer data from and to unauthorized devices, Denial of Service (DoS) attack, Distributed DoS (DDoS) attack, Escalation of privilege [16], man-in-the-middle (MITM) attacks, Eavesdropping, etc.). Security of Industrial Control Systems should be guaranteed to avoid these cyber-attacks. For that, various countermeasure methods can be taken such as particular actions and procedures within the target network, and techniques opposing potential threats or vulnerabilities.

SDN Approach In Industry 4.0 Application: SDN is an evolving technology that enables the implementation of a secure manufacturing environment. Indeed, low-level computing functions in SDN are more effective and authentication functions are embedded in the network rather than centralized in individual network component. As a result, the primary goal of implementing SDN is to reduce response time and provide continuous availability. This technology was applied to different domains including smart buildings, grids, healthcare, and industries, among others. Furthermore, research into security mechanisms and the development of enhanced confidentiality defense strategies to prevent multiple attacks in industrial networks are crucial for IIoT [17]. Indeed, SDN has brought very competitive advantages to industries in terms of management. This new network architecture consists of decoupling control plane and data plane while offering programmability that helps evolving networking services [9]. As we were particularly intrigued by resolving IIoT security threats, we aimed to deploy SDN to better manage cyber traffic passing through the multitudinous industrial systems. SDN controller provides a high-level view about the overall network. Therefore, IIoT attacks can be eliminated and prevented by minimizing the harm that might be caused and reporting it so that corrective action can be taken.

2.2 Literature Review

This section gathers related works in recent years discussing the concept of Industry 4.0 and its security challenges. Then, we presented studies focused on the approach of incorporating SDN in Industry 4.0 for security purposes as it safeguards the entire industrial network infrastructure and offers a rigorous network domain visibility.

These recent years, the development of manufacturing has increased the deployment of several Cyber Physical Systems (CPS) that improve production processes. Efficiency of these systems can be achieved by supporting the process of collecting and analyzing data from different distributed sources (machines, devices). In [18] contribution, authors cited some important criteria to control industrial processes such as: reliable and secure communication infrastructure, monitoring of the manufacturing process, and control and synchronization of work. Mazur et al. in [18] proposed a model of rapid distributed prototyping with greater emphasis on the control of the communication environment, which is built based on SDN model. A resilient network capable of self-monitoring, detecting problems, altering flows, doing calculations, and communicating with other components is critical to supporting Industry 4.0. As security is a very important criteria within a reliable factory, many of the technologies underlying this trend of industry, from Cyber Physical Systems (CPS) to the IIoT using machine-to-machine (M2M) communication protocols, need to be protected.

Traditional network designs have various limitations in terms of flexibility, and accessibility, which can be exacerbated in industrial contexts where diverse devices, machine tools, and industry-specific protocols must coexist. According to [22] work, the key limitations of traditional networks are the slowness in implementing new services and necessity to purchase dedicated hardware components to provide specific functionalities. However, difficulty in service utilization leads to duplication of labor and money. This is where SDN paradigm steps in. It improves the management [20] of security features of the whole industrialized infrastructure. Indeed, from its inception, one of its main goals is making security policies more controllable [11]. Also, it was presented in [38] that SDN with many controllers from the data layer to the control layer to the application layer, has the ability to ensure equal load allocation among devices, controllers, and efficiently to reduce packet losses. Recent studies in the literature have revealed a plethora of potential threats in the modern industrial environment. In this part, we have been inspired from [21] to provide an overview of Industry 4.0 vulnerabilities. Examples of possible cyber-attacks in this field are categorized into three target surfaces: devices, systems, and networks. Table 1 depicts the more important attacks in Industry 4.0.

Tsuchiya et al. [1] proposed an SDN Firewall that modifies filtering rules to implement distinct network segments based on application-level access control criteria. The Firewall employs the two filtering approaches: temporal filtering and spatial filtering, allowing only apps on a whitelist to connect to industrial control devices. This greatly simplifies network management responsibilities, but it is limited to ICS networks. Anichur et al. [2] proposed a model namely "DistB-SDoIndustry" based on developing technologies such as SDN-IoT and Blockchain for managing the numerous Industry 4.0 applications in a secure manner. However, this proposal needs to be evaluated and tested for more accuracy. Metrics than need to be considered are throughput, packet arrival rate, the response time of data, etc. Another work [17] discussed Industry 4.0 threats that may be faced while deploying Software defined IIoT as a centralized control system, with new data being forwarded to the controllers on a regular basis, which can cause forwarding delays and even packet loss. However, to guarantee the network programmability, system control apps must be given a lot of access privileges, which raises the chances of a system crash.

In summary, existing research have focused on many branches of IIoT-SDN technologies. But only a few numbers of researchers [40] have addressed security challenges in the context of Industry 4.0 in a dynamic manner. Through the analysis of literature, we can presume that very few researches have discussed the use of SDN to improve security in I4. In fact, related works mainly consider monitoring IoT from remote location through the SDN controller, or securing cloud storage through blockchain-based SDN, or adopting a policy checker approach to detect intrusions, or simply applying firewalling rules through SDN controller and OF switches. The gap in research appears in the lack of detection and mitigation methods of dynamic cyber threats in industry 4.0. For that, we attempt through this study to minimize challenges by proposing a secure architecture for Industry 4.0 using ML techniques. The following Table 1. Gives a summary of important attacks in Industry 4.0.

3 Proposed SDN-Assisted Approach (SSI4) for Securing Industry 4.0

This study proposes a new reference model namely "Secure-SDN-I4" to detect malicious behaviors in smart factories. We also address the issue of self-responsiveness to attacks as it can provide mitigation solution in a timely manner to secure I4 services. Figure 1 presents our proposed security framework. Basically, wired, and wireless IIoT sensors and actuators are capable of sensing data for specific applications. CPS such as robotics systems are working together to perform data processing. These systems that are intensively connected with the surrounding physical IIoT, are continuously exchanging traffic through the internal network system. Data traffic is handled by several SDN switches depending on the size of the production line. Then, OpenFlow switches are controlled by SDN controllers through Southbound Application Programming Interface (API) by injecting policy rules in OpenFlow switches.

Table 1. Important attacks in Industry 4.0.

Target Surface	Attack type	Explanation	References
Devices	Physical attack	Physical access to the manufacturing environment (change the location of the device, break the electric power of device)	[8]23
	Measurement Injection Attack	Injecting a falsified data to the sensors to modify the process measurements (e.g., Open Valve Attack)	[24]
	Side-channel attack	Gathering sensitive information from equipment by measuring side channel information (e.g., energy consumption, electromagnetic leaks) or recreating the same object by capturing physical-domain data (e.g., vibration, magnetic, power, etc.) of a 3D printing	[23]
	Time delay attack	Adding extra time delays into measurements of a sensor/actuator can make it crash which may disturb the stability of the whole industrial control system	[25]
	Application protocol attacks	Sending fake commands to damage devices through application protocol	[26]

(*continued*)

Table 1. (*continued*)

Target Surface	Attack type	Explanation	References
	The False logic attack	Injecting incorrect data values or modifying received data from sensors which may affect the execution logic of the system	[26]
	The Stuxnet attack	A complex computer worm targeting the industrial control execution by deviating the PLCs from its expected behaviors causing an entirely re-programming of micro-controllers	[27]
	The Deception attack	The attacker operates in a way that makes the worker accept as true an incorrect scenario to degrade system performance	[28] [29]
	The DOS attacks	Denial of Service could affect all control service devices such as SCADA servers, DCS controllers, OPC server, OPC client and smart meters, etc. (e.g., Slammer worm: a DOS attack targeting nuclear power plant in US that disabled the monitoring system for five hours)	[30]
	Zero-Day Attacks	The term "Zero-day" refers to an unknown system vulnerability that were recently discovered by hackers and were not disclosed publicly	[31]

(*continued*)

Table 1. (*continued*)

Target Surface		Attack type	Explanation	References
Network	Wired communications	Unauthorized access	It leads to: Report Server information, Force control devices into listen-only mode, Clear counters and diagnostic registers and remotely restart systems (e.g., Replay Attack, Brute Force Attack and Dictionary Attack)	[32]
		DoS	Unavailability of network resources due to the establishment of many network connections (e.g., TCP SYN Attack)	[26]
		Man in the middle attack (MITM)	When the attacker listens to the communication between two legitimate users and forges the exchanges in a way that allows him to pass as one of the legitimate parties	[33]
		Packet modification attack	Attacker can introduce abnormal operations if some packets have a function code less then, the normal function code. This causes system crash and buffer overflow by modifying the Manufacturing Message Specification (MMS) packet	[4]

(*continued*)

Table 1. (*continued*)

Target Surface		Attack type	Explanation	References
	Wireless communications	Jamming attack	It is a type of DoS attack that can chunk all communications by interfering with signal transmission. It involves directing electromagnetic energy at network infrastructure components	[34]
		Collision attack	This attack makes the destination request the re-transmission by modifying the checksum of a sent message	[35]
		Fake Location Injection	When attacker injects fake location coordinates in the network nodes which causes chaos in nodes trajectories	[36]
		Sybil attack	Malicious nodes can use fake identities to generate additional node identities through some devices. Then, attacker can use them to gain a disproportionately large influence on the network communication	[35]
		Node Replication attack	Replay attack can be used to build trust in network through inserting one or more cloned node to the network	[32]

(*continued*)

Table 1. (*continued*)

Target Surface		Attack type	Explanation	References
		Wormhole attack	A tunnel is established between two nodes and the packet is forwarded among each other. These remote malicious nodes pretend to be very close to each other so that neighbor nodes route packets through them	[37]
		Sinkhole attack	It happens when a compromised node sends fake information to its neighbors to redirect network traffic to himself	[27]
		False Routing Information attack	When an attacker impersonates another node by falsifying the identity field in routing messages. A malicious node can change the entire network topology. It allows to exhaust the node resources or increasing latency	[36]
		Selective Forwarding attack	It occurs when a malicious node drops some packets originated from some selected nodes and forwards the remaining traffic	[35]
		Information in Transit attack	The attacker can gather and listen in on the data stream transmitted between nodes. As a result of this assault, the system is exposed to sniffer, modification, injection…	[23]

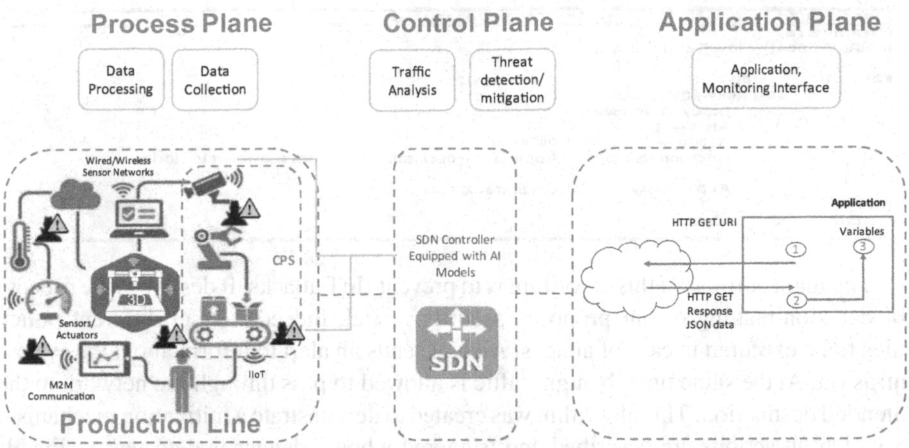

On the other hand, SDN controller is administered by applications through northbound APIs. They communicate behaviors and intended tasks to the controller to be then, processed by switches. When attackers gain access to devices or network, SDN helps to prevent them from harming the production line. It ensures data security through its flexibility and openness to new security features. In this model, we introduce a security module based on ML techniques to perform traffic analysis and threat detection. The primary objective of this module is to counteract Industry 4.0 cyber-attacks. Once IIoT threats are detected, it takes appropriate action. In other words, thanks to the SDN ability of centralization and programmability, it can prevent attacks from affecting the network behavior. For example, if traffic seems to be normal, the controller gives an order to the SDN switch to forward the data flow to its destination. However, if there is an anomaly in the traffic flow, a copy of the traffic flow is sent to the central controller to initiate the attack mitigation process. For that, the controller injects the suitable actions to the forwarding device to be performed to prevent the attack. Finally, to avoid manual configurations risks, we deployed rule automation using API scripts to better manage the huge number of cyber-attacks. Our security policy is based on articulating high-level policies in the way described in Algorithm 1. The controller analysis is regulated through policy rules to block attacks and allow forwarding benign traffic. For every attack, we set an alert followed by a specific action to be processed. For example, when a DoS attack is detected, the action is set to drop packets and close connection. Our proposal addresses these issues and offers high security solutions. It employs a system for detecting IIoT attacks using DT and RF classifiers, as well as a strategy for mitigating them using rule-based policy enforcement. It aids in the rapid detection of IIoT device assaults and the initiation of relevant mitigation procedures.

```
Algorithm 1 : Secure-SDN-I4 Threat Detection and Mitigation
Parameters
Input: Attack [] , Flow [] and Policy []

For i = 0, ...... , 3 do
        if (Attack== true) then
                policy_defense(i):
                Alert ← 1;
                Action ← Execute (Policy);
                Decision_Script(); // Apply Get/Post instructions from controller to Nodes
        Else
                Action ← Allow;  // Benign traffic flow
End
Output: Decision_script();
```

The main purpose of this algorithm is to prevent IIoT attacks. It describes the process for decision-making of our proposed security model. Indeed, we set different policy rules to be executed in case of attacks. Also, it sends an alert to inform about the system intrusion. At the same time, benign traffic is allowed to pass through the network to the intended destination. This algorithm was created to demonstrate a mitigation mechanism in which all actions are described and triggered when a danger is detected. In Fig. 1, the controller is in charge of the detection and mitigation process. The latter contains functions that make traffic-flow decisions. If the traffic is harmless, it is transmitted. When it is malignant, however, the right action is taken. Our threat detection modules detect several types of IIoT attacks, such as encryption assaults, network attacks, and software attacks, to do this.

4 Conclusion

This paper presents a model "Secure-SDN-I4" (SSI4) based on SDN technology and ML techniques for securing Industry 4.0 infrastructure. Basically, we have considered this work as a reference model to improve data security and confidentiality. Furthermore, this paper has implemented SDN for two main purposes. First, to guarantee a centralized control of traffic then to detect attacks transiting across CPS systems. Second, to prevent the attack from badly affecting the network through injecting rules in the OpenFlow switches from SDN controller. Still, the implementation of this model needs to be tested and prototyped in further stage with IIoT traffic. In the future, this study will be experimented with real traffic in order to test the performance of this framework. Moreover, we will analyze different types of attacks on it and evaluate parameters and metrics in various scenarios to reinforce security of this framework if needed.

References

1. Almusaylim, Z.A., Alhumam, A., Mansoor, W., Chatterjee, P., Jhanjhi, N.Z.: Detection and mitigation of RPL rank and version number attacks in smart internet of things (2020). https://doi.org/10.20944/preprints202007.0476.v1
2. Sisinni, E., Saifullah, A., Han, S., Jennehag, U., Gidlund, M.: Industrial internet of things: challenges, opportunities, and directions. IEEE Trans. Industr. Inf. **14**(11), 4724–4734 (2018)
3. Ghobakhloo, M.: Industry 4.0, digitization, and opportunities for sustainability. J. Cleaner Prod. **252** (2020). https://doi.org/10.1016/j.jclepro.2019.119869
4. Lee, J., Davari, H., Singh, J., Pandhare, V.: Industrial Artificial Intelligence for industry 4.0-based manufacturing systems. Manufact. Lett. **18**, 20–23 (2018). https://doi.org/10.1016/j.mfglet.2018.09.002

5. Pundir, S., Wazid, M., Singh, D.P., Das, A.K., Rodrigues, J.J.P.C., Park, Y.: esigning efficient sinkhole attack detection mechanism in edge-based IoT deployment. Sensors (Switzerland), **20**(5) (2020). https://doi.org/10.3390/s20051300
6. Rehman, A., Rehman, S.U., Raheem, H.: Sinkhole attacks in wireless sensor networks: a survey. Wireless Pers. Commun. **106**(4), 2291–2313 (2018). https://doi.org/10.1007/s11277-018-6040-7
7. AbdAllah, E.G., Zulkernine, M., Hassanein, H.S.: Preventing unauthorized access in information centric networking. Secur. Privacy **1**(4), e33 (2018). https://doi.org/10.1002/spy2.33
8. Lezzi, M., Lazoi, M., Corallo, A.: Cybersecurity for Industry 4.0 in the current literature: a reference framework. Comput. Ind. **103**, 97–110 (2018)
9. Correa Chica, J.C., Imbachi, J.C., Botero Vega, J.F.: Security in SDN: a comprehensive survey. J. Network Comput. Appl. **159**, 102595 (2020). https://doi.org/10.1016/j.jnca.2020.102595
10. Paraskevopoulos, A., et al.: Design of a secure software-defined access network for flexible Industry 4.0 manufacturing-The SESAM-project concept
11. Khalid, H., Hashim, S.J., Mumtazah, S., Ahmad, S., Hashim, F., Chaudary, M.A.: Cybersecurity in Industry 4.0 context: background, issues, and future directions
12. Kim, Y., Nam, J., Park, T., Scott-Hayward, S., Shin, S.: SODA: a software-defined security framework for IoT environments. Comput. Netw. **163**, 106889 (2019)
13. da Xu, L., Xu, E.L., Li, L.: Industry 4.0: state of the art and future trends. Int. J. Prod. Res. **56**(8), 2941–2962 (2018)
14. Yin, Y., Stecke, K.E., Li, D.: The evolution of production systems from Industry 2.0 through Industry 4.0. Int. J. Prod. Res. **56**(1–2), 848–861 (2018)
15. Baheti, R., Gill, H.: Cyber-physical systems. Impact Control Technol. **12**(1), 161–166 (2011)
16. Qiang, W., Yang, J., Jin, H., Shi, X.: PrivGuard: protecting sensitive kernel data from privilege escalation attacks. IEEE Access **6**, 46584–46594 (2018). https://doi.org/10.1109/ACCESS.2018.2866498
17. Rahman, A., Islam, M.J., Khan, M.S.I., Kabir, S., Pritom, A.I., Karim, M.R.: Block-SDoTCloud: enhancing security of cloud storage through blockchain-based SDN in IoT network. In: 2020 2nd International Conference on Sustainable Technologies for Industry 4.0 (STI), pp. 1–6 (2020)
18. Mazur, D., Paszkiewicz, A., Bolanowski, M., Budzik, G., Oleksy, M.: Analysis of possible SDN use in the rapid prototyping processas part of the Industry 4.0. Bull. Pol. Acad. Sci. Tech. Sci. **67**(1) (2019)
19. Melis, A., Berardi, D., Contoli, C., Callegati, F., Esposito, F., Prandini, M.: A policy checker approach for secure industrial SDN. In: 2018 2nd Cyber Security in Networking Conference (CSNet), pp. 1–7 (2018)
20. Alani, M.M., Alloghani, M.: Security challenges in the industry 4.0 era. In: Dastbaz, M., Cochrane, P. (eds.) Industry 4.0 and Engineering for a Sustainable Future, pp. 117–136. Springer, Cham (2019). https://doi.org/10.1007/978-3-030-12953-8_8
21. Jamai, I., ben Azzouz, L., Sa\"\idane, L.A.: Security issues in Industry 4.0. In: 2020 International Wireless Communications and Mobile Computing (IWCMC), pp. 481–488 (2020)
22. J. Sasiain, A. Sanz, J. Astorga, and E. Jacob, "Towards flexible integration of 5G and IIoT technologies in industry 4.0: A practical use case," *Applied Sciences*, vol. 10, no. 21, p. 7670, 2020
23. Tuptuk, N., Hailes, S.: Security of smart manufacturing systems. J. Manuf. Syst. **47**, 93–106 (2018)
24. Anton, S.D.D., Hafner, A.,Schotten, H.D.: Devil in the detail: attack scenarios in industrial applications. In: 2019 IEEE Security and Privacy Workshops (SPW), pp. 169–174 (2019)

25. Korkmaz, E., Davis, M., Dolgikh, A., Skormin, V.: Detection and mitigation of time delay injection attacks on industrial control systems with PLCs. In: International Conference on Mathematical Methods, Models, and Architectures for Computer Network Security, pp. 62–74 (2017)
26. Corbò, G., Foglietta, C., Palazzo, C., Panzieri, S.: Smart behavioural filter for industrial internet of things. Mob. Networks Appl. **23**(4), 809–816 (2018)
27. Ding, D., Han, Q.-L., Xiang, Y., Ge, X., Zhang, X.-M.: A survey on security control and attack detection for industrial cyber-physical systems. Neurocomputing **275**, 1674–1683 (2018)
28. Lu, A.-Y., Yang, G.-H.: Malicious attacks on state estimation against distributed control systems. IEEE Trans. Autom. Control **65**(9), 3911–3918 (2019)
29. Zhang, Q., Liu, K., Xia, Y., Ma, A.: Optimal stealthy deception attack against cyber-physical systems. IEEE Trans. Cybern. **50**(9), 3963–3972 (2019)
30. Qarabsh, N.A., Sabry, S.S., Qarabash, H.A.: Smart grid in the context of industry 4.0: an overview of communications technologies and challenges. Indonesian J. Electr. Eng. Comput. Sci. **18**(2), 656–665 (2020)
31. Prinsloo, J., Sinha, S., von Solms, B.: A review of industry 4.0 manufacturing process security risks. Appl. Sci. **9**(23), 5105 (2019)
32. Imtiaz, K., Arshad, M.J.: Security challenges of industrial communication protocols: threats vulnerabilities and solutions. Int. J. Comput. Sci. Telecommun. (2019)
33. Sebbar, A., Zkik, K., Baddi, Y., Boulmalf, M., Kettani, M.-C.: MitM detection and defense mechanism CBNA-RF based on machine learning for large-scale SDN context. J. Ambient. Intell. Humaniz. Comput. **11**(12), 5875–5894 (2020). https://doi.org/10.1007/s12652-020-02099-4
34. Zimmermann, M., Schellenberger, C., Schotten, H.D.: Dynamic live wireless communication monitoring for jamming and interference detection in industry 4.0. In: Mobile Communication-Technologies and Applications; 24. ITG-Symposium, pp. 1–6 (2019)
35. Baskar, R., Raja, P., Reji, M., Joseph, C.: Performance analysis of scalability in the sinkhole compromised topology of wireless sensor networks. Int. J. Pure Appl. Math. **117**(9), 35–39 (2017)
36. Januário, F., Carvalho, C., Cardoso, A., Gil, P.: Security challenges in SCADA systems over Wireless Sensor and Actuator Networks. In: 2016 8th International Congress on Ultra Modern Telecommunications and Control Systems and Workshops (ICUMT), pp. 363–368 (2016)
37. Deshmukh-Bhosale, S., Sonavane, S.S.: A real-time intrusion detection system for wormhole attack in the RPL based Internet of Things. Procedia Manuf. **32**, 840–847 (2019)
38. Rahman, A., et al.: Distb-sdoindustry: enhancing security in industry 4.0 services based on distributed blockchain through software defined networking-iot enabled architecture. arXiv preprint arXiv:2012.10011 (2020)
39. Brozzi, R., Forti, D., Rauch, E., Matt, D.T.: The advantages of industry 4.0 applications for sustainability: results from a sample of manufacturing companies. Sustainability **12**(9), 3647 (2020)
40. Lahlou, S., Moukafih, Y., Sebbar, A., Zkik, K., Boulmalf, M., Ghogho, M.: TD-RA policy-enforcement framework for an SDN-based IoT architecture. J. Netw. Comput. Appl. **204**, 103390 (2022)

Author Index

A. Mirzazadeh et al. (Eds.): SEMIT 2022, CCIS 1808, pp. 397–398, 2023.
https://doi.org/10.1007/978-3-031-40395-8

Printed in the United States
by Baker & Taylor Publisher Services

Printed in the United States
by Baker & Taylor Publisher Services